Perceiving Talking Faces

MIT Press/Bradford Books Series in Cognitive Psychology
Stephen E. Palmer, editor

A Dynamic Systems Approach to Development: Applications, edited by Linda B. Smith and Esther Thelen (1993)

A Dynamic Systems Approach to the Development of Cognition and Action, edited by Esther Thelen and Linda B. Smith (1994)

Cognition and the Visual Arts, by Robert L. Solso (1994)

Indirect Perception, edited by Irvin Rock (1996)

Perceiving Talking Faces: From Speech Perception to a Behavioral Principle, by Dominic W. Massaro (1998)

Perceiving Talking Faces

From Speech Perception to a Behavioral Principle

Dominic W. Massaro

A Bradford Book
The MIT Press
Cambridge, Massachusetts
London, England

This book was set in Palatino on the Monotype "Prism Plus" PostScript Imagesetter by Asco Trade Typesetting Ltd., Hong Kong and was printed and bound in the United States of America.

Library of Congress Cataloging-in-Publication Data

Massaro, Dominic W.
  Perceiving talking faces : from speech perception to a behavioral
principle / Dominic W. Massaro.
     p.   cm. — (MIT Press/Bradford Books series in cognitive psychology)
"A Bradford book."
Includes bibliographical references and index.
ISBN 0-262-13337-7 (hardcover : alk. paper)
  1. Speech perception. I. Title. II. Series.
BF463.S64M37   1997
153.6—dc21   97-1575
                                                                    CIP

a mia madre
til min kone
私の息子へ
filiae meae

Three so Divine

I love to feel the sun upon my back:
Farewell to clothes that used to weigh me down!
A heavy coat is something I don't lack.
Without my shoes it's nice to feel the ground.
The sky is blue with not a cloud in sight.
The water's crisp and cold, but is my kin.
To wade, to dive, to swim, to surf—I might,
I can entice the sea to bring me in.
The shore receives my exit from the sea,
But only after I escape the tide.
I'm cold, I'm wet, and drained of energy.
I fall on sand and think, "Oh, what a ride."
   The sky and the sea are grand, sand is fine:
   Together, though, the three are so divine!

—Pia T. Massaro

Contents

Series Foreword

This series presents definitive works on cognition viewed from a psychological perspective, including undergraduate and graduate textbooks, reference works, research monographs, and edited volumes. Among the wide variety of topics addressed are perception, attention, imagery, memory, learning, categorization, language, problem solving, thinking, and cognitive development. Although the primary emphasis is on presenting psychological theories and findings, most volumes in the series are interdisciplinary, attempting to develop important connections between cognitive psychology and the related fields of anthropology, computer science, education, linguistics, neuroscience, and philosophy.

Stephen E. Palmer

Preface

There are many reasons to write a book. Like the Norwegian bachelor farmers of Garrison Keillor's *Prairie Home Companion,* some scientists thrive on misery. Writing journal articles provides enough misery, though, that it cannot be the sole justification. Even so, a book is necessarily more exacting. A plausible "Just So" story can be woven easily enough for a research article reporting a few experiments. Publishers and readers of books, on the other hand, expect some overall theme to impose order on the myriad of scholarship that is presented. All kidding aside, the best reason for writing this book is perhaps most easily conveyed by the metaphor of climbing a mountain (or, in my case, cycling one). The proverbial answer is, "I climbed it because it was there." This book was written because a universal principle was there (along with an overwhelming array of support). Its existence demanded communication. The journals were not a satisfying venue for this enterprise because everything could not be organized and covered within the confines of a journal article. Furthermore, a book has a greater potential to inform an interdisciplinary audience. Most important, the writing of this book increased my faith in the possibility—one that sometimes seems unattainable—of gaining some understanding of how we work. I hope the reader experiences at least part of the excitement that enlivened this journey.

A project of this kind is a collaborative effort, and it is a pleasure to acknowledge the talented people who contributed to it in substantive ways. Michael M. Cohen, as always, was the quarterback who expertly managed the research environment that housed the many empirical projects, data analyses, and model tests, providing the backbone for the theoretical development. Early on, Michael had the foresight and initiative not only to envision the value of visible speech synthesis but to bring it to life in the form of Baldi, our cyberhead that talks. Michael Berger's knowledge of linguistics contributed significantly to the development and evaluation of Baldi. As we explain in part IV, co-authored by Cohen and Berger, the two Michaels built upon previous efforts at computer-animated synthetic speech and took it to a level approaching the real thing.

The communication channel of our research—that is, the book itself— has also been improved by several individuals. Michael Berger edited the manuscript with command and exigent expectations well beyond my previous experience. His input concerning the organization of the material and his effort in the development of an interdisciplinary message were uncompromising and rewarding in the outcome. Several scientists from various disciplines were kind enough to read and comment on an earlier version of the book. Christian Abry, Christian Benoit, Jaye Padgett, Bill Rowe, Jean-Luc Schwartz, Barry Stein, and J. D. Trout offered valuable advice on the empirical and theoretical research as well as its delivery. The sophisticated comments of Richard Golden and Daniel Friedman on part III were useful in the presentation of the intricacies of model building and testing. Lit-ze Hu helped me envision chapter 10 more securely in the context of statistical methods. Valerie Stone's guidance on the evolutionary perspective on the study of emotion in chapters 7 and 8 was extremely valuable.

The excitement and rewards of the study of mind and behavior were significantly enhanced by the presence of students. John Ellison's interest in studying emotion and his constant monitoring of the plethora of new findings helped guide me into that area, which until then had been ignored by this traditional cognitive experimentalist. Christopher Campbell expertly developed the study of the information in visible speech. Terry Bleizeffer helped study the processing of synthetic auditory sentences with the addition of visible speech. Anne Shin and Michael Shin tested subjects and helped in many day-to-day activities. Eric Berg and Jason Glass helped with the references. My appreciation of rewarding collaboration with many other students and colleagues is expressed in the discussions of our work sprinkled throughout the text. In particular, I want to recognize Ruth Campbell, Nelson Cowan, Uli Frauenfelder, Dan Friedman, Geoff Loftus, Harry McGurk, Gregg Oden, Steve Palmer, Fred Parke, Andrew Pearce, Laura Thompson, and Paul Verschure. The professionalism of Amy Pierce, Katherine Arnoldi, and the staff at MIT, and the help of Stevan de la Vaux, John Ellison, Lisa Menckhoff, and Cari Mercy on the page proofs, greatly eased the rigors of bringing this book to fruition. Finally, I am grateful to Pia for her poem that captures our theme of the richness of experience given multiple sensory inputs.

The research and writing were supported by continued funding from the National Institute of Deafness and other Communicative Disorders of the Public Health Service (PHS R01 DC00236), the National Science Foundation (BNS 8812728), Speech Technology Laboratory, AT&T Bell Laboratories, and the Social Sciences Division of the University of California, Santa Cruz. This brand of interdisciplinary research, with the technology it requires, is expensive, and the funds for it are greatly appreciated.

While reading the book, the reader is encouraged to experience the many intriguing phenomena in the accompanying CD-ROM, located in the back cover. Simply click on the README file for instructions.

I   Perceiving Talking Faces

1   Bimodal Speech Perception

Not chaos-like together crush'd and bruis'd,
But, as the world, harmoniously confused
Where order in variety we see,
And where, tho' all things differ, all agree.
—Alexander Pope, *Windsor Forest*

Pope's poem captures a persistent characteristic of human experience: people easily impose order on the blooming, buzzing confusion that bombards us. One of the themes of our research is that people have no trouble handling seemingly disparate inputs to arrive at a well-informed impression of the here and now. To give substance to this theme, we ask the reader to experience the puzzle that is at the heart of the monograph. We also rely on the belief that little else engages human endeavors more than experience.

An animated head will be our narrator for many of the demonstrations accompanying this monograph. This talking head is called "Baldi" for obvious reasons, but spells his name with an *i* because he lives on the West Coast. Baldi describes himself on band 1.1 on the CD-ROM. Baldi is a superficial person, to say the least. As he puts it, there is little beneath his attractive exterior. Figure 1.1 shows the underlying wire frame model and its appearance when the surface of each of the triangles is filled in and smooth shaded at the edges. In contrast to most studies of speech perception, our experiments present speech that can be both seen and heard. The way that most people experience this bimodal speech does not necessarily correspond to just the sound, or just the face; rather, the perception somehow emerges from the sound and sight of the face together.

To illustrate, watch and listen to band 1.2 on the CD-ROM. There are four sets of four syllables, and you should keep track of whether your auditory experience changes from syllable to syllable. You should play the demonstration before reading any further to avoid biasing your response.

If your perception changed from syllable to syllable, then the visible speech had a substantial influence on your perceptual experience. Within each set of four syllables, the *audible* syllable is identical. The *visible* syllable changes, however, from /ba/ to /va/ to /ða/ to /da/. The first set of four syllables always had an auditory /ba/, the second set had an auditory /va/, and so on. To

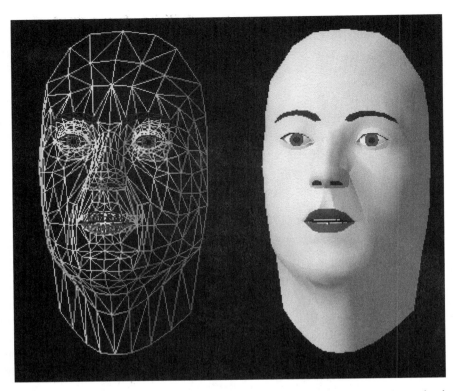

Figure 1.1 Framework (left) and Gouraud (1971) shaded (right) renderings of polygon facial model.

convince yourself, replay the band without looking at Baldi. You should now hear the auditory syllables correctly. You might finally watch and listen to the band again to convince yourself how robust this perceptual reaction is. I have been attending to conflicting auditory and visible speech for about 15 years and have not noticed any change in my percepts.

Band 1.3 is valuable because the auditory syllable is the fastest-moving variable, while the visible syllable is fixed for each set of four syllables. Your percept should again change from syllable to syllable, illustrating that the audible speech also has an important influence. These two bands challenge us to understand how we magically combine the two inputs to achieve an integrated perceptual experience. To anticipate the answer already adumbrated by Pope, our experience is well described by a very simple rule: we perceive the event that makes the most sense of the available auditory and visible inputs. We will present evidence supporting this conclusion in the discussion of our first experiment.

ANECDOTAL EVIDENCE OF BIMODAL SPEECH PERCEPTION

Many of us find the illusory experience demonstrated on the CD-ROM puzzling. With hindsight, however, we see that there is much anecdotal evidence to implicate an important role for the face in verbal communication. Hal, the intelligent computer in the movie *2001: A Space Odyssey*, successfully reads the lips of two space pilots who are plotting his demise. It is unlikely, however, that computers in the year 2001 will speechread as accurately as does Hal. Notwithstanding the 1937 movie *Charlie Chan at the Olympics*, we are skeptical that international secrets can be deciphered by simply reading lips across the stadium.

Although lipreading (referred to here as *speechreading* because it involves more than the lips) might not be sufficient to thwart international espionage, it is an important part of spoken language understanding. Many of us dislike talking over the phone and are irritated by poorly dubbed foreign films. Some people even comment that they hear the television better with their glasses on. Children who are born blind learn some speech distinctions more slowly than sighted children. Perhaps the following quotation from Benjamin Franklin will encourage teachers of second languages to place more emphasis on visible language.

I had formerly two pairs of spectacles, which I shifted occasionally, as in traveling I sometimes read, and often wanted to regard the prospects. Finding this change troublesome, and not always sufficiently ready, I had the glasses cut, and half of each kind associated in the same circle. By this means, as I wear my spectacles constantly, I have only to move my eyes up or down, as I want to see distinctly far or near, the proper glasses being always ready. This is I find more particularly convenient since my being in France, the glasses that serve me best at table to see what I eat not being the best to see the faces of those on the other side of the table who speak to me; and when one's ears are not well accustomed to the sounds of a language, a sight of the movements in the features of him that speaks helps to explain; so that I understand French better by the help of my spectacles. (Frank Donovan, *The Benjamin Franklin Papers* [New York: Dodd Mead, 1962])

It has been well known for some time that deaf and hearing-impaired persons can make valuable use of speechreading. Our demonstrations clearly show that even people with normal hearing are greatly influenced by the visible speech in face-to-face communication. Experimental investigations support this conclusion, and it is worthwhile to begin with an experiment that parallels the demonstration you have just experienced. As in the demonstrations, our study of speech perception usually involves the independent variation of several sources of information.

EXPERIMENTAL EVIDENCE

Experimental Strategy

Participants in the experiments are asked to watch and listen to our talking head and to identify the syllable presented on each trial. The participants are tested for many trials over the course of the experiment. In this design, the same stimulus event is repeated several times throughout the experiment. As has been known since the beginning of the study of the relationship between stimulus and response (psychophysics), the same stimulus event does not lead to the same response on each trial. Behavior is probabilistic rather than deterministic. Therefore, it is important to get a reasonable number of observations for each experimental condition to arrive at a reliable and sensitive estimate of the probability of a particular response to a given stimulus. (It took us some time to recognize the importance of accounting for this variability of response. That process now plays an important role in evaluating how well models describe the experimental results.)

Most participants find our experiment fairly boring. The first few trials might be considered interesting, but the repetition of trials with very similar stimulus events gets old very quickly. We tell the observers to simply do the best they can and to try to maintain a constant motivation throughout the task. Normally, no feedback is given in the experimental task because there is no single correct answer. There is no single correct answer to an audible /ba/ paired with a visible /da/. In many respects, the subjects' responses tell us what the perceptual event is. Thus this research bears some similarity to psychophysical scaling, in which the correspondence between stimulus input and perceptual output is described. In some experimental situations it is possible to define the accuracy of performance conditional upon one stimulus property or another. This dependent measure can be a valuable supplement to the analysis of the identification judgments. Finally, reaction times for the judgments can greatly inform our investigative work.

The data are analyzed with respect to each subject individually as well as using statistical tests done across subjects. Although we carry out our statistical tests by force of habit and demand, we give them very little weight. We follow Lord Ernest Rutherford's (1937) advice, "If your experiment needs statistics, you ought to have done a better experiment." We supplant traditional statistical tests with the testing of well-specified quantitative models, then determine their accuracy or goodness of fit. A model is evaluated both against other models and against an absolute criterion or standard.

We are also of the firm belief that averaging the results across subjects can be highly misleading (Massaro & Cohen, 1993b). In addition, our goal is to explain not the behavior of an average subject who does not exist, but rather the behavior of individual subjects who do exist.

Single-Factor and Factorial Designs   A necessary step in scientific inquiry is to disentangle variables that are normally confounded in the natural world. Experimentation in psychophysics has traditionally been characterized by single-factor designs in which all variables but one are eliminated or made neutral and the variable of interest is systematically varied. In speech perception, for example, the investigator might create a continuum between the alternatives /ba/ and /pa/ by manipulating the voice onset time. Seven to nine stimuli are synthesized in steps of 5 to 10 milliseconds. These test alternatives are presented randomly from trial to trial, and the subject is asked to identify the stimulus as the voiced or voiceless member of the pair. The prototypical results show that the proportion of "voiced" judgments decreases monotonically as the voice onset is delayed. In addition, the identification function is relatively sharp, which is one of the pieces of evidence people have used to support the idea of *categorical perception* (Massaro, 1987a).

There are several limitations inherent in the single-factor experiment. First, the single-factor experiment has little external validity in the sense that all the stimulus properties are neutralized except the one of interest. Although the participants might show themselves to be influenced by that particular property, such behavior is not representative of the real world, where many properties vary simultaneously. This discrepancy raises the important distinction between *ecological* and *functional* cues to behavior, a distinction first emphasized by Brunswik (1955, 1956). An ecological cue to behavior is one that is potentially useful in that it systematically varies with the perceptual event. For example, height in the visual field is an ecological cue to distance because, ceteris paribus, the higher an object is in the visual field, the farther away it tends to be. A functional cue, on the other hand, is a cue that is actually used by perceivers in the perceptual interpretation of an event. Brunswik recognized that not all ecological cues are necessarily used in perception (Massaro, 1985b).

The single-factor experiment thus may find a functional value for a cue that is greater than its actual utility in the real world. Most people are very cooperative participants; they might notice the design of the study and believe that they should respond differentially to the single property that is being varied. This limitation is not unique to single-factor designs and is one that all investigators face, but the single-factor design makes it more likely that the investigator might be misled. The *factorial* design, on the other hand, manipulates several cues independently of one another and, by simultaneously varying several cues, creates a situation that more closely resembles the real world. The greatest advantage of the factorial design, however, is that only such independent manipulation of input variables can address the issue of how two sources of information are used together.

The independent manipulation of the two cues in the factorial design means that opposing cues are sometimes presented. One might argue that this seldom occurs in the real world. However, because the world is variable or noisy and our perceptual systems are even noisier, it could be the case that observers normally are faced with several sources of information that conflict with one another. Another important advantage of the factorial design is that the investigator is challenged by a much larger data set. As is described later in this chapter in the section "A Down Side to the McGurk Effect," presentation of just a few experimental conditions does not sufficiently challenge and discriminate among current theories. The factorial design provides a more complete coverage of the behavior of interest, thereby allowing greater theoretical progress.

Visual

		/ba/	/va/	/ðˑa/	/da/	None
	/ba/					
	/va/					
Auditory	/ðˑa/					
	/da/					
	None					

Figure 1.2 Expanded factorial design with four auditory syllables crossed with four visual syllables.

Expanded Factorial Design   It is often true in life that the combination of two things, each of which is somewhat lacking, is necessary to produce an optimal situation. This is what we have done in joining the single-factor and factorial experimental designs in what is called an *expanded factorial design*. Figure 1.2 illustrates the expanded factorial design for bimodal speech with four levels each of two independent variables. (The term *level* refers to a setting of the independent variable.) As in the single-factor design, each of the syllables is presented unimodally. As in the factorial design, each of the four auditory syllables is combined with each of the four visible syllables. The presentation of all of these conditions provides an informative picture of how the two speech modalities are processed. More generally, the goal is to provide a theoretical description of the performance under the bimodal conditions as a function of performance under the unimodal conditions (or vice versa). As we will see, this expanded factorial design also provides a strong test of quantitative models because it includes both unimodal and bimodal conditions. Each candidate model must describe the relationship between unimodal and bimodal performance. We now describe the method and a subset of the results of a particular experiment using this research strategy (Massaro & Cohen, 1996).

Method

Synthetic visible speech and natural audible speech were used to generate the consonant-vowel (CV) syllables /ba/, /va/, /ða/, and /da/. Figure 1.3 shows a view of the talking head at the onset of articulation for each syllable. Using an expanded factorial design, the four syllables were presented auditorily,

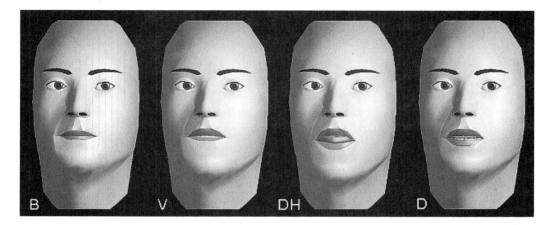

Figure 1.3 Synthetic visual syllables /ba/, /va/, /ða/, and /da/ at the onset of consonant articulation.

visually, and bimodally. Each syllable was present alone in each modality for $4 + 4 = 8$ unimodal trials. For the bimodal presentation, each audible syllable was presented with each visible syllable for a total of 4×4, or 16 unique trials. Thus, there were 24 types of trials. Twelve of the bimodal syllables contained inconsistent auditory and visual information.

The 20 participants in the experiment were instructed to watch and listen to the talking head and to indicate the syllable that was spoken. The subjects made their responses by pressing a key labeled as *b, v, th,* or *d* on the terminal keyboard for simple responses, or by pressing two keys successively for consonant cluster responses, such as the response /bda/. The 24 experimental conditions were presented in a randomized order without replacement to give a block of trials. There were four experimental sessions of six blocks each for a total of 20 experimental trials for each condition. The mean observed proportion of identifications for each subject for each of the 24 conditions was computed according to the relative frequency of response.

Performance on Unimodal Trials

In our task, the participants' goal was to perceive what was spoken by watching and listening to the talker. We can assess the influence of the auditory and the visual speech by evaluating performance in terms of accuracy of response with respect to each of the two modalities. The points in the left half of figure 1.4 show average performance scored in terms of accuracy with respect to the visible speech. The proportions of correct responses were .82, .94, .84, and .75, respectively, for the unimodal visible syllables /ba/, /va/, /ða/, and /da/. Thus, perceivers are fairly good at speechreading those syllables, and the more visually distinctive syllables, /ba/, /va/, and /ða/ are somewhat easier than the less distinctive /da/.

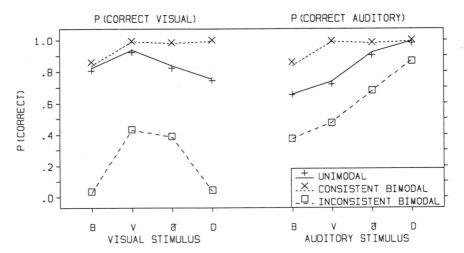

Figure 1.4 Probability correct visual (left panel) and auditory (right panel) responses as a function of visual or auditory level for unimodal, consistent, and inconsistent trials. The consistent condition is necessarily identical in the two panels because it represents the same results. The lines are the predictions of the fuzzy logical model of perception (FLMP; formalized in chapter 2).

Accuracy of response with respect to the auditory modality is given in the right half of figure 1.4. Correct identification averaged .66, .74, .92, and .99 for the unimodal auditory syllables /ba/, /va/, /ða/, and /da/. The auditory syllables /ða/ and /da/ were perceived more accurately than the syllables /ba/ and /va/. The different levels of performance for the auditory and visual syllables replicates a more general complementarity of the two modalities in speech perception. For whatever reason, several syllables that are easy to recognize in the visual modality tend to be difficult in the auditory modality, and vice versa (Benoit, Mohamadi & Kandel, 1994; Summerfield, 1987; see also chapter 14 of this volume). This is unlikely to be a rule in pattern recognition, but it does occur more generally for auditory-visual speech (e.g., Robert-Ribes, Schwartz & Escudier, 1995b).

Some readers might be surprised that the participants made errors on the unimodal trials. However, we are seldom expected to recognize isolated syllables; we usually have the benefit of supplementary contextual cues. In addition, these four syllables are fairly similar to one another and are therefore easily confused. I once received a phone interview from *Tanorama*, an Italian weekly magazine. Given my Italian heritage, I was embarrassed because I didn't know the magazine or even the meaning of the word. Only later did I learn that I had confused /t/ with /p/—the magazine was actually *Panorama*. This confusion probably would not have occurred if visible speech had also been available.

There were large differences in accuracy across the 20 participants, a finding that highlights the pervasiveness of individual variability. Some subjects in our task were completely accurate or at least almost perfect on the unimodal conditions. Other subjects were, of course, much worse. Such variability is not necessarily confounding, however; we can exploit it as did Darwin, taking advantage of the opportunity to observe what is consistent in the face of variability. Chapter 5 explores individual variability more systematically.

Performance on Bimodal Trials

Figure 1.4 also shows accuracy for bimodal trials. We partition these trials in terms of whether the two syllables (visual and auditory) are consistent or inconsistent with one another. The difference between the bimodal and unimodal curves in figure 1.4 indexes the degree of influence of a given source of information. The results show a strong influence of both modalities on performance. Overall performance was more accurate given two consistent sources of information than given just one of those sources. Analogously, given inconsistent information from the two sources, performance was poorer than that observed in the unimodal conditions.

The auditory source of information exerted a greater influence than the visual source. Figure 1.4 shows that inconsistent auditory information disrupted visual performance more than inconsistent visual information disrupted auditory performance. The difference between the unimodal and inconsistent conditions is much larger for the visual scoring (in the left panel) than for the auditory scoring (in the right panel). Consistent auditory information improved visual performance about as much as consistent visual information improved auditory performance. The latter result is probably due to the high accuracy of performance in the unimodal condition, which left very little room for improvement in the consistent conditions. Otherwise, we would expect consistent auditory speech to help visual performance more than consistent visual speech improves auditory performance.

The advantage of the auditory over the visual modality might be partially due to our use of natural auditory and synthetic visual speech; that is, perhaps the synthetic visual speech was of poor quality. Repp et al. (1983) used a female's natural visible and audible speech tokens of the same four syllables in a factorial design. Figure 1.5 gives the accuracy results plotted in the same manner as figure 1.4. Although Repp and colleagues did not include unimodal trials, it is still possible to determine whether the audible or visible speech was more influential in their study. As can be seen in figure 1.5, their participants were perfectly accurate on consistent trials, whereas ours made some errors on the syllable /ba/. For the inconsistent trials, the relative performance on the four syllables was comparable to our results. Relative to our findings, Repp et al. found a weaker effect of audible speech and a stronger effect of visible speech. Thus, we can conclude that our synthetic visible speech was probably less informative than natural speech. The quality of Baldi's visible speech has been improved gradually over the course of our project (see chapter 13), but at the time of the first study, Baldi's visible

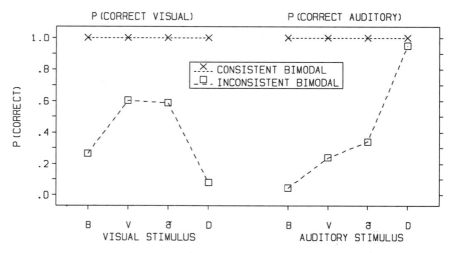

Figure 1.5 Probability correct visual (left panel) and auditory (right panel) responses for natural speech as a function of visual or auditory level for the consistent and inconsistent trials. (Observations from Repp et al., 1983.)

speech could not be speechread as well as a natural talker (Cohen, Walker & Massaro, 1996).

The strong effect of visible speech on the distinction between the four syllables /ba/, /va/, /ða/, and /da/ is not representative of all speech distinctions. Those four syllables just happen to be fairly distinctive visually and less so auditorily. More generally, audible speech is actually more informative than visible speech. As is well documented, some distinctions among speech segments are not conveyed visually. It is very difficult, if not impossible, to see voicing or nasality on the face. The words *bat, pat,* and *mat* are essentially indistinguishable from one another. For this reason, we can communicate effectively over the phone, but not very well via silent video. The second-class status of visible speech makes it even more impressive that it can have such a dramatic influence on our phenomenal impression and recognition of spoken language.

One concern is to what extent the influence of visible speech holds up for highly intelligible audible speech. Our participants differed with respect to their accuracy on unimodal auditory trials. One viable interpretation, the intelligibility hypothesis, is that visible speech has an influence only for unintelligible auditory speech. This point of view predicts no influence of visible speech unless the audible speech is unintelligible. The right panel of figure 1.6 gives the average results of three observers who were particularly accurate in the task of identifying the unimodal auditory speech. The three participants identified all four auditory syllables about perfectly, but they were still influenced by the visible speech, contrary to the expectations of the intelligibility hypothesis. The results shown in figure 1.6 are inconsistent with the idea that visible speech has an influence only when the auditory speech is unintelligible.

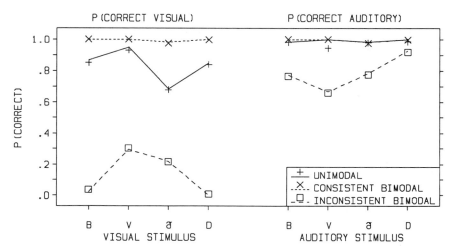

Figure 1.6 Probability correct visual (left panel) and auditory (right panel) responses as a function of visual or auditory level for unimodal, consistent, and inconsistent trials. The average results are shown for three participants who were very accurate in identifying the auditory speech. The consistent condition is necessarily identical in the two panels because it represents the same results. The lines are the predictions of the FLMP (formalized in chapter 2).

The group results shown in figure 1.4 also weaken the intelligibility hypothesis. When presented alone, auditory /da/ was misidentified only 2 out of 400 times, but it was identified correctly only 87% of the time when paired with inconsistent visual information (see right half of figure 1.4). Although auditory /da/ is relatively robust (Massaro, 1987f, p. 46), inconsistent visible speech can still have a substantial effect. Some participants identified several of the syllables perfectly on auditory-alone trials, and yet the identification of those syllables was influenced by visible speech on the inconsistent trials. If visible speech influences bimodal perception only when the auditory speech is unintelligible and we take perfect accuracy as indicating good intelligibility, then there should have been no influence of the visible speech in those cases. Thus, these results provide evidence against the hypothesis that visible speech has an influence only when the auditory speech is unintelligible.

For symmetry's sake, we should also assess the influence of audible speech when the visible speech is highly intelligible. Analogous to our analysis in figure 1.6, figure 1.7 gives the average results of three particularly accurate observers in the task of identifying the unimodal visible speech. Those three participants identified all four visible syllables almost perfectly but were still influenced by the audible speech. These results, like those shown in figure 1.6, reveal that a single source of information might be sufficient for identification and yet still be compromised when paired with another, inconsistent source of information. This outcome constitutes an important datum that will have to be described by any theoretical candidates.

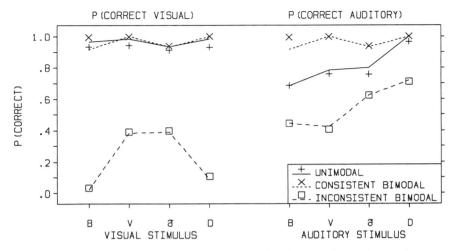

Figure 1.7 Probability correct visual (left panel) and auditory (right panel) responses as a function of visual or auditory level for unimodal, consistent, and inconsistent trials. The average results are shown for three participants who were very accurate in identifying the visual speech. The consistent condition is necessarily identical in the two panels because it represents the same results. The lines are the predictions of the FLMP (formalized in chapter 2).

Confusions among Test Alternatives

Although the results in figures 1.4–1.7 demonstrate the perceiver's use of both auditory and visible speech in perception, they do not indicate *how* the two sources are used together. There are many possible ways the two sources might be used. A finer-grained analysis of the results than that given in figures 1.4–1.7 is necessary to understand the processes involved in bimodal speech perception. The finer-grained analysis involves the proto-typical confusion matrix familiar to most psychophysicists. A confusion matrix gives results for all possible stimulus-response pairings. Figure 1.8 plots the confusion matrix for our results, giving the proportion of times each stimulus event was identified as a particular alternative.

According to the present theoretical framework, perception should correspond to the most reasonable alternative given the two inputs. We will sometimes appeal to psychophysical similarity to account for the confusion between two alternatives or for the fact that two sources of information lead to a particular percept. Although a detailed psychophysical analysis is beyond the scope of these studies, we can appeal to previous findings to support our claims. Perhaps the most informative study in this regard was one of the earliest such studies, carried out by Miller and Nicely (1955). Their listeners were asked to identify the initial consonant of auditory consonant-vowel syllables. There were 16 consonants, and the vowel was /a/ as in *father*. This seminal study had 17 listening conditions, which also made it a heroic one for the subjects. Noise was added in various amounts and low or high fre-

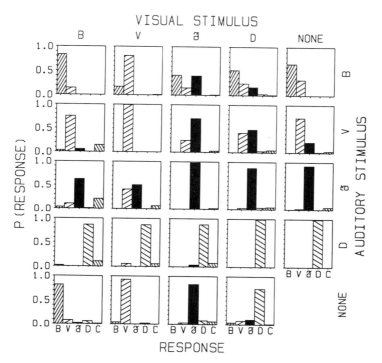

Figure 1.8 Proportion of /b/, /v/, /ð/, /d/, and consonant-cluster (C) responses as a function of the auditory and visual conditions for both the unimodal and bimodal trials.

quencies were filtered out. Shepard's (1988) multidimensional scaling of these data revealed two important dimensions, evidently corresponding to energy in the low and high frequencies (see chapter 4). By Shepard's analysis, there is more high-frequency energy as we move from /ba/ to /va/ to /ða/. Thus, auditory /ba/ is often categorized as /va/, and auditory /va/ is often categorized as /ða/. The syllable /da/, on the other hand, is fairly distant from the other three syllables and is categorized nearly perfectly.

Figure 1.8 shows that a visual /da/ paired with an auditory /va/ will often be identified as /ða/. Similarly, a visual /da/ presented with an auditory /ba/ will often be identified as /va/ or /ða/. The rationale for these judgments is also psychophysical similarity. Perceptual recognition will correspond to the alternative that is most similar to the conflux of audible and visible speech. A visual /da/ paired with an auditory /va/ provides one strong mismatch to each of the two alternatives. Visual /da/ is very different from a visual /va/. Similarly, auditory /va/ is very different from an auditory /da/. Thus, each of these two alternatives can be thought of as having one good match and one poor match. The alternative /ða/, however, is somewhat similar to both visual /da/ and auditory /va/. The response /ða/ is given to both unimodal auditory /va/ and unimodal visual /da/. In this case, /ða/ is a reasonable interpretation given a visual /da/ paired with an auditory /va/. The same argument can be made for why /va/ and /ða/ are reasonable responses to the combination of visual /da/ and auditory /ba/.

Figure 1.8 shows the proportion of times each response was given to each of the unimodal and bimodal conditions. These results give a finer-grained picture than would a simple accuracy statistic. Because participants were limited to /b/, /v/, /ð/, /d/, or some combination of those responses, the fifth category of responses necessarily corresponds to consonant clusters (C). The confusions in figure 1.8 show a substantial number of consonant clusters in the bimodal condition when a visual /ba/ is paired with any auditory syllable. For example, a visual /ba/ paired with an auditory /da/ was identified as /bda/ 10% of the time. These results also show that the same bimodal syllable can produce both so-called fusion and combination judgments (McGurk & MacDonald, 1976). For example, visual /ba/ paired with auditory /ða/ elicited 11% /va/ and 12% /bða/ judgments. The first consonant of the cluster response is not always one that is articulated more forward in the mouth than the second consonant. A visual /da/ paired with an auditory /va/ gave 3% /dva/ judgments.

Figure 1.8 shows that auditory /ba/ and auditory /va/ are more influenced by visible speech than are auditory /ða/ and auditory /da/, the latter being particularly robust. This result is easily understood in terms of the unimodal auditory conditions (shown in the right column of figure 1.8). Accuracy of identification of auditory /ba/ and /va/ is much poorer than that of /ða/ and /da/. Analogously, visual /da/ gave the poorest performance in the unimodal visual condition and had the least influence in the bimodal conditions. These results are qualitatively consistent with the principle that the influence of a source of information when combined with other sources is directly related to its potency when presented in isolation.

The configuration of responses reveals something about the psychophysical properties of the four syllables. The response /ba/ is given primarily to visual /ba/ with auditory /ba/ (V_bA_b), $V_ðA_b$, and V_dA_b. The response /ða/ is given primarily to V_vA_b, V_dA_b, V_bA_v, V_vA_v, $V_ðA_v$, V_dA_v, and $V_vA_ð$. The response /ða/ is given primarily to $V_ðA_b$, $V_ðA_v$, $V_bA_ð$, $V_vA_ð$, $V_ðA_ð$, and $V_dA_ð$. The response /da/ is given primarily to the syllables composed with auditory /da/. In all of these cases, the responses can be rationalized in terms of the degree of match between the auditory and visual components of the test item and the response that is made. To provide further insight into bimodal speech perception, we now use our synthetic speech to systematically vary the ambiguity of the audible and visible speech.

VARYING THE AMBIGUITY OF THE SPEECH MODALITIES

In our expanded factorial design with four alternatives, we were able to test unimodal as well as both consistent and inconsistent bimodal syllables. Although each modality was relatively unambiguous, their pairing helped reduce uncertainty about the processing responsible for the observed results.

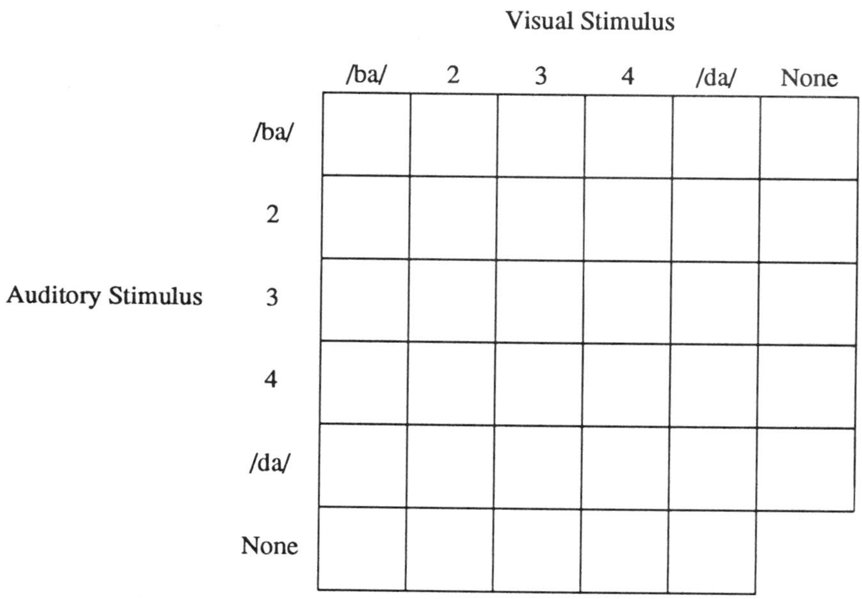

Visual Stimulus

	/ba/	2	3	4	/da/	None
/ba/						
2						
3						
4						
/da/						
None						

Figure 1.9 Expansion of a typical factorial design to include auditory and visual conditions presented alone. The five levels along the auditory and visible continua represent auditory and visible speech syllables varying in equal physical steps between /ba/ and /da/.

Another important manipulation is to systematically vary the ambiguity of each of the sources of information, that is, how much the stimuli resemble each syllable. Synthetic speech (or at least a sophisticated modification of natural speech) is necessary to implement this manipulation. We used synthetic speech to cross five levels of audible speech varying between /ba/ and /da/ with five levels of visible speech varying between the same alternatives. We also included the unimodal test stimuli to implement the expanded factorial design, as shown in figure 1.9. This design is illustrated on band 1.5.

Method

The properties of the auditory stimulus were varied to give an auditory continuum between the syllables /ba/ and /da/. In analogous fashion, properties of our animated face were varied to give a continuum between visual /ba/ and /da/. Figure 1.10 shows the five syllables at consonant articulation onset. Five levels of audible speech varying between /ba/ and /da/ were crossed with five levels of visible speech varying between the same alternatives. In addition, the audible and visible speech were each presented alone for a total of $25 + 5 + 5 = 35$ independent stimulus conditions. Six random sequences were determined by sampling the 35 conditions without replacement, giving six different blocks of 35 trials. An experimental session consisted of these six blocks preceded by six practice trials and with a short break between

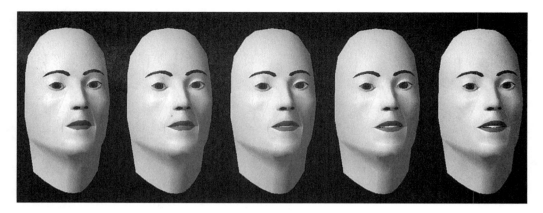

Figure 1.10 Five syllables on a continuum from /ba/ to /da/ at consonant articulation onset.

sessions. There were four sessions of testing for a total of 840 test trials (35 × 6 × 4). Thus there were 24 observations at each of the 35 unique experimental conditions. Subjects were instructed to listen and to watch the speaker, and to identify the syllable as either /ba/ or /da/. This experimental design was used with 82 participants (Massaro et al., 1993; Massaro, Cohen & Smeele, 1995), and the results will also serve as a database for testing models of pattern recognition in chapters 2 and 11.

Prototypical Results

The mean observed proportion of /da/ identifications was computed for each subject for the 35 unimodal and bimodal conditions. We first analyze the results for a subject who can be considered typical of the others in this task. The points in figure 1.11 give the observed proportion of /da/ responses for the auditory alone (left plot), the bimodal (middle plot), and the visual alone (right plot) conditions as a function of the five levels of the synthetic auditory and visual speech varying between /ba/ and /da/. We call these results prototypical because they are highly representative of many different experiments of this type. For the unimodal plots, the degree of influence of a modality is indicated by the steepness of the response function. By this criterion, both the auditory and the visual sources of information had a strong impact on the identification judgments. As illustrated in the left and right plots, the identification judgments changed systematically with changes in the audible and visible sources of information. The likelihood of a /da/ identification increased as the auditory speech changed from /ba/ to /da/, and analogously for the visible speech.

For the bimodal results in the middle plot, the degree of influence is again indexed by the slope of the function for the variable plotted on the x-axis, and by the spread among the curves for the variable described in the key or legend. By these criteria, both sources had a large influence in the bimodal

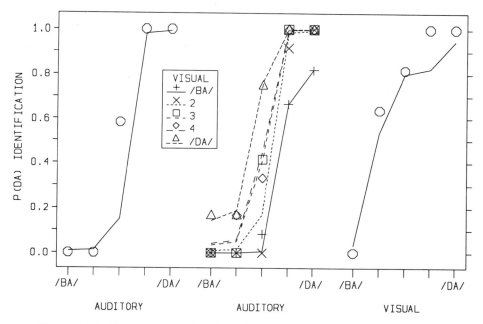

Figure 1.11 The points give the observed proportion of /da/ identifications for a typical observer in the auditory-alone (left panel), the factorial auditory-visual (center panel), and the visual-alone (right panel) conditions as a function of the five levels of the synthetic auditory and visual speech varying between /ba/ and /da/. The lines give the predictions of the FLMP.

conditions. The curves across changes in the auditory variable are relatively steep and also spread out from one another with changes in the visual variable.

Finally, the auditory and visual effects were *not* additive in the bimodal condition, as demonstrated by a significant auditory-visual interaction. The interaction is indexed by the change in the spread among the curves across changes in the auditory variable. Although the curves in the middle panel appear to be parallel to one another, that perception is illusory: we are biased to see the horizontal distances in the curves rather than the vertical ones, which give the true measure of the interaction. To see this, it is necessary to selectively focus on the vertical change at each level of the x-axis. The vertical spread between the curves is about four times greater in the middle than at the end of the auditory continuum. We will see that the same result is consistently obtained in this type of experiment. It means that the influence of one source of information is greatest when the other source is neutral or ambiguous. We now address how the two sources are used in perception.

How Two Sources of Information Are Used

Of course, an important question is how the two sources of information are used in perceptual recognition. An analysis of several results sheds light on this issue. Figure 1.12 gives the results for a given participant in the task.

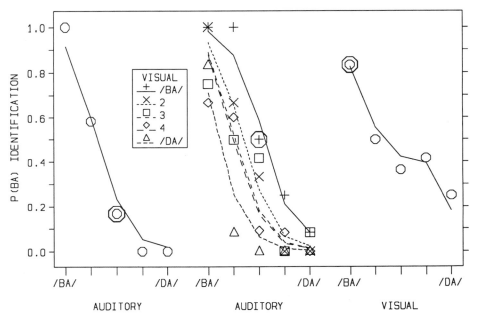

Figure 1.12 The points give the observed proportion of /ba/ identifications for a typical observer in the auditory-alone (left panel), the factorial auditory-visual (center panel), and the visual-alone (right panel) conditions as a function of the five levels of the synthetic auditory and visual speech varying between /ba/ and /da/. The three circled points give two unimodal conditions A_3 and V_1 and the corresponding bimodal condition. The relationship among the three points can be explained by the use of a single modality, an averaging of the two sources, or a multiplicative integration of the two sources. The lines are the predictions of the FLMP (formalized in chapter 2).

Three points are circled in the figure to highlight the conditions in which the third level of auditory information is paired with the first (/ba/) level of visual information. When presented alone, $P(/ba/|A_3)$ is about .2, whereas $P(/ba/|V_1)$ is about .8. When these two stimuli occur together, $P(/ba/|V_1A_3)$ is about .5. This subset of results is consistent with just about any theoretical explanation, for example, one that says only a single source of information is used on a given trial. Similarly, a simple averaging of the audible and visible speech predicts the same outcome.

Other observations, however, allow us to reject these alternatives. Figure 1.13 gives the results for another participant in the task. Three points are circled in the figure to highlight the conditions in which the second level of auditory information is paired with the second level of visual information. When presented alone, $P(/ba/|A_2)$ is about .8 and $P(/ba/|V_2)$ is about .8. When these two stimuli occur together, $P(/ba/|V_2A_2)$ is about 1. This so-called superadditive result (the bimodal response proportion is more extreme than either unimodal response proportion) is not easily explained by the use of a single modality or by a simple averaging of the two sources.

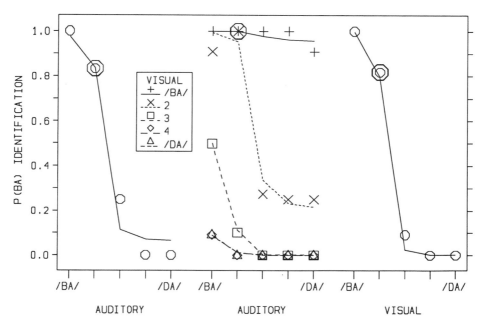

Figure 1.13 The points give the observed proportion of /ba/ identifications for a typical observer in the auditory-alone (left panel), the factorial auditory-visual (center panel), and the visual-alone (right panel) conditions as a function of the five levels of the synthetic auditory and visual speech varying between /ba/ and /da/. The three circled points give two unimodal conditions A_2 and V_2 and the corresponding bimodal condition. The relationship among the three points *cannot* be explained by the use of a single modality or an averaging of the two sources, but can be described by a multiplicative integration of the two sources. The lines are the predictions of the FLMP (formalized in chapter 2).

The lesson to be learned is that testing only a small set of conditions is unlikely to adequately distinguish the validity of different explanations; therefore, the full expanded factorial design should be used. The results given here are meant only to sufficiently engage the reader to continue to follow our search for a satisfying explanation.

FROM SYLLABLES TO MEANINGFUL SPEECH

An obvious criticism of our demonstration and our experimental findings is that what works for syllables might not work in the real world. We use language to communicate meaning, not to utter and recognize individual syllables. The importance of visible speech and its combination with audible speech might be limited to isolated syllables. If that were the case, however, this book would not have been written (or published). It certainly wouldn't include a CD-ROM demonstration package, which highlights the influence of visible speech.

Demonstration

A convincing demonstration at the sentence level is presented on band 1.6. Watch and listen to the sentence, and ascertain what is being said. If you don't succeed, repeat it a few times. As you will quickly discover, the auditory speech was "My bab pop me poo brive," and the visible speech was "My gag kok me koo grive." If the demonstration was successful, you actually heard "My dad taught me to drive" when you perceived these two pieces of nonsense together. In this example, created by Harry McGurk, the nonsense from each of the two modalities was selected to just approximate the meaningful sentence. Auditory *brive* provides strong support for *brive* but also some support for *drive*. Similarly, visual *grive* provides support for both *grive* and *drive*, and very little support for *brive*. In this case, *drive* is the best interpretation because it has substantial support from both the auditory and visual sources of information. A similar analysis can be given for the other segments that have conflicting auditory and visual information. The perceiver naturally combines the auditory and visual sentences into something meaningful because both the auditory and visual inputs are reasonably consistent with the meaningful sentence.

Experimentation

To explore the interaction of audible and visible speech in word recognition, we tested 12 subjects on a list of 420 one-syllable words. The words were played from a laser videodisc recorded by Bernstein and Eberhardt (1986) and included words from the Modified Rhyme Test (Kreul et al., 1968) as well as other familiar words. The words were presented either at a normal rate of presentation or at three times their normal rate. The speeded presentation was accomplished by presenting just every third frame of the word from the videodisc. The words were presented in auditory, visual, and bimodal conditions. Subjects wrote their answer for each presentation in a numbered box on a test sheet. At the normal rate of presentation, identification of the auditory word was almost perfect, therefore no advantage of the bimodal presentation was observed. At the speeded rate of presentation, however, the accuracy of word identification in the auditory condition was .55. Speechreading accuracy at the faster rate was only .04. A superadditive advantage of bimodal speech was found: performance improved to .73 when both audible and visible speech were presented. Thus, an influence of visual speech is not limited to meaningless syllables.

Nor is the important role for visible speech in sentence processing limited to inconsistent auditory and visible speech. It is well known that the intelligibility of sentences is improved when the talker's face is visible to the perceiver. MacLeod and Summerfield (1987) presented auditory sentences in a background of noise, with and without a view of the talker. Each sentence had three key words (here shown in uppercase); examples were as follows:

The WIFE HELPED her HUSBAND.

and

The BOY GOT into TROUBLE.

An *ascending method of limits* was used to determine the speech-reception thresholds for recognizing all three key words in the sentence. A view of the talker gave a benefit of an average of 11 dB, ranging from 6 to 15 dB across different subjects and from 3 to 22 dB across different sentences.

One does not have to stop at the sentence level. Reisberg, McLean, and Goldfield (1987) report similar findings for the processing of continuous text that is easy to hear but hard to understand. English-speaking participants repeated back (shadowed) text in a second language, an English text spoken with a slight foreign accent, or a difficult philosophical passage. In all cases, the percentage of words correctly shadowed was somewhat larger when the full face of the speaker was in view than when only sound was available.

THE REDISCOVERY OF BIMODAL SPEECH PERCEPTION

Illusions

What if everything is an illusion and nothing exists?
In that case, I really overpaid for my carpet.
—Woody Allen, *Without Feathers*

Psychologists, as well as their friends and neighbors, have traditionally been fascinated with illusions. An illusion is perhaps the quickest deterrent to naive realism—the belief that we experience the world exactly as it exists. There are several types of illusions. We can distinguish between physical and psychological illusions. Seeing a straight stick bent in the water is not the type of illusion that interests psychologists. It is known that light waves in water are bent relative to those in air, so in fact we are seeing the stick exactly as we physically should. We might not have a veridical perception of how the stick looks out of water, but we are experiencing the light rays correctly.

Psychological illusions are perceptual experiences that cannot be directly accounted for by the stimulus input. Most of us are familiar with the geometrical illusions named after some of our early psychologists: Müller-Lyer, Ponzo, and Ebbinghaus. Another popular illusion involves subjective or illusory visual contours, although some also classify such perception as not truly illusory because visual neuroscientists have observed activated neurons responding to the line that is not there. Thus, the perceptual experience of the line is not illusory because our sensory systems are delivering exactly this message: See a line right there where there isn't any. We can also experience illusory actions, not just perceptions, with vibration of the appropriate muscles (Roll et al., 1996).

Another important theoretical link with illusory experience is an old doctrine of Johannes Müller. As early as 1826 and also in 1838 (we know the value of repetition), Müller claimed some sort of specificity in the nerves serving the different sensations. Of course, little is totally new; Charles Bell anticipated Müller by at least a decade or so (Finger, 1994). Some of the strongest evidence for Müller's thesis showed that the same nerves stimulated by qualitatively different stimuli elicited the same qualitative sensation. Both light and pressure on the eye create visual experience. For Müller, different sensory experiences occur because the nerves themselves carry the message of the nature of the sensation. A specific nerve always gives rise to a specific sensation regardless of how it is stimulated. Yet in the case of bimodal speech perception, the visible speech has consequences for our auditory experience—which then must be illusory by Müller's doctrine.

Most illusions seem to occur within a single modality, however. A visual context creates an illusory visual impression; it does not change a visual experience into an auditory one. There might also be amodal influences on perceptual experience. Knowing or seeing the words to a rock song creates the impression of hearing a highly intelligible rendition of the words. Without this knowledge of the words, the listener often cannot make heads or tails of the message. The first demonstration of this kind that I know of was by John Morton, who played a song by the Beatles (see Norman, 1969). We can create the same effect with speech that is difficult to recognize, as demonstrated on band 1.7 of our CD-ROM. Another variation on this type of illusion is the so-called phonemic restoration effect, in which we claim to hear the /s/ in the word *legislatures* even when it is replaced by a cough, a buzz, or even a pure tone (Samuel, 1981; Warren & Warren, 1970).

The McGurk Effect: An Illusion for Speech Science

This circuitous tour of well-known illusions brings us to our prime exhibit, the recently described but famous McGurk effect, named for its discoverer, Harry McGurk. As far as I know, we have not been told how he discovered it. We might speculate that it was serendipitous, however. At the time of the finding, McGurk and other developmental psychologists were disturbing infants by creating sensory environments in which their different senses were given contradictory messages. For example, a talking image of an infant's mother might be projected to one location and the sound of her voice to another. As you might expect, infants did not appreciate this game experimenters were playing. (If some of today's young adults are less than trusting of their experience, we might blame these scientists).

Within this context, decorrelating the messages being conveyed by sight and sound is not much of a variation of the procedure of decorrelating their locations. Could babies detect discrepancies between what they see and hear a person saying? McGurk's own account provides a storybook example of serendipity in scientific endeavor (McGurk, 1996, personal communication).

We worked long and hard and spent a lot of money in the development of an accurate dubbing procedure. Once we had worked out how to achieve precise temporal synchrony in dubbing voices onto lips and had explained the procedures to the staff of the audio-visual unit at Surrey University, we did the basic filming and awaited the outcomes. I vividly recall going to the A-V workshop on the morning they told me that the dubbed tapes were ready. I had been disappointed by the standard of their work on a previous occasion and this time I was more than a little annoyed because as I watched the tapes they had prepared I was hearing stuff we had never recorded! I vented my anger at the technicians who had stuffed things up! They were totally perplexed because, since the dubbing strategy depended entirely on electronic wizardry, they had not even bothered to look at the final product. It was as we were engaged in a slanging match, the videotapes still running, that I realized that sometimes what you heard depended on whether or not you were watching the screen—birth of the McGurk effect.

In their published study with adults and young children, McGurk and MacDonald (1976) dubbed a visible /pa-pa/ with audible /na-na/. Their perceivers often reported hearing /ma-ma/. The experience of perceiving decorrelated auditory-visual speech is auditory. In our demonstration on band 1.2, a visual /da/ paired with an auditory /ba/ is sometimes heard as /va/. Contrary to Müllerian doctrine, a visual input appears to have auditory consequences. Admittedly, it also has a visual effect in that we see the talking head, but the visual information clearly modifies our auditory experience.

Should we be surprised by the finding that it is the auditory experience that is influenced by the visual input? Certainly the McGurk effect was not the first cross talk between modalities to be observed. We seem to have a little voice, not necessarily our own, in our heads as we read written language. Why do people watching a large screen in a movie theater hear an actor's voice coming from his face, even though the audio speakers are on the side of the screen? (This experience is equally powerful in theaters without stereoscopic sound, where indeed the auditory message has no information tying the sound to the actor.) This so-called visual capture is also exploited by ventriloquists, who, contrary to popular belief, do not throw their voices at their puppets. The visual input changes our auditory experience of the location of the sound we are hearing, a clear case of cross talk between modalities (Bertelson & Radeau, 1976, 1981).

We should be relieved that the McGurk effect resembles what we experience in other domains, such as localizing sound in space. That similarity offers the hope of a more general account of sensory fusion and modality-specific experience, rather than one unique to speech perception by ear and eye. Although visual information can bias auditory experience, it is not necessary to relinquish the Müllerian view of specific nerve energies. This result might simply mean that we cannot trust modality-specific experience as a direct index of processing within that modality. That is, it is not necessarily the case that the visual information invades the auditory pathways and confuses the auditory-specific nerves in terms of what is uniquely auditory and what is not. If there are neurons signaling lines that are not there in subjective contours, are there also necessarily auditory neurons being stimulated by the speaker's face? I prefer to think not. The invasion of the visual information might simply result from nonconvergent temporal integration (Zeki, 1993; see chapter 4). Speech information from two modalities provides a situation in which the brain combines both sources of information to create an interpretation that is easily mistaken for an auditory one. We believe we *hear* the speech because spoken language is usually heard. It is worthwhile to explain why we were attracted to bimodal speech perception as a paradigm for psychological inquiry.

Our Entry into the Field

One of the themes of our research is that people are influenced by multiple sources of information. This theme also captures, to some extent, the influences that led to our experimental investigations. I learned about Campbell's 1974 seminal study of phoneme recognition by ear and by eye while visiting the University of Nijmegen, the Netherlands, in the same year. Although I discussed that work in an earlier paper (Massaro, 1975b), I did not fully appreciate the valuable paradigm of manipulating audible and visible speech independently of one another as Campbell did in his dissertation research. I did not see McGurk and MacDonald's (1976) publication in *Nature*, nor did I see speech-is-special advocates or neo-Gibsonians racing through the streets and shouting with glee upon its publication. I encountered Harry McGurk at a conference in Edinburgh in 1979, when he challengingly described his findings that "disproved all current theories of speech perception." I was happy to learn about his research and tried to explain, over several beers, that our theoretical stance was generally compatible with his findings of a strong influence of visible speech. The following year I spent winding down my projects at the University of Wisconsin and preparing for my move to the University of California at Santa Cruz.

Armed with a new laboratory in Santa Cruz, I was stimulated by reviewing a paper by Easton and Basala (1982) for *Perception and Psychophysics*. The authors took issue with McGurk and MacDonald's conclusions; Easton and Basala found no influence of visible speech when the test items were words. When an auditory word was dubbed onto a different visual word, subjects always reported the auditory word rather than the visual. My reaction to this manuscript was that their findings did not necessarily support their conclusion that visible speech was ineffective when put in conflict with audible speech. The combined audible and visible speech did not support a meaningful word alternative, and therefore the auditory speech won out. Dubbing a visible *teeth* with an auditory *mouth* does not provide a meaningful word alternative because *nouth* and *neeth* are not words. The point was that one must consider the response alternatives that are supported by the two sources of information in order to understand the perceptual responses of the participants.

The bimodal speech task was attractive because the two sources of information could so easily be manipulated independently of one another. So, in a new location, in a new laboratory amid the redwoods of Santa Cruz, my graduate student, Michael Cohen, and I created videotapes with two cues: the mouth movements of a talker, which corresponded to /ba/, neutral, or /da/; and the synthesized auditory speech continuum between /ba/ and /da/. Our study showed that both audible and visible cues influenced the identification of the syllable. Because the two syllables differed only in place of articulation, these results provided strong evidence against McGurk and MacDonald's original idea that only the visible speech controls perception of place while the auditory speech controls perception of manner and voicing. In addition, the results of individual subjects were well fit by the fuzzy logical model of perception (FLMP), the guiding theoretical framework for this monograph. Our results were eventually published in the *Journal of Experimental Psychology: Human Perception and Performance* in 1983.

A Downside to the Investigation of the McGurk Effect

Many investigators have been misled by the traditional study of the McGurk effect. First of all, it is not reasonable for an investigator to study an effect. For example, it would be foolish for someone to say, "I study the Ebbinghaus illusion." One investigates illusions to gain insight into perceptual processing, not simply to study illusions. Similarly, it is important to keep in mind that the study of the McGurk effect should be aimed at understanding how we perceive speech. This subtle difference might seem underwhelming, but to focus on the illusion tends to compromise the type of experimental study that is implemented. Most studies of the McGurk effect use just a few experimental conditions in which the auditory and visual information is mismatched. Investigators also sometimes fail to test the unimodal conditions separately, so that there is no independent index of the perception of the single modalities.

The data analysis is also usually compromised because investigators analyze the data with respect to whether or not there was a McGurk effect, which often is simply taken to mean whether the visual information dominated the judgments. This approach is highly misleading, because it is well known after deep investigation that one modality does not dominate the other. Both modalities contribute to the perceptual judgment, with the outcome that the least ambiguous source of information has the most influence. McGurk's original interpretation—that place of articulation was cued by visual information and that manner and voicing were cued by auditory information—is categorically wrong. We have shown again and again that auditory information is important for perceiving place of articulation (Massaro & Cohen, 1983a,

1990). This is true even when the auditory information is paired with relatively unambiguous visible speech.

PHENOMENOLOGY AND CONSCIOUSNESS

Synesthesia

The influence of visible speech on our auditory experience is perhaps an instance of what is known as *synesthesia*. Synesthesia is in some sense a violation of the Müllerian doctrine, because it links one sensory experience with the stimulation of another sensory system. One common synesthetic experience is the inducement of color images by sound (called chromesthesia). Perhaps the most famous person with this syndrome was S, the mnemonist studied intensely by Luria (1968). Hearing an unfamiliar word, S would experience colored splotches, lines, or splashes (Luria, 1968, p. 31). These images would often distract him from the meaning of a spoken sentence. All linkages seem possible, however, and we even have recent documentation of a man who tasted shapes (Cytowic, 1993).

Pattern recognition of bimodal speech qualifies as synesthesia because visible speech influences our auditory experience. Yet we argue that the visible speech itself does not modify auditory processing per se. There seems to be independence between the visible and audible inputs at the level of representation in these two modalities. Their joint influence necessarily occurs at a later stage of processing. Our evidence for this interpretation comes from the repeated success of the FLMP, which assumes independence at the evaluation stage of processing. In addition, Stein and his colleagues provide good arguments for separable modalities for auditory and visual inputs (Stein, 1995).

Qualia

If we dare to, we might use these illusory situations to address issues in the theory of mind. A revived interest among cognitive and other scientists is consciousness, qualia, or experience. As Nagel (1974) argues, how could something physical explain "what it is like" say, to see red. Chalmers (1996) calls this the hard problem: how is our subjective experience caused by the brain? Dennett (1988, 1991), on the other hand, claims that there is nothing there. He either downright denies qualia or at least argues that arguments using qualia cannot be formulated coherently. Although there might be qualitative experience, qualia are nothing more than reactive dispositions. Searle (1990, 1992), in his convincing writings, claims that this subjective feel is every bit as real as any other physical thing. Searle appeals to our direct experience in the same way that Descartes did in his statement "Cogito, ergo sum" (I think, therefore I am). For Searle, it is "I have feelings, therefore, there are feelings." The experience of bimodal speech perception isn't always veridical, however. The auditory experience is influenced by the visible face. For Dennett, the hearing experience—at least as an indicator of an autonomous, distinctly psychological level of processing—is illusory to begin with, so it is not surprising that the hearer could be misled by a talking head. It could be that an automaton without qualia encoded the face along with the voice to infer something about what was said. Because the automaton "knows" that one hears spoken language, it necessarily thinks it heard the message. Searle, on the other hand, could still claim that the feeling is real, although wrong. By the same token, we couldn't weaken the Cartesian thesis by showing that we aren't really thinking but only thinking that we are thinking.

Perceptual Reports

What became of introspection? The common answer is that introspection was not viable so that it gradually became extinct. Another answer, however, is that introspection is still with us doing its business under various aliases, of which verbal report is one.
—Edmund G. Boring

In many respects Boring was correct in that perceptual reports might be criticized as simply being introspection in disguise. This is perhaps a special problem when there is no correct answer that can be defined by the experimenter. However, we can be less ambitious and simply direct our theories at explaining the identification judgments of the observers, while remaining neutral to what extent these identification judgments mirror the perceptual experience of the subject. Our feeling on this matter might also depend on where we stand with respect to qualia, the heart of our perceptual experience. If we are on the side of Searle, then we might be concerned about a slight mismatch between identification judgments and perceptual experience, whereas if Dennett has our ear, then qualia cannot be taken too seriously anyhow, and therefore we must simply concentrate on the identification judgments of the observers.

For most of our research we are satisfied with explaining the subjects' identification judgments as a function of changes in the stimulus conditions of the experiments. Traditionally, the McGurk effect has been studied by asking observers to report what they hear the talker to be saying, even though they must also look at the talker's face. We prefer simply to ask subjects to report what the talker says, because we include both auditory-alone and visual-alone trials. When we do give "auditory" instructions by asking observers to report what they *hear* the talker to be saying, we have to caution them that on some trials there will be only visual information, and therefore on those trials they must make their decision on the basis of the visual information. Given the well-documented limitations of introspective reports, the experimenter has no assurance that people are really reporting just their auditory representation, as opposed to what is available to them at some other juncture in their processing system.

Perceptual reports can be highly misleading, and therefore it is probably safest for the experimenter to concentrate on the actual identification judgments. This behaviorist stance is not unprecedented, but it still might be considered somewhat politically incorrect in view of the cognitive revolution of several decades ago. Even so, the instructions given to the subjects have been a part of our research program, and we are interested in to what extent attention and intentional set can influence subjects' perceptual reports. Experiments of this kind are described in chapter 8. Having laid this groundwork, we now face the challenge of how to think about what type of processing would produce bimodal speech perception. We begin with some general metaphors and then discuss a few extant theories.

METAPHORS FOR PROCESSING AUDIBLE AND VISIBLE SPEECH

Many of us have struggled to develop an appropriate metaphor for audible-visible speech perception. A simple metaphor derives from the use of visible information in speech recognition by machine (Petajan, 1985). The auditory information is the workhorse of the machine, and the visible information is used, mostly post hoc, to decide among the best alternatives determined on the basis of the auditory information. At a psychological level, this model is similar to the idea of auditory dominance, in which the perception is controlled by the auditory input unless it is ambiguous (Massaro, Cohen & Smeele, 1995). An ambiguous auditory input forces the system to use the visible information. This type of heuristic is not unreasonable: we have already seen that the audible speech is much more influential than the visible. Such a model is not new; it has been used in speech recognition by machine (Petajan, 1985) and also bears some similarity to the single-cue solution developed by Gigerenzer and Goldstein (1996) for decision making in more cognitive domains (see chapter 6).

In contrast to these views in which visible speech serves a backup function, other metaphors build on the idea of combination or integration. Somehow the visible and auditory information is combined, integrated, or joined together. The formalization of this operation is hotly debated. The two inputs are said to be fused (McGurk & MacDonald, 1976), morphed, or converged (Mattingly & Studdert-Kennedy, 1991). Fusion and morphing imply some type of blending of the two inputs. Convergence appears to be a metaphor describing how the different brain systems processing inputs from separate modalities converge at another brain area. The separate inputs are somehow combined at this convergence area. The nature of this putative blending and combination thus becomes a focal point for investigation and theorizing. Of course, these metaphors must be refined and quantified to specify the exact manner in which the two different modalities are combined.

In the next section, we assess extant theories of speech perception in the light of bimodal speech perception. The powerful influence that visible speech has been shown to have in face-to-face communication speaks to both traditional and extant theoretical accounts. The influence of several sources of information from several modalities provides a new challenge for theoretical accounts of speech perception. Most theories were developed to account for the perception of unimodal auditory speech, and it is not always obvious how they would account for the positive contribution of visible speech. We will learn that the theories in the field are not sufficiently formalized to be tested by our results, which leads us to the formalization and testing of specific models in the next chapter.

THEORIES OF SPEECH PERCEPTION

Psychoacoustic Accounts

One class of theory seems to be either contradicted by the findings in this chapter, or at least placed outside the domain of bimodal speech perception. Psychoacoustic accounts of speech perception are grounded in the idea that speech is nothing more than a complex auditory signal and that its processing can be understood by the psychophysics of complex sounds, without any reference to language-specific processes. Within this class of theories, the theory of acoustic invariance makes two claims: (1) each phonetic feature contains an invariant acoustic pattern that specifies the value of that feature, and (2) the perceptual system uses this information for speech perception (Blumstein, 1986; Blumstein & Stevens, 1979). The assumptions of this theory stand in sharp contrast to the predominant view that there is no orderly relationship between a perceived phonetic segment and its acoustic properties. According to this view it is unlikely that the acoustic properties of a segment could remain invariant across different speakers, phonetic contexts, and languages (Lindau & Ladefoged, 1986; Massaro, 1987d). A more modest claim is that the functional information is a conglomeration of auditory dimensions that provide a direct relationship between the acoustic signal and the appropriate percept (Diehl & Kluender, 1987, 1989).

Independently of the issue of acoustic invariance, a psychoacoustic account is no longer sufficient because speech perception is not strictly a function of auditory information. In addition to the convincing evidence for the influence of higher-order linguistic context in speech perception (Massaro, 1996c), we have presented overwhelming evidence for the influence of visible speech from a talker's (or even an animated character's) face. Moreover, it turns out that the psychoacoustic account fails even in the arena of auditory speech perception (Massaro, 1987d).

Advocates of the psychoacoustic account have modified their stance accordingly and now acknowledge the influence of visible speech (for example, Diehl & Kluender, 1987). They have not specified, however, how visible speech makes its contribution. It would appear that visible speech would somehow have to be secondary to audible speech, as, for example, in the auditory dominance model developed in the next chapter. For if these theorists propose that visible speech need not be secondary in their framework, then we might ask what is uniquely psychoacoustic about it.

Motor Theory

Two other theories have survived, even thrived on the findings of audible-visible speech perception. Traditionally, the motor theory assumes that listeners analyze the acoustic signal to generate hypotheses about the articulatory gestures that were responsible for it. The perceiver uses the sensory input to determine the set of articulatory gestures that produced the input (Liberman & Mattingly, 1985; Mattingly & Studdert-Kennedy, 1991). The main motivation and support for this theory comes from the observation that phoneme perception is more easily predicted on the basis of articulation than in terms of acoustic cues. Speech scientists learned that there did not appear to be a one-to-one correspondence between a set of acoustic properties and a phonetic segment. On the other hand, the phonetic segment could be more adequately described in terms of articulation. The best-known example is the difference between /di/ and /du/. The onsets of these two syllables have very different acoustic properties but have similar articulatory gestures, involving a constriction of the tongue against the alveolar ridge of the hard palate. The syllables with different vowels differ in their sound even at onset because the consonant and vowel are coarticulated. Thus motor theory appeared to solve the mapping problem from stimulus to percept by viewing articulation as a mediator of representation.

According to motor theory, the inadequate auditory input is assessed in terms of the articulation, and it is only natural that visible speech could contribute to this process. The motor theory is consistent with a contribution of visible speech because visible speech can be considered to be an integral part of the sensory input reflecting the talker's articulatory gestures. The motor theory has not been sufficiently formalized, however, to account for the vast set of empirical findings on the integration of audible and visible speech.

The early motor theory assumed that articulatory invariants existed whereas auditory invariants did not. Recognition occurred via the mapping of the auditory input to articulatory representations. However, research soon revealed that there was also a great deal of variability in peripheral articulatory movements, so the articulatory invariant could not be the commands to the muscles. The revised motor theory has not yet defined what the motor invariants are, but Liberman (1996, p. 31) remains confident that they are "the ultimate constituents of speech, as produced and as perceived."

The motor theory found new life in Fodor's notion of modularity, in which an input system operates in an encapsulated manner. Speech perception is viewed as a module with its own unique set of processes and information. As stated succinctly by Liberman (1996, p. 29), "The phonetic module [is] a distinct system that uses its own kind of signal processing and its own primitives to form a specifically phonetic way of acting and perceiving." To me, this statement implies that not only the information but the information *processing* should be qualitatively different in the speech domain than in other domains of perceptual and cognitive functioning. We will see that this expectation does not hold up to experimental tests. Furthermore, because of its notion of encapsulation, the motor theory has difficulty accounting for the strong effect of higher-order linguistic context in speech perception (see Massaro, 1996c, for a review of this literature). That is, there is nothing in the theory that would allow context to penetrate the assumed "innate vocal tract synthesizer."

Robert-Ribes, Schwartz, and Escudier (1995a) advocate an amodal motor representation to account for the integration of audible and visible speech (see also Robert-Ribes, Piquemal, Schwartz & Escudier, 1996). As we have argued, it is very difficult to determine the representation medium in which integration occurs. We see no reason, however, to postulate a motor representation for integration. Integration occurs in a variety of other domains, such as object recognition, that involve no analogous motor medium. This amodal motor representation account appears to suffer from many of the same problems posed for motor theories of speech perception more generally, such as accounting for the influence of higher-order linguistic context. It might seem reasonable to map auditory and visual speech into a motor representation, but the same cannot be said for linguistic context. Consider the striking perception of *My dad taught me to drive*, from meaningless auditory and visual inputs. It is difficult to see how the sentential constraints would be mapped into a motor medium in the same way as the audible and visible speech. Even if some representation is necessary to account for the joint influence of audible and visible speech, there is no compelling reason why that representation should be a motor one. There is a tradition of criticizing motor theory using evidence of people who perceive speech skillfully but are incapable of producing it (Fourcin, 1989). If indeed there is a parity between speech perception and production, as hypothesized by motor theory, there should be a closer correspondence between perception and production than is observed. Recent findings that weaken motor theory involve Kanzi, a bonobo (pygmy chimpanzee), who understands speech without being able to utter any coherent words of wisdom (Savage-Rumbaugh et al., 1993).

Direct Perception of the Vocal Tract

Although the direct perception theory also places articulatory gestures at center stage in speech perception, it "disagrees in almost every respect with the motor theory" (Fowler, 1996, p. 1731). Contrary to most extant views (e.g., Lindblom, 1996; Remez, 1996), Fowler claims that vocal tract gestures necessarily have invariant properties. These in turn cause specifying properties in the acoustic signal, and it is these properties that enforce direct perception. For Fowler and other neo-Gibsonians, direct perception is *not* mediated by inference or by mental representations (Fowler, 1996). In contrast to the motor theory and consistent with our view, the direct perception theory assumes that speech perception is not special. Thus, although gestures are the objects of speech perception, the speech motor system does not play a role. Furthermore, speech perception is just one of many different perceptual domains in which direct perception occurs. Thus, we would not expect a fundamentally different type of information processing in the speech domain, contrary to the implications of the modularity principles of motor theory.

The direct perception theory states that people perceive directly the causes of sensory input. In spoken language, the cause of an audible-visible speech percept is the vocal tract activity of the talker. Accordingly, it is reasoned that visible speech should influence speech perception because it also reveals the vocal tract activity of the talker. Speech perceivers therefore obtain direct information from integrated perceptual systems based on the flow of stimulation provided by the talker (Best, 1995). The observed influence of visible speech is easily predicted by this theory because visible speech represents another source of stimulation providing direct information about the gestural actions of the talker. However, we know of no convincing evidence for the gesture as the primary object of speech perception (see chapter 11, Processing Novel Sources of Speech Information). For now, it seems most parsimonious to assume that the objects of speech perception are relatively abstract symbols (Nearey, 1992).

On the basis of just this short review of extant theories of speech perception, it is apparent that they are stated in verbal rather than quantitative form. Although no one can deny that a qualitative fact is more informative than a quantitative one, qualitative theories do not appear to be sufficiently precise to be distinguished from one another. Very different theories make very similar predictions. Some quantitative refinement of the theories is usually necessary to create a chance for falsification and strong inference (Platt, 1964; Popper, 1959). Therefore, we attempt to quantify a family of specific models that represent the extant theories and also other reasonable alternatives. But first we give an overview of quantitative or computational modeling in general.

I hope our journey and demonstrations have convinced you that visible speech is an environmental source of information, and that it is a puzzle for psychological inquiry how the audible and visible sources are so naturally coordinated by the perceptual system. In chapter 2 we develop a general framework for pattern recognition to formalize models that can be tested against our observations of the influence of audible and visible speech. That work will lead to the development of a general principle of human behavior that accounts for these results and a variety of others.

2   Speech as Pattern Recognition

I never satisfy myself until I can make a mechanical model of a thing. If I can make a mechanical model I can understand it.
—Lord Kelvin

In chapter 1 we witnessed a powerful influence of visible speech in face-to-face communication. The influence of several sources of information from several modalities provides a new challenge for theoretical accounts of speech perception. It is not always apparent how theories developed to account for the perception of unimodal auditory speech would account for the positive contribution of visible speech. In addition, some extant theories view speech perception as a specialized process and not solely as an instance of pattern recognition. We take a different approach in this chapter by envisioning speech perception as a form of pattern recognition. After describing pattern recognition, we discuss computational modeling to set the stage for the formalization of a variety of quantitative accounts of speech perception by eye and ear.

PATTERN RECOGNITION

We use the term *pattern recognition* to describe what is commonly meant by recognition, identification, and categorization. Although these terms have different meanings, they are all concerned with roughly the same phenomenon. Recognition means re-cognizing something we experienced previously. Identification involves mapping a unique stimulus into a unique response. Categorization means placing several noticeably different stimuli into the same class. For example, a child sees a dog, recognizes it as a dog she has seen before, identifies it as "Fido," and categorizes it as a dog. Recognition, identification, and categorization appear to be central to perceptual and cognitive functioning. All three actions appear to entail the same fundamental processes. All can be characterized as situations in which the subject, given a stimulus, settles on one of a set of alternative interpretations. Pattern recognition has been found to be fundamental in such varied activities as playing chess, examining X rays, and reading text. Our operating assumption is that pattern recognition involves similar operations regardless of the specific nature of the patterns, and is thus equally appropriate for the description of speech perception.

What does pattern recognition accomplish? First, it reduces the complexity of a dynamic environment. As was said so eloquently by the Greek philosopher Heraclitus, no one sets foot in the same river twice. Although the river changes constantly, much about it does not change. Thus, it is appropriate to treat it more or less equivalently at different times. Categorization, in this case, would allow different instances to be treated identically. Second, categorization pigeonholes an event. Although each of us speaks the same word differently, a perceiver can interpret the different tokens as having the same form. Third, categorization facilitates learning by allowing us to transfer our experience from previous encounters with a given category. Fourth, categorization may specify an appropriate action that might not otherwise be carried out. For example, categorizing the intention of a large dog chasing you while you are bicycling determines whether or not some defensive action is necessary. Finally, categorization allows us to order and relate classes of events. Number categories enable us to order and relate a dozen (12) to a baker's dozen (13) irrespective of whether the objects involved are cookies or doughnuts. As these examples illustrate, pattern recognition is meaningful perception, and it is better understood if it is distinguished from sensory perception.

Sense Perception versus Meaningful Perception

Although dictionaries define perception as consciousness or awareness of the elements of the environment through physical sensation, it seems reasonable to make a distinction between two types of perception: sensory experience and meaningful recognition. For Dretske (1995), the early phase of the perceptual process that culminates in sensory experience is called "sense perception." Perception of the category of an object, on the other hand, is defined as meaningful perception. Dretske gives the example of his first encounter with an armadillo. He did not recognize it on the road in front of him, although he saw it clearly. In this way he had a sense perception of the armadillo but not a meaningful perception. After learning about the meaning of his sense perception, he became expert at recognizing armadillos. Thus, the accomplishment of meaningful perception was dependent on some prior experience that linked his sense perception with the knowledge of armadillos, or simply relied on an association between sensory experience and the category term and accompanying knowledge. An important aspect of Dretske's distinction is that the accomplishment of meaningful perception did not modify his sense perception of the armadillo. His experience of seeing the armadillo at the sensory level probably did not change, even though he now could recognize it successfully. Dretske's example is reminiscent of a passage from *Robinson Crusoe* that I have used to make the same point.

When, one morning the day broke, and all unexpectedly before their eyes a ship stood, what was was evident at a glance to Crusoe. But how was it with Friday? As younger and uncivilized, his eyes were presumably better than those of his master. That is, Friday saw the ship really the best of the two; and yet he could hardly be said to see it at all.

It is convenient to equate perception and pattern recognition. Category perception in this case allows the perceiver to impose meaning on the sensory information. Dretske is not the first to make this distinction (for example, Fodor, 1983, and Pylyshyn, 1984, on cognitive penetrability), which goes back at least to Thomas Reid in the eighteenth century. We should emphasize that sensory experience is seldom compromised by a lack of memory, whereas pattern recognition is highly dependent on knowledge stored in memory and as such goes well beyond initial sensory experience.

Although all sensation must in some sense be meaningful (Dennett, 1995), the distinction is useful to clarify a few controversial phenomena concerning pattern recognition. One has to do with the idea of categorical perception, defined as an inability to distinguish among members of the same category. We have argued previously that such categorical perception does not exist, because people have continuous sensory information. That is, their sense experience provides information about the degree to which an instance belongs to a given category—such as, for example, how prototypical it is of the category. Perceivers identify different events as belonging to the same conceptual class even though they notice the differences. We might then say that category perception is categorical (a tautology), but sense perception is not.

Another issue is whether pattern recognition occurs via specialized input systems, which are modular or encapsulated if they are influenced by only a narrow range of bottom-up information. Top-down constraints—for example, phonologic, syntactic, and semantic constraints in sentence processing—do not penetrate the input module in spoken language processing. There is good evidence that top-down information contributes to pattern recognition, but it might be convincingly argued that top-down information influences only category perception, not sense perception (Massaro, 1979b). That category perception, however, might easily be (mis)interpreted by the perceiver as sense perception. It is not obvious how we can interrogate someone to obtain a report of sense perception uncontaminated by category perception.

The final issue for our purposes is whether interactive activation is necessary for pattern recognition. Interactive activation occurs in a connectionist network of neuron-like units at different levels. Sensory or lower-level units feed activation forward to categorical or higher-level units, which in turn feed back and activate the lower-level units. The feedback supposedly drives the lower-level units to settle on discrete categories for recognition. However, there is no convincing evidence that the feedback is *necessary* for meaningful perception (Massaro, 1996c). As we will see, a simple feed-forward model can account for the influence of both bottom-up and top-down sources of information. For our purposes, meaningful perception may be the only data we can obtain from perceptual report, and this form of perception is what we equate with pattern recognition.

Pattern Recognition as Inductive Inference

Pattern recognition has been characterized by three basic claims: (1) pattern recognition is a process of inference; (2) this type of inference is not deductively valid (it is inductive inference); and (3) the inference process tends to be biased (Bennett, Hoffman & Prakash, 1989). Inductive inference means that pattern recognition goes beyond the information given; it cannot be deduced unequivocally. About a century and a half ago, Hermann von Helmholtz established the similar principle of unconscious inference, analogous to conscious logical inference, as a solution to perception, and he stressed how easily it could be fooled. Helmholtz was one of the most influential voices in a chorus of advocates of intelligent perception (Brunswik, 1955; Gregory, 1987; Rock, 1983).

The third claim, although not as familiar to psychologists as the other two, is that some interpretations are preferred relative to others. In visual perception, for example, we have a bias to see two-dimensional projections as three-dimensional scenes. In speech perception, we are biased to perceive the speech input in terms of the segments of our language and to perceive the segments as making up a meaningful utterance. These three claims capture one view of the perceiver's solution to the inverse mapping problem, that is, the problem of how to recover an event on the basis of sensory input. The perceiver's challenge is to determine what environmental situation exists given the current conflux of sensory cues. In speech perception, it is necessary to infer the utterance on the basis of the audible, visible, and other contextual sources of information. We now proceed to describe what processes appear to be necessary to accomplish that outcome.

Stages of Processing

We operate on the premise that language understanding is mediated by a sequence of processing stages. We refer to visual perception, a well-understood domain, to clarify the concept of stages of information processing (Banks and Krajicek, 1991; Wandell, 1995). There is evidence for at least three stages of visual processing: retinal transduction, sensory cues (features), and perceived attributes (DeYoe & Van Essen, 1988). Visual input is transduced by the visual system, a conglomeration of sensory cues is made available, and attributes of the visual world are experienced by the perceiver. Visual perception can be characterized by both a one-to-many and a many-to-one relationship between sensory cues and perceived attributes. As an example of the former, motion provides information about both the perceived shape of an object and its perceived movement. A case of the many-to-one relationship in vision is the way that information about the shape of an object is enriched not only by motion but also by perspective cues, picture cues, binocular disparity, and shading (e.g., chiaroscuro).

This same framework can be applied to speech perception and speech understanding. Speech perception involves transduction along the basilar membrane, sensory cues, and perceived attributes. A single cue can influence several perceived attributes. For example, the duration of a vowel provides information about vowel identity, prosodic attributes such as stress, and the syntactic role of the word in the sentence. Another example of several perceived attributes from a single cue is that the pitch of a speaker's voice is informative about both the identity of the speaker and intonation. There are also cases in which there are multiple cues to a single perceived attribute. The best-known example involves the many cues for the perceived voicing of a medial stop consonant (Cohen, 1979; Lisker, 1978). These include the duration of the preceding vowel, the onset frequency of the fundamental, the voice onset time, and the silent closure interval. An example at center stage in this monograph is the impressive demonstration that both the speech sound and the visible mouth movements of the speaker influence perception of place of articulation of speech segments (chapter 1; see also McGurk & MacDonald, 1976). Speech perception primarily involves the recognition of speech segments; sensory cues (features) and perceived attributes necessarily mediate perception of the segments of the speech input. Using this framework, we now address the issue of how speech segments are perceived.

COMPUTATIONAL MODELING

One of our goals is to understand how we perceive speech by ear and eye. We believe that our understanding grows when we can formulate a computational model of this behavior. What is a computational model? A model is usually considered to be a somewhat more constrained and specific form of a theory. *Computational* indicates a system that makes operations or computations. A computational model, then, is a theory that specifies its assumed operations exactly. Although there is some debate on this point (see Penrose, 1989, 1994), it is difficult to envision a theoretical explanation that would not be a computational one. The most familiar computational system is the computer. A computational model is not necessarily a computer model: a computational model might consist of a set of operations that are described in quantitative form, for example. Science is a precise discipline, and computational models constrain our theorizing to be more precise.

The computational models we develop are to be tested against empirical observations, which provide the final word about that which must be explained. The empirical data must be as detailed as possible, so that a model which predicts the results is more likely to be describing how humans arrive at that outcome. This forces us to develop a model "comprehensive enough" that predictions can actually be made with it. In this endeavor, we often discover that some important component was not specified or that it was not specified sufficiently, and that it is necessary to be more precise to allow some test of the model. Thus, computational modeling usually leads to greater detail and completeness, which in turn allows the model to be more easily tested in a broader range of situations.

Tests of a model either are consistent with its predictions or show them to be lacking. Having a completely specified model will sometimes reveal possible alternative models that differ in some specific way from the original one. This outcome usually leads to important experimental tests of specific assumptions of the model. Computational modeling, therefore, is a process of continual interplay between experimentation and modeling.

Component Processes in Speech Perception

To develop a computational model of pattern recognition and decision making, it is necessary to give an account of the psychological processes that lead from stimulus to response. Given a prototypical pattern recognition task, several psychological processes are necessarily involved. The simplest case would involve just a single feature that cues just a single attribute of the speech segment. This feature would be processed (evaluated) to obtain some perceived attribute, and a decision about the segment would be made. With just a single feature, we might postulate two psychological processes: evaluation and decision. To illustrate, consider a continuum of visible syllables ranging between /ba/ and /da/. The relevant feature might be degree of mouth opening at the onset of the stop consonant, which would provide information about perceived place of articulation. Given this information, some decision must be made to initiate a categorization response.

When multiple features, multiple perceived attributes, or both are present, however, it is necessary to deal with all of them. There are two major possibilities, which we refer to as *nonintegration* and *integration*. In nonintegration, only a single aspect of the input is relevant for decision. In integration, an additional operation combines or integrates the several features or sources of information before a decision is made. Evaluation is defined as the analysis of each source of information by the processing system. It can be thought of as the transformation of the physical value of each source into a psychological value. Integration is defined as a process that combines the representations made available by the evaluation process. Decision converts the outcome of integration into a response.

These three processes that may or may not occur are illustrated in figure 2.1. The processes are shown as overlapping because, although they are necessarily successive, one process could begin before a previous process is finished. Regardless of the type of model, something like each of the processes must be exactly specified in order to make predictions of performance. A theory must take a stand on whether each source of information is evaluated

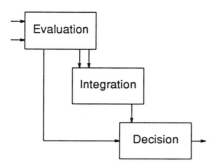

Figure 2.1 Schematic representation of the three processes that might be involved for perceptual recognition when given two or more sources of information. The three processes are shown to proceed left to right in time to illustrate their successive but possibly overlapping processing. The first stage processes the separate sources individually, and the second stage processes the multiple sources. It is also possible that the second stage would not be involved in the processing. The decision operation maps the outputs of this processing into some response alternative.

and whether integration occurs. When evaluation and integration are assumed, the nature of the processes must be specified. It is also necessary to formalize how a decision is made.

Models could be compared and tested more easily if our experiments could provide results that revealed the operations of one process in isolation from the others. If only a single source of information has been presented, it is safe to claim that evaluation has occurred and that there was no need for integration. Even in such a simple case, there are two processes to specify: evaluation of that source of information and decision. Figure 2.1 can also be misleading because it fails to acknowledge the important role of representation, or memory, which we now address.

Representation

The concept of representation plays a central role in psychological inquiry, as it does in other sciences and domains of discourse. As pointed out by Suppes, Pavel, and Falmagne (1994), most fundamental problems can be formulated as problems of representation. For us, the question is how audible and visible speech are represented to support spoken language understanding. We depend on representation at several levels. Each model we test can be considered to be a theoretical representation of the processes involved in perceiving speech. In these terms, the perceiver's mental representation of primitive segments of the spoken language is fundamental. For example, we could not even begin to understand cross-linguistic differences and similarities without acknowledging differences in perceivers' representations of these segments.

Representations in memory are an essential component of pattern recognition. The current stimulus input has to be compared to the pattern recognizer's memory of previous patterns. One type of memory is a set of summary descriptions of the meaningful patterns. These summary descriptions are called prototypes, and they contain an amalgamation of features of the pattern. Prototypes are central to cognition because, as Henry David Thoreau observed, "we hear and apprehend only what we already half know." The features of the prototype correspond to the ideal values that an exemplar should have if it is a member of that category. The exact form of the representation of these properties is not known and may never be known. However, the representation in memory must be compatible with the sensory representation resulting from the transduction of the input. Compatibility is necessary because the two representations must be related to one another. To recognize a speech segment, the perceiver must be able to relate or compare the input information to the prototypes in memory.

Given this general theoretical framework, we consider a variety of models of pattern recognition. The models can be characterized by whether or not integration occurs. Of these two classes, nonintegration is the simpler account of pattern recognition and we begin with these models.

NONINTEGRATION MODELS OF BIMODAL SPEECH PERCEPTION

We make a distinction between integration models and nonintegration models. According to nonintegration models, any perceptual experience results from only a single influence. Thus, the pattern recognition of any multimodal event is determined by only one of the modalities. Even this class of simple models involves a variety of alternatives that are worthy of formulation and empirical test. We will formulate and test such models. The details of the testing procedure are best described within the context of a specific model; that discussion is embedded in the next section on the first model to be considered.

Single Channel Model

Even when there are multiple inputs, it is possible that only one of them is used. This idea is in the tradition of selective attention theories, according to which only a single channel of information can be processed at any one time. The idea is also the antithesis of integration theories, but in the spirit of inquiry we attempt to leave no stone unturned. In addition, several more sophisticated models that we will develop contain, at some level, properties of this single channel model (SCM). So even if the reader is convinced that the SCM is a straw man, it might prove worthwhile to understand it to provide a basis for those other models.

In our bimodal speech situation, the auditory and visual modalities are two channels of information. Figure 2.2 illustrates the processes of the SCM in schematic form. Under the SCM, it is assumed that only one of the two sources of information determines the response on any given trial. The emitted

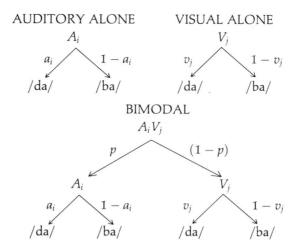

Figure 2.2 Processing trees for SCM for auditory alone, visual alone, and bimodal trials. Given a unimodal stimulus A_i, it is identified as /da/ with probability a_i. Given a bimodal stimulus A_iV_j, the auditory source is selected with probability p, which is identified as /da/ with probability a_i, and so on. The same tree diagram applies to the RACE model (discussed later in this chapter) except that the value of p is a function of the relative ambiguity of the A_i and V_j sources. See text for further explanation.

response is based on one source or the other, but not both. On unimodal trials, it is assumed that the response is determined by the presented modality. A unimodal auditory stimulus A_i will be identified as /da/ with probability a_i, and, analogously, the unimodal visual stimulus V_j will be identified as /da/ with probability v_j. The value i simply indexes the ith level along the auditory continuum, and j indexes the level of the visual input.

In our formulation of the SCM model, we assume that only one of the auditory and visual inputs is functional on bimodal trials. It is assumed that the auditory modality is selected with some bias probability p, and the visual modality with bias $1 - p$. As on unimodal trials, for a given bimodal stimulus the auditory information will be identified as /da/ with probability a_i, and the visual information with probability v_j. Thus, the predicted probability of a /da/ response given the ith level of the auditory stimulus, A_i, and the jth level of the visual stimulus, V_j, is

$$P(/da/|A_i \text{ and } V_j) = (p)(a_i) + (1 - p)v_j \tag{2.1}$$

Equation 2.1 predicts that a /da/ response can come about in two ways: (1) the auditory input is selected and is identified as /da/, or (2) the visual input is selected and is identified as /da/. This formalization of the SCM model assumes a fixed p across all conditions, an a_i value that varies with the auditory information, and a v_j value that varies with the visual information.

One might argue that the value p should be allowed to vary as a function of the stimulus conditions. For example, it seems reasonable that p should be a function of the ambiguity of the information along each modality. An optimal strategy would be to choose the modality that has the least ambiguous information. Determining the ambiguity of each modality, however, requires that both modalities be processed—which goes against the spirit of the model. Although we maintain the constraint of a fixed p in the SCM, the reader will learn about the value of a varying p in the context of the RACE model (see the section "RACE Model" later in this chapter).

We have learned that sometimes very different qualitative models make identical quantitative predictions. Such a quantitative identity holds for the SCM and a model based on the categorical perception of the audible and visible speech dimensions (Massaro & Cohen, 1990; Thompson & Massaro, 1989). In the latter model, both modalities are categorized and the perceiver reports one of them according to a bias. Thus, the categorical model can also be described by equation 2.1 describing the SCM.

We can assess the predictive power of the SCM and other models using the five-by-five expanded factorial design described in chapter 1. The points in figure 2.3 give the proportion of /da/ identifications for a prototypical participant in the task. Figure 2.3 also shows some predictions of the SCM, as represented by equation 2.1. Because the SCM is a very simple theory, it is not surprising that it makes very simple predictions. As can be seen in the figure, equation 2.1 leads to a set of parallel functions with this type of plot.

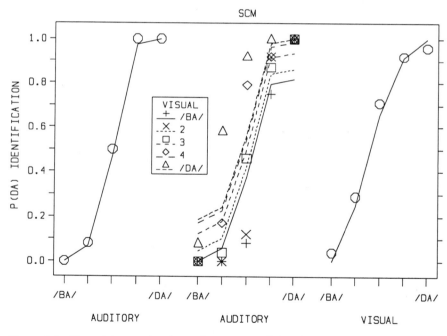

Figure 2.3 The points give the observed proportion of /da/ identifications for a prototypical observer in the auditory-alone (left panel), the factorial auditory-visual (center panel), and the visual-alone (right panel) conditions as a function of the five levels of the synthetic auditory and visual speech varying between /ba/ and /da/. The lines give the predictions of the SCM.

The equation and graph illustrate very nicely how a constant increase in a_i and v_j lead to a constant increase in $P(/da/)$. Before we evaluate empirical tests of the SCM, it is necessary to discuss estimation of the free parameters in a model.

Free Parameters and Their Estimation

We cannot expect a model's predictions of behavior to be exact or even very accurate without first taking into account what results are being predicted. For example, we cannot know exactly how often a given person will identify one of the visible speech syllables as a particular alternative. We saw in chapter 1 that individual participants give similar but not identical results for the same experiment. We can know that one syllable might be more likely to be identified as a /ba/ than another, but we do not know how *much* more likely. This uncertainty would preclude the quantitative test of models if we were not able to determine the values of (estimate) free parameters.

A free parameter in a model is a variable whose values cannot be exactly predicted in advance. The actual performance of the subject is used to set the value of this variable. When applied to empirical data, most computational or quantitative descriptions have a set of free parameters. We do not know what these values are, and we must use the results given by the subject to find them. The process is called parameter estimation.

The idea of free parameters has received a steady stream of bad press. Miller, Galanter, and Pribram (1960, p. 182) remarked that "a good scientist can draw an elephant with three parameters, and with four he can tie a knot in its tail." Although we can grant that too many free parameters elevates a model beyond falsifiability, they are still necessary for accurate prediction. To convince the reader that prediction is not possible without free parameters, we carried out the following exercise. The argument is that we cannot make an a priori prediction of how a given person will categorize a given source of information. To illustrate this, we computed the average probability of a /da/ response, $P(/da/)$, for each subject to each of our test conditions. Consider the third level of the unimodal auditory stimulus, A_3, and the third level of the unimodal visual stimulus, V_3. Figure 2.4 plots $P(/da/)$ for each of our 82 subjects to the unimodal V_3 as a function of $P(/da/)$ to the unimodal A_3. As can be seen in the figure, the response probabilities are distributed across the complete range of possible values for both A_3 and V_3. Given this variability across subjects, we cannot hope to predict a person's judgments without some type of parameter estimation based on their actual results. Figure 2.4 also shows that there is very little correlation between the two modalities. This result replicates in another way the earlier finding of independence between auditory and visual speech recognition tasks (Raney, Dancer & Bradley, 1984). Knowing a person's performance in one modality will not help predict his or her performance in the other modality. The

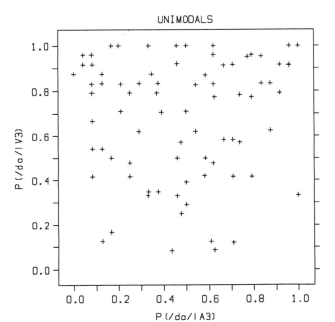

Figure 2.4 The probability of a /da/ response for each of 82 subjects to V_3 as a function of their probability of a /da/ response to A_3.

conclusion from this exercise is that we cannot have a parameter-free model of speech performance. As we will see in chapter 4, even traditional psycho-physical theories require free parameters. Similarly, speech scientists cannot be expected to predict categorization of a speech stimulus, even if all of its physical properties are known. This outcome also is strong evidence for our proposal that average results can be meaningless and that theories should be aimed at individual performance.

Some researchers are uncomfortable with any model whose predictions require free parameters. As a solution for the variability in figure 2.4, they might propose that a subject could be given two independent tests. Parameters could be estimated from the first test and used to predict the results of the second (Dijkstra & de Smedt, 1996). This is not an unreasonable sugges-tion, as long as it is recognized that the parameter estimates will not be as accurate as they would be if estimated from all of the data being predicted. As will be demonstrated in chapter 10, this method of testing a model against new results based on parameter estimates from old results must give a much poorer description of performance than the case in which all of the observa-tions being predicted are used to estimate the free parameters. Those uncomfortable with free parameters might also reconsider physical theories, sometimes used as ideal examples of prediction: Edmund Halley was able to predict the location of his comet more than 100 years later, for example. What is forgotten, however, is that he had a very reliable measure of the

Perceiving Talking Faces

comet's location at a given time in a highly deterministic physical system. The recent study of chaos has left even physical scientists less sanguine about chance and prediction (Casti, 1994; Waldrop, 1992).

In terms of the SCM, we do not know the a_i and v_j values because we cannot state ahead of time how the level along a stimulus continuum is related to the corresponding parameter value. We are predicting categorization as a function of some internal transformation of the stimulus, not of the stimulus directly. However, the SCM makes some strong assumptions that allow it to be quantitatively tested. In the model the probability of identifying the stimulus as /da/ when the auditory input is selected is dependent only on the physical characteristics of that modality, but not on the other modality. Without this *independence* assumption, the SCM would be essentially untestable. If a_i could change with the visible syllable as well as the auditory and v_j could change with the auditory syllable as well as the visible, then there could be unique a_i and v_j values at each of the 35 test conditions. This situation would give 35×2 free parameters for a task with only 35 independent data points to be predicted.

Even with the independence assumption, free parameters are necessary to test the SCM. The model does not predict in advance how often the syllable in each modality will be identified as /ba/ or /da/ (see table 2.1). According to the model, there can be a unique value of a_i for each unique level of audible speech. Similarly, there can be a unique value of v_j for each level of visual speech.

When the SCM is tested, equation 2.1 predicts $P(/da/)$ for each of the 35 conditions in the expanded factorial experiment. The 35 equations have five different values of a_i because audible speech i can vary between 1 and 5, and analogously, there are five values for v_j corresponding to the five levels of visible speech j. We also do not know the value of p on bimodal trials, which requires another free parameter. For unimodal trials, we assume that the presented modality is always used. We have 35 equations with 11 free parameters: the p value, the 5 a_i values, and the 5 v_j values. Finding values for these 11 unknowns allows us to predict the 35 observations. In the SCM, for example, the p, a_i, and v_j values are probabilities and thus must be between 0 and 1.

Because we want to give every model its best shot, our goal in parameter estimation should be to find the values of the parameters that will maximize how accurately the model is able to account for the results. This is called maximizing the goodness of fit of the model. When we compare competing models, each model should be predicting as well as it can to insure the fairness of the test.

Again, we want the values that maximize the fit of the observations, so not just any values will do. The optimal values can be found with a computer using a parameter search algorithm. This estimation procedure tries out a variety of values to find those that minimize the differences between the predicted and observed values. The search is made easier by restricting it to a permissible range of values.

Root Mean Squared Deviation Measure of Goodness of Fit

A factor that is often used to maximize the goodness of fit is the root mean squared deviation (RMSD) between the predicted and observed values. The best fit is that which gives the minimal RMSD. The RMSD is computed by (1) squaring the difference between each predicted and observed value, (2) summing across all conditions, (3) taking the mean, and (4) taking the square root of the mean. (Squaring the differences makes all differences positive and also magnifies large deviations compared to small ones.) The RMSD can be thought of as a standard deviation of the differences between the 35 predicted and observed values. The RMSD will increase as the differences increase. In general, the smaller the RMSD value, the better the fit of the model.

Some readers might wonder why RMSD is used, rather than some more popular statistical test. The most obvious candidate is Pearson's chi-square statistic, which could be used to test whether the observed and predicted results differ. For the use of chi-square to yield meaningful results, a number of assumptions must be met (Frank & Althoen, 1994). One requirement is that every cell should have at least five occurrences. This means that each judgment should be given to each stimulus at least five times. However, for our typical tasks, we seldom meet this requirement. Several of our test stimuli are relatively unambiguous, so that only one response tends to be given. Thus the use of chi-square would be inappropriate.

Another concern is that the differences used in the RMSD do not take into account the absolute values that contribute to those differences. Thus, a 4% difference between predicted and observed values when the observed proportion is 5% is weighted as much as the same 4% difference when the observed proportion is 50%. This concern is justified, but there is no easy solution for the computation of RMSD. We have developed a benchmark RMSD, however, that provides a standard to compare to the observed RMSD (see chapter 10). This benchmark is based on sampling variability, which takes into account the values of the observed proportions in addition to the number of observations per testing condition. When used with a benchmark, the RMSD provides a good index of a model's goodness of fit.

The quantitative predictions of the model are determined by using the program STEPIT (Chandler, 1969). The model is represented to the program in terms of a set of prediction equations and a set of unknown parameters. By iteratively adjusting the parameters of the model, the program minimizes the RMSD. The outcome of the STEPIT program is a set of parameter values that when put into the model, come closest to predicting the observed results. Thus, STEPIT maximizes the accuracy of the description of each model.

Predictive Power

The predictive power of a model is determined by considering how much can be predicted relative to how much must be assumed. We are impressed with the model to the extent that the number of independent data points being predicted exceeds the number of free parameters being estimated. Unfortunately, there is no accepted measure of how well a model describes some set of outcomes relative to the number of free parameters needed to predict those outcomes. For example, if we have two models, one with two free parameters and a second with three free parameters, the model with three parameters will usually do better in matching the results. But this is only because, in a sense, the three-parameter model is less specific and more open-ended in its predictions, and it can be adjusted more easily to any observed set of data. With our benchmark measure of goodness of fit, the observed RMSD of a model can be adjusted for its number of free parameters (see chapter 10). More generally, we are usually satisfied to say that a model is superior when it does better than other contenders and has the same number of or fewer free parameters.

Database and Model Tests

We have determined that a test of the SCM against the results of the expanded factorial design with 35 independent data points requires 11 free parameters. The 11 free parameters were estimated to minimize the RMSD between the observed and predicted results. The results for the present model tests come from the results from 82 participants, with 24 observations from each participant under each of the 35 conditions (Massaro et al., 1993; Massaro, Cohen, & Smeele 1995; see also "Varying the Ambiguity of the Speech Modalities" in chapter 1). The model fit was carried out separately on each subject's results. We have learned that individuals differ from one another and that averaging the results across individuals can be hazardous. The free parameters of a model should be capable of handling the individual differences. Fitting a model to single individuals should permit the model to describe individual subjects accurately while also accounting for between-subject differences, insofar as they can be captured by the differences among the 11 parameters.

Although average results can be misleading, we do not have the space to plot the results and predictions of all 82 participants. Therefore, we plot the results for a single representative subject and report the average RMSD across the 82 individual fits. The observations and predictions of the SCM for this representative subject were given in figure 2.3. The data points in the figures are the observations, and the lines correspond to the model predictions. We use lines for the predictions so one can see the form of those predictions. The distance between the observed points and the predictions gives a graphical measure of goodness of fit.

As can be seen in figure 2.3, the predictions of the SCM do not capture the trends in the data. Figure 2.3 also reveals that the failure of the SCM is systematic. The predictions are a set of parallel lines, whereas the observations resemble an American football—wide in the middle and narrowing at the ends.

The RMSD is used to evaluate the goodness of fit of a model both in absolute terms and in comparison to other models. Of course, the smaller the RMSD, the better the fit of a model. The RMSD for the subject shown in figure 2.3 was .1370. The RMSDs across all 82 subjects averaged .0969. There is no absolute criterion that can be used to evaluate an RMSD value. For this reason, we usually compare the RMSDs of different models. In addition, we have developed a benchmark RMSD that can be used as an absolute standard (see chapter 10). For now, our experience in this arena tells us that this is a poor fit, considering that the SCM is predicting 35 independent data points with 11 free parameters. We will now elaborate on the SCM to see if we can bring its predictions closer into line with the results. We do this with two different formulations: the postperceptual guessing model and the RACE model.

Postperceptual Guessing Model

The postperceptual guessing (PPG) model predicts that visual information has an effect on judgment only when the auditory information is not sufficient for a response. An important property of this model is that either recognition occurs via the auditory information or it does not. When it doesn't, visual information is used to make a judgment. This model appears to represent the view that speech perception occurs via the auditory modality and any visual effects are postperceptual. Our instantiation of the PPG model, illustrated in figure 2.5, assumes that visual speech has a possible influence *only* when the auditory input is not identified. There are two types of trials: the auditory input is identified or not. When auditory identification of the segmental source is successful, the perceiver responds with the appropriate alternative. In the case that no auditory identification is made, the perceiver uses the visual input to identify the test segment.

For bimodal trials, the predicted probability of a /da/ response is thus equal to

$$P(/da/|A_i \text{ and } V_j) = a_{Di} + (1 - a_{Di} - a_{Bi})v_{Dj} \tag{2.2}$$

where a_{Di} is the probability of identifying the auditory source as /da/, a_{Bi} is the probability of identifying the auditory input as /ba/, and v_{Dj} is equal to the probability of identifying the visual input V_j as /da/. The term $(1 - a_{Di} - a_{Bi})$ is the probability of not identifying the auditory source. Equation 2.2 represents the postperceptual theory that either the auditory source is identified or else visual speech is used.

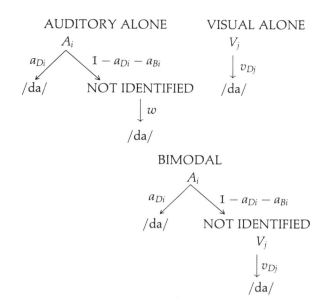

Figure 2.5 Processing trees for PPG for auditory-alone, visual-alone, and bimodal trials. The tree gives the paths to a /da/ response. An analogous diagram can be drawn for a /ba/ response. See text for further explanation.

For the unimodal auditory trials, the predicted probability of a /da/ response is given by

$$P(/\text{da}/|A_i) = a_{Di} + (1 - a_{Di} - a_{Bi})w \tag{2.3}$$

where w is equal to the bias to respond /da/ when the auditory speech is not identified. Given that the task is a two-alternative forced choice, the bias to respond /ba/ is necessarily $1 - w$. Therefore, the predicted probability of a /ba/ response is equal to

$$P(/\text{ba}/|A_i) = a_{Bi} + (1 - a_{Di} - a_{Bi})(1 - w) \tag{2.4}$$

For unimodal visual trials, it is simply assumed that the input is identified as /da/ with probability v_{Dj} and as /ba/ with probability $1 - v_{Dj}$. The model requires a_{Di}, a_{Bi}, w, and v_{Dj} parameters. For the five-by-five expanded factorial design, 16 parameters are necessary: 5 values of a_{Di}, 5 values of a_{Bi}, 5 values of v_{Dj}, and w.

The PPG is a departure from the SCM because the auditory input can be ambiguous (not identified as either /da/ or /ba/) in the PPG. In the SCM, if the auditory input is selected, it is identified as either /da/ or /ba/. In the PPG, the probability that the auditory input is not identified is a function of the auditory level. Thus, the PPG model can make the intuitive prediction that the visual speech is used more often at the intermediate levels along the auditory speech continuum between /ba/ and /da/.

The PPG modification of the SCM does not appear to salvage this type of nonintegration model. Although the PPG gave a significant improvement

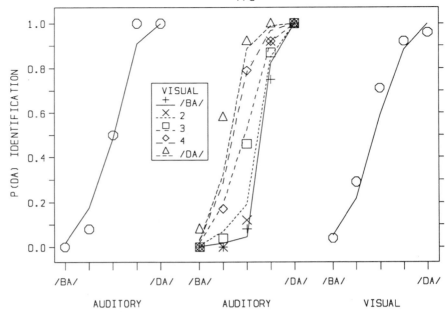

Figure 2.6 The points give the observed proportion of /da/ identifications for a prototypical observer in the auditory-alone (left panel), the factorial auditory-visual (center panel), and the visual-alone (right panel) conditions as a function of the five levels of the synthetic auditory and visual speech varying between /ba/ and /da/. The lines give the predictions of the PPG model.

over the SCM, it required five additional free parameters. Figure 2.6 gives the predictions of the results for our representative subject. The RMSD for this subject was .0713. This RMSD reflected the fits more generally, which averaged .067. Thus, we cannot call it an improvement.

RACE Model

Another way of dealing with multiple inputs is to treat them like horses in a race in which the winner takes all. That is, in a bimodal speech situation, the auditory and visual modalities could be in a race for control of speech perception. The best-known race model, which has been around for decades, is the dual-route model of reading. A written word is recognized either in terms of a spelling-to-speech translation or by a direct lexical lookup. The version that I develop here is an extension of a similar model that I formalized to account for bottom-up and top-down sources of information in language processing (Massaro, 1996c; Massaro & Sanocki, 1993). The present version is mathematically equivalent except that it is applied to auditory and visual sources in bimodal speech perception.

A critical feature of a RACE model is that the activation of a test alternative occurs at a discrete moment in time. In the spirit of a horse race, the

RACE model also must assume that discrete information about the test segment is made available at a discrete point in time. This assumption stands in sharp contrast to the idea that information is made available continuously.

The RACE model is fundamentally the same as the SCM given by equation 2.1 and figure 2.2, but it is claimed that p corresponds to the modality that is recognized first, that is, the winner in the race. Thus, p is *not* constant because the relative speed of the two routes will depend on their relative ambiguity. The value p is expected to decrease to the extent that the auditory source is ambiguous and the visual is unambiguous. Thus, it is necessary to index the value p by the subscripts ij that specify the auditory-visual combination on a given trial. Incorporating this assumption into equation 2.1 gives

$$P(/\text{da}/|A_i \text{ and } V_j) = (p_{ij})(a_i) + (1 - p_{ij})v_j. \tag{2.5}$$

Equation 2.5 shows that the probability that the auditory information controls the judgment depends on both the auditory and visual levels of the stimulus. The price paid for this assumption is a larger number of free parameters. This formulation of the RACE model requires 25 p_{ij} values for the 25 combinations of the auditory and visual information in the five-by-five expanded factorial design. These 25 parameters plus the 5 a_i and 5 v_j values make exactly 35 free parameters to predict 35 data points. Any test of such a model would be meaningless. Therefore, to provide a reasonable test of the model, it is necessary to reduce the number of free parameters. One possibility is to express p_{ij} in terms of the a_i and v_j values. Recall that p_{ij} represents the probability that the judgment is controlled by the auditory input. The value p_{ij} should be large to the extent that the auditory input is unambiguous and visual input is ambiguous. That is, p_{ij} should be large to the extent that a_i is near 0 or 1 and v_j is near 0.5. One reasonable formalization of this requirement is

$$p_{ij} = 2|a_i - 0.5| \times [1 - 2|v_j - 0.5|] \tag{2.6}$$

where $|x|$ means the absolute value of x.

Figure 2.7 gives the value of p_{ij} as a function of a_i and v_j. If a_i is small or large and v_j is near 0.5, then both terms in the equation will be near 1 and thus p_{ij} will be near 1. In this case, equation 2.5 predicts that the judgment will be controlled primarily by the auditory modality. If a_i is near 0.5 and v_j is small or large, then the first term would be near 0 and p_{ij} would approach 0. In this case, equation 2.5 predicts that the judgment will be controlled primarily by the visual input. This formalization requires no additional free parameters beyond the 5 a_i and 5 v_j values: a total of 10 free parameters are used to predict 35 data points.

Figure 2.8 presents the observed and predicted results of the RACE model for our representative subject. The fit was .0725, somewhat better than the average RMSD of .074 across all 82 subjects. Thus the RACE model comes close to the predictions of the PPG model without requiring the six additional

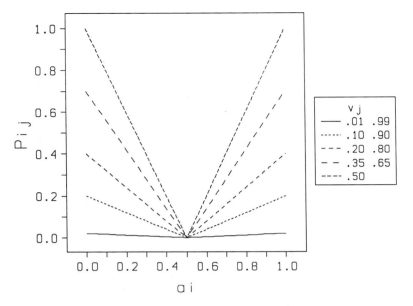

Figure 2.7 The value of p_{ij} as a function of a_i and v_j, according to equation 2.6.

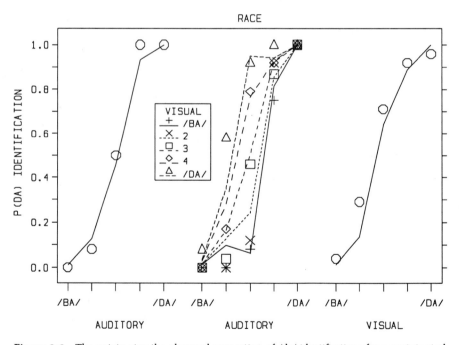

Figure 2.8 The points give the observed proportion of /da/ identifications for a prototypical observer in the auditory-alone (left panel), the factorial auditory-visual (center panel), and the visual-alone (right panel) conditions as a function of the five levels of the synthetic auditory and visual speech varying between /ba/ and /da/. The lines give the predictions of the RACE model.

parameters assumed by the PPG. At this point RACE is the best model, but a variety of other horses remain in the race.

Auditory Dominance Model

A fourth potential explanation of the influence of visible speech is that an effect of visible speech occurs only when the auditory speech is not completely intelligible (Sekiyama & Tohkura, 1991, 1993; Vroomen, 1992). Given the reasonable observation that speech perception is primarily auditory (Studdert-Kennedy, 1989), it would be only natural to conclude that visible speech plays a secondary role, influencing perception only when the auditory information is not intelligible. The hypothesis that auditory intelligibility determines whether or not visible speech will have an effect is difficult to test, primarily because intelligibility is not easily defined and incorporated in a model. Perfect identification in an auditory test might not mean perfect intelligibility. Given these limitations upon the measurement of intelligibility, we operationalize it by indexing correct identification of the auditory speech. This allows us to formulate one version of the intelligibility hypothesis, called the auditory dominance model (ADM).

The central assumption of the ADM is that the influence of visible speech given a bimodal stimulus is solely a function of whether or not the auditory speech is identified. We might expect this model to be similar if not identical to the PPG model, in which visible speech also played a backup role. In both models, either the auditory stimulus is identified or the visual information is used. In our formulation, however, the ADM is somewhat more general than the PPG, because it allows for a greater number of relevant response alternatives than just /ba/ and /da/.

It should be noted that the assumption of all-or-none auditory identification in the ADM is not inconsistent with intelligibility being a continuous measure. Intelligibility is determined from a set of identification trials. Even though identification is all-or-none on any given trial, the proportion of identifications over a set of trials would give a continuous measure of intelligibility.

Consider first an auditory-alone trial, as shown in the top left of figure 2.9. The probability of a response can be considered to arise from two types of response outcomes given a speech stimulus: the auditory speech is identified as one of the response alternatives r or is not identified. When the subject identifies the auditory stimulus as a given alternative r, he or she responds with that alternative. When no identification is made, the subject responds with a given alternative with some bias probability w_r. Therefore, the predicted probability of a response on auditory-alone trials is equal to

$$P(r|A) = a_r + \left(1 - \sum_r a_r\right) w_r \tag{2.7}$$

where a_r is the probability of the subject's identifying the auditory source as

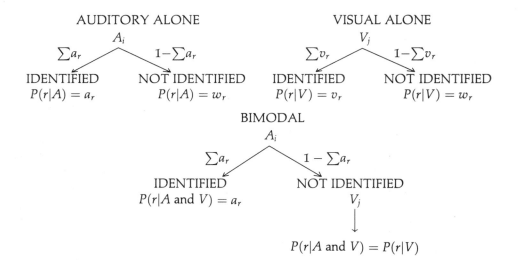

Figure 2.9 Processing trees for ADM for auditory-alone, visual-alone, and bimodal trials. See text for explanation.

response r. The term $\sum_r a_r$ is the sum across all a_r, which is the probability that the auditory source is identified as any of the response alternatives. Finally, the term $(1 - \sum_r a_r)$ is the probability that the auditory source is not identified.

The upper right panel of figure 2.9 gives the situation for visual-alone trials. This situation is analogous to the unimodal auditory one because the visual speech is identified as one of the response alternatives r or is not identified. When the subject identifies the visual stimulus as a given alternative r, he or she responds with that alternative. In the case that no identification is made, the subject responds with a given alternative with the bias probability w_r. Therefore, the predicted probability of a response on visual-alone trials is equal to

$$P(r|V) = v_r + \left(1 - \sum_r v_r\right) w_r \tag{2.8}$$

where v_r is the probability of the subject's identifying the visual source as response r, $\sum_r v_r$ is the probability that the visual source is identified as any of the response alternatives, and the term $(1 - \sum_r v_r)$ is the probability that the subject does not identify the visual source.

Finally, we consider the bimodal case, shown in the bottom panel of figure 2.9. For these trials the auditory speech is or is not identified as one of the response alternatives r. When the subject identifies the auditory stimulus as a given alternative r, he or she responds with that alternative. In the case that no identification is made, the subject responds according to the visual information, as described in the upper right panel of figure 2.9 for visual recognition. Therefore, the predicted probability of a response on bimodal trials is equal

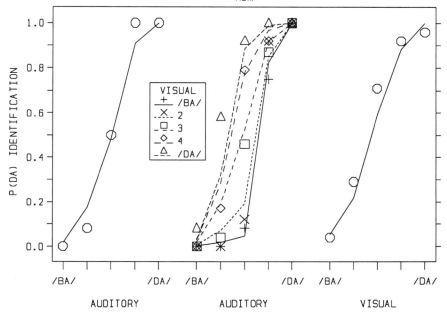

Figure 2.10 The points give the observed proportion of /da/ identifications for a prototypical observer in the auditory-alone (left panel), the factorial auditory-visual (center panel), and the visual-alone (right panel) conditions as a function of the five levels of the synthetic auditory and visual speech varying between /ba/ and /da/. The lines give the predictions of the ADM.

to

$$P(r|A \text{ and } V) = a_r + \left(1 - \sum_r a_r\right)\left[v_r + \left(1 - \sum_r v_r\right)w_r\right]. \tag{2.9}$$

Equation 2.9 represents the theory that either the auditory stimulus is identified or the subject bases his or her decision on the visual information. The visible speech has an influence only when the auditory speech is not identified as one of the alternatives in the task. The model requires a free parameter for a_r, v_r, and w_r for each response alternative. Given that the task requires participants to choose between /da/ and /ba/ test alternatives, free parameters are necessary for a_{Di}, a_{Bi}, v_{Dj}, and v_{Bj} for each of the five levels of a_i and v_j. Finally, a single parameter is necessary for w_D, for a total of 21 free parameters.

If perceivers use visible speech only when the auditory speech is not identified, then this model should give a good description of the results. It has the potential of accounting for the use of visual speech even though there is no integration of the two sources. Figure 2.10 gives the predictions of the ADM along with the observations for our prototypical subject. The fit of the ADM turned out to be mathematically equivalent to the fit of the PPG model. These two models make equivalent predictions for the five-by-five expanded factorial design with two response alternatives. For other tasks, the models could make differing predictions.

INTEGRATION MODELS OF BIMODAL SPEECH PERCEPTION

The models we have developed to this point can be classified as nonintegration models: they hold that for any perceptual experience there is only a single influence. We now consider integration models, which assume that the perceptual experience is influenced by both auditory and visible speech, that is, that both modalities contribute to pattern recognition. Both the audible and visible speech are evaluated and somehow must be used together—we call this process integration. The goal of recognition is to determine the overall goodness of match of each prototype with the stimulus as perceived through both modalities. In all of the models, the evaluation of each source occurs independently of the other source. The two outputs of evaluation are fed forward to the integration stage. The outcome of feature integration is a measure of how well each prototype matches the stimulus. The third operation, decision, must select a response given the outcome of integration. The exact operation of the integration stage is of central concern in our evaluation of this class of models. We begin with the simplest type of integration model.

Additive Model of Perception (AMP)

Additive models have been proposed and tested to explain perception and pattern recognition in several domains (Cutting et al., 1992; Massaro, 1988b; Massaro & Cohen, 1993a). In the additive model of perception (AMP), it is assumed that the sources of information are simply added together at the integration stage.

Each source of information is evaluated to determine how much support it provides for each alternative. The support for /da/ from the auditory stimulus at level i (A_i) can be represented by a_i, and support for /da/ from the visual stimulus at level j (V_j) can similarly be represented by v_j. (It should be noted that a_i and v_j now have different meanings than they did in the nonintegration models, such as the SCM. We prefer to use the same symbols because their notation clearly represents their role in the model of the experiment. The reader should simply interpret them in terms of the appropriate model.) This information is fed forward to the integration stage, where the two sources are added to give the overall support for /da/, $S(/da/|A_i$ and $V_j)$. For generality, it can also be assumed that one modality of information has more influence than another. To implement this assumption, the influence given each modality is represented by a weight parameter. Thus, the overall support given alternative /da/ can be expressed as

$$S(/da/|A_i \text{ and } V_j) = w_1 a_i + w_2 v_j \qquad (2.10)$$

where i and j index the levels of the auditory and visual modalities, respec-

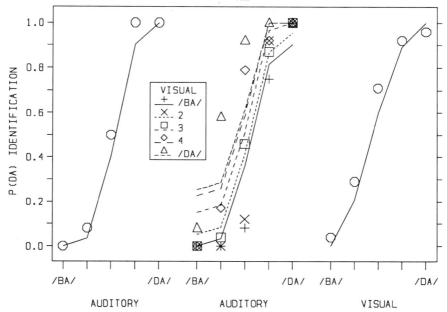

Figure 2.11 The points give the observed proportion of /da/ identifications for a prototypical observer in the auditory-alone (left panel), the factorial auditory-visual (center panel), and the visual-alone (right panel) conditions as a function of the five levels of the synthetic auditory and visual speech varying between /ba/ and /da/. The lines give the predictions of the AMP.

tively. The values w_1 and w_2 correspond to the emphasis or weight given the two sources of information.

The outcome of additive integration must be fed to the decision stage. The simplest decision rule is to equate the probability of a /da/ decision to the overall support for /da/, $P(/da/) = S(/da/|A_i \text{ and } V_j)$. More explicitly,

$$P(/da/|A_i \text{ and } V_j) = w_1 a_i + w_2 v_j. \tag{2.11}$$

Because the support for /da/ given by equation 2.10 can sometimes be greater than 1, it is also necessary to assume that $P(/da/)$ will be simply 1 whenever $S(/da/) > 1$.

The AMP requires 5 free parameters for the a_i values for the auditory source, 5 for the v_j values for the visual source, and 2 for w_1 and w_2. Figure 2.11 gives the predictions of the AMP applied to our prototypical subject. The RMSD for this fit with 12 free parameters was .132. The average RMSD across the 82 subjects was .091.

Averaging Model

A second integration rule that can be applied where there are two sources of information is a simple weighted averaging. If the goal is a weighted average of the support coming from the two sources of information, then the support given by equation 2.10 can be divided by $(w_1 + w_2)$ to give

$$S(/da/|A_i \text{ and } V_j) = \frac{w_1 a_i + w_2 v_j}{w_1 + w_2}. \tag{2.12}$$

Equation 2.12 can be rewritten with one fewer free parameter by defining w as $w_1/(w_1 + w_2)$. In this case, equation 2.12 reduces to

$$S(/da/|A_i \text{ and } V_j) = (w)(a_i) + (1 - w)v_j \tag{2.13}$$

where w now corresponds to the weight given the auditory source. If the same decision rule is used as for the additive model, then $P(/da/) = S(/da/)$. No additional assumption is needed because $S(/da/)$ will always lie between 0 and 1.

Another way the additive model can be transformed into an averaging model (AVM) is by changing the decision rule. The support value given by equation 2.10 can be mapped into the probability of a /da/ response by dividing by the weight values. In this case, we end up with the prediction that

$$P(/da/|A_i \text{ and } V_j) = \frac{w_1 a_i + w_2 v_j}{w_1 + w_2}. \tag{2.14}$$

The AVM has five free parameters for the a_i values for the auditory source, five for the v_j values for the visual, and one for w. Figure 2.12 dis-

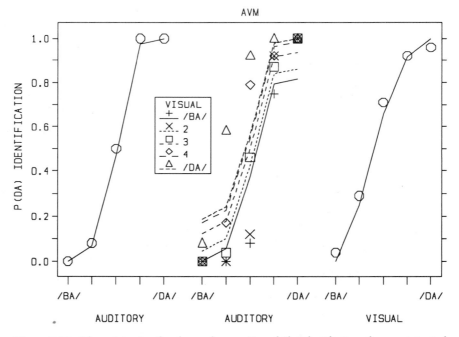

Figure 2.12 The points give the observed proportion of /da/ identifications for a prototypical observer in the auditory-alone (left panel), the factorial auditory-visual (center panel), and the visual-alone (right panel) conditions as a function of the five levels of the synthetic auditory and visual speech varying between /ba/ and /da/. The lines give the predictions of the AVM.

plays the predictions of this AVM for our representative subject, which gave an RMSD of .137. The average RMSD across all 82 subjects was .091.

It turns out that this averaging model is mathematically equivalent to the single channel model given by equation 2.1. The SCM, AMP, and AVM gave very similar descriptions that miss an important feature of the results—the American football shape.

The AVM is actually a *weighted* averaging model in that one modality can have a larger overall influence than another. In such a case, it is the modality that determines the overall influence. It is also possible to formulate a weighted AVM in which the weight is a function of the ambiguity of a source of information (Anderson, 1996). Thus we might expect that the contribution of a source of information would be inversely related to its ambiguity and positively related to the ambiguity of the other source of information. The reader might remember that this assumption was central to the RACE model (see equation 2.5 and figure 2.7). If the same quantification of relative ambiguity is made for this type of weighted AVM, then it is mathematically equivalent to the RACE model. So we can also reject this type of averaging model. We now turn to another form of integration that predicts exactly the American football shape of the observed results.

Fuzzy Logical Model of Perception (FLMP)

A central assumption of the fuzzy logical model of perception is that well-learned patterns are recognized in accordance with a general algorithm, regardless of the modality or the particular nature of the patterns (Massaro, 1987f). The reader should be forewarned that the FLMP is our favorite model because it has received support in a wide variety of domains. Like the general model outlined in figure 2.1, the FLMP consists of three operations: feature evaluation, feature integration, and decision. Continuously valued features are evaluated and integrated, and an identification decision is made on the basis of the relative goodness of match of the stimulus information with the relevant prototype descriptions. Figure 2.13 illustrates the three stages involved in pattern recognition according to the FLMP.

Central to the FLMP are summary descriptions of the perceptual units of the language. These summary descriptions are called *prototypes*, and they contain a conjunction of various properties called *features*. Soon after birth, if not while in utero, infants quickly acquire knowledge about the prototypical segments of their language. This knowledge can be thought of as a set of features that characterize each segment. Speech perception is greatly determined by this knowledge. Iverson and Kuhl (1995), for example, found that infants develop prototypical segments in the language but monkeys do not. Furthermore, consistent with our cross-linguistic findings with adults (see chapter 5), infants with different native languages have different prototypes. A prototype is a category, and the features of the prototype correspond to

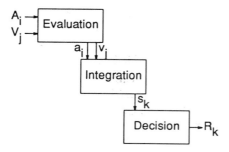

Figure 2.13 Schematic representation of the three processes involved in perceptual recognition. The three processes are shown to proceed left to right in time to illustrate their necessarily successive but overlapping processing. These processes make use of prototypes stored in long-term memory. The sources of information are represented by uppercase letters. Auditory information is represented by A_i and visual information by V_j. The evaluation process transforms these sources of information into psychological values (indicated by lowercase letters a_i and v_j). These sources are then integrated to give an overall degree of support, s_k, for each speech alternative k. The decision operation maps the outputs of integration into some response alternative, R_k. The response can take the form of a discrete decision or a rating of the degree to which the alternative is likely.

the ideal values that an exemplar should have if it is a member of that category. The exact form of the representation of these properties is not known and may never be known. However, the memory representation must be compatible with the sensory representation resulting from the transduction of the audible and visible speech. Compatibility is necessary because the two representations must be compared to one another. To recognize the syllable /ba/, the perceiver must be able to compare the information provided by the syllable itself to some memory of the category /ba/.

Prototypes are generated for the task at hand. In speech perception, for example, we might envision activation of all prototypes corresponding to the perceptual units of the language being spoken. For ease of exposition, consider a speech signal representing a single perceptual unit, such as the syllable /ba/. The sensory systems transduce the physical event and make available various sources of information called features. During the first operation in the model, the features are evaluated in terms of the prototypes in memory. For each feature and for each prototype, featural evaluation provides information about the degree to which the feature in the speech signal matches the featural value of the prototype.

Given the necessarily large variety of features, it is necessary to have a common metric representing the degree of match of each feature. The syllable /ba/, for example, might have visible featural information related to the closing of the lips and audible information corresponding to the second and third formant transitions. These two features must share a common metric if they are eventually going to be related to one another. That is, audible speech cannot be integrated with visible speech if the features are not represented in common terms. To serve this purpose, fuzzy truth values (Zadeh,

1965) are used because they provide a natural representation of the degree of match (Massaro, 1986). Fuzzy truth values lie between 0 and 1, corresponding to a proposition's being completely false and completely true. The value .5 corresponds to something completely ambiguous, whereas .7 indicates more true than false, and so on. Fuzzy truth values, therefore, not only can represent continuous rather than just categorical information, they also can represent different kinds of information, such as audible and visible speech.

It should be noted that fuzzy truth values are not probabilities, although both lie between 0 and 1. To say that a penguin is a bird to degree .85 is not the same as saying that the probability that a penguin is a bird is .85. The former represents some measure of the degree to which the concept *penguin* matches the concept *bird*, whereas the latter gives the probability that any given penguin exactly matches the concept *bird*. Thus, equivalent numerical values can correspond to different psychological representations. Although the FLMP might be mathematically equivalent to Bayes' theorem (Massaro & Friedman, 1990; see also chapter 4), the two formalizations are not equivalent psychological models.

Feature evaluation provides the degree to which each feature in the syllable matches the corresponding feature in each prototype in memory. The goal, of course, is to determine the overall goodness of match of each prototype with the syllable. All of the features contribute to this process, and the second operation of the model is called feature integration. That is, the features (actually the degrees of matches) corresponding to each prototype are combined (or conjoined, in logical terms). The outcome of feature integration consists of the degree to which each prototype matches the syllable.

The third operation during recognition processing is decision. During the decision stage, the merit of each relevant prototype is evaluated relative to the sum of the merits of the other relevant prototypes. This decision operation is modeled after Luce's (1959) choice rule, called a relative goodness rule (RGR) by Massaro and Friedman (1990). In pandemonium-like terms (Selfridge, 1959), we might say that it is not how loud some demon is shouting but rather the relative loudness of that demon in the crowd of relevant demons. This relative goodness of match gives the proportion of times the syllable is identified as an instance of the prototype. The relative goodness of match can also be mapped into a rating judgment indicating the degree to which the syllable matches the category. An important prediction of the model is that one feature has its greatest effect when a second feature is at its most ambiguous level. Thus, the most informative feature has the greatest impact on the judgment.

Prototypes are central to the description given by the FLMP. Defining the onsets of the second (F2) and third (F3) formants as the important auditory features and the degree of opening of the lips at the onset of the syllable as the important visual feature, the prototype for /da/ would be

/da/:   Slightly falling F2-F3 and Open lips.

The prototype for /ba/ would be defined in an analogous fashion,

/ba/: Rising F2-F3 and Closed lips.

Given a prototype's independent specifications for the auditory and visual sources, the value of one source cannot change the value of the other source. The integration of the features defining each prototype is performed by taking the product of the feature values. If a_i represents the degree to which the auditory stimulus A_i supports the alternative /da/, that is, has Slightly falling F2-F3; and v_j represents the degree to which the visual stimulus V_j supports the alternative /da/, that is, has Open lips, then the outcome of prototype matching for /da/ would be given by the product of a_i and v_j.

$$s(/\text{da}/) = a_i v_j \tag{2.15}$$

where $s(/\text{da}/)$ is the overall degree of support, s_k, for $k = /\text{da}/$. With just two alternatives, /da/ and /ba/, we can make the simplifying assumption that the degree to which the audible speech supports the alternative /ba/ is $1 - a_i$. Thus, the support for the alternative /ba/ would be

$$s(/\text{ba}/) = (1 - a_i)(1 - v_j). \tag{2.16}$$

The third operation that is necessary before a behavioral judgment is made is decision, which follows a relative goodness rule (RGR). According to the RGR, the probability of a particular categorization is assumed to be equal to the relative goodness of match. The RGR is related to Luce's (1959) choice axiom and to Shepard's (1957) view of generalization. In Luce's choice axiom, the choice objects are represented by scale values (analogous to the discriminal processes of case V of Thurstone, 1927). The choice axiom holds if and only if (1) the RGR holds, (2) the scale value representing an object does not change with changes in the response alternatives used in the choice task, and (3) the response alternatives defined as irrelevant do not enter into the RGR. Implementing the RGR in the FLMP, it is predicted that the probability of a /da/ response given A_i and V_j is equal to the total support for /da/ divided by the sum of the support for all relevant alternatives, in this case $s(/\text{da}/)$ and $s(/\text{ba}/)$:

$$
\begin{aligned}
P(/\text{da}/|A_i V_j) &= \frac{s(/\text{da}/)}{s(/\text{da}/) + s(/\text{ba}/)} \\
&= \frac{a_i v_j}{[a_i v_j + (1 - a_i)(1 - v_j)]}.
\end{aligned}
\tag{2.17}
$$

The fit of the FLMP is based on the estimation of 10 free parameters corresponding to the 5 a_i and 5 v_j values required by equation 2.17. Figure 2.14 gives the predictions of the FLMP to our representative subject. The fit of the FLMP to our representative subject was .040, whereas the fit averaged .051 across the 82 separate fits.

As can be seen in table 2.1, which summarizes the fits of all the models, the FLMP gives the best fit with the fewest free parameters. This conclusion

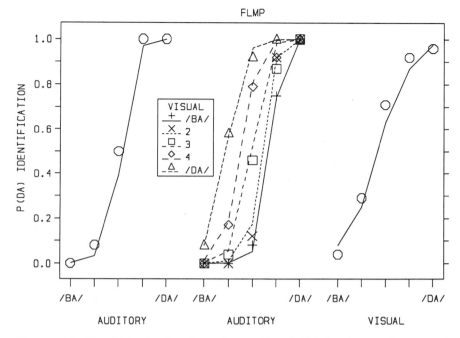

Figure 2.14 The points give the observed proportion of /da/ identifications for a typical observer in the auditory-alone (left panel), the factorial auditory-visual (center panel), and the visual-alone (right panel) conditions as a function of the five levels of the synthetic auditory and visual speech varying between /ba/ and /da/. The lines give the predictions of the FLMP.

Table 2.1 The RMSDs and numbers of free parameters (FP) for the fit of the nonintegration and integration models to the results of the five-by-five expanded factorial design in the /ba/-/da/ identification task

Model	FP	AVE RMSD	TYP RMSD
Nonintegration Models			
Single Channel Model (SCM)	11	.097	.137
Postperceptual Guessing (PPG)	16	.067	.071
Race Model (RACE)	10	.074	.064
Auditory Dominance Model (ADM)	21	.067	.071
Integration Models			
Additive Model (AMP)	12	.091	.132
Averaging Model (AVM)	11	.097	.137
Fuzzy Logical Model (FLMP)	10	.051	.040

The AVE RMSD is the average of the fit of the model over the 82 subjects, while TYP RMSD indicates the RMSD of the prototypical subject plotted in figures 2.3, 2.6, 2.8, 2.10, 2.11, 2.12, and 2.14.

is confirmed by statistical tests on the individual RMSD values. The FLMP also gives a good account of the experiment with four alternatives discussed in chapter 1. The lines in figures 1.4, 1.6, and 1.7 give the FLMP predictions. We will assess in chapter 10 how well the FLMP does in an absolute sense. Before closing this chapter, we describe a recent model that is very similar to the FLMP.

Prelabeling Model

More recently, Braida (1991) developed a prelabeling model (PRLM), in which information from multiple sources is integrated prior to labeling. In the taxonomy of Massaro and Friedman (1990) and Cohen and Massaro (1992), the PRLM is a multidimensional version of the theory of signal detectability (TSD). A presentation of a stimulus in a given modality locates that stimulus in a multidimensional space. Given that the process is noisy (Gaussian), the actual location may be displaced from the stimulus center. There is also a *response center* (prototype) in the multidimensional space. The multidimensional space for a bimodal presentation is simply the combination of the spaces for the two unimodal presentations. For example, if the auditory and visual sources are each represented in two-dimensional space, the bimodal information is represented in four-dimensional space. In all cases, the subject chooses the response alternative whose response center (or prototype) is closest to the location of the stimulus in the multidimensional space.

As shown by Massaro and Friedman (1990) and by Cohen and Massaro (1992), the PRLM bears a great deal of similarity to the FLMP. The PRLM model (called in those studies the TSD-N model) makes predictions almost identical to those of the FLMP. If we assume logistic rather than normal distributions in the binary response case, its predictions are identical to the FLMP. The models do make somewhat different predictions for the cases in which there are more than two response alternatives. When the FLMP and the PRLM have been directly compared in such cases, the FLMP has shown a significant advantage (Cohen & Massaro, 1995; Massaro & Cohen, 1993a; Massaro & Cohen, 1995c; Massaro, Cohen & Gesi, 1993). Because the PRLM requires computer simulation and Monte Carlo estimation, it is also the case that the PRLM is much more difficult and time-consuming to fit than the FLMP. For these reasons, our model of choice is the parsimonious form of the FLMP. Finally, we consider a popular model of speech perception that has been offered as an appropriate account of bimodal speech perception.

TRACE Model

We have considered several ways that a system could integrate auditory and visual speech. In all of the integration models, however, the two sources of information were treated as independent of one another at the initial evaluation stage. A contrasting candidate that has been considered is the TRACE model of speech perception (McClelland & Elman, 1986). Both Campbell (1988) and Vroomen (1992) have proposed that this model can account for the McGurk effect. TRACE is an interactive activation model in which information processing occurs through excitatory and inhibitory interactions among a large number of simple processing units. Three levels or sizes of units are used in TRACE: feature, phoneme, and word. Features activate phonemes, which activate words, and activation of some units at a particular level inhibits other units at the same level. In addition, activation of higher-order units activates their lower-order units; for example, activation of the /b/ phoneme would activate the features that are consistent with that phoneme.

A simple addition to TRACE is to include visual features as well as auditory ones, as assumed by Campbell (1988) and Vroomen (1992). That elaboration is consistent with the general scheme of integration models in which there is separate feature evaluation of the audible and visible sources of information. The important difference is that the integration models we have considered are feed-forward models whereas TRACE involves feedback. Activation of the phoneme level would in turn activate the feature level. Featural information in one modality would be sufficient to activate features in the other modality. Although this is a major difference between TRACE and the FLMP, a stochastic version of the model has been demonstrated to make predictions equivalent to those of the FLMP. Thus, our standard expanded factorial design cannot distinguish between the two models. More elaborate experimental tasks and manipulations are necessary to distinguish between the models (Massaro, 1989c; 1992b, 1996c; Massaro & Cohen, 1991). We describe some relevant tests in chapter 9.

Sine-Wave Speech and Convergence Theory

Remez, Rubin, and their colleagues (Remez, et al., 1994) use the perception of sine-wave speech to argue for a view of speech perception very similar to our own. To create sine-wave speech, these authors translate speech into a time-varying set of sinusoids (pure tones) that replace the formants (peaks of periodic energy concentration) of the original speech. When subjects are told simply to listen to it, they interpret the sine-wave speech as concurrently changing tones, modern music, electronic sounds, or even the tweeting of birds. When told that it is speech, however, the surprising result is that participants asked to listen to a sentence could understand it correctly. These linguistic impressions, however, do not replace or override the experience of hearing concurrently changing tones. This result is exactly analogous to our results on speech by ear and eye. Subjects naturally integrate auditory and visual information to arrive at some phonetic interpretation of what the speaker said, but they are also able to discriminate the nature of the information from the separate modalities. The integration does not replace the individual modality-specific representations. Similarly, in sine-wave speech, subjects are able to integrate the auditory information with linguistic constraints that limit the possible number of recognition alternatives; yet they input the two sources of information independently.

Although the authors tend to overinterpret their results as evidence against traditional approaches to speech perception, we see the results as simply consistent with the view that perceivers use multiple sources of information. Sine-wave speech can be thought of as providing a relatively coarse source of bottom-up information that can be combined with the top-down sources determining a well-structured sentence. Given the ambiguity of sine-wave speech, the information is naturally supplemented by phonological, semantic, syntactic, and pragmatic constraints in a speech comprehension task. Also, the sentences that are understandable in sine-wave speech must have most of their segments rich in periodic energy. Frication segments would be replaced with silence and would therefore be completely uninformative in the sine-wave format. Examples that are easily understood include *My TV has a twelve-inch screen* and *My dog Bingo ran around the wall*. Sine-wave speech can be viewed as analogous to a modification of written language in which just the outlines of the words' shapes are presented.

The theoretical framework proposed by Remez et al. (1994) is very similar to ours. For them the objects of perception are phonetic. We agree, but would replace *phonetic* with *linguistic* so as not to limit ourselves to a particular type of object or to preclude higher-order recognition at the word or sentence level without recognition at the phonetic level. People might easily perceive a word without being aware of the phonetic segments that make it up. Remez and colleagues also argue that there is an unlimited set of cues that can be used to perceive a message. These cues have no prior grouping relationship to one another: the meaningfulness of the input binds them together. In their view, neither the Gestalt laws of organization nor a schema-based grouping (Bregman, 1990) can account for the perceptual grouping of the cues. This accords with our view that features are selected for the recognition task at hand and are not fixed a priori.

The major difference between the view of Remez et al. and our view concerns the role of prototypes or standards in memory. In their framework, the appropriate sensory convergence takes place without reference to prototypes or standards in memory. In chapter 5 we will learn that speech perception is critically dependent on linguistic experience. Our native language guides our perceptual interpretation of linguistic input. The same speech signal has very different consequences for speakers of different languages. It is difficult to comprehend how that could be the case if memory did not play a central role in spoken language processing.

We were interested in the degree to which sine-wave speech would be integrated with the visible speech of a talking head. Therefore, Baldi was programmed to articulate the utterance as it was played in sine-wave form. Band 2.1 gives a few examples of sine-wave speech with and without Baldi's accompanying face. As can be observed in the demonstration, visible speech can contribute to the perception of sine-wave speech as it contributes to the perception of normal speech.

SPEECH THEORIES REVISITED

We closed chapter 1 with a review of several leading theories of speech perception. We can now ask how these theories stack up against the empirical findings and the good fit of the FLMP. Motor theorists are happy with the joint influence of audible and visible speech, and, in fact, the abundance of cues supporting speech perception has been interpreted as support for the articulatory gesture as the category or distal object of perception (Liberman & Mattingly, 1985). These authors note what many investigators have called "trading relations": variations in one cue can be compensated for by variations in another cue. Thus, for the voicing of a consonant in syllable initial position, a small change in voice onset time can be compensated for by a corresponding change in the fundamental frequency at the onset of voicing. In our framework, these trading relations are simply the *outcome* of the evaluation and integration of multiple sources of information. In the speech-is-special framework, however, this outcome is interpreted to mean that no cue could be assigned a characteristic setting (Liberman & Mattingly, 1985, p. 9). The justification for this conclusion is simply that trading relations would not be possible if the gesture did not define the speech category. However, we know that logically the speech category could be defined independently of the gesture. As evidence, we can point to so-called trading relations in other domains in which gestures cannot play a role (see chapters 4 and 6–8). As one reads more closely, and to some extent between the lines, it seems that even motor theorists are forced to assume a "front end" that accomplishes exactly what the FLMP does. That is, the conglomeration of cues must still be evaluated and integrated if it is to inform the perceiver about the gesture category. We believe that the same is true within the theory of direct perception. It is now incumbent on these gesture theorists to state how this process would differ from the universal principle of the FLMP. Until they do so, we see no reason to grant gesture a necessary role in speech perception.

At this point, the reader deserves both congratulations for persistence and apologies for the plethora of models and theories we have presented. One clear message did emerge, however: that an integration model is superior to nonintegration models. The consistently good fit of the FLMP makes viable the possibility that it might capture something universal about pattern recognition. In the next chapter, we confront a question about the temporal window of integration and how the two modalities of speech are treated when they do not occur together in that window.

3 Perceptual Events and Time

Time, initially, is no more intrinsic to our mind than it is to an hourglass.
—J. A. Michon and J. L. Jackson (eds.), *Time, Mind, and Behavior*

Time is defined so that motion looks simple.
—John Archibald Wheeler, *Gravitation*

Time is what prevents everything from happening at once.
—John Archibald Wheeler

When as a child I laughed and wept;
    Time crept.
When as a youth I waxed more bold;
    Time strolled.
When I became a full-grown man,
    Time RAN.
The older still I daily grew,
    Time FLEW.
Soon I shall find, in passing on,
    Time gone.
O Christ! wilt Thou haft save me then?
    Amen.
—Henry Twells, *Time's Paces*

We have witnessed repeatedly that multiple sources of information are available to the perceiver, who evaluates and integrates them to recognize a pattern. We have seen that the fuzzy logical model of perception (FLMP) describes pattern recognition in terms of three operations: feature evaluation, feature integration, and decision (see figure 2.13). After the stimulus is transduced to a featural representation, the continuously valued features are evaluated against prototype descriptions in memory, integrated, and an identification decision is made on the basis of the relative goodness of match of the stimulus information with the relevant prototype descriptions. Obviously, we cannot integrate every feature, nor would it be fruitful to do so. The concern of the present chapter is, What gets integrated and what doesn't?

THE BOUNDARIES OF INTEGRATION

Although it might be called a circular argument, it can reasonably be said that we integrate only those sources of information that specify or are related to a psychologically meaningful event. However, integration sometimes appears to occur even when it seems unreasonable to integrate. For example, integration occurs when there is a sex or location mismatch between the face and the voice (Green et al., 1991; Fisher, 1991). The mismatched face and voice must yield an integrated percept when they are producing the same message at the same time. Would asynchrony of the input from the face and that from the voice work against integration? How sensitive are we to temporal asynchronies?

An abundance of data appears to provide conflicting messages about our sensitivity to asynchrony between audible and visible speech. On the one hand, subjects are fairly good at detecting asynchronies when their task is aimed at detection (Dixon & Spitz, 1980). Furthermore, detection is better when the auditory speech leads the visual rather than the reverse. On the other hand, integration of the two sources of information seems relatively robust across relatively long differences in stimulus onset time (Massaro & Cohen, 1993a). Thus, the processing system is somewhat flexible in terms of how it deals with the temporal relations between multiple inputs.

Meaningful Objects

Central to our model of pattern recognition is the notion of a meaningful object or event. In order to integrate multiple sources of information as specified by the FLMP, it is necessary to relate them to the same event. Given a spoken syllable, perceivers quite naturally relate its auditory and visual consequences to the same event. The significant psychological event appears to be the syllable as a whole rather than its auditory and visual components. The perceiver integrates the sources of information made available by the event to achieve the best interpretation possible. This form of integration is a powerful phenomenon that occurs in a variety of domains (see Massaro, 1987c, 1991b, 1992a). Following the research strategy formulated by Greenwald and colleagues (1986), however, it is worthwhile to identify some limiting conditions for integration and to provide some boundary conditions on the phenomenon. According to their research strategy, finding situations in which integration does *not* occur should be as informative, if not more informative, than finding situations in which integration occurs. Boundary conditions also allow us to determine which environmental situations function as psychological events. If participants are asked to combine information from two different psychological events, the outcome might differ from that found when they integrate two sources of information from the same event.

Presentation of two successive auditory syllables separated by at least half a second of silence should be perceived as two different events. Two syllables separated by this period of silence are not usually articulated to convey the same message, but in fact should have two referents in natural discourse. (One possible exception might be a three-year-old child repeatedly exclaiming "more" or some other request.) In normal speech, a long silent period would mean, for example, that the two syllables are not likely to be part of the same word. Even so, the first syllable might provide some information about the second syllable and vice versa because both coarticulatory information and semantic and syntactic constraints might be present with successive syllables. By inserting a half-second of silence between nonsense syllables, however, we create separate, unrelated perceptual events. It is hypothesized that perceivers will be biased to interpret the two syllables independently of one another. This scenario contrasts sharply with how perceivers normally process the auditory and visual consequences of the same spoken syllable.

It should be noted that psychological events are probably hierarchical. Although two successive syllables might function as two separate events at the syllable level, they might also be integrated to form a single psychological event at a higher level such as in a word or a phrase. If /ba-ba/, /ba-da/, /da-ba/, and /da-da/ were four words, for example, we might expect the two syllables to be integrated in the manner described by the FLMP. In the present example, however, there is no meaningful word or phrase level, and we expect the two syllables to be treated as two separate events.

Participants given two successive syllables should not integrate them as they would two independent sources specifying the same syllable. If the results do not follow the predictions of the FLMP, what form might we expect the results to take? When participants do not integrate the two sources of information, they might base their judgment on the first syllable on some trials and on the second syllable on other trials. If this single channel algorithm is used, the results should follow the predictions of the single channel model developed in chapter 2. Even if the two asynchronous sources are integrated, they might be added or averaged or put together in some way other than that specified by the algorithm of the FLMP.

Previous Research Varying Synchrony

Manipulating the synchronization between the auditory and visual channels should provide information about the interval during which the auditory and visual speech sources can be integrated. Koenig (1965) carried out an early study of auditory-visual delay (see Pandey, Kunov & Abel, 1986). A single subject was tested with low-pass-filtered speech consisting of isolated words and sentences. Speech understanding was not disrupted until the delay exceeded 240 ms. McGrath and Summerfield (1985) assessed participants' accuracy at identifying key words in sentences in which the sound track was replaced by rectangular pulses corresponding to the closing of the talker's vocal folds. The sound track improved performance relative to the silent speechreading condition. However, a delay of the sound track by 80 ms disrupted performance relative to the no-delay condition, and a 160 ms delay eliminated the advantage completely.

Pandey, Kunov, and Abel (1986) presented audiovisual sentences using audio delays of up to 300 ms. They also degraded the auditory signal by mixing it with a multitalker babble. Although the results were somewhat variable, they found that accuracy in the audiovisual conditions at all delay values was significantly better than scores with either vision alone or audition alone. However, delays greater than 120 ms interfered with performance accuracy relative to the synchronous condition. Reisberg, McLean, and Goldfield (1987) had participants repeat back (shadow) a difficult philosophical passage taken from Kant. The percentage of words correctly shadowed was somewhat larger when the full face of the speaker was in view than when only sound was available. The advantage of having visible speech disappeared when the audible and visible speech were offset by about 0.5 seconds.

Campbell and Dodd (1980) presented subjects with consonant-vowel-consonant (CVC) words with visible speech preceding auditory speech by 400, 800, and 1,600 ms. Although phoneme identification was somewhat worse in these asynchronous bimodal conditions than in the synchronous condition, it was found that identification was invariably better in the asynchronous bimodal conditions than in the auditory-alone condition. In one of our studies, delays of up to 200 ms did not seem to disrupt identification of the CV syllables /ba/ and /da/ and the vowels /i/ and /u/ (Massaro & Cohen, 1993a). Munhall and coworkers (1996) found an influence of visible speech even when the audible speech lagged the visual by 180 ms.

Massaro and Cohen (1993a) looked for differences in the integration process with changes in stimulus onset asynchrony (SOA). A visual /ba/ or /da/ was combined with an auditory /ba/ or /da/ with an SOA of −200, −100, 0, 100, or 200 ms. The SOA in a bimodal syllable is defined as the difference between the onsets of the auditory and visual syllables. Participants were instructed to watch the talker and listen to what was spoken and to identify what was *heard*. Response buttons were labeled with eight alternatives (*ba, da, va, ða, ga, bda, dba,* and *other*). Band 3.1 on the CD-ROM gives a demonstration of sample trials from this experiment. Integration appears to occur at all of these SOAs. In the case of visual /ba/ and audible /da/, the reader may experience that the perception of a consonant cluster /bda/ is more likely when the visual /ba/ is presented some time before the audible /da/. This experience mirrors the experimental results. Figure 3.1 gives the probability of each response as a function of SOA. When the visual and auditory syllables were identical, the responses were mostly accurate (top curves in the lower left two plots). When visual /ba/ was combined with auditory /da/, the predominant responses were /bda/ (52%) and /da/ (31%) (curves with Xs in the two lower middle plots). The likelihood of a /bda/ judgment increased to

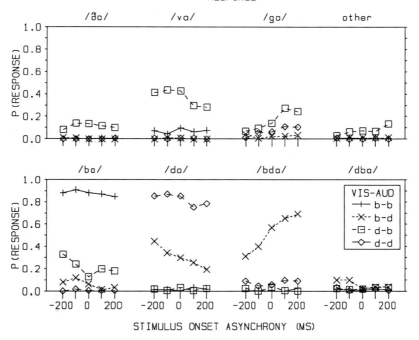

RESPONSE

Figure 3.1 Probability of each of eight possible responses (indicated at the top of each of the sets of plots) as a function of the SOA between the visible and audible syllables. The four possible combinations of the visual and auditory syllables is the curve parameter. For example, the b-d point (see key in lower panel) at −200 ms means that visual /ba/ occurred 200 ms after auditory /da/ (after Massaro & Cohen, 1993a).

the extent that the visual syllable preceded the auditory. The /bda/ responses increased from 31% to 69% as the SOA went from −200 to 200 ms.

Perceiving Two Consonants

We define a cluster judgment as one involving the report of two consonants as opposed to just one. Why do we perceive a visual /ba/ paired with an auditory /da/ as a consonant cluster /bda/? The answer could reveal something fundamental about pattern recognition. We envision pattern recognition as a process that yields the interpretation most compatible with *all* the relevant information. No source of information is ignored, but rather all sources are combined to arrive at a decision. The best interpretation is one that is reasonably compatible with all sources of information. A visual /bda/ is highly similar to a visual /ba/ articulation because both are initiated with closed lips and move to an open mouth. An auditory /bda/ would also be compatible with an auditory /da/ because the CV transition for /ba/ would be immediately followed by the transition for /da/. Thus, the alternative /bda/ is compatible with a visual /ba/ paired with an auditory /da/. On the other hand, the response alternatives /ba/ and /da/ would not be strongly supported because the visual /ba/ would conflict with the /da/ alternative and the auditory /da/ would conflict with the /ba/ alternative. It follows that a combination of visual /ba/ and auditory /da/ can lead to a /bda/ percept.

Another possible reason for cluster responses is that the information from visible /ba/ is available sooner than the information from audible /da/. Reaction times to unimodal syllables are somewhat shorter to visible /ba/ than to audible /ba/ (Massaro, 1987f, p. 160). It appears that some informative facial movement can be used for identification before actual release of the labial stop consonant. This temporal difference in processing the auditory and visual modalities might contribute to the perception of consonant clusters. Supporting this hypothesis is the experimental finding that the temporal difference between the two modalities can modulate the likelihood of a consonant cluster percept. The curve given by Xs for the /bda/ response condition in the lower middle right plot of figure 3.1 shows that the proportion of /bda/ judgments increased systematically as the delay increased between visual /ba/ and auditory /da/.

The curve given by □s in the lower right plot of figure 3.1 also shows that /dba/ judgments virtually never occurred when visual /da/ preceded auditory /ba/ by 100 or 200 ms. Because /dba/ responses rarely occurred in this condition, consonant clusters do not occur simply because of differences in arrival times of the two information sources during perceptual processing. Rather, clusters are perceived primarily when the information in both the visual and auditory syllables is consistent with the articulation of a consonant cluster. Judgments of /dba/ tend not to occur because a visual /da/ is highly dissimilar to a /dba/ articulation. However, differences in arrival time can modulate the degree to which clusters are perceived. Thus, both compatibility and arrival time influence cluster percepts. These results are consistent with the general premise that pattern recognition is influenced by multiple sources of information. Although informative, the findings of this research have not defined exactly the time window of integration. This is the goal of our new studies.

THE WINDOW OF INTEGRATION

The natural tendency to integrate audible and visible speech should be inhibited when these sources are sufficiently displaced in time to signify two different events. Although we do not believe that there will be an invariant SOA beyond which integration will break down, it should be valuable to examine how integration is modulated by SOA. The studies we just reviewed do not establish boundaries for the SOA at which integration breaks down. The major reason is that previous researchers did not design the experiments or use the results to test extant models of bimodal speech perception. We show that the issue of the integration window is more directly addressed when the empirical research is combined with model testing.

The Value of Model Tests

Integration is one of the central assumptions of the FLMP, so a good fit of this model to the results more or less signifies that integration has occurred (Massaro, 1987f). A good fit of the FLMP would imply integration, whereas we would expect a poorer description of performance by the model if integration did not occur. Integration might break down with SOAs greater than some minimal duration; it follows that the FLMP should give a poor description at SOAs larger than that value.

In our framework, we expect integration across asynchronies as long as the two inputs are perceived as belonging to the same perceptual event. At large asynchronies, different perceptual events should be perceived and the integration predicted by the FLMP should not occur, therefore the model should necessarily give a poor description of the results.

One versus Two Perceptual Events

Of course, we predict that the FLMP provides the best description of bimodal speech perception. The goal of the study we describe first was to test the hypothesis that the FLMP will no longer give the best description of performance if the SOA is sufficiently large to create two perceptual events. Thus, we are using tests of the FLMP to indicate when integration does and does not occur. In terms of our discussion of meaningful objects, it is predicted that the FLMP should give a good description when a single perceptual event is perceived, and possibly a poorer description when two perceptual events are experienced. To illustrate, band 3.2 varies the SOA to give the impression of either one or two perceptual events.

Method In two of our unpublished experiments, an expanded five-by-five factorial design was used to test the FLMP and alternative models. Five levels of audible speech varying between /ba/ and /da/ were crossed with five levels of visible speech varying between the same alternatives. The audible and visible speech were also presented alone, giving a total of $25 + 5 + 5 = 35$ independent stimulus conditions. In the first experiment, with 9 participants, the presentation of the auditory synthetic speech was synchronized with the visible speech for the bimodal stimulus presentations. In the second experiment, with 16 observers, two asynchronous conditions were used: the auditory syllable either led the visual by an SOA of 800 ms or lagged the visual by the same SOA. Half of the participants performed under the auditory-lead condition in the first session and the auditory-lag condition in the second session. For the other half of the participants the order of the sessions was reversed.

For the auditory-lead condition, the participants were instructed as follows:

On some trials, you will be presented with a sequence of two syllables. The first syllable will be auditory in the form of a speech sound, and the second syllable will be visual in the form of lip movements of the speaker. The two syllables might be the same, might appear to be different by a little, or might appear to be different by a lot. Your task is simply to decide whether (the single response) /ba/ or /da/ is the best description of the two syllables. Think of the two syllables as having two observations to help you make your decision. Simply make the best choice you can based on your perception of both syllables. . . . On some other trials, you will be presented with a single syllable, either visual or auditory. In this case your task is to identify the single syllable as /ba/ or /da/.

The instructions were the same for the auditory-lag condition, except that the observers were told that the visible speech would occur first.

All of the test stimuli were recorded on videotape for presentation during the experiment. Six unique test blocks were recorded with the 35 test items presented in each block. Each of the 35 possible stimuli was presented a total of 12 times during two sessions, and the participants made a /ba/ or /da/ judgment on each trial.

Results The proportion of /da/ responses, $P(/da/)$, was computed for each participant for each of the 35 conditions. Three separate analyses were carried out, for the auditory, visual, and auditory-visual conditions. The points in figure 3.2 show the average results for the synchronous experiment. We did not have the luxury of a pilot study to devise a good visual continuum, and the three most /da/-like syllables had very similar effects. This result makes the experiment somewhat less sensitive, but it should be informative nonetheless. As in our many other studies, there were large main effects of the audible and visible speech and a significant interaction between the auditory and visual levels. Figure 3.2 shows that one variable had larger effects at the more ambiguous levels of the other variable; that is, the spread among the visual levels is larger in the middle of the auditory continuum than at the extremes. Thus we might expect the FLMP to be more successful than other models at describing these data.

Figure 3.3 gives the corresponding results for the asynchronous experiment. In contrast to our prototypical findings, there were main effects of the two modalities but no significant interaction between them. Given these additive results, we do not expect the FLMP to give a better fit than some competing models such as the SCM or AVM.

Comparing figures 3.2 and 3.3 we see a significantly smaller effect of the visible speech in the asynchronous than in the synchronous condition. The spread among the curves in figure 3.2 is much greater than the spread in figure 3.3. It would not be surprising that the judgments were primarily influenced by the auditory modality in the asynchronous condition if no integration occurred. As we saw in chapter 1, the auditory influence is normally larger than the visual influence. In the case in which the sources are

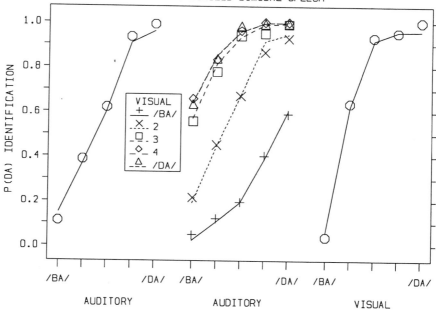

Figure 3.2 Observed (points) and predicted (lines) proportion of /da/ identifications as a function of the auditory and visual levels of the speech event for the synchronous visual-auditory condition. The left panel gives the auditory-alone condition, the right panel gives the visual-alone condition, and the center panel gives the bimodal condition. The predictions are given by the FLMP.

separated in time, we might expect the perceiver to respond on the basis of just the auditory information. Audition is the modality of speech that is most familiar and informative, and without integration the perceiver is free to use that source exclusively.

Model Tests   In our introduction to this experiment, we hypothesized that the FLMP would give the best description of the synchronous condition whereas the SCM might do better (or at least as well) for the asynchronous condition. The models were tested against the results using the formulations and logic described in chapter 2. Ten free parameters (5 a_i and 5 v_j) were needed for the FLMP, and 11 parameters (5 a_i and 5 v_j plus p) were needed for the SCM. For the synchronous experiment, the average RMSD across the nine participants was .0612 for the FLMP versus .1243 for the SCM. An analysis of variance, carried out on the RMSD values for the fits of the two models, showed that the FLMP gave a significantly better fit than the SCM.

The results of the asynchronous condition were also fit by the same two models. The mean RMSD for the FLMP was .0840, versus .0796 for the SCM. In contrast to the synchronous condition, the FLMP provided a somewhat poorer fit to the asynchronous results. The lines in figures 3.2 and 3.3

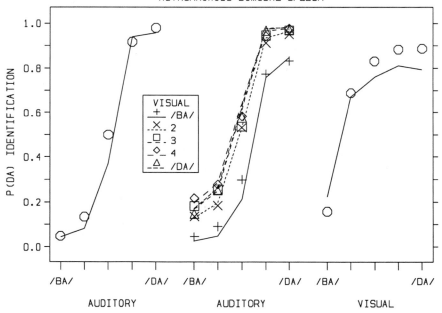

Figure 3.3 Observed (points) and predicted (lines) proportion of /da/ identifications as a function of the auditory and visual levels of the speech event for the asynchronous visual-auditory conditions. The left panel gives the auditory-alone condition, the right panel gives the visual-alone condition, and the center panel gives the bimodal condition. The predictions are given by the FLMP.

illustrate the predictions for the FLMP. As can be seen in the figures, the FLMP gave a better description of the synchronous than the asynchronous condition. Particularly noticeable was its poor description of the visual-alone condition in the asynchronous condition.

Figures 3.4 and 3.5 give the results from a typical observer in each of the two conditions. As can be seen in these figures, the conclusions reached from the group results hold up for individual subjects. Thus, our experiments were successful in showing that the natural tendency to integrate multiple sources of information can be disrupted when the sources of information are separated in time sufficiently to signify two separate events.

Quantifying the Temporal Period of Integration

In the previous section, we studied simultaneous inputs or inputs separated by 800 ms. Of course, the territory in between should be explored. How close together in time must the syllables occur for integration to take place? To quantify the temporal window of integration, we recently carried out several experiments systematically varying the relative time of occurrence of audible and visible CV syllables (Massaro, Cohen & Smeele, 1996).

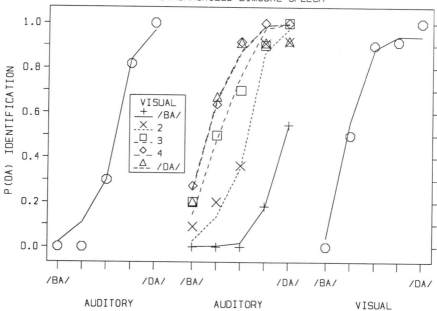

Figure 3.4 Observed (points) and predicted (lines) proportion of /da/ identifications as a function of the auditory and visual levels of the speech event for the synchronous visual-auditory condition. The left panel gives the auditory-alone condition, the right panel gives the visual-alone condition, and the center panel gives the bimodal condition. Results for a typical subject. The predictions are given by the FLMP.

Method The participants were 28 native speakers of American English. The expanded factorial design with the four alternatives /ba/, /va/, /ða/, and /da/ was used, as described in chapter 1. Audiovisual stimuli were created by combining the auditory speech of the four syllables with the visual speech of each of those syllables. The asynchronous conditions were created by offsetting the auditory and visual syllables by the specified duration relative to their normal co-occurrence at the simultaneous condition.

In each of two experiments, the auditory and visual syllables were presented at seven SOAs. Given that the range of asynchrony used in the first experiment did not have much effect on identification performance, the experiment was replicated with new participants using more extreme SOAs. The visible syllable onset is defined as the reference point, and the SOA as the difference between this reference point and the time of occurrence of the auditory onset. In the short SOA experiment, the SOAs were −267 ms, −167 ms, and −67 ms when audition preceded vision; 0 ms when the syllables were synchronous; and 67 ms, 167 ms, and 267 ms when vision preceded audition. Band 3.3 gives sample trials from the short SOA experiment. In the long SOA experiment, the SOAs were −533 ms, −267 ms, −133 ms, 0 ms, 133 ms, 267 ms, and 533 ms. Band 3.4 gives sample trials from the long

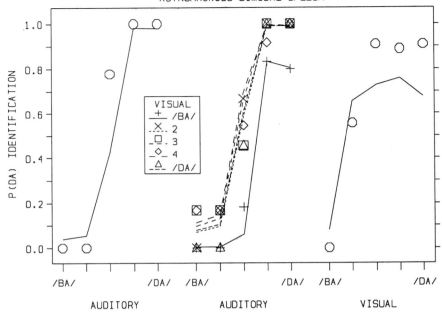

Figure 3.5 Observed (points) and predicted (lines) proportion of /da/ identifications as a function of the auditory and visual levels of the speech event for the asynchronous visual-auditory conditions. The left panel gives the auditory-alone condition, the right panel gives the visual-alone condition, and the center panel gives the bimodal condition. Results for a typical subject. The predictions are given by the FLMP.

SOA experiment. For the unimodal auditory condition the video monitor was blank during the trial, and during the unimodal visual condition there was no sound.

Subjects were instructed to listen to and watch the talker on the video monitor, and to identify the consonant presented as either /b/, /v/, /ð/, or /d/, or as a combination of two of those alternatives (a consonant cluster).

Results: Short SOAs   The results were analyzed as a function of accuracy with respect to each of the two modalities, as was done in chapter 1. Figure 3.6 presents accuracy of performance scored with respect to the visual (left panel) and auditory (right panel) speech stimuli. The seven levels of desynchronization are plotted on the x-axis of each panel.

The solid straight line in both the left and right plots shows performance on the unimodal trials. Performance averaged about 90% correct for both unimodal conditions. As expected from the results in chapter 1, performance under the synchronous condition was most accurate when the subject was given two sources of consistent information. The new result is that consistent information improved accuracy across all SOAs. Thus, the advantage of two sources of information over just one is replicated and is shown to be robust at asynchronies up to 250 ms.

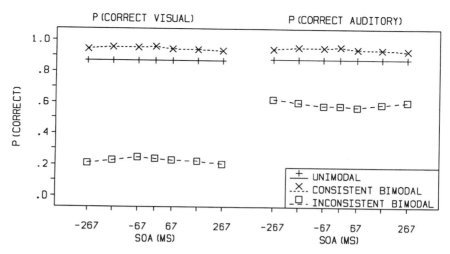

Figure 3.6 Probability correct visual (left panel) and auditory (right panel) responses as a function of stimulus onset asynchrony (SOA) for unimodal, consistent, and inconsistent trials. The unimodal results are necessarily a straight line because SOA is meaningless for those conditions. The consistent condition is necessarily identical in the two panels because it represents the same results. Negative SOAs indicate that the auditory speech occurred before the visual speech, whereas the visual speech preceded the auditory for the positive SOAs.

Both panels in figure 3.6 show that inconsistent information disrupted performance accuracy. Comparing the left and right panels shows that this interference was also more or less independent of SOA. Figure 3.6 also shows that inconsistent auditory information decreased visual accuracy much more than inconsistent visual information decreased auditory accuracy. This result was roughly the same order of magnitude across all SOAs. These results replicate the results described in chapter 1, while showing that integration appears to be robust across differences in arrival time of roughly 250 ms. Of course, these accuracy data could be camouflaging some systematic effect of SOA, and we will provide a more fine-grained analysis after we present the same type of results for the long SOAs.

Results: Long SOAs   The analysis of this experiment was similar to that done for the short SOA experiment. Figure 3.7 presents the results in the same format used in figure 3.6. Performance on the unimodal syllables was somewhat poorer with long SOAs, averaging about 75% correct. For bimodal syllables, unlike the short SOAs, longer SOAs had a substantial effect on the accuracy of identification performance. Accuracy on consistent trials decreased significantly as SOA became very positive or very negative. In other words, consistent information improved accuracy over the unimodal condition, but only at the shorter SOAs. Consistent information did not help at the 533 ms SOA.

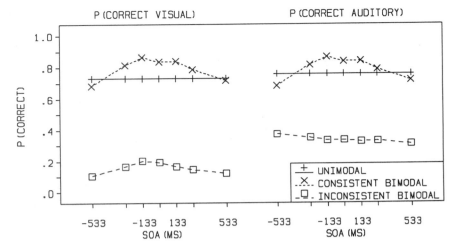

Figure 3.7 Probability correct visual (left panel) and auditory (right panel) responses as a function of stimulus onset asynchrony (SOA) for unimodal, consistent, and inconsistent trials. The unimodal results are necessarily a straight line because SOA is meaningless for those conditions. The consistent condition is necessarily identical in the two panels because it represents the same results. Negative SOAs indicate that the auditory speech occurred before the visual speech, whereas the visual speech preceded the auditory for the positive SOAs.

Inconsistent information disrupted performance accuracy, and inconsistent auditory information decreased visual accuracy more than inconsistent visual information decreased auditory accuracy. Performance on inconsistent trials was roughly the same order of magnitude across all SOAs, with a slight improvement in visual accuracy at short SOAs. One should ask why SOA had no effect on inconsistent trials. Inconsistent information from the two modalities is necessarily disruptive at short SOAs. At longer SOAs, however, it would not necessarily be less disruptive because observers would still have to deal with two conflicting sources of information, even if they are not integrated. So inconsistent information is disruptive at both long and short SOAs.

In summary, the measure of performance accuracy indicated that performance is relatively robust across short but not long asynchronies. However, robustness in performance is not sufficient to conclude that integration occurred. The tests of the FLMP provide a more direct test of integration and therefore produce a more revealing picture of its disruption by temporal asynchrony.

Tests of the FLMP The FLMP was tested against the experimental data for its predictions of five response types: the four syllables plus a general cluster category. The FLMP was fit separately to each experiment, each subject, and each SOA condition. The same unimodal trials were used in the fit at each of the seven unique SOA conditions. This constraint instantiates our belief that a good theory should describe both the unimodal and the bimodal

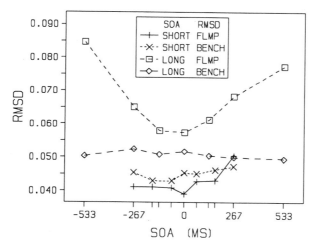

Figure 3.8 The average RMSD for the fit of the FLMP and the average benchmark RMSD as a function of SOA. Negative SOAs indicate that the auditory speech occurred before the visual speech, whereas the visual speech preceded the auditory for the positive SOAs.

results. Thus, each fit involved 32 bimodal and 12 unimodal trials, with 5 response categories for a total of 220 data points. Each fit required 4 visual and 8 auditory parameter values for each of the 5 response categories (Massaro et al., 1996). These values indicate the degree to which each unimodal source of information supports each response alternative. Thus, the FLMP required a total of 12 × 5, or 60 parameter values for each fit.

Because of our previous results (e.g., chapter 1), we expect the FLMP to give a good description at short SOAs. If integration breaks down at longer SOAs, the FLMP should correspondingly give a poorer description. Because we are using the fit of the FLMP as a measure of integration, it is necessary to determine how good the fit is in an absolute sense. As will be discussed more fully in chapter 10, a benchmark measure has been developed to provide an absolute index of a model's goodness of fit. We can then ask if the fit of a model is poorer than this benchmark. A benchmark RMSD was computed for each subject as the index to assess the goodness of the FLMP fit.

The question of central interest is whether the goodness of fit of the FLMP differed across the different SOAs. In this case, it is assessed against its yoked benchmark. Figure 3.8 gives the average observed and average benchmark RMSDs. First, note that the benchmark RMSDs are smaller for the experiment with short SOAs than for the one with long SOAs. This difference reflects the fact that the response proportions were more extreme (closer to 0 or 1) in the short SOA experiment (see chapter 10). The benchmark RMSDs make it easier to compare results across experimental conditions with necessarily different levels of performance.

For each experiment, an analysis of variance was carried out comparing the observed RMSD to the benchmark RMSD with SOA and subjects as factors. In the experiment with short SOAs, the benchmark RMSDs tended to be somewhat larger than the observed RMSDs, but there was no statistically significant difference between the observed and benchmark RMSDs and no effect of SOA. Given that the goodness of fit changed very little across SOAs, we can conclude that integration of audible and visible speech can occur even with SOAs as large as 250 ms. This analysis confirms the conclusion based on performance accuracy.

The RMSDs for the longer SOA experiment, however, not only indicate when the good fit can break down, they also show that the results might be somewhat context dependent. With long SOAs, there was a difference between the observed and benchmark RMSDs that interacted with SOA. As can be seen in the top two curves of figure 3.8, the FLMP gave a poorer fit at the more extreme SOAs.

One potentially troubling result is that the overall performance on both auditory and visual unimodal trials was significantly poorer in the experiment with longer SOAs. In principle, the longer SOAs should not have changed performance on unimodal trials. However, there are very large individual differences in these speech perception tasks, and we are reluctant to pay too much attention to an overall difference in performance accuracy across the two experiments. The average accuracy was .88 for the unimodal auditory trials in the short SOA condition and .76 for the long SOA condition. The average accuracy was .87 for the unimodal visual trials in the short SOA condition and .73 for the long SOA condition. To ensure that this overall performance difference was not responsible for the different effects of SOA in the two experiments, we separated the 18 subjects in the long SOA experiment into high and low accuracy groups. The high-accuracy group achieved the same level of performance accuracy as the subjects in the short SOA experiment. Figure 3.9 shows the same results seen in figure 3.8 except that it represents only the high-accuracy group. The statistical analyses of these results and tests of the FLMP replicated what was found for the complete group. Thus, the overall level of performance cannot account for the difference between the two experiments.

In summary, we were successful in inducing a disruption of integration with sufficiently long SOAs. The combined results of these two experiments provide a reasonably coherent specification of the temporal window for integrating auditory and visual speech. As in almost every other type of behavioral situation, behavior does not show catastrophic breakdowns across environmental variation. In our case, there is no sharp boundary separating integration from nonintegration. An asynchrony of 500 ms is clearly disruptive, whereas integration does not appear to be disrupted at around 150 ms asynchrony. There also appears to be an influence of the test context, in that repeated tests with extreme SOAs might lead to some disruption of integration even at SOAs that would normally produce integration. It appears that subjects are able to integrate audible and visible speech more easily if most of the bimodal speech events have fairly short SOAs, as they do in natural

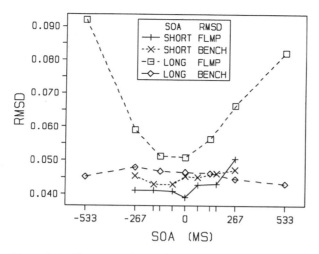

Figure 3.9 The average RMSD for the fit of the FLMP and the average benchmark RMSD as a function of SOA. The results for the long SOAs are based on a subset of nine subjects whose overall accuracy was similar to that of the short SOA subjects. Negative SOAs indicate that the auditory speech occurred before the visual speech, whereas the visual speech preceded the auditory for the positive SOAs.

speech. Presenting many bimodal speech events with very long SOAs tends to disrupt the integration process.

Cluster Judgments   The change in cluster responses across SOA also supports the hypothesis that integration tends to deteriorate at longer SOAs. Cluster responses normally occur only under a small set of conditions, such as a visual /ba/ paired with an auditory /da/ (V_bA_d), which produces /bda/. However, a visual /da/ paired with an auditory /ba/ seldom produces /dba/. On the other hand, if the SOA is sufficiently large, the two syllables might be interpreted as two successive syllables. In that case, their properties would not have to be consistent with the characteristics of a single syllable. Responses in such a situation would be better described as being two-syllable responses, such as /bada/ or /daba/, rather than consonant clusters. Table 3.1 gives the proportion of /bada/ and /daba/ judgments as a function of SOA for V_bA_d and V_dA_b in the experiment with long SOAs. As can be seen in the table, SOA had a large effect on performance. For example, /bada/ judgments are seldom given to V_dA_b unless the auditory syllable is presented much earlier than the visual syllable. Similarly, /daba/ is seldom given to V_dA_b unless the visual syllable is presented much earlier than the auditory syllable.

In summary, the results speak to the issue of whether our perceptual world is tuned to perceptual events or to the properties that make up the events. People appear to find it easy to integrate multiple sources of information that specify a single event, whereas they have trouble with integration if the sources specify different events (Massaro, 1985a). Thus, the FLMP gives a good description of performance when the two sources arrive sufficiently

Table 3.1 The proportion of /bada/ and /daba/ judgments as a function of SOA for visual /ba/–auditory /da/ and for visual /da/–auditory /ba/ in the long SOA experiment (with natural auditory speech)

SOA	V_bA_d		V_dA_b	
	/bada/	/daba/	/bada/	/daba/
−533	.06	.37	.27	.02
−267	.19	.22	.24	.07
−133	.39	.08	.14	.08
0	.43	.02	.08	.16
133	.43	.04	.06	.18
267	.50	.00	.08	.23
533	.48	.00	.01	.24

close in time that they are treated as belonging to a single event. Separating the sources in time, however, disrupts integration, leading to a poor description of performance by the FLMP. A mirror image of this view comes from Kahneman and Treisman (1984) and Neisser (1976), who claim that we attend to objects (events) and not to properties that make them up (Massaro, 1985a).

ASYNCHRONIES IN NATURAL SPEECH

The SOA experiments might be considered to be somewhat contrived, but in fact asynchrony is the rule rather than the exception in bimodal speech. Even when the two inputs are perfectly correlated in the natural world, they cannot be simultaneous in terms of their perceptual processing. Given the physics of auditory and visual stimuli and the physiology of their respective sensory systems, it would be miraculous if they arrived at the relevant processing sites at the exact same time. Light travels faster than sound and will arrive at the sensory surface sooner. For stimuli at 10 meters, the light arrives about 30 ms before the sound. On the other hand, because the chemical process by which the retina transduces light is somewhat slower than that by which the basilar membrane transduces sound, we can expect a faster neural reaction to sound than to light. In an ideal world, these opposing tendencies might simply cancel one another to give complete synchrony. Our world is not ideal, however, and asynchronies between audible and visible speech are typical. It is also well known that the physiological travel time to neural centers varies inversely with stimulus intensity (Kohfeld, 1971). The influence of intensity can be substantial; McGill (1961) observed that increasing the amplitude of a test tone from 30 to 100 dB decreased simple reaction time by about 100 ms. Thus, for a loud command in a soldier's face the commander's voice might be processed much sooner than his face, whereas the auditory speech received at the back of a large classroom might lag behind a soft-spoken lecturer's facial movements by the same duration. All of these influences require that a successful integration process be relatively immune to substantial differences in the arrival time of the audible and visible speech.

Given the adaptive value of utilizing information from several modalities, an interesting problem to be solved is how information from the two modalities is integrated when the inputs are subject to relatively large differences in arrival times at the appropriate neural sites—differences of tens or even hundreds of milliseconds.

How has nature solved this problem? Obviously, she could not simply allow indiscriminate multimodal integration across too wide an interval, because only meaningfully related features should be integrated. It turns out that there is evidence from both the neural and information-processing domains that points to a likely solution. At the neural level, activity outlasts stimulation. The sensory systems seem to have solved the problem of integrating multisensory stimuli arriving at different times by extending the neural activation resulting from stimulation beyond the stimulation period. Thus, stimuli that co-occur at roughly the same time in the world will tend to have overlapping neural activation patterns. This observation meshes with the concept of a sensory storage that has played an important role in information processing theory for the last three decades (Massaro & Loftus, 1996).

That sensory storage allows both auditory and visual processing to continue after the relevant stimulation is removed. A ballpark estimate of the duration of the storage is around 250 ms. If sensory storage allows auditory and visual processing to continue after the relevant stimulation is finished, then integration of asynchronous events can occur as long as some sensory storage remains. Neurological findings support these conclusions (Stein & Meredith, 1993). For the localization of objects in space, it is not surprising that multisensory interactions are not dependent on matching the onsets of the two different sensory stimuli, or their latencies, but on how much the neural activity patterns resulting from the two inputs overlap (Stein, Meredith & Wallace, 1994). Similarly, as we have seen in speech perception, integration occurs with onset asynchronies of up to roughly 250 ms.

Audible-Visible Asynchrony as a Multimodal Feature

We have been concerned with the integration of asynchronous modalities, but perceivers also appear to use the information conveyed by the asynchronies themselves. It is well known that voice onset time (VOT) is an important cue to the voicing feature in stop consonants. Within the auditory modality, the length of the delay between the release of the stop and the onset of the vocal cord vibration in the following vowel indicates whether the stop is voiced (as in /b, d, g/) or voiceless (as in /p, t, k/): a short interval signifies a voiced stop whereas a longer interval cues a voiceless stop. This information might also be conveyed bimodally by the interval between seeing the stop release and hearing the vocal cord vibration. Similarly, nasal stops might be distinguished from nonnasal stops by hearing auditory nasality before seeing the stop release (see Erber & DeFilippo, 1978).

McGrath and Summerfield (1985) were interested in whether differences in arrival time of the audible and visible speech could cue voicing and nasality differences in stop consonants. These differences are not easily seen on the face. A Lissajou interference pattern mimicking a pair of opening lips was presented with an auditory triangle wave. The stimuli were made to resemble /ma/, /ba/, and /pa/ by offsetting the onset of the auditory and visible components. Observers were asked to judge whether the auditory or visual signal occurred first to determine how well they could detect stimulus onset asynchrony (SOA). The results showed an overwhelming insensitivity to SOA. For 71% correct performance, the visible signal had to lead by 138 ms and the auditory had to lead by 79 ms. The authors concluded that we are insensitive to the intermodality timing differences that could potentially cue VOT and nasality in bimodal speech.

For whatever reason, this conclusion might have been overly pessimistic. Earlier research by Hirsh and Sherrick (1961) found much better resolution of auditory-visual asynchrony. Stimulus duration, onset abruptness, and learning all have an important influence on sensitivity, and it may be that bimodal onset differences can be informative in a typical speech situation. In fact, there is some direct evidence that perceivers can use the onset differences between the visual and auditory (or tactile) sources as a cue to voicing of stop consonants (Breeuwer & Plomp, 1984, 1986). Breeuwer & Plomp (1986) asked their participants to speechread visible vowel-consonant-vowel (VCV) sequences with /a/ as the vowel and with 18 possible consonants. For our discussion, we will restrict the analysis to the three consonants /b/, /p/, and /m/. The experimenters documented the difficulty of speechreading voicing and manner information in the visible speech of the consonants. As can be seen in the visual (V) condition in figure 3.10, speechreading the differences between these three labial stop consonants is very difficult and results in near chance performance.

The researchers were then interested in the bimodal condition, specifically whether the temporal relationship between the auditory and visual speech could be sufficient to provide information about voicing. To eliminate all other information in the auditory signal, they transformed the voiced speech into a sequence of filtered pulses. Each glottal pulse period was replaced by one filtered pulse. This auditory signal is heard as a simple buzz. When the simple buzz is presented alone, the listener should have no information at all about the voicing of the stop consonant. He or she hears the sections of voiced speech but does not know whether the stop was voiced or voiceless. Even so, it would have been valuable to test the auditory-alone condition. As can also be seen in figure 3.10, when this transformed source of auditory information was combined with the visual information, performance improved dramatically.

Band 3.5 on the CD-ROM gives stimuli analogous to those in the McGrath and Summerfield (1985) and Breeuwer and Plomp (1986) experiments. The three indistinguishable visual syllables /ma/, /ba/, and /pa/ are paired with

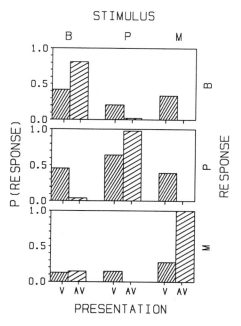

Figure 3.10 Probability of /b/, /p/, and /m/ responses as a function of visual (V) or auditory/ visual (AV) presentations of /b/, /p/, and /m/ (after Breeuwer & Plomp, 1986).

an uninformative auditory signal (corresponding to the onset of voicing in a subsequent vowel). The bimodal stimuli were made to resemble /ma/, /ba/, and /pa/ by offsetting the onset of the auditory and visible components by the appropriate amount. Because the visual signal alone provided only a weak cue and the auditory signal alone was completely uninformative about voicing, it was necessarily the combination of the two inputs that provided the informative cue to voicing. In this case, the information could not be derived from the independent evaluation of the two modalities. For this reason, Breeuwer and Plomp's (1986) results were cited by Bernstein (1989) as evidence against the FLMP assumption of independent evaluation of auditory and visible speech. At that time (Massaro, 1989b), I agreed that the voicing information being conveyed was necessarily a function of the asynchrony between the auditory and visual speech. This implies a bimodal feature, in the sense that it is derived from both sources of information.

Elaborated FLMP with Multimodal Features

The FLMP necessarily assumes multiple cues that are evaluated independently of one another. A cue corresponding to the onset differences between the audible and visible speech does not violate this independence assumption. In figure 3.11, the schematic form of the FLMP has been elaborated from previous representations (see chapter 2) to clarify the assumptions of the model and to account for this important finding in bimodal speech per-

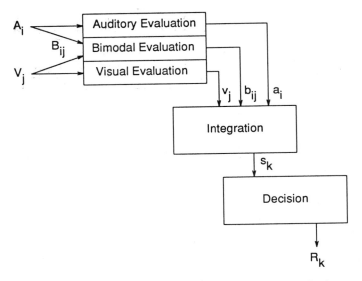

Figure 3.11 Schematic representation of the three stages involved in perceptual recognition. The three stages are shown to proceed left to right in time to illustrate their necessarily successive but overlapping processing. The sources of information are represented by uppercase letters. Auditory information is represented by A_i and visual information by V_j. In addition, information about the temporal asynchrony between the auditory and visual information is indicated by B_{ij}. The evaluation process transforms these sources of information into psychological values (indicated by lowercase letters a_i, v_j, and b_{ij}). These sources are then integrated to give an overall degree of support for a given alternative, s_k. The decision operation maps this value into some response, R_k, such as a discrete decision or a rating.

ception. First, evaluation of the auditory features and visual features occurs independently and thus is shown as occurring in separate boxes. Simultaneously, there is cross-modal information available, which includes the feature of voicing even though other features of speech such as place of articulation can occur independently along the auditory and visual modalities. This cross-modal information would be integrated with the modality-specific sources of information in the same multiplicative manner as is already assumed by the FLMP.

The cross-modal information about voicing does not violate the independence assumption at the evaluation stage. By independence at evaluation we simply mean that the evaluation of one cue is independent of the evaluation of all other cues. In our previous research, the cues were defined as the auditory and visual modalities providing information about place of articulation. The important point, however, was that visible place features were evaluated independently of audible place features. Similarly, other modality-specific features would be evaluated independently of information along another modality. This independence does not preclude the possibility of some bimodal relationship functioning as yet another independent feature. What is important for our purposes is that the evaluation of the bimodal cue is carried out independently of the modality-specific cues. For the many additional applications of the FLMP in this book, the reader should be warned that it is not necessary to assume such a bimodal source of information. In many tests, voicing is not relevant, and in those where it is, cross-modal information about voicing is not functional in perception.

Much of this chapter was concerned with the temporal window of integration, but we have noted that perceivers are not necessarily blind to time differences even though asynchronous inputs are being integrated to impose meaning on a perceptual event. The use of the temporal relationship between the bimodal inputs again highlights the multiplicity of the sources of information perceivers make use of in language processing, and how these sources can be processed simultaneously. Although perceivers normally integrate asynchronous information from different modalities, they are also sensitive to the time differences and can exploit them to identify the input. Given this illustrative foundation, we are now prepared to address our new principle or law of information integration in greater depth.

4   A Universal Law

With my two algorithms, one can solve all problems—without error, if God wills!
—Al-Khorezmi (780–850)

My mind seems to have become a kind of machine for grinding general laws out of large collections of facts.
—Charles Darwin

[On two pieces of evidence]
Each is suggestive; together, they are conclusive.
—Sherlock Holmes

In 1956, George Miller published one of psychology's most influential articles, in which he documented the ubiquitousness of the number 7 plus or minus 2, in describing psychophysical outcomes and memory results. As engagingly described by Miller, texture mapped onto our talking head on band 4.1 on the CD-ROM, a constancy of behavior forced itself upon him. This constancy in some aspect of performance was deemed important because it putatively corresponded to some universal principle of human behavior. We describe Weber's law, the power law of learning, and exponential laws of forgetting and generalization as a few examples of universal principles of behavior. These laws also have the advantage of being illustrated in graphical terms rather than just verbally. We value the visual representation of scientific principles because it crystallizes and helps to communicate our under-standing. This background sets the stage for our new principle of integra-tion. To facilitate our presentation, we discuss levels of explanation, the concept of algorithm, and another law of generalization. We then illustrate our new principle and contrast its predictions against those of other models. The reader should not be surprised to learn that our new principle is nothing more or less than the FLMP account of pattern recognition. The optimality of our law of pattern recognition is then addressed. We end the chapter with three alternative ways in which integration might be implemented in the brain.

SOME PSYCHOLOGICAL LAWS

Weber's Law

One of the best-known laws of perception is Ernst Weber's. It is also one that is readily experienced. Our ability to identify one stimulus as different from another is dependent on the overall magnitude of the stimuli. We require a larger stimulus difference when the overall magnitude of the stimulus is large than when it is small. In fact, the regularity is that the just-noticeable difference needed for discrimination is some constant proportion of the overall stimulus magnitude. By how little, for example, can two lights be made to differ in intensity and yet still be seen as different? Weber's significant observation was that the just-noticeable difference was dependent on the overall intensity of the lights being discriminated. We are much more sensitive to small intensity changes in dim lights than in bright lights. This is easily observed using a three-way bulb of, say, 50, 100, and 150 watts. The noticeable change from 50 to 100 watts is much greater than that from 100 to 150. To experience a difference similar to the change from 50 to 100 watts, the 100 watts would have to be increased to 200.

Weber observed an exact relationship between the just-noticeable difference for a particular stimulus and its absolute magnitude. This relationship has come to be known as Weber's law and is expressed both verbally and quantitatively. Verbally, the law is that an increment in the intensity of a stimulus becomes just noticeable when it is made a fixed percentage more intense than the original stimulus. That is, the just-noticeable difference is a constant when measured relative to the absolute intensity of the stimuli. In mathematical terms, this form of Weber's law can be expressed as

$$\frac{dI}{I} = K \tag{4.1}$$

where dI is the just-noticeable intensity change in a stimulus of original intensity I, and K is a constant value for a given intensity continuum. Thus, if K were equal to 0.05 for brightness sensation, the intensity of a light must be increased or decreased by 5% (0.05 = 5%) to be noticed.

Weber's law captures the fact that a weaker stimulus requires a smaller absolute stimulus change in order for the change to be noticed. An observer notices a smaller absolute change in a weak than in a strong stimulus. Equation 4.1 can be rewritten as

$$dI = KI \tag{4.2}$$

which is a linear function of the form $y = ax$. As can be seen in figure 4.1, the just-noticeable difference in line length predicted by Weber's law follows a linear equation. The slope of the function as measured by the amount of change in y (the vertical axis) divided by the amount of change in x (the horizontal axis) gives Weber's constant K.

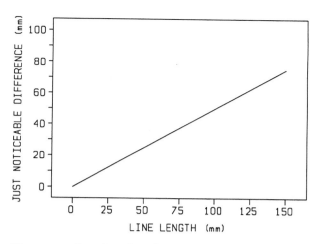

Figure 4.1 Hypothetical results illustrating the just-noticeable difference in line length as a function of the length of the line.

Weber's law is a good example of how laws require free parameters. We expect that the value of K would depend on the sensory modality and the observer in addition to a host of other factors. The just-noticeable difference varies for different modalities, but in all cases it follows the linear relationship predicted by Weber's law. This general principle—we know that a given proportional difference can be noticed but we cannot specify what the proportion will be—is parallel to a distinction we will repeatedly make between information and information processing. In Weber's law, the information processing involved in noticing a difference appears to be universal in terms of requiring a proportional change. What that proportion is, however, depends on a variety of factors.

Power Law of Learning

One of the best-known laws in learning theory is the power law of learning. In their seminal study, Bryan and Harter (1897, 1899) documented learning in the transmission and reception of telegraphic messages. Written English text is translated into Morse code, which is transmitted to a receiver. The sender taps a telegraph key for short and long durations separated by pauses, which are transmitted over a wireless telegraph. The receiver, with no storage device other than memory, translates the message back into written English. As anyone could have predicted, performance improved with practice, but one could not have predicted that the improvement would proceed according to a very orderly relationship. It was found that the time to perform a skill decreases as the number of practice trials increases, following a concave or negatively decelerating function. This relationship between practice and performance has been found in a broad range of domains, including Morse code, cigar making, arithmetic, and geometry proofs. The systematicity

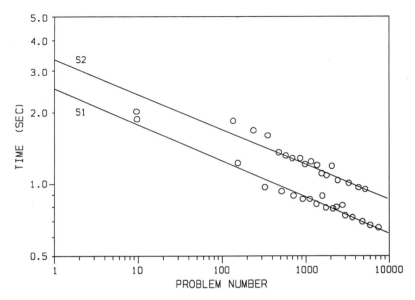

Figure 4.2 The time required to complete addition problems as a function of the number of practice problems. (Points taken from Crossman, 1959, after a study by Blackburn, 1936.)

of this quantitative relationship is most apparent if the time to complete the task and the number of practice trials are plotted logarithmically. The logarithm of response time is a decreasing linear function of the logarithm of the number of practice trials. Expressed quantitatively,

$$\log T = \log B - A \log n \qquad (4.3)$$

where T is the time to complete the task, B is a base time at the start of practice, n is the number of practice trials, and A is a constant reflecting the rate of learning.

Blackburn (1936) found two heroic participants who practiced addition problems for 10,000 trials. He recorded the time required for each problem as a function of practice. Figure 4.2 shows the results plotted on a log-log scale. As can be seen in the figure, the time to complete a problem decreased linearly on the logarithmic plot.

Exponential Law of Forgetting

Forgetting, under very controlled conditions, is also systematic and can be described by a fairly straightforward law. The law is transparent only under conditions in which both the acquisition of memory and its loss are quantified. We can understand this orderliness in the framework of an important study carried out by Waugh and Norman (1965). They employed a probe recall study in which subjects were presented with a list of items (the learned items) followed by a repetition of one of those items (the test item) and had to report the item that had followed the test item in the list. The subjects

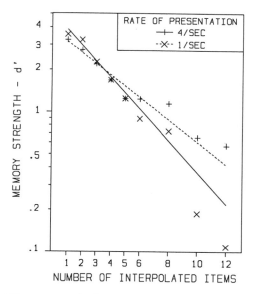

Figure 4.3 The d' transformation of percentage of correct recall as a function of the number of interpolated items between presentation of the digit and its test under two rates of presentation (after Waugh & Norman, 1965). The lines are predicted functions given by an exponential forgetting rule (after Massaro, 1970a).

were explicitly instructed to concentrate on the current item being presented and not to rehearse earlier items in the list. This instruction was given in order to eliminate differences in rehearsal for the different serial positions, so that any differences in memory performance as a function of serial position could be attributed to some variable other than amount of rehearsal.

The list was a set of 15 digits. Waugh and Norman varied the rate of presentation of the list and compared the forgetting functions under two rates, 1 or 4 digits per second. The forgetting function was determined by systematically testing the subjects for different items in the list. There were 1, 2, 3, 4, 5, 6, 8, 10, or 12 digits between the presentation of the tested item and its prior presentation in the list. It was found that the percentage of correct recall decreased as a function of the number of interpolated digits between a digit's original presentation and its test under both rates of presentation.

The law of forgetting is best captured when accuracy of performance is translated to a memory strength measure, d', and this measure is plotted on a log scale as a function of the number of interpolated test items. An exponential law translates into a linear one when the dependent measure is transformed in a log scale. As can be seen by the points in figure 4.3, the log of observed memory strength decreased linearly with the number of items intervening between learning and test. The two lines in figure 4.3 give the predictions of the law of exponential forgetting. As can be seen in the figure, the two lines give a good description of the observed points. Forgetting is exponential with the constraint that the rate of forgetting (the slope of the function) is dependent on the rate of presentation of the test items. The results in figure 4.3 show how quickly forgetting occurs and reveal a systematic difference between the forgetting functions under the two rates of presentation.

The predicted function describing forgetting at a rate of presentation of four items per second starts out lower and ends up higher than the function describing forgetting when the items are presented at a rate of one per second. The predicted value at 0 interpolated items provides some measure of the original perception of the digits, whereas the slope of the curves should provide an index of the retention or rate of forgetting. According to this analysis, the items presented at one per second were better perceived but were forgotten faster than the items presented at four per second. Every memory task contains both perception and retention stages that must be isolated in order to reveal the underlying law of forgetting.

Shepard's Law of Generalization

A recent seminal contribution to psychological inquiry provides a helpful foundation for the development of our universal law of pattern recognition. It is the universal law of generalization proposed by Roger Shepard (1987). When a response learned to one stimulus is also made to a similar stimulus, this result could signify either a failure of discrimination, in which the difference between the two stimuli is not perceived, or a generalization, demonstrating the natural tendency to behave similarly in response to a similar but noticeably different event. Shepard is concerned with the latter case. Although we notice change in Heraclitus's river, we tend to respond in the same way to similar rivers. Shepard's law of generalization is that the probability of generalization decays exponentially with the distance between the original stimulus event and the new event in a psychological space of variable dimensionality. The psychological space can follow either a Euclidean metric or a city-block metric, depending on the relations between the dimensions along which the stimuli vary (Shepard, 1962).

Shepard's predecessors had reached the discouraging conclusion that an invariant law of generalization was not possible. Shepard's leap in the understanding of the process of generalization was the idea that one needed a psychological measure of the difference between two stimuli rather than a measure of the actual physical difference. What this does is to normalize or put on equal footing our perception of the different stimuli under consideration. By formulating potential laws on the basis of physical differences, scientists were trying to do the impossible: such laws would have to assume that people would respond similarly to stimulus differences that were not psychologically equivalent. By first deriving a psychological measure of difference, we can then impose the appropriate constraint that people should behave equivalently in response to differences that are psychologically equivalent. For example, I will generalize from a red light to a pink light in the same way that I would generalize from a loud tone to a somewhat softer

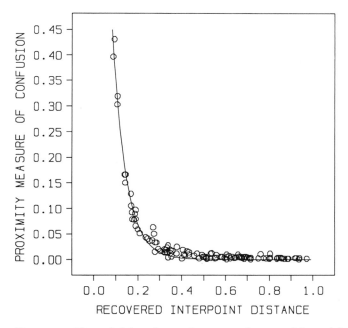

Figure 4.4 The probability of generalization as a function of the Euclidean distance among the consonants in English obtained in the two-dimensional representation. (Results from Miller and Nicely, 1955, taken from Shepard, 1987.)

tone when the psychological difference is equivalent in the two cases. If I perceive the pink light to be half as red as the red light, and the softer tone to be half as loud as the loud tone, then I will generalize equivalently in the two situations.

It is instructive to review an example of Shepard's law, particularly because there is one from speech science. Shepard (1988) reanalyzed Miller and Nicely's (1955) comprehensive study of confusions in auditory speech perception, which was discussed briefly in chapter 1. He found that 16 consonants of English could be represented along two dimensions. The psychological distance between all consonant pairs could therefore be represented by the Euclidean distance in this two-dimensional space. As can be seen in figure 4.4, the observed confusion measure of similarity among the test consonants is well described by an exponential function of the Euclidean distance obtained in the two-dimensional representation.

Shepard's innovative analysis of the process of generalization anticipates exactly the strategy that we have used in our work. In the application of our universal principle of pattern recognition, we necessarily make a distinction between information and information processing. The law of information processing concerning how multiple sources of ambiguous information are integrated is revealed only when the information available to the perceiver is taken into account. This is exactly analogous to Shepard's distinction between the physically measured differences between stimuli and the psychological differences between those same stimuli. Shepard imposed order on unorderly data by making this distinction. We must do the same: unless we have measured the information, the information processing is not apparent. Shepard's analysis of a broad range of data across different domains produces a highly consistent and universal function that describes generalization. When generalization between stimuli is predicted from distances between points in a psychological space, the resulting generalization function is exponential. This precedent for our work gives us much greater confidence in the strategy that we have applied to understanding how people impose meaning on a world with multiple sources of ambiguous information.

Shepard also lists some exceptions to his general rule. The behavior of primitive organisms in response to similar stimuli, for example, does not support the distinction between generalization and failure of discrimination. After protracted discrimination training with highly similar stimuli or delayed test stimuli, Shepard's generalization principle does not hold. If there are multiple learning trials, for example, then differential reinforcement schedules can shape the generalization function in a variety of different ways. The fact that only in sentient organisms can we make the distinction between the failure of discrimination and the ability to generalize indicates that this is a law that applies to sentient organisms, perhaps organisms that have a theory of mind beyond age four. Although it is beyond the scope of our endeavor, that question raises the interesting issue of whether this type of generalization is involved in the acquisition of speech.

Shepard's work on generalization makes apparent once again that believers in categorical perception have failed to see the broader picture involved. What researchers interpret as categorical perception is really nothing more than generalization. What has to be emphasized repeatedly is that categorical perception is not a failure to discriminate. We simply generalize from one experience to similar experiences and treat them in similar ways. If we have a speech continuum between /ba/ and /da/, it should not be surprising that we tend to treat instances within a category as more similar to one another than instances between categories, in both categorization and discrimination tasks.

Finally, Shepard's law of generalization offers a potential clarification of our prototypical representations that mediate pattern recognition. We have defined these representations as summary descriptions of the ideal values for each feature for each test alternative. Given that the ideal values seldom occur in the stimulus to be recognized, how is the goodness of match determined? Normally, we would have to claim that some additional representation of the distribution of feature values is included in the summary description. With Shepard's principle, however, we could assume that only the ideal value is maintained in memory; the truth value indicating goodness of match decays exponentially with the psychological distance between the feature in the stimulus and its ideal value in memory. We now discuss universal principles more generally.

UNIVERSAL PRINCIPLES

Our approach seeks more universal principles that cut across qualitatively different domains. The principles we seek might be considered less specific than most theories, in that any universal principles that are substantiated across domains will necessarily be more globally relevant. For example, the perception of speech and emotion probably involve different sources of information and different neural machinery, but those differences do not necessarily preclude common principles that describe their function. To justify this approach, we can point to the usefulness of universal principles in other disciplines, such as the emerging science of complexity. An example is the concept of increasing returns, which is applied to such widely disparate areas as economics, technology, and evolutionary biology. It is well captured by the biblical proverb, "To them that hath shall be given," or the common man's adage, "The rich get richer." Engineers are also familiar with this principle in the form of positive feedback.

In the economic and technological domains, increasing returns help to explain why the VHS video format now dominates the market even though the Beta was technically superior. The VHS was a little more popular early on, and this encouraged the production of more video recordings in the VHS format, which in turn encouraged the purchase of VHS tape players, and so on, to produce increasing returns for VHS and a diminishing market for Beta. More currently, the same analysis might lead to the prediction that the Macintosh platform, with its decreasing market share, will travel the same road as the Beta video tape player. Increasing returns might also help to make sense of the origin of life. Some molecules in the "primordial soup" might have formed a structured self-reinforcing network of reactions. Those molecules in the network would catalyze new members so that eventually members would outnumber nonmembers, and as the membership became rich enough, life could have emerged. Increasing returns is also integral to chaos theory's notion of the butterfly effect, that is, that small influences early on can lead to dramatic consequences later. The twentieth-century proverb is that a butterfly's activities (or at least those of a 747) in the far Northwest can influence the weather in Santa Cruz a few days later.

Level of Explanation

Another issue in the formulation of new laws is the level of description or explanation. A behavioral principle might be expressed in neurophysiological terms. Mind and behavior are believed to emerge from neurological mechanisms in the brain, and any description would necessarily be at that reductionist level. As defended by Nelson Goodman (1984) and others, however, there is nothing inherently valid about reductionism (see also Uttal, 1990). More global levels of description might be preferable. If we accept Hume's view of causality as nothing more than succession of events, then causality at one level cannot be considered more basic or fundamental than causality at another level. Do Searle and other reductionists actually believe that causality at the molecular level is somehow more real than causality at other levels?

Algorithm

Our principle of behavior operates not at the biological level but rather at the algorithmic level. What is an algorithm and why is it the appropriate form for laws of nature? An algorithm is nothing more than a recipe. Most recipes or formulas promise a particular result if the instructions are followed; but even experienced chefs or potters will tell you that there are no guarantees. Conscientious adherence to the recipe does not insure that today's bread will be identical to yesterday's or that the surface of a pot will be consistent from firing to firing. Contrary to most definitions of algorithms, we do not impose the restriction that the algorithm guarantees a particular outcome. What is essential for the algorithm (as essential as anything can be for a fuzzy theorist) is that the procedure or recipe is well specified. In today's parlance, an algorithm might be equated with a set of computational operations. (We must also reject the false dichotomy between algorithm and heuristic, because both can be well specified.)

More importantly, however, we need to be clearer about the algorithm we are proposing for pattern recognition. How do we discover whether our algorithm is represented in the brain? Is it neurologically plausible? Neither of these questions is appropriate once we clarify what we mean by algorithm. To facilitate that explanation, we make a direct analogy to natural selection. Natural selection is Darwin's description or explanation of how we and other living creatures have come to be in existence. If organic beings vary in several parts of their organization, if there is a struggle for life, and if variation is useful for a being's welfare, then those individuals with the best chance of survival will produce offspring with the same advantage.

As expressed so elegantly by Dennett (1995), "the algorithmic level *is* the level that best accounts for the speed of the antelope, the wing of the eagle, the shape of the orchid, the diversity of species, and all the other occasions for wonder in the world of nature." Any explanation can be given in substrate-neutral terminology. Evolution implemented by natural selection is an algorithmic process. That's all there is to it. Life as we know it emerged from a procedure that is easily described in algorithmic terms. There was no way to predict the current outcome of the procedure and there is no way to predict the future outcomes. However, the procedure alone was and is sufficient. There is no creator, guiding hand, or other influence outside of the algorithm itself. The algorithmic level seems to this writer to be the right level of explanation because it is a necessary one to understand how natural selection works.

The algorithmic level is abstract in the sense that it is only a recipe or a procedure. Although natural selection is an algorithm, we do not expect to find it instantiated in the biology of living systems. Only biology is found in living systems, not algorithms (Searle, 1992). The biology might help explain why variability, a necessary ingredient of the natural selection algorithm, is inherent in life-forms. But a biological explanation cannot represent and therefore replace the algorithm. Biology is only biology.

Similarly, we do not expect to find our law of pattern recognition in the brain. We expect to observe only chemical and electrical activity, not the algorithm itself. Of course, that observed activity can be interpreted in different ways. For example, neuroimaging can give us a picture of blood flow or electrical charges that might be interpreted as activations in neural networks. But there is no algorithm that can be seen in this activation, only biological activity. The law being proposed gives a universal algorithm for how patterns are recognized, but don't look for it in the brain. A model can never be the thing that is being modeled, although some models might be more abstract than others. We forget this too often and must be chided by critical philosophers such as John Searle, who convincingly argues that the information-processing or functional level of explanation has no material or phenomenological existence. With this prelude, it is now time to articulate a new principle of pattern recognition.

A NEW PRINCIPLE

One might ask why a new behavioral principle can still be discovered after more than 100 years of psychological inquiry. Two reasons might be offered. First, most research in psychology is highly domain-specific; investigators do not usually look outside their field for explanatory principles. For example, one would not expect attitude change and the perception of depth to have any principles in common. Second, the dominance of the single-variable experiment precluded the establishment of any principles having to do with more than one variable. Thus, there has been little impetus for the emergence of global or multimodal principles.

Unidimensional versus Multidimensional Laws

Weber's law is a unidimensional law: it describes how our discrimination behavior changes as a function of the overall magnitude of the stimulus. Analogously, exponential forgetting and the power law of learning are one-dimensional laws. George Miller's 7 plus or minus 2 rule is also unidimensional: it simply puts a cap on the size of short-term memory. We might expect laws to diminish in number as their complexity increases. (Maybe this is a law.) Each of the laws we have described boils down to a unidimensional relationship between two variables. Our proposed psychological law, the FLMP, is multidimensional in that it describes how several factors impact behavior. Another component that adds to the complexity of the law is that pattern recognition behavior can be measured in several ways.

Discrimination versus Meaningful Perception

Pattern recognition is concerned with meaning, whereas Weber's law is about sensory discrimination. The simplicity of Weber's law about sensation is not easily extended to meaning. Consider the discrimination of differences in line length. Our ability to notice a difference in line length is systematically related to the overall length of the line. We appear to be able to just notice a proportional difference regardless of line length. Now let's place the same line in a context in which it has meaning, as in marking the difference between lowercase e and c, or between v and y. The meaning of line length with respect to the formation of a pattern, as well as its discriminability, affect the decision. The perceiver not only has to distinguish lines of different lengths, but also must correctly infer or categorize the letter on the basis of line length.

There is also good reason to distinguish between perceptual experience and meaning; the latter is much more flexible and less stimulus-determined than the former. (This duality of discrimination and categorization might have an analogy in perception and Gibson's [1979] concept of affordance. Cutting [1987] makes a similar point that affordance is not sufficiently constrained by the perceptual event.) The meaning of a pattern across stimulus changes does not follow Weber's law, although it is clearly systematic. For illustrative purposes, consider a continuum of "letters" between lowercase c and e, made by increasing the length of the horizontal line (Massaro, 1979a; see also chapter 9). We notice changes along the continuum between e and c, but the meaning of these changes is determined by our categories or prototypes in memory. Before describing our universal principle, we discuss universal principles more generally.

Hindsight Bias

The principle we propose here is one that many will claim is obvious, mundane, nonessential, and peripheral to the goals of inquiry. We must adamantly disagree. It is commonplace for an answer, once given, to have been known all along. Brunelleschi was aware of hindsight bias more than five centuries ago. He proposed to the town fathers of Florence a design for the dome of the duomo Santa Maria de Fiore, which had remained uncovered for about eight decades. No one had been able to provide an innovative design to bridge the immense distance between the walls of the cathedral without intermediate supports. The story is told that when the town fathers wanted to see Brunelleschi's design before offering him the commission, Brunelleschi replied that they might consider the design obvious once they had seen it and hence feel no obligation to pay him the commission. To convince the town fathers of this possibility, he offered that he could also stand an egg on end. They were skeptical of this claim, but Brunelleschi slightly crushed an end of the egg and stood it on end. Of course, the town fathers replied, "That's obvious!" They quickly comprehended Brunelleschi's point and awarded him the commission, and the duomo remains protected by Brunelleschi's roof even today.

Illustration of the Principle

The principle, substantiated in a wide variety of domains, involves several components: (1) People (and nonhuman animals) are influenced by multiple sources of information in pattern recognition; (2) those sources are simultaneously influential, (3) their influence follows a quantitative pattern; and (4) that pattern can be described by the law that the influence of a given source of information is directly related to its information relative to the information in other sources. This principle is illustrated by experiments in which several independent variables are manipulated in a systematic way and their influence on behavior is measured in terms of some perceptual report or action.

Before we illustrate our principle, we cannot pass up the opportunity to insert a sports analogy. Baseball fans often complain that the umpire at first base has made a wrong call, but they don't have access to the auditory information indicating the ball hitting the glove or the foot hitting the bag. The umpire uses both the visual and auditory sources of information and thus is able to be more accurate.

On the experimental side, the most straightforward illustration of this principle involves an expanded factorial design with two independent variables. We call upon the same paradigm discussed in the previous chapters to assess the form of the interaction between the variables. Auditory and visual speech continua were made between the alternatives /ba/ and /da/, and the dependent variable is the proportion of /da/ responses. An analysis of variance shows significant main effects of both variables and a significant interaction between them.

The principle is that the interaction between the two variables takes a unique form regardless of the magnitude of the main effects. Graphically, the interaction takes the shape of an American football when plotted as a two-factor plot with the dependent variable proportion choice or relative rating on the ordinate, the levels of one factor plotted on the abscissa, and the levels of the other as the parameter of the graph. The football shape reflects the principle that the influence of one factor is larger in the middle, ambiguous range of the other factor. It should be noted that the complete football will not always be observed because the levels of one or both of the factors might not cover the complete range between the two alternatives.

Figure 4.5 gives the observed results from a typical participant in the experiment. The points in figure 4.5 are connected by lines to make the graph easier to read. The proportion of /da/ judgments is plotted as a function of the auditory and visual independent variables. The graph is a bit complicated because it includes both the bimodal and unimodal conditions. For example,

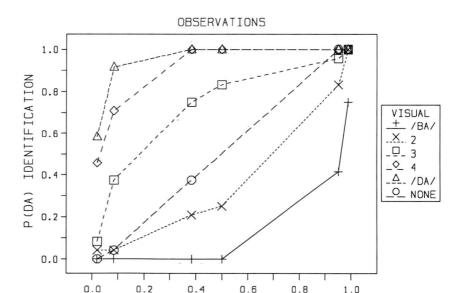

Figure 4.5 The points give the observed proportion of /da/ identifications in the unimodal and factorial auditory-visual conditions as a function of the five levels of synthetic auditory and visual speech varying between /ba/ and /da/. The auditory levels are plotted along the x-axis in terms of their corresponding parameter values from the fit of the FLMP. The unimodal visual condition is plotted at .5 (completely neutral) on the auditory scale. Results for subject 79. The lines are drawn through the observed points.

the unimodal auditory results are given by the open circles (the visual None condition). We have also plotted the auditory levels in terms of the auditory parameter values from the FLMP fit for each level. Thus, in figure 4.5, the first (most /ba/) auditory level is plotted at 0.08 on the auditory axis, which is the corresponding auditory parameter value for this subject. The unimodal visual conditions are plotted at 0.5 (completely neutral) on the auditory axis because the predictions for these conditions are equivalent to bimodal trials with completely ambiguous (0.5) auditory information. This type of plot gives a direct index of the influence of the auditory variable by showing the parameter values. The influence of the visual variable is given by the spread between the points at a given auditory level.

As developed in Chapter 2, our universal principle can be quantified to make exact predictions of each observer's results. Figure 4.6 gives another set of observations along with the predictions of the FLMP. Several character-istics of figure 4.6 are worth noting. First, it should be observed how closely the predicted lines come to the observed values. Second, the predicted per-formance for the unimodal auditory condition (visual None) is a straight line in this type of plot, simply because the outcome of the unimodal auditory performance is predicted to be equal to the auditory parameter value. Sim-ilarly, the points plotted at 0.5 on the auditory scale can be taken as a direct

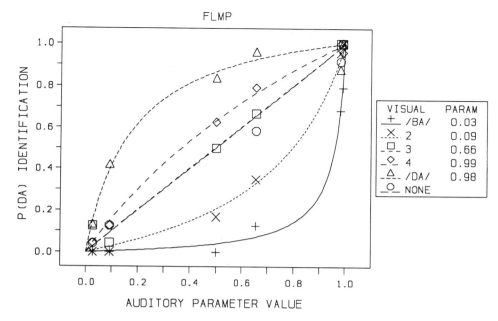

Figure 4.6 The points give the observed proportion of /da/ identifications in the unimodal and factorial auditory-visual conditions as a function of the five levels of synthetic auditory and visual speech varying between /ba/ and /da/. The auditory levels are plotted along the x-axis in terms of their corresponding parameter values from the fit of the FLMP. The unimodal visual condition is plotted at .5 (completely neutral) on the auditory scale. Results for subject 7. The lines give the predictions of the FLMP.

measure of the visual parameter values. Finally, the predicted point at (0.5, 0.5) corresponds to the missing cell in the lower right-hand corner of our expanded factorial design.

Figure 4.7 presents the results from a third subject to give the reader some feeling for the individual variability that permeates this inquiry. Although the subjects in figures 4.6 and 4.7 differ from one another, their performance is accounted for equally well by our principle.

TESTING ALTERNATIVE PREDICTIONS

We have seen that it is informative to plot observed and predicted performance as a function of the parameter values on the x-axis. This type of plot revealed more directly the predictions of the FLMP. Given this finer-grained microscope, it should also be worthwhile to expose other models through its lens. The single channel model claims that only one source influences a given percept. Figure 4.8 shows the performance of that model when the auditory levels are plotted along the x-axis in terms of their corresponding parameter values, taken from the model's best fit.

As can be seen in figure 4.8, the single channel model fails miserably. The SCM predicts parallel straight lines when the auditory parameter values are

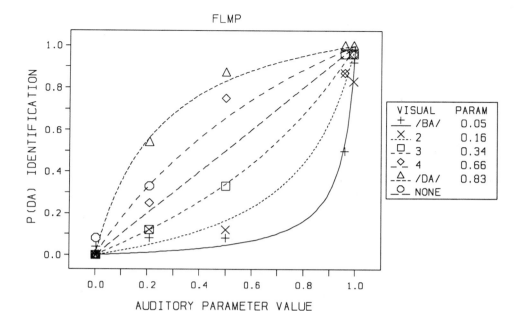

Figure 4.7 The points give the observed proportion of /da/ identifications in the unimodal and factorial auditory-visual conditions as a function of the five levels of the synthetic auditory and visual speech varying between /ba/ and /da/. The auditory levels are plotted along the x-axis in terms of their corresponding parameter values from the fit of the FLMP. The unimodal visual condition is plotted at .5 (completely neutral) on the auditory scale. The lines give the predictions of the FLMP.

plotted along the x-axis. We have witnessed, however, that the observed results follow the shape of the American football. When the results are plotted in this way, the difference between the FLMP and the SCM fits is much more noticeable than it is in the traditional plots given in chapter 2.

The same type of plot is also given for the RACE model in figure 4.9. The predicted results for the RACE model are counterintuitive because they show a nonmonotonic relationship between the two sources of information. Such a result is never observed—a fact that provides a strong disconfirmation of the RACE model. Although the RMSDs for the RACE model might not be all that much bigger than those for the FLMP, this type of prediction by the RACE model forces us to reject the model out of hand.

There is no easy way to interpolate between the predicted points in the postperceptual guessing (PPG) model and those of the auditory dominance model (ADM), so those two models are not plotted in this form.

The predictions of the additive model (AMP) are given in figure 4.10. Not surprisingly, the AMP also gives a poor approximation of the American football–shaped results because it, like the SCM, predicts parallel straight lines in this type of plot. The averaging model makes predictions equivalent to those of the SCM (see figure 4.8).

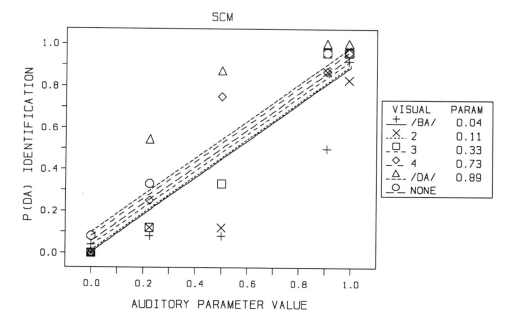

Figure 4.8 The points give the observed proportion of /da/ identifications in the unimodal and factorial auditory-visual conditions as a function of the five levels of the synthetic auditory and visual speech varying between /ba/ and /da/. The auditory levels are plotted along the x-axis in terms of their corresponding parameter values from the fit of the SCM. The unimodal visual condition is plotted at .5 (completely neutral) on the auditory scale. Results for subject 26. The lines give the predictions of the single channel model (SCM) or, equivalently, of the averaging model (AVM).

Falsifiability of the Principle

One concern that readers might have experienced is that our universal principle might be too powerful or flexible—a characteristic we have called superpower (Massaro, 1988b). It is the case, however, that the FLMP can be falsified by data that do not follow its principle. We saw in the previous chapter that the FLMP gives a poor description of the processing of audible and visible speech syllables when these sources are offset in time by a quarter of a second or so. When sources are not integrated, the FLMP fails as it should. Furthermore, the FLMP is not capable of predicting the results generated by most of the competing models we have considered (Massaro, 1987f; Massaro & Friedman, 1990). We explore the topic of superpower in more depth in chapter 11. For now, the reader can be assured that the success of the FLMP is not simply due to its superpower.

Affect from the Face and the Voice

Our claim is that the FLMP is a universal law, so to substantiate this claim we will want to demonstrate it in action in several different domains. In this

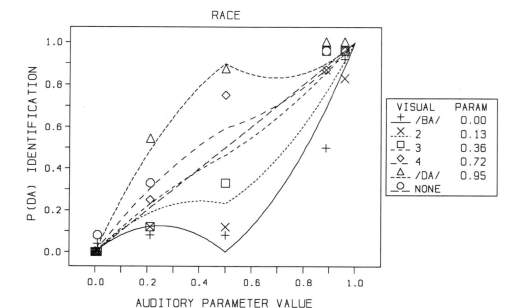

Figure 4.9 The points give the observed proportion of /da/ identifications in the unimodal and factorial auditory-visual conditions as a function of the five levels of the synthetic auditory and visual speech varying between /ba/ and /da/. The auditory levels are plotted along the x-axis in terms of their corresponding parameter values from the fit of the RACE model. The unimodal visual condition is plotted at .5 (completely neutral) on the auditory scale. Results for subject 26. The lines give the predictions of the RACE model.

chapter we will not give an exhaustive survey of the universality of the principle. That is the charge of chapter 6, in which we explore the universality of the principle in a broad range of behavioral domains. Chapter 6 addresses the issue of how well the FLMP withstands situational variability. One aspect of situational variability is domain variability, and we will see the principle in action in several more domains in chapter 6. For now, we apply the principle to data concerning the bimodal perception of affect from the face and the voice. Rather than asking people to make a decision about speech, we ask them about the apparent emotional state of our talking head. For example, people are asked whether our talking head appears happy or angry. The face is made to convey various degrees of anger or happiness and so is the voice.

Figure 4.11 gives the results of an experiment in which the face could be happy, neutral, or angry and the voice could be happy, neutral, or angry. The factorial combination of these two variables produces 9 conditions. The unimodal conditions were also presented, giving a total of 15 conditions. The observed results are plotted in a four-by-four plot with one missing entry. As can be seen in figure 4.11, both sources of information contribute to the perception of affect, just as both audible and visible speech influence speech perception. More important, the same American football pattern is

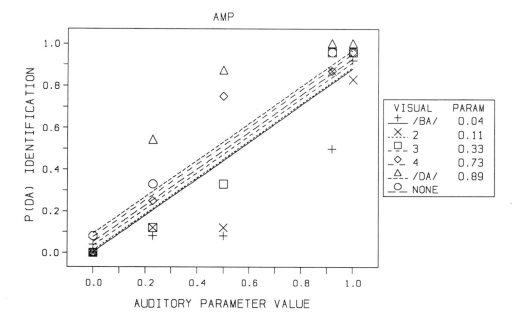

Figure 4.10 The points give the observed proportion of /da/ identifications in the unimodal and factorial auditory-visual conditions as a function of the five levels of the synthetic auditory and visual speech varying between /ba/ and /da/. The auditory levels are plotted along the x-axis in terms of their corresponding parameter values from the fit of the AMP. The unimodal visual condition is plotted at .5 (completely neutral) on the auditory scale. Results for subject 26. The lines give the predictions of the additive model of perception (AMP).

observed in the affect domain as in the speech domain. We explore the perception of affect from the face and the voice in more detail in chapters 7 and 8.

Sensory Integration within Modalities

As we have evaluated our universal principle, we have focused on the integration of information from different sensory modalities, such as audible and visible speech or emotion in the face or voice. We actually began our investigation with studies of sensory integration within the auditory modality (Massaro & Cohen, 1976, 1977; Oden & Massaro, 1978). Our early auditory studies were successful tests of the FLMP, and because multiple cues can occur within a modality, we view sensory integration within a modality as being *as* central if not *more* central than sensory integration between modalities. However, auditory-visual speech perception is ideal for experimentation and theory testing because these two sources of information are so easily manipulated independently of one another. Given our promotion of a universal principle of pattern recognition and the hypothesized relevance of our framework to speech perception more generally, it is valuable to confirm the FLMP within a sensory modality.

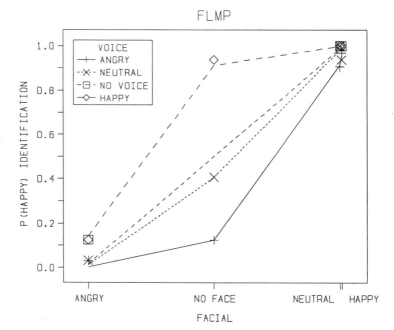

Figure 4.11 Observed (points) and predicted (lines) proportion of "happy" judgments as a function of facial and voice levels: a happy, neutral, or angry face and a happy, neutral, or angry voice. The factorial combination of these two factors produces 9 conditions. The unimodal conditions were also presented, giving a total of 15 conditions. The auditory levels are plotted along the x-axis in terms of their corresponding parameter values from the fit of the FLMP.

We anticipate the research to be reported in chapter 7, which addresses the recognition of facial emotion. To implement the expanded factorial design, it was necessary to choose two features to vary systematically to create a range of emotions between happy and angry. We chose two features that seem to differ somewhat in happy and angry faces: brow displacement and mouth corner displacement. A five-by-five expanded factorial design was used. Five levels of the upper face conditions and five levels of the lower face conditions were factorially combined, along with the ten half-face conditions presenting the upper face or lower face alone. Thus, we created a task exactly parallel to our speech task except that it measures the recognition of facial emotion rather than of speech by ear and eye. The points in figure 4.12 give the observed average results for a typical subject as a function of the mouth and brow variables. Also shown in the figure are the predictions of the FLMP. As the figure illustrates, our universal principle seems to apply to facial emotion as well as to bimodal speech and emotion from the face and the voice.

Thus, we can conclude that the FLMP is equally capable of describing pattern recognition within a modality and between modalities. The results discussed in chapter 6 build toward a truly universal principle by stretching the

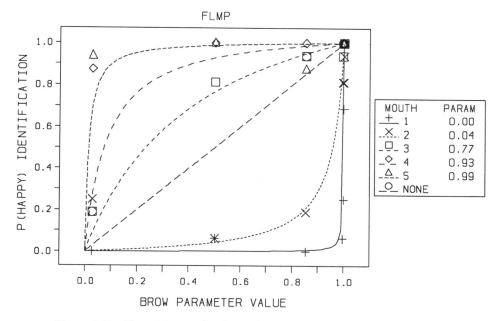

Figure 4.12 The points give the observed proportion of "happy" identifications in the half-face and full-face conditions as a function of the five levels of the mouth and brow varying between angry and happy. The brow levels are plotted along the x-axis in terms of their corresponding parameter values from the fit of the FLMP. The mouth half-face condition is plotted at .5 (completely neutral) on the brow scale. The lines give the predictions of the FLMP.

boundaries of the FLMP's application even further. In addition to robustness across domains, the results in chapter 5 will reveal the law's ability to describe pattern recognition across many different types of individual variability. At this point, it is valuable to address the optimality of our universal principle. If indeed the principle is ubiquitous, then we would expect it to be maximally adaptive.

OPTIMALITY OF THE FLMP ALGORITHM

The FLMP provides an optimal algorithm for integrating several sources of information in pattern recognition, learning, and judgment (Massaro, 1987f). Optimal integration requires that all sources contribute to a decision but that more ambiguous sources be given less of a say in the decision. Some time after the development of the FLMP, it was determined that it corresponded to an optimal integration rule (Massaro, 1987f). That optimal integration rule was developed more than two centuries ago by a Nonconformist minister who never published a mathematical paper but nonetheless was a Fellow of the Royal Society. Bayes' theorem, as it was eventually dubbed, was formulated in a paper called "An Essay toward Solving a Problem in the Doctrine of Chances." A friend discovered the paper after Bayes' death and had it published in the influential voice of the Royal Society, *Philosophical Transactions*.

Basically, Bayes' theorem gives the optimal (the most accurate) solution for determining the probability of an event given several pieces of evidence.

We now prove that the FLMP can be viewed as mathematically equivalent to Bayes' theorem. Bayes' theorem states that

$$P(H_1|E) = \frac{P(E|H_1) \times P(H_1)}{\sum_i P(E|H_i) \times P(H_i)} \tag{4.4}$$

where $P(H_i|E)$ is the probability that some hypothesis H_i is true given that some evidence E is observed; $P(E|H_i)$ is the probability of the evidence E, given that the hypothesis H_i is true, and $P(H_i)$ is the a priori probability of the hypothesis H_i. The likelihood of hypothesis H_1 given some evidence E is equal to the likelihood of the evidence given the hypothesis times the a priori likelihood of the hypothesis divided by the sum of analogous likelihoods for all possible hypotheses. If the a priori probabilities of all possible hypotheses are equal, Bayes' theorem reduces to

$$P(H_1|E) = \frac{P(E|H_1)}{\sum_i P(E|H_i)} \tag{4.5}$$

If each hypothesis corresponds to a particular response alternative, R, equation 4.5 is similar in form to the predictions of the FLMP.

$$P(R_1|E) = \frac{t(E|R_1)}{\sum_i t(E|R_i)}, \tag{4.6}$$

which gives the probability of choosing a particular hypothesis (response alternative, R_1), as equal to the truth value (t) indicating the support for that alternative divided by the sum of the truth values for all relevant alternatives.

The important question that remains is how different sources of evidence are combined according to Bayes' theorem. Given two pieces of evidence E_1 and E_2, the likelihood of a hypothesis H_1 is expressed as follows:

$$P(H_1|E_1 \text{ and } E_2) = \frac{P(E_1 \text{ and } E_2|H_1)}{\sum_i P(E_1 \text{ and } E_2|H_i)}$$

$$= \frac{P(E_1|H_1) \times P(E_2|H_1)}{\sum_i P(E_1|H_i) \times P(E_2|H_i)} \tag{4.7}$$

The equation with two sources of evidence follows from probability theory, in which the likelihood of the joint occurrence of two independent events is the multiplicative combination of the likelihoods of the separate events. The likelihood of two heads in two tosses of a coin is the multiplicative combination of the likelihood of a head on each toss. A psychological model of Bayes' theorem could simply assume that the probability of a response corresponding to hypothesis H_i is equal to the right-hand expression in equation 4.7. We also assumed a multiplicative combination of the auditory and visual evidence in the FLMP (see equation 2.15). Thus, a multiplicative combination of independent sources of evidence in the FLMP is identical in form to a probability model based on Bayes' theorem. The two models could be applied to experimental results in the same manner. In the FLMP, a parameter is estimated for each level of each source of evidence. The same parameter estimation would be used for the probabilities assumed by Bayes' theorem.

Given that previous research has rejected Bayes' theorem in a variety of judgmental situations, why has the mathematically equivalent FLMP been so successful? Two possibilities must be considered. The first is that the rejections of the Bayesian model have been premature, and the second is that the models have been tested in very different domains. Both appear to be true to some extent. Previous tests of Bayes' theorem did not distinguish between information and information processing; predictions were derived on the basis of objective measures of information. In contrast, tests of the FLMP allow for the assignment of subjective values to the various objective sources of information. Consider the test of the model in situations in which the prior probability, or base rate, of an alternative is varied. When subjective base rates are assumed to be equal to objective base rates, performance falls short of the predictions of Bayes' theorem (Leon & Anderson, 1974). Our principle, however, simply states that the information-processing algorithm will be optimal; the information derived from a source could be less than optimal. It could be the case that participants incorrectly estimated the base rates but still integrated that information with that from other sources in the manner described by the FLMP. Thus, performance could fall short of the optimally objective prediction but still be described by the FLMP algorithm.

The second possibility is also valid, because the FLMP and Bayes' theorem have been tested in very different domains. Most tests of Bayes' theorem have focused on estimates of probability in some variant of the two-urn task. Subjects see two urns and are told the proportion of red to blue beads in each urn. One urn is picked with some probability, and a sample of beads is drawn. Given the sample, the subject estimates which urn was in fact chosen. The probability of picking an urn, the relative proportion of beads in each urn, the sample size, and the sample makeup can be varied. Even in these situations, however, it is the normative Bayesian model that has been rejected. It remains an empirical question whether the FLMP can survive in situations where the Bayesian model has supposedly failed. We address this issue of domain variability in chapters 6–8.

Category-Conditional Independence

We postulate independent evaluation followed by integration of the sources of information in bimodal speech perception. Our assumptions imply that although the sources emanate from the same external event, it is not possible to predict the degree of support one source will provide for a given category

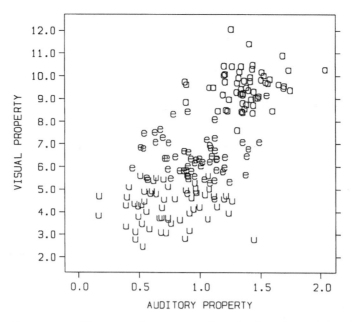

Figure 4.13 Illustration of category-conditional independence. Each point represents a measure of auditory goodness and visual goodness of an audiovisual signal belonging to one of three vowels /e/, /a/, and /u/. Taken as a whole, there is strong correlation—dependence—between the auditory and the visual signals. Nevertheless, within a vowel category the signals are roughly independent.

on the basis of the degree of support that another source provides. The combination of both sources is necessary to make a judgment. However, the claim of noncorrelation between the two sources must be conditional, because it is true in some respect that two sources from the same event tend to be correlated in terms of the information they provide. Specifically, we expect them to support the same category identification rather than different categories. Thus, if a token of auditory speech supports the alternative /ba/, we can expect that the visual speech will support the same alternative. To illustrate the concept of category-conditional independence, figure 4.13 gives a plot of tokens of the vowels /e/, /a/, and /u/ as a function of a hypothetical auditory and a hypothetical visual property. As can be seen in the plot, the audible and visible properties of each category are correlated, in that the same general properties will occur together for any token of a given category. However, within the property space defined by the category, the plot shows that the two properties are independent. This is what we call category-conditional independence.

There are two ways to ascertain category-conditional independence in bimodal speech. One is to measure the characteristics of the auditory and visible speech, as done in figure 4.13, and look for any correlation within a speech category. Marcus Hennecke and David Stork (1996) measured some auditory and visual properties of bimodal signals belonging to one of four speech categories. No correlation between the audible and visible properties was found within each speech category. The second method is to determine whether speech recognition is poorer when category-conditional independence is assumed; if it is poorer, then the assumption was erroneous. Movellan and Chadderdon (1996) recognized that one could never exhaust all possible measures of the audible and visible characteristics to test the property of independence in bimodal speech perception. Their strategy was to test hidden Markov models (HMMs) using separate HMMs for each modality, with and without independence between the two. There was no advantage in performance when the strict constraint of independence was relaxed. Similar results were found by Adjoudani and Benoit (1996). Separate HMM classifiers for the auditory and visual speech mimicked human performance better than did a single classifier for both modalities. These two studies and the measurements by Hennecke and Stork provide some evidence that category-conditional independence exists for bimodal speech. If this is indeed the case, we have another source of evidence that the FLMP assumption of the independence of the two sources at evaluation is reasonable. If the audible and visible speech are objectively independent within a speech category, then processing should treat it that way. Nonindependence of processing would *not* lead to better performance.

One reason Bayesian integration might have evolved is that many situations might be characterized by category-conditional independence. In such situations the only given is that if one source of information supports a given alternative, then the other source will also support that alternative. What is not known, due to category-conditional independence, is how good a visible /e/ can be expected given some observation of the goodness of an audible /e/. The information available is not sufficient to allow the perceiver to implement some cross talk in processing the auditory and visual speech, as is assumed by interactive activation models. For cross talk to have evolved, it would have to be possible to predict the degree to which one modality supports a category on the basis of the degree of support from the other modality.

Probabilities versus Truth Values

Given the mathematical equivalence between a probability model and the FLMP based on fuzzy truth values, it is important to determine whether one can be justified over the other. Traditionally, the use of probabilities in psychology has been associated with threshold or categorical models (Massaro, 1975a). The use of fuzzy truth values represents a shift away from those models to continuously valued states of information. In a strict sense, however, the Bayesian probability theory makes use of continuous information if the evidence is continuous. Both representations are therefore also equivalent in their assumption of continuous rather than categorical states of information. Given the formal identity of the FLMP to a model based on Bayes' theorem, either of the two models is adequate to formally account for the results (Cheeseman, 1986).

A healthy wave of controversy has arisen over whether fuzzy logic offers anything more than what can be easily described by probability (see McNeill & Freiberger, 1993, for a summary). For us, what is different is that Bayes' theorem computes the *probability* of a given hypothesis whereas the FLMP computes the *truth value* of the hypothesis. Truth values can more easily represent the degree of fit between a stimulus and a category, whereas probabilities most naturally represent the likelihood of the category given the stimulus. Consider the question of whether a pillow is a piece of furniture. We want to represent a person's belief that a pillow is a piece of furniture to degree .4, not a .4 probability of its being furniture. The latter representation would seem to mean that 40 out of 100 pillows would qualify as furniture whereas 60 would not. But pillows are not either furniture or not; they are furniture to some degree. Given the pattern recognizer's ability to transmit continuous information about the alternatives, the representation in terms of fuzzy truth values appears more reasonable than a representation in terms of probabilities.

The Constrained Model with Two Alternatives

In cases in which a feature is evaluated against two mutually exclusive response alternatives, H_1 and H_2, we make the simplifying assumption that $t(H_2)$ is equal to $1 - t(H_1)$. In Bayesian terms, when considering only a single source of information, this equivalence means that $P(E|H_2)$ is equal to $1 - P(E|H_1)$. Obviously, this assumption is an additional constraint imposed on Bayes' theorem, and, therefore, this form of the FLMP is no longer equivalent to Bayes' theorem. It turns out, however, that this constrained version of the FLMP and the general version of Bayes' theorem make the same predictions in a task with two mutually exclusive alternatives. The constrained version of the FLMP (equation 2.17) can be written as

$$\frac{x_i y_j}{x_i y_j + (1 - x_i)(1 - y_j)}, \tag{4.8}$$

whereas Bayes' theorem (equation 4.7) can be expressed as

$$\frac{u_i v_j}{u_i v_j + (a_i)(b_j)}. \tag{4.9}$$

A demonstration of their mathematical equivalence reduces to a verification that

$$\frac{x_i y_j}{x_i y_j + (1 - x_i)(1 - y_j)} = \frac{u_i v_j}{u_i v_j + (a_i)(b_j)} \tag{4.10}$$

for all values of $x_i, y_j, a_i, b_j, u_i,$ and v_j in [0,1]. Multiplying both the numerator and denominator of the left and right terms of equation 4.10 by $1/x_i y_j$ and

$1/u_i v_j$, respectively, gives

$$\frac{1}{1 + \frac{(1 - x_i)(1 - y_j)}{(x_i)(y_j)}} = \frac{1}{1 + \frac{(a_i)(b_j)}{(u_i)(v_j)}}. \tag{4.11}$$

The equivalence of the right and left sides of equation 4.11 can be seen by noting the parallel forms of $1/(1 + z)$ on each side. That is, it is sufficient to show that the value of z is the same on each side, or,

$$\frac{(1 - x_i)(1 - y_j)}{(x_i)(y_j)} = \frac{(a_i)(b_j)}{(u_i)(v_j)}, \tag{4.12}$$

which can be viewed as two simple ratios on each side of the equal sign. Given that each ratio is indexed by a single subscript, a single parameter is sufficient to specify each of their values. That is, for example, there is a value of x_i in [0,1] such that $(1 - x_i)/x_i$ is equal to a_i/u_i for all values of a_i and u_i in [0,1]. Thus this implementation of the FLMP does not decorrelate its predictions from those given by Bayes' theorem. They are mathematically equivalent, but we still prefer the FLMP for the reasons just outlined.

Although our law is formulated at the algorithmic level, it seems appropriate to end this chapter with a brief discussion of several brain metaphors for our universal principle.

IMPLEMENTATION IN THE BRAIN

The title of this section might surprise some readers given our earlier argument that the FLMP algorithm is not to be found in the brain. The brain activity taking place during pattern recognition, however, might be informative about different algorithms. Therefore it is worthwhile to consider how the FLMP algorithm might be implemented in the brain. We consider three different neurologically plausible solutions. In all three cases, modality-specific information is sent forward to other neurons from auditory and visual neurons. The three interpretations differ with respect to how the auditory and visual information is shared during the chain of processing from input to output. In the first case, the processing of one modality activates the location that is normally activated by the other modality. In the second case, the activation from the two modalities is sent to a third location that combines their inputs. In the third case, the activation from the two modalities is simultaneously sent forward but there is no location at which the separate modality-specific information is integrated. Only the last two cases are consistent with the FLMP.

Sensory Penetration

Integration can occur when the processing of one modality is shunted to a location that is normally activated by the other modality. We call this sensory

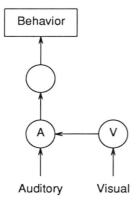

Figure 4.14 Schematic representation of the neural processing involved in sensory penetration, in which information from one modality affects the actual neurological hardware devoted to the other modality.

penetration because the idea is that somehow information from one modality has an impact on the actual neurological hardware devoted to processing some other modality. As illustrated in figure 4.14, the activation from the visible speech is sent to a location that receives activation from the auditory modality.

Given that speech is primarily auditory, we might expect that the visual speech eventually ends up at the location of auditory speech processing. A few researchers of brain imaging have interpreted their results in this way (Sams et al., 1991). Earlier measurements seemed to have shown activation of the auditory cortex with visible speech. More recently, however, Sams and Levänen (1996) learned that the magnetoencephalograph signals are highly complex, showing a significant amount of individual variability. (In our framework, we would have expected variability in information but not in information processing.) The investigators hoped to show differential activation of the auditory cortex by visible speech. However, several findings suggest that visible speech does not influence early stages of auditory information processing. First, visible speech alone does not activate auditory cortex. Second, the influence of visible speech in bimodal presentations is very late, occurring 200 ms after the onset of the auditory syllable. This late activation could reflect processing well after the processes of pattern recognition have been completed. In that case the outcome of speech perception would emerge from the auditory pathways. This interpretation would at least give a satisfying account of why perception of visible speech affects our auditory experience. On the other hand, it seems inconsistent with the many findings that the processing of audible and visible speech is well described by the FLMP law, which represents the two modalities independently of one another. Thus, we claim that sensory penetration could not underlie the FLMP algorithm. The next two implementations, on the other hand, are consistent with the FLMP.

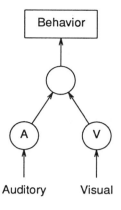

Figure 4.15 Schematic representation of the neural processing involved in simple feed-forward convergent integration.

Convergent Integration

A second type of brain integration involves simple feed-forward convergence. As illustrated in figure 4.15, the neural activation from the auditory and visible speech activates a third location that is sensitive to the inputs from both modalities. An important set of observations from single cell recordings in cats could be interpreted in terms of convergent integration (Meredith & Stein, 1985, 1986; Stein & Meredith, 1993). Neurons in the superior colliculus can be made to respond with presentation of just a single sensory cue, such as a light spot or a brief hissing sound. The combination of both stimuli, however, produces a much more vigorous response. This enhancement (given two modalities relative to either one) offers a potentially valuable neural parallel to our behavioral findings.

There are some differences between multisensory interactions at the neural level in the superior colliculus and integration in speech and other domains of pattern recognition. In the superior colliculus, maximal enhancement (given two modalities relative to either one) occurs with minimally effective unimodal stimuli (Stein & Meredith, 1993, fig. 10.19). In speech, maximal enhancement occurs when two modalities are each intermediate in their support for a given alternative (Massaro, 1987f, p.185, fig. 7). If both sources are completely ambiguous in the FLMP, then their combination is also completely ambiguous. If both sources are maximally informative in the FLMP, then their combination cannot be more informative than either one alone. The condition of truth values of .75 on both gives lots of enhancement.

In the superior colliculus, maximal enhancement (given two modalities relative to just one) occurs with multimodal stimuli. Neural activity given two stimuli in the same modality is always less than the sum of the activity given each stimulus (Stein & Meredith, 1993, Figure 10.18). In speech, however, one also observes enhancement or superadditive integration with several auditory cues. For example, duration and formant quality are two auditory cues that are integrated for the perception of vowel identity. Another example is the integration of consonant duration and vowel duration for perception of voicing in final stops.

Spatially coincident multisensory stimuli tend to produce response enhancement, whereas spatially disparate stimuli produce either depression or no interaction. This makes sense for locating events in space. If the auditory and visual sources agree, there is enhancement. If they disagree, there is attenuation, as one would expect. This pattern is confirmed in behavioral studies with cats. The localization task is a choice of *where* (recognition) not simply *whether* something occurred (detection). The behavioral studies also show disruption on disparate trials or those with conflicting information. If a cat learns to respond to a visual source and is never rewarded for responding to an auditory source, then if both are presented together with the auditory source dislocated 60 degrees away from the visual there is a disruption of performance (Stein & Meredith, 1993, figures 11.1–11.5).

In speech perception, on the other hand, the spatial location of the auditory and visual speech can differ and yet integration still occurs (Fisher, 1991; Bertelson et al., 1994).

One of the similarities between the two domains is that auditory and visual sources are integrated even though their relative onset times differ by tens or even hundreds of milliseconds. Given the physics of auditory and visual stimuli and the physiology of their respective sensory systems, the senses must be prepared for temporal differences in their neural consequences. In the previous chapter, we learned that audible and visible speech are integrated even if they are offset in time by roughly 250 ms. Stein and Meredith (1993) have carried out similar studies.

As pointed out by Stein (1995) and by Stein, Meredith, and Wallace (1994), the sensory systems seem to have solved the problem of integrating multisensory stimuli arriving at different times by extending the neural activation resulting from stimulation beyond the stimulation period. Thus, stimuli that occur at nearly the same point in time will tend to have overlapping activation patterns. This solution provides a valuable independent substantiation of the concept of a sensory storage, which has played an important role in information-processing theory for the last three decades (Massaro & Loftus, 1996). In summary, there appear to be some similarities and some differences between multisensory interactions in the superior colliculus and the bimodal perception of speech. Notwithstanding the differences, convergent integration offers a potential implementation of the FLMP.

Nonconvergent Temporal Integration

A third type of implementation involves integration-like behavior, but there is no location at which the separate modality-specific information is integrated. Figure 4.16 gives a schematic form for this type of neural processing.

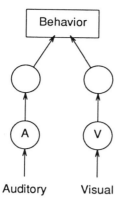

Figure 4.16 Schematic representation of the neural processing involved in nonconvergent temporal integration.

Liederman (1995) and Zeki (1993) describe a highly plausible process, which they call "nonconvergent temporal integration" and "confluent convergence", respectively, in which there is a temporal synchronization of segregated areas. As can be seen in figure 4.16, this type of integration involves the combination of information from two or more remote regions of the brain. Cortico-cortical pathways (pathways that connect regions of the cortex) synchronize the outputs of these regions and enable them to feed forward, independently but synchronously, to other areas. There is no terminating Cartesian theater (Dennett, 1991), but rather only temporal integration. Such integration would influence some output process rather than producing some higher-order integrated representation for storage or further processing by other parts of the brain.

According to Zeki (1993), input systems are domain specific, as are sub-systems within a domain like color, motion, and form. He proposes three brain processes that involve integration. The first process enlarges the receptive field of cells in order to integrate information from a larger part of the sensory surface. The second process utilizes cells that have more specific properties, such as orientation-specific cells. The third process integrates information from different attributes such as form and motion. (Zeki does not address the important issue of multimodal integration.) What is important for our purposes is that, according to this model, information from two separate areas does not necessarily converge to the same third area. The simultaneous activation of different areas could produce the experience of a single object with multiple perceptual attributes. This type of brain process-ing appears to be most consistent with the findings that an integrated per-cept can exist simultaneously with and independently of representations of the separate sources of information.

One fairly well documented example of nonconvergent temporal integra-tion involves the dorsal and ventral streams of visual information. Goodale and Milner (1992) state that "the set of object descriptions that permit identification and recognition may be computed independently of the set of descriptions that allow an observer to shape the hand appropriately to pick up an object" (p. 20). Evidence for this point of view comes from dissociations shown by brain-injured patients. One patient with Balint's syndrome had good object perception but could not use the size, shape, and orientation of the object to control the hand and fingers during a grasping movement. A visual agnostic patient with ventral stream damage could not recognize the object but could use its information to guide the hand and fingers to pick up the object. The dorsal and ventral systems seem to control behavior relatively independently of one another. They need not converge to or be integrated at a single location. As pointed out by Liederman (1995), "it seems unlikely that a region will be discovered that consists of a map of 'where' the object is superimposed on 'what' the object is. Synchronization may be the best way to get independent maps to cohere" (p. 479).

The control of behavior by the dorsal and ventral systems might not be the appropriate analog of the integration of auditory and visual information in speech perception. It is not clear whether the two visual systems actually control behavior together or whether one system is responsible for one type of behavior and the other system responsible for the other. In the framework of formal models we have developed and tested, this type of control might be implemented by a nonintegration model. In such a model a behavioral consequence is then the result of either one system (source of information) or the other. At any given time, behavior does not reflect the combined influence of the two sources. We have called this model a single channel model (SCM). Testing between integration and nonintegration alternatives is no easy matter and requires quantitative models. The predictive ability of the FLMP has shown, on the other hand, that speech perception reflects the simultaneous influence of both audible and visible speech. Thus, what is required for an implementation of the FLMP is neural activity along two independent channels that simultaneously influences behavior.

RETROSPECTIVE

Although we advocate a componential analysis of behavior, it is always possible that we are dividing up the phenomena in places where no divisions actually exist. Psychology has certainly operated on the premise that the different sensory modalities are encapsulated, or at least relatively isolable from one another. This strategy appears to have been reasonably successful both in experimental psychology and in neuroscience. We know that almost all of the primary projection pathways in the visual cortex are modality specific, even though there are a few multisensory neurons—neurons that can be activated by several different modalities. Multisensory neurons are found in other locations, however, including visual-somatosensory, visual-auditory, and visual-auditory-somatosensory cortex.

Stein (personal communication) offered a neuroscientist's perspective that is very similar to the one I was led to by our experimental studies. "I believe that higher organisms have evolved an interesting duality—to simultaneously hold sensory experiences apart from one another in some parts of the brain, and to integrate the information they provide in others. This happens at every level in the CNS: midbrain, thalamus, cortex." This point of view offers the best understanding of our identification and discrimination experiment (see chapter 11). Participants were easily capable of discriminating two different bimodal speech events even though they were categorized equivalently.

Armed with a general principle, we now proceed to push the boundaries to assess exactly how general and robust it is. In part II, we explore how well the principle holds up across broad individual and situational variability.

II Broadening the Domain

5   Individual Variability

The preservation of favorable variations and the rejection of injurious variation, I call Natural Selection, or Survival of the Fittest. Variations neither useful nor injurious would not be affected by natural select[ion] and would be left a fluctuating element.
—Charles Darwin, *Origin of Species*

Experience in the methodological and theoretical intricacies of bimodal speech perception has led me to formulate some productive strategies for psychological inquiry, which I express in various sets of prescriptions. The prescriptions are a productive route to the formulation and test of general principles within some research domain. In the previous chapter we explored a universal principle describing speech perception by eye and ear. This second part of the book follows those prescriptions to provide a rigorous test of that principle. One set of prescriptions involves analyzing the influence of well-known variables having to do with the differences between individuals. These variables differ from the typical independent variables that are aimed at influencing psychological processes. Variability among individuals is usually considered to be orthogonal to the questions of interest. Individual variability plays a central role in evolutionary theory and inquiry: one viable hypothesis is that psychology—the study of the behavior that has necessarily evolved—should be no different. The proposed variables having to do with individual variability are (1) development and aging, (2) languages, (3) sensory impairment, (4) brain trauma, (5) personality, (6) sex, and (7) experience and learning. We begin with a presentation of our treatment of individual variability.

UNDERSTANDING INDIVIDUAL DIFFERENCES

In the next sections, the processing of bimodal speech is assessed in the context of different sources of individual variability. We will see that individual variability modulates the phenomena of interest. However, these modulations are well described within our theoretical framework. Thus, the variability we see actually highlights that which is consistent in the information processing of bimodal speech. Before we assess the influence of variables having to do with individual differences, it is important first to assess the variability found within a random sample of individuals—in our case, students from the university community. An assessment of individual variability makes clear that results of experiments cannot be pooled across subjects, as is usually the case. We begin with an illustration of the dangers of pooling.

The Sins of Averaging across Individuals

It is well known that individual differences exist, and usually our experimental investigations are aimed at reducing them as much as possible. Often the chosen strategy is to average the results across individuals and consider only the average performance. This is still true for much of psychological inquiry, so I sometimes worry that we might have an explanation for an average subject but one that does not apply to any of the actual individuals making up the average. Thus the averaging procedure may preclude the discovery of important properties of the processes of interest.

Individual variability is the reason we emphasize individual-subject analyses rather than group analyses. Group results can be highly misleading, as can be seen in some recent tests of the fuzzy logical model of perception (FLMP) and of an additive model of perception (AMP). In contrast to the FLMP, the AMP predicts that the absolute contribution of one source of information to performance is independent of the ambiguity of the other sources of information. Replicating Massaro's (1988a) analyses, Cutting and coworkers (1992) found that model tests based on individual data did not unambiguously discriminate between the FLMP and the AMP. The average results and the individual data appeared to be somewhat inconsistent. Considering the individual fits of all 44 subjects across three experiments, the FLMP did show a slight edge. When the two models were fit to the group data, averaged across the individual subjects, the AMP gave a better fit than the FLMP.

Cutting's research team noted a larger variability in the individuals than in the average data across the three experiments and so interpreted the average functions as more meaningful than those from individuals. However, this finding has little to do with differences between individuals and groups, but is simply a function of the number of observations per data point. The law of large numbers states that variance decreases with increases in the number of observations (see chapter 10). One can also obtain smoother curves for individuals if the number of observations is increased.

Furthermore, it is well known that a group function might not correspond to any of the individual functions making up the group function. For this reason, previous investigators (Sidman, 1952; Massaro, 1989a) have cautioned against the use of group functions. Our goal should be to describe individual behavior, rather than an average behavior that is not necessarily exhibited by any real person. Describing average behavior is analogous to having a theory of planetary motion that predicts where the average planet is without any hint of the locations of the individual planets (or, for baseball fans, to a league-wide earned run average). Although there are many examples of the sins of averaging in the psychological literature, we will focus in particular on how averaging the results across individuals can distort the results in favor of the AMP. Individual functions conforming to the predictions of the FLMP, when averaged together, might give a function that is more consistent with those of the AMP.

To illustrate the dangers of averaging across subjects, we have implemented for the AMP and the FLMP what previous investigators have demonstrated for all-or-none and incremental models of learning. Given a learning experience, learning of some target behavior occurs either completely or not at all, or else some incremental improvement in the target behavior is obtained. Different individuals who each learn in an all-or-none manner, when averaged together, can give results predicted by the incremental model. For our demonstration, we generated hypothetical predictions of a model because we do not know what model actually accounts for the data of real subjects. We created four FLMP subjects performing in a factorial design with two independent variables A and B with seven levels each. These individual FLMP results are shown as the points in figure 5.1 and their group results as the points in figure 5.2.

Figure 5.1 also illustrates the predictions of the AMP when fit to the results from the four different FLMP subjects. As can be seen in the figure, the AMP gives a poor description of the individual results, with an average RMSD of .070 across the four fits. As expected, the fit of the FLMP gave an essentially perfect description of each of the four individual results. The right panel of figure 5.2 gives the fit of the AMP to the average group data. As can be seen, the AMP gave an almost perfect description of the average results (RMSD of .004). In contrast, the right panel of figure 5.2 shows that the FLMP fit of the group results was significantly poorer (RMSD of .023). The predictions of the FLMP are nonlinear, and averaging several FLMP subjects will not necessarily yield an ideal FLMP subject. Thus, the fit of the AMP to the group average was five times better than the fit of the FLMP, even though the individual results were FLMP subjects who were very poorly described by the AMP. Admittedly, the individual FLMP subjects were contrived to make this point, but we found it very easy to find examples with the same outcome. Thus, a good fit of the AMP to group data should not be interpreted as evidence for additive integration.

The sins of averaging are seldom ecumenical. Averaging across individual all-or-none learning curves can always bias the outcome to support incremental learning, but averaging across incremental curves will never falsely favor all-or-none learning. Similarly, it is important to note that pooling across different AMP individuals can never give average results that are more accurately described by the FLMP. Average AMP results will always give ideal AMP results and will necessarily be more poorly fit by the FLMP

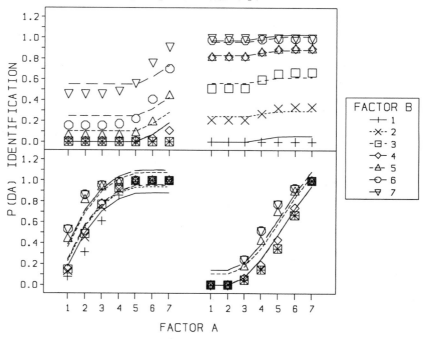

Figure 5.1 Simulated FLMP data (points) and predicted AMP fits (lines). The four panels give the individual results for four pseudosubjects as a function of seven levels of two factors A and B.

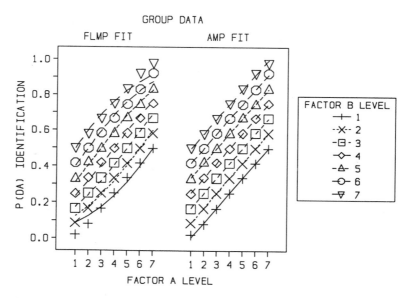

Figure 5.2 Average group data (points) and predicted FLMP (left panel) and AMP (right panel) fits (lines) as a function of arbitrary factors A and B. Average group data derived from the four simulated FLMP pseudosubjects shown in figure 5.1.

than the AMP. Given the necessity of individual analyses, understanding individual differences becomes central to our endeavor. Such understanding is enhanced by a distinction between information and information processing.

Information versus Information Processing

We all know that individuals differ, but we want to know how they differ. To answer this question, the investigator must have available a good process model of the task. Our process model makes a distinction between *information* and *information processing*. The separate sources of information make contact with the individual at the evaluation stage of processing. The reduction in uncertainty effected by each source is defined as *information*. In the fit of the FLMP, for example, the a_i and v_j values correspond to information. These parameter values represent how informative each source of information is. *Information processing* refers to how the sources of information are processed. In the FLMP, that processing is described by the evaluation, integration, and decision stages.

The distinction is central to the analysis of individual differences and of variables that influence individual variability. The variability in the information is analogous to the variability of the weather. There are just too many previous contributions and influences to allow quantitative prediction. In addition, small early influences can lead to dramatic consequences at a later time (the butterfly effect in chaos theory). However, once we account for the variability by estimating free parameters in the fit of the model, we are able to provide a convincing description of how the information is processed and mapped into a response. Although we cannot predict, a priori, how /ba/-like a particular audible or visible speech syllable will be for a given individual, we can predict how the two sources of information will be integrated and how a decision will be made. In addition, the model does take a stand on the evaluation process in the sense that it is assumed that the sources of information are evaluated independently of one another. Individuals might differ simply with respect to the information they have, or they might differ in how they process the information. In previous papers, we have concluded that individual differences could be attributed solely to information differences and not to information-processing differences (Massaro, 1992a; Massaro & Ferguson, 1993). We provide a more rigorous test of this hypothesis by analyzing the results of our database of 82 subjects.

Model Tests

In chapter 2, the FLMP and a variety of other models were fit to our database of 82 subjects. We concluded that the FLMP gave the best fit based on the average goodness of fit (RMSD) derived from the 82 individual fits. We can now provide a finer-grained analysis by determining the range of predictive accuracy across all subjects. Figure 5.3 gives a frequency distribution

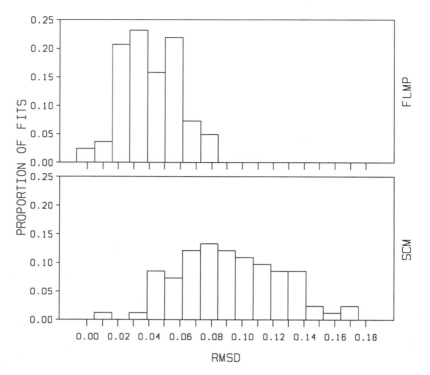

Figure 5.3 Frequency distribution of the RMSD values for the fit of the FLMP (top plot) and SCM (bottom plot) across the 82 subjects.

of the RMSD values for both the FLMP and the single-channel model (SCM). As the figure shows, the distributions overlap to some extent. The roughly single-peaked functions show that the RMSD values are fairly evenly distributed around the average RMSD. The spread of RMSD values is somewhat larger for the SCM than for the FLMP. One might conclude from the overlapping distributions that the FLMP fits better for some subjects and the SCM for others. However, that conclusion would not be justified because one must compare the goodness of fit for each subject individually.

The best check on individual variability in information processing is to compare the range of predictive accuracy for the FLMP against the range for some other model. We choose the SCM for this comparison because its mathematical instantiation represents several different forms of information processing (see chapter 2). So, if any of these alternative models described an individual, the fit of the SCM would be better than the fit of the FLMP. Figure 5.4 plots the RMSD value for each subject as a function of his or her corresponding RMSD value for the SCM. As can be seen in figure 5.4, all but five of the points are below the diagonal, indicating that the FLMP provided the better fit for 77 of the 82 subjects. This result supports our faith in the robustness of the FLMP across different individuals. Given no individual differences in information processing, we expect to find them in information.

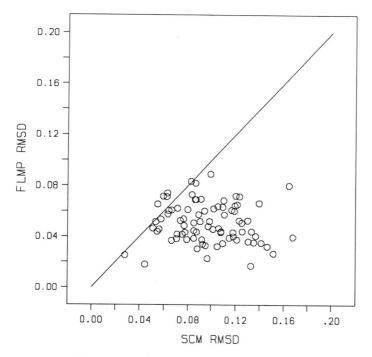

Figure 5.4 The RMSD value for the fit of the FLMP on the ordinate as a function of the RMSD value for the SCM for each of the 82 subjects.

Relative Influence of Visible and Audible Speech

If people do not differ in how they process bimodal speech, how else might they differ? Our unique sensory systems, life histories, and current resources guarantee that a source of information will have different consequences for each of us. In bimodal speech perception, those different consequences will be seen in individual differences in the relative influence of the audible and visible speech.

One index of the magnitude of a modality's influence can be given by the difference in response probabilities for the two endpoint stimuli from that modality. An example is the difference in average probability of a /da/ response to the /da/ and /ba/ endpoint stimuli of the visual continuum. This marginal-range difference was computed for each subject for both the audible and visible endpoints. For example, an average .9 probability of /da/ given the visual /da/ endpoint stimulus and an overall .2 probability of /da/ given the visual /ba/ endpoint stimulus would render a visual effect of .7. An auditory effect and a visual effect were computed for each subject in the experiments that made up our database of 82 subjects.

Figure 5.5 plots the size of the visual effect as a function of the size of the auditory effect for the 82 subjects. There are several points of interest in figure 5.5. First, the size of the auditory and visual effects varied significantly

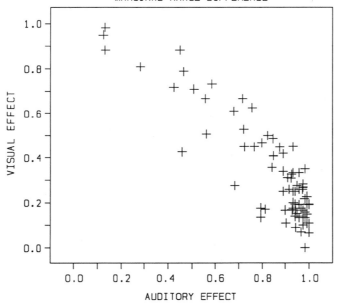

Figure 5.5 The visual effect plotted as a function of the auditory effect for the 82 subjects.

across subjects. The points are not clustered together but spread across the graph. Second, the fact that the points are at or above the negative diagonal means that there was a strong combined influence. Third, only one subject at zero visual effect showed no influence of visible speech. Fourth, there is trade-off between the influence of audible and visible speech. Figure 5.5 shows that there was a strong negative correlation between the two effects. To the extent that one modality had a large effect, the other had a small effect. Fifth, audible speech had a larger influence than visible speech. As can be seen in figure 5.5, only 10 of the 82 participants are located above the positive diagonal, which is the area in which a participant gave a larger effect of visual than auditory speech. Many of the observers are also clustered at the lower right-hand corner of the graph, indicating a larger influence of audible than visible speech.

The consistently good fit of the FLMP and the large differences in figure 5.5 support the hypothesis of individual variability in information but not in information processing. To illustrate the huge variability that exists in the information, and the constancy of the information processing, figures 5.6 and 5.7 give the results for two subjects tested in this same task (Massaro, 1990). The participant whose results are shown in figure 5.6 was influenced primarily by the visual information, whereas the opposite was the case for the participant represented in figure 5.7. Given these large differences, one might expect that the information processing would also be very different for the two participants. This was not the case, however: the FLMP gave about

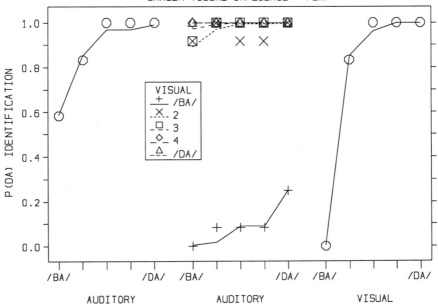

Figure 5.6 The points give the observed proportion of /da/ identifications in the unimodal and factorial auditory-visual conditions as a function of the five levels of the synthetic auditory and visual speech varying between /ba/ and /da/. Results for a participant influenced primarily by visible speech. The lines give the predictions for the FLMP.

equally good descriptions of both sets of results. The RMSD values were .0269 and .0447.

The parameter values a_i and v_j index information in the FLMP. Figure 5.8 gives the parameter values determined in the fit of the FLMP to their results. It is impressive that the FLMP is able to give a good account of both observers' results with simply a change in parameter values to reflect the information value of each source. These differences should refute the common belief that a good theory should necessarily be parameter-free or have a fixed set of parameter values. I do not see how any parameter-free theory or a theory with a single set of parameter values can describe the results in both figures 5.6 and 5.7. Results of this type inform us about what we can expect to predict (information processing) and what cannot be specified in advance (information). Armed with our scalpel to dissect information from information processing, we initiate an exploration of the dimensions of individual variability by evaluating differences across the life span.

LIFE-SPAN VARIABILITY

One question of importance in the present chapter is whether bimodal speech is processed in the same manner across the life span. The study of bimodal speech perception has been limited primarily to the study of young adults

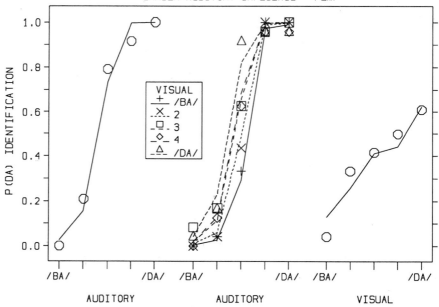

Figure 5.7 The points give the observed proportion of /da/ identifications in the unimodal and factorial auditory-visual conditions as a function of the five levels of the synthetic auditory and visual speech varying between /ba/ and /da/. Results for a participant influenced primarily by audible speech. The lines give the predictions for the FLMP.

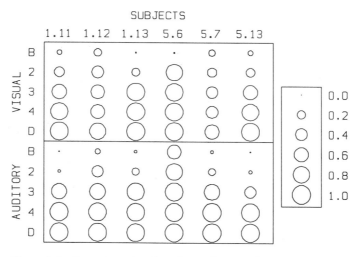

Figure 5.8 Parameter values for subjects shown in figures 1.11, 1.12, and 1.13 and in figures 5.6, 5.7, and 5.13. The parameter values give the degree of support for the response alternative /da/ as a function of the five levels along the visual and auditory speech continua. The parameter value is represented by the area of each circle.

(Massaro & Cohen, 1990; Summerfield, 1979, 1983). It is important to determine to what extent the results obtained to date are dependent on the subject population. Our empirical findings, theories, and models tend to be limited to highly specific situations. Developmental and aging studies allow us to assess the degree to which we can generalize our conclusions. As in our study of individual differences and similarities, a process model is valuable for the evaluation of the influence of development and aging (Massaro, 1984, 1994b; Massaro, et al., 1986). There are significant overall differences in the perception of bimodal speech across the life span. However, when performance is accounted for by a process model of the task, the differences appear to be accounted for completely in terms of the information from the auditory and visual sources, rather than differences in how that information is combined. We first look at developmental influences and then at the effects of aging.

Developmental Changes

To illustrate the value of the FLMP framework in the study of developmental changes, we point to an experimental study reported in Massaro (1987f, chap. 8). A two-by-five expanded factorial design was used with six different groups. Subjects were presented with two levels of visual information (/ba/ or /da/) and five levels of an auditory continuum between /ba/ and /da/. For illustrative purposes, we will describe only the preschool children (average age 3 years, 5 months) and fourth-grade students (9 years, 7 months). For the speechreading condition, the child watched the experimenter's mouth as she demonstrated silent articulations of the two alternatives.

The points in figures 5.9 and 5.10 give the observed results for the two groups of subjects. Both groups of children were influenced by both the audible and visible speech. The lines give the predictions of the FLMP. The good fit of the FLMP to both sets of results suggests that preschool children integrate independent and continuous sources of information in the same way as we have observed for adults. The good fit of the FLMP for both age groups argues against a developmental change from one type of process to another in the recognition of speech. At every age, performance is appropriately described as following the operations of the FLMP, which in turn provides a framework for assessing differences in information value.

Using the FLMP, we ask whether the information values for the auditory and visual sources change with age and whether the processes involved in the perceptual recognition of speech differ with age. The measure of information we use is identical to the relative influence of auditory and visual speech described in the previous section. The auditory effect was .48 for the preschool children and .85 for the fourth-graders. The visual effect was .18 for the preschool children and .30 for the fourth-graders. Thus, the fourth-graders had significantly more information about both auditory and visual

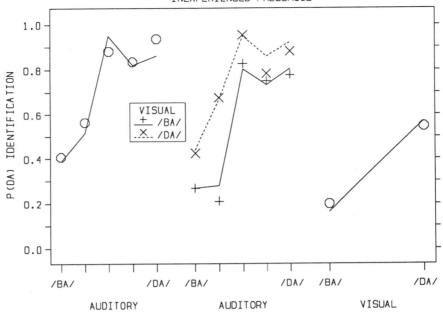

Figure 5.9 The points give the observed proportion of /da/ identifications for inexperienced preschool children in the auditory-alone (left panel), the factorial auditory-visual (center panel), and the visual-alone (right panel) conditions as a function of the five levels of the synthetic auditory and the two levels of natural visual speech. The lines give the predictions for the FLMP.

speech than did the preschool children. This result and the good description by the FLMP of both groups' results suggest that the developmental differences are due only to information differences. Previous studies found developmental differences, but their paradigm could not pinpoint whether information or information-processing differences were responsible (McGurk & MacDonald, 1976). Our studies unambiguously locate the developmental differences at information.

Several other results of our study are important for understanding language development. The increase in information between preschool and fourth grade shows that learning the functional features for audible and visible speech is a slow process that continues at least until adolescence. This conclusion about bimodal speech perception is consonant with the more general view that psycholinguistic development is an instance of skill acquisition. With experience, for example, infants develop prototypical representations of the speech segments of their language (Iverson & Kuhl, 1995). "What differs between the adult and child is the richness of their experiences with and their knowledge about their native language." (Nusbaum & Goodman, 1994, p. 329). On the other hand, the FLMP algorithm appears to be already in place by age three and is consistently used throughout development and during adulthood.

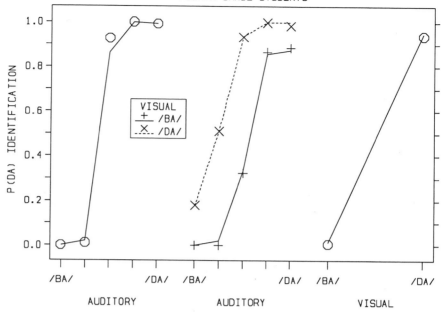

Figure. 5.10 The points give the observed proportion of /da/ identifications for fourth-grade students in the auditory-alone (left panel), the factorial auditory-visual (center panel), and the visual-alone (right panel) conditions as a function of the five levels of the synthetic auditory and the two levels of natural visual speech. The lines give the predictions for the FLMP.

It is well known that higher-order context influences perceptual recognition, and we can ask to what extent that phenomenon varies across development. Results presented in chapter 11 indicate that children are influenced by phonological context in the same manner that adults are. Similar results across development also seem to be the norm for lexical and sentential context. Nittrouer and Boothroyd (1990) had children between 4.5 and 6.5 years old identify consonant-vowel-consonant (CVC) syllables and four-word sentences presented in auditory noise. The results were compared to those of an earlier study with adults (Boothroyd & Nittrouer, 1988). Although the children performed more poorly overall—as we would expect—they benefited as much from lexical and syntactic context as did the adults. The children showed somewhat less of a benefit from semantic constraints, a result that was taken to reflect their relative lack of semantic knowledge. All of the results were successfully analyzed using the assumption that the stimulus and context provide independent channels of information. In our framework, it appears that the children were integrating the stimulus characteristics and the higher-order context in the same manner as adults. Thus we have some evidence that the integration of bottom-up and top-down sources of information is constant across development. We now assess the influence of aging.

Aging Changes

Given the changes that affect the sensory organs as we age, it seems unlikely that a given speech stimulus will be perceived equivalently by populations of different ages. For example, some hearing loss occurs with aging (Corso, 1959, 1963; Van Rooij, Plomp & Orlebeke, 1989; Working Group on Speech Understanding and Aging, 1988), and the hearing loss occurs earlier for men than for women (Corso, 1963). There is also some evidence for age-related differences in the use of visual information. Van Rooij and coworkers (1989) found that elderly adults were slower than young adults at reaction tasks. This result may be of particular interest in light of evidence that the visual evoked response is positively correlated with speechreading skill (Samar & Sims, 1983; Shepherd, 1982). However, Rönnberg et al. (1989) were unable to replicate these findings, and it seems unlikely that fast visual-neural processing could account for speechreading skill. Farrimond (1959) found changes in speechreading skill across aging, with a decline after middle age.

It might be expected that a loss of hearing with aging might lead to an enhanced ability in speechreading. If perceivers somehow attend more to the visual information in situations that afford less auditory information, then the aging person, who probably has some degree of hearing impairment, might develop increased speechreading ability. However, Farrimond (1959) found a decrease of about 8% per decade in the speechreading ability of men after about age 35. Similarly, Shoop and Binnie (1979) found a decline of the visual perception of speech across the adult life span (see also Binnie, Montgomery & Jackson, 1974). Finally, Ewertsen and Nielsen (1971) found a decline between ages 20, 50, and 70 years in auditory, visual, and auditory-visual speech perception. Thus, the evidence reveals a loss of information across the life span; it remains to be determined whether there is also a degradation in information processing. Our FLMP framework allows us to address that important question.

To address the question, we refer to a study using a five-by-five expanded factorial design with young and old subjects, with median ages of 19 and 69, respectively (Massaro, 1994b). The test items were the synthetic auditory and visible speech syllables varied between /ba/ and /da/. Subjects were instructed to listen and to watch the talker, and to identify the syllable as /ba/, /da/, /bda/, /dba/, /ða/, /va/, /ga/, or "other."

The points in figures 5.11 and 5.12 give the observed results for the college students and senior citizens, respectively. The overall pattern of results is very similar for the two groups. The most frequent responses were /ba/, /da/, /bda/, /ða/, and /va/, and each of those responses is plotted in a separate panel. As can be seen in the left-most set of plots, judgments changed in preference from /ba/, to /va/ and /ða/, and then to /da/ across the visual /ba/-to-/da/ continuum. Judgments also changed from /ba/ to /da/ along the auditory continuum, with a significant number of /va/ and /ða/ judgments

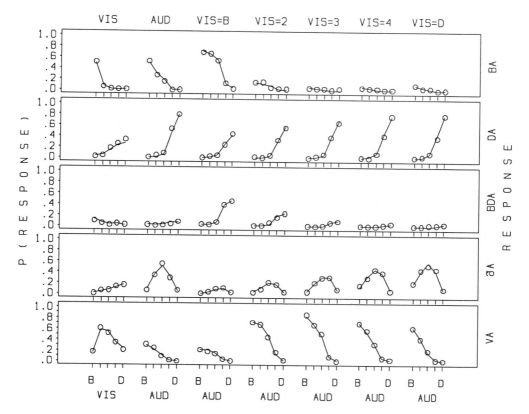

Figure 5.11 Observed (points) and predicted (lines) proportion of identifications for the visual-alone condition (left panel), auditory-alone condition (second from left panel), and the factorial auditory-visual conditions (other five panels) as a function of the five levels of the synthetic auditory (AUD) and visual (VIS) speech varying between /ba/ (B) and /da/ (D). Results for college students. The lines give the predictions for the FLMP.

for the intermediate syllables. The judgments of the bimodal speech syllables can be understood in terms of the unimodal responses, which show that the audible and visible syllables were relatively ambiguous. We use these results to address the question of whether the groups differ on information, information processing, or both.

Age-Related Differences in Information We computed the auditory and visual influence as before, but in this case we limited the measure to just the unimodal conditions. This measure should be a more direct index because there is no opportunity for an influence from the other source. By these measures, senior citizens had less information than college students for both the auditory and visual modalities. The magnitude of the visual effect averaged .31 for the seniors and .40 for the college students, showing somewhat less visual information with aging. This finding agrees with those of earlier studies (Ewertsen & Nielsen, 1971; Shoop & Binnie, 1979). The average

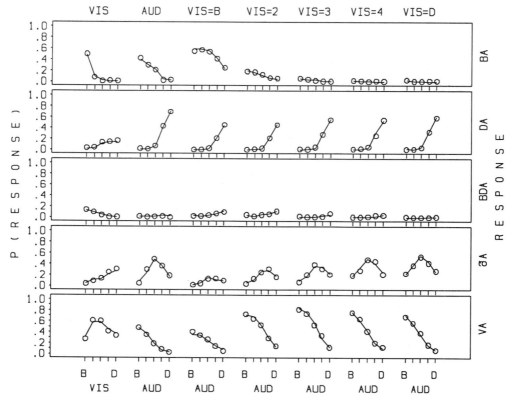

Figure 5.12 Observed (points) and predicted (lines) proportion of identifications for the visual-alone condition (left panel), auditory-alone condition (second from left panel), and the factorial auditory-visual conditions (other five panels) as a function of the five levels of synthetic auditory and visual speech varying between /ba/ and /da/. Results for the senior citizens. The lines give the predictions for the FLMP.

auditory effect was .52 for the college students and .39 for the senior citizens, consistent with the general finding of a decrease in auditory sensitivity with aging (Van Rooij, Plomp & Orlebeke 1989; Working Group on Speech Understanding and Aging, 1988).

Tests of the FLMP   The lines in figures 5.11 and 5.12 show that the FLMP provided a good description of the identifications of both the unimodal and bimodal syllables for both age groups. The average RMSD was .053 and .047 for the college students and senior citizens, respectively. As predicted, there appears to be consistency in processing of bimodal speech across the life span. This conclusion is exactly analogous to what was observed across development. Thus, we conclude that information changes across development and aging but information processing remains constant. We close the aging question with an assessment of cluster judgments.

When the stimulus was an auditory /da/ paired with a visible /ba/, a frequent response was the syllable with consonant-cluster onset /bda/. This perceptual judgment is reasonable because visible /bda/ is almost identical in appearance to visible /ba/, and audible /da/ sounds similar to audible /bda/. The alternative /dba/ is not reasonable because of the huge mismatch between visible /dba/ and visible /ba/ (see chapter 3).

As can be seen in figures 5.11 and 5.12, senior citizens give fewer /bda/ judgments than did college students. It turns out that a given subject responded /bda/ either frequently or not at all. Only 3 of the 13 old subjects gave /bda/ responses, but they gave them about as frequently as did the typical young adult. In like fashion, 4 of the 13 young students did not respond /bda/. Thus, in terms of whether /bda/ judgments occurred, there were a few college students who resembled senior citizens and a few senior citizens who resembled college students. Most important, however, the FLMP gave a good description of the individual subjects independently of whether they tended to give /bda/ responses.

There are several determinants of whether /bda/ percepts emerge. Aging appears to decrease the likelihood of a person's giving /bda/ judgments. Prototypes play a role in recognition, and there may be age differences in the quality of the prototype for the consonant cluster /bda/. On the other hand, older adults may simply have been less willing to give cluster responses in the task. There is also some literature that supports the distinction between fluid and crystallized processing, corresponding to a difference in flexibility of behavior. Older adults tend to be more crystallized than younger adults, and this characteristic might account for fewer adults giving /bda/ judgments. Although we are not sure why a young adult relative to an elderly adult is more likely to respond with /bda/ given a visible /ba/ and an auditory /da/, the fundamental processes seem to work equivalently across these different response patterns.

There is a body of research supporting the idea of a mental slowing among the elderly. We take this slowing as representative of a loss in information derived from the senses and from memory. In our view, mental slowing is not due to a change in information processing (by which we mean the mental processes responsible for speech perception).

Both children and older adults are at a disadvantage with respect to the information they have available for speech recognition. Luckily, the availability of multiple sources of information usually precludes a catastrophic breakdown. For example, visible speech from the talker's lips appears to compensate for hearing loss with age. Some older adults report that they hear the television better with their glasses on, for example. This compensation occurs as a natural consequence of having the visible speech as an additional source of information, not because older people speechread better. We saw that old adults actually have less visible information than young adults. The value of the FLMP is that it not only describes how speech perception might be accomplished, it provides a framework for understanding how it changes with development and aging. These findings have developmental implications both within and outside the field of speech perception (Massaro, 1992a; Massaro & Burke, 1991).

LANGUAGE VARIABILITY

Related to the work on developmental differences, the next source of individual variability is linguistic differences. Perceivers accustomed to different languages might differ with respect to information or information processing. Consider the second level along a synthetic auditory speech continuum between /ba/ and /da/. The stimulus might support the alternative /ba/ for one language significantly more than for another language. This is an example of a difference in information. In experimental studies, we cannot hope to equate the amount of support for a given category across different linguistic groups. To solve this problem, we simply synthesize the same range of speech stimuli for the different languages and have the subjects categorize the stimuli in their native languages.

It has been claimed that Japanese talkers process bimodal speech differently from American English talkers. This is an intriguing hypothesis, particularly for students of cultural differences. In traditional Japanese society it is impolite to look directly at the talker. For this reason it has been hypothesized that the Japanese know a lot less about visible speech than do individuals in Western "in your face" societies. I am skeptical of this thesis for several reasons. Japanese advocates of oral language training for hearing-impaired children were every bit as optimistic about visible speech as were their counterparts in the West. Many hours on Japanese trains convinced me that face-to-face conversations in Japan were not different from those in the West. Even if the Japanese culture did prohibit facial contact, there would be many other opportunities to learn about visible speech, such as watching television or surreptitiously monitoring other conversations. Finally, as will be described in chapter 14, it appears that information about visible speech does not require a direct foveal view of the talker—one might both be polite and obtain a good deal of peripherally visible speech.

Although I am skeptical of culturally based differences, we should not be surprised if linguistically based differences are found. Given the unique phoneme inventories and phonologies of the different languages, we can expect to observe different response patterns from the different linguistic groups. Such results would reflect differences in information. The FLMP, however, makes a very strong prediction concerning information processing. Regardless of the evaluation value for /ba/-ness of a given source of information, it will be combined with other sources of information as prescribed by the integration and decision operations. Thus, tests of the FLMP determine whether linguistic differences can be located entirely at the evaluation stage of processing.

Phonetic Realizations, Phonological Inventories, and Phonotactics

This research was carried out by Massaro, Tsuzaki, Cohen, Gesi, and Heredia (1993) and by Massaro, Cohen, and Smeele (1995). In addition to English talkers, Japanese, Spanish, and Dutch informants were tested. All four languages have /b/ and /d/ segments (Maddieson, 1984). Although bilingual talkers of any two of these languages usually claim that each of the segments has roughly equivalent articulation across the two languages, we can be sure that there are differences in the ideal auditory and visual speech. The /d/ is more dental for Spanish talkers, for example. Differences in phonetic realizations across the languages should have some influence on performance in our task.

The phonological inventories of the four languages also differ from one another. In contrast to English, Japanese does not have the phonemes /ð/ or /v/, American Spanish does not have /v/, and Dutch does not have /ð/. These differences have important consequences for the outcome of bimodal speech perception. We have just seen in the previous section that the syllables /va/ and /ða/ are frequently the alternatives identified by English talkers when auditory and visual speech are varied along a /ba/ to /da/ continuum. These alternatives are reasonable because of the auditory and visible properties of the segments. Talkers whose language does not have the segments /v/ or /ð/ should therefore perceive the same continuum differently.

We would expect cross-linguistic differences in syllable recognition performance not only because of the different phoneme inventories, but also because of the differences in phonotactics—that is, restrictions on the possible sequencing of sounds. For example, a frequent response for English talkers is /bda/ when the stimulus is a visible /ba/ paired with an auditory /da/. In English, the /bd/ cluster occurs at syllable, morpheme, and word boundaries, in words such as *abdicate* and *subdue* and in phrases such as *crab dish*. Although in the syllable /bda/ in our task the cluster occurs not across a syllable boundary but as the onset of a single syllable, it might still be a reasonable alternative for English talkers, given that other consonant clusters do occur initially.

Initial consonant clusters do not occur in the Kansai dialect of Japanese spoken by our subjects. In addition, consonant clusters do not occur across word boundaries because in Japanese, most words end in vowels. Spanish has fewer consonant clusters than English. Consonant clusters are also less likely to occur across word boundaries in Spanish because a greater proportion of Spanish words end in a vowel. Although there are /bd/ clusters across morpheme boundaries in Dutch, they are usually pronounced /pd/ or /pt/; there is an assimilation rule in Dutch. Thus, we might expect that Japanese, Spanish, and Dutch talkers would be less likely to respond /bda/ given a visible /ba/ and an auditory /da/.

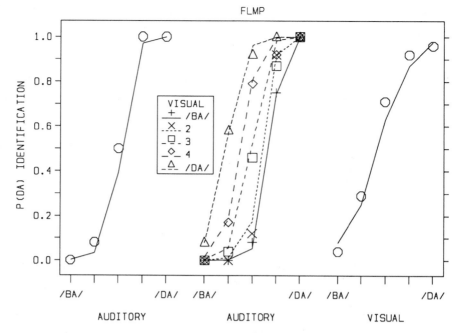

Figure 5.13 The points give the observed proportion of /da/ identifications for a typical Japanese observer in the auditory-alone (left panel), the factorial auditory-visual (center panel), and the visual-alone (right panel) conditions as a function of the five levels of the synthetic auditory and visual speech varying between /ba/ and /da/. The lines give the predictions for the FLMP.

Two-Alternative Task

It can be argued that the phoneme inventories should play less of a role if subjects are limited to just two responses, /ba/ and /da/. In that case there should be no difference across languages with respect to the number of prototypes that are functional in the task. All four languages have /ba/ and /da/ syllables. So with just two choices, the additional /va/, /ða/, and /bda/ prototypes for the English talkers should have no influence. There were no significant differences across the four language groups. Figure 5.13 gives the results for a prototypical Japanese participant. As can be seen in the figure, the results show a strong effect of both audible and visible speech. In addition, the joint influence on bimodal trials follows the predictions of the FLMP. This simple two-alternative task shows consistency of performance across languages when the differential influence of unique features of the languages is eliminated. Of course, we are also interested in whether we can account for cross-linguistic differences when the unique features of each language are permitted to play a role. We do this by allowing the participants to choose their responses freely.

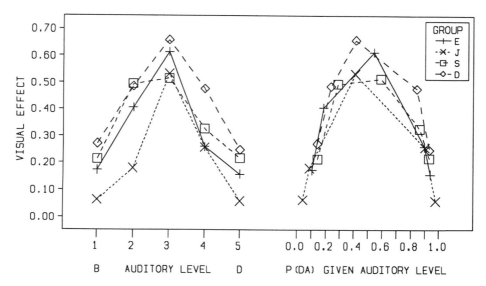

Figure 5.14 Average visual effect in the bimodal condition as a function of the auditory level (left plot) and as a function of the probability of a /da/ response given the auditory level (right plot) for American English (E), Japanese (J), Spanish (S), and Dutch (D) talkers.

Influence of Visible Speech

As we have stated, our framework allows us to measure differences in information independently of whether there are differences in information processing. In the present case, we computed each modality's effect at each of the five levels of the other modality. The left plots of figure 5.14 show the effect of the visual level as a function of the auditory level in the bimodal condition for the English, Japanese, Spanish, and Dutch talkers. As can be seen, the visual effect was highest at the more ambiguous central auditory levels than at the unambiguous endpoints. When the visual effect is replotted in the right plot in figure 5.14 as a function of the marginal P(/da/) in the bimodal trials, the curves for the four language groups come more closely into agreement. Notwithstanding the similar results shown in figure 5.14, the average visual effect (.322, .219, .354, and .428 for the English, Japanese, Spanish, and Dutch talkers, respectively) differed somewhat across the four groups. Although it appears that there might be some differences across the four groups, it should be stressed that we do not predict that the size of the effect of a given modality will be equivalent across the four languages. There is no guarantee that a given unimodal stimulus will match the prototypical values of the /ba/ and /da/ alternatives equally well for the different languages. Thus, for example, the visible speech might have been a poorer match to the /ba/ and /da/ prototypes for the Japanese than for the Dutch talkers. However, a good fit of the FLMP for all groups would indicate that visible and audible speech are processed in the same manner independently of language.

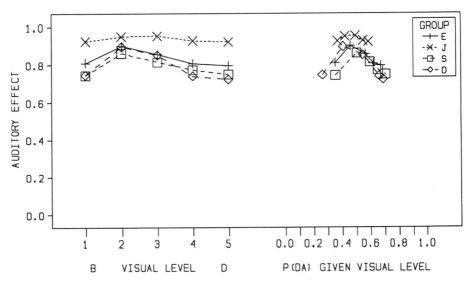

Figure 5.15 Average auditory effect in the bimodal condition as a function of the visual level (left plot) and as a function of the probability of a /da/ response given the visual level (right panel) for the English (E), Japanese (J), Spanish (S), and Dutch (D) talkers.

Figure 5.15 shows the analogous analysis for auditory effects. As can be seen in the left plot, there was a larger auditory effect for the more ambiguous visual levels. Like the visual effect in figure 5.14, the auditory effect is replotted in figure 5.15 as a function of the marginal $P(/da/)$ in the bimodal trials. In contrast to the visual effect, the average auditory effect (.834, .936, .788, and .791 for the English, Japanese, Spanish, and Dutch talkers, respectively) was somewhat more constant across the four groups. Although there is a hint that the Japanese perceivers were somewhat more influenced by audible speech, the auditory endpoints might have been more prototypically like Japanese /ba/ and /da/ than the visual endpoints, which would account for the larger auditory effect and smaller visual effect.

Another way to consider the relative sizes of the visual and auditory effects is shown in figure 5.16. That figure plots the size of mean auditory effect as a function of the size of the mean visual effect for the subjects in each of the four groups. Figure 5.16 illustrates that audible speech had a larger influence than visible speech across the four languages. As can also be seen in the figure, the size of the effects varied significantly across subjects within each group. As we observed in earlier plots of this type, there was a strong negative correlation between the two effects. To the extent that one modality had a large effect, the other had a small effect. Most important, figure 5.16 shows that the individual differences within a language are much larger than any differences between languages.

Using a videotape made in our laboratory, de Gelder and Vroomen (1992) tested native Dutch speakers and native Chinese speakers in our bimodal speech perception task (Massaro & Cohen, 1983c). The results indicated

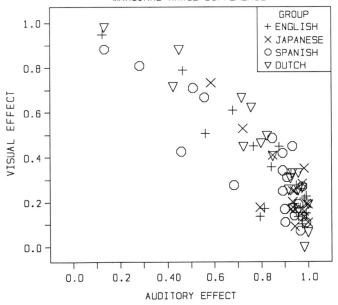

Figure 5.16 Visual effect plotted as a function of the auditory effect for the 82 subjects identified by their native language.

a larger influence of visible speech for the Dutch than for the Chinese subjects. In addition, Chinese subjects who had learned an alphabetic writing system revealed a larger visual influence than Chinese subjects who were readers of solely logographic Chinese. In unpublished tests of the FLMP and other models against these results, the FLMP gave the best description of all three groups of subjects. Thus, the observed differences reflect differences in information only and not information processing. In summary, the two-alternative task shows that visible speech is a powerful source of information in all languages that have been tested, with some differences in information but with constancy in information processing.

Free-Response Task

A task with open-ended response alternatives is still useful for several reasons. First, the nature of the responses in different languages is of interest. We have seen that English talkers respond with the alternative that gives the best match to both the auditory and visual information. Will the same hold true for speakers of other languages? Second, will the FLMP continue to give a better description than the other models when talkers are permitted an open-ended set of alternatives? Finally, it is of interest whether visible speech will still have an important influence in other languages when open-ended alternatives are permitted.

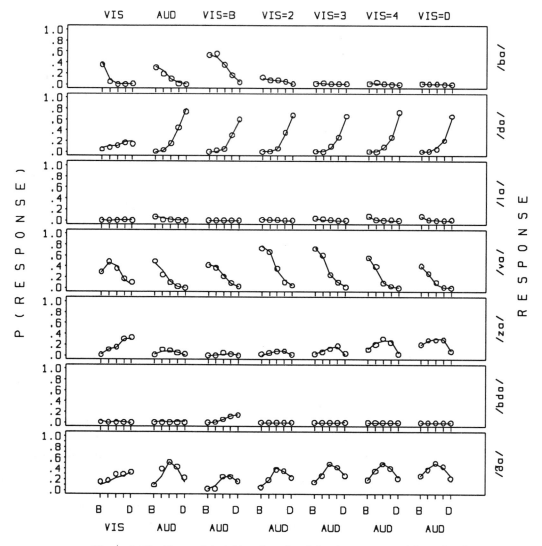

Figure 5.17 Observed (points) and predicted (lines) proportion of /ba/, /da/, /la/, /va/, /za/, /bda/, and /ða/ identifications by the English talkers for the visual-alone (left plot), auditory-alone (second plot), and bimodal (remaining plots) conditions as a function of the five levels of the synthetic auditory (AUD) and visual (VIS) speech varying between /ba/ (B) and /da/ (D). The lines give the predictions of the FLMP.

The same five-by-five expanded factorial design was used, but subjects were permitted to give any response in their language (Massaro et al., 1993; Massaro, Cohen & Smeele, 1995). Figures 5.17–5.19 give the results for the English, Japanese, and Dutch talkers. The English talkers gave 29 alternatives. Voiceless responses occurred on about 23% of the trials; because the auditory and visual modalities were varied to influence perception of place of articulation, voicing was irrelevant, and the voiceless responses were pooled

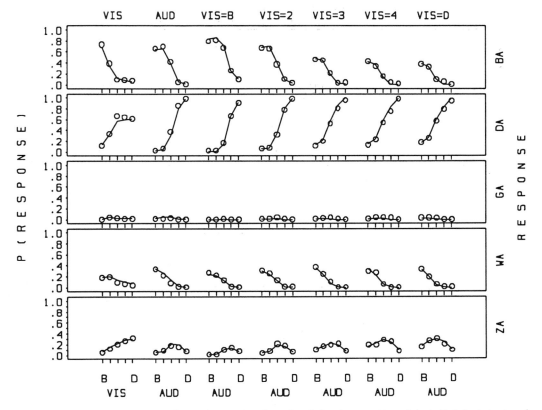

Figure 5.18 Observed (points) and predicted (lines) proportion of /ba/, /da/, /ga/, /wa/, and /za/ identifications by the Japanese talkers for the visual-alone (left plot), auditory-alone (second plot), and bimodal (remaining plots) conditions as a function of the five levels of the synthetic auditory (AUD) and visual (VIS) speech varying between /ba/ (B) and /da/ (D). The lines give the predictions for the FLMP.

with their voiced counterparts. After this pooling, /ba/, /da/, /va/, /ða/, /za/, /bda/, and /la/ judgments accounted for about 97% of the responses.

Figure 5.17 gives the results for the English talkers. Contributions of both audition and vision can be observed in their responses. Visual information (especially the second and third levels) rendered increased /va/ judgments when paired with the /ba/ end of the auditory continuum. More /za/ judgments were given to visible /da/ when it was paired with an auditory syllable from any level of the continuum other than the /da/ endpoint. Visual /ba/ yielded increased /bda/ responses only at the /da/ end of the auditory continuum.

Figure 5.18 gives the results for the Japanese talkers. The Japanese talkers mainly responded /ba/ and /da/, but also gave frequent /wa/ and /za/ judgments. The response /ga/ was infrequently given. These five judgments accounted for 98.8% of the responses. Japanese talkers were also influenced by visible speech, even when open-ended alternatives were permitted. In

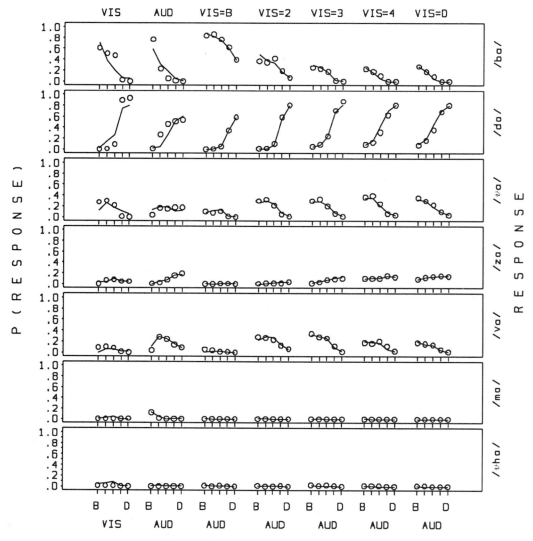

Figure 5.19 Observed (points) and predicted (lines) proportion of /ba/, /da/, /ʋa/, /za/, /va/, /ma/, and /ʋha/ identifications by the Dutch talkers for the visual-alone (left plot), auditory-alone (second plot), and bimodal (remaining plots) conditions as a function of the five levels of the synthetic auditory (AUD) and visual (VIS) speech varying between /ba/ (B) and /da/ (D). The lines give the predictions of the FLMP.

figure 5.18, the top left plot of the visual-alone condition shows that the likelihood of a /ba/ judgment decreased as the visible stimulus went from the /ba/ end to the /da/ end of the continuum. This effect of the visible speech also occurred in the bimodal condition, as shown in the top right five plots of figure 5.18. Similarly, the second panel from the top shows that the likelihood of a /da/ judgment increased from the /ba/ end to the /da/ end of the visual continuum. There were more /za/ responses for the visible speech at the /da/ end of the continuum. The number of /wa/ responses increased at the /ba/ end of the visible continuum.

The Dutch subjects gave a variety of responses (24 alternatives). Voiceless responses occurred on about 4% of the trials. Like the English subjects' data, these responses were pooled with their voiced counterparts. After the pooling of judgments, the syllables /ba/, /da/, /ʋa/, /za/, /va/, /ʋha/, and /ma/ accounted for 98.84% of the responses. The proportion of /ba/ and /da/ judgments changed systematically in the expected direction across the levels of the visual and auditory continua. Synthetic visible speech at the /ba/ end of the visible continuum also gave some support for the alternative /ʋa/. The number of /za/ responses increased somewhat at the /da/ end of the auditory continuum. There were very few /ma/ and /va/ responses. The bimodal judgments reflect the contribution of both auditory and visual speech. As was the case for the English and Japanese talkers, the judgments were more or less in line with the psychophysical similarity between the test stimuli and the response alternatives.

The results from English, Japanese, and Dutch talkers supports our analysis of the differences in the phonemic repertoires, phonetic realizations of the syllables, and phonotactic constraints in the three languages. English talkers tended to respond /da/ or /bda/ when a visual /ba/ was paired with an auditory /da/. Japanese talkers, on the other hand, responded /da/, /ba/, or /za/, whereas Dutch talkers tended to respond /ba/ or /da/. When the audible and visible speech came from the /ba/ side of the continuum, English and Dutch talkers sometimes responded /va/ where Japanese talkers would respond /wa/. Although different responses were given, talkers of all three languages were influenced by visible speech.

The FLMP was tested against the results shown in figures 5.17–5.19. For each group, an "other" response category was made from the responses not shown in the figures. The fit of the FLMP requires 10 free parameters for each response alternative R, unless the response probabilities are constrained to add to 1, in which case only $10(R - 1)$ free parameters are necessary. Thus, 70 free parameters are necessary for the English and Dutch talkers with 8 alternatives, and 50 free parameters must be estimated for the Japanese talkers with 6 alternatives. The RMSD values for the fit of the FLMP to the English, Japanese, and Dutch talkers were .051, .044, and .073, respectively. The details of the judgments are well captured in the predictions of the FLMP.

An important consideration in our cross-linguistic experiments is that all of the Japanese, Spanish, and Dutch talkers had various degrees of English experience. However, there are several reasons why we expect the same results with truly monolingual talkers of those languages. The experiments were carried out in their native languages, and the results revealed large differences due to the language of the talker. Furthermore, we would expect similar results even if the talkers were attempting to interpret the speech as English. Mills and Thiem (1980) tested native German talkers who had learned English as a foreign language on English CV syllables with conflicting auditory and visual information. In contrast to English talkers, the German participants gave very few identifications of the phoneme /ð/, which does not occur in German. This difference illustrates how the influence of both audible and visible speech is modulated by the prototypes of the perceiver's native language, even when he or she interprets the stimulus as a foreign language. We also believe that information differences, as mediated by prototype differences, can account for cross-linguistic differences in segmental processing (Cutler et al., 1986). Similar conclusions can be reached at the sentence level (MacWhinney & Bates, 1989; Massaro, 1987f).

Summary

The methodology of the Massaro et al. (1993) and Massaro, Cohen, and Smeele (1995) experiments allows us to separate information differences from those in information-processing. The experiments with native English, Spanish, Japanese, and Dutch talkers revealed interesting differences in performance across the four languages. The experiments substantiate the distinction made between information and information processing. The information made available by evaluation naturally differs for talkers of different languages, whereas the information processing involved in integration and decision is identical. The differences observed are primarily between the response categories used by the different linguistic groups, which can be attributed to differences in the phonemic repertoires, phonetic realizations of the syllables, and phonotactic constraints in the different languages. Talkers of different languages are similarly influenced by visible speech, whose contribution is larger to the extent that the other source is ambiguous. The details of these judgments are nicely captured in the predictions of the FLMP. These results also provide some of the first findings to confirm that the FLMP provides a good account of bimodal speech perception for talkers of languages other than English.

SENSORY IMPAIRMENT

Sensory impairment is a source of individual variability, and it is worthwhile to determine the extent to which the processing of information changes with this variable. We use the FLMP to describe two thorough experimental studies of unimodal and bimodal speech perception in individuals with hearing impairments.

Hearing Impairment in Children

Erber (1972) tested three populations of children (adolescents and young teenagers): normal hearing (NH), severely impaired (SI), and profoundly deaf (PD). All of the children with impaired hearing had sustained their loss before the acquisition of speech and language. They also had extensive experience with hearing aids and had at least four years of experience with the oral method of multimodal speech perception. The hearing-impaired children used their hearing-assistance devices during the test. None of the children with normal hearing had any training in speechreading. The test consisted of a videotape of the eight consonants /b, d, g, k, m, n, p, t/ spoken in a bisyllabic context /aCa/, where C refers to one of the eight consonants. It is important to note that the talker's face was intensely illuminated so that the inside of the oral cavity was visible. The test was presented under auditory, visual, and bimodal conditions.

The results for the three groups under the three presentation conditions are shown in figure 5.20 in the form of confusion matrices. These data are not as overwhelming as they seem at first glance. First, the results for the NH subjects replicate what we already know: auditory speech is easier to perceive than visible speech. Persons in the NH group were perfect in the auditory and bimodal conditions and made within-viseme-class errors with visible speech alone. Given the unimodal auditory speech, the SI group made

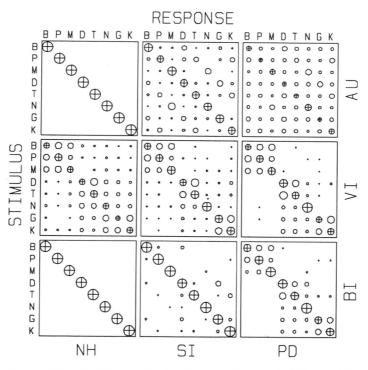

Figure 5.20 Confusion matrix for three populations of children (adolescents and young teenagers): normal hearing (NH), severely impaired (SI), and profoundly deaf (PD). The area of the circle is proportional to response probability. The results should be interpreted as both the observations and the predictions of the FLMP because they were essentially equivalent to one another; the small differences are not noticeable in this type of plot.

many errors and the PD group made even more, performing at near chance for some of the test items. The SI and PD groups, however, appeared to speechread somewhat better than the normal population—a result that is not always found. What is important for our purposes is the tremendous performance gain these two groups showed in the bimodal condition relative to either of the unimodal conditions. The SI subjects did better with bimodal speech than the PD subjects because the former group had much more auditory information.

The FLMP was applied to the results from all three groups and gave an excellent description of the confusion errors of all three groups of children. The predicted values are not plotted in figure 5.20 because they would not be noticeably different from the observed values. Erber's results also reveal a strong complementarity between the audible and visible modalities in speech, which is discussed more fully in chapter 14.

Hearing Impairment in Older Adults

Walden et al. (1990) provide some comprehensive results on adults who became hearing-impaired with aging. These subjects had bilateral hearing loss predominantly in the high frequencies. They did not wear hearing aids during the experiment. The test items were synthetic auditory speech syllables along a /ba/–/da/–/ga/ continuum for a total of 14 syllables. The auditory syllables were presented either alone or paired with a visual /ba/ or a visual /da/. The subjects responded with /ba/, /da/, or /ga/.

The average observed results are shown in figure 5.21 along with the predictions of the FLMP. As can be seen in the figure, both sources of information had a large impact on performance. Although the task was more complicated than our standard two-response task, the results are easily understood. There is a very large impact of visible speech, but the auditory speech had an important and orderly influence. Changes along the auditory continuum had the expected effect. Stimuli at the /ba/ end of the auditory continuum were sometimes called /da/ or /ga/, indicating that auditory /ba/ was not as robust as auditory /da/ or /ga/. This difference seems responsible for the finding that the visual effect was larger at the /ba/ end of the auditory continuum. A visual /ba/ almost always produced /ba/ judgments for such auditory stimuli, and a visual /ga/ eliminated /ba/ judgments. Visual /ba/ had a huge impact on performance. A visual /ba/ yielded a large number of /ba/ judgments, which tapered off across the continuum from /ba/ to /da/ to /ga/. A visual /ga/ produced both /da/ and /ga/ judgments and very few /ba/ judgments.

The predictions of the FLMP capture the joint influence of the two modalities. The parameter values of the model are consistent with the observed and predicted results. The auditory parameter values more or less follow the visual None curves in figure 5.21. The visual /ba/ provided about 20 times more support for the alternative /ba/ than it did for /da/ and /ga/ combined. The visual /ga/ supported the alternative /ga/ to degree .54 and the alternative /da/

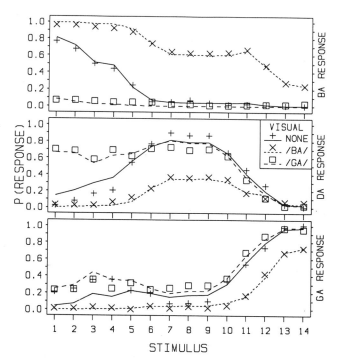

Figure 5.21 Observed (points) and predicted (lines) proportion of /ba/, /da/, and /ga/ identifications as a function of auditory stimulus ranging from /ba/ to /da/ to /ga/ and the visual stimulus. Observed results from Walden et al. (1990). The lines give the predictions of the FLMP.

to degree .42. The similarity between these two values is consistent with the general finding that /d/ and /g/ belong in the same viseme class and are difficult to distinguish unless the inside of the talker's mouth is well lighted. Walden et al. (1990) also tested observers with normal hearing using both normal and degraded auditory speech. Those subjects showed much less of a visual influence with normal auditory speech but a much larger influence when the auditory speech was degraded. According to our perspective, this result is entirely understandable. Hearing-impaired people integrate information in the same manner as those with normal hearing, but they have less auditory information. One group's performance can be made to resemble that of the other if the appropriate quality of information is assigned.

The good fit of the FLMP illustrates that it accounts for speech perception in both normal and sensory-impaired individuals. We would expect visually impaired individuals to be less influenced by visible speech, but we do not know of any relevant experiments. As mentioned in our anecdotal evidence for the influence of visible speech, however, nonsighted children appear to have some difficulty learning those speech distinctions that are visibly salient and auditorily difficult. Our paradigm thus offers a potentially useful framework for the assessment and training of individuals with hearing impairment (Grant & Walden, 1995).

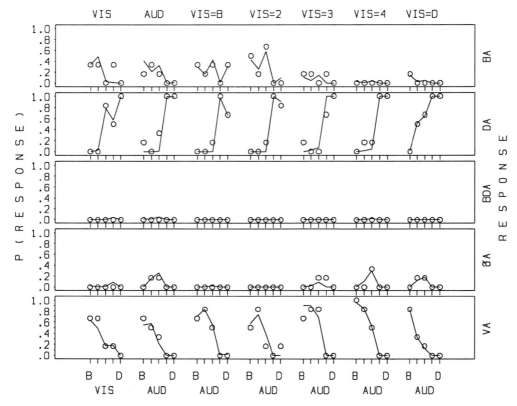

Figure 5.22 Observed (points) and predicted (lines) proportion of /da/ identifications for the visual-alone (left panel), auditory-alone (second from left panel), and factorial auditory-visual (other five panels) conditions as a function of the five levels of the synthetic auditory (AUD) and visual (VIS) speech varying between /ba/ (B) and /da/ (D). Results for prosopagnosic participant HJA. The lines give the predictions for the FLMP.

BRAIN TRAUMA

Brain trauma provides another source of individual variability to be assessed. Seven years after his stroke, a visual agnosic patient, HJA, still cannot recognize the faces of his closest relatives by sight. Ruth Campbell tested him in bimodal speech perception, using a videotape of our five-by-five expanded factorial design. The results indicated that his speech perception by ear and eye appears to be representative of normal adults at his age. His results, shown in figure 5.22, are representative of the results found for other senior citizens (shown in figure 5.12). Figure 5.22 indicates that HJA was influenced by visible speech as well as by audible speech. Most important, his results were well described by the FLMP.

We have collaborated on testing three other prosopagnosics in our task. Each of them showed no influence of visible speech. In such individuals, the information about visible speech is not available, making the question of FLMP integration moot.

HJA has difficulty recognizing faces but can perceive visible speech; thus he exhibits a dissociation between face recognition and speech perception. We attribute this dissociation to the fact that different sources of information are probably used in the two domains. As we will see in chapters 7 and 8, different features are used for facial affect than for speech. We expect that the same is true for facial identity and speech. Unfortunately, we were not able to test HJA on our facial affect task to see whether he could integrate facial and vocal information about affect.

PERSONALITY

All scientists adhere to some form of modularity: no matter how open they are to potential influences, some things are ignored. Although we don't expect personality to influence fundamental processes in pattern recognition, it is unkind to quell the enthusiasm of an undergraduate. Erika Ferguson told me about category width, which refers to the range of instances included in a cognitive category (Pettigrew, 1982). Individuals have been shown to vary significantly in their category widths: narrow categorizers will accept exemplars of the category "table" only if they are ideal instances with the appropriate attributes (flat top, reasonable size, and four legs of appropriate length), whereas broad categorizers will accept less ideal instances (curved top and no legs). Category width is usually measured by Pettigrew's (1958) test of 20 questions. Each question states the average value of a property for members of a given category and asks for the largest and smallest values possible for members of that category. Four possible answers are given for each property. The categories chosen for the test were intentionally obscure so that the answers would reflect a person's general processing strategy rather than situation-specific knowledge. For example, subjects might be asked about the average width of windows.

We used Pettigrew's test to find extreme broad and narrow categorizers and tested them in our speech perception task (Massaro & Ferguson, 1993). Our goal was to test the hypothesis that category width would influence how subjects behave in different speech perception tasks. Given our framework, if there were differences, then we could locate whether the differences were due to information or to information processing. In this endeavor, the distinction was superfluous because absolutely no differences could be attributed to category width. The results were analyzed in terms of (1) discrimination and feature evaluation of auditory and visual speech information, (2) integration of these sources of information, and (3) the process of decision, and revealed no effects attributable to category width. As can be seen in figure 5.23, the results from both broad and narrow categorizers supported the predictions made by the FLMP. It appears that the common processes involved in speech and other pattern recognition tasks are unlikely to vary with personality measures such as category width.

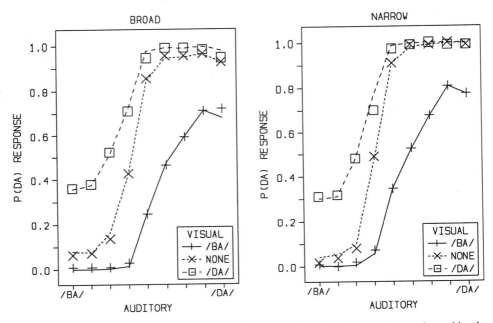

Figure 5.23 The probability of a /da/ judgment as a function of the auditory and visual levels of the speech syllable as a function of the audible and visible speech for the broad and narrow categorizers. The points give the observations, and the lines give the predictions of the FLMP.

SEX DIFFERENCES

Although sex differences are an important distinction in other domains of psychological inquiry, they have not been given much consideration in pattern recognition. Because data are usually pooled for groups of subjects, it is only natural to ignore any question of sex differences. Given our emphasis on individual subject analyses, however, we can address the issue of sex differences in a straightforward manner. Of our pool of 82 subjects, we had records of the sex of the 21 English and 20 Spanish talkers. There were 24 female and 17 male participants. As with other sources of variability, we measured information differences by analyzing the magnitude of the influence of the audible and visible speech. Given that we had already carried out this analysis in figure 5.5, we replotted in figure 5.24 those subjects whose sex could be identified. Nine of the 14 subjects showing the largest visual effect were female. However, there were no statistically significant sex differences with respect to the information value of audible and visible speech.

We assessed information processing by comparing the fit of the FLMP to the male and female groups of subjects. The RMSDs of males were contrasted with the RMSDs of females. The RMSD averaged .0549 for the females and .0568 for the males—not significantly different. Because the male and female

Broadening the Domain

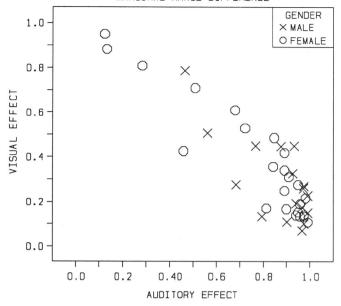

Figure 5.24 The visual effect plotted as a function of the auditory effect for the male and female subjects.

populations of subjects necessarily differ with respect to their response proportions and therefore their expected goodness-of-fit values, a direct comparison between the RMSDs may not be valid. The most useful assessment normalizes the RMSDs by their corresponding benchmarks (see chapter 10). For each subject, his or her benchmark was subtracted from the RMSD of the fit of the FLMP. An analysis of variance on these values indicated no significant difference between the male and female subjects. Thus, we were unable to uncover any sex differences in either information or information processing in the bimodal speech perception task. This confirms the findings of an earlier study by Massaro and Ferguson (1993). Our framework has the potential to provide a measure of the exact nature of any language differences between males and females, if any are found.

EXPERIENCE AND LEARNING

All of the applications of the FLMP have been to relatively static situations in which the prototype representations remain relatively constant throughout the course of the experiment. A more powerful model would specify exactly how the feature values used at evaluation change with experience. Following the presentation in Friedman et al. (1995), learning in the FLMP can be described by the following algorithm. The feature value representing the support for an alternative is initially set to .5 (because .5 is neutral

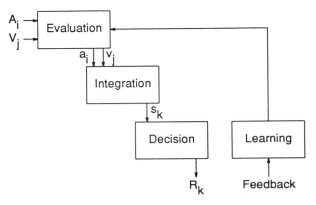

Figure 5.25 Schematic representation of the FLMP to include learning with feedback. The feedback is assumed to tune the prototypical values of the features used by the evaluation process.

in fuzzy logic). A learning trial consists of a feature (such as closed lips at onset) occurring in a test item followed by informative feedback (such as the syllable /ba/). After each trial, the feature values are updated according to the feedback, as illustrated in figure 5.25. Thus, the perceiver uses the feedback to modify the prototype representations, and these in turn become better tuned to the informative characteristics of the patterns being identified.

Given the importance of the visual modality for spoken language understanding, a significant question is to what extent skill in speechreading can be learned. In addition, it is important to determine whether the FLMP can describe speech perception at several levels of skill. A long-term training paradigm in speechreading was used to test the FLMP across changes in experience and learning (Massaro, Cohen & Gesi, 1993). The experiment provided tests of the FLMP at several different levels of speechreading skill.

Subjects were taught to speechread 22 initial consonants in three different vowel contexts. Training involved a variety of discrimination and identification lessons with the consonant-vowel syllables. Throughout their training, subjects were repeatedly tested on their recognition of syllables, words, and sentences. The test items were presented visually, auditorily, and bimodally, and at normal rate or at three times normal rate.

Subjects improved in their speechreading ability across all three types of test items. Figure 5.26 gives their individual performance on the syllables across seven sessions. The results are plotted in terms of correct viseme classifications, which group similar visible consonants together. As can be seen in the figure, all six participants improved with training. Replicating previous results, the present study illustrates that substantial gains in speechreading performance are possible.

The FLMP was tested against the results at both the beginning and the end of practice. According to the model, a subject would have better infor-

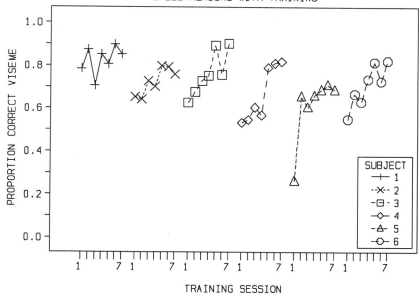

Figure 5.26 Proportion of correct viseme recognition of the initial consonant in the visible presentation of consonant-vowel syllables, as a function of the seven sessions of training in speechreading for each of the six subjects.

mation after training than before. To implement this gain in information, we simply assume more informative feature values after than before training. However, the audible and visible sources should be combined in the same manner regardless of training level. Consistent with these assumptions, the FLMP gave a good description of performance at both levels of speechreading skill. Thus, the FLMP was able to account for the gains in bimodal speech perception as the subjects improved their speechreading and listening abilities. This success suggests that the FLMP and its distinction between information and information processing would provide a valuable framework for the study of language learning.

Psychologists tend not to spend much time or effort emphasizing how individuals differ. I am not opposed to this tradition; our concern with individual differences had the primary purpose of revealing the universalities that hold across those differences. However, I believe that theorists should challenge their hypotheses by confronting individual variability. In our case, the distinction between information and information processing is the key to imposing order on the superficial disorder.

Many individual differences can apparently be attributed to information, which must necessarily be different because of our unique life histories. It might be convincingly argued that information is meaningful only when referenced to some memory representation in a sentient being. I prefer the term *information* rather than *representation*, however, because it is more neutral with respect to how life experiences shape our behavior. Information processing, of course, is equated with the pattern-recognition algorithm of the FLMP. This distinction between information and information processing will keep us afloat in the next chapter when we explore the variety of behavioral domains in which our universal principle seems to hold.

6 Ecological Variability

If we wish to give a definition of "knowing," we ought to define it as a manner of reacting to the environment.
—Bertrand Russell, *Outline of Philosophy*

Our goal is to confront the fuzzy logical model of perception with a broad range of variability. This tack allows us to assess how general the model is and to what extent variability can be accounted for by differences in information only. The hypothesis is that information processing should remain invariant across various sources of variability. In the previous chapter we saw that the FLMP was successful when measured against individual variability. We now take the same approach with respect to *ecological variability*, which refers both to different perceptual and cognitive situations involving pattern recognition and to variations in the tasks themselves.

Thus we will be manipulating additional well-known variables having to do with the environmental situation. The reader might question the sanity of this endeavor because psychologists tend to believe that we are plagued by variability. Broadbent (1987) called this the "problem of observational fragility," or the too-frequent experience that a small variation in experimental conditions changes the outcome. This perceptive scientist, who was at the forefront of psychological research during the last half of the twentieth century, also anticipated the present analysis of variability. He showed how small changes in a model's parameters could provide an adequate description of different patterns of results. This solution is analogous to assuming differences in information and not information processing. In the previous chapter we saw how different parameter values in the FLMP could account for individual differences. In this chapter we take the same tack with respect to situational differences.

Specifically, it is important to know to what extent the processes uncovered in the situation of interest generalize across (1) sensory modalities, (2) environmental domains, (3) items, (4) behavioral measures, (5) instructions, and (6) tasks. The processes involved in bimodal speech perception might be clarified by addressing these six variables in addition to those traditionally manipulated. The hope is that the interactions with these six variables will inform and constrain the kinds of processing mechanisms used to explain the observations.

One of the most engaging proposals of the last two decades has been the modularity of mind (Fodor, 1983). This thesis makes the very strong prediction that processing mechanisms used to describe performance in one perceptual domain will not be adequate to describe performance in a different domain. The claim of modularity entails that neither information nor information processing can be described the same way across different domains. Recognizing speech in conversation will be governed by different processes than those used to recognize three-dimensional objects. No one can dispute the modularity of information (Massaro, 1994c). For example, the cues for identifying speech are very different from those used to recognize objects. On the other hand, it is an open question whether these different cues are processed in the same way. That question is tested most directly by studying behavior as a function of modality and domain variability. In the first case, we evaluate pattern recognition in communication modalities other than auditory and visual speech. In the second case, we evaluate pattern recognition in domains other than linguistic communication.

MODALITIES

The evidence we have harnessed for the FLMP algorithm comes from speech perception by eye and ear. Our work, in fact, began with the integration of multiple auditory cues in speech perception (Massaro & Cohen, 1976, 1977; Oden & Massaro, 1978). There is substantial evidence that the processes described by the FLMP in speech perception by ear and eye generalize to such modalities as electrical stimulation of cochlear implants and tactile stimulation on the skin (Tyler & Moore, 1992; Waldstein & Boothroyd, 1995).

There are several powerful modes of communication that function very much like audiovisual speech. In addition to the widely used sign language, there are other forms of communication that supplement rather than replace speech. Cued speech (Mohay, 1983), for example, supplements lipread information with manual hand movements for communicating to the hearing-impaired. For individuals who lack sight as well as hearing, a method known as the Tadoma method involves the receiver placing his or her hands on the face and neck of the talker (Norton et al., 1977; Reed et al., 1989).

McNeill (1985) argues that manual gestures during speaking appear to have properties and functions that are strikingly similar to those of speech. McNeill's thesis is that manual gestures and speech are aspects of a single linguistic system. The two work together to express the same meaning. If this thesis is correct, then gestures and speech should function as two sources of information to be integrated by the perceiver. To test this hypothesis, we extended our framework to study the integration of a pointing gesture with audible speech (Thompson & Massaro, 1986, 1994). Following the strategy of an expanded factorial design, preschool and fourth-grade children were presented with gesture, speech, and both sources of information together (Thompson & Massaro, 1994). An auditory continuum of five levels was made between the words *ball* and *doll*. The gestural information, also with five levels, was varied between pointing to the ball or doll objects. Band 6.1 on the CD-ROM shows the experimental setup and a few example trials. The task was to determine whether a ball or a doll was indicated by the talker. "Sometimes the woman just points to the thing you should choose," the instructions went, "sometimes she just says it, and sometimes she both points and says which thing you should choose. Each time though, she wants you to choose one thing, either the ball or the doll."

As occurs in too few studies, we were initially surprised by the results. The children, although instructed to respond "ball" or "doll," often responded with "wall." We quickly realized that auditory "wall" is similar to the sound of "ball," and that the intermediate pointing gestures were aimed at a wall. Given this "speech on the wall," we incorporated that response alternative into the data analysis and model tests.

Figure 6.1 gives the results only for the fourth-graders; the preschoolers behaved more or less equivalently except that they showed a somewhat

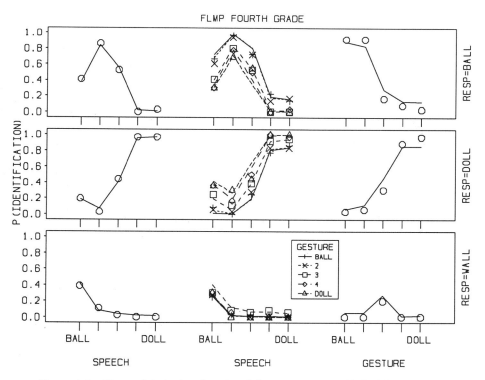

Figure 6.1 Observed (points) and predicted (lines) proportion of ball, doll, and wall identifications for speech (left panel), speech-gesture (center panel), and gesture (right panel) trials as a function of the speech and gesture levels of the speech event for fourth-grade children. The predictions are for the FLMP.

smaller influence of gesture. Both auditory speech and gestures influenced performance, and the results were essentially identical in form to those found in experiments with audible and visible speech. Each source of information presented alone had some influence, and their joint influence followed the predictions of the FLMP. The top two middle panels of figure 6.1 reveal the American football trademark of the FLMP, showing that the amount of gesture influence is greatest when the auditory speech is ambiguous.

The present perspective makes apparent the value of providing supplementary sources of information for disabled individuals. One such source of information that has been used for profoundly deaf individuals is cochlear prosthesis (Schindler & Merzenich, 1985). The technique involves electrical stimulation of residual auditory nerve fibers using intracochlear electrodes (Shannon, 1983; Simmons, 1985). Usually, some parameters of the speech signal are used to drive the location, amplitude, and rate of electrode stimulation. Although this information is not usually sufficient for complete communication, remarkably good performance can be obtained when it is combined with speechreading.

In a prototypical study, a patient with a multiple-channel cochlear implant was tested with just electrical stimulation, just speechreading, or both sources of information (Dowell et al., 1982). Twelve consonants were presented in a VCV context with the vowel /a/, spoken by a female talker in one test and by a male talker in the other. Twenty observations were made on each consonant for each test. The results are of the form of a 12-by-12 confusion matrix under each of the three presentation conditions. The FLMP was applied to the results of the female and male talkers separately and gave a very good description of the results. Thus, the model is capable of describing the integration of speechread information with electrical stimulation to the cochlear implant in the same manner as with auditory information. Although beyond the scope of this analysis, the present approach offers a promising framework for the assessment and treatment of communication disorders. In chapter 14 we discuss several different modalities and dimensions within a modality that could be used to convey linguistic information.

ENVIRONMENTAL DOMAINS

Modularity of mind has been the center of much controversy, and the issue of the modularity of speech perception is equally interesting (Mattingly & Studdert-Kennedy, 1991). Do the processes uncovered in speech perception occur analogously in other environmental domains? We have learned that the FLMP generalizes very nicely across different communication and perceptual modalities. It is also of interest to determine to what extent the theoretical framework generalizes across widely disparate performance domains. Table 6.1 lists the different domains that have supported the processes assumed by the FLMP. In addition to speech perception, the FLMP has given a good description in a variety of domains such as letter and word recog-

Table 6.1 Domains of Evidence for FLMP

Speech Perception	
Audible & visible speech	Massaro, 1996
Acoustic features	Smits, ten Bosch & Collier, 1996
Visible features	Campbell & Massaro, 1996
Phonological constraints	Massaro, 1989c
Lexical constraints	Massaro & Oden, 1995
Syntactic constraints	Massaro, 1987f, pp. 34–36
Semantic constraints	Massaro, 1996b
Semantic & syntactic information	Massaro, 1987f, pp. 261–272
Speech & gestures	Thompson & Massaro, 1994
Reading	
Letter features	Massaro & Hary, 1986
Orthographic constraints	Massaro & Cohen, 1994
Spelling-to-speech constraints	Massaro & Cohen, 1994
Lexical constraints	McDowell & Oden, 1995
Categorization	
Cups & bowls	Oden, 1981
Arbitrary categories	Massaro, 1987f, pp. 251–261
Visual Perception	
Cues to exocentric distance	Massaro & Cohen, 1993b
Cues to figure-ground perception	Palmer et al., 1995
Localization	
Auditory & visual cues	Massaro, 1992a
Memory Retrieval	
Letters & semantic cues	Massaro, Weldon & Kitzis, 1991
Explicit memory	Massaro, Weldon & Kitzis, 1991
Implicit memory	Weldon & Massaro, 1996
Priming	Weldon & Massaro, 1996
Social Events	
Person impression	Massaro, 1987f, pp. 245–251
Judgment	
Conjunction fallacy	Massaro, 1994a
Learning	
Medical diagnosis	Friedman et al., 1995
Emotion	
Facial cues to affect	Massaro & Ellison, 1996
Facial and vocal cues to affect	Massaro & Egan, 1996

The citation listed for each domain is a more recent publication that contains a description of the experiment and data, the model tests, and similar analyses of earlier experiments, if relevant. Many of the domains are also analyzed in this book.

nition in reading, object identification, sentence interpretation, the perception of depth, memory retrieval, judgment, learning, and the recognition of affect. We end this section by questioning whether the same type of integration also occurs naturally in the domain of reasoning.

Pattern Recognition versus Reasoning

Perhaps we have viewed our "universal principle" as more universal than it really is. We have argued for a strong role of the principle in perceptual recognition situations ranging from spoken and written language processing to the categorization of artificial and natural stimuli. We have even claimed that this algorithm might describe cognition in more complex decision-making and reasoning domains. Admittedly, there has been much less evidence about perceptual than about cognitive domains. However, we were recently successful in applying the framework in the model to the now infamous Linda task (see chapter 9).

It would be ironic if a so-called rational algorithm were to successfully describe sensory and perceptual performance, over which we have very little intentional control, and yet fail to describe situations that allow relatively slow, cautious thinking, reasoning, and decision making. But this seems to be the case. At a cognitive level it appears to be very difficult to devise situations in which people can perform Bayesian reasoning. The major limitation appears to be the difficulty that we all have with probability. Steven J. Gould, a natural scientist writing in a psychological domain, supports Tversky and Kahneman (1983) in their conclusion that "our minds are not built (for whatever reason) to work by the rules of probability."

Gigerenzer and Hoffrage (1995) make an important distinction between *cognitive algorithm* and *information format*, which is very similar to our distinction between information processing and information. They criticize previous theoretical and empirical studies of decision making as focusing on cognitive processes and ignoring the nature of the information presented to the observers. They argue convincingly that the cognitive algorithm is necessarily entwined with the information format. As an example, they ask us to imagine how our pocket calculators would work if we entered binary numbers for the calculations. The algorithms of the calculator are designed to work with decimal numbers. It doesn't take great imagination to see that they would fail with binary numbers. Therefore we should not expect people to behave optimally, even though they may have optimal algorithms, if the information being presented is inappropriate for those algorithms. In a way this argument is closely analogous to my interpretation of the conjunction effect in the Linda problem (Massaro, 1994a). I argued that people could indeed have been using an optimal algorithm for decision, but the Linda problem was formulated in such a way that the experimenters interpreted the behavior of their subjects as being nonoptimal, or in violation of the rules of probability theory.

Gigerenzer and Hoffrage ground their approach in evolutionary theory. If the design of the mind evolved in a specific environment, then the algorithms of the mind have necessarily evolved to process the information that that environment provided. For decision making and judgment, they argue that the mind was tuned to actually experienced frequencies of events rather than to some summary statistics such as probability or percentage. That is, we easily understand that a bin has 10 blue balls and 90 red ones, but have difficulty with the statistic that .10 of the balls are blue. Testing observers with probabilities and percentages therefore would expose nonoptimal behavior because the information format would necessarily violate the format appropriate for the cognitive algorithm.

Information Formats   The authors contrast two types of information formats: probability and frequency. They tested individuals under both formats and found that the frequency format gave performance that was much more consistent with Bayesian computation whereas the probability format was more likely to violate Bayesian computation. Although Gigerenzer and Hoffrage demonstrate that the frequency format leads to Bayesian reasoning and calculation, they point out that the frequency format may not be sufficient for Bayesian algorithms in more complex situations where hypotheses, data, or both are multinomial or continuous, or when there is not only one datum but several sources of information. Furthermore, they propose that people might actually be using more parsimonious algorithms rather than Bayesian ones, and that those algorithms might actually lead to better performance.

"Take the Best" Algorithm   In an important paper, Gigerenzer and Goldstein (1996) offer a set of cognitive algorithms that can outperform the algorithms proposed by the classical models of rationality. Their paper is a striking challenge to our approach, in which people supposedly integrate multiple sources of information in an optimal way to impose patterns upon the world around them. They develop a number of shortcut algorithms and compare the performance of those algorithms to that of rational decision-making procedures.

The Gigerenzer and Goldstein "take the best" algorithm performs a subjective rank ordering of cues according to their validities. In our perceptual tasks, cues may differ in validity but on any given trial one cue may be much more informative than another. Thus it would be a mistake to ignore the least informative cues. For example, we might argue that cues to place of articulation are more valid in the visual than in the auditory domain whereas voicing cues are more valid in the auditory domain. This would lead us to McGurk and McDonald's (1976) original but incorrect hypothesis that place of articulation is perceived visually and voicing is perceived auditorily.

One limitation of contrasting the Gigerenzer and Goldstein research with the present approach is that the task they use seems to be far removed from our prototypical pattern recognition task. Their task involves tests concerning the relative population size of about a hundred cities in Germany. Which city of two randomly chosen ones has the larger population—for example, Hamburg or Cologne? They list nine properties characteristic of large cities that can be used to predict how large a city is. Cities are scored for these properties in a binary way—either they possess each property or they do not. For example, every city is scored with respect to whether it has a soccer team. A soccer team is evidence that the population of that city is large. So-called rational algorithms would involve an integration of all of the cue values to indicate the degree to which the city can be assumed to be large. Such integration would have to occur for both cities in the comparison, and the decision maker would supposedly have to choose the one with the highest probability of being large.

A critical issue is whether there is an integration algorithm in the two-city task that can lead to better performance than what the researchers observe with their shortcut cognitive algorithms? Gigerenzer and Goldstein simply assumed that parallel processing is more demanding than serial processing and that limiting the number of cues is necessarily more efficient than using all of the sources of information. Without this assumption, however, the integration algorithm would be better. Although their assumption seems reasonable in the context of cognitive decision making, it may not be so easily rationalized in the domain of bottom-up pattern recognition.

Given the frequency alternative, we can ask whether there is a frequency-based representation of multiple sources of information that would promote a simpler algorithm in the pattern recognition situation. As will be demonstrated in the next section, there is no way to optimally combine the frequencies from the two features in a way that is necessarily less complex than the FLMP algorithm. There is an easier solution, but it dispenses with combining sources of information and simply concentrates on the frequency of occurrence of all possible combinations of the two features. This solution is equivalent to an exemplar model of categorization (see Massaro, 1987f, pp. 258–261). We envision exemplar models as being unwieldy for speech recognition, however, given the large number of potential exemplars. Thus, the "take the best" algorithm can be rejected for speech recognition. We now demonstrate that it does not appear to be feasible for cognitive decision making situations.

Frequency Algorithms and Integration Consider the "take the best" algorithm for the auditory-visual speech task. Depending on the specific assumptions, this idea leads to a single channel model (SCM) of some form. Given that the audible speech is usually more informative than the visual, one might claim that the percept is controlled by the audible speech. This claim is similar to the auditory dominance model (ADM), which has been falsified in several experiments (see chapter 2).

Gigerenzer and Hoffrage (1995) argue that Bayesian algorithms are easier for people to follow in frequency formats than in probability formats. For the

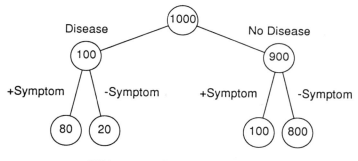

P(Disease | +Symptom) = 80 / (80 + 100)

Figure 6.2 Schematic representation of a situation in which a doctor has observed 1,000 people, 100 with the disease and 900 without. Eighty of the 100 with the disease had the symptom A, whereas 100 of the 900 without the disease had the same symptom.

sake of argument, assume there are two binary features and two response categories. Figure 6.2 illustrates the possible outcomes in frequency terms for a hypothetical situation.

Assume that a doctor has observed 1,000 people, 100 with the disease and 900 without. Eighty of the 100 with the disease had a symptom A, whereas 100 of the 900 without the disease had the same symptom. Now the doctor observes a new patient with the symptom. What is the likelihood that the new patient actually has the disease? This question can be solved by the frequency algorithm.

$$P(H|A) = \frac{(d \text{ and } h)}{(d \text{ and } h) + (d \text{ and } -h)} \tag{6.1}$$

where d (data) is the number of people who have the symptom and h is the number of people who have the disease, and $-h$ is the number of people who do not have the disease. Equation 6.1 simply says that the probability of disease given a symptom is the number of people who had both the symptom and the disease divided by the total number of people who had the symptom.

$$P(H|A) = \frac{(d \text{ and } h)}{(d \text{ and } h) + (d \text{ and } -h)} = \frac{80}{(80 + 100)} \tag{6.2}$$

Things become much more complicated, however, with two symptoms. As illustrated in figure 6.3, assume again that the doctor has observed 1,000 people, 100 with the disease and 900 without. Assume that 60 of the 100 with the disease had symptom B, whereas 200 had the same symptom even though they did not have the disease. Sixty of the 100 with the disease had symptom B, whereas 200 had the same symptom even though they did not have the disease. If the doctor had only symptom B available, then the accurate solution would take the same form as equation 6.1.

$$P(H|B) = \frac{(d \text{ and } h)}{(d \text{ and } h) + (d \text{ and } -h)} = \frac{60}{(60 + 200)} \tag{6.3}$$

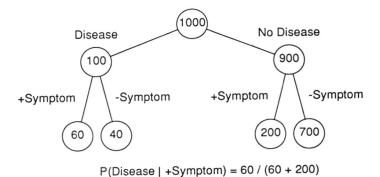

P(Disease | +Symptom) = 60 / (60 + 200)

Figure 6.3 Schematic representation of a situation in which a doctor has observed 1,000 people, 100 with the disease and 900 without. Sixty of the 100 with the disease had the symptom B, whereas 200 of the 900 without the disease had the same symptom.

However, when the doctor is faced with a new patient who has both symptoms, there is no easy way to make the judgment on the basis of these frequencies. How does the doctor combine the frequency information across the two symptoms to determine $P(H|A$ and $B)$? A frequency algorithm will not work. In this case, there is no valid way to combine $80/(80 + 100)$ and $60/(60 + 200)$ to give the correct answer.

If the information is in this form, then the only way to compute the correct probability is to follow something algorithmically equivalent to Bayes' theorem—a probability algorithm.

$$P(H|A \text{ and } B) = \frac{P(A|H) \times P(B|H)}{P(A|H) \times P(B|H) + [1 - P(A|H)] \times [1 - P(B|H)]} \qquad (6.4)$$

Although Bayes' theorem solves the combination problem, this exercise made apparent a potential limitation of a combinatorial algorithm based on probabilities. When the probabilities from several sources of information are combined, there is no corresponding information relevant to the reliability of the respective probabilities. One symptom might have occurred more frequently than another, as in the case of audible speech being experienced more often than visible speech. In the Bayesian computation, however, the probabilities corresponding to these two sources of information would not be differentially weighted as a function of their base rate frequency of occurrence. The influence of each source would be solely dependent on the conditional information of a speech category given the source information. As far as I know, this limitation has not been previously acknowledged. The FLMP could compensate for reliability by maintaining more ambiguous truth values for less reliable sources of information.

A computation mathematically equivalent to Bayes' theorem is not the only way to solve the problem, of course. An exemplar algorithm can solve the problem using frequencies, as demonstrated in figure 6.4. It might not be reasonable to assume that people can maintain exemplars of all possible symp-

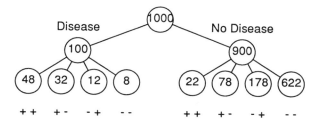

P(Disease | ++Symptom) = 48 / (48 + 22)

Figure 6.4 Schematic representation of a situation in which a doctor has observed 1,000 people, 100 with the disease and 900 without. In this case, the doctor keeps track of each of the four symptom combinations separately, contingent on having the disease or not having the disease.

tom configurations, however. With 9 binary symptoms, as in Gigerenzer and Goldstein's example data, there are 2^9 or 512 possibilities. In this case, a simple algorithm is dependent on an intensive memory load, a trade-off that may be too big a price to pay. In this case, the cognitive algorithm would have to operate on continuous information representations—something similar to probabilities.

More generally, the FLMP framework appears to offer a valuable approach to cognitive functioning. We refer the reader to two other domains where it has shown reasonable success. The first involves a simulated medical diagnosis task in which subjects categorize hypothetical patients on the basis of symptom configurations. Learning and asymptotic categorization are both described by the FLMP (Friedman et al., 1995). The second situation involves incidental and intentional retrieval from memory. In this application, memory retrieval is viewed as a form of pattern recognition. Subjects are asked to retrieve a word, given orthographic, conceptual, and/or episodic information at test. Accuracy of retrieval improves with increases in the amount of each source of information and with increases in the number of sources. In tests of a variety of retrieval models, an extension of the FLMP provided the best description of the integration of the influences on memory retrieval (Massaro, Weldon & Kitzis, 1991; Weldon & Massaro, 1996; Wenger & Payne, 1997). Having addressed the ecological variable of the type of information being processed, we now turn to variation in the experimental format. The sources of variability include test items, behavioral measures, instructions in the task, and tasks.

TEST ITEMS

It is important to know to what extent some observed phenomena generalize across all items and to what extent they are limited to the few items tested in most experiments. Thus it is of interest to determine to what extent the FLMP supported in bimodal speech perception of syllables can be generalized to perceptual recognition of higher linguistic units—words, sentences, and discourses. Also of interest is recognition of the subordinate units that compose the syllable—consonant and vowel segments. With respect to the segmental level, we can ask to what extent the contribution of visible speech varies as a function of different speech segments. We have already seen that our results hold for a variety of consonant contrasts in bimodal speech perception. In chapter 1, the results were found for the alternatives /ba/, /va/, /ða/, and /da/ in one task and for /ba/ and /da/ in another. FLMP integration of audible and visible speech has also been documented for all of the visibly distinctive consonants in English (Massaro, Cohen & Gesi, 1993). Similar results have been found for some vowels (Massaro & Cohen, 1993a).

Consonants versus Vowels

It is valuable to determine whether the recognition of consonants and vowels can be described by the same processing algorithm. We questioned whether people process these two classes of segments differently in bimodal speech perception (Cohen & Massaro, 1995). Analyzing differences between consonants and vowels in auditory speech perception has a long tradition. At one time, vowels were believed to be perceived differently from consonants (Liberman et al., 1967). For example, the "categorical perception" observed for consonants did not occur for vowels unless the vowels were made relatively short (Pisoni, 1973). In fact, the two classes of sounds also appear to differ in terms of their auditory memory (Fujisaki & Kawashima, 1970), their discriminability along the respective speech continua (Ades, 1977), their psychophysical boundaries (Pastore, 1987), and the presence of perceptual anchors (Macmillan, 1987). Finally, a major difference between the auditory form of vowels and consonants is that the acoustic information for vowels is not as dynamic as that which defines consonant sounds (Studdert-Kennedy, 1976).

A common property of all of these differences is that there is less auditory information for consonants (at least stop consonants) than for vowels. Thus, all of these accounts of consonant-vowel differences would seem to predict that visible speech would have a smaller effect on perception of vowels than of stop consonants. The reason is the known trade-off between auditory and visible speech: the contribution of one source is attenuated to the extent that the other source is unambiguous. If vowels provide more robust auditory information, then the perception of bimodal vowels might not be influenced very much by visible speech (Summerfield & McGrath, 1984). On the other hand, one might argue that the visual influence should be greater for vowels than for consonants. There tends to be a larger perceptual range between one endpoint and another along an auditory continuum between two vowels relative to a continuum between two consonants (Ades, 1977). Thus, there should be a larger range of ambiguity along a vowel continuum than along a consonant continuum. Given that the influence of one source of information is greater to the extent that the other source is ambiguous, this would imply a larger effect of visible speech for vowels than for consonants.

Vowels and consonants also differ in terms of their visible characteristics. Vowels involve slower articulatory gestures and less specific articulator positions than stop consonants. The first property should result in better discrimination of visible vowels relative to visible consonants, whereas the second property implies the opposite. Compared to consonants, it is easier to articulate the same vowel with different vocal tract configurations (Ladefoged et al., 1978), which often occurs because of coarticulation. This flexibility occurs in part because it is possible to reduce lip movement without altering the acoustic form of vowels. Thus, one might expect fairly poor identification of visible vowels. When context is held constant, however, as with the fixed context /h-g/ used by Montgomery and Jackson (1983), all vowels can be recognized at better than chance accuracy. Thus, both audible and visible characteristics point to potential information differences for vowels and consonants. The question is whether these two classes of items are processed in the same manner. That is, will the processes in the FLMP that describe auditory-visual perception of consonants also describe vowel perception?

In one study, bimodal speech perception of two consonants, /b/ and /d/, was compared to two vowels, /i/ and /u/. The consonants were presented in a CV syllable with /a/ as the fixed vowel. Although that study was necessarily limited because there were only two alternatives in each category, it offers a direct comparison between the two classes of segments. The left and right panels of figure 6.5 give the results for the consonants and vowels, respectively. The results for consonants and vowels were not equivalent. Figure 6.5 shows a larger spread between curves for the consonants than for the vowels. These results indicate that visible speech had a larger impact in the perception of consonants than of vowels (Massaro & Cohen, 1993a; Cohen & Massaro, 1995). Although the two panels in figure 6.5 are obviously different from one another, the FLMP predictions allow us to see what is similar about them. The interaction of the two sources appears to follow the same form for vowels as for consonants. The American football shape is apparent in both panels, and the predictions of the FLMP capture the observations for both consonants and vowels.

We might expect that the degree of influence will vary within each class depending on the set of items in the test, and that the influence being conveyed by each modality will necessarily depend on which segments are in the test. The strong prediction supported by these results, however, is that the FLMP will give an adequate description of the information processing involved.

Words and Beyond

The expected outcome of the FLMP is found not only for nonsense syllables but also for meaningful items. In a study described in chapter 1, we found

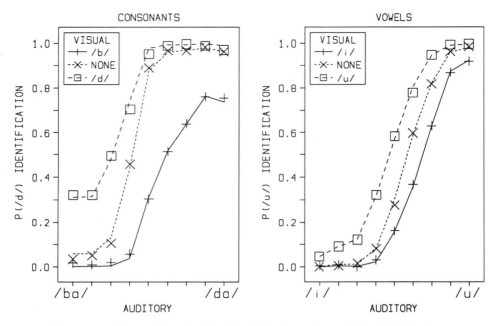

Figure 6.5 Observed (points) and predicted (lines) proportion of /d/ and /u/ identifications as a function of the auditory and visual levels of the speech event for a stop consonant continuum between /ba/ and /da/ (left panel) and a vowel continuum between /i/ and /u/ (right panel). The lines give the predictions of the FLMP.

that word recognition can be more informative given two sources of information relative to just one. The stimuli were one-syllable English words. Presented at a fast presentation rate, two sources of information were clearly superior to just one. Other evidence described in chapter 1 shows an advantage of having visible speech at the sentence and even the text level. Having demonstrated the integration of visible and auditory speech across test items, we test the FLMP's ability to predict several dependent measures.

BEHAVIORAL MEASURES

It is easy for the investigator who is interested in how the input is processed to neglect the role of behavioral measures. Our goal, however, is to assess to what extent the FLMP can predict performance across different types of behaviors (responses). Most speech perception work uses traditional psychophysical tasks with a fixed number of discrete alternatives and using response probability as the dependent measure. Our work has continued this tradition, but we also initiated the use of graded judgments in speech perception research (Massaro & Cohen, 1976, 1977). We extend the number of discrete response alternatives beyond just two, use response accuracy as the primary dependent measure, and measure RT (reaction time) of the response. Thus, to challenge the FLMP, we consider its description of the following different dependent measures: rating responses, multiple response alternatives, response accuracy, and RT. We begin with rating responses.

Ratings

In a graded response task, subjects are asked to grade a stimulus for its resemblance to two alternatives. They might locate the stimulus on an actual presented continuum between the two alternatives, or they might use a more abstract scale of integers 1 through 9 to describe the similarity of the stimulus to the two alternatives.

As noted in the development of the FLMP, the output of the integration stage is the overall goodness of match between the integrated stimulus and each of the category alternatives being considered. In the framework of the FLMP, we assume that the subject's rating is a direct measure of the relative goodness of match between the stimulus and the categories. When participants rate the item on a nine-point scale, the responses are directly normalized to be between the values 0 and 1—no transformation of the rating judgments is necessary. For example, an average rating of 5.5 on a scale between 1 and 9 would be equal to $(5.5 - 1)/(9 - 1)$, or 0.56. This rather strong assumption has been supported in a variety of previous experiments (Anderson, 1981, 1982; Oden, 1978). Following in the same tradition, we assume that the rating judgment gives the relative degree of support for each of the test alternatives. In every case, the rating of a /da/ response given $A_i V_j$ is equal to the total support for /da/ divided by the sum of the support for all relevant alternatives, in this case $s(/da/)$ and $s(/ba/)$.

$$
\begin{aligned}
R(/da/|A_i V_j) &= \frac{s(/da/)}{s(/da/) + s(/ba/)} \\
&= \frac{a_i v_j}{[a_i v_j + (1 - a_i)(1 - v_j)]}
\end{aligned}
\tag{6.5}
$$

where $R(/da/|A_i V_j)$ is the predicted rating of /da/-ness for the syllable $A_i V_j$.

According to equation 6.5, people have information about the degree to which a given alternative is supported by the stimulus rather than just information about which of the alternatives is supported. The empirical question, then, is whether the outcomes of rating studies follow equation 6.5. In one study, participants were asked in one task to identify the test item as either /ba/ or /da/, and in another task to rate the degree to which the test item corresponded to /ba/ or /da/ on a nine-point scale (Massaro & Ferguson, 1993). The results of both types of tasks are shown in figure 6.6. The results are very similar for both types of dependent measures. Both show the American football signature, although the rating judgments converge less at the endpoints. Thus, the FLMP accurately predicts the finding that rating judgments follow the same form as identification judgments (Massaro & Ferguson, 1993).

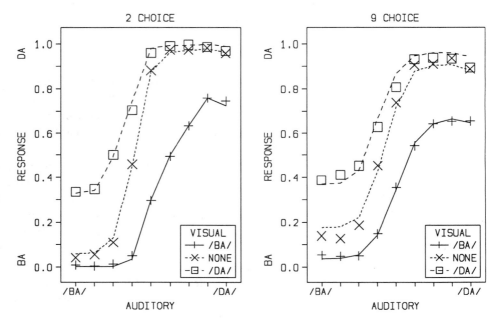

Figure 6.6 Proportion of /da/ identifications in the two-choice (/ba/ versus /da/) task (left panel) and average rating between /ba/ and /da/ alternatives (on a nine-point scale linearly normalized to be between the values 0 and 1). The lines give the predictions of the FLMP.

Number of Response Alternatives

Our next challenge for the FLMP is to assess performance as we increase the number of response alternatives. We replicated our basic five-by-five expanded factorial design with eight rather than just two response alternatives. The basic task was carried out in four different experiments to give a total of 36 subjects in this data set. Each of the 35 stimulus conditions was tested 12 times. Subjects were instructed to listen to and watch the talker, and to identify the syllable as /ba/, /da/, /bda/, /dba/, /ða/, /va/, /ga/, or "other." The category "other" was to be used by the subject whenever none of the other seven responses seemed suitable. The eight response alternatives were determined through pilot studies in which the responses were not constrained.

Figure 6.7 gives the average proportion of responses across the 36 participants. Although the test continua were between /ba/ and /da/, we obtained many tokens of other response alternatives. The most frequent responses were /ba/, /da/, /va/, /ða/, and /bda/. The alternatives /dba/, /ga/, and "other" were seldom used. The results showed a strong contribution of both audible and visible speech. The number of /ba/ judgments increased toward the /ba/ end of the visible continuum. The /bda/ judgments occurred primarily when a visible /ba/ was paired with an auditory syllable from the /da/ end of the

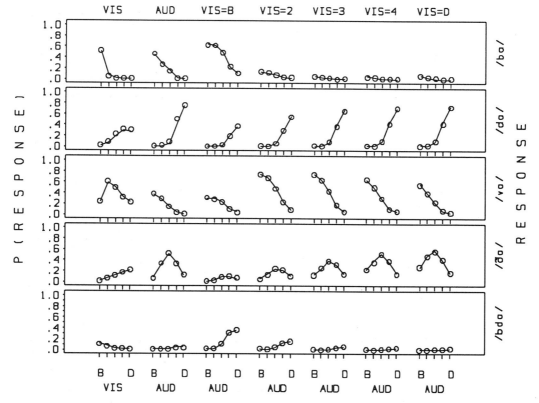

Figure 6.7 Observed (points) and predicted (lines) proportion of /ba/, /da/, /va/, /ða/, and /bda/ identifications for the visual-alone (left plot), auditory-alone (second plot), and bimodal (remaining plots) conditions as a function of the five levels of the synthetic auditory (AUD) and visual (VIS) speech varying between /ba/ (B) and /da/ (D). The lines give the predictions of the FLMP for the task with a fixed set of eight response alternatives.

continuum. Visible /da/ articulations increased the likelihood of /da/, /ða/, and /va/ responses. The visual information influenced the likelihood of a /va/ judgment primarily at the /ba/ end of the auditory continuum. The visual /ba/ endpoint stimulus decreased the number of /va/ responses, whereas the other four visual levels increased the number of /va/ judgments at the /ba/ end of the auditory continuum. These judgments point to a contribution of both auditory and visual speech even when observers are permitted a larger permissible set of response alternatives.

The FLMP is tested against results from tasks with multiple response alternatives in the same manner as with just two response alternatives. With more than two alternatives, it is necessary to estimate a unique parameter to represent the degree to which each source of information supports each alternative. We use a_{Bi} to represent the degree to which the audible speech supports the alternative /ba/. The term v_{Gj} would represent the degree to which the visible speech supports the alternative /ga/, and so on for the other alternatives. Given both audible and visible speech, the total support for the alternative /ba/ would be

$$s(/\text{ba}/) = a_{Bi}v_{Bj},$$

(6.6)

and so on for the other test conditions and the other alternatives.

As in the case of just two alternatives, the probability of a particular categorization is assumed to be equal to the relative goodness of match.

$$P(/\text{da}/|A_iV_j) = \frac{s(/\text{da}/)}{\sum_r s_r}$$

(6.7)

where s_r corresponds to the goodness of match for alternative r, and $\sum_r s_r$ corresponds to the sum of the goodness-of-match values of all eight alternatives.

The fit of the model requires 5 a_i and 5 v_j parameters for each of the 8 response alternatives, for a total of 80 free parameters. This might seem like a large amount, but we have increased the number of data points to be predicted by the same factor. We are now predicting $35 \times 8 = 280$ data points. The fit of this model to each of the 36 subjects produced an average RMSD of .0507. Figure 6.7 also gives the average of the predicted results. To assess whether the FLMP maintains its advantage with multiple response alternatives, we compared this fit with that of a single channel model (or, equivalently, a weighted averaging model). The fit of the competing model was about two times poorer, giving an RMSD of .1049. We now compare these results to a situation with a completely open-ended set of responses.

Not Specifying Response Alternatives

Most experiments, including investigations of speech perception, use a fixed set of response alternatives. Will similar results be found when observers are able to respond with an unlimited response set? To explore the robustness of the results, English talkers were given a completely open-ended response task. We expect to find that the same theoretical framework can explain results in both fixed-alternative and open-ended tasks. Identification of the speech segments should be influenced by both the auditory and visual sources of information. More important, the FLMP should give an equally good description of both tasks.

The same experiment was already presented in chapter 5 concerning robustness across languages. The participants were students at the University of California at Santa Cruz (UCSC). All procedural details were similar to experiments using the five-by-five expanded factorial design with a fixed number of response alternatives. The only difference was that subjects were allowed to give any possible response.

With an open-ended set of alternatives, we can expect a much more varied set of responses. Much of this variability is generated by the lack of information in visible speech. Distinctions in voicing and manner are particularly difficult to see on the face. Thus subjects could just as easily call our visual /ba/ the alternative /pa/ or even /ma/. The English-speaking subjects gave 29 alternatives. Voiceless responses occurred on about 22% of the trials. Because the auditory and visual modalities were varied to influence perception of place of articulation but there was no manipulation of the perception of voicing, the voiceless responses were pooled with their voiced counterparts. After this pooling, /ba/, /da/, /va/, /ða/, /za/, /bda/, and /la/ judgments accounted for more than 97% of the responses. The remaining alternatives formed the "other" category.

We were initially surprised that there were several other frequent responses besides /ba/ and /da/ in the unimodal conditions. The audible and visible speech tended to also support the alternatives /va/, /ða/, and /za/. We should not have been very surprised, however, because of the psychophysical similarities among these alternatives. With an open-ended set of alternatives, such responses are natural.

As evident in figure 6.8, contributions of both audition and vision can be observed in the responses. Visual information from the second and third levels increased the number of /va/ judgments at the /ba/ end of the auditory continuum. The proportion of /ða/ responses was largest at the middle levels of the auditory continuum. There were /ða/ judgments when visible /da/ was presented alone or paired with an auditory syllable. Visual /ba/ increased the number of /bda/ responses only at the /da/ end of the auditory continuum.

Rather than pool the responses into just eight response categories as we did in chapter 5, we fit the FLMP to all 29 response alternatives. Recall that the fit of the FLMP requires $N(a + v)$ parameters, where N is the number of response alternatives with a levels of auditory and v levels of visual stimuli. Thus, with 29 alternatives and five levels each of auditory and visual stimuli, 290 free parameters are necessary. The lines in figure 6.8 give the predictions of the FLMP for the seven most frequent responses. The FLMP gave a good description of performance, yielding an average RMSD across the individual fits of .027. In comparison, the fit of the SCM was .094, or about 3.5 times larger. Thus, we can be confident that the FLMP describes performance equally well with an unconstrained response set. The richness of the data, however, should encourage investigators to explore the role of response specification more intensely.

The study with open-ended responses illuminates some influence of specifying response alternatives in advance. Although subjects will make a wider variety of responses, they will also make responses in the task with specified alternatives that they would not have given in the open-ended task. For example, significantly more /bda/ judgments were given when /bda/ was given as one of the eight possible response alternatives, compared to the present study in which the response alternatives were unspecified. Also, a small proportion of /dba/ and /ga/ judgments were given when these were specified alternatives but not in the completely open-ended task. On the other hand,

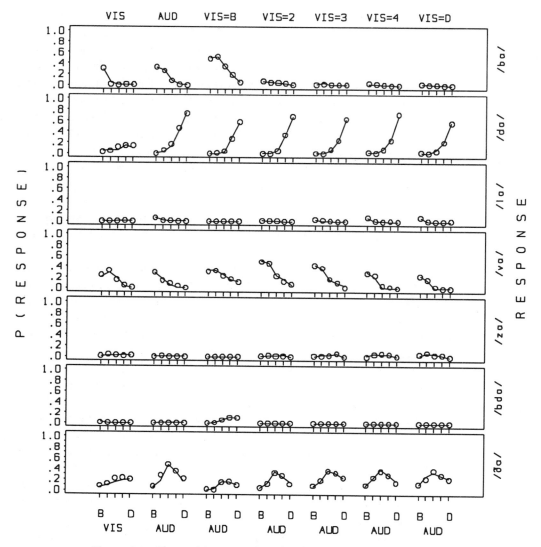

Figure 6.8 Observed (points) and predicted (lines) proportion of /ba/, /da/, /la/, /va/, /za/, /bda/, and /ða/ identifications for the visual-alone (left plot), auditory-alone (second plot), and bimodal (remaining plots) conditions as a function of the five levels of the synthetic auditory (AUD) and visual (VIS) speech varying between /ba/ (B) and /da/ (D) for the English talkers. The lines give the predictions of the FLMP for the task with an open-ended set of response alternatives.

more /la/ and /za/ responses were given in the open-ended study. These results show that the differences between the two methods were quantitative and not qualitative. Apart from these differences, the two response profiles bear a great deal of similarity. Based on the good fit of the FLMP to both experiments, we can conclude that the nature of speech processing is not changed in any fundamental way by constraints upon the number of possible response alternatives.

Accuracy of Response

We began our argument for the influence of visible speech by demonstrating its distortion of the accuracy of our phenomenal experience. When the auditory and visual speech conflicted, the visible speech changed our percept. The FLMP gave a good prediction of a multitude of accuracy results in chapter 1. The FLMP made strong predictions about the accuracy of performance in that it predicted that two sources of consistent information can be more informative than just one. Accuracy was greater given bimodal speech than given the unimodal presentation of audible or visible speech. Furthermore, two inconsistent sources of information are expected to disrupt performance relative to either one presented alone. Congruent with this prediction, we found less accurate performance given inconsistent information sources relative to either unimodal presentation. We continue our investigation of various behavioral measures by analyzing the time it takes to make a judgment.

Reaction Times

Finally, reaction times can be an informative independent variable: they have the potential to provide converging evidence for the process of integrating auditory and visual speech. Of the 82 participants in our two-alternative five-by-five expanded factorial design (see chapter 2), we recorded reaction times from 41. There were 24 observations for each subject for each of the 35 experimental conditions. In this task, subjects were told to identify each test stimulus as /ba/ or /da/ the best they could.

Figure 6.9 shows the average proportion of /da/ judgments for the 35 conditions as a function of the levels of the auditory and visual information. As expected, these 41 subjects show the same pattern that was observed for the complete set of 82 participants.

Figure 6.10 shows the mean reaction times averaged across /ba/ and /da/ judgments for the 35 conditions as a function of the levels of the auditory and visual information. (Evaluating reaction time as a function of response type for each trial type is not feasible because one of the two responses could be very infrequent. For example, there are very few /da/ responses to the /ba/ endpoints.) Although the results might appear to be complex at first glance, they follow a fairly simple pattern: reaction time tends to increase with increases in the overall ambiguity of the test stimulus. For the unimodal conditions, reaction time is longest in the ambiguous middle range of the stimulus continuum. For the bimodal conditions, reaction time increases when both modalities are ambiguous or when the information from the two modalities differs.

To illustrate the importance of ambiguity, we define it in terms of how consistently subjects identify a given speech stimulus. Stimuli that are identified more consistently are necessarily less ambiguous. Quantitatively,

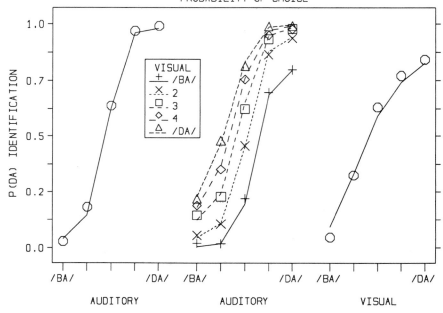

Figure 6.9 Observed (points) proportion of /da/ responses as a function of auditory-alone (left plot), visual-alone (right plot), and bimodal (middle plot) conditions as a function of the five levels of the synthetic auditory and visual speech varying between /ba/ and /da/. Lines give the predictions of the FLMP.

ambiguity is defined as the extent to which $P(/da/)$ approaches .5.

$$A = 1 - 2[|.5 - P(/da/)|] \tag{6.8}$$

where $|x|$ is the absolute value of x. Thus, ambiguity varies between 0, when $P(/da/)$ is 0 or 1, and 1, when $P(/da/)$ is .5. This definition of ambiguity appears to give a good account of the observed reaction times. A reaction time (RT) averaged across all subjects was computed for each of the 35 stimulus conditions and correlated with the A values computed from the average identification results. Figure 6.11 shows that there was a strong positive correlation between A and RT, $r = .834$, $p < .001$.

The FLMP is a stage model that assumes some processing time for each of the three stages (Massaro & Cohen, 1994). Categorization reaction time will include some time for each stage and also time for other processing not accounted for by these stages. In chapter 9 we propose that the evaluation process follows a negatively accelerating growth function of processing time. This function can be described by its rate of processing and its asymptotic value. The rate of processing is assumed to be constant across the different test stimuli, although their asymptotes will necessarily differ. To illustrate these assumptions, consider the rate of processing a visual source of information V_j. It is assumed that this rate does not depend on whether or not other sources of information are present or on whether the other sources

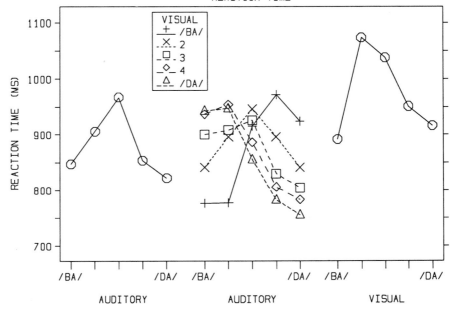

Figure 6.10 Reaction time (RT) as a function of auditory-alone (left plot), visual-alone (right plot), and bimodal (middle plot) conditions as a function of the five levels of the synthetic auditory and visual speech varying between /ba/ and /da/.

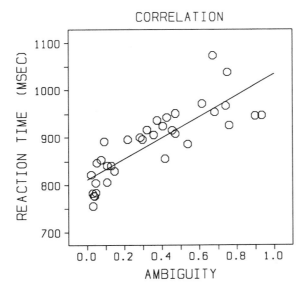

Figure 6.11 Observed reaction time (points) averaged across 41 subjects as a function of ambiguity for the averaged 35 experimental conditions, with best-fitting linear correlation line.

agree with or conflict with the visual source. Evaluation continuously transmits its outcome to integration, and it is assumed that integration time does not depend on the number of sources of information or on whether the sources agree with or conflict with one another. Thus, it is assumed that evaluation and integration processes consume time but that the amount of time is independent of the stimulus conditions. It is a constant.

Although the times for evaluation and integration are constant, their outputs do influence reaction time. The outcome of integration is made available to the decision stage, and its ambiguity is assumed to influence the time required for decision. Decision time is assumed to be a direct function of the relative goodness of match given by the relative goodness rule (RGR). The RGR gives the predicted probability of a response, in this case, $P(/da/)$. Thus, the reaction time to a given speech event is assumed to be a function of $P(/da/)$.

$$RT = E + f[P(/da/)],\qquad(6.9)$$

where E is some constant expected time for all processes not related to decision, and $f(\ )$ is the function that relates $P(/da/)$ to RT. Although we don't know the function $f(\ )$, we can obtain an idea of it by looking at the relationship between RT and $P(/da/)$ in the two-choice identification task. That relationship is illustrated in figure 6.12, in which the plus symbols plot average reaction times across subjects and responses as a function of $P(/da/)$. As can be seen in the figure, RT increases as $P(/da/)$ approaches .5 and diminishes as $P(/da/)$ approaches 0 or 1. This empirical finding shows that reaction time

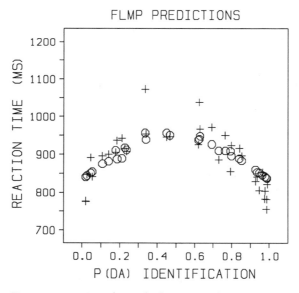

Figure 6.12 Mean observed (plus signs) and predicted (circles) RT (reaction time) as a function of $P (/da/)$ identifications for 41 subjects.

increases to the extent that a subject responds equally often with the two response alternatives.

The relationship between RT and $P(/\text{da}/)$ shown in figure 6.12 shows the maximum RT at $P(/\text{da}/) = .5$ and a roughly linear decreasing function as $P(/\text{da}/)$ approaches 0 or 1. If a linear falloff from the maximum is assumed, then the FLMP can predict the RTs by equation 6.10.

$$RT = a - b[|(P(/\text{da}/)) - .5|] \tag{6.10}$$

Basically, equation 6.10 says that reaction time is a linear function of ambiguity. We include two free parameters a and b because we do not know the intercept or slope of this assumed function. The values a and b are necessarily greater than or equal to 0, and $|x|$ means the absolute value of x. To predict the reaction times, the predicted $P(/\text{da}/)$ values given by equation 2.17 were taken from the FLMP fit of the identification judgments to the 35 stimulus conditions. These predicted values of $P(/\text{da}/)$ were used in equation 6.10. Values of a and b were then estimated to maximize the fit of the RTs. The estimated value of a was 1062 ms; the estimated value of b was 447 ms. The RMSD for the fit of the observed RTs of each of the 41 individual subjects averaged 84 ms. As can be seen in figure 6.12, the predictions of this model (represented by circles) provide a fairly good description of the changes in reaction time.

It is assumed that the goodness of match is continuously passed forward from the evaluation to the integration to the decision stage. The decision stage computes the relative goodness of match (RGM). In terms of the model, the time for the decision process increases to the extent that RGM is less extreme. It is assumed that the decision process does not initiate a response until the RGM values reach asymptote (that is, have a small change over some time period). Following the algorithm of the FLMP, the decision-stage probability matches, in the sense that the relative frequency of a response is equal to the RGM. Thus, the time required for initiating a response is an increasing function of the ambiguity of the RGM. The decision process finds it more difficult to settle on a choice to the extent that the choices are less clear-cut.

This FLMP analysis of reaction time is in the spirit of other recent quantitative models (e.g., Link, 1992; see also Norman & Wickelgren, 1969; Thomas & Myers, 1972). The reaction times increase with increases in the ambiguity of the speech event. Reaction times are very long to stimuli in the middle of a unimodal continuum where there is maximum ambiguity or when the two sources of information support different alternatives, creating an ambiguous event. On the other hand, very fast reaction times are predicted (and observed) with two consistent sources of unambiguous information.

In summary, the FLMP has been successful in predicting the time required for the identification judgments solely as a function of the predicted proportion of judgment. This should be considered an impressive prediction because only two additional parameters are necessary to predict another 35 independent observations. One could easily have believed that conflicting sources of information would increase RT beyond that expected simply from the ambiguity that is necessarily present. However, no additional processing time is required when sources of information conflict (Massaro, 1987a, 1987f). The critical variable is the output of integration, not the sources of that output. To date, most of the research in speech and other domains of pattern recognition has not directly measured the time course of information processing. In chapter 3 we gained some evidence on the time course of integration by varying the relative onset time of the audible and visible speech. A challenge for future work in speech is to broaden the experimental design and analyses to measure the time course of pattern recognition more directly.

INSTRUCTIONS IN THE PATTERN RECOGNITION TASK

To what extent does pattern recognition change with variations in instructions? The value of instructional manipulations is apparent in our study of bimodal speech perception. In particular, we have investigated whether one of the processes in speech perception entailed by the FLMP—integration—can be prevented through instructional manipulation. In the FLMP, the two sources of information are integrated and both influence perceptual judgments. A strong test of the robustness of integration is to assess the extent to which subjects can bypass integration. Can subjects voluntarily identify the speech event on the basis of just a single source of information when both are available? If subjects cannot selectively attend to a single source, we have strong evidence for the robustness of integration. Subjects have been tested in the bimodal speech recognition task under two selective-attention conditions: the subjects identified only what they saw or only what they heard. Even with these instructions, subjects were influenced by the modality they were trying to ignore (Massaro, 1987f; see also chapter 8).

Experimenters should worry when small changes in instructions bring about very different results. An implicit assumption in our research is that we are studying processes not easily modified by any intentional set of the participant. Our results support the notion that integration is a natural form of processing bimodal speech.

TASKS

Investigators should be concerned with whether their findings generalize across variations of the experimental task. The study of performance on different tasks improves the chances of gaining insights into underlying mechanisms. We do not expect the results to be identical, but we do expect our theories to account for performance across variability in the task domain. Our understanding of psychological mechanisms is good to the extent that we can predict behavior across different tasks.

In particular, we should like to know whether our view of bimodal speech perception holds up over a wide variety of tasks. We therefore look for tasks other than the ones we have employed to further challenge the FLMP. In *selective adaptation*, listeners are exposed to a number of repetitions of an "adapting" syllable, and then are asked to identify syllables taken from a continuum between two categories. Relative to the baseline condition of no adaptation, the identification judgments of syllables along the speech continuum are pushed in the opposite direction of the adapting syllable (a contrast effect). If subjects are adapted to the syllable /ba/, they will tend to categorize intermediate members of a /ba/–/da/ continuum as /da/.

Roberts and Summerfield (1981) used selective adaptation to obtain a somewhat indirect measure of the influence of visible speech. They employed auditory, visual, and bimodal adaptors to evaluate auditory adaptation along an auditory /be/ to /de/ continuum. They found no evidence for cross-modal adaptation. The visual adaptors presented alone produced no adaptation along the auditory continuum. Similarly, equivalent levels of adaptation were found for an auditory adaptor and a bimodal adaptor with the same phonetic information. The most impressive result, however, was the adaptation obtained with the conflicting bimodal adaptor. The auditory /be/ paired with visual /ge/ produced adaptation equivalent to the auditory adaptor /be/. This result occurred even though the subjects supposedly experienced the bimodal adaptor as /de/. Although the authors did not provide an exact measure of the subjects' identification of the adaptors, the result has been replicated by Saldana and Rosenblum (1994) with an auditory /ba/ and visual /va/ adaptor. Their subjects always identified this combination as /va/, and yet the adaptation led to an increase in /va/ judgments. Thus, adaptation follows the auditory information and is not influenced by the visual information or the phenomenal experience of the bimodal syllable.

The adaptation results provide strong support for the FLMP assumption that there is no cross talk between the auditory and visual sources. By cross talk we mean the modification by one source of information of the representation of the other. If there were cross talk at evaluation, then there should have been an influence of cross-modal adaptation. For example, the auditory /be/ paired with visual /ge/ should *not* have produced adaptation equivalent to the auditory adaptor /be/ because the auditory /be/ representation would have been changed by the visual /ge/.

These same results might provide evidence against competing accounts of bimodal speech perception. The interactive activation model of McClelland and Elman (1986) predicts that the bottom-up activation of the phoneme /d/ should provide top-down activation of the features representing that phoneme. Because of this top-down activation, it might be predicted from their model that a bimodal syllable composed of an auditory /be/ and a visual /ge/ should produce a different type of adaptation than an auditory /be/ adaptor. The auditory /be/ and visual /ge/ adaptor should function more or less as a /de/ adaptor, and both the auditory and the visual features should have adapted to be more like /d/. The auditory /be/ adaptor, on the other hand, should have driven both the auditory and visual features toward /b/. It follows that subjects should not have adapted to the bimodal syllable experienced as /de/ in the same manner as they adapted to the unimodal auditory /be/.

In a study described in chapter 11, we have also demonstrated that observers have access to undistorted modality-specific information from the evaluation stage even after integration has occurred. In that study, participants performed both a categorization task and a discrimination task. Participants found it easy to discriminate two syllables that they categorized as the same syllable. This result is similar to the finding that observers can report the degree to which a stimulus resembles some syllable even though they categorically label it as one syllable or another. These findings support the FLMP assumption that continuous auditory and visual information from the evaluation stage is maintained in unaltered form even after the two sources have been combined for identification at the integration stage. A system is perhaps more flexible when it has multiple representations of the events in progress and can draw on the different representations when necessary.

SENSORY INTEGRATION WITHIN MODALITIES

In broadening the domain of our universal principle, the focus has been on the integration of information from different sensory modalities, such as audible and visible speech or speech and gesture. We actually began our investigation with studies of sensory integration within the auditory modality (Massaro & Cohen, 1976, 1977; Oden & Massaro, 1978). Because multiple cues are present within a modality, we view sensory integration within a modality as being just as central as sensory integration between modalities, if not more so. However, auditory-visual speech perception is ideal for experimentation and theory testing because the two sources of information are so easily manipulated independently of one another. In view of our promotion of a universal principle of pattern recognition and the hypothesized relevance of our framework to speech perception more generally, it is valuable to confirm the FLMP within the auditory modality.

Our early auditory studies were successful tests of the FLMP (e.g., Massaro & Oden, 1980a), and it should be sufficient to describe a single recent test. For the expanded factorial design, the goal is to find cues that can be manipulated independently of one another and cues that can be present or absent in the speech signal. Because this is not so easily accomplished within the auditory modality, we were pleased to find a recent study of the perception of place of articulation of stop consonants in Dutch carried out by Smits, ten Bosch, and Collier (1996). A persistent issue in auditory speech perception has concerned the relative contribution of burst and transition cues to the identity of place of articulation of stop consonants (Dorman, Studdert-Kennedy

& Raphael, 1977). The procedure used by Smits and coworkers involved the manipulation of the acoustic cues by deleting and cross-splicing the burst and formant transition cues as well as testing the original utterances. Although the authors did not formulate their experimental design and data analysis as such, their study actually involved an expanded factorial design. Stimuli were made that had just the burst information, just the transition information, and all combinations of the burst and transition.

Smits et al. tested the three stops /p/, /t/, and /k/ in consonant-vowel syllables with four different vowel contexts. In addition, the experiment was replicated using two different tokens from each of two speakers. This procedure gives a total of 16 replications of the expanded factorial experiment. Figure 6.13 gives the results for one of these conditions in terms of the probability of a /p/, /t/, or /k/ response as a function of the transition and burst cues. As can be seen in the left and right plots, both the transition and burst alone were informative. In addition, both cues influenced perceptual identification when both were present in the speech segment. The contribution of a cue when both cues were present was fairly well predicted

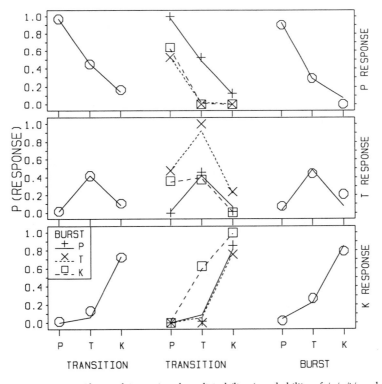

Figure 6.13 Observed (points) and predicted (lines) probability of /p/, /t/, and /k/ judgments as a function of the burst and transition cues. Results from Smits, ten Bosch, and Collier, 1996; the stimulus condition is second token by speaker 1 for the vowel context /i/; predictions for the FLMP.

by their respective contributions when presented in isolation. The FLMP provided a fairly good description of this condition and of each of the 16 different conditions that were tested. The RMSD averaged .053 for the fit of the FLMP, compared to an average RMSD of .129 for the SCM.

Although the FLMP easily outperformed its competitors, the fit was not as good as our comparable fits to auditory-visual speech. Hence, it might be claimed that the FLMP is better suited to integration between modalities than to integration within a modality. However, the difference seems to lie in failing to meet the requirements of the expanded factorial design within the auditory modality. The manipulation of several auditory cues in an expanded factorial design raises an issue not apparent in the bimodal speech situation. The experimental elimination of an auditory cue might actually provide information, and that information could support one alternative more than others. For example, a transition presented without a burst might actually provide support for /p/ independently of the support from the transition itself because this consonant does not have much of a burst to begin with. To check on this possibility, we included an additional three parameters to represent the support for the three alternatives when only the transition was presented. This embellishment of the model improved its fit significantly. Thus, we can conclude that the FLMP is equally capable of describing pattern recognition within a modality —even though the assumptions required by the expanded factorial design might not always be met.

ROBUSTNESS OF FLMP INTEGRATION

We presented many experimental findings that substantiate the robustness of the FLMP for integration of audible and visible speech. By robustness we mean that FLMP integration occurs across a broad range of ecological conditions, and that the FLMP gives a good account of this integration. Integration is also robust across relatively large temporal asynchronies between the audible and visible speech (see chapter 3). The robustness of the FLMP algorithm held up across changes in intention as manipulated by instructions, as did its robustness across individual and situational variability. This type of integration holds up even when the two sources being integrated are not ecologically joined. For example, natural auditory speech is integrated with synthetic visible speech in the same way it is combined with natural visible speech (Massaro & Cohen, 1990). Furthermore, auditory and visual speech are combined in a natural fashion even when the sex of the voice differs from the sex of the face doing the talking (Green et al., 1991). Similarly, differences in the spatial location of the auditory and visual speech do not disrupt the integration process (Bertelson et al., 1994; Fisher, 1991; Massaro, 1992a). Our next detailed description of a test of robustness involves the integration of audible speech with an inverted face, which has been shown to interfere with face processing.

Inverting the Face

We have seen that the face is a powerful source of information in speech perception, and it is of interest to what extent integration is disrupted when the face is presented in an unusual orientation. It is well known that recognition of faces is disrupted when they are viewed upside down (Valentine, 1988). This raises the question of whether rotations of the face would also disrupt speech perception. In previous research, several investigators have explored the influence of facial rotation on speech recognition. Campbell (1994) reports a significant but weaker McGurk effect (an influence of visible speech) with an inverted projection of the face. Jordan and Bevan (1997) found that the McGurk effect decreased to the extent that the face was rotated from the upright. Bertelson and colleagues (1994) varied both the spatial separation between the auditory and visual speech and whether or not the face was inverted, to test the robustness of the combining of the two sources. Inverting the face did not interfere with the tendency to locate the speech at the face of the speaker. However, consistent with the Fisher (1991) study, even though the McGurk effect did not depend on the spatial separation between auditory and visual speech, it did decrease with facial inversion. Green (1994) likewise found a significantly weaker McGurk effect when an auditory syllable /ba/ was presented with a visible /ga/ spoken by a face in the inverted position. Green (1994, p. 3014) concluded that "inverting the face ... impacts on the integration of phonetic information from the auditory and visual modalities." What is not clear, however, is whether that impact is due to a decrease in the visual information from an inverted face or to a weakening of the actual integration of the visual information with auditory speech.

Information versus Information Processing

Given the framework of the FLMP, we can test whether the smaller influence of visible speech from an inverted face is due to interference with the visual information or with the integration of the auditory and visual information. An expanded factorial design was used to carry out this test (Massaro & Cohen, 1996). We crossed 4 auditory syllables with 8 visual syllables—4 from an upright face and 4 from an inverted face. This produced 32 bimodal conditions and 12 unimodal conditions, making a total of 44 conditions, each of which was tested 20 times. The participants were ten native speakers of American English. Identification judgments were recorded for each stimulus. The mean observed proportion of identifications was computed for each participant for each of the unimodal and bimodal conditions by pooling across all 20 replications of each condition.

Our manipulation was successful: inverting the face disrupted the identification of the visible syllables. Accuracy of lipreading for the visual-alone condition was .82 with the upright face and .72 with the inverted face. We can thus conclude that there is in fact a decrease in visual information due to inversion of the face.

Of theoretical interest is to what extent the inversion of the face changed the nature of processing bimodal speech in addition to influencing the information available in visible speech. To make this determination, we compared the separate fits of the FLMP for the upright and inverted faces. If inverting the face disrupts the processes postulated by the FLMP, then the fit of the model should be significantly poorer for the inverted than for the upright face. The RMSD values for the fit of the FLMP to the upright and inverted face were .014 and .016, respectively. The difference was not statistically significant, indicating that inverting the face does not disrupt information processing as postulated by the FLMP. Apparently, it is only the visible information that is degraded by inverting the face: people tend to integrate the auditory and visual sources even under relatively strange and novel conditions such as facial inversion.

Inverting the face did not appear to change the nature of processing bimodal speech, but simply influenced the information available from the face. Thus, inverting the face can be viewed as simply a method of degrading visual information, in the same way that auditory noise and band-pass filtering have been used to degrade the auditory information. Analogous to these results with visual degradation, the FLMP has also been successful in describing bimodal speech perception under different levels of auditory noise (Massaro, 1987f, chapter 2). The same conclusion was reached: auditory noise did not change the nature of processing bimodal speech.

The distinction between information and information processing clarifies the interpretation of findings in face processing. It is often assumed that different psychological systems perform different aspects of pattern recognition in the face. For example, there appears to be a hemispheric asymmetry between face identification and speech perception. That asymmetry might simply reflect differences in information as opposed to differences in information processing. In addition to the systems used for face identification and speech perception, there are also different systems putatively used for face and emotion identification (Etcoff & Magee, 1992; Tanaka & Farah, 1993). However, there is no reason to assume that dissociations among these various behaviors necessarily reflect different processing systems (Levine, Banich & Koch-Weser, 1988; Sergent, 1994). It might instead be the case that different types of information are used. For example, different cues would be used for determining sex and identifying the person. Thus, observed dissociations might be due to differences in information rather than to differences in information processing.

In summary, the distinction between information and information processing raises important theoretical questions that must be addressed both experimentally and theoretically. We applied our framework to a broad range of ecological niches and were successful in accounting for their behavior in terms of the FLMP. Information will necessarily differ across these situations, but the information processing appears very similar. We hope that researchers will be encouraged to apply this framework to new situations to challenge the model even further. We continue to expand the horizons of our paradigm and universal principle by pursuing an exciting area of inquiry: the processing of emotion as communicated by the face and the voice.

7 Emotion in the Face

Emotions are the life force of the soul, the source of most of our values.
—R. C. Solomon, *The Passions*

The face of man is the index to joy and mirth, to suffering and sadness.
—Pliny the Elder

The face is the mirror of the mind—and eyes without speaking confess the secrets of the heart.
—St. Jerome

In the previous chapter, the fuzzy logical model of perception was shown to be capable of describing pattern recognition across a broad variety of content domains. Because of space limitations, we could not describe all of the content domains in which the FLMP has been successful. In this chapter and the next, we turn to a seemingly improbable domain for success—that of emotion. "Emotion is special and unique," is the common refrain from colleagues expressing the received wisdom in the field. Emotion in the face is the concern of this chapter; chapter 8 addresses emotion in the face and voice.

Face recognition and the perception of facial expression are now being studied intensively by cognitive scientists and neuroscientists. The field is at a stage of development similar to that of the study of speech perception about two decades ago. Only a handful of hard-nosed experimental psychologists brought the phenomenon of face perception into the laboratory and subjected it to the disinterested scrutiny of empirical inquiry. Much of the previous literature was also burdened by a casual and less than well informed application of evolutionary theory.

In spite of our belief in universal rather than domain-specific processes, we acknowledge that the information sources available for perception of emotion belong to a different family than those available for speech perception. Nonetheless, our successes in chapters 4 and 6 in demonstrating common principles of information processing across various domains encourages us to expect that these principles will hold up in the domain of emotion.

We operate under the assumption that multiple sources of information are also used to perceive a speaker's emotion. These consist of a variety of paralinguistic signals that co-occur with the verbal content of the speech. They may be aspects of voice quality, facial expression, and body language. In order to study how multiple paralinguistic sources of information are used, it is important first to define those sources. In our research we choose two sources of paralinguistic information, facial expressions and vocal cues, to create a situation analogous to that of bimodal speech. We begin with a review of the study of facial cues to emotion.

FACIAL AND OTHER CUES TO EMOTION

There is no doubt that the production of facial expressions is an effective means of communicating emotion. Darwin (1872) argued that facial expressions have their origins in basic acts of self-preservation common to human beings and other animals, and that those acts were related to the emotional states now conveyed by the descendent expressions. Research by Meltzoff and Moore (1977) suggests that we are biologically prepared from birth to respond to facial expressions. Infants only a few days old are able to imitate adult facial expressions. If a picture is worth a thousand words, a face must communicate much more, even if what is perceived is sometimes difficult to express in words. Although many facial movements are possible, we tend to behave as if there are only a few emotional categories. Some evidence exists, based on the studies of animals, children born deaf and blind, and preliterate and isolated societies, that the production of some facial expressions such as those associated with rage, startle, fear, and pleasure, are reliably developing (innate) and universal.

Although production of emotion might be universal and reliably developing, the story is more muddled for the recognition of emotion. Fridlund (1991, 1994) argues that behavioral and ecological factors have been the main influence in the development of the ability to recognize facial expressions. For example, there is an ecological explanation for why smiling is usually interpreted as a friendly gesture. Small things tend to produce higher frequencies than large things. Smiling while speaking raises the fundamental frequency and formant frequencies of speech, which can then be interpreted as coming from a smaller and less threatening organism (Ohala, 1984).

We recognize and characterize facial expressions of emotion in other humans with a high degree of accuracy and consistency (Ekman, 1984, 1993; Ekman & Friesen, 1975; Ekman, Friesen & Ellsworth, 1972; Collier, 1985). The face is not unique in this regard; we are also attuned to various nonfacial displays of emotional arousal. Hand and body gestures are well-known communicators of affective states (Archer & Silver, 1991). Even other species produce and respond to visible displays of emotion. Parakeets, for example, are sensitive to the size of the iris. Evidently, this cue is functional: male parakeets constrict the iris as part of their courtship display (Brown & Dooling,

1993). This cue is only one of several that parakeets use to signal relevant information, such as sex, age, and emotional arousal. These cues were shown to be highly functional—that is, they were discriminated more quickly than other, nonfunctional features.

Facial Emotion versus Facial Identity

The recognition and identification of emotional expressions has usually been isolated in the literature from the processing of facial identity. One testable assumption, however, is that the identity of faces is derived from the features that make them up in the same manner that the expression on a face is computed from facial features. In other words, the difference between the two domains may be one of information rather than information processing. Although it is necessarily the case that the features analyzed for facial expression differ from those that reveal facial identity, the processing involved in the two domains could be similar. Previous findings of dissociations between emotion and identity, such as segregated processing in the brain (e.g., Sergent et al., 1994), might reflect only differences in information.

One important difference between these two domains is the number of categories. We can recognize and identify a small number of emotional categories and a boundless number of people. Therefore, any differences found between the two domains might be due to differences in the number of distinguishable categories rather than between the two types of category. A second difference is the nature of the variability within and between categories. For emotion, there is a good deal of variability within an emotional category and, of course, significant differences between categories. For identity, there is less within-category variability. A good working premise is that studies of facial identity and facial emotion are equally informative about how we process and categorize facial information.

Face Recognition versus Object Recognition

Farah (1995) has provided some evidence of a dissociation between face recognition and object recognition. Within our scheme, she locates this difference at information processing rather than just information. By different systems for face and object recognition, she means that "two different systems must: (1) be functionally independent, such that either can operate without the other; (2) be physically distinct ...; and (3) process information in different ways, so that [one system] is not merely a physical duplicate of another" (p. 102). Farah's criteria for different systems are consistent with our belief that previous arguments for modular systems have meant differences in information processing, not simply differences in information. As evidence, Farah studied a man, called LH, who was prosopagnosic. People with this neurological disorder have difficulty recognizing the faces of loved ones and well-known celebrities. In one study, LH recognized faces and eyeglass frames about equally poorly whereas normal subjects showed a significant 20% advantage for faces over eyeglass frames. Furthermore, inverting faces disrupted performance somewhat for normal subjects but actually improved performance for LH. These results could have resulted from differences in information and not information processing. One way of distinguishing between the two possibilities would be to utilize the microscope of the expanded factorial design and model testing. This will tell us whether face recognition conforms to the FLMP.

Previous research into emotion recognition and classification has usually tested either highly schematic stimuli (i.e., line drawings) or exemplar photographs of persons either naturally displaying emotional expressions or feigning (as an actor might) the expression in question. These artificial stimuli might not be representative of naturally occurring emotions. Most important, faces with incomplete, ambiguous, or contradictory features are not usually tested, even though they are potentially the most challenging to information-processing models. Our talking head offers the potential to achieve both stimulus control and naturalism in experimentation.

VARYING AMBIGUITY IN THE RECOGNITION OF EMOTION

Baldi makes available for research a set of quite realistic faces that are standardized and replicable as well as controllable over a wide range of feature dimensions. Displays of ambiguous or contradictory features and partial face presentations can be made more easily than with earlier types of facial stimuli (see figures 7.2 and 7.14 later in the chapter).

Thus, it quickly became apparent that we could initiate a cottage industry in the study of facial and vocal cues to emotion. There was no shortage of literature on facial cues to emotion, but we found a tremendous void in the domain of vocal cues. We also learned that Baldi had to be given increased resolution in certain parts of the face and that we needed additional controls over those parts (see chapter 12).

Method

We use the expanded factorial design illustrated in figure 7.1 to study the pattern recognition of emotion (Ellison & Massaro, 1997). The affective categories *happy* and *angry* were chosen because they represent two of the basic categories of emotion. Of course, happy and angry faces are not discrete, nonoverlapping emotional displays; rather, a face can vary in the degree to which it represents one emotion as opposed to the other. To implement the expanded factorial design, it was necessary to choose two features and vary them systematically to create a range of emotions between happy and angry.

We chose two features that seem to differ somewhat in happy and angry faces. The features varied were brow displacement (BD) and mouth corner displacement (MD). As can be seen in figure 7.2, BD was varied from slightly

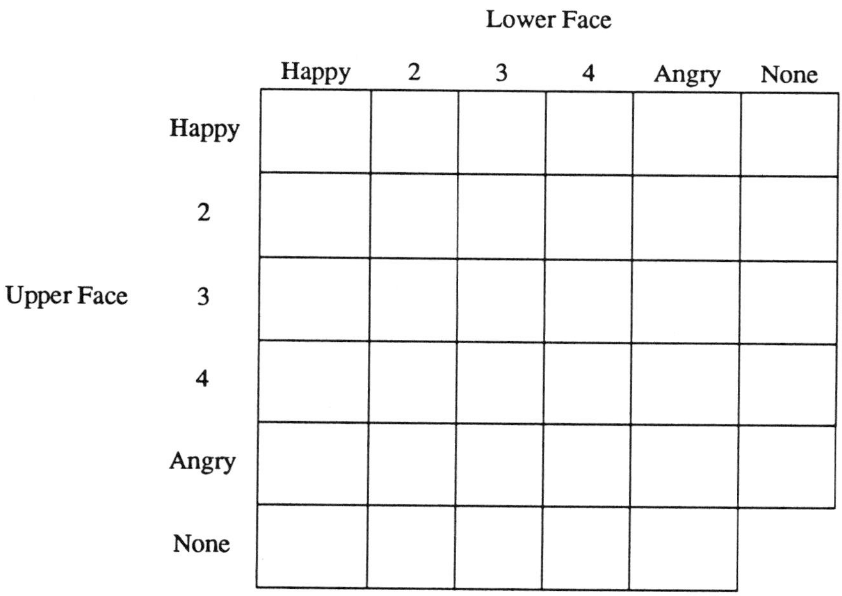

Figure 7.1 Expansion of a typical factorial design to include upper-face and lower-face conditions presented alone. The five levels along the upper and lower face continua represent displacements of the displayed feature along five physical steps from upward displacement to downward displacement.

elevated and arched for a prototypically happy expression to fully depressed and flattened for a prototypically angry expression. MD was varied from fully curled up at corners for a prototypically happy emotion to fully curled down at corners for a prototypically angry emotion. An important criterion for the choice of two features to manipulate is that they can be varied independently of one another. Varying one cue in the upper face and one cue in the lower face was an ideal solution. Furthermore, there appear to be motor neurons from the neocortical motor strip that serve the upper and lower face differentially (Fridlund, 1994, pp. 92–94). Five levels of the upper-face conditions and five levels of the lower-face conditions were factorially combined, along with the ten half-face conditions presenting the upper face or lower face alone. The feature values were obtained by comparison to features displayed in exemplar photographs in Ekman and Friesen (1975). Band 7.1 presents the different faces in the expanded factorial design. The levels change from the most happy to the most angry. The upper half is the fastest-moving variable and the half-face condition is the sixth level. Band 7.2 gives the same demonstration with the lower half of the face as the fastest-moving variable.

These two features are neither necessary nor sufficient for happy or angry faces; rather, they are simply correlated with those emotional categories. Like other categories, emotional categories are fuzzy in that no set of necessary and sufficient features characterizes a particular emotion. Even for natural

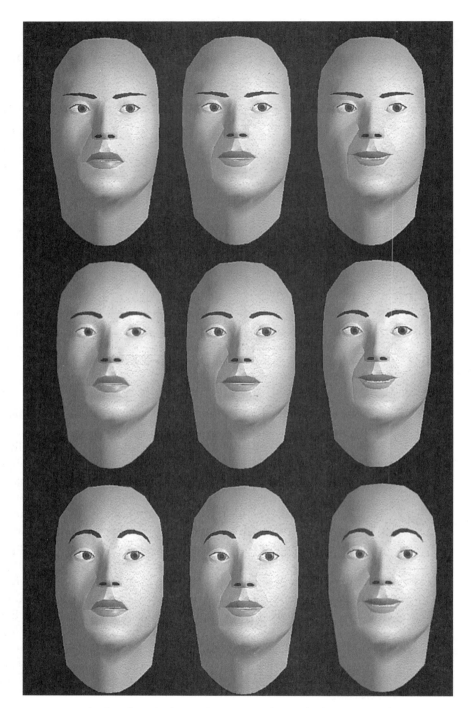

Figure 7.2 The four faces displaying the maximum feature displacements (at the corners) as well as faces displaying "neutral" displacements. The center face is the "neutral baseline" face, with both mouth and brow at the neutral values. Note that some faces are quite ambiguous and incongruent in their expressions. The unimodal (half-face) conditions displayed only the upper or lower half of the stimulus face.

faces, there is some controversy concerning the degree to which observers can accurately categorize different emotions. As concluded by Fridlund (1994, p. 237), there is no evidence for the claim that a given facial expression is unambiguously linked with a single emotion category. In addition, several other features are also correlated with these affective categories. For example, there is a tendency for a tightening around the eyes and a lifting of the cheeks in spontaneous smiling (Allen & Atkinson, 1981; Duchenne & de Boulogne, 1862; Ekman, Hager & Friesen, 1981). We limited our study to just two features in order to keep the number of unique faces reasonably small and the number of test observations relatively large.

Our task was a two-alternative forced choice between *happy* and *angry*. There were 35 different test faces. Participants were not shown any exemplar faces, nor were they given any feedback. After 10 practice trials, each stimulus face was randomly presented 16 times to each of 26 participants for identification.

Results

The points in figure 7.3 give the observed average results as a function of the mouth and brow variables. The left panel shows performance when just the upper half of the face was presented. Changes in the displacement of the brow were effective in changing the identified emotion in the expected direction. Similarly, the lower half of the face influenced the number of "happy" judgments in the anticipated way. The steeper curve for the mouth variable illustrates that it was somewhat more influential than the brow variable. The middle panel gives the factorial combination of the two halves of the face. As the figure shows, each of the two variables continued to be influential even when paired with the other variable.

The average results show most conclusively how two sources of information are more informative than just one. The probability of a "happy" judgment was about .80 when just the most upward deflection of the brow was presented and was about .88 for the most upward deflection of the mouth. However, when the two features were presented together in the whole face, the probability of a "happy" judgment was near 1. An analogous result was found for the most downward deflection of the two variables. These superadditive outcomes are consistent with our general view of pattern recognition. We now derive the predictions of the FLMP in order to test the model quantitatively against all of the results.

Fuzzy Logical Model of Perception   Because of the close analogy to speech, we give only a short description of the implementation of the FLMP for emotion perception. Participants are assumed to have prototypes corresponding to happy and angry faces. A happy face is characterized by the eyebrows slightly elevated and arched and the mouth corners fully curled up. An angry face is represented as having the eyebrows fully depressed and flattened and

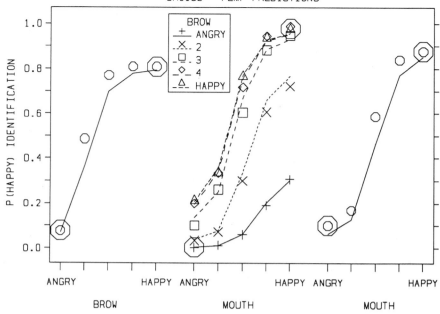

Figure 7.3 Predicted (lines) and observed (points) proportion of "happy" judgments as a function of the levels of the brow and mouth variables. The left panel shows performance for just the upper half of the face and the right panel for just the lower half. The middle panel gives performance for the factorial combination of the two halves. Average results across 26 subjects. The circled points show the superadditivity predicted by the FLMP. Predictions are for the FLMP. (From Ellison & Massaro, 1997, experiment 1.)

the mouth corners fully curled down. Of course, there are other sources of information described in the prototypes, but these do not require our attention because they should not be influenced systematically by the two independent variables. If B_i represents the brow information, then feature evaluation would transform B_i to b_i, the degree to which the brow supports the alternative *happy*. With just two response alternatives, *happy* (H) and *angry* (A), we can assume that the degree to which the evaluation of the brow supports the alternative A is $1 - b_i$ (Massaro & Friedman, 1990). The mouth information M_j is evaluated analogously: its support for H is m_j and its support for A is $1 - m_j$.

Feature integration consists of a multiplicative combination of the feature values supporting a given alternative. Given that b_i and m_j are the values of support for alternative H, then the total support for this alternative, $s(H)$, would be given by their product,

$$s(H) = b_i m_j. \tag{7.1}$$

The support for the alternative A would be

$$s(A) = (1 - b_i)(1 - m_j). \tag{7.2}$$

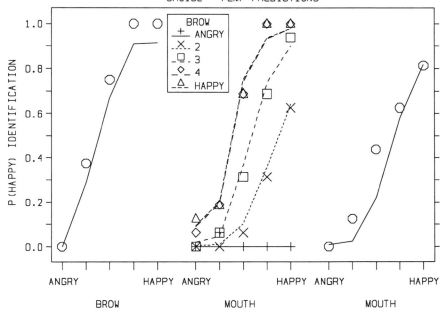

Figure 7.4 Predicted (lines) and observed (points) proportion of "happy" judgments as a function of the levels of the brow and mouth variables. The left panel shows performance for just the upper half of the face and the right panel for just the lower half. The middle panel gives performance for the factorial combination of the two halves. Results for a subject who is representative of the average results. Predictions are for the FLMP. (From Ellison & Massaro, 1997, experiment 1.)

The third operation is decision, which uses a relative goodness rule to give the relative degree of support for each of the test alternatives. In the two-alternative choice task, the probability of a "happy" choice given stimulus B_iM_j is given by equation 7.3.

$$P(H|B_iM_j) = \frac{s(H)}{s(H) + s(A)} \tag{7.3}$$

where $s(H)$ and $s(A)$ are given by equations 7.1 and 7.2.

As in the case of bimodal speech, the FLMP requires ten free parameters for the five levels of brow displacement and the five levels of mouth displacement. In the two-choice identification task, the FLMP's RMSDs for the participants ranged between .047 and .128, averaging .082.

Figure 7.4 gives the FLMP's predictions for a typical subject who is highly representative of the group results. As the figure shows, the FLMP gives a good account of the results. Thus, when both the brow and the mouth are deflected upward, the face is perceived as happy. The reader might have also noticed that only half of the American football shape (see chapter 4) is present in the factorial part of the design. This simply means that the mouth

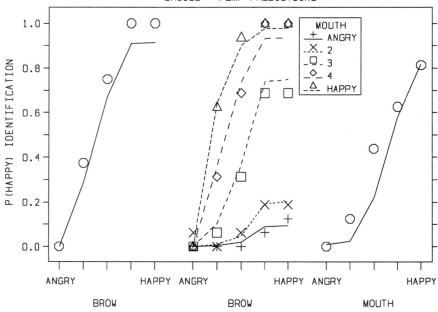

Figure 7.5 Predicted (lines) and observed (points) proportion of "happy" judgments as a function of the levels of the brow and mouth variables. The left panel shows performance for just the upper half of the face and the right panel for just the lower half. The middle panel gives performance for the factorial combination of the two halves. These are the same results plotted in figure 7.4 except that the brow variable is plotted on the x-axis in the factorial graph. Predictions are for the FLMP. (From Ellison & Massaro, 1997, experiment 1.)

variable did not give enough support for *happy* to dominate the judgments at the right side of the factorial plots. Figure 7.5 plots the results with the brow variable on the x-axis and the mouth as a parameter of the graph. The same half of the football is seen. Thus, the brow variable also did not provide unambiguous support for the happy emotion. The half-football is consistent with the asymmetry of the parameter values. The average parameter values for the brow variable were .05, .35, .71, .79, and .80 as that variable was changed from angry to happy. The analogous values for the the mouth variable were .05, .11, .48, .82, and .88. In both cases, the parameter values are more extreme at the *angry* than at the *happy* end of the continuum. In this case, a downward deflection of the brow carries more influence than the upward deflection of the mouth, and analogously for the reverse pairing.

Figures 7.6–7.8 give the results for three other observers in the task. The subject in Figure 7.6 shows a slight nonmonotonicity of responses to the brow variable. For this subject, an upward deflection actually provides somewhat less support for *happy*. This result only highlights one of our main premises: that we cannot predict exactly how an individual will be influenced by a given source of information. We have also found nonmonotonic results

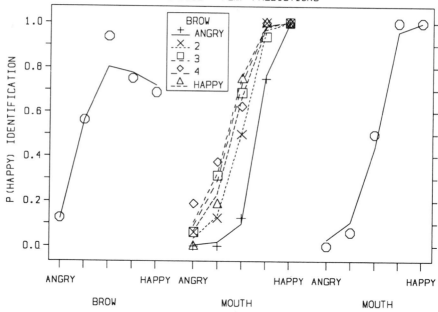

Figure 7.6 Predicted (lines) and observed (points) proportion of "happy" judgments as a function of the levels of the brow and mouth variables. The left panel shows performance for just the upper half of the face and the right panel for just the lower half. The middle panel gives performance for the factorial combination of the two halves. Observed results for a subject who showed a slight nonmonotonic effect of the brow variable. Predictions are for the FLMP. (From Ellison & Massaro, 1997, experiment 1.)

in the speech domain, so this type of finding is not unique to emotion. Figure 7.7 illustrates observed and predicted performance for a person who was highly influenced by the brow variable. Figure 7.8 shows the outcome for a subject more highly influenced by the mouth variable. The FLMP is capable of describing all of these different configurations of influence.

The reader might have noticed that the RMSD values given above are larger than those obtained in the analogous five-by-five expanded factorial design in speech recognition (see table 2.1). It is not valid, however, to compare the absolute value of RMSDs across experiments. We devote much of chapter 10 to this limitation and how it can be solved with a benchmark goodness of fit. For now, the reader is asked to accept that the fit of the FLMP to emotion in the face is acceptable.

Reaction Times Reaction times (RTs) of the identification judgments in the Ellison and Massaro (1997) study were also analyzed. The reaction times of the identification judgments can be used to test the FLMP's prediction that RT should increase to the extent that the facial information is ambiguous. Recall that ambiguity is defined as the extent to which the probability of a judgment, in this case the probability of "happy" $P(H)$, approaches .5.

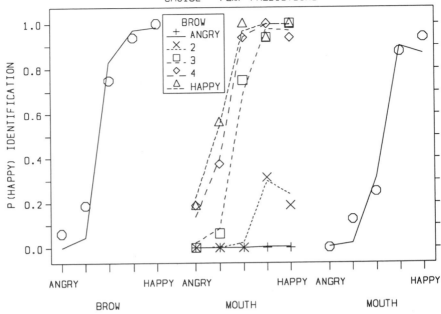

Figure 7.7 Predicted (lines) and observed (points) proportion of "happy" judgments as a function of the levels of the brow and mouth variables. The left panel shows performance for just the upper half of the face and the right panel for just the lower half. The middle panel gives performance for the factorial combination of the two halves. Observed results for a subject who was highly influenced by the brow variable. Predictions are for the FLMP. (From Ellison & Massaro, 1997, experiment 1.)

$$A = 1 - 2[|.5 - P(H)|] \tag{7.4}$$

where $|x|$ is the absolute value of x. Thus, ambiguity varies between 0, when $P(H)$ is zero or one, and 1, when $P(H)$ is .5. A reaction time averaged across all subjects was computed for each of the 35 stimulus conditions and correlated with the A values computed from the average results of the identification task. Figure 7.9 shows the strong relationship between this measure of ambiguity and RT. There was a strong positive (.83) correlation between A and RT. This reaction-time analysis supports the conclusions reached from the identification judgments. Both dependent measures provide support for the FLMP account of the processing of facial emotion.

As can be seen in figure 7.9, ambiguity predicts RT for both the bimodal and unimodal conditions. For the unimodal condition, when a half-face is made more ambiguous, its identification RT increases. For the factorial conditions, RTs appear to increase to the extent that the two half-faces are both ambiguous or when they conflict with one another (e.g., a "happy" brow and an "angry" mouth, which creates an ambiguous stimulus).

These RT results are consistent with recent findings that the time required to match unfamiliar faces was longest when some features matched and

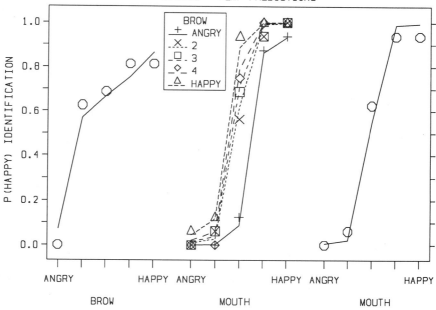

Figure 7.8 Predicted (lines) and observed (points) proportion of happy judgments as a function of the levels of the brow and mouth variables. The left panel shows performance for just the upper half of the face and the right panel for just the lower half. The middle panel gives performance for the factorial combination of the two halves. Observed results for a subject who was highly influenced by the mouth variable. Predictions are for the FLMP. (From Ellison & Massaro, 1997, experiment 1.)

some did not (Nachson, Moscovitch & Umiltà, 1995). A complete match or a complete mismatch led to the fastest reaction times. This result occurred even when subjects were instructed that some of the features were irrelevant to the decision. The subjects' inability to prevent the influence of a source of information anticipates our findings on the limited role of intentionality and instructional set in perceiving emotion from the face and the voice (see chapter 8).

Rating Judgments Rating judgments also provide a valuable dependent measure of pattern recognition. Ellison and Massaro (1997) also obtained rating judgments. The procedure was identical to the identification task except that the 22 participants received instructions to rate the emotion on a scale from 1 to 9. Faces that clearly exhibited the *happy* or *angry* emotion were to be rated as a 1 or a 9, respectively; faces that were perfectly ambiguous between the emotions were to be rated 5, and intermediate faces were to be rated using the 2, 3, 4 or 6, 7, 8 keys depending on the degree of perceived correspondence to the *happy* or *angry* emotions. Figure 7.10 shows the ratings, averaged across the participants, along with the predictions of

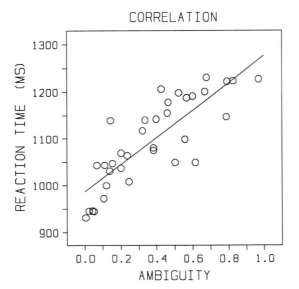

Figure 7.9 Reaction times (RT) averaged across all subjects and plotted as a function of ambiguity (*A*, given by equation 7.4) for each of the 35 conditions of the expanded factorial design. (From Ellison & Massaro, 1997, experiment 1.)

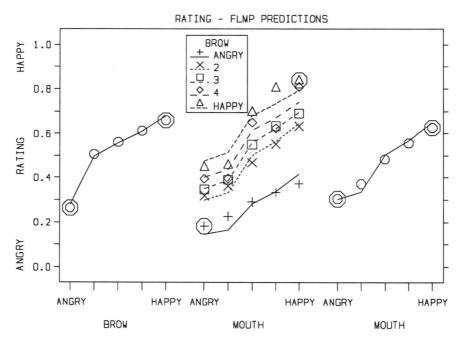

Figure 7.10 Predicted (lines) and observed (points) rating of "happy" judgments as a function of the brow and mouth conditions. The left panel shows performance for just the upper half of the face and the right panel for just the lower half. The middle panel gives performance for the factorial combination of the two halves. Predictions are for the FLMP. The circled points illustrate the superadditivity predicted by the FLMP. (From Ellison & Massaro, 1997, experiment 2.)

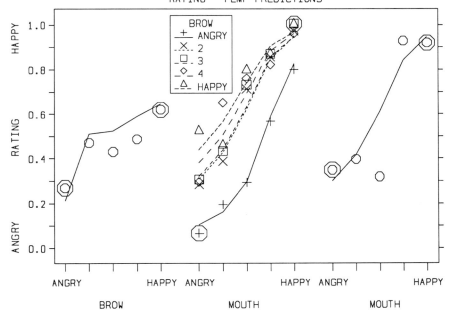

Figure 7.11 Predicted (lines) and observed (points) rating of "happy" judgments as a function of the brow and mouth conditions. The left panel shows performance for just the upper half of the face and the right panel for just the lower half. The middle panel gives performance for the factorial combination of the two halves. Results for a single subject. Predictions are for the FLMP. The circled points illustrate the superadditivity predicted by the FLMP. (From Ellison & Massaro, 1997, experiment 2.)

the FLMP. The independent variables influenced performance in the same manner as in the two-choice task.

Figures 7.11 and 7.12 give the observed and predicted ratings for two subjects in the task. The ratings for individual subjects follow the predictions of the FLMP. We have circled six points in each figure to illustrate that the superadditivity predicted by the FLMP holds for rating judgments as well as for identification judgments. We circled brow and mouth events at the extremes of the continua. As can be seen in the figures, the rating judgment when the subject was given the two sources of information combined is more extreme than the judgment based on either one of the sources presented alone. These results are strong evidence against an averaging model (AVM) or a single channel model (SCM) in which the rating for two sources of information cannot be more extreme than the rating for either source presented alone. Consistent with this observation, the model tests for the rating judgments gave the same conclusions they gave for the identification judgments. The RMSD for the FLMP fit to average rating data was .047 compared to an RMSD of .076 for the fit of the AVM and SCM.

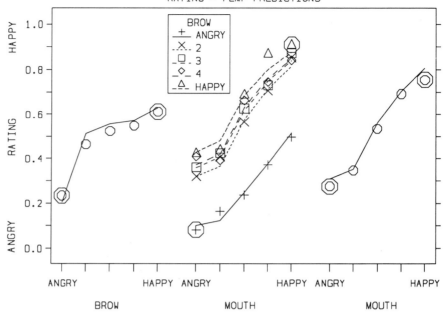

Figure 7.12 Predicted (lines) and observed (points) rating of "happy" judgments as a function of the brow and mouth conditions. The left panel shows performance for just the upper half of the face and the right panel for just the lower half. The middle panel gives performance for the factorial combination of the two halves. Results for a single subject. Predictions are for the FLMP. The circled points illustrate the superadditivity predicted by the FLMP. (From Ellison & Massaro, 1997, experiment 2).

QUESTIONS FOR FACE PROCESSING

The success of our tree of wisdom concerning speech perception by ear and eye (Massaro, 1987e, 1987f) encourages us to apply it to face processing. Ellison and Massaro (1997) took the same game of "playing twenty questions with nature" (Newell, 1973) we have used in speech research and extended it to emotion processing. Figure 7.13 illustrates a tree of wisdom, which consists of a number of binary oppositions about how facial emotion is processed. These questions are not necessarily hierarchical but are simply arranged to anticipate the answers proceeding from the top down and along the right side. At the top of the tree, we ask whether just a single holistic cue or multiple cues are used in processing a face. That is, to what extent can the identification and rating of a face be described by the processing of the parts that make it up? If not, we have holistic processing. At the next branch, we ask whether a feature of the face is perceived continuously or categorically. Next, are separate parts of the face evaluated independently of one another or is there cross talk (called dependence)? Fifth, how are the parts of the face used together or integrated to achieve recognition of facial emotion? Although these questions have been addressed in the literature, the answers have

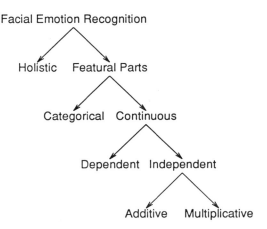

Figure 7.13   Tree of wisdom illustrating binary oppositions central to the differences among theories of emotion recognition.

usually differed from the conclusions reached in our research. We have seen that the identification, RT, and rating results are well described by the FLMP. We now discuss how those results contradict competing models. We begin with the single channel model (SCM).

Single Channel Model (SCM)

The single channel model serves as the antithesis of the FLMP with respect to the first binary opposition. For the SCM, only a single source of information is functional on any trial. Following the logic in chapter 2, the predictions for this model of the probability of a *happy* response, $P(H)$, can be given by

$$P(H|B_iM_j) = pb_i + (1 - p)m_j \tag{7.5}$$

where b_i and m_j are the respective probabilities of identifying the brow and mouth as happy. The value p is the probability of using the brow source of information. On single-feature trials, $P(H)$ is equal to simply b_i for the brow or m_j for the mouth. In light of the large interaction shown in figure 7.3, it is not surprising that the SCM gave a very poor description of the two-choice identification results, with an average RMSD of .155. In addition, the RMSD for the SCM fit to average rating data was .076, almost twice as large as the .047 fit of the FLMP.

Holistic Models

Next to the indeterminacy principle, I have learned in recent years to loathe most the term "holistic," a meaningless signifier empowering the muddle of all the useful distinctions human thought has labored at for two thousand years.
—Roger Lambert, in *Roger's Version,* by John Updike

In view of our success in predicting pattern recognition as a function of a pattern's component parts, it should come as no surprise that I abhor holistic models. For face processing, however, holistic processing is almost synonymous with theories of facial identity perception. Although holistic models have been formulated in the domain of facial identity recognition, the processes they propose could also be assumed for facial affect recognition. Thus, it is worthwhile to describe these models and evaluate their potential for describing our results.

Holistic processing is a loaded term that is easily criticized; fortunately, researchers have begun to clarify what they mean by holistic processing (Farah, 1995). Farah, Tanaka, and Drain (1995) and Carey and Diamond (1994) articulate two different characterizations of holistic processing of the face. The terms *holistic encoding* and *configural encoding* are used to describe the two viewpoints. In holistic encoding, the parts of the face are not separately represented and utilized. Rather, the face is represented as a whole. As evidence, Tanaka and Farah (1993) found that individual facial features were recognized more easily when displayed as part of a whole face than when displayed in isolation. Whereas recognition of individual features of faces was facilitated by the context of the whole face in normal orientation, recognition was not facilitated in the context of scrambled faces, inverted faces, or houses. These findings suggested to Tanaka and Farah that facial recognition is in some sense a holistic process, differing qualitatively from the recognition of other types of images. They claim that "the representation of a face used in face recognition is not composed of representations of the face's parts, but more as a whole face" (p. 226). In this view, parts of the face are not the atoms of face analysis or representation. This viewpoint is closest to the traditional version of holistic processing in that it bears great similarity to a template matching scheme of pattern recognition (Massaro, 1998). According to this viewpoint, the parts of the face would not be as accessible as the complete face.

On the other hand, we wonder whether this prediction of holistic models is falsifiable or whether it is simply like the untestable claim that a boy will grow up to either love or hate his father. It seems almost as reasonable to expect the holistic view to predict that the complete face would camouflage one of its parts rather than facilitate its perception. In fact, an advocate of holistic processing in word perception has continuously argued exactly this point (Johnson, 1975; Johnson & Blum, 1988; for an early critique, see Massaro & Klitzke, 1977). Thus it seems that an advocate of this version of holistic perception could have predicted either outcome, facilitation or inhibition.

The second characterization of holistic processing, called configural encoding, refers to the possibility that the spatial relations among the parts of the face are more influential than the parts themselves. The parts are represented, but it is the relations among the parts that are critical for analysis. This interpretation of holistic processing is also consistent with Tanaka and Farah's finding that individual facial features were more easily recognized when part of the complete face than when presented alone. According to this view, the complete face would provide spatial relations that would not be available from a part of the face presented in isolation. We have no objection to this possibility. In the framework of the FLMP, a relation between two parts of the face could function as an additional source of information. Such a relational function would be analogous to a temporal bimodal feature in speech perception by eye and ear (see figure 3.9).

A commendable goal of formalizing models is to prepare them for experimental tests. Unfortunately, we know of no holistic model that can be tested quantitatively against the results. Holistic encoding models would assume that each unique feature combination would create a unique emotion that could not be predicted from its component features. This formulation captures the idea that somehow the whole is more than some combination of its parts. We are not able to test a specific quantitative formulation of this holistic model because it requires as many free parameters as observed data points. Every face is unique, and its identification cannot be predicted on the basis of its components. This model remains untestable until there is some implementation of its principles with fewer free parameters. However, regardless of whether a particular holistic encoding model can be tested, an adequate fit of the FLMP provides evidence against the class of holistic encoding models. If the emotion of the whole face is not a function of its component features, then a model assuming that the value of the whole is derived from the values of its parts should fail. The fact that the FLMP does not fail in predicting emotion judgments from brow and mouth features is therefore evidence against this form of holistic perception in the domain of affect perception.

The second type of holistic model, configural encoding, is not so easily falsified. It is certainly possible that the brow and mouth features are better described in terms of their spatial relations than in terms of isolated features. Spatial relations must be used at some level. For example, the displacement of the corner of the mouth is probably evaluated relative to the center of the mouth. The displacement of the eyebrows could be evaluated relative to the eyes and nose. However, our research does eliminate the possibility that the spatial relation between the upper and lower half of the face is a functional feature for affect recognition. If spatial relations were functional, the identification of the whole and half faces could not have been predicted with the same parameter values, which are necessarily based on the component features.

In summary, the expanded factorial design provides a very strong test of both forms of holistic processing. Half of a face should be processed differently when presented alone relative to its processing when combined with the other half. Thus our research paradigm is rich enough to investigate what information is actually being used by the perceiver, even if a spatial relation among features is involved. The displacement of the eyebrows could be varied orthogonally to the distance between the eyebrows and eyes. Experimental manipulations of this nature would allow the investigator to zero in on the actual information being used. The current results, however, falsify the use of spatial relations between the upper and the lower half of the face, and the same test could be done for other features. So, we move down the right branch of the tree of wisdom toward compositional rather than holistic processing.

Categorical Models

The categorical model claims that emotion perception is discrete in that gradations of emotion are not easily perceived within an emotion category. We have underemphasized categorical perception in speech because it has now taken on the status of a straw man. Categorical perception means that perceivers do not distinguish among instances within a category. Speech theorists currently seem to agree that perceivers have within-category information that is functional in speech perception. This extant viewpoint did not emerge easily, and sometimes a bit of theoretical regression reaches the airwaves; but when pushed, virtually no speech theorist would defend categorical perception. Unfortunately, this progress has not transferred to research on the processing of faces. We review and criticize a few recent experimental claims for categorical perception to set the stage for the categorical model.

Etcoff and Magee (1992) presented computer-generated faces created by a weighted averaging of line drawings of exemplar faces displaying different emotional expressions. Following the tradition in speech perception studies, they carried out both identification and discrimination tasks. The former requires a categorization, whereas the latter asks the subject to notice a difference. The identification task presented faces in random order in a two-alternative forced-choice task. The identification results showed a systematic change in the identification judgment as the face changed from one emotion category to another. In the discrimination task, three faces were presented of which the first two differed, and the participant was asked to tell which one was identical to the third face. This is known as an ABX task. Discrimination performance was better for pairs of faces that tended to be identified as different emotions than for pairs identified as the same emotion. Given that categorization appeared to undermine discrimination, Etcoff and Magee concluded that these facial expressions were perceived categorically. Pairs of faces equally spaced along a stimulus continuum did not appear to produce equivalent perceptual differences. Two stimuli within a category were supposedly more poorly discriminated than two stimuli from two different categories. These results are similar to previous findings of "categorical perception" in speech, but we now know that other, better explanations exist.

It is now known that some discrimination tasks underestimate discrimination capacity (Massaro, 1987a). Many discrimination tasks have memory limitations, and performance is easily influenced by the participant's use of category labels. The ABX task, for example, makes it difficult to compare the third stimulus, X, to the first stimulus, A. In this task, participants often encode the stimuli categorically and base their discrimination decision on these category labels. Furthermore, categorical models were not explicitly developed by Etcoff and Magee nor tested against continuous models—maintaining the poor tradition established in early speech perception research. Better discrimination between items from a different category than between items from the same category does not conclusively demonstrate categorical perception.

Given a continuum of stimuli between two alternatives, a typical result is that the identification judgments change rather abruptly around the category boundary. Several researchers, like Etcoff and Magee (1992), have interpreted these prototypical findings as evidence for categorical perception. One error in this interpretation, however, is that the dependent measure, proportion of judgments, is being treated as a linear measure of perception. In fact, it has been shown that the observed identification function follows directly from continuous perception (Massaro, 1987a, 1987f). Sharp identification boundaries between categories follow naturally from a system with continuous information and a decision criterion (see Massaro, 1987a, 1987f, pp. 115–117).

In the Ellison and Massaro two-feature emotion perception study, for example, we find that perceivers have continuous information about each of the two facial characteristics being varied. Both the identification and rating judgments are well described by the FLMP, which assumes continuous information about each of the two features. Even though the results are best described by the FLMP with continuous information at evaluation and integration, the results show the same "discontinuous" identification functions that have previously been interpreted in favor of categorical perception. The lesson from this demonstration is that the shape of the identification functions alone is not sufficient to determine whether perception is continuous or categorical. Discrimination functions are also limited in interpretation because they could always result from the use of category labels. The most direct measure of whether perception is continuous or categorical involves comparing quantitative tests of models that assume either continuous or categorical information (Massaro, 1998).

Unfortunately, like holistic theories, most categorical theories do not allow compositional determination and are therefore not easily formalized to make testable predictions for our task. For both types of theories, it might be claimed that perception of each face is unique and cannot be predicted from performance on the parts that make it up. On the other hand, there are several other ways categorical perception can be tested. There is a specific categorical model of perception (CMP) in which the participant categorizes information from each feature or modality and responds with the outcome of the categorization of only one of the features (e.g., the brow) with a certain probability or bias toward that feature. Because the CMP is mathematically equivalent to the SCM, the poor fit of the SCM relative to the fit of the FLMP also provides evidence against the model. Of course, other categorical models are possible, and one of them might provide an adequate description of the results. Obviously, one cannot reject all possible categorical models, but there are no known quantitative formulations of this theoretical notion other than the CMP. In the spirit of scientific inquiry, however, another investigator is always free to develop another version and test it against the present results. In light of these findings, we choose the right branch of the tree of wisdom in favor of continuous over categorical perception.

The final two branches of the tree of wisdom are answered by the good fit of the FLMP. The brow and mouth features were assumed to be independent of one another and combined in a multiplicative manner. As we saw in the rating results of individual subjects, the rating given two sources of consistent information (the mouth and the brow) could be more extreme than the rating given to either source alone. Equipped with a successful framework for inquiry, we pursue the influence of culture on emotion recognition.

CULTURAL INFLUENCES ON EMOTION RECOGNITION

A controversial issue is whether the recognition of facial expression is universal or culturally dependent (Ekman, 1993, 1994; Fridlund, 1994; Russell, 1994). With the use of the FLMP paradigm, we can ask whether the processes involved in emotion recognition differ on the basis of the apparent cultural (racial) affiliation of the face or on the basis of the culture of the observer. Once again of key importance is the FLMP distinction between information and information processing. Information can be considered to be equal to the outputs of the evaluation process—the b_i and m_j of equation 7.1. Information processing, on the other hand, refers to the nature of the integration and decision operations. Given this distinction, our inquiry breaks down into the following questions: (1) whether the same information is used in the recognition of affect from faces associated with different cultures and (2) whether this information is the same for observers across cultures; (3) whether the same processes occur in the recognition of faces from different cultures and (4) whether information processing is the same for observers across cultures.

Previous Research

In a classic study, Ekman and Friesen (1975) asked college students in the United States and Japan to view stress-inducing films either alone or in view of a research assistant. When alone, the Japanese and Americans appeared to make identical facial expressions. When in view of another person, however, the Japanese appeared to mask their facial expression more than the Americans. Although these results are highly controversial (see Fridlund, 1994), they provide a starting point for the present study. If indeed there are cultural differences in the display of facial expression, we would also expect to find cultural differences in the information value of the features used for recognition. If the Japanese tend to attenuate their facial expression, for example, then we might expect that Japanese students would tend to judge a Japanese facial feature as having a more extreme emotion than the equivalent American face. On the other hand, Japanese students might tend to be less extreme in their judgments overall relative to the American students if they tend to attenuate their own overt interpretations of emotion. Furthermore, in Ekman's (1973) neurocultural model, learned culture-specific habits can influence the specific emotional expression associated with a face. It follows that the cues that perceivers use to recognize facial expression in one culture might differ somewhat from those used in another. All of these potential differences would qualify as differences in information and not information processing.

In addition to and independently of these possible differences in information, however, the theoretical framework of model testing allows us to ask whether the information processing involved in the recognition of facial expression differs between cultures. Although the features used to categorize facial expression might vary somewhat across cultures, information processing might be invariant across cultures and thus be uniformly consistent with the predictions of the FLMP. On the other hand, it is possible that the FLMP is capable of describing the information processing of individuals from one culture but not another. Based on the findings of support for the FLMP in a variety of pattern recognition tasks across development, aging, and different languages, we predict that the information processing used in emotion recognition should be universal across race and culture.

Experimental Test

To test this prediction, Massaro and Ellison (1996) compared Japanese and American subjects using the expanded factorial design with two facial features. The Japanese participants were 16 native Japanese students who were attending a three-week English-language course at UCSC. Although the students understood some English, the experimental instructions were written in Japanese Kanji and were explained in Japanese by a Japanese interpreter. The American participants were 14 UCSC undergraduate students. All participants were unaware of the procedures and hypotheses of the study; none had seen the synthetic face stimuli prior to the experimental sessions.

Because the skin surface texture of Baldi is chosen arbitrarily, we can use digitized images of actual persons, wrapping the features closely around the polygons of the face frame. This capability, combined with the facial motion simulation attained by varying polygon vertex angles and edge lengths, allows the program to simulate motion of features in realistic face images in a quantifiable and reproducible manner. An American face and a Japanese face were formed, using digitized images of an adult male American face and an adult male Japanese face for the texture-mapped skin. Twenty-four face stimuli were constructed to portray affective expressions that varied along

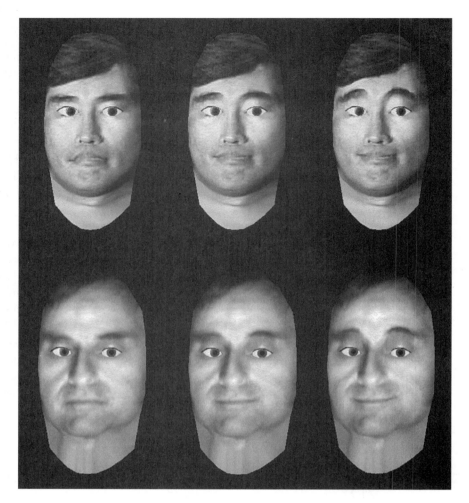

Figure 7.14 The Japanese and American face types displaying the maximum displacements of the brow and mouth features (at the corners of the figure) as well as faces displaying relatively neutral displacements of each of the features.

two feature dimensions in an expanded factorial design. The features manipulated in the stimulus set were the same brow and mouth characteristics used before, but with only four steps to each feature rather than five. The stimulus set, then, incorporated 24 faces—16 in the whole-face condition and 4 in each half-face condition for each of the two face types, for a total of 48 unique faces. Figure 7.14 depicts some of the faces at their target values for the Japanese and American faces. This experiment employed dynamic facial expression rather than the static expressions used in the previous experiment by Ellison and Massaro (1997). Each face stimulus began with a neutral expression and moved to the target feature value(s) during the first 600 ms, then remained on without motion for an additional 400 ms. Bands 7.3 and 7.4 illustrate the different face stimuli in the expanded factorial design for the American and Japanese faces, respectively. The levels change from the most

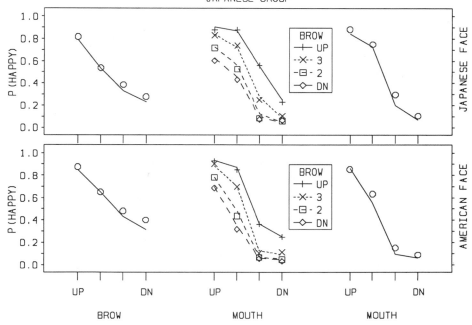

Figure 7.15 Predicted (lines) and observed (points) proportion of "happy" judgments by the Japanese group as a function of the brow and mouth conditions, for both the Japanese face (top panel) and the American face (bottom panel). The left and right portions of the graph give the single-factor half-face conditions, whereas the middle portion gives the factorial full-face conditions. Predictions are for the FLMP. (From Massaro & Ellison, 1996.)

happy to the most angry. Within each illustration, the upper half is the fastest-moving variable. The half-face condition is the fifth level of each variable.

Participants were required to respond to each stimulus face with either "happy" or "angry" by pressing a correspondingly labeled key on either the left or right edge of the keyboard. The keys were labeled in Kanji for the Japanese. Participants were tested for a total of 12 observations for each of the 48 unique stimuli.

Figure 7.15 gives the average proportion of "happy" results for the Japanese participants identifying the Japanese and American faces. The results for both faces replicate the earlier study with Baldi. The average results for the American participants identifying the Japanese and American faces are similar; they are shown in figure 7.16. At this coarse level of analysis, it appears that there are no large ethnic or cultural differences. The model tests confirm these conclusions. The models were fit separately to each of the individual participants and to the mean participant, computed by averaging the results across participants. Given the four-by-four expanded factorial design, 8 free parameters are necessary to fit the FLMP to the 24 conditions for each face (Japanese or American): 4 parameters for each level of brow displacement and 4 for mouth displacement for each face, for a total of 16. The parameter values represent the degree to which these features match those in the happy

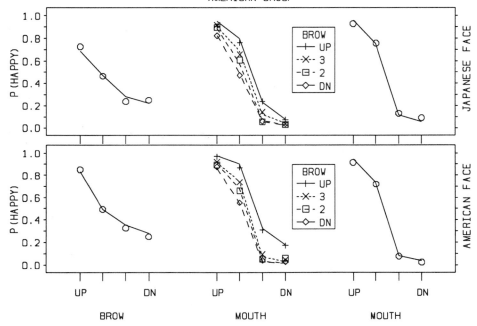

Figure 7.16 Predicted (lines) and observed (points) proportion of "happy" judgments by the American group as a function of the brow and mouth conditions, for both the Japanese face (top panel) and the American face (bottom panel). The left and right portions of the graph give the single-factor half-face conditions, whereas the middle portion gives the factorial full-face conditions. Predictions are for the FLMP. (From Massaro & Ellison, 1996.)

prototype. The FLMP predictions of the average results are given in figures 7.15 and 7.16. As can be seen in the figures, the FLMP gives an equally good description of the recognition of emotion in both faces by both groups.

The theoretical framework we employ also allows us to assess information differences across the two cultures and the two faces. As can be seen in figures 7.15 and 7.16, the single-factor half-face mouth condition is steeper for the American than for the Japanese group. In addition, the spread among the curves in the factorial full-face condition is smaller for the American relative to the Japanese group. These results indicate that the mouth variable was somewhat more influential overall for the American group than for the Japanese group. The influence of the brow variable did not differ across the two cultures.

The two faces provided more or less the same information to both groups of observers. The only (small) difference was that the brow of the American face was evaluated as happier overall than the brow of the Japanese face. Thus, there were only a few small differences in information from faces associated with different cultures and from observers across different cultures.

There is a good deal of literature (and debate) asking whether the cues for facial emotion are universal across cultures. The present research goes further by asking whether the information processing of facial cues is universal. We have shown how the distinction between information and information processing can be formalized within the framework of the FLMP. Using that framework we were able to address not only whether the cues are cross-culturally valid but also whether the cues are combined in the same manner across cultures and for faces of different races. The results indicate that the perceptual processing of facial emotion follows well-established principles of pattern recognition, independently of the ethnicity and culture of the perceiver and of the perceived face.

Summary

One of the goals of our experiments on emotion recognition is to broaden the domain of the application of our framework. For many, moving from speech to emotion is a great leap indeed, but the theoretical edifice seems to stand firm. Two features of the face were evaluated and integrated to achieve perceptual recognition of emotion. Both brow displacement and mouth displacement were effective in changing the judgment from *happy* to *angry*. In addition, the influence of one of these features was larger to the extent that the other feature was ambiguous, as described by the FLMP. Given that the FLMP assumes independent features, its good fit to the experimental results challenges holistic models (Tanaka & Farah, 1993). The FLMP also assumes continuous features, which poses a problem for theories of categorical perception of emotion (Etcoff & Magee, 1992). Finally, the multiplicative integration of the FLMP, along with the poor fit of the SCM, weakens additive models of feature integration (Huber & Lenz, 1993).

The RTs of the judgments also increased to the degree that the test face displayed an ambiguous expression. In accord with the predictions of the FLMP, participants took longer to respond when the two features were displayed in conflicting directions, when the two features were only slightly displaced (ambiguous), or when one of the features was missing and the other was ambiguous. The fastest responses occurred when features were congruent and unambiguous. These RTs pose a great problem for categorical models, which assume that within-category differences are not perceptually relevant.

The present results in the facial expression domain are highly analogous to those found in speech perception. We have learned that multiple sources of information are influential in speech perception. In addition, the FLMP gives a good description of performance when multiple speech cues are varied in an expanded factorial design. Furthermore, there appear to be information (but not information-processing) differences across different individuals, across age, and across language. In the facial expression domain, we have inferred information differences as a function of both individuals and ethnicity.

However, information processing was invariant across individuals, ethnicity of the perceiver, and ethnicity of the face being judged.

As with all research, additional empirical evidence is necessary to determine the generality of the conclusions. Two obvious limitations are that our experiments to date have used just two emotions and that they have limited judgments to just two possible response alternatives. Our paradigm is easily extended to other emotions and to multiple response alternatives, however, and findings in the speech domain give us confidence that the present conclusions are applicable well beyond the present task. We encourage other scientists to use the expanded factorial design to help provide a much-needed database on the perception of facial emotion.

To pursue the analogy between speech perception and emotion even further, we now turn to the perception of emotion from the face and the voice. The studies described are exactly analogous to our studies of speech perception by eye and ear.

8 Emotion from the Face and the Voice

There is a kind of universal language, consisting of expressions of the face and eyes, gestures and tones of voice, which can show whether a person means to ask for something and get it, or refuse it and have nothing to do with it.
—Augustine, *Confessions*, 1–8.

We usually think of the face as providing the dominant window into emotion, in the same way as we think of the voice as providing the linguistic message. We have learned, however, that visible speech also helps to convey the linguistic message. Analogously, there is an abundance of affective information in the voice. The multimodal nature of emotion perception allows us to carry out empirical research exactly parallel to our studies of bimodal speech perception. The previous chapter addressed facial cues to emotion. We begin here with a review of the literature on what aspects of the voice are cues to emotion.

VOCAL CUES TO EMOTION

The voice conveys a variety of paralinguistic sources of information. Among other attributes, a person's age, intelligence, and emotional state can be determined from the voice alone (see reviews by Kramer, 1963; Archer & Silver, 1991). As for emotion, voice quality can change directly with physiological changes induced by different emotional states (Ohala, 1981). Three changes that can affect the voice are dryness in the mouth or larynx, accelerated breathing rate, and muscle tension. There is no doubt that the voice is a powerful source of information about emotion. In a forced-choice experiment, subjects were almost perfect at recognizing joy, sadness, anger, and fear when listening to a semantically neutral sentence spoken in different simulated emotional states (Johnson et al., 1986). It is surprising how little is known, however, about the auditory cues that are actually responsible for the perception of emotion in the voice. Scherer (1986, 1995) and Murray and Arnott (1993) review many studies, revealing that there is very little consensus on what the fundamental emotion categories are and what unique acoustic properties cue those categories.

Williams and Stevens (1972) concluded that the pitch contour over the course of a sentence is the best indicator of its emotional content. Cues to voice quality, however, also seem to be available in single words, syllables, and phonemes, and even in smaller segments. Tartter and Braun (1994) asked speakers to produce syllables while smiling, while frowning, or in a neutral manner. The auditory utterances were then played in pairs to listeners, who were to identify the happier one of each pair. Listeners were able to select the appropriate utterance in both normal and whispered speech. Pollack, Rubenstein, and Horowitz (1960) showed that emotion can be conveyed in speech segments as short as 60 ms. In their review of the literature, Murray and Arnott (1993) noted that the most commonly referenced vocal parameters are pitch (i.e., both the average value and range of the fundamental frequency), duration, intensity, and the undefined term "voice quality."

Although we derive emotional information from auditory speech, that information is not easily synthesized. One of the most common reactions to synthetic auditory speech is that it sounds mechanical. That mechanical sound has become the trademark of synthetic speech. In light of the immense effort dedicated to speech synthesis and the attendant progress, we might ask why achieving realism in the voice has been out of reach. *Toy Story*, the first completely computer-animated film, used the voices of live actors. Although the film represents an innovative milestone in animation, it makes apparent the poor state of the art for realistic speech synthesis. Speech synthesis appears to be able to capture the phonetic quality of the meaningful segments in our language, but somehow without the concomitant naturalism of real speech.

Facial versus Vocal Cues to Emotion

We believe that both the face and the voice influence the perception of emotion. As expected, research on whether facial or vocal cues are more effective in communicating emotion is inconclusive. In her literature review, Noller (1985) concluded that the issue is far too complex for general claims to be made about the relative importance of verbal and nonverbal channels. Relative importance is affected by too many variables, including the type of emotion, the sex of the encoder, the sex of the decoder, and the age of the decoder. In the present framework, one modality is not necessarily more effective than the other. Rather, the relative effectiveness of the two modalities will fluctuate as a function of context. In general, however, we can expect the effectiveness of one modality to increase to the extent that the other modality is ambiguous. We will present two experiments to explore the role of the face and the voice in communicating emotion. These studies of emotion are exactly parallel to our speech studies described in chapter 1. In the first experiment, an expanded factorial design is used to present unimodal, consistent, and inconsistent bimodal information. The ambiguity of the two sources of information is varied in the second experiment. Finally, we assess the degree to which instruction and intentionality can modify the joint processing of facial and vocal sources of information. Before describing the studies, we hope to engage the reader with a demonstration of bimodal communication of emotion.

Demonstration

In face-to-face communication, perception of speech does not necessarily result from just the sound, but somehow emerges from the sound and sight of the face, collectively. We ask whether the same is true of judgments of emotion. Watch and listen to band 8.1 on the CD-ROM. Our talking head will repeatedly say the word *please* with different emotions in the face and in the voice. Given the poor state of the art in the synthesis of vocal emotion, we used the voice of a real person simulating the emotion. Try to determine the emotion being conveyed during each articulation. There are four sets of four utterances of the word, and you should keep track of whether the emotion you perceive changes within each set. For the best effect, you should experience the demonstration before reading further.

If your perception of the emotion did change within each set, then the audible speech had a substantial influence on your experience. Within each set of four utterances, the auditory word was articulated to be happy, angry, surprised, and fearful. However, each set had a constant visual stimulus. The first set of four always had a happy face, the second set always had an angry face, the third surprised, and the fourth fearful.

Band 8.2 makes the facial emotion the fastest-moving variable, and the audible emotion is fixed for each set of four words. Does your perception again change from word to word? We believe that this perceptual experience exactly parallels what we have learned about the bimodal perception of speech. If we use the speech situation as a model, then we have a working hypothesis about how processing the face and the voice leads to an integrated perceptual experience of emotion.

Experiment: Unimodal, Consistent, and Inconsistent Information

As in our studies of speech perception, a particularly valuable experimental paradigm is to independently vary the two modalities in an expanded factorial design. Figure 8.1 illustrates the design for the four emotion categories used in the demonstration.

Method Using an expanded factorial design, the four emotions were presented auditorily, visually, and bimodally. For the bimodal presentation, each audible word was presented with each visible word for a total of 4 × 4, or 16 unique conditions. Twelve of the bimodal words had inconsistent auditory and visual information: a necessary condition to achieve an informative picture of how these two modalities are processed. More generally, the goal is

Visual

	Happy	Angry	Surprised	Fearful	None
Happy					
Angry					
Surprised					
Fearful					
None					

Auditory (label to the left of the row headers)

Figure 8.1 Expanded factorial design with four auditory emotion categories crossed with four visual emotion categories.

to arrive at a theoretical account that can describe or explain the performance on the bimodal conditions as a function of performance on the unimodal conditions.

In this experiment, we paired the synthetic face with natural audible speech. Due to the current inability of synthetic voice programs, such as DECtalk, to adequately portray emotion in isolated words, the vocal stimuli are produced by recording a male amateur actor speaking a semantically neutral stimulus word, *please*, in four different simulated emotional states: happy, angry, surprised, and fearful. Some noticeable differences across the three different emotions were the pitch contour during the vowel /i/, the word duration, and the amount of frication in the final segment /s/. To make the cues somewhat less obvious, the words were standardized for length and intensity during the vocalic (vowel) portion across the four emotions. In the bimodal condition, the auditory /p/ burst release was synchronized with the mouth opening of the visible /p/ articulation.

A set of four stimuli was constructed from our synthetic face to portray affectual expressions representing happy, angry, surprised, and fearful states. The face maintained its emotional expression during the articulation of the test word *please*, which lasted about one second. Figure 8.2 shows a view of the talking head expressing each of the four emotion categories during the articulation of the test word.

The nine participants were instructed to watch the talking head and listen to the voice on each trial and to indicate which of the four emotion categories was being communicated. The subjects made their responses by pressing a labeled key. All of the experimental conditions were randomized and presented repeatedly for identification. The mean observed proportion of iden-

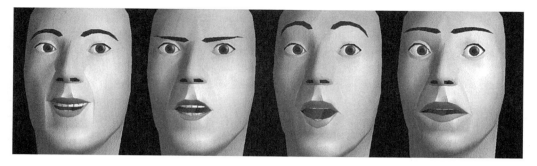

Figure 8.2 The four facial emotions during the articulation of the word *please*.

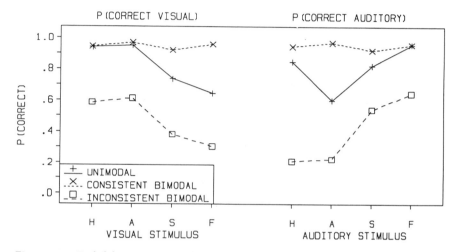

Figure 8.3 Probability correct visual (left panel) and auditory (right panel) responses as a function of happy (H), angry (A), surprised (S), and fearful (F) level of visual and auditory stimuli for unimodal, consistent, and inconsistent trials. The consistent condition is necessarily identical in the two panels because it represents the same results.

tifications was computed for each of the 24 conditions for each subject by pooling across all of the 18 experimental trials for each condition.

Results The analysis of the results parallels that carried out for speech in chapter 1. Given that the participants' goal was to perceive the emotion, it is informative to evaluate performance in terms of accuracy with respect to each of the two modalities. The points in the left half of figure 8.3 show average performance scored in terms of accuracy with respect to the visible emotion. For unimodal trials, the average correct performances given just the face were .94, .95, .73, and .64, respectively, for the emotion categories happy, angry, surprised, and fearful. Thus, perceivers are fairly good at identifying emotion from just the face even in a synthetic face.

Performance scored in terms of accuracy with respect to the auditory emotion is given in the right half of figure 8.3. On the basis of unimodal trials, correct identification given just the auditory information averaged .85, .60, .82, and .96 for the auditory emotion categories happy, angry, surprised, and fearful. Happy, surprised, and fearful were relatively easy to identify in the voice, whereas angry was somewhat more difficult.

Just as in speech recognition, we can ask whether there is a general complementarity of these two modalities in emotion perception. In speech, we found that one modality tended to be informative when the other modality was not (see also chapter 14). As described in chapter 1, several syllables that are easy to identify in the visual modality tend to be difficult in the auditory modality and vice versa. The auditory syllable /da/ is relatively easy to identify, whereas its visible counterpart is not. The syllable /ba/ shows just the opposite relationship. Angry and to some extent happy appear to be easier to see in the face than to hear in the voice. Surprised and fearful, on the other hand, give the opposite relationship. In agreement with our general principle of commonalities across domains, there appears to be some hint of a complementarity that is analogous to that proposed for speech. Perhaps in every domain there are alternatives whose difficulty happens to be complementary across modalities or sources of information. For other alternatives, however, we might expect to find no correlation or even a positive correlation.

Accuracy is also given for bimodal trials, separately according to whether the two modalities are consistent or inconsistent with one another. When measured relative to the unimodal results, the bimodal results show a large influence of both modalities on performance. Bimodal performance was close to perfect for all four emotion categories in the consistent condition. Thus, overall performance was more accurate with two sources of consistent information than with either source of information alone. Conversely, given inconsistent information from the two sources, performance was poorer than that observed in the unimodal conditions. The disruptive effect of inconsistent sources held strongly for all four emotion categories.

In speech, we found a larger influence from the auditory than the visual source of information. That is, inconsistent auditory speech disrupted visual accuracy more than inconsistent visible speech disrupted auditory accuracy. Figure 8.3 shows that the overall amount of disruption from inconsistent information was about equal for the two types of accuracy, which indicates about equal influences from the two modalities.

As observed in the speech task, the participants made errors on the unimodal trials. There were also large individual differences. Some subjects in our task were completely accurate or at least almost perfect on the unimodal conditions. Other subjects, of course, did much worse. Again, we can observe what is consistent in this variability. Figure 8.4 gives the results of a particularly accurate observer in the task. As the figure shows, inconsistent information from the face and the voice was highly disruptive, resulting in poorer performance than in the unimodal condition. Thus, conclusions reached from the average results in figure 8.3 hold even in the case where the observer accurately identifies the emotion when each source is presented separately.

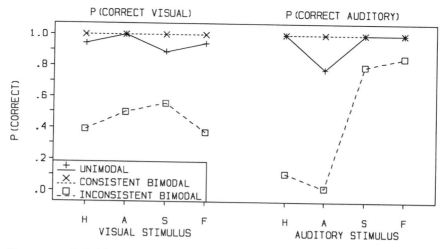

Figure 8.4 Probability correct visual (left panel) and auditory (right panel) responses as a function of happy (H), angry (A), surprised (S), and fearful (F) level of visual or auditory stimuli for unimodal, consistent, and inconsistent trials. The consistent condition is necessarily identical in the two panels because it represents the same results. Results for a particularly accurate observer in the task.

Although the results in figures 8.3 and 8.4 demonstrate that both the face and the voice are used in emotion perception, they do not indicate how the two sources are used together. There are many possible ways the two sources might be treated. As in the speech domain, a finer-grained analysis of the results helps reveal the underlying process. The confusion matrix in figure 8.5 plots the proportion of times each stimulus event was identified as each alternative emotion.

This analysis provides a measure of what alternatives are perceived given the different experimental conditions. Recall that a rough approximation of the FLMP prediction is that perception will consist of the most reasonable alternative given the two inputs. The bimodal emotion judgments are best understood in terms of the degree of support from each of the two modalities (as approximately estimated from the unimodal conditions). This degree of support from the two modalities is a better predictor of bimodal performance than are other variables such as, for example, what modality is providing the support.

An illustrative example involves the surprise and fear alternatives. As can be seen in figure 8.5, when auditory surprise is paired with visual fear, surprise is the dominant judgment. On the other hand, when auditory surprise is paired with visual anger, anger is the dominant judgment. The difference between these two cases can be completely understood by the information available in the various inputs. In both cases, the dominant response is that which agrees with the least ambiguous source of information. Auditory surprise is less ambiguous than visual fear, hence when they are combined surprise is the dominant judgment; auditory surprise is more ambiguous than

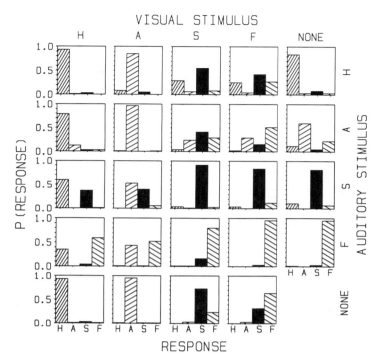

Figure 8.5 Proportion of happy (H), angry (A), surprised (S), and fearful (F) judgments as a function of the auditory and visual levels for both the unimodal and bimodal trials.

visual anger, hence anger is the dominant judgment. These results are qualitatively consistent with the principle that the influence of one source of information when combined with another source is related to their relative ambiguity when presented in isolation.

Of course, the true test of the influence of the two sources involves model testing. The FLMP and a variety of other models were fit to each of the nine subjects. To fit the 24 independent conditions, the FLMP requires four free parameters for the four auditory inputs and four for the visual. The RMSDs of the fits ranged between .0168 and .0501, averaging .0311. The SCM, on the other hand, gave a much poorer description. That model, even with one additional parameter, gave a range of RMSDs between .0724 and .1683, averaging .1207. The SCM is mathematically equivalent both to a weighted averaging of the two sources of information and to a specific categorical model. The poor fit of the SCM thus also weakens interpretations of the results based on either weighted averaging or categorical perception.

Given our interest in analogous processes in different domains, it is useful to compare the fits of the models in the emotion domain to those in the speech domain. The four-alternative experiment is exactly analogous to the one described in chapter 1 on bimodal speech. As developed in chapter 10, RMSDs cannot be directly compared unless they are evaluated relative to a

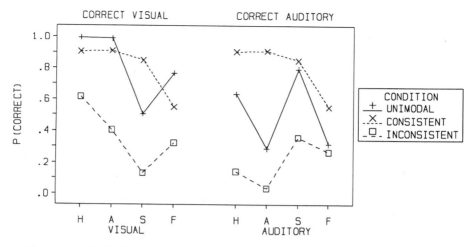

Figure 8.6 Probability correct visual (left panel) and auditory (right panel) responses as a function of happy (H), angry (A), surprised (S), and fearful (F) level of visual or auditory stimuli for unimodal, consistent, and inconsistent trials. The consistent condition is necessarily identical in the two panels because it represents the same results.

benchmark. As a first approximation, however, we found that the advantage for the FLMP over the SCM is about equally pronounced for emotion and for speech. Thus we seem to have further evidence for analogous processes across the speech and emotion domains. We now explore the influence of increasing the number of response alternatives in the task (see Rosenberg & Ekman, 1995).

Replication with More Response Alternatives

The previous experiment was replicated with ten new subjects, but this time the subjects were given six emotion categories as well as the category "other." The categories *sad* and *disgusted* were added to the response set. The response "other" was to be used when none of the six emotion categories seemed appropriate.

Figure 8.6 plots the accuracy with respect to the visible and audible emotions, as was done in figure 8.3. As can be seen in the figure, increasing the number of response alternatives lowered performance significantly, but only for the auditory stimuli. The average correct performance given just the face was .81 for the emotion categories happy, angry, surprised, and fearful. This overall level of performance was comparable to an accuracy of .82 from the experiment with just four alternatives.

Performance scored in terms of accuracy with respect to the auditory emotion is represented in the right half of figure 8.6. Correct identification given just the auditory information averaged .51 for the auditory emotion categories happy, angry, surprised, and fearful. Thus, this performance was much worse than performance (.81) in the task with four response alternatives.

Emotion from the Face and the Voice

It seems that we were more successful at animating emotions in a synthetic face than at producing them in a natural voice.

Accuracy is also given for bimodal trials, separately according to whether the two stimulus modalities were consistent or inconsistent with one another. When measured relative to the unimodal results, the bimodal results continued to show a large influence of both modalities on performance. In contrast to the results shown in figure 8.3 with just four response alternatives, however, performance was still somewhat poor even with two sources of information. The main reason was that auditory information was not very helpful. Inconsistent information from the two sources produced poorer performance than that observed in the unimodal conditions.

Figure 8.7 gives the confusion matrix. The auditory emotion of anger was often identified as fearful, disgusted, or "other." The auditory emotion of fearful was twice as often identified as sad as it was fearful. The facial emotions were identified fairly accurately, except that surprised and fearful were once again confused with one another.

Summary

An expanded factorial design with unimodal and consistent and inconsistent bimodal stimuli illuminated how emotion is communicated via the face and

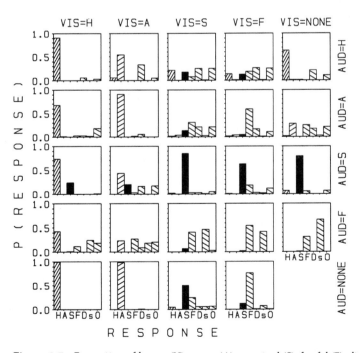

Figure 8.7 Proportion of happy (H), angry (A), surprised (S), fearful (F), disgusted (D), sad (s), and other (O) judgments as a function of the auditory and visual levels for both the unimodal and bimodal trials.

the voice. Emotion communicated through two modalities is more influential than just one. Furthermore, these two sources appear to be processed in accordance with our universal law, the FLMP algorithm. These conclusions about emotion derived from both the face and the voice are consistent with those reached about emotion derived from two features of the face (see chapter 7). We continue our exploration by varying the ambiguity of the two modalities.

AMBIGUITY OF VISIBLE AND AUDIBLE SOURCES

Massaro and Egan (1996) created happy, neutral, and angry expressions in both the face and the voice and used them in an expanded factorial design. This gives 3 unimodal auditory, 3 unimodal visual, and 9 factorial test stimuli, for a total of 15 conditions. Fifteen participants judged the faces, the voices, and the combinations of face and voice as happy or angry. This study also allows us to address the question of how facial expression and vocal cues are evaluated and integrated in the judgment of two specific emotions, happiness and anger.

For facial expression, two features were changed together (eyebrow displacement and mouth corner displacement) to create the three levels. Figure 8.8 shows that the brows were lowered and flattened and the corners of the mouth downturned for angry, the brows were raised and arched and the mouth corners upturned for happy, and both features were intermediate for the neutral expression. The face maintained its emotional expression during the articulation of the test word *please*, which lasted about one second altogether. For vocal expression, the three types of emotion were simply recorded from a human speaker. In the experiment, the 15 participants were instructed

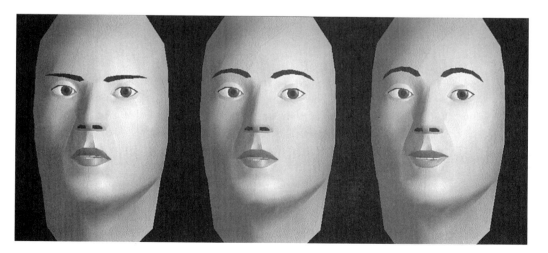

Figure 8.8 The three faces representing (from left to right) angry, neutral, and happy during the articulation of the word *please*.

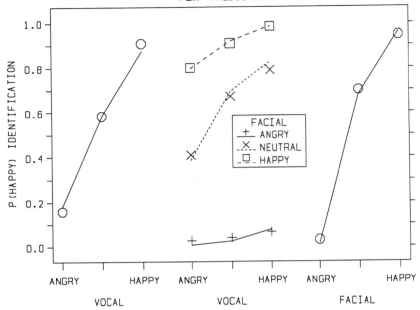

Figure 8.9 The observed (points) and predicted (lines) proportion of "happy" judgments as a function of the visual and auditory variables. The left panel shows performance for just the face and the right panel for just the voice. The middle panel gives performance for the factorial combination of the two modalities. Predictions are for the FLMP. (From Massaro & Egan, 1996.)

to watch the face and listen to the word and to identify the emotion as happy or angry. There were 24 observations for each of the 15 test conditions.

Band 8.3 illustrates the 15 test stimuli in the expanded factorial design, with the face as the fastest-moving variable. Band 8.4 repeats this design with the voice as the fastest-moving variable.

Results

The two independent variables influenced performance as expected. As can be seen in figure 8.9, the face had a larger effect on the judgments than the voice. This is evident from the fact that the probability of a happy judgment changed by a larger amount across the three unimodal levels of facial emotion than across the three unimodal levels of vocal emotion. In addition, the bimodal results show that the voice had a minor effect when paired with the angry or the happy face. The voice had a substantial influence only when the face was neutral. As expected, figure 8.9 also reveals a significant interaction between the variables: the influence of one variable was larger to the extent that the other variable was ambiguous.

The observed data were used to test the FLMP and the SCM. The FLMP required six free parameters and the SCM required seven to fit the 15 independent data points. Figure 8.9 shows the good fit of the FLMP to the aver-

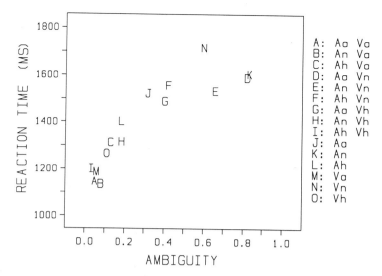

Figure 8.10 Reaction times (RT) of the 15 test conditions averaged across all subjects and plotted as a function of ambiguity. The letters in the graph specify the experimental conditions; for example, A: Aa Va corresponds to auditory angry and visual angry. (From Massaro & Egan, 1996.)

age results. The RMSDs for the FLMP fit of individual participants ranged from .0081 to .1200 with an average RMSD of .051. The fit of the SCM produced larger RMSDs with a range of .007 to .192 and an average RMSD of .086. The FLMP thus provided a significantly better overall fit than the SCM.

An average reaction time (RT) was also computed for each of the 15 stimulus conditions. To assess the influence of ambiguity on reaction time, we computed a measure of ambiguity between 0 and 1, as in chapter 7. Figure 8.10 shows RT plotted as a function of ambiguity. The RTs show that participants were significantly faster at making a choice when the stimulus was unambiguous. When the emotional cues are contradictory or ambiguous, more time is required before a sufficient degree of support accumulates and a response is emitted. Average RT correlated strongly (.881) with the average ambiguity of the 15 test conditions. This high correlation provides additional strong support for the FLMP, which assumes that decision time increases as the degree of support for one alternative becomes more similar to the degree of support for the other alternative. As noted in chapter 7, categorical perception cannot easily explain any change in reaction time because perceivers putatively have information about only the discrete category (angry or happy), not the degree of category membership.

Summary

The present experiment helps us understand how facial and vocal cues are evaluated and integrated in the perception of emotion. Both variables (facial and vocal cues) were effective in changing the judgments of emotions from "happy" to "angry." The ability to perceive emotion appears to be enhanced by the use of multiple sources of information. Each modality was more influential to the extent that the other variable was ambiguous.

Both the good fit of the FLMP to the results and the poor fit of the SCM argue against additive models. The good fit of the FLMP is also evidence against categorical models, simply because the FLMP assumes continuous evaluation of features. Also, categorical models cannot easily explain why reaction times increased when the stimuli were ambiguous. The FLMP, however, can explain that phenomenon.

The recognition of emotion on the basis of facial and vocal cues is analogous to pattern recognition in a wide variety of other domains, such as bimodal speech perception. Pursuing the analogy with speech perception, much research has shown that observers integrate auditory and visual information in an optimal manner, as described by the FLMP. That is, they can arrive at a relatively unambiguous percept even though both modalities are somewhat ambiguous (Massaro, 1987f, p. 65). When the two sources of information conflict, on the other hand, an ambiguous percept is obtained.

The facial synthesis program provides a standardized set of faces that can be controlled precisely. However, as noted by Scherer and coworkers (1991), research on vocal expression of emotion lags behind the study of facial emotion expression, and as a result vocal cues are difficult to define and to manipulate accurately. The recent interest in developing speech synthesis programs to signal attitudes and emotions carries the promise that we will someday be able to manipulate the acoustic signal directly to convey emotion (Cahn, 1990; Carlson, Granström & Nord, 1993).

Future research involving the expanded factorial design applied to other sources of information about emotion, such as hand movements and body posture, would help us to understand better how various features are combined in the perception of emotion. In the next section, we report some new research on instructions in the emotion and speech tasks.

INTENTIONALITY AND INSTRUCTIONS

In the bimodal speech perception task, instructions appear to play only a relatively minor role. One observes a large influence of visible speech even when the observers are instructed to report only what they hear (Massaro, 1987f, pp. 66–83). One of the characteristics of our integration law is its naturalness or automaticity. When multiple sources of information are present, we cannot help but integrate them. The consequence of this automaticity of integration is the difficulty of ignoring a source of information. This lack of control over integration has been previously demonstrated in speech (Massaro, 1987f), so it is valuable to question whether the same is the case in the emotion domain.

An extension of this earlier research was, therefore, implemented to assess how easily people could filter out one of the sources of information about emotion. We replicated the three-by-three expanded factorial design (discussed in the previous section) using different sets of instructions. Three types of instructions were given to direct the intentional set or goal of the participant. For all instructions, participants were instructed to watch the face and listen to the word and to identify the emotion as happy or angry. For the auditory instructions, they were instructed to "make the judgment on the basis of what you hear the voice to be expressing." Of course, it was necessary to warn the participants that sometimes only the face would be presented and in those cases they would have to make their judgments on that basis. For the visual instructions, they were instructed to "make the judgment on the basis of what you see the face to be expressing." The reader might want to view bands 8.3 and 8.4 again but with different intentions. Is it possible to focus completely on one modality and shut out any influence from the other (without closing your eyes or turning off the auditory input, of course)?

The same task was carried out in auditory-visual speech to allow a direct comparison of how instructions influence performance in the speech and emotion domains. One of the themes of our framework is that there are analogous processes across a broad range of domains. Thus, we expect to find similar results for emotion and speech. The speech stimuli were chosen from the audible and visible synthetic speech. We created a good /ba/ and a good /da/ and an ambiguous syllable between those alternatives. These syllables were used in a three-by-three expanded factorial design exactly like that of the emotion conditions. Although band 1.5 is a five-by-five design, it provides an opportunity for the reader to explore the influence of intentional set in the speech domain. Of interest is whether control over processing differs between the two domains.

Each participant was tested under the three instruction conditions in either the speech or emotion task. Fifty students were recruited from the undergraduate psychology subject pool at UCSC. There were 24 participants in the speech experiment and 26 in the emotion study.

Results

In the emotion task, the probability of a happy judgment, $P(H)$, is the dependent measure. The average $P(H)$ judgments under the bimodal instructions ("use the information from both the face and the voice") are shown in the top panel of figure 8.11. As expected, the influence of the two independent variables replicated the Massaro and Egan (1996) study. The middle of the top panel reveals a significant interaction because the influence of one variable was larger to the extent that the other variable was ambiguous. As can be seen in figure 8.11, the face had a larger effect on the emotion judgments than did the voice.

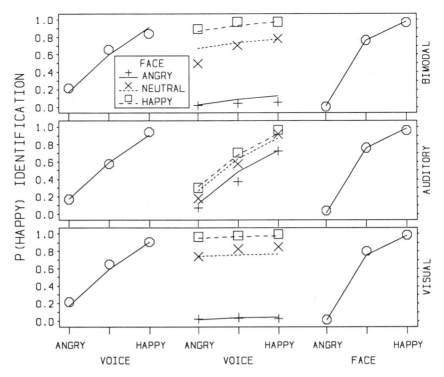

Figure 8.11 The observed (points) and predicted (lines) proportion of "happy" judgments as a function of the facial and vocal variables. The top, middle, and bottom panels give performance for the bimodal, auditory, and visual instructions, respectively. Within each panel, the left graph gives performance for the vocal-only, the right graph for the facial-only, and the middle panel for the bimodal condition. Predictions are for the FLMP.

Instructions had a significant impact on performance in the emotion task. With the bimodal instructions ("use the information from both the face and the voice"), the face had a much larger influence in the bimodal stimulus condition than did the voice (see top panel of figure 8.11). The voice had very little influence when the face was either happy or angry, and it had a relatively small influence when the face was neutral. With the auditory instructions ("make the judgment on the basis of what you heard the voice to be expressing"), the voice had a large influence across all three levels of facial emotion. This result can be seen in the middle panel of figure 8.11, where the three curves change significantly across the three auditory levels. The auditory instructions also produced somewhat more extreme judgments than the bimodal instructions in the unimodal auditory condition. In contrast, performance on the unimodal face was fairly consistent across the bimodal and auditory instructions.

With the visual instructions ("make the judgment on the basis of what you saw the face to be expressing"), there was much less room for changing the results because the face already had a much larger influence than the voice in

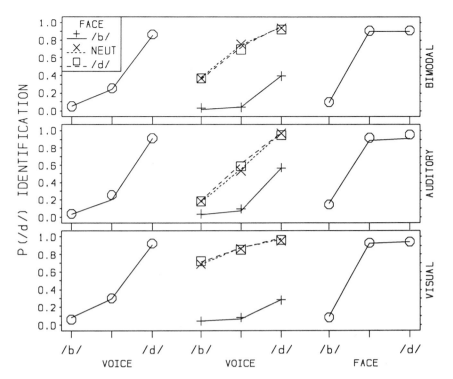

Figure 8.12 The observed (points) and predicted (lines) proportion of /da/ judgments as a function of the facial and vocal variables in the speech task. The top, middle, and bottom panels give performance for the bimodal, auditory, and visual instructions, respectively. Within each panel, the left graph gives performance for the vocal-only, the right graph for the facial-only, and the middle panel for the bimodal condition. Predictions are for the FLMP.

the bimodal condition. Visual instructions did have an impact, however, particularly in that the auditory stimulus when paired with the neutral face was less influential under visual instructions than under bimodal instructions. Contrast the top and bottom panels of figure 8.11; the flatter the line for the neutral face, the less the auditory influence. Another difference with the visual instructions was that the neutral visual level of the face was judged to be more happy overall than with the bimodal instructions. More generally, it appears that modality-specific instructions enhance perceivers' sensitivity to small differences along that modality.

Similar results were found in the speech perception task. The average $P(/da/)$ judgments given the bimodal instructions ("use the information from both the face and the voice"), are shown in the top panel of figure 8.12. Replicating previous research, the two independent variables influenced performance in the expected direction. Figure 8.12 also reveals a significant interaction because the influence of one variable was larger to the extent that the other variable was ambiguous. For example, as can be seen in the top middle panel of figure 8.12, the face had a larger influence when the auditory speech was at the neutral level.

Emotion from the Face and the Voice

One slightly unlucky result is that both variables were influential but the neutral facial level was much too /da/-like and gave roughly the same performance as the endpoint /da/. Fortunately, this equivalence does not necessarily weaken the test of the hypotheses of interest. Even with the equivalence, the face had about the same amount of influence in the bimodal condition as did the voice.

The middle panel of figure 8.12 shows performance under the auditory instructions. Although these results are similar to those observed under bimodal instructions, there are clear and significant differences. With the auditory instructions ("make the judgment on the basis of what you heard the voice to be saying"), the voice had a larger influence across all three levels of the face. This result is apparent in the somewhat steeper curves that result from the auditory rather than the bimodal instructions in the bimodal stimulus conditions.

With the visual instructions ("make the judgment on the basis of what you saw the face to be saying"), the influence of the face was enhanced and the influence of the voice was attenuated relative to the bimodal instructions. The middle bottom panel of figure 8.12 shows a spread among the three curves under the visual instructions that is larger than the spread under the bimodal instructions (shown in the middle top panel). Furthermore, as in the emotion task, the modality-specific instructions heightened the sensitivity to that modality in the unimodal condition. The middle left panel of figure 8.12 shows a somewhat larger influence of the voice under auditory instructions compared to the bimodal instructions, shown in the top left panel. Analogous but smaller differences can be seen for the influence of the face under the visual instructions (top and bottom right panels).

In summary, both variables influence emotion and speech judgments regardless of instructions. Instructions do modulate the degree of influence, however. In order to get a proper assessment of this interaction, a process model is necessary. Not surprisingly, we use the framework of the FLMP.

FLMP Analysis

We evaluate the influence of instructions and any performance differences between emotion and speech tasks within the context of the FLMP and the information versus information processing distinction. The FLMP was fit to the results of each of the 50 participants individually. Each fit required the estimation of three a_i values for the three levels of the auditory information and three v_j values for the three levels of the visual information. Our hypothesis is that changes in instructions change the cue value of the information but do not change the information processing—the manner of combining the cue values to arrive at an overall judgment. Assuming that only information is changed by instructions, there should be a unique set of parameters for each of the three instruction conditions. If the FLMP is tested with the same parameter values across all three instruction conditions, a very poor fit should be obtained. Consistent with prediction, the RMSD for this six-parameter (three a_i and three v_j) FLMP fit was .154 for the speech task and .192 for the emotion task.

The poor fit assuming the same parameters across instructions can be contrasted with the fit when a different set of parameters is estimated for each instruction condition. When the parameters can vary with instruction, the FLMP provides a very good description of the results under each instruction condition. The average fit of the FLMP is shown in figure 8.11 along with the average results in the emotion task. The RMSDs for the FLMP fit of individual participants ranged from .006 to .109 with an average RMSD of .057. These fits were significantly better than the fits by the six-parameter FLMP for both the speech and emotion tasks. The fact that this model is a good description of the results shows not only that there must be an informational difference between the three instructional conditions, but also that there is no difference in information processing.

A similar outcome was observed in the speech task. Figure 8.12 shows the average of the individual fits of the FLMP along with the average results in the speech task. As the figure shows, the FLMP gave a good description of the results. The RMSDs for the FLMP fit of individual participants ranged from .024 to .106 with an average RMSD of .054.

This model-fitting exercise shows highly analogous findings in the emotion and speech domains. Because comparisons are being made across subjects and tasks, a direct comparison between the observed results is not justified. A more reliable comparison requires the use of a benchmark goodness of fit, which is discussed in chapter 10. We should await that development before proceeding with such a comparison. To preview the outcome, however, the results and the FLMP description were found to be equivalent in the emotion and speech domains. The emotion and speech domains thus gave very similar outcomes for the influence of instructions on pattern recognition.

Although previous results had shown that auditory and visual information contribute to both types of pattern recognition, no study had shown that the information processing is equivalent in the two domains. The FLMP, which assumes continuous independent features for each source, a multiplicative integration function, and a decision based on a relative goodness of match, gave an excellent description of both domains. Within this framework, the ability to perceive speech and emotion accurately usually requires the use of multiple sources of information. The good fit of the FLMP to the results, and the poor fit of the SCM, are evidence against categorical models of perception as well as additive models. Nor can categorical models easily explain why RTs increased when the stimuli were ambiguous (Massaro, 1987f, pp. 110–114). The FLMP, however, can explain this phenomenon. When the emotional cues are contradictory or ambiguous, more time is required before a sufficient degree of support accumulates and a response is emitted.

We found that instructions and intentional set can modulate the relative influence of the modalities in bimodal speech perception. Thus, intentional set seems to play a role in processing. Other evidence for a contribution of intentional set comes from a very creative study that displaced a talking head away from a noisy auditory message (Driver, 1996). Two verbal messages were spoken in the same voice and presented at the same time and—unknown to the subjects—at the same location in auditory space. A video of a talker articulating one of the messages was shown either at the location of the two messages or displaced to the other side. Subjects were instructed to report the target words that agreed with the talker's mouth movements. The displacement facilitated recognition of the to-be-attended message relative to presentation of the video at its actual location. Displacing the talker away from the location of the auditory messages led to about a 20% increase in accuracy of identification of the target words. Participants were evidently able to use the talking head to perceptually locate the relevant message away from the location of the distracting message, and thus facilitate their processing of the to-be-attended message.

We have seen that instructions can modulate the influence of a modality, so we might expect that the influence of a cue might also be modified in other ways. Gordon, Eberhardt, and Rueckl (1993) showed that the contribution of auditory speech cues could be modulated by a secondary task. The secondary task involved the arithmetic processing of numbers or the perceptual evaluation of lines. Subjects identified auditory speech stimuli that were varied along two dimensions. In one test, the voice onset time (VOT) and the fundamental (F0) onset frequency of consonant-vowel syllables were varied. The secondary task attenuated, but did not eliminate, the influence of F0 onset frequency. In another test, subjects identified vowels varying in formant pattern and duration. The secondary task attenuated, but did not eliminate, the influence of formant pattern.

This result probably reflects the output of the evaluation process in the FLMP. The competing task probably degrades the information value of a particular cue. Such degradation would be analogous to some form of lowering the quality of the information, such as by adding noise to the cue. However, it appears that the secondary task does not disrupt the integration process. Information is integrated in the same manner with and without the secondary task. This interpretation requires a formal theoretical analysis of the results, which Gordon, Eberhardt, and Rueckl (1993) did not apply. Such an analysis could easily be carried out in our bimodal speech perception task using an expanded factorial design. This type of study could indicate whether the influence of audible or visible speech is more easily attenuated by a secondary task. It would also be of interest to see whether the influence of a secondary task is dependent on the modality of the distractor.

Summary

In addition to testing for analogous processes in the two domains, the instruction experiment was also aimed at finding out whether instructions and intention would affect the two domains differently. As far as we can tell, instructions and intention modulate the impact of a given source of information but cannot preclude its influence completely. People are not able to filter out completely the influence of a to-be-ignored modality. On the other hand, they can attenuate its influence; some degree of control is possible. It remains to be seen to what extent increasing a subject's practice in the task or the use of some particular intentional strategy can lead to successful use of just a single source of information (see Massaro, 1987f, pp. 75–82). Future research using expanded factorial designs and the theoretical framework of the FLMP should be able to provide more definitive understanding of the role of intention in pattern recognition.

To estimate the free parameters corresponding to the evaluation of the auditory and visual sources, the FLMP assumed different parameter values in the different instruction conditions. Different parameter values were sufficient to capture the results. In terms of the distinction between information and information processing, intention can thus be accounted for in terms of information, with no qualitative changes in information processing. Why would the evaluation of the sources change with instructions? Subjects might simply learn more about the attended-to dimension over the course of the experiment and thus show a larger influence of that dimension at evaluation. Within the framework of the FLMP, the fundamental pattern recognition algorithm is changeless. Bearing out this assumption, intention can enhance or attenuate the information contribution of sources that are available, but intention does not seem capable of enforcing another type of pattern recognition algorithm.

The robustness of the FLMP algorithm across changes in intentional set is consistent with its robustness across individual variability, task variability, and domain variability. Perhaps the most important contribution of these results is the evidence that speech perception and emotion perception can be described by the same information-processing model. These results are taken as a strong disproof that information processing is modular even though there is a necessary modularity of information. It is obvious that the information is different for speech and emotion, but the results simultaneously indicate that the information processing is identical across domains. More generally, there is no question of modularity of information across different domains (Massaro, 1994c). On the other hand, information processing appears to be highly similar, if not identical, across the different domains.

RETROSPECTIVE

In this second part of the book, we explored the universality of the law of pattern recognition proposed in the first section. We discovered that perceivers tend to integrate several sources of information in many different circumstances. The integration process conforms to the FLMP, a quantitative law of pattern recognition. Surprisingly, perhaps, people tend to integrate sources of information even when it might be claimed that it is unreasonable to do so. Many individuals will make a conjunction error by interpreting a question incorrectly as one involving pattern recognition (Massaro, 1994a). Given a description of Linda, they claim it is more likely that she is a bank teller and a feminist than only a bank teller. The reason is that "bank teller and feminist" matches her description more aptly than just "bank teller." People overextend their tendency to recognize patterns, committing an error in terms of the question that was asked. Correspondingly, we experience visual illusions when cues to three dimensions actually come from two-dimensional displays.

The same type of processing occurs even when the two sources being integrated are not ecologically joined. For example, natural auditory speech is integrated with synthetic visible speech in the same way it is combined with natural visible speech (Massaro & Cohen, 1990). Furthermore, auditory and visual speech are combined in a natural fashion even when the sex of the voice differs from the sex of the face doing the talking (Green et al., 1991). Similarly, differences in the spatial location of the auditory and visual speech do not disrupt the integration process (Bertelson et al., 1994; Fisher, 1991; Massaro, 1992a).

The proposed law of pattern recognition is found to be valid across development and aging, different languages, sensory impairments, brain trauma, personality differences, males and females, and differences in experience and learning. The law given by the FLMP has also held up across different modalities, situational domains, and task differences. We saw in chapter 6 that audible speech is integrated with an inverted face, which has been shown to disrupt face processing. Finally, the FLMP algorithm can be verified in a variety of behavioral outcomes. This strong support for the FLMP sets the stage for an elaboration of the FLMP, its empirical tests, and the account of the challenges it has faced.

III Broadening the Framework

9   Broadening the Model

A crystal lacks rhythm from excess of pattern, while a fog is unrhythmic in that it exhibits a patternless confusion of detail.
—Alfred North Whitehead, *The Principles of Knowledge*

All chance, direction, which thou canst not see.
—Alexander Pope, *Essay on Man*

We have developed and tested a specific form of our universal principle, the fuzzy logical model of perception (FLMP), with great success. In this chapter we broaden the model in a variety of directions. First, we explicitly formalize the model to account for the dynamics of perceptual processing. Until now, the time course of pattern recognition has not received much emphasis. Some investigators have claimed that our theoretical framework speaks only to the output of processing rather than addressing the processing itself (McClelland, 1996). For the life of me I cannot understand what is meant by this claim, but I know it appears to be less than complimentary. In all cases, students of behavior are faced with some observable behavior in some environmental situation, and their task is to describe the behavior in terms of the way that hidden processes operate in the environmental situation.

Second, we analyze the integration stage with more scrutiny. We show that our universal principle of how two sources of information interact in pattern recognition follows not only from the integration algorithm but also from the decision operation. Third, we decompose the decision operation into two component operations that were implicitly assumed by the relative goodness rule. We call these *assessment* and *response selection*, respectively. Assessment involves consideration of the multiple outcomes of integration corresponding to all of the response alternatives under consideration. Response selection maps the assessment into an actual response. There are two competing candidates for assessment: absolute goodness or support, and relative support. Response selection also has two primary contenders: a probability matching rule implicitly assumed by our relative goodness rule, and a criterion rule. With a criterion rule, the outcome of assessment is compared to a criterion to completely determine the response that is selected. This deterministic selection is more compatible with current thinking about response selection in psychophysical situations than is the probability matching rule.

In the course of this broadening of our model, some new types of independent and dependent variables will be used. The time available for perceptual processing will be systematically varied in the standard pattern recognition task. We will also depend on rating judgments to provide a more direct measure of the information available to the perceiver. Finally, the FLMP will be extended to account for the relationship between identification and rating judgments. We begin with the presentation and test of the dynamic FLMP.

THE DYNAMIC FLMP

According to our description of the evaluation process, each feature of the stimulus gives some support for relevant alternatives. That support, of course, is not arrived at instantaneously. In the information-processing approach every process takes time, and the evaluation process is no different. The time available for processing simply has not been an issue. The output of evaluation has been expressed in terms of truth values, such as the auditory support of level i for the alternative /da/, written as a_{Di}. Time enters into evaluation because we expect that a more informative outcome will result from more processing time. Recall that in fuzzy logic, .5 is ambiguous, and the truth value conveys more information to the extent that it approaches 0 or 1. Thus, we expect the truth value to begin at .5 before any evaluation processing has occurred and to move toward either 0 or 1 as more processing time is available. The sixty-four-dollar question, of course, is, what function describes this relationship? We take advantage of the developments in another research area to answer this question (Massaro & Loftus, 1996).

The research of interest employs a backward recognition masking (BRM) task. The backward masking paradigm is sketched in figure 9.1. A brief test stimulus is presented, followed after a variable interstimulus interval (ISI) by a second stimulus (the mask). The time between the onset of the test stimulus and the onset of the mask is called the stimulus onset asynchrony (SOA).

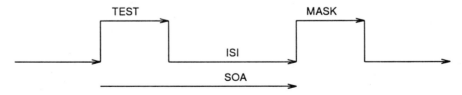

Figure 9.1 Schematic diagram of a backward masking task.

Backward Recognition Masking Study

For illustrative purposes, we describe one of the first studies of auditory backward recognition masking (Massaro, 1970b). The two test stimuli were brief tones (20 ms) differing slightly in frequency and presented at a normal loudness level. The task of the subjects was to identify the test tone as high or low in pitch. The test tones were randomly presented over many trials and followed by a masking tone after one of seven different ISIs. The masking tone was presented at the same normal loudness level. On some trials, no masking tone was presented. An interesting outcome of this experiment is that the masking tone makes recognition of the test tone difficult. The subject hears a test tone on every trial, but the sooner the masking tone arrives the more difficult it is to accurately identify the pitch of the test tone as high or low.

Figure 9.2 gives the results for three young adults. For each of the three observers, accuracy of performance improves dramatically with delays in the presentation of the masking tone. The improvement corresponds to a negatively accelerated function of the ISI. This means that more information is gleaned early than late in the processing of the test tone. Also noticeable in figure 9.2 are the individual differences in overall performance. We can describe the rate and asymptote of each function. The rate represents how quickly performance reaches the asymptote, which is the maximum level of

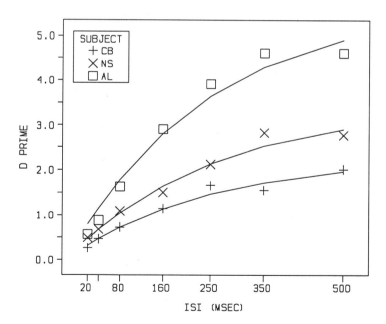

Figure 9.2 Observed (points) and predicted (lines) recognition accuracy (measured in d') as a function of the interstimulus interval (ISI) between the test tone and the masking tone (after Massaro, 1970a).

performance. The observers differ in terms of asymptote but not rate, a result that we claim represents a difference in information and not information processing (Massaro, 1972, 1975a; Massaro & Burke, 1991).

These backward masking results have been explained within the framework of a model of auditory information processing in which the target sound is transduced by the listener's sensory system and stored in a preperceptual auditory store that briefly holds a single auditory event (Massaro, 1972, 1975a). Processing of this preperceptual sound representation involves resolving the features of the sound to produce a synthesized representation of some auditory event. A second sound replaces the first in the preperceptual auditory store and terminates any further reliable processing of the first sound. Because of the transient nature of preperceptual memory, and because of backward masking when a second sound occurs before resolution of the first sound is complete, the duration of preperceptual memory and the rate of processing together place a limit on how much can be perceived.

The amount of time that the target information is available in preperceptual memory can be controlled by carefully manipulating the duration of the SOA. The accuracy of target identification increases as SOA lengthens (Massaro, 1970b). The amount of improvement with processing time reflects the rate of processing the stimulus information. The performance function typically has its asymptote at an SOA of roughly 250 ms, and that interval is believed to reflect the duration of the preperceptual auditory store (Cowan, 1984; Kallman & Massaro, 1983). That is, after 250 ms the mask no longer affects performance because the preperceptual trace is no longer available for processing.

According to this theory, subjects accumulate information about the test tone gradually during the processing time available before the onset of the mask. Perceptual recognition cannot be considered to be completely accurate or inaccurate at any time during the processing interval. Rather, accuracy increases systematically with increases in processing time. The masking stimulus serves to terminate any additional processing of the test, but it does not work retroactively; it does not reduce the amount of processing that has occurred before the mask.

Remarkably, the changes in accuracy with increases in processing time can be described accurately by a relatively simple mathematical function. The function assumes that information is accumulated as a negatively accelerated exponential growth function of processing time,

$$d' = \alpha(1 - e^{-\theta t}), \tag{9.1}$$

where α and θ are free parameters of the function, e is the natural logarithm (2.718), and t is the SOA. The parameter α corresponds to the asymptote (maximum) of the function, and θ is the rate of growth toward this asymptote. The function can be conceptualized as representing a process that resolves some fixed proportion of the potential information that remains to be resolved per unit of time. The same increment in processing time thus contains a larger absolute improvement in performance the earlier it occurs in the processing interval.

Dynamic Feature Evaluation

A reasonable assumption is that feature evaluation should follow the same negatively accelerating growth function found in backward recognition masking tasks. Early in feature evaluation, the perceiver would have some information about each feature, but the information would not be sufficient to identify the stimulus. Integration of the separate features would be updated continuously as the featural information is being evaluated. Similarly, decision could occur at any time after the stimulus presentation. For example, a response could be initiated before sufficient information is accumulated, as might occur in speed-accuracy experiments.

According to the theoretical analysis of backward masking, a masking stimulus would terminate any additional processing of the test stimulus. Although the masking function given in equation 9.1 represents the time course of only a single feature's evaluation, this dynamic model can be combined with the FLMP to describe how multiple sources of information are evaluated and integrated over time. There is evidence for the parallel evaluation of multiple sources of information in the BRM task. Moore and Massaro (1973), for example, asked subjects to identify both loudness and timbre in the BRM task. On each trial, the subject was asked to identify either the loudness (loud or soft), the timbre (dull or sharp), or both dimensions of the test tone. Typical backward masking functions were found under each of the instruction conditions. In addition, the subjects were able to identify the two dimensions of the test tone (loudness and timbre) about as accurately as they could identify one.

We have illustrated the three stages—evaluation, integration, and decision —as sequential stages of processing; an earlier stage must begin before a later stage can start. This means that each stage of processing occurs over time, and therefore it should be possible to specify the time course of the processing. Given the analogous behavior of pitch identification in the BRM task and feature evaluation in the prototypical pattern recognition task, it is reasonable to assume that evaluation of a source of information would also follow equation 9.1. The truth value x_A of a source of information x supporting a given alternative A increases or decreases over time t toward some final asymptotic value α from an ambiguous initial value (.5). This value of x_A over time, $x_A(t)$, can be described as the sum of a negatively accelerated transition from 0 to the asymptotic truth value α and a negatively accelerated transition from the initial value .5 to 0.

$$x_A(t) = \alpha(1 - e^{-\theta t}) + .5(e^{-\theta t}). \tag{9.2}$$

The output from evaluation would be fed continuously to the integration process, which would operate in the same manner as assumed in the FLMP.

The overall goodness values at integration would be fed forward to decision, which would compute the relative goodness of match of the alternatives. To account for the dynamics of processing, an additional process must be implemented. This process would determine when a subject would actually initiate a response in the task. In most identification tasks with unlimited response time, it seems reasonable to assume that the subject waits until evaluation of the sources of information is near asymptote. With limited processing time, the decision system would initiate a response when no additional information is being accumulated. Thus, the decision system could maintain some running memory of the change in goodness values, and, if this change is less than some minimum in a given time period, a response could be initiated. In tasks that require speeded responses, the decision system would simply initiate a response at the designated time based on the relative goodness values at that time. We now test this dynamic FLMP against empirical results.

Context Effects and Backward Masking

In an experiment reported by Massaro (1979a), readers were asked to read lowercase letter strings with an ambiguous test letter between c and e. It is possible to gradually transform the c into an e by extending the horizontal bar. To the extent that the bar is long, there is good visual information for an e and poor visual information for a c. Now consider the letter presented as the first letter in the context $-oin$ and the context $-dit$. Only c is orthographically admissible in the first context because the sequence $eoin$ is not a recognizable word, and because the three consecutive vowels eoi are in general violation of English orthographic patterning. Only e is admissible in the second context because $cdit$ does not form a word and the initial cluster cd is not an English pattern. In this case, the context $-oin$ favors c, whereas the context $-dit$ favors e. The contexts $-tsa$ and $-ast$ can be considered to favor neither e nor c. The first remains an inadmissible context whether e or c is present, and the second is orthographically admissible for both e and c.

The experiment factorially combined 6 levels of visual information with these 4 levels of orthographic context, giving a total of 24 experimental conditions. For the 6 levels of visual information, the bar length of the letter took on 6 values progressing from a prototypical c to a prototypical e. The 4 orthographic contexts were favoring c, favoring e, favoring neither, and favoring both. The test letter was also presented at each of the 4 letter positions in each of the 4 contexts. Thus, there were actually 96 ($6 \times 4 \times 4$) unique displays. Subjects were told that there was a test letter in each display and were instructed to identify it as e or c on the basis of what they saw. The results of the experimental test are shown in figure 9.3. As the figure shows, both the test letter and the context influenced performance in the expected direction. In addition, the effect of context was larger for the more ambiguous test letters along the stimulus continuum.

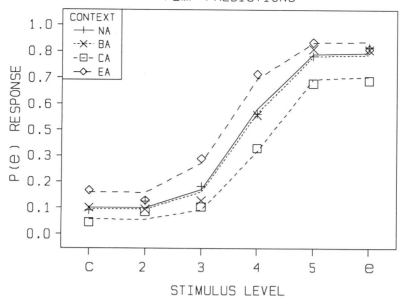

Figure 9.3 Probability of *e* identifications as a function of the bar length of the test letter and the orthographic context: NA = neither, BA = both, CA = c, and EA = e admissible (after Massaro, 1979a).

The same study also evaluated context effects as a function of processing time controlled by backward masking. The test display was presented for a short duration, followed after some short interval by a masking stimulus composed of random letter features. The test stimulus was presented for 30 ms. Four SOAs (35, 70, 125, and 240 ms) were tested in that task at each of the other experimental conditions. The points in figure 9.4 show the probability of an *e* response as a function of the bar length in the test letter and of the four contexts at each of the four masking intervals. Each point represents an average of data from 176 trials (16 observations from each of 11 subjects). As can be seen in the figure, performance was more chaotic at the short masking intervals. That is, less processing time led to less orderly behavior —as expected from research on the time course of perceptual processing. Even for unambiguous test letters, subjects did not make consistent identification judgments at short masking intervals. As predicted by perceptual processing theory, there was not sufficient time for feature evaluation and integration to take place before the onset of the masking stimulus.

Both the test letter and the context influenced performance at all masking intervals. The effect of test letter was attenuated at the short relative to the long processing time. That is, with increases in processing time, the identification functions covered a larger range across the *e*–*c* continuum. The spread among the four curves in each plot in figure 9.4 shows that context had a significant effect at all masking intervals. Furthermore, the spread at the

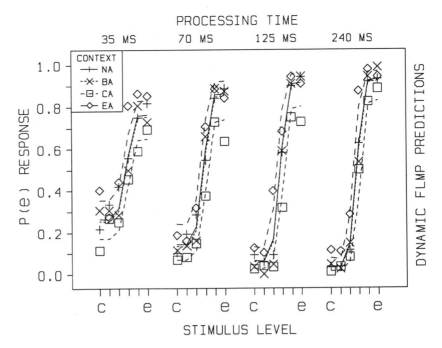

Figure 9.4 Observed (points) and predicted (lines) probability of *e* identifications as a function of the bar length of the test letter, the orthographic context, and the processing interval (SOA) between the onset of the test stimulus and the onset of the masking stimulus for the dynamic FLMP model (results after Massaro, 1979a).

endpoints of the *e–c* continuum shows that the context effect was larger for these endpoint test letters at the short than at the longer masking intervals. This result follows naturally from the FLMP prediction that context has a smaller influence to the extent that the stimulus information is unambiguous.

It is possible to describe performance in terms of the change in featural information *F* and contextual information *C* across the four masking intervals in the task. Implementing equation 9.2 for both context and featural information, the featural information across time *t*, *F(t)*, can be described by

$$F(t) = \alpha_{Fi}(1 - e^{-\theta t}) + .5(e^{-\theta t}) \tag{9.3}$$

and the contextual information *C(t)* by

$$C(t) = \alpha_{C_j}(1 - e^{-\theta t}) + .5(e^{-\theta t}) \tag{9.4}$$

for the processing time *t* (the sum of the masking interval and the 30 ms stimulus duration).

In fitting the FLMP, 11 parameters were used: 6 α_{Fi} values for the 6 levels going from *c* to *e*, 4 α_{C_j} values for the 4 contexts, and 1 additional parameter for θ. Figure 9.5 shows how the predicted feature values (left panel) and context values (right panel) changed with processing time. The points in figure 9.5 give the predicted values that are inserted into the integration and

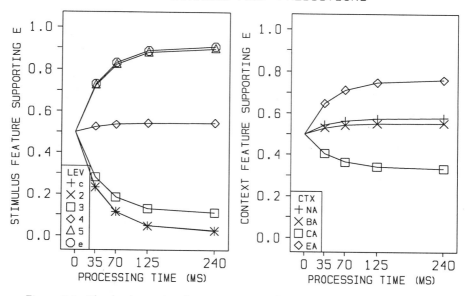

Figure 9.5 The development with processing time of feature values for e–c level (left panel) and context (right panel) for the dynamic FLMP model. Points correspond to the predicted values. The lines connect the points.

decision algorithm for each of the 96 conditions. Figure 9.4 gives the resulting predictions of response probability for the FLMP (lines) along with the observed data (points). The RMSD between the observed and predicted points was .050.

Although the test was in the reading rather than the speech domain, we were successful in extending the FLMP to account for the dynamics of pattern recognition. We extended the model parsimoniously by incorporating theoretical constructs derived from the research on the time course of information processing. Although somewhat more arduous, it will be important to replicate these results in the speech domain. Because speech varies over time and time serves as a source of information, the backward masking task is made more complicated. We now turn to further broadening the FLMP by decomposing the decision stage.

DECOMPOSING THE DECISION PROCESS

The decision stage takes as input the overall degree of support for each of the relevant alternatives. Following tradition, we have postulated a relative goodness rule (RGR) for decision in which the probability of responding with a particular alternative is equal to its support divided by the sum of support for all alternatives. This RGR is parsimoniously expressed in a simple ratio (see equations 9.5–9.7). A decomposition of the decision process exemplifies one of the distinguishing features of information-processing

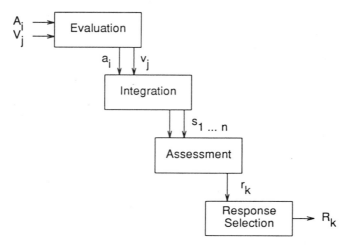

Figure 9.6 Schematic representation of the FLMP in which the decision process is decomposed into two processes, assessment and response selection. The four processes are shown to proceed left to right in time to illustrate their necessarily successive but overlapping processing. The two processes that replace decision are (1) assessment of the degrees of support for all of the relevant alternatives and (2) response selection given that assessment. The sources of information are represented by uppercase letters. The evaluation process determines the support from each source of information. The support values from those sources are then integrated to give the total support, s_k, for each of the speech alternatives k. The assessment operation uses these to arrive at some overall measure of support for a given alternative. The response selection maps that value into some response alternative, R_k. The actual response can take the form of a discrete decision or a rating of the degree to which a given alternative is supported.

models. Each process can be decomposed into component processes (Palmer & Kimchi, 1986).

Figure 9.6 illustrates that this decision process in fact includes two important component processes. These two subprocesses are the assessment of the degrees of support for all of the relevant alternatives and the selection of a response based on that assessment. This formulation of the process makes clear that there are several possibilities for each of the two subprocesses. The assessment process might use absolute goodness rather than relative goodness as the input to send on to the response selection stage. For response selection, the input from assessment might be compared to a decision criterion rather than used for probability matching. Distinguishing between these two subprocesses in decision is valuable because the possibilities for each subprocess can be considered independently of the possibilities for the other process. We begin with the issue of the nature of the output from the assessment stage.

ASSESSMENT: RELATIVE VERSUS ABSOLUTE GOODNESS

Spinoza once claimed that "every decision is, at the same time, the rejection of all other possibilities." We will see that pattern recognition could not be accurately predicted if we strictly followed Spinoza's claim. Within the framework of the FLMP (and many other models), his claim might be interpreted to mean that we act on the basis of absolute goodness of match rather than relative goodness of match. Within this same framework, absolute goodness of match would be characterized by an assessment of which alternative has the largest amount of support given the outcome of the integration process. As we have said, relative goodness of match assesses the goodness of each alternative relative to the sum of the goodness values for all alternatives.

There is an intuitive reason why absolute goodness of match is an implausible assessment rule. Our natural tendency is to impose meaning on each event we experience, and yet some events have much more ambiguity than others. If absolute goodness were the standard for choice, we would fail to act appropriately in the more ambiguous situations. Appropriate action follows, however, if we interpret the situation in terms of relative rather than absolute goodness of match. Thus, pattern recognition could not succeed if we demand an absolute goodness of match to be exceeded. Relative goodness is a more flexible assessment: what seems important is the relative goodness of the competing candidates rather than their absolute goodness of match.

In addition to this intuitive argument, there is strong empirical and theoretical support for relative goodness. That support—in the form of evidence that pattern recognition occurs in situations with varying numbers of relevant alternatives and with one or more sources of information—will be discussed in the next two sections. We consider each of these situations in the context of the FLMP.

Variable Number of Relevant Alternatives

Perhaps the most direct illustration that assessment involves relative rather than absolute goodness is the change in performance that is observed when the number of relevant response alternatives is systematically varied. Across our experiments, we have varied the number of possible alternatives in the five-by-five expanded factorial design. Participants were given two response alternatives in one set of experiments and eight in another. (The two-alternative task was discussed in chapter 1 and the eight-alternative task in chapter 6.) Figure 9.7 plots the observed /da/ response probabilities in these two sets of experiments. As can be seen in the figure, /da/ judgments are much more frequent when /ba/ and /da/ syllables are the only response alternatives than when there are also six other permissible responses.

We have seen that the FLMP gives a good description of both the two-alternative and the eight-alternative tasks when the model is fit to each task independently. To achieve these fits, a different set of free parameters is estimated for each of the two response conditions. As figure 9.7 shows, predictions were accurate as expected. The FLMP gave a good description of the average results in the two experiments with an RMSD of .026. In principle, however, the FLMP should be capable of predicting the results even

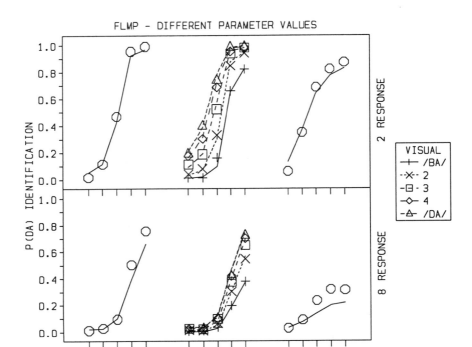

Figure 9.7 The points give the average observed proportion of /da/ identifications in the auditory-alone (left panel), the factorial auditory-visual (center panel), and the visual-alone (right panel) conditions as a function of the five levels of the synthetic auditory and visual speech varying between /ba/ and /da/. The top panel gives performance for the two-alternative response task, and the bottom panel gives performance for the eight-alternative task. The lines give the predictions of the FLMP (a different set of free parameters is estimated for each of the two response conditions).

when the same parameter values are used in the two response conditions. If the same stimulus conditions are used in both experiments, then a single set of parameter values should be sufficient to describe a subject's performance.

It is worthwhile to describe this additional application of the FLMP to these results with two or eight response alternatives. In our previous formulation of the FLMP (see chapter 2), the equations were written to be specific to a set number of alternatives. Here we give more general equations. With only a single source of information, such as the auditory one A_i, the probability of a /da/ response, $P(/da/)$, is predicted to be

$$P(/da/|A_i) = \frac{a_{Di}}{\sum_k a_{ki}}, \qquad (9.5)$$

where a_{Di} is the auditory support at level i for the /da/ alternative and the denominator is equal to the sum of support for all relevant alternatives (k). With the alternatives /da/ and /ba/, the denominator would be the sum of a_{Di}

and a_{Bi}, where a_{Bi} is the auditory support for the /ba/ alternative. With eight alternatives, eight degrees of support would be summed in the denominator.

Similarly, the probability of a /da/ response given just the visual source of information is predicted to be

$$P(/\text{da}/|V_j) = \frac{v_{Dj}}{\sum\limits_{k} v_{kj}},$$
(9.6)

where v_{Dj} is the visual support for the /da/ alternative and the denominator would be the sum of visual support for all relevant alternatives.

Given two sources of information A_i and V_j, $P(/\text{da}/)$ is predicted to be

$$P(/\text{da}/|A_i \text{ and } V_j) = \frac{a_{Di} \times v_{Dj}}{\sum\limits_{k} (a_{ki} \times v_{kj})}.$$
(9.7)

These equations express general predictions of the FLMP regardless of the number of response alternatives. With two response alternatives, the denominator in the equations would be the sum of the support for /ba/ and /da/ alternatives. With eight response alternatives, the denominator would be the sum of the support for all eight response alternatives.

Thus, to test the FLMP predictions it seems essential that response choice should be accurately described with the same parameter values. Unfortunately, different subjects were tested in the two response conditions, and we have made the case that models cannot be definitively tested on group data. In the present application, we would not only have to test group data, we would also have to assume the same parameter values across two different groups of subjects. With this caveat in mind and in the absence of data from the same subjects on both tasks, it is worthwhile to test this prediction of the FLMP.

The results of the two experiments were fit with a single set of free parameters that were estimated from both experiments. Figure 9.8 gives the same observed results as figure 9.7 along with the predicted response probabilities in the two experiments based on this combined fit with a single set of parameter values. The good fit with a low RMSD value of .028 compares favorably to the RMSD of .026 when different parameter values were estimated in the two experiments. This outcome indicates that the FLMP nicely describes performance with both two and eight response alternatives even when constrained to a single set of parameter values.

Although it never hurts to document another success of your favorite model, the goal of this exercise is actually to illustrate the necessity of relative goodness rather than absolute goodness at the assessment stage. If absolute support is taken as the critical information, then the responses in the two response conditions cannot be accurately predicted. To illustrate, consider the most /da/-like level of visual information. The observed $P(/\text{da}/)$ was .87 and .31 with two and eight alternatives, respectively. In the two-alternative task, predicted $P(/\text{da}/)$ is .85, whereas it is predicted to be .28 in the eight-alternative task. The parameter estimate for that level's support for the

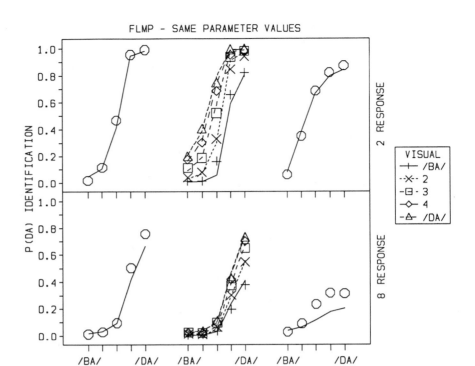

Figure 9.8 The points give the average observed proportion of /da/ identifications in the auditory-alone (left panel), the factorial auditory-visual (center panel), and the visual-alone (right panel) conditions as a function of the five levels of the synthetic auditory and visual speech varying between /ba/ and /da/. The top panel gives performance for the two-alternative response task, and the bottom panel gives performance for the eight-alternative task. The lines give the predictions of the FLMP with the constraint that the same parameter values are used in the fit of both response conditions.

alternative /da/ is .65. The support for /ba/ in the two-alternative case was .12, which gives .77 as the denominator in equation 9.5. In the eight-response case, the denominator was equal to 3.23, and so predicted $P(/da/)$ is much smaller than in the two-response case. These two predictions are so different from one another because of the use of relative goodness. Thus, relative goodness allows very different predictions depending on the number of relevant alternatives. Absolute goodness alone would not allow different predictions to be made for the two response conditions, and so could not achieve accuracy. We find that relative goodness is also functional in semantic memory.

Relative Goodness in Semantic Judgments

An experiment by Oden (1977a) provides a test of relative versus absolute goodness at assessment in the domain of semantic memory. Subjects were given two statements such as

An eagle is a bird.
A pelican is a bird.

and asked, "Which of the following statements is truer and how much more true is it?" Subjects made their judgments along a linear scale between true and false. If subjects used absolute goodness of match, then they would have available the absolute truth of each of the two statements. When asked to indicate which statement is truer and by how much, they might simply subtract the truth values of the two statements. Thus, we might expect the judgments to follow a simple subtractive model:

$$J(A) = t(A) - t(B) \tag{9.8}$$

where $J(A)$ would be equal to the truthfulness of statement A minus that of statement B and $t(A)$ and $t(B)$ represent the truth values of the individual statements. However, this subtractive model based on absolute goodness gave a poor description of the results. On the other hand, relative goodness gave an adequate account of the judgments. Thus, the results were described by

$$J(A) = \frac{t(A)}{t(A) + t(B)} \tag{9.9}$$

where the statement A is judged to be more true in terms of the truthfulness of A relative to the sum of the truthfulness values of A and B. Any judgment appears to contain a relative aspect. We now consider a third justification for relative goodness: the number of sources of information used to categorize an event varies widely.

Integration Necessitates Relative Goodness

Pattern recognition occurs in situations with varying numbers of sources of information. We saw that two sources of information can lead to more reliable categorization than just one. In the context of the FLMP, integration involves a multiplicative combination of the respective truth values of the two information sources (Oden, 1977b). Because the truth values are less than one, their multiplicative combination will necessarily be less than the value of either one individually. This observation has been taken by Osherson & Smith (1981, 1982) to be an inconsistency in fuzzy logic, but neither their analysis nor Zadeh's reply (1982) considered the role of using the relative degree of support for the different alternatives. As we have seen in the example varying the number of response alternatives, relative goodness normalizes the predicted outcomes in the FLMP. An analogous principle holds for the number of information sources. Consider, for example, the case in which audible and visible speech each support /ba/ to degree .7 and /da/ to degree .3. On bimodal trials, the total degree of support for /ba/ would be .7 × .7 = .49. On unimodal trials, the degree of support should be .7. If the decision is based on absolute support, then the likelihood of a /ba/ judgment would necessarily be greater on unimodal than bimodal trials—an incorrect prediction. If relative goodness is used, however, then the total degree of support for /ba/ on bimodal trials would be .49 divided by (.49 + .09) = .85 —a correct prediction. In chapter 1 we saw that two sources of consistent information resulted in more accurate judgments than just one of those sources.

It is hoped that the reader has gained from this section an appreciation of the value of relative goodness at decision. The idea of relative goodness is not new. As early as 1959, Oliver Selfridge introduced the idea of relative goodness in his Pandemonium model of letter recognition. He proposed that the decision demon listened to the relative loudness of shouting of the letter demons, not their absolute level of shouting. This assumption resonated with the theorizing in experimental psychology (Clarke, 1957; Luce, 1959; see Massaro, 1987f, for a discussion of this work in the context of the FLMP). For our purposes, it is important to know that relative goodness is the best assessment rule for decision independently of how it is finally mapped into an actual response. Having gained insight into the assessment component of our original decision stage, in the next section we consider the response selection component.

RESPONSE SELECTION RULE

Variability in Processing Models

An important factor in settling on a response selection rule is where to include variability or noise in a model. Some models have noise from the very start of processing, whereas other models do not include variability until very late in processing. Most important, however, is that variability be present at some point, because the behavior being modeled is indeed vari-able. A person given the same stimulus situation will respond in one way at one time and in another way at another time. In the FLMP, the evaluation and integration processes have been assumed to be noise-free. For example, at evaluation, the second level of the auditory speech continuum supports the /ba/ alternative to degree a_{B2} (where a is the feature or truth value, the subscript B refers to the alternative /ba/, and the subscript 2 corresponds to the second level). This value is supposedly the same each time the second level of the auditory speech is presented. Similarly, no variability is intro-duced at the integration stage. The values obtained from evaluation are simply multiplied together. Until the current modification, variability was introduced at the decision stage by the relative goodness rule (RGR).

As currently formulated, the FLMP predicts probabilistic rather than deterministic behavior. Probabilistic behavior means that the same situation leads to one response at some times and to another response at other times. Deterministic behavior, when the term is used in contrast with probabilistic behavior, means that the same behavioral outcome always occurs in response to a specific environmental event. In the context of the FLMP, a deterministic response selection rule would fail miserably. Given the same stimulus event—for example, the second level of the auditory speech continuum—a person does not respond consistently to each repetition of the event. He or she might call it a /ba/ on some trials and a /da/ on others.

It might seem strange that the same information would elicit different behaviors, but further reflection should reveal that nature could have it no other way. The sight of my refrigerator, the ring of the telephone, and the smell of freshly brewed coffee all have different consequences for my actions depending on a variety of factors. As these examples reveal, the indeterminacy of behavioral action might characterize not only psychophysical tasks but also cognitive domains of decision making and judgment. Needless to say, there is a fuzzy boundary between perception and cognition, but we might safely argue that response selection can be viewed as a cognitive function. If this is the case, we should be concerned with whether response choice is indeterminate in cognitive as well as in perceptual situations. To explore this question, we review response selection in a few experimental paradigms in domains involving cognitive decision making.

Cognitive Decision Making

In the study of cognitive decision making, participants are given descriptions of fictitious persons and asked to rate how likely those persons are to have various vocations, avocations, or some combination. In one experiment (Massaro, 1994a), participants were given descriptions of Linda and Joan.

Linda is 31 years old, single, outspoken, and very bright. She had a double major in philosophy and music. As a student, she was deeply concerned with issues of discrimination and social justice, and also participated in antinuclear demonstrations.

Joan is 29 years old, married, athletic, and intelligent. She majored in economics, and graduated with honors. She was a writer for the conservative campus newspaper, and participated in intramural sports.

On each trial, an avocation, a vocation, or an avocation-vocation pair was presented. There were 35 test questions and each test question was repeated a number of times, as in prototypical experiments on pattern recognition. (In fact, a five-by-five expanded factorial design was used, with 12 trials for each of the 35 unique conditions.) Subjects were instructed to indicate whether Linda or Joan was more likely to have some avocation, vocation, or avocation and vocation. For example, is Linda or Joan more likely to be an IBM executive in charge of computer programs and a violin player in an amateur chamber group?

Figure 9.9 gives the results for a prototypical observer in this task. To repetitions of the same question during the experiment, this typical participant

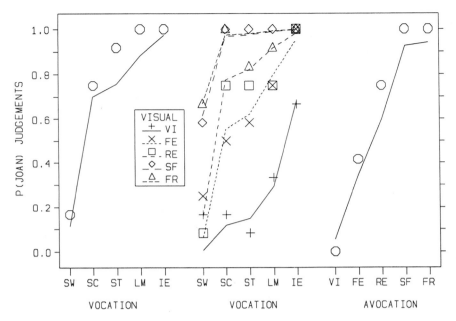

Figure 9.9 Proportion of "Joan" judgments as a function of unimodal vocation (left panel), unimodal avocation (right panel), and combined avocation and vocation (center panel) as a parameter for a prototypical observer. The lines give the fit of the FLMP. The vocations were social worker, sales clerk, schoolteacher, loan manager, and IBM executive; the avocations were violinist, feminist, Republican, frisbee player, and science-fiction reader.

responded "Linda" on some of the trials and "Joan" on other trials. Clearly, a deterministic response selection rule in the FLMP would have been as incapable of describing these results as those of any of the pattern recognition experiments we have analyzed.

Probability Matching Rule for Response Selection

As we have said, there is a general heuristic for predicting probabilistic judgments: either add noise before response selection or use a probabilistic rule. In the FLMP, there is no noise before response selection, so the indeterminacy problem is solved by making a probabilistic choice at response selection. If the relative goodness of /ba/ is .8 and that of /da/ is .2, then the perceiver responds /ba/ exactly .8 of the time and /da/ .2 of the time. This is a probability matching rule (PMR), in which the assessment that is input to this rule is matched to the probability of a response. Basically, the PMR says that a biased coin is flipped on each trial to determine the response. The bias is equal to the output of the assessment process: .8 and .2 in our example. The PMR has been observed in many probability learning experiments in humans and other animals (Davison & McCarthy, 1988; Estes, 1984; Myers, 1976; Thomas & Legge, 1970). In these tasks, people are instructed to predict which of two events, such as the flashing of two lights, will occur. They go through a series of prediction trials and receive feedback on each trial. If one light occurs with probability .8, people tend to predict that light about 80% of the time. Although some overshooting is sometimes observed, people clearly are not responding with the more frequent alternative all of the time. We now discuss a couple of reservations that have been expressed about the PMR.

Nonoptimality of the Probability Matching Rule

Probability matching behavior can be considered to be nonoptimal because it does not maximize the likelihood of being correct. Consider our example in which the more frequent light occurs 80% of the time. If participants always choose the more frequent event, which occurs on 80% of the trials, they will be 80% correct in the task. If they probability match, however, they will be only 68% correct. (They will be correct $.8 \times .8$ when they choose the more frequent light and $.2 \times .2$ when they choose the less frequent light.) This early research convinced many psychologists that people were nonoptimal decision makers long before the more recent assault on our everyday rationality (Gilovich, 1991; Tversky & Kahneman, 1983).

A nonoptimal process should not necessarily be discarded just because it is nonoptimal. But probability matching perhaps suffers from another limitation. Although probability matching can make quantitatively correct predictions in our tasks, its psychological underpinnings are limited (George Sperling, personal communication; Townsend & Landon, 1982). Probability matching predicts only the expected value of choice performance. It does not predict the actual response outcome on a particular trial because it is necessarily assumed that the choice is probabilistic. On any given trial, the response selection process must essentially flip a (biased) coin in order to arrive at the judgment response. This state of affairs might bother some scientists, because it seems to violate the type of deterministic prediction that science values. For some, it is bothersome to postulate that the elaborate processing at evaluation and integration is followed by the use of a response selection rule that in essence flips a biased coin. On the other hand, some loss of information must occur when continuous information is mapped into a discrete alternative.

Independently of this nondeterminism, however, the putative nonoptimality of probability matching has been troublesome. If several alternatives are supported to different degrees, why would a rational process ever choose an alternative other than the best? If the PMR is so unreasonable, why has it been so successful? We might simply argue that behavior doesn't have to be reasonable. However, such an argument could be criticized on the basis of evolutionary principles. Why would nonoptimal behavior evolve, let alone survive? Luckily, it is possible to have our cake and eat it too. There are two alternative solutions that allow us to salvage probability matching without relinquishing optimality. The first provides a rationalization for probability matching results, and the second shows how an optimal deterministic decision rule can also lead to a probability matching result.

Probability Learning

The probability learning task presents a random sequence of events. A choice of the least likely alternative doesn't necessarily mean that the participant believed it was least likely. The choice might have been made because it seemed the most probable given the recent history of occurrences (e.g., the participant might believe that the expected event sequence calls for the least frequent event on this trial). Alternatively, a few negative rewards for choosing the more likely event could be sufficient inducement for choosing the least likely one (Real, 1991). We might argue that similar inducements influence response selection in the prototypical pattern recognition situation, even though no feedback is given in the task.

There might also be downsides to always predicting the most frequent event. Such deterministic behavior would be more easily predicted by or "second-guessed" by others, and thus would not represent an evolutionarily appropriate strategy. Completely predictable behavior could more easily be exploited by predators or enemies—maybe even by friends. Our evolutionary history and experience may not have prepared us for repeated situations in which there is always the same best choice. More typical would be situations in which the alternatives change in value. Finally, persons may intend to pick the more frequent event but memory or other behavioral limitations might prevent them from doing so.

We have woven several rationales for why the PMR might be a good behavioral strategy. More generally, deterministic behavior is more characteristic of less intelligent behaviors or of simpler organisms. A spider will react to my finger touching its web in the same manner it reacts to a fly or other insect. This deterministic behavior is appropriate for the fly but not for the finger. If intelligence is what Piaget described as what you do if you don't know what to do, people might be responding intelligently when they are inconsistent in their predictions of random events.

In the second solution, we will show that an accurate description of probability matching performance can be provided by a model that is grounded in optimality. Thus, the PMR might be so successful because it predicts almost, if not exactly, the same results as an optimal response selection rule.

A Criterion Rule for Response Selection

The PMR has been shown to be mathematically related to the criterion rule (CR), assumed by Thurstone's law of comparative judgment and by signal detection theory. The criterion rule satisfies the goal of specifying a response on each trial and that of optimal response selection. Figure 9.10 illustrates

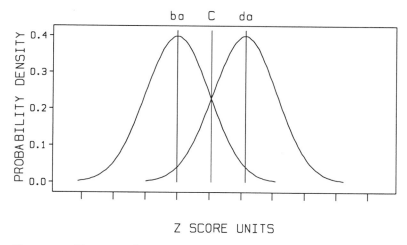

Figure 9.10 Illustration of the criterion rule for response selection, when the outputs of assessment are noisy. As noted below, noise is added to the input so that response selection is faced with a variable input, even though the stimulus is constant.

this response selection rule for a choice between /ba/ and /da/. According to the rule, for two response alternatives the decision process maintains a criterion along the psychological dimension of degree of support. The support is passed from the assessment process to response selection. Given the constraint that relative support rather than absolute support is necessary, the response selection or categorization would be based on where the relative goodness of match falls in relation to the criterion value. If the relative goodness of match falls on one side of the criterion, one response is made; if it falls on the other side of the criterion, the other response is made.

Consider a situation in which there is a stimulus continuum between *not A* and *A* that is perceived continuously—that is, the observer has information about the degree of support for the two alternatives. The left panel of figure 9.11 gives an example by showing degree of support at the assessment stage for the alternative *A* as a linear function of a stimulus continuum. Now the observer is asked to categorize the stimulus as *not A* or *A*, and a criterion rule is used. This response selection rule with two response alternatives would set the criterion value at the midpoint of the two alternatives and classify the pattern as *A* for any value greater than that value. Otherwise, the pattern would be classified as *not A*. Given this response selection rule, the probability of an *A* response would take the step-function form shown in the right panel of figure 9.11. That is, with a fixed criterion value and no variability, the criterion operation changes the continuous linear function given by the perceptual operation into a step function. Choice is deterministic with this criterion rule, in the sense that the relationship between the observation and the criterion completely determines the response. However, our observed response function does not resemble this step function.

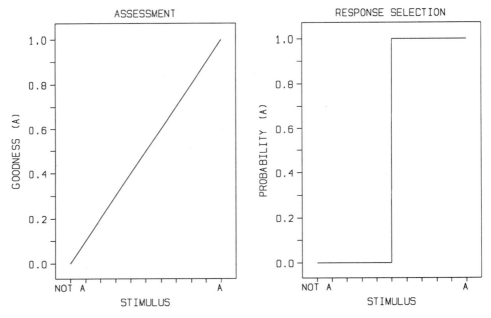

Figure 9.11 Left panel: The degree to which a stimulus represents the category A, called GOODNESS(A), as a function of the level along a stimulus continuum between not A and A. Right panel: The probability of an A response, PROBABILITY(A), as a function of the stimulus continuum if the subject maintains a decision criterion at a particular value of GOODNESS(A) and responds A if and only if the GOODNESS(A) exceeds the decision criterion.

To bring the predictions of the criterion rule into line with the observations, some variability has to be assumed. Within the framework of the FLMP, variability can come from the processing at evaluation, integration, and assessment. Variability can also occur at response selection, based on the momentary location of the criterion value (Carterette, Friedman & Wyman, 1966). Figure 9.12 illustrates a hypothetical response function when there is normally distributed noise with a mean value of 0 added at some point before the deterministic decision is made. If there is noise in the mapping from stimulus to identification, a given stimulus level cannot be expected to produce the same identification judgment on each presentation. It is reasonable to assume that a given level of the stimulus continuum produces a normally distributed range of GOODNESS(A) values with a mean that is a function of the stimulus continuum and a variance that is equal across all levels of the stimulus continuum. With noise somewhere in the chain of processing, the prediction given by the criterion rule is thus probabilistic, as it should be if we want it to conform to actual behavior. We now review evidence that the criterion rule can make predictions that are equivalent to those of the PMR.

Equivalence of the Probability Matching and Criterion Rules

We have learned that the PMR and the CR can make very similar predictions. What type of variability added to the CR produces mathematical

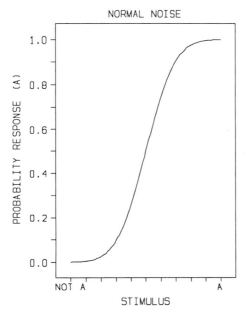

NORMAL NOISE

Figure 9.12 Probability(A) as a function of Stimulus A given the linear relationship between Goodness(A) and Stimulus A and the decision criterion represented in figure 9.11, but with normally distributed noise added to the mapping of Stimulus A to Goodness(A).

equivalence between the RGR and the CR? It turns out that the answer to this question has been available for some time. The CR has its foundation in Thurstone's (1927) theory of comparative judgment, which describes how two different objects or events are compared. Two different objects are discriminated when their respective discriminal processes react differently to them. Thurstone proposed that each discriminal process is associated with a distribution of variability. Luce (1959) proved that PMR (his choice axiom) is equivalent to a version of Thurstone's theory in which the differences between the discriminal processes have a logistic distribution instead of the normal distribution implied by Thurstone's Case V. The logistic distribution is almost identical to the normal, as illustrated in figure 11.4 (see chapter 11). There is equivalence between the two models if and only if the differences between the discriminal processes are logistic random variables.

Yellott (1977) observed that it is important to know what is the distribution of the discriminal processes themselves, not simply the distribution of the differences. In addition, can the relationship between the two models be generalized to sets of alternatives greater than two? If the discriminal processes are assumed to have the double exponential distribution, then the differences will be logistic and thus the two models are equivalent for any choice experiment, not simply for pair comparisons (Yellott, 1977). It also turns out that for pair comparisons, distributions other than the double exponential yield equivalence between the two models. For three or more alternatives, however, the double exponential distribution is the only one. It is relevant to our concern with the response selection rule that the mathematical predictions of the PMR are equivalent to a CR with logistically distributed noise. Thus we see that the PMR and the CR can make equivalent predictions at the response selection stage. The question we now pursue is whether it is still possible to devise a test that will distinguish between them.

Distinguishing between the Probability Matching and Criterion Rules

We are faced with the fact that the PMR and the CR (with noise) make essentially equivalent predictions in the pattern recognition task. Given the close correspondence between these two alternative rules, it might appear impossible to distinguish between them. In keeping with our theme of utilizing variability, however, we can test between them by comparing the observed variability of response with that predicted by the two theoretical possibilities. In other words, the two decision rules make equivalent predictions about the expected probability of choice but differ in terms of their predictions about the variance of repeated choice judgments to the same stimulus.

The PMR predicts that the observed variability is equivalent to sampling variability, which is the variability due to having only a finite number of test trials. When averaged over the test trials, an output of .8 for the PMR in a two-alternative task predicts that the response probability should be equal to a mean of .8 with a sampling variability equal to that expected from a binomial distribution. The variance of the mean of a binomial distribution (with two outcomes) is equal to the square root of the distribution's variance.

$$\sigma^2 = \frac{pq}{N} \tag{9.10}$$

where p is the probability of one outcome, q is the probability of the other (where $q = 1 - p$), and N is the number of observations. With this prediction, we can ask if the observed variance is larger or smaller than what would be expected from binomial variability.

For the five-by-five expanded factorial design, the predicted root mean square deviation, RMSD, is determined by computing the binomial variance for each of the 35 experimental conditions, averaging those 35 values, and taking the square root.

$$\text{RMSD} = \left(\frac{\sum_{1}^{k} pq/N_k}{k} \right)^{1/2} \tag{9.11}$$

where k is the number of experimental conditions (35 in this example) and N_k is the number of observations for the kth condition. Thus, the PMR predicts that the variability of responses should be equal to the sampling variability given by equation 9.11.

The CR with noise, on the other hand, assumes that the variability of responses could be either larger or smaller than the predicted binomial variance. The only variance is due to noise in one or more of the processes because the CR itself is deterministic. Given their different predictions about response variability, a test between these theoretical alternatives is possible. If the observed variability is less than that predicted by sampling variability, we have an unambiguous victory for the CR over the PMR. We now attempt to test between the two alternatives by empirically measuring the response variability.

Measuring Response Variability

In our five-by-five expanded factorial design, we recorded six observations per session across four sessions for each of the 35 test conditions. An overall probability, p_o, for each of the 35 test conditions was set equal to the observed $P(/da/)$ averaged across all four sessions. An individual session value, p_s, was also computed for each of the four sessions by computing $P(/da/)$ for each test session. The RMSD was determined between p_o and p_s using our standard computation, described in chapter 2. To test the PMR, we asked whether this RMSD is larger than what would be expected from simple binomial sampling variance. To assess this question, we created a simulated subject yoked to a real subject. An expected p_s value for a given session was computed by random sampling of six observations, setting the p_o value equal to the real subject's observed $P(/da/)$ averaged across all four sessions. The simulation was carried out for each of the 35 test conditions for each session and for each subject. Thus, each simulated subject provided a p_s value for each session based on only sampling variability. These simulated values were used to give an expected RMSD for each session for each subject. So we ended up with observed and expected measures of RMSD for each subject. Is the observed RMSD significantly larger than the expected (based on only sampling variance)?

The logic of this analysis is actually straightforward, even though the analysis itself is somewhat tedious. We had the results from separate sessions available from the 21 English and 20 Spanish talkers (see chapter 2). The analysis computed an RMSD for each real subject and for each subject's yoked simulated subject, and a comparison between the two values was made. The observed variability was larger than the simulated variability based on just sampling variance (.0857 versus .0702). Unfortunately, these results do not resolve the issue of the CR versus the PMR. As with every attempt at elucidation, there are hidden assumptions that might actually make the waters muddier. In our case, probability matching might still have occurred even if the results indicate that the observed variability is larger than that expected from sampling variance. The actual output from the assessment stage, corresponding to the p value in equations 9.10 and 9.11, might have changed from session to session. Changes could have occurred because of adaptation, learning, fatigue, motivation, or a variety of other factors. If that were the case, the observed variability might be larger than the simulated variability even if probability matching occurred. Thus, we cannot unambiguously reject the PMR, and the issue of the PMR and the CR remains unsettled. However, the possibility of a criterion rule in the FLMP raises the question of where variability would exist, if it did exist.

Locating Variability in the Model

It would be valuable to find the location of variability in the chain of information processing. In the FLMP, we distinguish between evaluation, integration, and decision stages. Given three possible locations for variability, to locate it is no small task. We can ask, however, to what extent the integration process adds variability. We can measure the variability of the unimodal judgments relative to the variability of the bimodal judgments. A necessary claim is that integration of audible and visible speech occurs in the bimodal but not the unimodal conditions. The difference between the variability on bimodal trials and the variability on unimodal trials should therefore be informative. If there is no variability in the integration process, then the variability of bimodal trials should not be any larger than that predicted from the unimodal trials.

On the other hand, if variability is found to be larger on the bimodal trials relative to the unimodal trials, this fact does not necessarily locate the additional variability at the integration stage. The reason is that two sources of information are being evaluated and integrated on the bimodal trials, and just one source of information is being evaluated on the unimodal trials. If only evaluation contributes to the variability, then the variability on a bimodal trial should actually be equal to the sum of the variability on the two corresponding unimodal conditions. However, if there is no difference in the variability between unimodal and bimodal trials, we have evidence that integration does not add any additional variability; and in fact there may be very little variability at evaluation either, in the sense that an additional evaluation does not add to variability.

To implement this test, we must evaluate the measured variability relative to the expected, as we did in our tests in the previous section concerning the presence of variability beyond that expected from sampling variance. We repeated those analyses for the unimodal and the bimodal trials separately. The results were unambiguous: the observed variability was larger than the simulated variability in both the unimodal and the bimodal trials. If anything, the discrepancy was slightly larger for the unimodal visual condition than for the unimodal auditory and bimodal conditions. We can conclude that the integration process does not seem to add any additional variability beyond that contributed by other processes. To date, then, we have not been successful in locating variability in the FLMP. We believe, however, that trying to locate the sources of variability in the pattern recognition task should be given a high priority in research.

One of the barriers in our inquiry might be the use of a discrete categorization judgment as a dependent measure. Categorical responses do not seem to provide an ideal window into the processes involved in pattern recognition. We now describe research using rating judgments to determine whether that dependent measure can better reveal the inner workings of pattern recognition.

RATING JUDGMENTS

Notwithstanding the popularity of categorization behavior and research, there is much that could be learned by measuring and analyzing continuous rather than categorical judgments. We do not expect that a continuous rather than categorical judgment will change the underlying perceptual processes. Compared to categorical judgments, however, continuous judgments may provide a more direct measure of the observer's perceptual experience. A categorical response might even prove insensitive to the manipulation of an independent variable whereas continuous ratings would reveal significant effects of the same variable. We might call two different animals "dog" even though we see large differences between them. Categorical judgments do not literally mirror the processes or the perceptual experience underlying the report. As a graduate student, I was struck by this limitation when I was able to make undergraduates call a low tone "high" and a high tone "low" simply on the basis of the feedback they were given after each categorical judgment (Massaro, 1969). Clearly, it would have been a mistake to assume that the subjects' perception was accurately described by their categorization. We now illustrate the value of rating judgments within the context of written language.

Reading Words

The study of reading is composed almost entirely of questions about how information on the written page is combined with the reader's knowledge. Our goal is to present some new, unpublished research on reading to illustrate how rating judgments can provide a more direct measure of perceptual processing. The reason is that the response selection for ratings might not camouflage the perceptual processing as much as do categorization judgments. Consider the situation described in the earlier section "Context Effects and Backward Masking," in which a reader is asked to read lowercase letter strings with an ambiguous letter between *c* and *e*. The *c* is transformed into the *e* by extension of the horizontal bar. The letter is presented in different letter strings to give contextual support for one alternative or the other. On each trial, a test string containing a test letter was presented, and the subject's task was to rate the degree to which the test letter was *e* or *c* on a scale between 1 and 9. Subjects were instructed to make the rating on the basis of what they saw. The experiment factorially combined 7 levels of visual

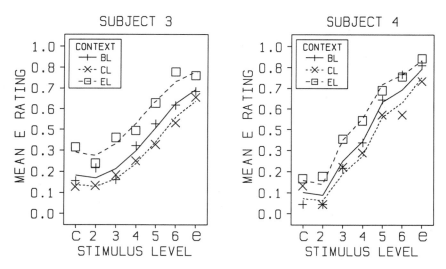

Figure 9.13 The points give the average rating judgments between e and c alternatives (on a nine-point scale linearly normalized to be between the values 0 and 1) as a function of the level of the ambiguous letter and the letter-string context. The context "BL" is neutral, "CL" is favoring c, and "EL" is favoring e. Results for two typical subjects. The lines give the predictions of the FLMP.

information (the test letter) with 3 levels of orthographic context (e-favoring, c-favoring, and neutral), giving a total of 21 experimental conditions. For the seven levels of visual information, the bar length of the letter took on seven values going from a prototypical c to a prototypical e. The test letter was presented at each of the four letter positions in each of the three contexts. The test string was presented for a short duration (30 ms) followed after some short interval by a masking stimulus (also 30 ms) composed of random letter features. Nine participants were tested for 336 experimental trials, giving a total of 16 ratings at each of the 21 test conditions.

The rating judgments made on the nine-point scale were directly normalized to be between the values 0 and 1. Thus, the rating judgment is assumed to give a direct measure of the relative degree of support for each of the two test alternatives. Figure 9.13 gives the average rating judgments for two prototypical subjects as a function of the level of the ambiguous letter and the letter-string context. The ambiguity of the test letter and the context had significant effects on rating performance. In addition, there was a significant interaction revealing that the influence of context was largest when the test letter was most ambiguous.

As described in chapter 6, the FLMP is easily formalized to predict rating judgments. In this case, the rating of e-ness is predicted to be equal to the total support for e divided by the sum of the support for both e and c.

$$R(e|L_iC_j) = \frac{l_ic_j}{[l_ic_j + (1 - l_i)(1 - c_j)]} \tag{9.12}$$

where $R(e|L_iC_j)$ is the predicted rating of e-ness for the letter-context test stimulus L_iC_j; and l_i and c_j give the support for e from the letter and from the context, respectively. To fit the model, ten free parameters (seven values of l_i and three values of c_j) were estimated to fit the average ratings of each of the nine participants individually. Figure 9.13 also gives the predictions of the FLMP for the two prototypical subjects. As the figure shows, the FLMP provides a good description of the rating results; the average RMSD across the individual fits of the nine participants was .046.

The results in figure 9.13 are usually sufficient to convince most researchers that perceivers have available continuous rather than just categorical information (Miller, 1995). The fact that the average rating judgment changes gradually with changes in the independent variables would seem to indicate that the observer's percept also changes gradually. However, we know that this cannot be sufficient evidence of continuous information because the categorization judgments can also change gradually and yet they supposedly reflect a discrete categorization. In fact, average rating judgments that vary continuously with variation in the stimulus conditions can be predicted by a model that assumes that only categorical information is available. The average rating could simply be the result of a mixture of two types of ratings generated from two different discrete percepts. The change in the mean rating is a function of the number of ratings generated from one percept or the other.

To distinguish between the availability of continuous and categorical information, we must analyze the distribution of the individual ratings (Massaro & Cohen, 1983a, 1995a). Figure 9.14 presents that analysis by plotting the proportion of ratings at each of the nine rating categories. The results cannot be explained by a mixture of ratings generated by two discrete percepts. If this were the case, there should have been a bimodal distribution of ratings in those conditions that gave an average rating somewhere in the middle of the rating scale. Consistent with previous results (Massaro & Cohen, 1983a, 1995a), the distribution of rating judgments for each test condition is more accurately described by a continuous than a categorical model.

Ratings of Bimodal Speech

We have only recently employed rating judgments in our five-by-five expanded factorial design. We replicated the design used for our database of 82 subjects (see figure 1.9 and the corresponding "Method" section in chapter 1). The only difference was that we made the syllables somewhat more ambiguous and more similar to one another. With the original continuum, subjects tended to rate the stimuli as good instances of either /ba/ or /da/ and tended not to use the middle region of the scale. The rating judgments were made on a nine-point scale between /ba/ and /da/. Subjects were instructed to

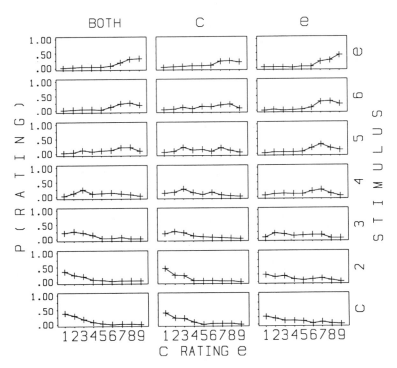

Figure 9.14 The mean proportion of rating judgments in each of the nine rating categories between the *e* and *c* alternatives as a function of the level of the ambiguous letter stimulus and the letter-string context. The context "Both" is neutral, "c" is favoring *c*, and "e" is favoring *e*.

rate visual, auditory, or visual-auditory syllables on a nine-point scale from *ba* to *da*. Your task is to indicate on this scale where you think each syllable falls between a perfect *ba* and a perfect *da*. You will make your response using only these nine buttons *ba*-1,2,3,4,5,6,7,8,*da*-9 on the top row of your keyboard. The *ba*-1 button would be used to indicate the best *ba*, and the *da*-9 button would be used to indicate the best *da*. The other seven buttons would be used to indicate intermediate degrees of the syllable between these extremes. For example, the 3 button would be used for a syllable perceived to be a fairly good *ba*, but not as good as *ba*-1 or 2. The 7 button would be used for a syllable perceived to be a fairly good *da*, but not as good as *da*-9 or 8, and so on for the other buttons. The 5 button would be used in the case of a syllable which falls exactly in the center between *ba* and *da*. The syllables that you will observe might be presented visually or auditorily, or in both senses, but your task remains the same. Simply tell us where on the nine-point scale each syllable is. You should experience a whole range of syllables between *ba* and *da*, so you should find yourself using all nine of the buttons to make your judgments.

The 35 test conditions were randomized within a trial block, and participants were tested for eight blocks of trials.

For the dependent measure, the ratings were directly normalized to be between the values 0 and 1. The average ratings were computed by averag-

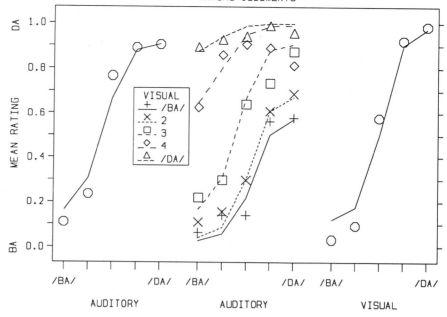

Figure 9.15 The points give the average rating judgments between /ba/ and /da/ alternatives (on a nine-point scale linearly normalized to be between the values 0 and 1) in the auditory-alone (left panel), the factorial auditory-visual (center panel), and the visual-alone (right panel) conditions as a function of the five levels of the synthetic auditory and visual speech varying between /ba/ and /da/. Results for a typical subject. The lines give the predictions of the FLMP.

ing across the eight observations at each experimental condition. Figures 9.15 and 9.16 give the average rating judgments for two subjects in the task. As can be seen in the figures, the results are qualitatively similar to the binary judgments. In general the average ratings are somewhat less extreme than the binary choice judgments. This result might reflect the fact that none of the test items were ideal /ba/ and /da/ stimuli and, therefore, subjects were reluctant to respond 1 or 9. Recall that we made the test continua more ambiguous by shrinking the differences between adjacent syllables.

Figure 9.17 gives the distribution of rating judgments via a plot of the proportion of ratings at each of the nine rating categories. The distribution cannot be explained by a mixture of ratings generated by two discrete percepts. If the ratings were mixed in such a way, there should have been a bimodal distribution of ratings in those conditions that gave an average rating somewhere in the middle of the rating scale. Figure 9.18 gives similar results for another subject on the task. Consistent with the results in the reading experiment, the distribution of rating judgments for each test condition is more accurately described by a continuous than a categorical model.

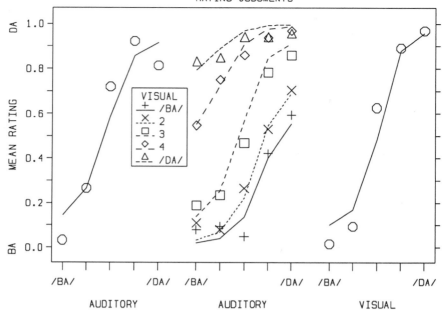

Figure 9.16 The points give the average rating judgments between /ba/ and /da/ alternatives (on a nine-point scale linearly normalized to be between the values 0 and 1) in the auditory-alone (left panel), the factorial auditory-visual (center panel), and the visual-alone (right panel) conditions as a function of the five levels of the synthetic auditory and visual speech varying between /ba/ and /da/. Results for a typical subject. The lines give the predictions of the FLMP.

Relationship between Ratings and Identification

Given that relative goodness of match mediates both the rating judgments and the categorization judgments, there should be an orderly relationship between the two types of judgments. If we assume that ratings provide a direct measure of the relative goodness of a response alternative, then we should be able to predict the categorization judgments from the rating judgments. This follows from the stage model shown in figure 9.1, in which the output of the assessment process is passed on to the response selection process. Using this logic, a strong claim of the PMR is that the average rating and the proportion of categorization judgments should be equivalent. If the expected probability of a /da/ response is .8, then the rating response should be equal to .8 when scaled linearly between the two test alternatives. According to the PMR, there is an equivalence relationship between the relative goodness, the rating, and the response probability.

The rating, R, indicating the relative goodness of match for /da/, is given by the FLMP to be

$$R(/da/) = \frac{s(/da/)}{s(/da/) + s(/ba/)} \tag{9.13}$$

VISUAL STIMULUS

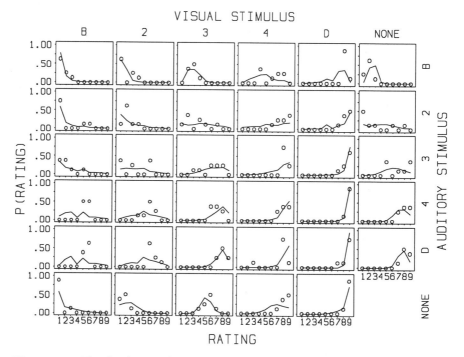

Figure 9.17 The distribution of rating judgments between /ba/ and /da/ alternatives (on a nine-point scale linearly normalized to be between the values 0 and 1) in the auditory-alone (right panels), the factorial auditory-visual (center panels), and the visual-alone (bottom panels) conditions as a function of the five levels of the synthetic auditory and visual speech varying between /ba/ and /da/. Results for the same typical subject shown in figure 9.15. The lines give the predictions of the FLMP.

where $s(*)$ is the overall goodness of match for each of the two test alternatives.

Most experiments employ only one type of judgment, and it has not been possible to test this predicted relationship between the two types of judgments. More recently, however, McDowell and Oden (1995) used these two types of judgments and provided a direct test in two experiments. Subjects were presented with words in cursive writing ambiguous between the words *eat* and *lot*. They were asked to make both binary identification judgments and relative ratings indicating where the stimuli fell on a continuum between the two words. The rating was made on a touch tablet and had a resolution of 1/639. The ratings were linearly transformed into values between 0 and 1. Separate sessions with just the two-choice response indicated that including the rating judgment did not change the results of the two-choice task.

A schematic form of the results is shown in figure 9.19, which illustrates the systematic relationship between the rating and categorization judgments. At the ends of the scales, there is a small change in the identification probability with larger changes in the rating. In the middle of the scale, just the

VISUAL STIMULUS

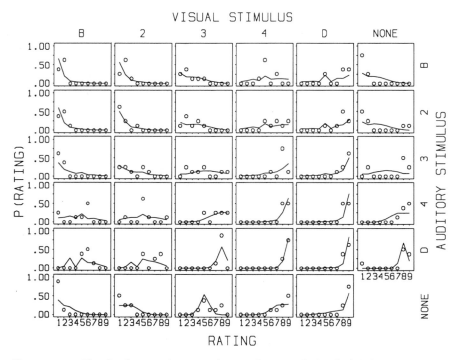

Figure 9.18 The distribution of rating judgments between /ba/ and /da/ alternatives (on a nine-point scale linearly normalized to be between the values 0 and 1) in the auditory-alone (right panels), the factorial auditory-visual (center panels), and the visual-alone (bottom panels) conditions as a function of the five levels of the synthetic auditory and visual speech varying between /ba/ and /da/. Results for the same typical subject shown in figure 9.16. The lines give the predictions of the FLMP.

opposite occurs: a larger change in identification accompanies a somewhat smaller change in rating. The form of this functional relationship makes clear that the rating judgments give higher resolution within a category. As figure 9.19 shows, changes along the test continuum have a larger influence near the endpoints for the rating task than for the categorization task. As we have seen, categorization necessarily dispenses with some information about what the subject perceives (and knows). This information tends to be preserved by the rating judgments. This observed relationship between the rating judgments and the identification judgments is very convincing and represents an important advance in our knowledge of how categorical decisions and ratings are made in a pattern recognition situation. Many authors have argued against interpreting rating judgments as an interval scale of perception (Poulton, 1989). The ratings obtained by McDowell and Oden (1995) and their systematic relationship to the categorization judgments provide strong supporting evidence for observers' ability to use an interval scale. Investigators should be encouraged, therefore, to ask for both rating and categorization judgments to double the number of dependent measures and to provide a finer-grained measure of speech perception.

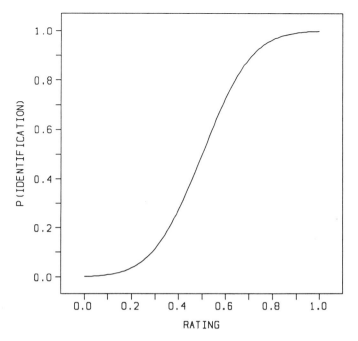

Figure 9.19 Schematic form of the observed probability of identification as a function of rating judgments (linearly scaled to be between 0 and 1).

Although we have rationalized the use of a criterion rule for the FLMP's predictions of categorization judgments, in practice, equations 9.5, 9.6, and 9.7 are used to predict the results. Given the mathematical equivalence between the PMR and the CR with logistic noise, it is simply more practical to use the closed form of these equations rather than a logistic transformation, which would be required for the CR (analogous to the z-score transformation of signal detection theory).

10 Broadening the Tests

Science, viewed as competition among theories, has an unmatched advantage ... the winner succeeds not by superior rhetoric, not by the ability to convince or dazzle ... but by the support of data.
—Herbert A. Simon, *Models of My Life*

How often things occur by the merest chance!
—Terence, *Phormio*

In the course of the previous chapters, we have developed a universal principle of perceptual cognitive performance to explain pattern recognition. We found that people are influenced by multiple sources of information in a diverse set of situations. In many cases, these sources of information are ambiguous and any particular source alone does not usually specify the appropriate interpretation. The perceiver appears to evaluate the multiple sources of information in parallel for the degree to which each supports various interpretations, integrate them together to derive the overall support for each interpretation, assess the support for each alternative based on all of the alternatives, and select the most appropriate response. Research from a variety of experiments was well fit by the implementation of our universal principle. We now explore some potential limitations concerning the tests of this principle that might compromise the conclusions we have reached about its universality. Our goal is to broaden the domain of the techniques of model testing to confirm the robustness of the FLMP account of pattern recognition.

In the present chapter we discuss the meaning of prediction in scientific inquiry. We illustrate how we fit the FLMP to results and discuss the role of free parameters and how they are estimated in the model fit. We face the challenge that experimental psychology is plagued with variability in a variety of guises. That challenge follows from the fact that behavior is not deterministic, in the sense that the same stimulus situation does not always lead to the same behavior. In our experiments, we give repeated tests of the same stimulus to estimate the likelihood of particular responses to the stimulus. Such estimation has sampling variability, which makes exact prediction more difficult. For this reason, we develop a benchmark for goodness of fit that provides a standard for determining a model's accuracy. We then examine different methods of fitting models to observed results. Finally, we consider reasons why a correct model might fail to meet the benchmark criterion.

PREDICTION IN SCIENTIFIC INQUIRY

A popular strategy in the scientific process is to take turns focusing on the doughnut and the hole. Investigators most easily focus on the doughnut, whereas their competitors or audience are often attentive to the hole (as they should be, in the spirit of falsification and strong inference; Massaro, 1987b, 1987f). Our doughnut is the good fit of the FLMP to a variety of experimental tasks. The hole has been pointed out by a variety of others but also has been confronted by ourselves; it consists in the fact that the predictions of the FLMP require some prior knowledge of what is being predicted. The need to know something about the results before prediction is possible is not new to scientific inquiry.

Nor is it new to psychological theorizing. Weber's law, discussed in chapter 4, does not claim to predict our discrimination behavior before its measurement—it states only that our sensitivity is proportional to the absolute magnitude of the stimulus (see chapter 2). This constant proportion differs for different senses and for different individuals. If a new sense were discovered, the law would not be expected to predict its constant of proportionality; the constant would be most efficiently estimated from an experiment that systematically varied the absolute magnitude of the stimulus.

We find no shortage of theoretical endeavors that have involved an interdependence between observation and prediction. The science of experimental psychology evolved in part from the early astronomers' belief that the heavens functioned in a systematic (and predictable) manner. One of their goals was to place the stars in time and location. Their log books should have revealed a consistency of measurement across different astronomers. In hindsight—with our knowledge of individual variability—we should not be surprised to learn that their results did not agree. One scientist was even fired for recording measurements that disagreed with those of his superior. These two were not the only astronomers who disagreed in their measurements; thus, very little predictive ability was achieved. It was necessary to somehow take into account the individual differences of the astronomers. Using both the log books and actual experimental studies, a scientist was able to correct each astronomer's results. It was then possible to predict when a given star would be seen in a given location when a correction was made for the particular astronomer making the observation. In this case, it was necessary to know an astronomer's previous measurements to predict some later ones.

Although historical examples are valuable and engaging, our situation bears greater similarity to that of Shepard's universal law of the generalization of behavior. The law predicts an exponential generalization function, but one that does not emerge until the stimulus values are transformed to psychological values. In the case of Shepard's law, multidimensional scaling is used to transform the stimulus space into a psychological space before the exponential law is applied. The psychological space can be determined only from prior measurements.

The FLMP predictions are fit to the individual data points from each of the subjects in an experiment. In our prototypical five-by-five expanded factorial design with two response alternatives—/ba/ and /da/, for example—there are 35 independent response probabilities, and equations are formulated to predict each of them. The predictions for the unimodal auditory and unimodal visual trials are given by equations 10.1 and 10.2, respectively.

$$P(/\text{da}/A_i) = \frac{a_i}{a_i + (1 - a_i)} = a_i \tag{10.1}$$

$$P(/\text{da}/|V_j) = \frac{v_j}{v_j + (1 - v_j)} = v_j \tag{10.2}$$

where a_i and v_j correspond to the degree of auditory and visual support for the alternative /da/.

The bimodal observations are predicted to follow equation 10.3:

$$P(/\text{da}/|A_iV_j) = \frac{a_iv_j}{a_iv_j + (1 - a_i)(1 - v_j)}. \tag{10.3}$$

The a_i and v_j values in equations 10.1–10.3 are unspecified, although they are constrained to be between 0 and 1. Using these equations with free parameters, no predictions are possible without first replacing the free parameters with actual numbers. In this case, the values must be estimated before any predictions are made. As in the application of Shepard's law, we require an analogous transformation of the stimulus space into a psychological space. The levels of the stimulus continua have to be transformed into degrees of support for the test alternatives (during the evaluation stage). We do not attempt to predict this transformation exactly. We know enough to expect that one speech stimulus along the stimulus continuum will be more /ba/-like than /da/-like, but we cannot say a priori how much more.

In practice, this requirement of having the appropriate stimulus transformation usually means that we need to know what the results of an individual are before we predict them. Stated in this manner, the requirement appears to justify the opinion of some researchers in the field that the strategy is blatantly illegitimate. Reviewers of our papers have been particularly critical of this practice: "How can you claim that you are predicting results when in fact you need the results to predict them? Wouldn't it be a more convincing state of affairs if you could predict results without first knowing the form that those results take? Why not use the parameters from one experiment to predict the results of another?"

Even if we convince our colleagues that it is necessary to obtain observations in advance to adequately test the models or principles, they might still object to our description of the resulting activity as prediction. In a more pejorative light, the determination of the predicted points might be tagged "postdiction." To split hairs, we might say that we are *predicting* the exact *form* of the results, but *postdicting* the actual quantitative *values* that make up the overall predictions. We use the term *prediction* loosely and will explore a variety of different predictive techniques. Before doing so, we consider the role of free parameters in model testing.

The Role of Free Parameters

Our method of utilizing observed results to make predictions follows in the tradition of mathematical psychology. The prototypical procedure in that field is to formulate a mathematical model and then "fit" it to some empirical data. In order to fit, however, the model must make definite (quantitative) predictions. To achieve these predictions, all of the values in the predictive equations must be known. Those values that are not known are free parameters and must thus be estimated. The estimation of the free parameters is derived from the data. For example, the well-known learning theories of the 1950s specified a function describing how performance changed with experience. A theory would give only the learning function, however. The absolute amount of performance change with a particular experience was considered to be a free parameter, and accordingly it was estimated from the data that were observed.

It might be claimed that with ten free parameters the model could predict just about anything. As with most things in life, opinions are subjective; however, we can usually provide some widely acceptable criteria by which to make an unbiased judgment. Our guiding criterion is parsimony, operationalized in terms of degrees of freedom. Clearly, estimating 35 parameters to predict the 35 data points would be unfair. On the other hand, predicting all 35 data points without any free parameters would be an achievement far beyond our reach. Ten free parameters is somewhere between 0 and 35, and, perhaps to our credit, closer to 0 than to 35. The sole justification for ten free parameters, however, is that there are ten different sources of information (five levels each of the auditory and visible speech continua). We have made the case, in chapter 2 and elsewhere, that these values cannot be predicted in advance. One could easily hypothesize functions relating the feature values to the stimulus levels, but that would represent a model of information in addition to one of information processing. For the present, we stick to the latter and estimate the values as free parameters.

Estimating Parameters

Our approach to estimating parameters is to select the values that will optimize the fit of whatever model is being tested. The goal is to have every model perform at its personal best. A variety of routines can be used to discover the parameter values that will maximize goodness of fit, including an exhaustive search of the parameter space, Newtonian methods of minimization, and even neural networks. We use the program STEPIT (Chandler, 1969), which is a highly efficient and proven method of searching the parameter space. In practice, a model is represented to the STEPIT program by a prediction equation for judgment at each experimental condition. These equations are expressed in terms of the set of unspecified parameters. Each parameter is constrained by a parameter space; in the FLMP, for example, the parameter values corresponding to the different degrees of support must necessarily fall between 0 and 1. Each parameter is also given a starting value. Needless to say, our guess at the starting values for each parameter cannot be expected to give a very good set of predictions. In practice, we actually start each value at .5, which guarantees an absolutely horrible initial prediction. The program searches for the parameter values that best reproduce the description of the observed values (i.e., an optimal result). What seems miraculous is that the program, with no knowledge of psychological theory, converges on a reasonable set of predictions. In most cases, the estimation routine finds the optimal parameter values in just a few hundred iterations.

In retrospect, this estimation routine should have sensitized us to the possibility of minimization techniques as possible candidates for learning. But here is a case in which the principle of statistical tools mutating into theories (Gigerenzer & Murray, 1987) did not rule. That is, we did not try to adopt this type of adaptive minimization (a statistical tool) as a learning model (a theory). This experience did, however, make me more skeptical of the excitement in the mid-1980s over neural networks. I questioned the many propositions that the learning algorithms in neural networks were somehow innovative and psychologically plausible (Massaro, 1988a). Neural networks converge on ideal estimates by using a local rather than a global measure of goodness of fit; in all other respects, they parallel the more traditional Newtonian methods of estimation.

The minimization program used to estimate the parameters also has to be given some standard that describes goodness of fit. Of course, we want the predicted values to come as close as possible to the observed values. Our measure of a model's goodness of fit is the root mean squared deviation (RMSD), the square root of the average squared deviation between the predicted and observed values. The RMSD is computed by (1) squaring the difference between each predicted and observed value (this makes all differences positive and also magnifies large deviations compared to small ones), (2) summing the squared differences across all conditions, (3) taking the mean of these differences, and (4) taking the square root of that mean. In equation form,

$$\text{RMSD} = \left(\frac{\sum_1^N (p - o)^2}{N} \right)^{1/2}$$

(10.4)

where p is the predicted value, o is the observed value, and N is the number of conditions. This RMSD can be thought of as a standard deviation of the differences between the 35 predicted and observed values. The RMSD would increase as the differences increase. In general, the smaller the RMSD value, the better the fit of the model.

This measure constrains STEPIT to seek a compromise by predicting each point about equally well rather than predicting some points much better than others. Squaring the deviations punishes a set of predictions in which some points are fairly well predicted and other points are very poorly predicted. Each experimental condition is given equal weight in the RMSD computation because we usually have the same number of trials for each experimental condition.

To summarize, by iteratively adjusting the parameters of the model, STEPIT minimizes the root mean squared deviation between the observed and predicted points. The STEPIT program and a tutorial on its use is available at http://mambo.ucsc.edu/psl/stepit.html. Because of the speed and ease of using STEPIT, one can be somewhat frivolous in choosing the family of models to test, the parameter space to be searched, and the starting values for the parameters. Within literally minutes after the subjects have finished testing, we can have completed tests of all of the models currently in competition. Such quick analysis stands in sharp contrast to the time-intensive tests of various extant theories implemented using neural networks and Monte Carlo simulations (Massaro & Cohen, 1991; Braida, 1991). We now describe our standard procedure of fitting models, along with several alternative procedures.

COMPUTING BENCHMARKS: SAMPLING VARIABILITY

One characterization of behavior is that it is variable: the same stimulus is identified as /da/ on some trials and as /ba/ on other trials. Given that our theories cannot predict the exact response on each trial, the next-best goal is to predict the proportion of each judgment across a series of trials. That proportion can be assumed to represent the probability of that judgment given the stimulus. Because there are necessarily a finite number of observations contributing to each data point, we cannot expect a theory to predict the proportion of judgments exactly. The reason is sampling variability: a finite sample cannot be expected to match the actual probability of an event. If we flip an unbiased coin 10 times, heads will occur on exactly 5 of the tosses with a probability of only about .246. If the same coin is flipped 11 or any odd number of times, our estimate of its underlying probability will necessarily be wrong. We can come close with very large samples, as the casinos know only too well, but in everyday practice we can only approximate the underlying probability. That is, even if there were a true predicted probability for some experimental condition and we knew what that probability was, it would be unlikely that we would observe the probability in any given experiment. Thus, the problem is to know what the sampling variability is in a given experiment; without that knowledge we do not know how close to the observations our predictions should be in order to be considered accurate.

Many readers will not be surprised by variable outcomes and the resulting ambiguity of predictive accuracy. Those growing up in the tradition of psychological science are not greatly bothered by this assumption of the variability of data. They are well aware of the elaborate statistical techniques that have been developed to account for this variability in the testing of hypotheses and models. However, such tests address primarily the statistical significance of a particular hypothesis. That is, the conclusion concerns whether or not the hypothesis can be rejected or determined to be false (J. Cohen, 1994; Loftus & McLean, 1997). With regard to model testing, however, our goal is to determine how closely a model describes the results.

As was pointed out by David Grant (1962) more than 35 years ago, with enough observations we can use statistical tests to reject any hypothesis. While I was writing this section, a graduate student (not one of mine) came by and lamented that his significance level had been .06 and the subject he had just tested had brought it up to .2. Although he had heard my sermon on the sins of statistics, they evidently took second place to a statistically significant and therefore publishable result. Most of us have been guilty of either taking more observations or testing additional subjects in order to achieve statistical significance. Similarly, some of us might have been negligent in acquiring enough data to truly test—and reject—a pet hypothesis. To overcome the limitations of the traditional statistical test, we have developed a benchmark measure of goodness of fit, which is described in the following section.

It might be observed that the use of a benchmark is also statistics, but we point out that it is a different type of statistics. Standard statistical tests usually involve a concern with the variability of the dependent measure under different experimental conditions. However, there is seldom any worry about the causes of the variability involved in the generation of the dependent variable. If probability of response is the primary dependent variable, then how it varies across experimental conditions is of central interest. The benchmark, on the other hand, is concerned with the variability behind that response probability for a given subject for a given experimental condition. Thus, this benchmark should help provide a solution to Grant's perceived limitation of statistical tests.

BENCHMARK MEASURE OF GOODNESS OF FIT

Even if a model that predicts probability of response is perfectly correct, we cannot expect it to fit results perfectly. For example, assume that the response selection process of the FLMP predicts the probability of a /da/ judgment,

P(/da/), to be .8. Given that probability, we cannot expect to be able to predict the exact judgment the subject will make on any given trial. Furthermore, because any experiment necessarily involves only a finite number of observations, we cannot expect from our prediction that the actual proportion of responses will be precisely .8. There will be some mismatch between the predicted and observed values, even if the prediction is correct. Luckily, there are methods to determine how accurate the prediction has to be to be considered correct. These involve a computation of the variability in our predictions, in terms of a benchmark RMSD. This makes transparent the pivotal role played by RMSD. We have seen how the RMSD provides a measure of the deviation of a model's predictions from a set of observed results. The benchmark RMSD gives an analogous measure of the deviation of two sets of results in repeated experiments or of the deviation of a model's predictions from simulated results generated by the model. We now discuss two techniques to compute this benchmark—a closed form equation and Monte Carlo simulation.

Closed-Form Equation

Our benchmark measures are measures of variability. For experiments with just two response outcomes, there is a computation that allows us to estimate sampling variability directly. This direct estimation is given by a closed-form equation based on binomial variance. Binomial variance is simply the expected variability for two-outcome experiments; it is a function of the probability of each outcome and the number of repeated observations. The probability of each outcome is estimated from the observed response proportions, and the number of observations is equal to the number of trials. The binomial variance must be averaged over all conditions of the experiment, and its square root is the benchmark RMSD.

As we have said, the observed variability should be equal to that expected from probability theory—binomial variability in this case with two response alternatives. It is possible to determine the expected binomial variability as a function of the observed response probabilities and the number of observations of each experimental condition. With this prediction of the expected variability we can ask whether the fit of a model is poorer than what would be expected from chance binomial variability.

The standard deviation of the mean of a binomial distribution (with two outcomes) is equal to the square root of its variance.

$$\sigma = \sqrt{\frac{pq}{N}} \tag{10.5}$$

where p is the observed probability of one outcome, q the observed probability of the other ($q = 1 - p$), and N is the number of observations.

Consider a subject from our data set of 82 subjects in the two-alternative five-by-five expanded factorial design. The benchmark RMSD is determined by computing the variance for each of the 35 experimental conditions, averaging these 35 values, and taking the square root.

$$\text{RMSD}(b) = \left(\frac{\sum\limits_{1}^{k} pq/N}{k} \right)^{1/2} \tag{10.6}$$

where k is the number of experimental conditions (35 in this example). The value for p would be the proportion of /da/ responses, q the proportion of /ba/ responses, N would be 24, and $\text{RMSD}(b)$ is defined as the benchmark RMSD. This $\text{RMSD}(b)$ value can be compared to the observed RMSD value, $\text{RMSD}(o)$, from the fit of the competing models.

Monte Carlo Simulation

We will not always have the luxury of having just two response outcomes and hence the convenience of binomial variance. However, it is also possible to compute a benchmark RMSD by simulating the experimental events, which will be necessary when a closed-form equation is not available. We therefore use this computation when there are more than two response alternatives because we know of no closed-form equations to estimate multinomial variability for three or more alternatives. Late in this chapter, we will employ these analyses in the same five-by-five expanded factorial design with eight response alternatives and in a four-by-four expanded factorial design with four or more response alternatives. It is also worthwhile to describe this technique because it provides some help in understanding the cause(s) of variability.

The Monte Carlo simulation involves creating simulated subjects for each real subject. Our simulated subject will have some probability of each response for each experimental condition that is set equal to the proportion of the same response in a real subject. For example, the probability of a /da/ response for the real subject might be .75 for a given condition. In our two-alternative task, the probability of a /ba/ response would consequently be .25. For each simulated subject, a uniform random number between 0 and 1 is drawn. If the number is less than or equal to .75, then the simulated response would be a /da/. If the number is greater than .75, then the simulated response would be a /ba/. This computation was carried out 24 times to simulate the 24 observations in the experiment. Because it uses the same number of trials, the simulation should have the same sampling variability as was present in the data set being modeled. The same procedure would be carried out for each of the 35 conditions of the experiment, resulting in a set of results for a simulated subject. Because any one simulated subject does not provide a good estimate of the variability, the procedure is used to create several simulated subjects and to average their estimates. In our analyses, we simulate 20 subjects for each real subject.

Finally, we need to determine the degree to which the simulated results deviate from the original observed response probabilities. We simply compute an RMSD between these observed probabilities and the simulated probabilities. We do this for each simulated subject and take the average RMSD across the 20 simulated subjects. This procedure produces a benchmark RMSD that can be directly compared to that subject's observed RMSD for the fit of the FLMP (or any model).

It should be noted that this procedure, as well as the closed form, can be carried out using either the actual observed probabilities or the predicted probabilities from a given model. In the closed form, the p and q values would correspond either to the observed $P(/da/)$ and $P(/ba/)$ or to the corresponding predicted values. In the Monte Carlo simulation, the sampling probabilities would be set equal to either the observed probabilities or the predicted probabilities for that subject. These benchmarks are labeled RMSD(bo) and RMSD(bp) for benchmark observed and benchmark predicted, respectively.

The Monte Carlo method offers another advantage over the closed-form method of computing benchmarks. It provides a procedure for generating a hypothetical set of results given some set of assumptions. For example, it can be used to generate a sample set of results for a subject in a specific task as though that subject has been behaving according to a given model. To give the reader a feeling for sampling variability, we took the observed results for a given subject and treated those observations as the predictions of a degenerate theory. It is degenerate because it is predicting no more than it is assuming. A new simulated subject under the same experimental conditions was generated from these predicted response probabilities. If there were no sampling variability, then the results for the simulated subject would be equal to the original results. Figure 10.1 gives the two sets of results. As can be seen in the figure, the results generated from the correct theory come close but do not exactly describe the original results. Visually, they seem to come about as close as the FLMP predictions. Thus, inexact predictions are to be expected, but we will learn that we have to determine how inexact they are.

Correcting for Free Parameters

The benchmark measures that we have developed can be at a disadvantage relative to an observed RMSD of a model fit. The reason is that fitting the model involves the setting of free parameters whereas calculating a benchmark does not. To illustrate, assume that we have a correct model for all of the observed points but one (that is, $k - 1$ points). Because we have a correct model, the RMSD(o) based on the predictions of these $k - 1$ points should be equal to the RMSD(b) for these points. What about the kth point that is not predicted correctly by the model? Assume that a free parameter is used in the model to allow this point to be predicted exactly. If the free parameter is used to predict this point exactly, and the model correctly predicts the

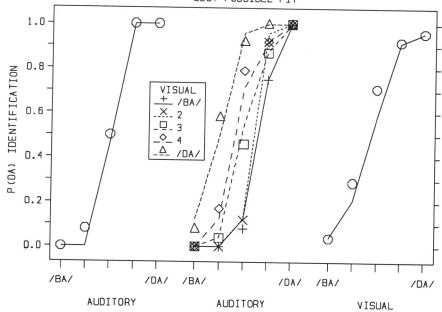

Figure 10.1 The points give the observed proportion of /da/ identifications for a typical observer in the auditory-alone (left panel), the factorial auditory-visual (center panel), and the visual-alone (right panel) conditions as a function of the five levels of the synthetic auditory and visual speech varying between /ba/ and /da/. The lines correspond to a new simulated subject generated from predicted response probabilities equal to those observed from the same subject. For obvious reasons, we call this a degenerate set of predictions.

other points without any free parameters, then the RMSD(*o*) for all of the predictions would necessarily be somewhat less than the RMSD(*b*). Extending this logic, the more free parameters there are, the smaller we can expect the RMSD(*o*) to be relative to the RMSD(*b*). If there are as many free parameters as data points, then the observed RMSD would be 0.

According to this line of argument, it is necessary to adjust the RMSD(*o*), corresponding to the fit of a given model, on the basis of the number of free parameters assumed by that model. The correction we propose is rationalized in terms of the logic of statistics. The fundamental assumption is that each free parameter could allow one data point to be perfectly predicted. Thus the corrected RMSD(*o*), RMSD(*co*), is the RMSD(*o*) adjusted upward for each free parameter,

$$\text{RMSD}(co) = \frac{k}{(k-f)} \times \text{RMSD}(o) \tag{10.7}$$

where *f* is the number of free parameters and *k* is the number of independent data points being predicted. This adjustment in the observed RMSD agrees with current thinking about the evaluation of goodness-of-fit indices. "One loses a degree of freedom for each parameter estimated" (Muliak et al., 1989, p. 438).

The reader might rightly have some reservations about this adjustment, and luckily we are not dependent on it in any critical way. In most cases, we also measure the observed RMSD against a benchmark in which no correction is necessary. In these cases, predictions of a model are generated with sampling variability and the model is refit to those predictions. We will reach the same conclusions using these two different benchmarks.

Use of the Benchmark and the Adjusted RMSD

We will use four different data sets with a total of 82 subjects to illustrate the use of the benchmark in model testing. We will then use the same data to evaluate how well the models hold up when other procedures are used to test them. The observed values come from an expanded factorial design with five levels each of audible and visible speech (Massaro et al., 1993; Massaro, Cohen & Smeele, 1995). These data are particularly valuable because a fairly large number of observations (24) were recorded under each of the 35 experimental conditions. The participants were instructed to watch and listen to the talker on the monitor and to identify the syllable presented on each trial as either /ba/ or /da/.

As we have discussed, several different types of benchmarks can be computed. First, a benchmark can be determined on the basis of the observed values or on the basis of the predicted values of a given model. The resulting two benchmarks might not be identical to one another because the observed and predicted probabilities are not necessarily equal to one another. The second option has to do with how the benchmark is computed from the observed and predicted values. Sometimes, it is possible to compute the benchmark directly, as given by equation 10.6 (the closed-form method). In other cases it is necessary to simulate the variability and then refit the model to the simulated results (the Monte Carlo method). We will provide the exact form of the calculations in the following analyses.

We begin with tests of the FLMP against the 82 individual subjects' results. The FLMP was fit to each subject's data separately and gave an average RMSD for the fit, RMSD(o), of .0509. Given ten free parameters, the corrected RMSD(co) is equal to 35/25 times .0509 or .0713 (see equation 10.7). We may compute each type of benchmark to compare with this RMSD. First, we will compute the benchmarks that are based on observed proportions, RMSD(bo). Following equations 10.5 and 10.6, we can compute a direct closed-form benchmark based on the observed proportions, RMSD(dbo). This RMSD(dbo) is equal to .0571. Or, we can simulate the variability of the observed proportions and obtain a measure of the simulated values against the observed values, RMSD(sbo). This RMSD(sbo) is equal to .0561. These two RMSDs are more or less identical (as they should be) and substantially smaller than the RMSD(co).

We can also compute these two benchmarks on the basis of the predicted rather than the observed probabilities. The direct closed-form benchmark based on the predicted proportions, RMSD(*dbp*), is .0567. The simulated benchmark for the predicted results, RMSD(*sbp*), is .0557. The near equivalence of these benchmarks indicates that the procedures appear to be fundamentally sound and should make their comparison to the observed RMSDs much easier.

For the last benchmark, RMSD(refit, *sbp*), we refit the FLMP to its original predictions after sampling variability has been added. In other words, we have the FLMP make predictions about the simulation of its own predictions. The predictions of the FLMP for each subject can be considered to be a new subject. Sampling variability is added to this new subject's results. Thus we have created a simulated subject who represents a true FLMP subject with sampling variability. This is done for 20 simulated subjects for each real subject, because a single simulation might not provide a representative measure. The FLMP is then fit to the data of each of the 20 simulated subjects by estimating new parameter values to give the best possible fit. The average of the 20 RMSDs from these 20 fits serves as RMSD(refit, *sbp*). The average across the 82 subjects gave an RMSD(*sbp*) equal to .037. Given that free parameters were used both in the fit of the real data and in the fit of the noisy predicted data, this value can be compared directly to the original RMSD(*o*) of .0509. Table 10.1 summarizes the RMSD computations (see p. 312).

A closed-form computation and a Monte Carlo form of the benchmark give similar estimates of the expected sampling variability. Very similar results are also obtained whether the sampling variability is computed from the actual observed or from the predicted response probabilities. In all of these four variations on computing the benchmark there was no refitting of the model, and therefore no free parameters were estimated. Thus, these values are at a disadvantage when compared to the observed RMSD—hence our need to upgrade the observed RMSD by equation 10.7. However, it is also possible to refit the FLMP to the simulated subjects. This benchmark RMSD is computed by estimating free parameters as in the original fit of the FLMP, and its value can be compared directly to the observed RMSD. Both in the case of the benchmarks that do not involve free parameters and in the case of the one that does, the observed RMSD is substantially larger than the benchmark. In the case without free parameters for the benchmark, the comparison is $7/5 \times .051 = .071$ versus .056. In the case with free parameters for the benchmark, the comparison is .051 versus .037. In the first case the observed RMSD was 1.27 times larger than the benchmark, whereas it was 1.39 times larger in the second. This impression is confirmed by an analysis of variance comparing the observed RMSDs to the benchmark RMSDs across the 82 participants. Thus, the FLMP does not perform as well as it conceivably could. We will address this discrepancy after we assess the rationale of our method and those of other methods of model testing.

METHODS OF MODEL FITTING

Standard Procedure: Full Fit

In our prototypical procedure, we fit the FLMP to the individual data points of a single individual and estimate the free parameters based on those points. In our expanded five-by-five factorial design, for example, we estimate ten parameters to predict 35 data points. The critical property of the standard full fit is that all 35 data points are used to estimate the parameters. Each data point has equal say about what the parameter values should be.

For the full fit, the FLMP predictions were determined for each of the 82 subjects. The fit to each subject can be considered to represent an FLMP subject. Now sampling variability is added to this subject in the manner described previously. For a given predicted point we generated a simulated observed point by sampling 24 trials using the Monte Carlo method. In this way we created a simulated subject that contained the same variability that a real subject would be expected to have if their data followed the form of the FLMP. This was done for 20 simulated subjects for each real subject.

The FLMP was then fit for the data of each of the 20 simulated subjects by estimating new parameter values to give the best possible fit. The RMSD of this fit serves as a benchmark, specifically a simulated benchmark based on the predicted proportions, RMSD(sbp). We average this expected variability or benchmark across the 20 simulated subjects to give a benchmark corresponding to each real subject, which can be directly compared to the RMSD(o) for the real subject, derived from the FLMP's predictions of the real data. The average across the 82 subjects gave an RMSD(sbp) equal to .0366. Given that free parameters were used in both the fit of the real data and the fit of the simulated predicted data, this value can be compared directly to the original RMSD(o) of .0509. Once again, we conclude that the FLMP gave a significantly poorer fit than should have been expected from a correct model. Figure 10.2 gives the predictions of the FLMP for one of the 82 subjects determined by the standard full fit. As can be seen in a comparison to figure 10.1, the FLMP fit for this subject is not quite as good as could be expected. That is, the differences between observed and predicted points are somewhat larger than the differences obtained from a degenerate model in which the predictions were assumed to be equal to the original response probabilities.

Unimodals Used to Fit Bimodals

We choose free parameters by choosing those values that maximize the goodness of fit between the model and the results. We have demonstrated the practice of maximizing fit by using all of the results, both unimodal and bimodal, in estimating the parameters. However, we have also developed model tests based on a different procedure, first used by Braida (1991), in which unimodal

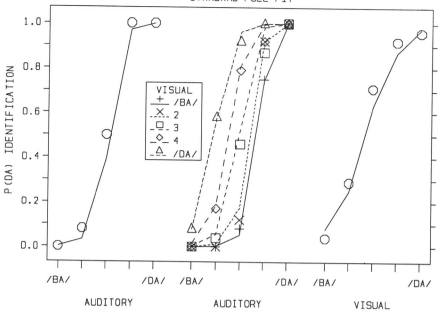

Figure 10.2 The points give the observed proportion of /da/ identifications for a typical observer in the auditory-alone (left panel), the factorial auditory-visual (center panel), and the visual-alone (right panel) conditions as a function of the five levels of the synthetic auditory and visual speech varying between /ba/ and /da/. The predicted results were determined by the standard full fit method of model testing.

conditions were used to predict bimodal conditions. As can be seen in equations 10.1 and 10.2, the predicted P(/da/) in each unimodal condition is simply equal to a free parameter, a_i or v_j. With Braida's technique, then, the observed P(/da/) is taken to be the corresponding parameter value. These values are used to predict the 25 bimodal conditions. Some investigators, such as Grant and Walden (1995), have argued that predicting the bimodal results from the unimodal observations is the only appropriate method for testing models such as the FLMP. We have argued that this is an inappropriate strategy because it is grounded in the false assumption that the unimodal results are necessarily variance-free measures of the parameter values (Massaro, Cohen & Gesi, 1993). There must be variability in the unimodal results in the same way that there is variability in the bimodal results.

Figure 10.3 gives the observed and predicted P(/da/) for our prototypical participant in the five-by-five expanded factorial design. The predicted results were determined using the unimodal observations. Given that the parameter values are set equal to the unimodal P(/da/), there is a perfect fit in the unimodal condition. As can be seen in figure 10.3, however, the fit to the bimodal results is much worse than what was obtained with the standard "full fit" procedure.

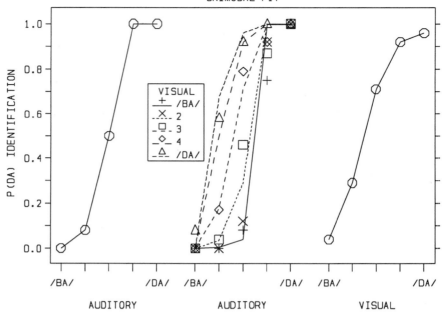

Figure 10.3 The points give the observed proportion of /da/ identifications for a typical observer in the auditory-alone (left panel), the factorial auditory-visual (center panel), and the visual-alone (right panel) conditions as a function of the five levels of the synthetic auditory and visual speech varying between /ba/ and /da/. The predicted results were determined by using the unimodal observations to predict the bimodal results.

Although we have criticized predicting bimodal results from unimodal observations because it is not optimal, it can be used as long as an appropriate benchmark is derived to evaluate goodness of fit. For the reasons outlined previously, we cannot expect the fit to be as good as the full fit in which all of the results are used to estimate the parameter values. In the full fit, we are predicting 35 data points with 10 free parameters. In the unimodal fit, we are essentially predicting 10 unimodal points exactly and 25 bimodal points with no free parameters. At first glance, these two types of fit seem comparable. The latter fit, however, is much more influenced by the variability in the results. To illustrate this difference, we derived two benchmarks corresponding to the full and unimodal fits. The benchmarks for the full fit can be derived from either the observed or the predicted results. Unfortunately, we cannot compute a benchmark for the unimodal fit on the basis of the observed data because all 35 data points are not given equal weight. The actual predictions of the model are necessary to compute the benchmark for a unimodal fit. To provide a direct comparison between the full and unimodal fits, we used the FLMP predictions to derive a benchmark in both cases. The benchmark for the full fit was described in the previous section.

For the unimodal fit, in which the unimodal results are used to predict the bimodal results, the benchmark was based on the following procedure. Recall that, in determining the benchmark for the full fit, the FLMP's predictions for a given subject are subjected to sampling variability. These simulated predictions can be expected to be what real data would look like if the FLMP were correct. In the full fit, the FLMP is refit to these simulated FLMP predictions to give the appropriate benchmark. The benchmark for the unimodal fitting procedure uses only the unimodal results to predict the bimodal outcomes. Thus, the variability at the unimodal conditions makes it difficult to make very good predictions for the bimodal conditions. To simulate a unimodal fit, we fit these simulated results with a procedure that takes into account only the fit of the unimodal data. That is, the unimodal results are used to predict the bimodal results directly. The RMSD for this fit was then considered as the benchmark for the unimodal fits. In this case, the average value of the benchmark RMSD, for the unimodal fitting procedure, is equal to .1159, which is significantly larger than the comparable benchmark RMSD for the full fit (.0561).

We may now compare the observed RMSDs to these benchmarks. The FLMP, when fit to the original observed results with the constraint that the unimodal proportions are equal to the ten parameter values, gives a much worse description of the results than does the normal full FLMP fit. The observed RMSD for the unimodal fit to the original results was .1683, which is much larger than the .0509 RMSD for the full fit. Neither of these RMSDs has to be corrected to compare to its respective benchmark because both benchmarks use free parameters. For the full fit, the observed RMSD of .0509 is significantly larger than the benchmark of .0366. For the unimodal fit, the observed RMSD of .1683 is also significantly larger than the benchmark of .1159.

Readers might be surprised that the benchmark for the unimodal fits would be so much larger than that for the full fits. The reason is that the variability inherent in the unimodal results magnifies the variance involved in predicting the bimodal conditions. To illustrate this point, we give the following example, which the reader can easily graph. Assume a theory that predicts a linear relationship between two variables. There are four points to be fit by the line. In one case, all four observed points can be used to maximize the placement of the straight line. In the other, only two of the observed points can be used. In the first case, the best placement draws a line close to all four points, whereas the best way to draw the line in the second case is to place it through the two points that are known. Clearly, the sum of the squared deviations between the four points and the line would be much less in the first case than in the second.

The same holds for more complex predictions. Assume that the audible and visible unimodal conditions have true parameter values of .7 each. However, because of sampling variability, the observed proportions of a /da/ response are observed to be .75 each. According to the FLMP algorithm, the predictions for the bimodal condition using these true parameter values should be given by $(.7 \times .7)$ divided by $(.49 + .09)$, or .84. The predictions using the unimodal conditions to predict the bimodal conditions would be $(.75 \times .75)$ divided by $(.56 + .06)$, or .90. Sampling variability might lead to an observed value of less than the predicted value of .84, say .80. In this case, the predicted value of .90 misses the mark of .80 by a large margin. If all of the conditions are used to estimate the parameters, however, the parameter values can be estimated to be less than .75, which would bring the prediction of the bimodal condition much closer. For example, the parameter values might be estimated to be .7. The RMSD would then be less for the full than for the unimodal fit. For the unimodal fit, only the bimodal condition $(.90 - .80)$ would contribute to the RMSD, which is .0577 by equation 10.4. For the full fit, the deviations are $(.7 - .75)$, $(.7 - .75)$, and $(.84 - .80)$, for an RMSD of .0469. As can be seen in this example, predicting the bimodal results from the unimodal observations magnifies the deviations between predicted and observed values. This procedure can be used, but the investigator must then compare the observed RMSD with the appropriate benchmark.

Training/Test Procedure

We have just described two model-fitting procedures, the full fit and the unimodal fit, to provide an absolute measure of the goodness of fit of a particular model. We now describe another model-fitting procedure, called the training/test procedure. The full procedure, in which we use all of the data to estimate the parameters used in the model description, is the traditional mathematical psychological technique. In computer science and artificial intelligence, on the other hand, and especially in work with neural networks, another method has been developed: the so-called training and test procedure. By this procedure, evaluation of a model usually consists of training the model on a particular set of experimental conditions and then testing the model on some new conditions. The training of the model establishes the value of the free parameters, and the testing with those parameters against new data is taken to assess the model's goodness of fit. In the spirit of broadening our inquiry, and to address our concern about the robustness of the goodness of fit of the FLMP, we explored this training/test procedure.

The training/test procedure involves training the model on some of the results and testing it on the rest. This procedure can be said to encompass the unimodal fit as a special case. Having the unimodal results predict the bimodal results is equivalent to training the model on the ten unimodal results and testing it on the remaining conditions. As we learned in the comparison of the full fit to the unimodal fit, the unimodal benchmark is necessarily much larger. We thus expect larger benchmarks for the training/test procedure also.

We explored the training/test procedure to evaluate the FLMP. We picked a mixed subset of 10 of all of the 35 conditions as training stimuli and used the remaining 25 for test stimuli. In one test, we used the 10 training conditions shown in figure 10.4. These 10 conditions were used to find the best-

Auditory	/ba/	2	3	4	/da/	None
/ba/		X				X
2	X				X	
3			X		X	
4	X					X
/da/				X		
None		X				

Figure 10.4 Expansion of a typical factorial design to include auditory and visual conditions presented alone. The five levels along the auditory and visual continua represent audible and visible speech syllables varying in equal physical steps between /ba/ and /da/. For the training/ test procedure, the 10 cells indicated by Xs are the 10 trial types used to train the model; the 25 empty cells correspond to the subset of data used to test the model. These 25 cells were also used to test the FLMP as a comparison to the fit of the same model to the 25 factorial conditions.

fitting values for our 10 free parameters in the FLMP. Those parameter values were then used to predict the remaining 25 conditions. Figure 10.5 gives the observed and predicted results for our prototypical participant in the task. The predicted results were determined by the training/test method of model testing, with 10 training trials and 25 test trials (indicated in figure 10.4). As in the other methods, the RMSD is computed from all 35 conditions. The fit of the observed results using this training/test procedure gave an RMSD of .2402. That fit is significantly worse than both the full and unimodal fits. We therefore expect that a larger benchmark will also be found for the training/ test procedure.

A benchmark for the training/test procedure was derived in the same manner as those for the other fitting procedures. We began with the FLMP predictions for a given subject and made them variable by adding sampling variability. The new simulated results were then refit by the FLMP using the same training/test procedure used in the fit of the observed results. The parameter values were estimated in the training of the ten points shown in figure 10.4. Those parameter values were used to predict the remaining 25 conditions. The RMSD for this fit was computed from all 35 conditions and was considered to be the benchmark for the training/test procedure. The

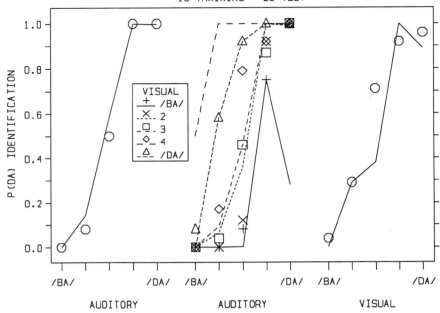

Figure 10.5 The points give the observed proportion of /da/ identifications for a typical observer in the auditory-alone (left panel), the factorial auditory-visual (center panel), and the visual-alone (right panel) conditions as a function of the five levels of the synthetic auditory and visual speech varying between /ba/ and /da/. The predicted results were determined by the training/test method of model testing, with 10 training trials and 25 test trials (indicated in figure 10.4).

average RMSD(*sbp*) was equal to .2245, which is significantly larger than the comparable benchmarks for the full fit (.0561) and for the unimodal fit (.1159).

The training/test procedure performs so much more poorly than the unimodal fit because it is not able to predict even the ten training conditions exactly. For the unimodal fit, the unimodal conditions are predicted exactly, whereas exact prediction is not possible for a sample of 10 of the 35 experimental conditions. We can make the training/test procedure give a better fit by increasing the number of training conditions. The full fit can be considered to be a degenerate training/test fit with 35 training trials and no test trials. We repeated the training/test procedure with 18 training and 17 testing conditions. The 18 training conditions are indicated in figure 10.6. In this case, the fit of the FLMP gave an RMSD(*o*) of .1252, whereas the benchmark RMSD(*sbp*) was .1067. Once again, the FLMP gave a poorer fit than what should have occurred if the model were correct. Figure 10.7 gives the observed and predicted results for our prototypical participant in the task. As can be seen in a comparison with figure 10.5, increasing the number of training trials improves the fit considerably.

Visual

Auditory	/ba/	2	3	4	/da/	None
/ba/	X		X		X	
2		X		X		X
3	X		X		X	
4		X		X		X
/da/	X		X		X	
None	X		X		X	

Figure 10.6 Expansion of a typical factorial design to include auditory and visual conditions presented alone. The five levels along the auditory and visual continua represent audible and visible speech syllables varying in equal physical steps between /ba/ and /da/. For the training/test procedure, the 18 cells indicated by Xs are the 18 trial types used to train the model; the other cells are the subset of data used to test the model.

Summary of Model-Fitting Procedures

The results of the exercise described in this section have revealed that the benchmark measure is much larger for the unimodal and training/test procedure results than for the full test procedure. The reason is very easy to understand. We know that sampling variability limits the accuracy of a model's predictions, but that variability hurts a lot more when some of the observations are assumed to have no variability. For example, when the FLMP settles on the parameter values equal to the observed unimodal observations, a small error in that estimation can be devastating for prediction of the bimodal conditions. A similar but even more problematic situation exists for the training/test procedure. Allowing the model to use all of the data to estimate the free parameters, as in the full fit procedure, attenuates the troublesome influences of sampling variability as much as possible. The more conditions that are used to estimate the free parameters, the better the fit to all of the conditions.

Comparing the full fit, the unimodal fit, and the training/test procedure shows that the evaluation of the model is more or less the same in the three cases—as long as the model is assessed relative to the appropriate benchmark. Table 10.1 gives the observed RMSDs and benchmarks for the three procedures. Understandably, the goodness of fit is much worse in the unimodal and training/test procedures than in the full procedure. However, the

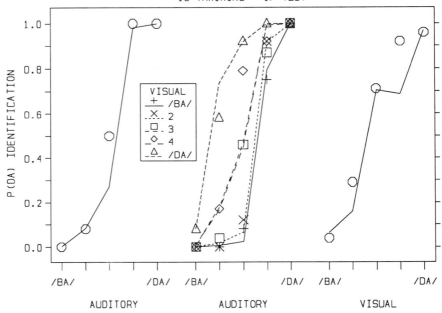

Figure 10.7 The points give the observed proportion of /da/ identifications for a typical observer in the auditory-alone (left panel), the factorial auditory-visual (center panel), and the visual-alone (right panel) conditions as a function of the five levels of the synthetic auditory and visual speech varying between /ba/ and /da/. The predicted results were determined by the training/test method of model testing, with 18 training trials (indicated in figure 10.6) and 17 test trials.

Table 10.1 RMSD values for the fit of the 35 points in the five-by-five expanded factorial design

Fit	Full	Unimodal	Train 10	Train 18
RMSD(o)	.051	.168	.240	.125
RMSD(sbp)	.037	.119	.225	.107
F(1,81)	87.89	51.57	4.72	10.71
p	<.001	<.001	.031	.002

The RMSDs are the averages across the individual fits of 82 subjects in the two-response condition. The fitting procedures (Fit) and the benchmarks are described in the text. The F statistics and probabilities compare the RMSD(o) and RMSD (sbp) results for each fitting procedure.

benchmark is also significantly larger in those procedures. Thus, the ability of the FLMP to predict the results can be considered to be roughly the same across all three fitting procedures. The benchmark standard precludes us from being misled by the absolute goodness of fit of a model because it points out that what is important is not the absolute goodness of fit of a model, but how well the model does compared to a benchmark that indicates how well we can expect an accurate model to do. The only qualification is that a very large benchmark could be a poor standard, in that an incorrect model might give an RMSD close to a very large benchmark. Thus, we have to be alert for highly variable data with very few observations or inefficient model testing. If the benchmark RMSD is too large to begin with, then it does not provide a good standard. Given its effectiveness, we hope that investigators will explore the strategy of using benchmarks in model testing. We now address the failure of the FLMP to meet its benchmarks.

MEETING BENCHMARKS

Given that the FLMP is fit to each individual's results and a benchmark is computed for each individual, an analysis of variance can be carried out comparing the observed goodness of fit to the benchmark goodness of fit. This comparison was statistically significant, indicating that the FLMP did not perform as accurately as it should have if it were indeed the correct model. There are at least two possible reasons for this discrepancy: (1) the FLMP is not correct for the expanded factorial design; or (2) the adjusted benchmark RMSD is an overly demanding measure of goodness of fit. We will explore both possibilities.

Expanded Factorial versus Factorial Design

Perhaps it is not reasonable to expect the same set of parameter values to describe both the unimodal and bimodal results. It could be the case that there is a slight loss or distortion of information in the bimodal relative to the unimodal conditions, for example. Another possibility is that the unimodal trials might not really be neutral with respect to the missing source of information. The missing visual information might be encoded as supporting one alternative more than another rather than as being completely neutral. This might be the case, for example, in the use of auditory burst and transition cues in recognizing stop consonants. A missing burst might be taken to be more representative of a labial than an alveolar stop consonant (Smits, ten Bosch & Collier, 1996).

In such a case the FLMP might still provide a good description of the results of the factorial (bimodal) conditions, even though it is not an adequate description of the expanded factorial design. To test this possibility, we carried out the model fit and benchmark analysis on data from just the 25 factorial conditions and also on data from a subset of 25 conditions from the expanded factorial design. The latter subset of 25 conditions included both unimodal and bimodal conditions; they were chosen to be directly comparable to the factorial test. The success of the model in these two situations is informative about the extent to which the model can handle unimodal and bimodal results simultaneously, as opposed to doing better with just the factorial data.

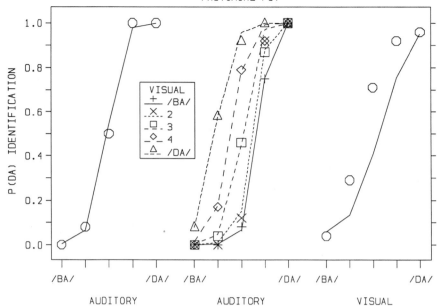

Figure 10.8 The points give the observed proportion of /da/ identifications for a typical observer in the auditory-alone (left panel), the factorial auditory-visual (center panel), and the visual-alone (right panel) conditions as a function of the five levels of the synthetic auditory and visual speech varying between /ba/ and /da/. The predicted results were determined by fitting only the 25 factorial conditions, using our standard method of model fitting.

One way to test this idea is to fit the FLMP to only the bimodal results. Figure 10.8 gives the observed and predicted results for our prototypical participant in the task. The predicted results were determined by fitting only the 25 factorial conditions using our standard method of model fitting. Although we are now fitting just 25 data points with ten parameters, we have the benchmark procedure that putatively will place the two types of fit on an equal footing. The full fit of the FLMP to the factorial design improves to an average RMSD(o) of .031 when just the bimodal results are fit. This RMSD(o) can be compared directly to the RMSD(sbp) of .029, which corresponds to a simulated benchmark based on the 25 predicted factorial proportions. In this case, there was no statistically significant difference between the goodness of fit and its corresponding benchmark.

Table 10.2 gives the RMSDs of the factorial conditions for both the full and the two training/test fits. The two training/test fits led to the same conclusion as the one obtained from the full fit. The FLMP performed as accurately as a correct model could when tested against only the factorial conditions. This result lends credence to the benchmark comparison and simultaneously highlights a possible shortcoming in the FLMP: its potential failure to provide an adequate description of the complete expanded factorial design.

Table 10.2 RMSD values for the fit of the 25 points in the factorial conditions of the five-by-five expanded factorial design (Factorial) and in a control condition (Control) of the subset of 25 points from all 35 conditions shown in figure 10.4

Fit	Full	Train 10	Train 13
Factorial			
RMSD(o)	.031	.134	.091
RMSD(sbp)	.029	.131	.094
$F(1,81)$	4.71	.22	.51
p	.031	.644	.517
Control			
RMSD(o)	.042		
RMSD(sbp)	.028		
$F(1,81)$	95.22		
p	<.001		

The RMSDs are the averages across the individual fits of 82 subjects in the two-response condition. The fitting procedures (Fit) and the benchmarks are described in the text. The F statistics and probabilities compare the RMSD(o) and RMSD(sbp) results for each model.

One doubt about this conclusion is that the difference might be due to predicting 35 data points in one case and just 25 in the other. Although both sets of predictions involve the same number of parameters, they differ in the number of predictions, and the fit may be improved by making fewer predictions. To provide an independent test of this possibility, we carried out the same test on 25 data points chosen from the expanded factorial design. If the good fit of the FLMP is simply due to predicting just 25 data points, it should fit these 25 mixed unimodal and bimodal points as well as it fit the 25 factorial conditions. The full fit of the FLMP to these 25 points gave an RMSD(o) of .042. Following our logic, a benchmark was also computed. There was a significant difference between this goodness of fit and its corresponding benchmark, RMSD(sbo) of .028. This test indicates that the FLMP does not fit the mixed subset of results as well as the benchmark criterion. Thus, the FLMP appears to have some difficulty predicting the unimodal and bimodal conditions simultaneously. We can conclude that the elegant form of the model, which assumes that the same parameter values are functional on unimodal and bimodal trials, falls somewhat short of providing a complete description.

Softening the Benchmark

The second possible explanation for why the FLMP does not perform as accurately as it should might also be correct, even though there appears to be some evidence for the first. It could still be the case that the benchmark, as currently formulated, provides an unreasonable standard for evaluating goodness of fit. This benchmark assumes that the only variability is due to sampling variability, the variability that arises from having just a finite number of trials to estimate the underlying probabilities (see the section "Computing Benchmarks" earlier in this chapter). However, there might be additional variability due to the presence of noise in the information processing involved. In the FLMP, there might be noise at evaluation, at integration, at decision, or at more than one stage. It is possible to compute new benchmark measures based on the assumption of additional noise during processing. One question is, can the addition of noise to some processing stage account for the observed RMSD being somewhat larger than the benchmark? If so, how much noise must be added to bring the fits of the model in line with the benchmark measure? Similarly, can noise salvage any of the models that were rejected in favor of the FLMP?

The Addition of Noise

Recall that we can fit the FLMP to a subject by estimating parameters to maximize its fit. These parameters can then be used to predict some probability of response for each experimental condition. This creates an FLMP subject, and to add sampling variability, a Monte Carlo simulation can be employed to create simulated subjects for this FLMP subject. For example, the probability of a /da/ response might be predicted to be .75 for a given condition. For each simulated trial, a uniform random number between 0 and 1 is drawn. For this example, if the number is less than or equal to .75, then the simulated response will be a /da/.

To accomplish the addition of noise, each stage of processing in the FLMP is specified and noise is added at some stage of processing. To explore the influence of noise, we generated simulated subjects based on the idea that noise during the FLMP processing was added (1) at feature evaluation, (2) at the outcome of integration, and (3) at the decision stage. At the evaluation stage, the auditory and/or visual information is evaluated to determine how much the alternatives /ba/ and /da/ are supported. For example, the value a_i would index the auditory support for /da/ and $(1 - a_i)$ the auditory support for /ba/. For evaluation noise, normally distributed noise was added to the output(s) of the feature value(s). On a typical simulated trial, the noisy auditory feature value, na_i would be equal to $a_i + e$, where e is the noise added on that trial. The noise had a mean of 0. In addition, the value na_i was limited to values between 0 and 1. The predicted probability of a response would follow the algorithm of the FLMP as usual, but now the feature values would include a noise component.

The standard deviation of the noise was systematically varied to determine whether noise could bring the benchmark into line with the RMSD of the fit of the FLMP to the observed results. If it could, we asked what level of noise would be necessary to bring it into line. In this analysis, the benchmark has both sampling variability and processing noise. Thus, a series of simulation trials was carried out for each experimental condition to produce a simulated subject but with noise added at a given stage of processing. These simulated data for our subject would then be fit by the FLMP to determine the RMSD for the best fit when a given amount of noise is added. This RMSD would serve as a new benchmark for a noisy FLMP.

In the first test, we assume feature noise at the evaluation stage, and we incorporate it by adding normally distributed noise to the feature values (the a_i and v_j values subsequently limited between 0 and 1) before using them directly for a decision on unimodal trials or before integrating the features together using FLMP multiplication. For noise added at evaluation, it was determined that adding noise with a standard deviation of .14 was sufficient to give a benchmark equivalent to the observed RMSD. Thus, a noisy FLMP may still be the correct model even though its RMSD is higher than a benchmark based on just sampling variance.

Similar analyses were carried out by adding noise to the integration and decision stages. For integration, the noise was added to each output of integration, that is, to the measures of total support for the /da/ and /ba/ alternatives. The benchmark RMSD with this noisy data was brought in line with the observed RMSD by assuming that there was .07 standard deviation of noise added to the total support for each alternative at the outcome of integration. For decision, the noise would be added to the ratio of the goodness of /da/ relative to the sum of the goodness of /da/ and /ba/. A standard deviation of .10 added to the output of the relative goodness was sufficient to give a benchmark equivalent to the RMSD. The smaller amount of noise at integration might be artifactual, that is, due to the fact that the integration values will tend to be reduced in range because the multiplicative combination of the two values is less than 1. The evaluation and decision values necessarily occupy the complete interval between 0 and 1.

The reader should be concerned about the addition of noise because it might seem that one could always add additional noise to bring any model in line with the observations. That is not always the case, however, as we will see in the next section. It was not possible to improve the fit of the SCM with the addition of noise. Evidently, when the model is totally wrong to begin with, no amount of noise can salvage it. Another justification for adding noise is provided when one considers where a contribution of noise might enter into the processing. As the reader might suspect by now, there could be noise from information rather than from information processing. Recall that subjects were tested for a total of 24 observations at each experimental condition across two days with two sessions of trials per day. We might expect that the feature values could have fluctuated somewhat between days, between sessions, or even within a session. Such fluctuation would have effects equivalent to adding noise at the evaluation stage. We can ask how much fluctuation in the feature values would be necessary to produce the level of noise that brings the FLMP into line with the observations. We found that noise with a standard deviation of .14 was necessary. This means that there would have to be a fairly wide variation in the feature values during the experiment. As we just noted, the presence of variability in the feature values is expected, and future work is planned to assess whether the amount of noise required by the model is reasonable.

Single Channel Model of Perception

Following our dictum of falsification and strong inference, it is also incumbent upon us to carry out the different methods of estimating parameters on other models. We chose the single channel model (SCM) of perception as an ideal model to compare because it represents so many different types of psychological models: a categorical model, a weighted averaging model, and an additive model. We found the SCM to be equally deficient under each of the different methods of estimating parameters. Thus, we can be confident that the poor showing of the SCM is not due to a particular type of parameter estimation.

The most interesting result with the SCM, however, was that its soul could not be saved no matter how much noise was added. That is, the model's predictions are inherently wrong, so that no amount of noise can bring them into line with the observed results. Adding noise drives the predicted response probabilities to .5, but it never produces the additive outcome that is predicted by the model. In all cases of noise in the FLMP, a sufficient amount of noise can bring the benchmark RMSD into line with the observed RMSD. That is not the case for the SCM. We now extend the analyses developed in this chapter to additional databases.

ADDITIONAL DATABASES

Eight-Alternative Task

Our analyses have been carried out on our database of 82 subjects in a five-by-five expanded factorial design with two response alternatives. We also composed a database from the same task but with eight response alternatives: There were 36 subjects in this database and 420 observations per subject, giving 12 observations per subject for each of the 35 test conditions. Table 10.3 gives the average observed RMSDs and their corresponding benchmarks for the different methods of model fitting. As can be seen in the table, the unimodal and training/test procedures are particularly poor methods when there are eight response alternatives. Only the standard procedure gives a reasonable fit and benchmark.

As in the two-alternative case, the FLMP fell somewhat short of the benchmark. The average RMSD for the fit of the FLMP was .051, compared to an average benchmark of .040. However, the predictions of the model could be brought into line with the addition of just the smallest amount of noise. Noise with just a .005 standard deviation brought the goodness of fit of the model into line with the benchmark. Again, the SCM gave a very poor fit:

Table 10.3 RMSD values for the fit of the 35 points in the five-by-five expanded factorial design

Fit	Full	Unimodal	Train 10	Train 18
RMSD(o)	.051	.292	.370	.206
RMSD(sbp)	.040	.268	.365	.165
F(1,35)	64.46	7.46	3.08	46.33
p	<.001	.010	.084	<.001

The RMSDs are the averages across the individual fits of 36 subjects in the eight-response condition. The fitting procedures (Fit) and the benchmarks are described in the text. The F statistics and probabilities compare the RMSD(o) and RMSD(sbp) results for each model.

Table 10.4 Average of the RMSD values for the fit of the 25 points in the factorial conditions of the five-by-five expanded factorial design (Factorial) and in a control condition (Control) of the subset of 25 points from all 35 conditions shown in figure 10.4

Fit	Full	Train 10	Train 13
Factorial			
RMSD(o)	.035	.217	.141
RMSD(sbp)	.030	.230	.147
F(1,35)	17.24	1.40	2.08
p	<.001	.244	.155
Control			
RMSD(o)	.038		
RMSD(sbp)	.031		
F(1,35)	23.46		
p	<.001		

The RMSDs are the averages across the individual fits of 36 subjects in the eight-response condition. The fitting procedures (Fit) and the benchmarks are described in the text. The F statistics and probabilities compare the RMSD(o) and RMSD(sbp) results for each model.

RMSD of .105 relative to a benchmark of .064. As in the two-alternative case, no amount of noise could bring the predictions of the SCM into line with the benchmark.

It could be the case that the FLMP falls short in predicting the results of the expanded factorial design with eight response alternatives but not those of the factorial design, as was the case with two response alternatives. To assess this possibility, we refit the results for just the 25 factorial conditions and compared that fit to a new benchmark based on the same conditions. We also included a control of 25 points from the full design, using the same 25 points that were used in the two-alternative task (see figure 10.4). Table 10.4 gives the outcomes of these analyses. The outcome of this comparison indicated that the FLMP did not appear to do any better on the factorial than on the expanded factorial conditions. Because the amount of noise required to bring the model's predictions into line with the observed results is small,

Table 10.5 RMSD values for the fit of the 35 points in the five-by-five expanded factorial design

Fit	Full	Unimodal	Train 10	Train 18
RMSD(o)	.082	.235	.302	.196
RMSD(sbp)	.049	.134	.294	.106
$F(1,25)$	40.06	47.62	0.20	27.68
p	<.001	<.001	.666	<.001

The RMSDs are the averages across the individual fits of 26 subjects in the two-response condition in the emotion task. The fitting procedures (Fit) and the benchmarks are described in the text. The F statistics and probabilities compare the RMSD(o) and RMSD(sbp) results for each model.

Table 10.6 Average of the RMSD values for the fit of the 25 points in the factorial conditions of the five-by-five expanded factorial design (Factorial) emotion recognition study and in a control condition (Control) of the subset of 25 points from all 35 conditions shown in figure 10.4

Fit	Full	Train 10	Train 13
Factorial			
RMSD(o)	.037	.157	.108
RMSD(sbp)	.035	.154	.109
$F(1,25)$	1.17	0.05	0.10
p	.290	.822	.757
Control			
RMSD(o)	.079		
RMSD(sbp)	.042		
$F(1,25)$	43.89		
p	<.001		

The F statistics and probabilities compare the RMSD(o) and RMSD(sbp) results for each model.

however, we believe that the fit of the FLMP to the eight-alternative task is acceptable.

Four-by-Four Expanded Factorial Design

We presented two four-by-four expanded factorial designs, one in speech in chapter 1 and one in emotion in chapter 8. In both cases, four alternatives were cued by the face and the voice. Thus, we can directly compare two different domains. For the speech task, the FLMP was fit to the five response alternatives /ba/, /va/, /ða/, /da/, and other. For the emotion task, the FLMP was fit to the four response alternatives "happy," "angry," "surprised," and "fearful." The average RMSD for the individual fits to the 20 subjects in the speech task was .021, which was only somewhat larger than the average benchmark RMSD of .015. For the emotion task, the average RMSD for

8 subjects was .031. The average benchmark RMSD was .027, which was not significantly different from the fit of the FLMP. Thus this task provides convincing evidence for the FLMP description of both speech perception and the perception of facial emotion.

Emotion Recognition

We postponed the assessment of the absolute goodness of fit of the FLMP to the perception of facial emotion until we had our benchmark in hand. Table 10.5 gives the average observed RMSDs and their corresponding benchmarks for the different methods of model fitting. As the table shows, the observed RMSD falls short of the benchmark for all methods of model fitting, with the exception of the Train 10 condition, in which the benchmark is very large. The average RMSD for the 26 participants in the five-by-five design with brow and mouth variables was .082. The corresponding benchmark averaged .049, which was significantly smaller than the fit of the FLMP.

Like the speech results, the predictions of the FLMP fall somewhat short of an ideal prediction for emotion recognition. We found that the predictions could be brought into line by the addition of integration noise with a standard deviation of .226. That amount of noise is almost identical to the amount needed to bring the FLMP in line for the comparable speech data.

As in the speech domain, it could be the case that the FLMP falls short in predicting the results from the expanded factorial design but not the factorial design. To assess this, we refit the results for just the 25 factorial conditions and compared that fit to a new benchmark based on the same conditions. We also included the same control of 25 points from the full design. Table 10.6 shows that the FLMP does as well as the benchmark for the factorial conditions but not for the control condition. As was found in speech, the FLMP falls somewhat short of simultaneously predicting the single-factor and factorial conditions with two response alternatives.

Summary

The analyses of our additional databases along with our main database do not provide a completely consistent picture. Sometimes, but not always, the fit of the FLMP fell somewhat short of meeting the benchmark criterion. The FLMP fit to just the factorial conditions brought the model in line with the benchmark for the speech and emotion tasks with two responses. With eight responses the FLMP fit was very close to the benchmark in both the expanded factorial and factorial fits. For the four-by-four expanded factorial design, the FLMP appeared to give a respectable account of both bimodal speech and bimodal emotion perception. Most important, when the fit of the FLMP did come up short, it could be explained by a small amount of noise added to the feature values or to the output of a processing operation. This type of account could not salvage the poor fit of the competing SCM. To conclude, this fine-grained analysis offers the potential of more stringent tests and further insights into the fundamental processes responsible for pattern recognition.

We have trekked another laborious path to measure the accuracy of our universal principle of pattern recognition. Dissatisfied with standard statistical tests, we developed a benchmark standard of model accuracy based on the fact of sampling variability. We then described various methods of model fitting, found that the FLMP remains the superior model across the different methods, and concluded that our standard full fit method provides the most sensitive test. We learned that the FLMP fell somewhat short of our strict criterion of model accuracy, but also recognized that there are unavoidable factors in experimentation that could degrade ideal performance. Armed with additional confidence in our enterprise, we turn to addressing various critiques of our paradigm.

11 Addressing Critiques

When specific publications of mine have been criticized as technically flawed, however, I have often responded.... I have never felt quite comfortable in leaving wrong mathematics unchallenged.
—Herbert A. Simon, *Models of My Life*

It is in keeping with the spirit of scientific inquiry to embrace disagreement. Scientific progress is almost synonymous with the cycle of disagreement, controversy, and resolution. I am told by my colleagues that how we handle disagreement depends on our discipline. When two physicists cannot agree, they go away worrying a lot. Two social scientists who disagree, on the other hand, both go on their merry way. As for myself, I have spent my share of time worrying. As expected, it took several seasons of experimental and theoretical work before our paradigm for inquiry attracted enough attention that it could boast both advocates and critics. We are grateful for the contributions of our competing colleagues, even though we respectfully find fault with many of their criticisms. In this chapter we describe the critiques and offer our perspective in return. The reader is promised much more than unresolved controversy, however, because this forum presents the opportunity to describe new tasks and results that further substantiate our paradigm. The difficulty of basing model tests on transformed data and traditional statistical tests is one concern. Another issue involves the uniqueness of the parameter values in the fit of the FLMP. Finally, we deal with the question of whether the FLMP fails to account for the use of novel information in speech perception. We begin with the idea that the FLMP is superpowerful and therefore not capable of falsification.

SUPERPOWER OF FLMP

Some investigators have questioned why the FLMP has been so successful at describing behavior across a broad range of different situations. We interpret this success as support for a universal principle of perceptual and cognitive functioning, whereas others have viewed the outcome as artifactual. One of the most critical claims is that the FLMP is superpowerful, or in principle capable of predicting any result. We are already highly sensitive to this possibility, and we have explored the limits of predictive power not only in the FLMP but in other models as well. I published a series of demonstrations showing that neural network models with hidden units are capable of fitting highly different response functions (Massaro, 1988b). The conclusion from these demonstrations, that neural network models with hidden units are capable of describing almost any result, was supported by a formal analysis in later work by Hornik, Stinchcombe & White (1989).

Cutting, Bruno, Brady, and Moore (1992) make the potentially devastating charge that the FLMP is superpowerful. According to their critique, the FLMP seems capable of predicting any function and even has the ability to absorb random data. The authors speculate that the advantage of the FLMP is due to nothing more than equation length. We begin with the question of whether the FLMP can absorb random noise.

Absorbing Random Noise

If, as the challengers claim, the FLMP somehow absorbs random noise better than the other models, it will have an advantage with noisier data. In chapter 10 we learned that the sampling variability inherent in a data point decreases with the number of observations contributing to that data point. Thus, the goodness of fit of any reasonably accurate model should improve with increases in the number of observations per data point. To provide an empirical test of whether the FLMP absorbs random variability and the AMP does not, we evaluated the goodness of fit of these models as a function of the number of observations per data point. We tested the models against our database of 82 subjects from the expanded factorial design with two test alternatives.

As mentioned in the description of that study, the subjects were tested in four sessions of six blocks of 35 trials in each block. We were interested in the goodness of fit of the models as a function of the number of observations per data point. Therefore, we tested the models with 6, 12, and 24 observations per data point. For each subject, there were seven sets of data. Four sets had 6 observations per data point, two sets had 12 observations, and one set had 24 observations. The sets were created by simply pooling the observations across the appropriate number of trials. The FLMP and the AMP were fit to the results. An RMSD value was determined for each subject at each of the three observation quantities. An analysis of variance was carried out on these RMSD values with number of observations and choice of model as two independent variables. The FLMP gave a significantly better fit than the AMP, and the goodness of fit of both models improved with increases in the number of observations. Figure 11.1 shows the predicted and observed results for the three conditions and the two models. As can be seen in the figure, the FLMP improved more, and its advantage increased, with increases in the number of observations. Our challengers would have to predict that, on the con-

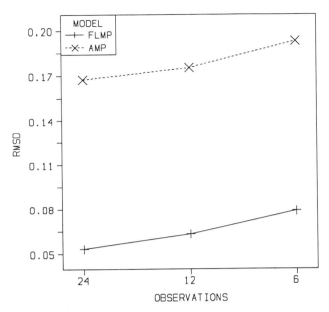

Figure 11.1 The average RMSD values of the fit of the FLMP and the AMP to results based on 24, 12, or 6 observations per condition from the 21 subjects in the Massaro et al. (1993) study.

trary, the advantage of the FLMP over the AMP should have been larger with fewer observations. The fact that it was not casts doubt on the premise that the FLMP absorbs random variability.

Fitting Random Data

Another claim is that the FLMP is good at fitting random data. Cutting and coworkers generated 1,000 sets of random data and fit them with the FLMP and AMP. The mean RMSD was .240 for the FLMP and .241 for the AMP. The FLMP showed a very slight advantage over the AMP in the model fits. Their simulations were interpreted to mean that the noisier the data, the better the FLMP fares. However, that conclusion is unjustified. Both models gave unacceptably large RMSDs for all of the sets of random data. The FLMP does not fit random data, as evidenced by the fact that the fits of the random data were about eight times poorer than the fits of real data. No model has ever given such a poor description of actual results (with optimal parameter estimation as in the present case). Thus, the simulations actually show that the FLMP is not superpowerful, because it does not give an acceptable description of random data and so cannot be said to be capable of predicting any possible result.

We replicated the findings of Cutting et al. on the fit of the models to random data in a factorial design with two factors and seven levels per factor. We questioned further whether the results would differ for an expanded factorial design. As in the Cutting et al. analysis, 1,000 random data sets were generated and were fit by the FLMP and the AMP. The FLMP gave a better fit of 527 of the 1,000 data sets. The average RMSD was only slightly smaller for the FLMP than for the AMP (.25407 versus .25463). We see no significance in this small difference relative to the RMSD values of fits to real data.

What is extremely interesting about fitting the FLMP and the AMP to random data, however, is that their RMSDs stay very close to each other even across the large range of RMSD values for the different data sets. The correlation between the fit of the FLMP and the fit of the AMP was .971, a result that appears to contradict the conclusion that the FLMP absorbs variability better than the AMP. The FLMP is offended by variability in the same way as is the AMP. Random data take on a variety of forms, and what is generally good for the FLMP is also good for the AMP and vice versa. The FLMP does not have magical powers to fit various sets of random data that cannot be fit by the AMP. Just the opposite must be the case. Very orderly data with small amounts of variability are necessary to distinguish between the FLMP and the AMP.

In much of our previous research, we have contrasted the FLMP with a weighted averaging model (AVM) or a categorical model of perception (CMP) (Massaro, 1987b, 1987f; Massaro & Cohen, 1990). (It should be noted that the "full averaging model" of Cutting et al. is *not* a weighted averaging model but an additive model with the additional constraint that the parameters corresponding to the manipulated variables sum to 1.) The AVM and the CMP are mathematically equivalent to one another and equivalent to the SCM. However, all of these models have an additional free parameter that allows a differential weighting of the two sources of information. Therefore, it should be worthwhile to fit them to random data and evaluate how they compare to the FLMP. In this case, the FLMP had the disadvantage. The SCM gave a better fit for 839 of the 1,000 sets of random data. The average RMSD was also smaller for the SCM than for the FLMP (.24757 versus .25407). Thus, the previous victories of the FLMP over the AVM, CMP, and SCM in the fit of real data cannot have been due to a magical ability of the FLMP to absorb random variability. The FLMP has been a clear winner over models that should have had the advantage according to the criteria of Cutting et al.

Fitting Different Functions

Cutting and colleagues also compared the AMP and the FLMP in terms of their ability to predict responses as a function of the number of sources of information. In their comparison, each source of information is assumed to have the same effect as every other source; therefore, the only variable of importance is the number of sources of information. They reduce the four-factor design to a plot of responses as a function of 0 through 4 sources of information. Hypothetical functions describe how the responses change with additional sources of information. The functions are assumed to be negatively accelerating, linear, or positively accelerating. The FLMP and the AMP were then fit to these results. The researchers found that the FLMP gave a better description of a majority of these functions relative to the AMP. They took this outcome as an illustration of an inherent flexibility in the FLMP that is not shared by the AMP.

We are not surprised by the outcome just described because the authors simply generated data sets that were more consistent with the FLMP than with the AMP. As noted by the authors, the AMP predicts that the change in scale values should be a linear function of the number of sources of information. Most of the functions they generated were clearly nonlinear and therefore better fit by the FLMP than the AMP. We could easily perform an analogous exercise with different functions and show an advantage for the AMP. Thus, their outcome does not show that the FLMP is superpowerful.

Massaro and Friedman (1990) had previously demonstrated that the FLMP and the AMP were distinguishable from one another (see also Cohen & Massaro, 1992). A comparison between the models requires that data generated by one model be fit by the predictions of the other model, as carried out by Massaro (1987f, 1988b). It was determined that neither model is capable of describing the results of the other model. The one exception is in the middle range of the response scale, where the predictions of the two models are not identifiably different. In the middle range, both models predict relatively additive results, so the results of the AMP in the middle range can be well described by the FLMP and vice versa. Only data that give extreme responses (close to 0 or 1) provide a strong test between the two models.

The outcome of these exercises showed that the FLMP and AMP were in principle distinguishable from one another, because data points generated by the one were not well fit by the other. The predictions of each model being thus limited, neither can be considered superpowerful. One of the limitations of these demonstrations was that the cross fitting of models was always carried out on noise-free data. Massaro and Cohen (1993b) extended these earlier exercises to use data to which variability had been added. Figures 11.2 and 11.3 give the RMSD values as a function of the number of observations per simulated data point. The figure shows that the models are clearly distinguishable from one another. It is true that the FLMP does have a little more flexibility than the AMP (see Myung & Pitt, in press). With just six observations per data point, the FLMP fit AMP data about as well as the AMP fit its own data. With more observations, however, the AMP was clearly the winner on AMP data. Even in that case, however, both models made unique predictions that were falsified by the other model's data.

Equation Length

Cutting et al. hypothesize that equation length somehow accounts for the magical ability of the FLMP to fit results. However, they must remember

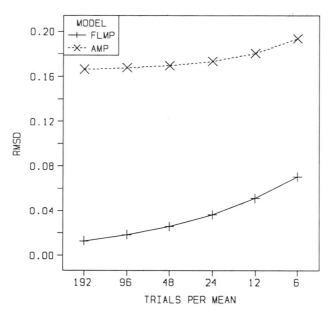

Figure 11.2 The expected average RMSD values of the fit of the FLMP and AMP to simulated results based on the predictions of the FLMP, as a function of the number of observations per data point. The predictions were generated for 1,050 hypothetical subjects based on the parameter values obtained from the fit of the FLMP results to the 21 subjects in the Massaro et al. (1993) study. Fifty hypothetical subjects were generated for each of the 21 sets of parameters.

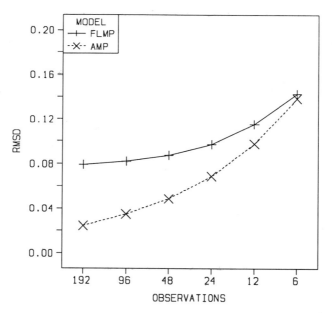

Figure 11.3 The expected average RMSD values of the fit of the FLMP and AMP to simulated results based on the predictions of the AMP, as a function of the number of observations per data point. The predictions were generated for 1,050 hypothetical subjects based on the parameter values obtained from the fit of the AMP results to the 21 subjects in the Massaro et al. (1993) study. Fifty hypothetical subjects were generated for each of the 21 sets of parameters.

that correlation does not imply causation. The curiously significant correlation between Superbowl outcomes and the economy does not imply any causal link between the two. The FLMP gives the better fit and also is the longer equation, by their count. Thus, it cannot be surprising that equation length will be correlated with goodness of fit. This does not make a case for equation length *causing* goodness of fit.

Furthermore, equation length is not necessarily even a fixed measure. The FLMP predicts additivity when the antilogistic transform of the response probabilities is taken. It is perfectly reasonable to have both models predict these transformed values. If equations of the FLMP and the AMP are now derived to predict these transformed values, the AMP will necessarily have the greater length. Hence, equation length is to some extent flexible and can have very little relevance to the issues at stake. If the investigator desires a measure of equation length for each model, then it seems fair to allow each model to choose the optimal response measure. In this case, the AMP and the FLMP would have identical equation lengths (for linear and logistic data, respectively) and a direct comparison between them would be justified.

Summary

We appreciate the concern that investigators have expressed about the possible superpower of the FLMP. Models should definitely be falsifiable, and it is important that a model as successful as the FLMP indeed be one that is capable of being rejected. We saw that the FLMP is indeed capable of failing. Similarly, in chapter 3 we saw that the FLMP fails when the auditory and visual speech fall outside of the temporal period of integration. Future work on the flexibility of models (Myung & Pitt, in press) affords the promise of a continuing increase in our understanding of the properties of psychological models of behavior. We now turn to the difficulties one faces when data are transformed before being used in model tests.

TESTING MODELS WITH TRANSFORMED DATA

Although we encourage model testing, it is a delicate endeavor, especially when it involves transformed data. In brief, transformations involve a rescaling of the data into a more meaningful or more predictable (understandable) dependent measure. A well-known transformation is the standard correction for guessing in multiple-choice tasks (Massaro, 1975a). Another, more reasonable transformation is the measure of sensitivity used in signal detection theory (Green & Swets, 1966). Sensitivity refers to how well one event or stimulus characteristic can be discriminated from another. Because they are relevant to the issues raised in this section, figure 11.4 shows transformations of a proportion of choice judgments into normal and into logistic values. As can be seen in the figure, these transformations map the proportion of choices between 0 and 1 into the complete set of real numbers. The mapping

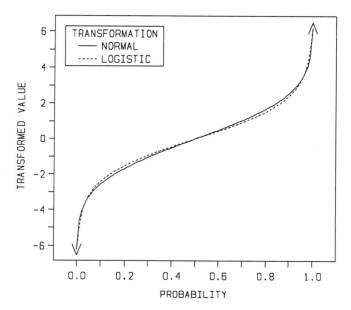

Figure 11.4 Normal and logistic transformations of probability are shown to illustrate their similar functions, which magnify the differences near 0 and 1.

is nonlinear: small differences near 0 or 1 are transformed to much larger differences on the normal and logistic scales.

Transformations carry with them a number of implicit assumptions that might not hold. The pitfalls of transforming data are revealed in a recent study by Pitt (1995). Although he collected enough observations to allow the analysis of individual subjects, his conclusions were based on the plots of data averaged across subjects and on statistical analyses of these results. Dependence on transformed data and an unquestioning application of traditional statistics led Pitt to conclude falsely that the results of his research argued against the FLMP in favor of an interactive activation framework. His transformation, to be discussed in the section "Lexical Context," is not justified for several reasons. Chief among them is that, ultimately, models must hold up when tested directly against observed behavior.

Pitt (1995) studied the joint influence of phonological information and lexical context in an experimental paradigm developed by Ganong (1980). Participants are asked to identify a segment in an auditory test item when the segment varies ambiguously between two test alternatives and the context of the segment is also systematically varied. In Pitt's task, the initial consonant segment was varied along six steps between /g/ and /k/ and the following context was either the phonemic string /Ift/ or /Is/. In this case, the context /Ift/ would bias subjects to perceive /g/ as in *gift*, and the context /Is/ would bias subjects to perceive /k/ as in *kiss*. That is the result that was observed, and Pitt's next question was whether the FLMP or the TRACE model would give the better description of the results. Pitt's analysis of that issue was derived from some earlier work of my own in which I illustrated how the TRACE model fails empirical tests. Before going into a critique of Pitt's analysis, it will be worthwhile to review that earlier examination of the model.

Test of the TRACE Model

The TRACE model is structured around the process of interactive activation. That is, it predicts that the representation over time of one source of information is modified by another source of information. Or, conceptualized within the theory of signal detection, the TRACE model predicts that the *sensitivity to* (or discrimination of) one source of information is influenced by another source. Signal detection theory distinguishes between sensitivity (d') and bias (β). The concept of sensitivity is tied to the discriminability of two different stimulus events, whereas *bias* refers to the tendency to make a particular perceptual judgment. It is claimed that the concept of interactive activation, as implemented in TRACE, should affect sensitivity.

Phonological Context   I varied a top-down and a bottom-up source of information in a speech identification task to determine whether sensitivity to the bottom-up source is modified by the top-down source. Top-down and bottom-up refer to hierarchical levels of linguistic structure. Within this framework, the question is whether the top-down context of several segments modifies the sensitivity to another segment, whether it creates a biased judgment, or both. For example, consider the following top-down effect. Subjects were asked to identify a liquid consonant in different phonological contexts (Massaro, 1989c). Each test item was a consonant cluster syllable beginning with one of the three consonants /p/, /t/, or /s/ followed by a liquid consonant ranging (in five levels) from /l/ to /r/, followed by the vowel /i/. The onset of the third formant (F_3) of the liquid was changed from high to low to create the continuum between /l/ and /r/. Thus, 15 test stimuli were created from the factorial combination of five stimulus levels with three initial-consonant contexts. Eight elementary school children were instructed listen to each test syllable and to respond whether they heard /l/ or /r/.

Figure 11.5 gives the average probability of an /r/ response as a function of the two factors. As the figure shows, both factors had a strong effect. The probability of an /r/ response increased systematically with decreases in the F_3 transition. Phonological context also had a significant effect on the judgments. Subjects responded /r/ more often given the context /t/ than given the context /p/. Similarly, there were fewer /r/ responses given the context /s/ than given the context /p/. Finally, the significant interaction reflected the fact that the phonological context effect was greatest when the information about the liquid was ambiguous.

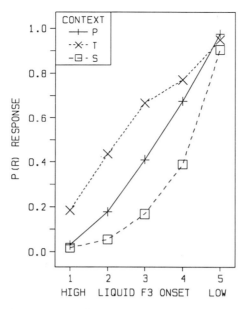

Figure 11.5 Observed probability of an /r/ response as a function of the liquid F_3 onset level and context (after Massaro, 1989c).

Subjects are influenced not only by the information specifying /l/ or /r/, but also by the initial-consonant context (Massaro & Cohen, 1983d). Without the appropriate experimental design and data analysis, however, we do not know whether this result is due to sensitivity or to bias. One technique is to provide a continuum of stimulus conditions and to analyze performance across the continuum (Braida & Durlach, 1972). Such an analysis was used successfully by Massaro (1979a) in testing for top-down sensitivity effects in written-word recognition. Sensitivity effects would be reflected in changes in the discriminability of two adjacent levels along the liquid continuum as a function of context. Bias would be reflected in a change in overall response probability as a function of context. The computation of sensitivity and bias within the framework of signal detection theory is based on the proportion of responses. To determine whether the presence of top-down connections also modifies sensitivity, the observed proportions were translated in d' values as in Braida and Durlach (1972) and Massaro (1979a). There was no systematic effect of phonological context on sensitivity as measured by d'.

Given the absence of sensitivity effects in the actual results, we ask whether they exist in the TRACE model. Because the TRACE model is formalized as a computer simulation, it cannot be tested directly against the results. It is thus necessary to simulate the experiment with TRACE and to compare the simulation with the observed results. Two simulations of TRACE were run, with and without top-down connections. If top-down activation modifies sensitivity, then we should get differences in a sensitivity measure with these two simulations. The results of the simulations were analyzed for sensitivity and bias effects. As expected, the presence of top-down connections influenced sensitivity. Context had systematic effects on sensitivity as measured by d'. Thus the simulation was consistent with the expectation that interactive activation between the word and phoneme levels in TRACE produces sensitivity changes at the phoneme level (Massaro, 1988b). Because TRACE showed sensitivity effects and human subjects did not, we have evidence against the model.

Lexical Context   Pitt carried out the same type of analysis on his observed results in the Ganong task, but he did not carry out any simulations or tests of the FLMP or TRACE. He greatly simplified the empirical question by simply asking whether changes in d' would occur with changes in lexical context. If they did, it would constitute evidence for TRACE and evidence against the FLMP. This simplification is dangerous because it fails to ask what the size of the sensitivity differences are and whether they are consistent with those predicted by TRACE and necessarily inconsistent with the predictions of the FLMP. In our earlier studies, we carried out specific tests to check on these points in addition to the d' analysis (Massaro, 1989c; Massaro & Cohen, 1991).

As you probably expect, if you do not already know, Pitt did find a sensitivity effect (in contradiction to the findings of Massaro, 1989c) and concluded in favor of TRACE and against the FLMP. Pitt placed all of his chips on the putative demonstration of a sensitivity effect. However, even assuming that this finding is valid (which I am inclined to doubt) the analysis does not adequately address what kind of sensitivity effect is found and whether any models, such as interactive activation, can predict the type that was observed. As an example, simulations of TRACE could easily be carried out to see if the same effect of sensitivity is found. Without specific tests of interactive activation models such as TRACE, even if the result were valid, we would have no idea what it means with respect to interactive models.

Model testing aside, Pitt's appraisal of the data, which led him to conclude the presence of sensitivity effects, rests on a questionable methodology grounded in the theory of signal detectability. There are many reasons this methodology might not be completely valid. The d' transformation can be dangerous because the z-score (and the logistic) blow up small differences when the proportions are close to 0 and 1 (see figure 11.4). The methodology requires a response transformation, which carries with it some unproven assumptions. On a practical level, there are usually several data points for most subjects that are 0 or 1, and these values cannot be transformed to d' values. The common solution is to make these slightly larger and smaller, respectively, so that a transformation is possible. For example, Macmillan and Creelman (1991) recommend that the 0 and 1 proportions be changed to $1/2N$ and $(2N - 1)/2N$, respectively (where N is the number of observations), before being transformed. Although such slight tampering with the data seems innocuous, it does provide a distortion even before a transformation is made.

This might be considered a minor point, but in fact, 42 of the 144 total data points in Pitt's experiment 2 were either 0 or 1. A second danger is that the d' transformation assumes that the variance is normally distributed and equal for the two types of trials. Experiments of this type don't incorporate an independent assessment of these assumptions.

For these reasons, the use of the signal detection transformation clouds the theoretical issues. It is now accepted that the signal detection story is more complicated than originally envisioned. One cannot equate d' with perception and β with response bias (see Massaro & Cowan, 1993, pp. 406–408; Massaro, 1989c, pp. 222–223). Furthermore, the use of other measures of sensitivity does not necessarily solve the previously noted problems with d'. Finally, the d' analysis of Massaro (1989c) was considered only an approximation with respect to the predictions of the FLMP, because the FLMP actually predicts no sensitivity effects when the analysis uses the logistic rather than the d' transformation (Massaro & Oden, 1995). In light of these potential pitfalls, it would be preferable to have the models predict the responses directly without any transformation. As we have seen, that procedure is the usual accepted manner of testing the FLMP and related models.

Fit of the FLMP

Given the controversy with respect to sensitivity effects, it seemed appropriate to fit Pitt's results with the FLMP. A large number of observations were recorded for each subject, providing an opportunity to test formal models against individual performance. Massaro and Oden (1995) tested the FLMP against the identification results of the 12 individual subjects in Pitt's experiment 3a. The points in figure 11.6 give the observed results for each of the 12 subjects in the task. For most of the subjects, the individual results tend to resemble the average results reported by Pitt and by earlier investigators. Ten of the 12 subjects were influenced by lexical context in the appropriate direction. Subject 1 gave an inverse context effect, and subject 7 was not influenced by context.

When producing predictions for the FLMP, it is necessary to estimate parameter values for the six levels of bottom-up information and the two lexical contexts. Thus, eight free parameters are used to predict the 12 independent probabilities of a voicing judgment: six values of s_i and two values of c_j. The lines in figure 11.6 give the predictions of the FLMP. The good description of the results is apparent in figure 11.6 and in the small RMSD between predicted and observed values. The RMSD is .017 on the average across all 12 independent fits.

Subject 1 showed a context effect in the opposite direction to the other subjects (and to reasonable expectation). The FLMP gave a very poor description of this subject's results, yielding an RMSD of .066. That poor fit is impressive because it demonstrates in another way that the FLMP is not so powerful

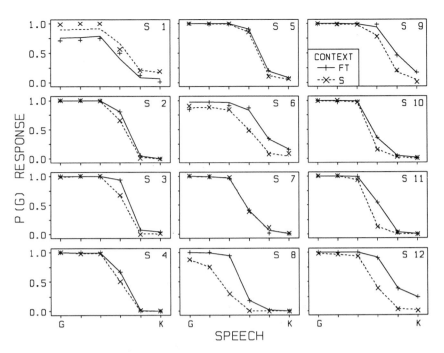

Figure 11.6 Observed (points) and predicted (lines) probability of a /g/ judgment, P(G), as a function of VOT and lexical context. The 12 panels correspond to 12 different subjects. Predictions for the FLMP.

that it can fit any possible result. The average of the 12 benchmarks for the results in figure 11.6 was .024, not significantly different from the observed RMSDs, which averaged .017. Thus, we can conclude that the FLMP described the results as accurately as could be expected of any correct model.

DIFFERENT PROCESSES FOR DIFFERENT TYPES OF CONTEXT?

Faced with the putative discrepancy between Massaro's and his results as to whether there is a sensitivity effect, Pitt tries to resolve it by pointing to two different types of linguistic context: phonological and lexical. Constraints based on phonological context, which are operant in the Massaro study, limit the possible sequencing patterns of phonemes in the language, whereas lexical constraints, relevant to Pitt's study, are dictated by what sequences of phonemes actually take place in the inventory of words. Pitt claimed that phonological constraints must necessarily operate differently from lexical context but gave no rationalization of why this should be the case. However, we have fit the FLMP successfully to the original Ganong finding of lexical context effects (Massaro & Oden, 1980b), and even to Pitt's own data. Pitt was forced into his position because he putatively found a sensitivity effect with lexical context whereas Massaro (1989c) did not. A more parsimonious position is that there was no sensitivity effect in either case.

To pursue whether the type of context might be responsible for whether sensitivity effects occur, we analyzed the results of three different experiments. All three experiments independently varied bottom-up speech information and top-down context, but the type of top-down constraint could be phonological, lexical, or syntactic. The results of the phonological context study come from Massaro & Cohen (1983d) and are similar to the results plotted in figure 11.5. The results of the lexical context study come from Ganong's original experiment, in which he created a VOT continuum between /d/ and /t/ that served as the initial consonant placed before the contexts *urf* and *irt*. The consonant /t/ makes a word in the context *urf*, whereas /d/ makes a word in the context *irt*. The results parallel the results in figure 11.6. The third set of results come from an experiment on the influence of syntactic context.

Syntactic Context

Isenberg, Walker, and Ryder (1980) created a speech continuum between the function words *the* and *to* and placed each of the test stimuli in two different sentence contexts. One context was appropriate for *the* and the other for *to*. This independent variation of the test word and sentential context allows a direct test of the FLMP.

The speech continuum was created by beginning with a natural utterance of the word *to* and attenuating the onset energy between 14 and 36 dB in steps of 2 dB. With little attenuation, the word is heard consistently as *to*; with a lot of attenuation, the word is heard as *the*. Intermediate levels of attenuation give more ambiguous percepts. The test word was placed as the initial word in one of two sentence contexts:

... go is essential.

... gold is essential.

The only difference between the sentences is whether *go* or *gold* follows the test word. Subjects were presented with the 12 versions of the test word in the two sentence contexts and were asked to identify the test words as either *the* or *to*. The appropriate syntactic constructions are *to go* and *the gold*, and the experimental question is how the sensory information and sentential context influence perceptual recognition of the test word.

Figure 11.7 gives the observed results. As expected, the probability of a *the* identification increased systematically with increases in the attenuation of the onset of the test word. Sentential context also had an effect, especially at the intermediate levels of attenuation of the test word. In terms of the FLMP, the acoustic features in the test word and the syntactic constraints given by the sentence provide independent sources of information for identification of the test word. The predictions of the model are identical in form to those it gives in the studies of phonological constraints and lexical con-

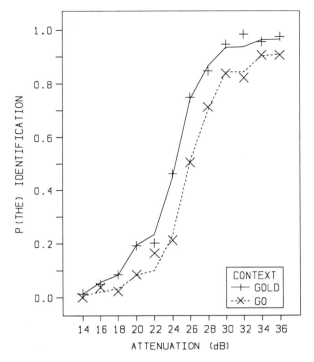

Figure 11.7 Observed (points) and predicted (lines) proportion of *the* identification as a function of the onset attenuation of the test stimulus and the sentential context (observations from Isenberg, Walker & Ryder, 1980).

straints. The model gave a good description of the results, with an RMSD of .020. The fit of the SCM was about twice as poor, with an RMSD of .041.

A Comparison of Three Types of Context

Our goal is to determine whether phonological, lexical, and syntactic context operate differently from one another. Figure 11.8 shows the results of these three analogous studies plotted on the same graph, along with the predictions of the FLMP. As can be seen in the figure, the three sets of results are fundamentally identical in form, and the form is the American football shape of the FLMP. The most parsimonious conclusion is that these results can be described by the same principles across the three domains. As a Gedanken experiment, you might envision trying to convince introductory-level students that these results really do differ from one another. All you would have to do is perform some magical transformation and look for some statistically significant difference somewhere. We would hope that even beginning students would be skeptical of such an enterprise.

Although the results are described by the same model, they contain several differences worth pursuing in future research. First, the two curves do not converge completely on the left side of the phonological context. In terms of

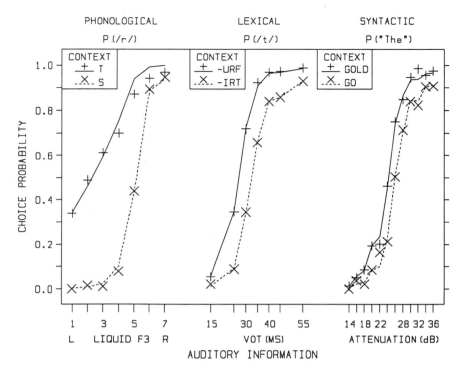

Figure 11.8 Observed (points) and predicted (lines) choice probability as a function of auditory information and three different types of top-down context. Predictions for the FLMP.

the model description, the liquid F_3 was still ambiguous enough even at the endpoint to allow a large effect of context. We expect that a more unambiguous F_3 at the /l/ end of the stimulus continuum would diminish the influence of context and result in convergence. Actually, the elementary school children showed more convergence, as can be seen in figure 11.5. More important, the size of the context effect appears to diminish with the higher-order linguistic contexts. This effect, if real, can be explained in terms of information rather than information processing. One might justifiably argue that the perceiver has more information about lower-order than about higher-order context. The algorithm combining context with bottom-up information, however, is invariant across different types of context. We end this section with a few comments on methodology.

The Downside of Statistical Hypothesis Testing

Pitt's conclusion was that lexical context produces sensitivity effects, whereas Massaro and Oden reached the opposite conclusion. I believe that this disagreement arose because of too much reliance on statistical outcomes. Considering only statistical tests, it appears that phonological constraints necessarily operate differently from lexical context because there was statistical significance in one case but not in the other. Unfortunately, statistics provides no rationalization of why this should be the case. It is necessary at least to make some attempt to estimate the magnitude of the statistical differences that are observed. Furthermore, null hypothesis testing does not demand a specific alternative. The null hypothesis for the analysis in Pitt's study was that there would be no sensitivity effect. However, no specific alternative hypothesis was specified: no prediction was made as to where sensitivity effects would be found. We know that with this kind of strategy we can always reject the null (see J. Cohen, 1994, for a damning critique of this research strategy). Thus a small effect anywhere along the continuum—which might easily be due to a type 1 error—would be taken to inappropriately reject the null hypothesis.

Null hypothesis significance testing is, in Paul Meehl's (1967) terms, "a potent but sterile intellectual rake who leaves in his merry path a long train of ravished maidens but no viable scientific offspring" (p. 265). As pointed out so convincingly by Cohen, significance testing cannot tell us the answer to the question, Given these data, what is the probability that the null hypothesis, H_0, is true? In our model testing, we formulate the null hypothesis in terms of the FLMP and show that it can accurately describe the results within the range of measurement error (as measured by our benchmark RMSDs). Therefore, it would be wrong to reject H_0. Our approach is in the spirit of Tukey's (1962, 1977) goal of understanding the set of data in hand.

Experimental Designs for Model Testing

An experiment with just two levels of lexical context is very weak for the testing of different formal models of language processing (Massaro, 1996b). It is preferable to have more symmetrical experimental designs. For example, it is possible to create more levels of the lexical context factor by varying the ambiguity of the lexical context. In the /Ift/-/Is/ study, one could also make a continuum between /Ift/ and /Is/ to create different degrees of lexical support. Admittedly, the amount of influence of lexical context is small to begin with, and the ambiguous levels would necessarily lie between those two extremes. Another possibility is to increase the ambiguity of the segmental continuum to increase the magnitude of the lexical context effect. This more symmetrical paradigm should provide a stronger test of extant models.

ADDITIONAL TEST OF INTERACTIVE ACTIVATION

We have seen that a critical prediction of interactive activation models such as TRACE is sensitivity effects. Those predictions do not hold up against many different empirical investigations (Massaro, 1989c). Given that failure, it is only reasonable to revise the model to attempt to bring it into line with the results. McClelland (1991) placed the blame for TRACE's failure on the absence of variability in the model rather than on some other process such as interactive activation. TRACE was modified by (1) making the initial processing in the model variable by adding noise, and (2) changing the RGR decision rule to a best-one-wins (BOW) rule in which the response alternative corresponding to the most active unit would always be chosen (McClelland, 1991). With these two modifications, McClelland showed that that predictions of TRACE are consistent with the experimental results and with the predictions of the FLMP. In light of this development, it is necessary to distinguish between the models in other venues. In one, Massaro and Cohen (1991) showed that the FLMP better described the time course of the influence of stimulus information and context. An interactive activation model could not accurately describe the time course of pattern recognition in a situation where the time for processing was controlled by a backward masking task (see chapter 9).

In addition to evaluating the time course of processing, another way to test the concept of interactive activation is to use rating rather than categorization judgments. According to interactive activation, there are sensitivity effects during processing *before* the BOW decision rule is introduced. The BOW decision rule nullifies any appearance of these sensitivity effects in the observed results. A rating task should provide a direct measure of the processing without having been modified by the BOW decision rule. Supposedly, subjects would not be able to use the BOW decision rule in a rating task in which they had to rate the degree to which the stimulus was one alternative or another. McDowell and Oden (1995) tested this question using the reading of test words in which two letters of the test word were manipulated independently of one another. Subjects were presented with ambiguously written words and had to make binary word judgments (*eat* or *lot*) and then give a relative rating indicating the degree to which the stimulus fell between the two words. The rating was made on a touch tablet and had a resolution of 1/639. These ratings were directly transformed to values between 0 and 1, by defining one end of the scale 0 and the other 1. Separate sessions with just the two-choice response indicated that adding the rating judgment did not change the nature of the two-choice response.

The form of the rating results was essentially identical to typical categorization results. Both have the characteristic form of the FLMP predictions. If the rating response is a direct mapping of the predecision processing, then sensitivity effects should be discernible in the results. The results should therefore be well predicted by interactive activation and poorly predicted by the FLMP. Unfortunately, there is no closed-form prediction of interactive activation to test. However, the interactive activation must claim that the predictions of the FLMP must fail because the model predicts no sensitivity effects. In fact, the results were well described by our universal principle, the FLMP. We saw similar good fits of the FLMP to rating judgments in our bimodal speech task (see figures 9.15 and 9.16). Thus we take the good fit of the FLMP to rating judgments both as evidence for this model and as a falsification of interactive activation. It is encouraging that the equivalent predictions of the two models for steady-state categorization judgments can be overcome by the use of rating judgments.

MODEL AND PARAMETER IDENTIFIABILITY

The previous exercises have convinced us that the FLMP is identifiably different from other models. It makes unique predictions and cannot predict just any type of result. Crowther, Batchelder, and Hu (1995) provide a formal analysis of the FLMP with two response alternatives (chapter 2, equation 2.17). We expand on their observations by discussing the concepts of parameter identifiability and model identifiability. We also cover expanded factorial designs, the relationship to other extant models, and evidence for the fuzzy logic interpretation of the parameters of the FLMP.

Crowther and colleagues show that a factorial design with two response alternatives estimates fuzzy truth values with properties that fail to hold under permissible rescalings. For this reason, the parameters are not identifiable. For the parameter values to be identifiable, there can be one and only one set of values to optimize the predictions of the model. In our previous writings, we used the term *identifiability* to mean that one model's predictions differ from another model's predictions. Thus, we have two types of identifiability: parameter identifiability and model identifiability. Both types are universal issues in model building and testing (Restle & Greeno, 1970; Wickens, 1982). We have always known that the fit of the FLMP to results from nonexpanded factorial designs does not give a set of unique parameter values. We never thought this to be much of a problem because STEPIT always seemed to converge on a set of meaningful parameter values that were readily interpretable. One reason for this is probably that we set the starting values at .5 in the STEPIT parameter estimation routine. For example, the parameter values tended to be consistent with other analyses, such as direct comparisons of the response proportions or the outcome of an analysis of variance. Even so, since the mid-1980s, most of our designs were expanded factorial, and for that type of design the parameters are identifiable (in the two-alternative choice task).

Although the Crowther team proved the nonidentifiability of the parameters of the FLMP in factorial experiments with two response categories, with respect to model identifiability the FLMP is identifiably different from a variety of other models (see figure 11.2; Massaro and Friedman, 1990). For example, in their equation 26, Crowther and colleagues prove that the FLMP is equivalent to a logit model without an interaction, which is distinguishable from a logit model with an interaction, and these two models necessarily make different predictions that are testable.

Other Extant Models

Crowther, Batchelder, and Hu addressed primarily the FLMP and its equivalents, although their observations are much more general. Parameter nonidentifiability exists for a variety of other models. Equivalence issues (in terms of distinguishing among models) and identifiability issues (in terms of the uniqueness of parameter values) are not unique to the FLMP but rather pervade computational modeling (Anderson, 1990; Cohen & Massaro, 1992; Massaro, 1998; Massaro & Cowan, 1993; Massaro & Friedman, 1991a, 1991b; Restle & Greeno, 1970; Wickens, 1982). Most of our analyses have focused on model identifiability, and it is of value to be alerted to the issue of parameter identifiability.

Parameter nonidentifiability in the factorial two-response design is not limited to the FLMP, but is a general problem for all models. Massaro and Friedman (1990) proved that the FLMP, Bayes' theorem, and a two-layer connectionist model make equivalent predictions for the two-factor, two-response design, along with a one-to-one mapping between their parameter values. Thus, it can be concluded that the parameter values for these other models are also not unique for the two-factor, two-response factorial design. Crowther and coworkers (p. 31) do not see parameter nonidentifiability as a problem for models that do not require the parameters to be invariant under rescaling. More generally, however, parameter identifiability would seem to be a necessary goal for psychological models, especially when the parameters serve as dependent measures (Massaro, 1975a). For example, parameter identifiability appears to be a necessary ingredient of Batchelder and Riefer's (1990) multinomial processing models. It is therefore worthwhile to prove that the two-factor, two-response design also produces parameter nonidentifiability for other extant models that are not mathematically equivalent to the FLMP. I begin with an additive model of perception.

Additive Model of Perception

The FLMP assumes a multiplicative combination of truth values representing the different sources of information. Additive models have also been proposed to explain performance in various domains of pattern recognition (Cohen & Massaro, 1992; Cutting et al., 1992; Huber & Lenz, 1993). In an additive model, the sources of information available to the participant are assumed to be added, rather than multiplied as in the FLMP. One instantiation of this model is exactly the same as the FLMP except that the truth values are added rather than multiplied. Adding the values at integration and using a relative goodness rule (RGR) at decision reduces this adding model to an averaging model (Massaro, 1987f, chap. 7). Using the notation of the Crowther team, the additive model can be written as

$$p_{ij} = \frac{(c_i + o_j)}{2}. \tag{11.1}$$

To prove that the parameter values are not unique in the two-factor, two-response design, let $c_i^* = c_i + B$, and $o_j^* = o_j - B$. In this case, equation 11.1 becomes

$$p_{ij} = \frac{(c_i^* + o_j^*)}{2} = \frac{(c_i + B + o_j - B)}{2}. \tag{11.2}$$

Because the B values cancel out, equation 11.2 reduces to equation 11.1, which shows that the parameter values are not unique.

The additive model can be made more general by allowing one factor to have more influence than the other, producing a weighted averaging model:

$$p_{ij} = wc_i + (1 - w)o_j, \tag{11.3}$$

where w is the weight given to one factor and $(1 - w)$ is the weight given to the other. The same type of proof can be used to show that the parameter values of this model are also not unique.

It should be noted that the equation 11.3 is also the mathematical form of a single channel model (SCM), in which the participant attends to information from just one modality or feature on a particular trial (Thompson & Massaro, 1989, 1994). Equation 11.3 also expresses a categorical model, in which the participant categorizes information from each feature or modality and responds with the outcome of the categorization of only one of the features with a certain probability (or bias). Thus, the parameters of these models are not unique for a two-factor, two-response design. Because of their close relationship to equation 11.2, the same lack of parameter uniqueness exists for the two other theories discussed by Massaro and Friedman (1990): the theory of signal detectability (TSD) and multidimensional scaling (MDS) (see also Cohen & Massaro, 1992).

Nonidentifiability and Number of Free Parameters

We have considered models in which parameter values are not identifiable for the two-factor, two-response design. In some cases, the same predictions can be made with a different *number* of free parameters. As demonstrated in chapter 4 and in an earlier paper (Massaro & Friedman, 1990), the FLMP is mathematically equivalent to Bayes' theorem for the two-factor, two-response paradigm. It turns out that the FLMP is capable of making the same predictions as Bayes' theorem with half the number of parameters (see chapter 4). This example and the one to follow reveals that not only are parameter values not unique, the number of parameters for a set of predictions is also not unique.

To compare the FLMP and Bayes' theorem, consider the case in which a feature is evaluated against two mutually exclusive alternatives, T_1 and T_2. According to Bayes' theorem, the support a_i of a feature for T_2 is independent of the support u_i of that same feature for T_1. It follows that an n-by-n

factorial design would require $2n + 2n$ free parameters. In the FLMP, on other hand, we use the rule for negation from fuzzy logic (Zadeh, 1965). That rule allows the support of the feature for T_2 to be defined as 1 minus its support for T_1. With just two alternatives, /ba/ and /da/, if a visual feature supports /da/ to degree c_i, then it supports alternative /ba/ to degree $(1 - c_i)$. The assumption of negation by the FLMP is an additional constraint imposed on the Bayesian formulation, and therefore the FLMP is no longer the same form as Bayes' theorem. It can be proven, however, that this constrained version of the FLMP and the general version of Bayes' theorem make the same predictions in a two-factor design with two mutually exclusive alternatives. The predictions of the FLMP can be written as

$$p_{ij} = \frac{c_i o_j}{c_i o_j + (1 - c_i)(1 - o_j)},$$ (11.4)

as also expressed in the Crowther team's equation 1. The predictions of Bayes' theorem can be expressed as

$$p_{ij} = \frac{u_i v_j}{u_i v_j + a_i b_j},$$ (11.5)

where all of the terms on the right side of equation 11.5 are conditional probabilities. The a priori probabilities are assumed to be equal and are not represented in the equation (Massaro & Friedman, 1990). A demonstration of the mathematical equivalence of the FLMP and Bayes' theorem reduces to verifying that

$$\frac{c_i o_j}{c_i o_j + (1 - c_i)(1 - o_j)} = \frac{u_i v_j}{u_i v_j + a_i b_j}$$ (11.6)

for all values of c_i, o_j, a_i, b_j, u_i, and v_j in [0,1]. Multiplying both the numerator and denominator of the left and right terms of equation 11.6 by $1/c_i o_j$ and $1/u_i v_j$, respectively, gives

$$\frac{1}{1 + \dfrac{(1 - c_i)(1 - o_j)}{(c_i)(o_j)}} = \frac{1}{1 + \dfrac{a_i b_j}{u_i v_j}}.$$ (11.7)

The equivalence of the right and left sides of equation 11.7 can be proven by simply showing the equivalence of the right-hand terms in the denominators of both sides of the equation. That is, it is sufficient to show that

$$\frac{(1 - c_i)(1 - o_j)}{(c_i)(o_j)} = \frac{a_i b_j}{u_i v_j}.$$ (11.8)

Each side of equation 11.8 can be interpreted as the multiplicative combination of two ratios (Cohen & Massaro, 1992).

$$\left(\frac{1 - c_i}{c_i}\right) \times \left(\frac{1 - o_j}{o_j}\right) = \left(\frac{a_i}{u_i}\right) \times \left(\frac{b_j}{v_j}\right).$$ (11.8a)

Given that each ratio is indexed by a single subscript, a single parameter is sufficient to specify each of the values of each of the four ratios. There is, for example, a value of c_i in [0,1] such that $(1 - c_i)/c_i$ is equal to a_i/u_i for all values of a_i and u_i in [0,1]. Thus this implementation of the FLMP gives the same predictions as those given by Bayes' theorem. This proof illustrates that even the actual number of parameters is not unique in two-factor, two-response designs. So both the number of parameters and their uniqueness are problematic in two-factor, two-response designs.

The literature contains proofs of similar equivalences for other non-expanded factorial designs. With two levels of each of four factors, for example, the full Bayes model can be expressed in nine free parameters (see Friedman et al., 1995). Eight of the parameters are necessary for the likelihoods of the two response categories and the ninth for their prior odds. However, this full model can be mimicked with five parameters (Friedman et al, 1995; Nosofsky, 1990). With this design, then, not only are the parameters not unique, the number of parameters can differ for equivalent models.

One might conclude that the parameter values, because of this nonidentifiability, cannot give a measure of factor impact—the relative influence of an independent variable on the results. With Crowther, Batchelder, and Hu's equations 11–13, however, there is now a meaningful measure of factor impact (even in two-factor experiments with two response categories). That measure gives meaningful comparisons between the respective influences of two factors. In actual fact, in nonexpanded designs we have usually used the changes in response probabilities, rather than the parameters of the FLMP, as measures of factor impact (e.g., Massaro, 1992a). Other recent studies in which parameter values have been important have all used the expanded factorial design, in which the parameters are unique (Massaro, 1987f, chap. 8; Massaro, 1994a, 1994b; Massaro & Cohen, 1990; Massaro et al., 1993; Massaro, Cohen & Smeele, 1995). I now discuss the value of expanded factorial designs.

Expanded Factorial Designs

As acknowledged by Crowther and colleagues, the nonidentifiability of the parameter values does *not* hold for expanded factorial designs, in which the single factors are also presented in isolation. To overcome model nonidentifiability is one of the reasons we have used expanded factorial designs in our research during the last decade or so (Massaro, 1987f, chapters 3 and 8; Massaro, in press; Massaro & Cohen, 1990; Massaro et al., 1993). An added benefit is that this design also allows parameter identifiability. The description given by the Crowther team for their equation 16 might give the impression that both factors of the two-factor design must be presented in a single-factor condition in order to have parameter uniqueness. However, if only one level of either of the two factors is presented alone, parameter uniqueness is insured. The proof of this assertion is justified by their corollary 1

(p. 12), where in fact only a single parameter assures parameter uniqueness. A single-factor condition can be thought of as an empirical method for uniquely setting the value of the parameter corresponding to that condition.

To overcome parameter nonidentifiability, experimenters should try to include at least one single-factor condition. In some cases, one independent variable cannot be eliminated from the stimulus whereas the other one can. With respect to variables that influence grouping in perceptual organization (Palmer, 1992), for example, the presentation of two visual objects always has some level of proximity (distance between the objects). However, the factor of a boundary (common region) can be present or absent, thus allowing proximity to be tested in a single-factor condition. Including only one of the two factors as a single-factor condition insures that the parameter values will be unique.

It is valuable to address two reservations that Crowther, Batchelder, and Hu express concerning the expanded factorial design. First, they claim that the expanded factorial design requires the assumption that the parameter values in the single-factor design must also apply in the two-factor situation. This assumption can be tested, however. As emphasized in our research, the expanded factorial design provides a much more challenging test of the contending models. A good fit of a model provides strong support for this assumption. One can test the assumption directly by evaluating the goodness of fit of the FLMP to the complete factorial design versus its fit to just the factorial conditions, as we did in chapter 10.

Secondly, Crowther and coworkers observe that it is not always feasible to present a single factor in isolation. For example, one cannot present the frequency of a tone without also presenting a particular intensity. Garner (1974) has called these "integral dimensions." In many situations, however, single-factor trials are highly feasible. In the G-Q experiment of Massaro and Hary (1986), for example, in which participants are asked to identify the stimulus as either a G or a Q, it is reasonable to present the oval and straight-line features in isolation, and in fact Townsend, Hu, and Ashby (1981) have carried out a similar manipulation with productive results. Experimental psychology is grounded in the paradigm of presenting unusual events for processing—and isolated features are no more unusual than the variety of other stimulus events found in typical studies. For example, isolated features are not really any more unusual than stimulus events containing contradictory values of two features, such as an open oval paired with an oblique straight line in the Q-G task, or—in speech—an auditory /ba/ paired with a visual /da/.

It has been shown that the expanded factorial design insures the identifiability of parameters in addition to providing a strong test of multifeatural processing. A further property of parameter values in the FLMP toward which Crowther and colleagues express reservations is their interpretation as fuzzy logical truth values. In the next section we take advantage of those reservations to provide evidence for the psychological reality of fuzzy logic.

Crowther, Batchelder, and Hu have reservations about the usefulness of fuzzy logical interpretation even if the FLMP provides a good fit to data from an expanded factorial design. They are not comfortable interpreting the "observable proportions as scale-invariant fuzzy logic truth values" (p. 22). To address this skepticism, I will now present some evidence for the logical operations assumed by fuzzy logic.

The authors rightly expect empirical evidence for the specific operations assumed by fuzzy logic. I agree with their goal to "encourage more work designed to uncover the underlying processing events that give rise to the success of the equation in fitting data from classification tasks" (p. 36). I describe one empirical and one logical source of evidence in support of fuzzy logic as a psychologically real medium of processing. Oden (1977b) accumulated some early evidence for the fuzzy logic rules for conjunction and disjunction. Subjects were given pairs of statements and asked to rate the truth of the statement that both statements were true on a continuous line scale between false and true. To test for disjunction, the same subjects were asked to rate the truth of the statement that either of the statements was true. The results for both tasks were consistent with the fuzzy logic predictions. Like Oden, we will use both conjunction and disjunction tasks, but ours are in the domain of bimodal speech processing.

Same-Different Task

In the Massaro and Ferguson (1993) study, participants performed both a perceptual identification task and a same-different discrimination task. There were three levels of visual speech (/ba/, neutral, /da/) and two levels of auditory speech (/ba/, /da/). This design gives $2 \times 3 = 6$ unique bimodal syllables for the identification task. In the identification task, participants identified the syllables as /ba/ or /da/. For the same-different discrimination task, two of the bimodal syllables were presented successively, and the task was to indicate whether the two syllables differed on either the auditory or visual channels. There were 20 types of discrimination trials: 6 "same" trials, 6 trials with auditory different, 4 trials with visual different, and 4 trials with both auditory and visual different.

Band 11.1 illustrates the same-different task. Pairs of syllables are presented. Simply watch and listen and determine whether either the audible or visible speech differed for a given pair. It is also possible to identify each syllable for the identification task. Syllables that are identified equivalently can still be distinguished from one another.

FLMP Predictions

The predictions of the FLMP were derived for both tasks, and the observed results of both tasks were described with the same set of parameter values. The predictions for the identification task were derived in the standard manner. At the evaluation stage, truth values (of fuzzy logic) are assigned to the auditory and visual sources of information, indicating the degree of support for each of the response alternatives /ba/ and /da/. The truth values lie between 0 and 1, with 0 being no support, 1 being full support, and .5 being completely ambiguous. The degree of auditory support for the alternative /da/ can be represented by a_i, and the degree of visual support for /da/ by v_j. With just two alternatives /ba/ and /da/, if the visual feature supports /da/ to degree v_j, then it supports the alternative /ba/ to degree $(1 - v_j)$, and the same is true for the auditory feature (Massaro, 1987f). Integration computes the overall support for each alternative. It follows that the overall support for alternative /da/, $s(/da/)$, is given by

$$s(/da/) = a_i v_j.$$
(11.9)

Analogously, the support for /ba/, $s(/ba/)$ is equal to

$$s(/ba/) = (1 - a_i)(1 - v_j).$$
(11.10)

The decision operation in the identification task determines the support for the /da/ alternative relative to the sum of support for each of the /ba/ and /da/ alternatives, and translates relative support into a probability. The probability of a /da/ judgment, $P(/da/)$, is thus equal to

$$P(/da/) = \frac{a_i v_j}{a_i v_j + (1 - a_i)(1 - v_j)}.$$
(11.11)

Given the FLMP's prediction for the identification task, its prediction for a same-different task can be derived. Participants are instructed to respond "different" if a difference is perceived along either or both modalities. Within the framework of fuzzy logic, this discrimination task is a disjunction task. The perceived difference, d_v, between two levels j and $j + 1$ of the visual factor is given by the difference in their truth values assigned at the evaluation stage:

$$d_v = v_j - v_{j+1}.$$
(11.12)

Analogously, the perceived difference, d_a, between two levels of the auditory factor is

$$d_a = a_i - a_{i+1}.$$
(11.13)

Given two bimodal speech syllables, the difference, d_{va}, between them can be derived from the assumption of a multiplicative conjunction rule for integration in combination with DeMorgan's law (Enderton, 1972).

$$d_{va} = d_v + d_a - d_v d_a.$$
(11.14)

It is also assumed that the participant computes the degree of sameness from the degree of difference, using the fuzzy logic definition of negation. In this case, the degree of sameness, s_{va}, is equal to

$$s_{va} = 1 - d_{va}.$$
(11.15)

The participant is required to select a "same" or "different" response in the discrimination task. The actual "same" or "different" response is derived from the relative goodness rule used at the decision operation. The probability of a "different" response, $P(\text{diff})$, is thus equal to

$$P(\text{diff}) = \frac{d_{va}}{d_{va} + s_{va}} = d_{va}, \tag{11.16}$$

where d_{va} is given by equation 11.14 and s_{va} by equation 11.15.

The joint identification-discrimination paradigm also overcomes the parameter nonidentifiability in the factorial design. A straightforward proof can be seen in the predictions when the two syllables differ on just a single modality. Consider two adjacent levels along the visual factor, for example. In this case, the predicted proportion of "different" judgments is equal to the difference in the fuzzy logic truth values that are used to predict the identification judgment. Thus, the discrimination task appears to provide the same type of constraint on the parameter values as does the expanded factorial design.

In the identification task, the probability of a /da/ identification varied systematically with the auditory and visual levels. When paired with an auditory /ba/, $P(/\text{da}/)$ for the visual /ba/, neutral, and /da/ was equal to .01, .11, and .50, respectively. These same visual conditions gave .63, .97, and .99 when paired with an auditory /da/.

The predictions of the FLMP were determined for both the identification and discrimination tasks. There were 6 unique syllables in the identification task, and there were 14 types of different trials and 6 types of same trials in the discrimination task. These 26 independent observations were predicted with just five free parameters, corresponding to the three levels of the visual factor and the two levels of the auditory factor. The simultaneous prediction of identification and discrimination with the same set of free parameters insures parameter identifiability, even when only the factorial conditions are tested. Values of the five parameters were estimated to give the optimal predictions of the observed results, with the goodness of fit based on the RMSD between predicted and observed values. The model was fit to the average results (pooled across the 20 participants). The best fit of the FLMP to the average results gave an RMSD of .081, a good fit considering that 26 data points are being predicted with just five free parameters. Figure 11.9 plots the observed versus the predicted outcomes of the FLMP for those 26 observations.

As we have noted, the application of the FLMP to the results carries the assumption that the output of the evaluation stage is identical in both the identification and discrimination tasks. This assumption captures the proposal that integration of the audible and visible sources does not modify or eliminate the representations of them given by the feature evaluation stage. If it did, then the model could not have accurately predicted the results with the same parameter values for identification and discrimination. According to the application of the model, the only difference between the two tasks is how

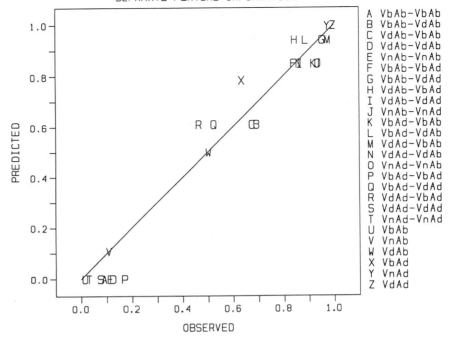

Figure 11.9 Observed and predicted probability of a /da/ identification in the identification task and the observed and predicted probability of a different judgment in the discrimination task, as a function of the different test events. The points are given by letters: the letters A through T give the discrimination performance; the letters U through Z give identification. The conditions are listed to the right of the graph. For example, A corresponds to a visual /ba/ auditory /ba/ followed by a visual /ba/ auditory /ba/. Predictions are of the FLMP, which assumes maintenance of separate auditory and visual feature information beyond the evaluation stage.

the truth values provided by evaluation are combined. They are conjoined in the identification task and disjoined in the discrimination task.

Holistic Model Prediction

To further test the assumption that the feature values produced by evaluation are maintained throughout integration and decision, we formulated an alternative model carrying the opposite assumption and tested it against the same data. That model assumes that auditory and visual sources are blended into a single representation, and there is no separate access to the auditory and visual representations. According to this holistic model, the only representation that remains after a bimodal syllable is presented is the overall degree of support for the response alternatives. What is important for this model is the overall degree of support for /da/, independent of how much the auditory and visual modalities contributed to that support. According to both the FLMP and the holistic model, it is possible to have two bimodal

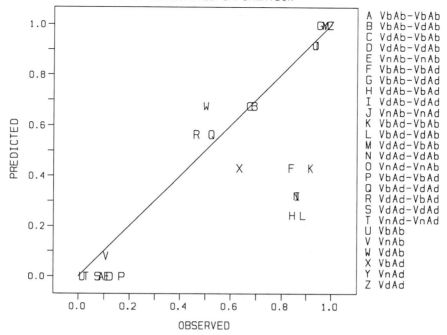

ONLY INTEGRATED INFORMATION

A	VbAb–VbAb
B	VbAb–VdAb
C	VdAb–VbAb
D	VdAb–VdAb
E	VnAb–VnAb
F	VbAb–VbAd
G	VbAb–VdAd
H	VdAb–VbAd
I	VdAb–VdAd
J	VnAb–VnAd
K	VbAd–VbAb
L	VbAd–VdAb
M	VdAd–VbAb
N	VdAd–VdAb
O	VnAd–VnAb
P	VbAd–VbAd
Q	VbAd–VdAd
R	VdAd–VbAd
S	VdAd–VdAd
T	VnAd–VnAd
U	VbAb
V	VnAb
W	VdAb
X	VbAd
Y	VnAd
Z	VdAd

Figure 11.10 Observed and predicted probability of a /da/ identification in the identification task and the observed and predicted probability of a different judgment in the discrimination task, as a function of the different test events. The points are given by letters: the letters A through T give the discrimination performance; the letters U through Z give identification. The conditions are listed to the right of the graph. For example, A corresponds to a visual /ba/ auditory /ba/ followed by a visual /ba/ auditory /ba/. Predictions are of the holistic model, which assumes no maintenance of separate auditory and visual feature information.

syllables that are made up of different auditory and visual components but give the same overall degree of support for /da/. For example, a visual /ba/ paired with an auditory /da/ might give a similar degree of overall support for /da/ as an auditory /ba/ paired with a visual /da/. The FLMP predicts that those two bimodal syllables could be discriminated from one another. On the other hand, the holistic model predicts that only the output of integration is available, therefore the two different bimodal syllables could not be discriminated from one another. Figure 11.10 plots the observed versus the predicted outcomes for the holistic model for these 26 observations. When formulated, the holistic model gave a significantly poorer ($p < .001$) description of the results, with an RMSD of .176.

The results shown in figure 11.10 substantiate the claim that information from evaluation maintains its integrity and can be used independently of the output of integration and decision. Thus, it is inappropriate to believe that perceivers are limited to the output of integration and decision. Perceivers can also use information at the level of evaluation when appropriate. A related result consistent with this conclusion is the observed difference between the ability to detect temporal asynchrony between auditory and visual speech and the interval over which integration occurs. An observer can detect asynchrony at relatively short asynchronies, whereas integration can occur across much longer asynchronies (Massaro & Cohen, 1993a; Massaro, Cohen & Smeele, 1996; see also chapter 3).

From the results of the identification-discrimination task, it appears that observers maintain access to information gained at evaluation even though integration has occurred. Furthermore, the integration process does not modify the representation that corresponds to evaluation. Based on a perceptual identification judgment that reflects the influence of both audible and visible speech, it is often concluded that a new representation has somehow supplanted the separate auditory and visual codes. However, we learned that we can tap into those separate codes with the appropriate type of psychophysical task. This result is similar to the finding that observers can report the degree to which a syllable was represented by a given stimulus even though they categorically labeled it as one syllable or another (Massaro, 1987f). If we grant that integration of audible and visible speech produces a new representation, then we see that multiple representations can be held in parallel. On the one hand, this result should not be surprising because a system is more flexible when it has multiple representations of the events in progress and can draw on the different representations when necessary. On the other hand, the simultaneous existence of multiple representations makes the study of behavior much more challenging because a psychophysical report might reflect one of several or some combination of multiple representations. We end this chapter with an account of a unique result that supposedly cannot be described by the FLMP.

PROCESSING NOVEL SOURCES OF SPEECH INFORMATION

As noted in chapter 2, the direct perception theory states that persons directly perceive the causes of sensory input, and in speech the cause is the vocal tract activity of the talker. According to this view, visible speech should influence speech perception because it reveals the vocal tract activity of the talker. Furthermore, vocal tract activity should also be picked up directly from touching the speaker's mouth. To test this idea, Fowler and Dekle (1991) asked college students to place their hands on a talker's mouth while she silently uttered one of the two syllables /ba/ and /ga/. An auditory syllable selected from a continuum between /ba/ and /ga/ was simultaneously presented. The observers were instructed to report the auditory syllable. The results indicated that the articulated syllable influenced the perceiver's interpretation of the auditory speech. The researchers interpreted these results as exactly analogous to the McGurk effect found in auditory-visual speech perception.

Fowler and Dekle interpret their results as evidence against the FLMP because there should be no tactile information available in the perceivers' prototype descriptions. Normal perceivers supposedly have not directly experienced tactile information about speech, nor have they experienced acoustic and tactile speech information occurring together. Accordingly, they should have no experience that would have led to the development of the appropriate prototype descriptions.

We offer an alternative point of view. Although we may never have actually touched the mouth of a talker while hearing speech, it is only natural to relate experience in one modality to potential experience in others. As speakers and perceivers of language, we can easily infer what tactile differences would exist between /ba/ and /ga/, for example. It should not be surprising if perceivers are influenced by tactile information when tactile and acoustic information are presented jointly in a speech identification experiment.

Even though we would not view an influence of tactile information as inconsistent with the FLMP, it is not obvious that perceiving speech by ear and hand is exactly analogous to speech perception by ear and eye. As with most questions, it is best to begin with their data. The talker uttered /ba/ or /ga/ or nothing during the presentation of an auditory syllable chosen from a /ba/ to /ga/ continuum. Unfortunately, their design was not completely expanded because it did not include tactile-alone trials. (In their defense, tactile-alone trials were probably seen as incompatible with the auditory instructions.) Figure 11.11 presents the observed proportion of /ba/ judgments. The figure shows a relatively small influence of the talker's utterance

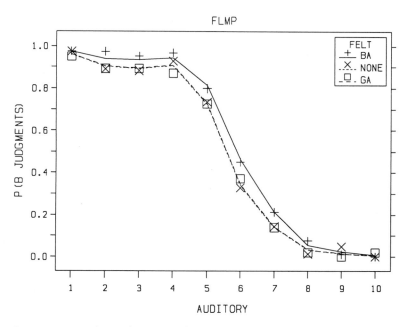

Figure 11.11 Observed (points) and predicted (lines) probability of /ba/ judgments as a function of the auditory and tactile information. Predictions of the FLMP.

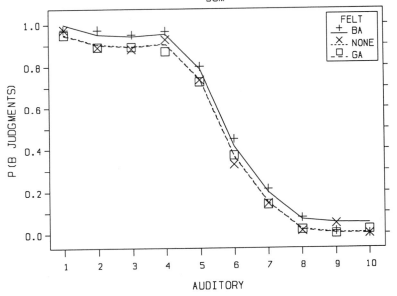

Figure 11.12 Observed (points) and predicted (lines) probability of /ba/ judgments as a function of the auditory and tactile information. Predictions of the SCM.

and a large effect of the auditory speech. The tactile information also had an asymmetrical influence in that a tactile /ba/ increased the probability of /ba/ judgments relative to unimodal auditory trials but a felt /ga/ had no noticeable influence. The lines in figure 11.11 give the predictions of the FLMP. At first glance, the fit of this model appears to be reasonable, and the parameter values also show that tactile /ga/ had no influence. The degree of support of tactile /ga/ for the /ba/ alternative was .505, when .5 signifies no support. The degree of support for the /ba/ alternative was .657 for the tactile /ba/ stimulus. Notwithstanding what seems to be a reasonable fit of the FLMP, figure 11.12 shows that the single channel model (SCM) actually does almost as well in describing the results. The RMSDs were .022 and .018 for the SCM and the FLMP, respectively. Thus it is possible that a tactile situation with naive observers is not analogous to the audible-visible speech situation at all. My feeling is that some learning is probably necessary to develop the ability to use a novel source of information. Early in the use of a new source of information, perceivers might not be able to integrate it with another source. Instead, they might use just the new source or other familiar sources on a given trial, as prescribed by the SCM.

Given their compatibility with both the FLMP and the SCM, the results do not unambiguously support the idea that it is the events of the articulatory tract that are the objects of speech perception. The influence of tactile information no more supports articulatory objects than the influence of auditory speech supports auditory objects. Furthermore, people are adept at utilizing many different kinds of information, even types never before experienced. If an uppercase letter is drawn on a person's back, it can be recognized even though the person has never experienced such an event before. Its accurate recognition does not mean that reading letters involves direct perception of the hand movements that produce the letters. The stimulation on the back simply informs the perceiver about some event; whether perception is direct or mediated by information processing is another question.

Rosenblum and Fowler (1991) state that the FLMP cannot predict an influence of visible effort on perceived loudness because the model does not include loudness prototypes. However, they interpret the use of prototypes in the model much too rigidly. As stated in several venues, "Prototypes are generated for the task at hand" (e.g., Massaro, 1987f, p. 17). Our experience as perceivers of speech in face-to-face communication includes the positive correlation between loudness and the perceived vocal effort of the talker. This information can be used in pattern recognition.

Fowler (1996) is not troubled by the fact that animals other than speaking humans perceive actions of the human vocal tract. Given that chinchillas, quail, and chimpanzees have auditory systems like ours, they should be capable of recovering the causes of the acoustic events. As Fowler puts it, "Perceiving sounding events specified by acoustic signals promotes survival more than does hearing structured air itself." (p. 1738). Given this account of nonhuman perception, I do not think there is a possible way to test between the FLMP and direct perception. Fowler's "evidence" for direct perception now seems arbitrary. Some fascinating aspect of human speech perception, such as the influence of tactile information, is no longer fascinating because the same results in nonhumans could be explained just as easily. For example, we wouldn't be too surprised if Kanzi, a bonobo (pygmy chimpanzee) who understands language, showed a McGurk effect. As suggested by O'Shaughnessy (1996), there is no proof (or even strong evidence) that listeners exploit articulatory features in speech perception. I believe the argument boils down to the issue of what representation is used to process the multiple sources of information provided in the speech event. The challenge for these gestural theories is to formulate some quantitative predictions that could be contrasted with other viewpoints such as the FLMP. Until that is done, few will accept articulation as a necessary mediator of speech perception (Lindblom, 1996; Remez, 1996).

RETROSPECTIVE

In this section of the book, we learned that broadening the FLMP was a productive strategy. We extended the model to account for the dynamics of information processing. The decision process, which has received less attention than the other processes up to now, was decomposed to include two component operations: assessment and response selection. Appropriate behavior in pattern recognition seems to require consideration of all of the viable response alternatives. This relative assessment is followed by a mapping into an actual response. We learned that a criterion rule could be employed in the FLMP to make the same predictions as a probability matching rule. These extensions of the FLMP reveal the productive framework of computational modeling.

The FLMP held up fairly well when challenged with a broader range of test criteria. The benchmark measure provides a productive analysis of the accuracy of models of performance. The superiority of the FLMP relative to other models was not compromised by different methods of model testing. This inquiry also showed how actual experimentation might not meet all of the assumptions required in the tests of the competing models. More specifically, the repeated testing of subjects across some period of time might introduce some fluctuation in the information that is used. Thus the picture obtained about information processing might be somewhat camouflaged by additional noise.

We should state again that we value the reactions of our colleagues to our work within the framework of the FLMP. We have learned a great deal from their input and we look forward to continued dialogue and progress. The challenges have stimulated us to further refine the lens of our microscope for inquiry. As we learned in chapter 10 as well, challenges remain and there is much to keep us occupied in the near future. We now turn to the final part of the book, in which our talking head takes center stage.

IV Creating Talking Faces

with Michael M. Cohen and Michael A. Berger

12 Synthesizing Talking Faces

The discovery of appropriate variables for biology is itself an act of creation.
—Brian Carey Goodwin, *Towards a Theoretical Biology*

Most of our research in visual speech perception described in the preceding chapters was carried out using a synthetic talking head. A synthetic stimulus was considered crucial to this enterprise because it enabled us to have a level of control over the stimulus not possible by natural means—for example, building continua of precise, equal steps between pairs of syllables or systematically manipulating some property of the speech signal. Development and refinement of the talking head has thus been as important a part of our research as our use of it in psychological experiments; the ultimate goal of this development is to create a synthetic speaking face that is as realistic as a natural face in the movements of speech. The next three chapters deal with the synthesis, evaluation, and alternative applications of our talking head. We hope this discussion will be informative and useful to readers in a variety of fields, including psychology, speech synthesis, animation, psycholinguistics, human—machine interaction, hearing-impaired communication, and numerous other fields that also share this fruitful intersection.

Our early studies of bimodal speech perception involved the dubbing of videotapes of real talkers. Although there was no shortage of experimental questions that could be asked (and even answered) with this procedure, the experimental, theoretical, and applied value of a synthetic face was too obvious to be ignored. In many ways, we were surprised when we learned that the seminal work had been done more than a decade earlier (Parke, 1974), and that only a little had been done since that time (e.g., Platt & Badler, 1981). One group of investigators, however, implemented Parke's animation to give phoneme-by-phoneme control of the targeted animation sequence (Pearce et al., 1986). Although we did not have the hardware technology ourselves, our colleagues in mathematics and computer sciences were kind enough to give us a few sessions of the graveyard shift on their Silicon Graphics Inc. IRIS 3030 computer (Cohen & Massaro, 1990). We were able adapt the Pearce et al. software to synthesize test phonemes for use in psychological experiments. We synthesized a test continuum of five visible syllables between /ba/ and /da/, which took several hours of rendering time because each frame required about one minute to render before recording on videotape. The syllables were then employed along with synthetic auditory speech in an expanded factorial design in 1986. We were intrigued that the synthetic speech was fairly realistic and influenced bimodal speech perception in the same manner as natural visible speech (Massaro & Cohen, 1990). However, with our limited technology, we were not able to study the perception of other contrasts and of larger units such as words and sentences. It took another four years of active participation in the research world before we finally obtained support to purchase the necessary hardware to create a full-fledged talking face.

Many of us agree that much of what we know about auditory speech perception has come from experimental studies using synthetic speech. Although some research questions can be answered in part using natural speech stimuli, our overall progress in understanding speech perception has been critically dependent on the use of synthetic speech. Extending this approach to the visual dimension of speech, we have developed a high-quality visual speech synthesizer—a computer-animated talking face—which incorporates coarticulation (the assimilating influence of neighboring speech segments on one another) through a model of speech production that takes into account the relative dominance of speech segments (Cohen & Massaro, 1993, 1994). Our goals for this technology include gaining an understanding of the visual information that is used in speechreading and of how that information is combined with auditory information in language perception and understanding; we also foresee its use as an improved channel for human–machine communication, as a useful aid in education and language training, and as a synthetic actor in entertainment. These and other application ideas will be the focus of chapter 14.

The value of synthetic speech is usually unquestioned because it is important that psychophysical studies have good control over the stimulus. Before describing our animation and synthesis system, we briefly address the issue of the value of synthetic speech in speech science.

THE VALUE OF SYNTHETIC SPEECH

Given the nature of our research, it is important to defend the experimental, theoretical, and applied value of synthetic speech. We believe that auditory synthetic speech has proven to be valuable and will continue to be valuable in all three of these domains. As noted, synthetic speech gives the experimenter control over the stimulus in a way that is not always possible when natural speech is used. Synthetic speech also permits the implementation and testing of theoretical hypotheses, as for example in manipulating articulatory cues to determine which ones are critical for some particular speech distinction. The applied value of auditory synthetic speech is apparent in the multiple everyday uses for text-to-speech systems. Given the benefit that many sight-impaired people have obtained from text-to-speech technology, it is reasonable to speculate that synthetic visible speech will play an equally important role in alleviating some of the communication disadvantages faced by deaf and hearing-impaired people.

Research Applications

Originating with the innovative use of the pattern playback, speech synthesis has long been an essential trademark of speech research in the auditory domain. For example, the acoustic properties responsible for particular speech distinctions could be determined by surgically manipulating whether or not the properties of interest were present in the synthetic speech. The recognition of speech categories could also be more easily investigated. Researchers could assess differences between sounds as within-category or between-category differences by creating synthetic speech tokens that varied in linear steps between two speech segments. Early studies used speech continua between voiced and voiceless sounds to study the perception of those phonetic categories (see Liberman, 1996, for a retrospective review). It seems that the facts of auditory speech perception as we know them have often been uncovered through the use of synthetic speech.

Synthetic visible speech likewise allows the visual signal to be manipulated directly, an experimental feature central to the study of psychophysics and perception. Typical features manipulated include jaw opening, the horizontal and vertical opening of the lips, tongue movements, and visibility of the teeth. In addition, the combination of synthetic visual and auditory speech permits the use of symmetric expanded factorial designs, which provide the most powerful test of quantitative models of perceptual recognition. Synthetic speech provides a more fine-grained assessment of theoretical questions than is possible with natural speech. For example, testing subjects with synthesized syllables intermediate between several alternatives provides a more powerful test of nonintegration and integration models, compared to the use of unambiguous natural stimuli (see chapters 2 and 11). The first chapters of this book are testimony to that fact.

Synthetic speech allows a flexibility not permitted by natural speech, and natural speech has several characteristics that limit its use in psychophysical inquiry. For example, unnatural utterances, such as ambiguous syllables or syntactic or semantic violations, are more easily produced and controlled using synthetic speech. A seminal study by Miller and Isard (1963) presented strings of words that varied in grammaticality. When subjects were asked to repeat back (shadow) the word strings, performance improved with increases in grammaticality. Because the sentences were read by a human talker, however, segmental and prosodic properties of the words might have contributed to the differences that were observed. That is, the talker could have provided segmental and prosodic cues in his reading of the grammatical strings that were not present in the ungrammatical strings. This type of information could more easily be controlled using synthetic speech, as in the more recent study of Benoit (1990).

In spite of these merits and advantages, some respected investigators have challenged the value of synthetic speech. They have claimed that research with synthetic speech may have misled us about the information and processes supporting speech perception. However, when the phenomena uncovered using synthetic speech can be tested using natural speech, the same results are found. In our initial studies of a /ba/–/da/ continuum using synthetic visible speech, we found very similar results for the endpoint stimuli /ba/ and /da/ to those found in earlier studies using natural speech tokens (Massaro, 1987f; Massaro & Cohen, 1990). Band 12.1 gives the same demonstration of the influence of visible speech as given in band 1.1, but with a real face rather than a synthetic one. As the reader can see, the influence of visible speech is roughly comparable in the two situations. In the next section we will present a few studies confirming that what is found with synthetic speech is not only theoretically informative but is also externally valid—that is, applicable to the everyday world of natural speech.

Evidence for Validity

Challenges to the validity of synthetic speech for speech perception research call into question the state of our knowledge resulting from that research. The goal of this section is simply to assess the validity of both synthetic speech and the findings based on it, by asking to what extent those findings hold for natural speech. To the degree that the same facts emerge from both synthetic and natural speech, we have extended the validity of the findings to include natural speech and simultaneously provided support for the value of synthetic speech. If the same facts are also revealed in natural speech, one might then challenge the experimental need for synthetic speech. However, as emphasized above, synthetic speech does more than simply corroborate what can be found with natural speech; the superior level of control over the synthetic stimulus makes it a more flexible and accurate tool for psychophysical inquiry.

Although there have not been many direct comparisons between synthetic and natural speech perception, many phenomena have been investigated with both synthetic and natural speech, and we can compare the results observed. Differences as a function of this variable would speak to the argument that research with synthetic speech might be highly artifactual and therefore might not generalize to natural speech. Our reading of the literature offers just the opposite conclusion. Well-known facts about speech perception appear to hold up for both synthetic and natural speech. Because these facts are straightforward and well documented, we give just a few examples in detail and then list a variety of others in table 12.1.

Changes in the stimulus effect changes in perception, and we would expect the same correspondences between stimulus and perception to hold

Table 12.1 Domains of evidence for the equivalent findings using synthetic and natural speech

Finding	Natural Speech	Synthetic Speech
VOT continua	Rudnicky & Cole, 1977	Liberman, Delattre & Cooper, 1958
Vowel identification	Klein, Plomp & Pols, 1970	Delattre et al., 1952
Suffix effect	Crowder & Morton, 1969	Crowder & Cheng, 1973
Selective adaptation	Rudnicky & Cole, 1977	Roberts & Summerfield, 1981
Backward recognition masking	Massaro, 1974	Newman & Spitzer, 1987
Vowel trading relations	Denes, 1955	Derr & Massaro, 1980
Top-down context effects	Isenberg, Walker & Ryder, 1980	Ganong, 1980

The citations listed for each domain are representative publications.

for both natural and synthetic speech. One of the best-known correspondences is between voice onset time (VOT) and the perception of voicing in stop consonants in initial position. The earlier the onset of voicing relative to the release of a stop consonant, the greater the likelihood that the consonant will be perceived as voiced. The later the voicing starts—say, in the region of the following vowel—the more likely the perception of the consonant as voiceless. VOT is easy to vary using formant speech synthesis, which has a periodic energy source feeding into formant resonators. Changes in VOT involve delaying the periodic voicing source and substituting aperiodic energy at the onset of an initial stop consonant. A voicing continuum can also be made by editing natural speech, as illustrated by Rudnicky and Cole (1977). A voiceless syllable is modified to become voiced by removal of successively larger portions of the initial burst and aspiration of the syllable. Judgments change from voiceless to voiced as larger portions of the initial segments are removed. Perception results for continua of this type created from natural and synthetic speech are highly similar to one another. Their differences are usually no larger than what would be observed between two different studies using synthetic speech or two different studies using natural speech.

Another comparison can be made between identification of synthetic and natural vowels. Early research at Haskins Laboratories revealed that the first two formants were sufficient for fairly good recognition of synthetic vowels (Delattre et al., 1952). Researchers have also studied vowel perception using natural speech by assessing identification of several vowels spoken by several speakers (Klein, Plomp & Pols, 1970). Acoustic analyses were carried out, and identification was again found to be related to the first and second formants (see also Peterson & Barney, 1952). Thus, studies using synthetic and natural vowels are in agreement on what elements of the signal are functional in vowel identification.

Further evidence of parallelism comes from memory research. One of the best-known characteristics of short-term memory is the modality effect: a sequential list of items is better remembered if it is presented in spoken rather than in written form (Murray, 1966). However, a suffix spoken at the end of the list disrupts the advantage for words at the end. This so-called suffix effect holds up for both synthetic and natural speech. Most studies have used natural speech, but Crowder and Cheng (1973) used synthetic speech in their study of suffix effects varying with the similarity of the test list and the suffix. They replicated the standard result found with natural speech.

A variety of other phenomena appear to hold up for either synthetic or natural speech. Table 12.1 lists some representative phenomena in speech research and representative studies using natural and synthetic speech. These include VOT continua, vowel identification, suffix effects, selective adaptation, backward recognition masking, trading relations among acoustic cues, and top-down context effects in speech perception.

More generally, synthetic speech is an important component of the scientist's arsenal in the study of spoken language (Bailly, Benoit & Sawallis, 1992). In chapter 13, we provide a more direct performance comparison between our visible speech synthesis and natural speech. For now, we proceed to the primary charge of this chapter, the technology of visible speech synthesis.

FACIAL ANIMATION AND VISUAL SPEECH SYNTHESIS TECHNIQUES

Visible speech synthesis is a subfield of the more general area of computer facial animation. Table 12.2 summarizes some representative work that has been done in that area. We discriminate two general classes of facial animation techniques—physically based (PB) and terminal analog (TA). The PB class involves the use of physical models of the structure and function of the human face. The typical approach here is to use multilayer tissue models with quasi-muscular controls to change the shape of the face. For the TA class, the goal has been to arrive at the terminal end of the process (a face surface) without resorting to physically based constructs. The typical approach is to employ a polygon surface with keyframe or parametric controls. Let us first consider PB models.

Physically Based Synthesis

Figure 12.1 shows the facial muscles as seen from the inside out, as though one were peeling off a mask. As described by Fridlund (1994), the musculature of the human face can be thought of as a mask. It portrays our attitudes to the world around us in much the same way as the masks that covered the faces of actors in ancient Greece and Rome—the kind still used today in Japanese Kabuki and No. The face we present to the outside world appears

Table 12.2 Facial animation techniques

Project	Class	Surface	Control	Speech
Parke Models				
Parke (1972)	TA	polygons	keyframe	no
Parke (1974, 1975, 1982, 1991)	TA	polygons	parametric	manual natural
Lewis & Parke (1987)	TA	polygons	parametric	automatic natural
Pearce et al. (1986)	TA	polygons	parametric	semiautomatic synthetic
Cohen & Massaro (1990, 1993)	TA	polygons	parametric	automatic synthetic
Le Goff et al. (1994)	TA	polygons	parametric	natural with noise
Le Goff & Benoit (1996)	TA	polygons	parametric	automatic synthetic
Beskow (1995)	TA	polygons	parametric	automatic synthetic
Petajan & Graf (1996)	TA	polygons	parametric	automatic natural
2D TA Models				
Montgomery (1980)	TA	2-D vectors	key-points	no
Brooke (1989)	TA	2-D vectors	key-points	no
Brooke & Summerfield (1983)	TA	2-D vectors	key-points	no
Other TA Models				
Nahas, Huitric & Saintourens (1988)	TA	b-spline	keyframe	manual natural
Bergeron & Lachapelle (1985)	TA	polygons	keyframe	manual natural
Kleiser & Walczak (1989)	TA	polygons	keyframe	manual natural
Elson (1990)	TA	polygons	s-dynamics	manual natural
Patterson, Litwinowicz & Greene (1991)	TA	polygons	mapping	manual natural
Henton & Litwinowicz (1994)	TA	images	disemes	automatic synthetic
Yau & Duffy (1988)	TA	polygons	key-frames	manual natural
Kurihara & Arai (1991)	TA	polygons	wraphot texmap	no
Saulnier, Viaud & Geldreich (1995)	TA	polygons	parametric?	automatic natural
PB Models				
Platt & Badler (1981)	PB	3-layer skin	FACS	no
Platt (1985)	PB	1-layer skin	FACS	no
Waters (1987)	PB	polygons	FACS	no
Terzopoulous & Waters (1990, 1991)	PB	3-layer skin	FACS	no
Waters & Levergood (1993)	PB	2-D polygons	keyframe	automatic synthetic
Harashima, Aizawa & Saito (1989)	PB	polygons	FACS	no
Vatikiotis-Bateson et al. (1996)	PB	3-layer skin	EMG driven	no
Pelachaud, Badler & Steedman (1991)	PB	1-layer skin	FACS	manual synchronization
Cassell et al. (1994)	PB	1-layer skin	FACS	automatic synchronization
Kalra et al. (1991)	PB	polygons	AMAS	manual natural
Patel & Willis (1991)	PB	bone & skin	FACS	no
Wang & Forsey (1994)	PB	b-spline	FACS	manual natural
Reeves (1990)	PB	Catrom patches	muscle actions	just babbling
Lasseter & Daly (1995)	PB	patches	muscle actions	manual natural

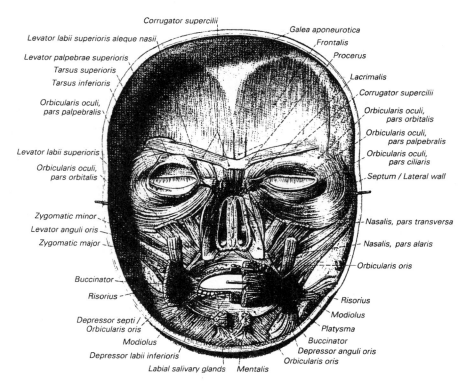

Corrugator supercilii
Levator labii superioris aleque nasii
Levator palpebrae superioris
Tarsus superioris
Tarsus inferioris
Orbicularis oculi, pars palpebralis
Levator labii superioris
Orbicularis oculi, pars orbitalis
Zygomatic minor
Levator anguli oris
Zygomatic major
Buccinator
Risorius
Depressor septi / Orbicularis oris
Modiolus
Depressor labii inferioris
Labial salivary glands
Mentalis

Galea aponeurotica
Frontalis
Procerus
Lacrimalis
Corrugator supercilii
Orbicularis oculi, pars orbitalis
Orbicularis oculi, pars palpebralis
Orbicularis oculi, pars ciliaris
Septum / Lateral wall
Nasalis, pars transversa
Nasalis, pars alaris
Orbicularis oris
Risorius
Modiolus
Platysma
Buccinator
Depressor anguli oris
Orbicularis oris

Figure 12.1 The facial muscles as seen from the inside of the head. Our natural tendency is to perceive this representation as if we are viewing from the outside, as in the mask illusion, when we see the outside of a face while viewing the inside of a mask.

to be much simpler than its underlying musculature. There are putatively hundreds of muscles that control the face, and it is mind-boggling to imagine how all of them could be simulated to achieve control of a synthetic face. However, only a small subset of the facial muscles control the speech articulators, so this technique might be feasible for the synthesis of visible speech. In fact, one motivation cited for the use of physically based (PB) rather than geometric models is that the physiological controls might *reduce* the number of degrees of freedom required. With regard to speech synthesis with PB models, we should also note a potential advantage in the intrinsic simultaneity of visual and auditory synthesis based on the same physical structure.

Using the PB approach, computer-animated human faces are made by construction of a computational model for the skin surface, muscle, and bone structures of the face (e.g., Platt & Badler, 1981; Waters, 1987; Waters & Terzopoulous, 1990). At the foundation of this type of model is an approximation of the skull and jaw including the jaw pivot. Simulated muscle tissues and their insertions are placed over the skull; the process requires complex elastic models for the compressible tissues. A covering surface layer then changes shape according to the underlying structures. The dynamic information for such a model is defined by a set of contraction-relaxation muscle commands. Many of the PB systems use Ekman and Friesen's (1977) Facial Action Coding System (FACS) to control the facial model. The codes are based on about 50 facial actions ("action units," or AUs) defined as combinations of muscle actions. Band 12.2 on the CD-ROM illustrates an example of musculoskeletal synthesis. The animation was done using Takeuchi and Franks's (1992) version of Waters's algorithm.

Recently, Pelachaud, Badler, and Steedman (1996) have extended and updated Platt's (1985) seminal PB model, adding manually synchronized natural auditory speech as well as the display of paralinguistic information. A related project (Cassell et al., 1994) incorporated synchronized speech synthesis and automatic gesture production by two automatons negotiating a bank transaction.

Facial animation has also appeared in popular entertainment. In a relatively early effort, Reeves (1990) presented us with a babbling, toy-abusing synthetic baby in *Tin Toy*. The facial animation used was based on a head consisting of four-sided Catrom patches, controlled by 43 linear and 4 sphincter muscles that pulled on the patch control points. A hierarchical control strategy utilized about 12 higher-level macro muscle command groups. The baby's head also included a tear-shaped tongue consisting of 12 bi-cubic patches. The same group later produced the massive project *Toy Story*, an entirely animated feature film (Lasseter & Daly, 1995). Facial animation was based on a cubic patch face with muscle controls. For the character Woody, the hero of the film, a very large number of such controls was used—712, including 212 on his face and 58 for his mouth alone. The face was synchronized with the natural speech of actors using largely manual adjustment.

Some researchers have attempted to derive the muscle commands for driving a PB face from measurements of human muscle actions. For example, Vatikiotis-Bateson and colleagues (1996) have embarked on a project to drive a PB face utilizing information obtained through neural-net analysis of EMG and facial motion measurements. So far their project has yielded mixed results.

A project of more immediate application from the PB school is Waters and Levergood's (1993) DECface software. In order to achieve real-time performance (15 frames per second with texture mapping) on a DEC Alpha workstation, their approach compresses Waters's 3-D tissue model to a simple 2-D mesh. A set of 55 "viseme" mouth shape key positions is utilized, and a physically motivated nonlinear interpolation algorithm is used between these positions. Only this nonlinearity and the previous research of the workers qualifies the approach as physically based. It might also be viewed as a system in the TA class, which we now discuss.

Terminal-Analog Synthesis

The goal of our synthesis has been to obtain a realistic mask, not to duplicate the musculature of the face to control the mask. Our choice was to develop visible speech synthesis in the manner that has proved most successful for audible speech synthesis. We call this technique terminal-analog synthesis because its goal is to mimic the final speech product rather than the physiological mechanisms that produce it. In auditory speech synthesis, this is the difference between articulatory (e.g., Flanagan, Ishizaka & Shipley, 1975) and terminal-analog formant (Klatt, 1979, 1980, 1987) synthesizers for auditory speech (see Boves & Cranen, 1996). Auditory articulatory synthesizers require several orders more computation than do terminal-analog ones.

In a seminal development, Parke (1972, 1974, 1975, 1982, 1991) modeled the facial surface as a polyhedral object composed of about 900 small surfaces arranged in three dimensions, joined together at the edges and smooth shaded. In his original work (Parke, 1972), keyframes were used to change the shape of the face, but in subsequent work he animated the face by altering the location of various points in the grid under the control of 50 parameters. About 10 of those parameters were used for speech animation, such as jaw rotation, mouth width, lip protrusion, and lower-lip "f" tuck. Parke (1974) selected and refined the control parameters used for several demonstration sentences by studying his own articulation frame by frame and estimating the control parameter values. Band 12.3 on the CD-ROM gives an example of the original Parke synthesis.

One advantage of the polygon topology strategy is that calculations of the changing surface shapes in the polygon models can be carried out much faster than those for the muscle and tissue simulations. It also may be easier to achieve the desired facial shapes directly rather than in terms of the constituent muscle actions.

Our own current software (Cohen & Massaro, 1993, 1994; Cohen, Walker & Massaro, 1996) is a descendant of the Parke software and of his particular 3-D talking head. Our modifications over the last three years have included additional and modified control parameters, a tongue (which was lacking in Parke's model), a new visual speech synthesis control strategy, controls for paralinguistic information and affect in the face, text-to-speech synthesis, and bimodal (auditory-visual) synthesis. Most of our current parameters move points on the face by geometric functions such as rotation (e.g., jaw rotation) or translation of the points in one or more dimensions (e.g., lower and upper lip height, mouth widening). Other parameters work by interpolating between two alternate faces. Many of the face shape parameters, such as cheek shape, neck shape, and forehead shape, as well as some affect parameters, such as smiling, employ this strategy. More detailed discussion of our algorithms used to drive the speech synthesis will be found thouhout the rest of this chapter. Consisting of about 20,000 lines of C code, the synthesis program runs in real time on an SGI Crimson-Reality Engine.

Instead of these 3-D models, a number of speech scientists have used 2-D vector facial models for perceptual studies (Montgomery & Soo Hoo, 1982; Brooke, 1989, 1992; Brooke & Summerfield, 1983; Summerfield et al., 1989). Individual key-points define vector-based shapes on the face such as the mouth outline. These controlling key-points move on the basis of articulatory trajectories measured from human speech. Typical of this approach is a study by Summerfield and coworkers (1989), who used faces with and without teeth to examine lipreading performance.

The TA approach has also been used in entertainment. An early example was the animated story "Tony de Peltrie" (Bergeron and Lachapelle, 1985) in which a polygon-based model was animated using manually synchronized keyframes for speech and expression. A similar approach was used in "Sextone for President" (Kleiser & Walczak, 1989). We now consider in greater detail the various approaches for facial control during speech animation.

CONTROL MECHANISMS FOR ANIMATED SPEECH

The Communication Coding Perspective

The problem of designing control mechanisms for synthesis is one aspect of the much broader problem of communication coding. The problem to be solved in communication coding is how one can most economically code information—such as the visual (and auditory) appearance of a talking face—transmit the information, and reconstruct the image at another location. There are many levels of coding, which differ in terms of how much of the output information is a specific reproduction of the input information and how much is reconstructed on the basis of abstract, repeatable tokens that are drawn from a permanent system. In general, the more abstract the coding, the more control the user has over the resulting image. At the highest levels of analysis-resynthesis techniques, synthesis can acquire a life of its own and be performed independently of any originally analyzed image. Thus, the methodology of communication coding ultimately merges with that of pure synthesis.

A very direct form of coding would be simply to transmit a video signal and display it at the far end. This technique, however, requires a considerable amount of expensive bandwidth. Various coding schemes, such as JPEG encoding of each image and MPEG-1 & 2 encoding of image sequences, have been developed to reduce the amount of information transmitted, at some computational cost for the encoding and decoding processes. Related approaches include the transmission of only image subsections of a talking face, such as the area around the mouth, and reinserting them in a facial image at the far end (Yau & Duffy, 1988); the display of a sequence of a very limited set of synthetic facial images (e.g., Nahas, Huitric & Saintourens, 1988); and the concatenation of short diseme (two-viseme sequence) video clips (e.g., Henton & Litwinowicz, 1994).

A higher level of coding facial image sequences, more closely related to the approaches to pure synthesis discussed in the preceding two sections, is the concept of model-based coding (Harashima, Aizawa & Saito, 1989), in which information regarding a scene is transmitted through parametric descriptions of objects in the scene. A new coding standard currently under study, MPEG-4, will use this general approach, including facial models (Doenges et al., 1996). One interesting characteristic of this approach (at an image, point-mapping, or parametric coding level) is that it can bypass issues such as the need to determine the size or identity of the transmitted speech segments. A number of researchers have carried out work in this area, and some demonstrations of facial analysis, parameter transmission, and resynthesis are worth mention.

Pure PB facial animation is not feasible with analysis-resynthesis techniques. It is not currently practical to carry out the accurate real-time measurements of the muscle commands (e.g., using EMG) that would be needed to drive a remote PB animation. Even if it were possible, most talkers would not consent to wearing the necessary electrodes. On the other hand, the TA approach has already been used for analysis-resynthesis. One interesting example, albeit not in real time, was the use of facial point measurements to drive cross-species facial animation (Patterson, Litwinowicz & Greene, 1991). A human actor was the source of an animated circus dog's performance. Fluorescent spots on the actor's face were tracked in 3-D and used to alter corresponding control points to warp a 3-D model of the dog's face. At a more abstract level of analysis, one can extract parametric information (e.g., mouth width and height) from a talker for transmission and resynthesis (Le Goff et al., 1994; Petajan & Graf, 1996). Le Goff et al. (1994) studied how well such resynthesized information (lips alone or lips on a synthetic face) is perceived relative to the original face on video. For 18 VCVCV stimuli presented silently, they found approximately 23% correct for synthetic lips alone and 41% correct for synthetic lips and face, compared to 62% correct for the original face. A complete survey of techniques for the automatic tracking of facial information is outside the scope of this chapter (see Stork and Hennecke, 1996, for some historical and current approaches).

It is interesting to note here some auditory speech coding analogs. Corresponding with low-level video transmission would be simple acoustic digitization. At a higher level, corresponding to image-coding techniques, LPC (linear predictive coding) allows lower-bandwidth transmission with the possibility of some synthetic modifications, such as changes in the pitch or rate of speech. Still higher levels of analysis (e.g., formant analysis and resynthesis) would allow additional modifications of the signal, such as changing the speaker's voice.

Higher levels of visual and auditory speech coding involve the identification of abstract linguistic objects such as segments, words, and ideas. The use of these linguistic objects allows the most parsimonious transmission of information, as well as allowing synthesis to take place independently of analysis so that the machine itself might be able to generate and understand speech. When considering such higher levels of coding, a preliminary question that must be answered is what are the appropriate units of representation for analysis and synthesis.

Units of Speech Synthesis

Paralleling much of the work in auditory speech synthesis, we use phonemes as the basic unit of speech synthesis. Readers familiar with our work might wonder why we settled on phonemes rather than syllables, when we have so adamantly defended the syllable as functional in speech perception (Massaro, 1972, 1996b). There is no reason why perception should mirror production, however; and, more important, we make no claims about the psychological reality of our speech synthesis. Because many utterances are completely novel, one of the most important decisions is to choose a unit of synthesis that allows the necessary flexibility to simulate all possible utterances. Clearly, the sentence level would be inappropriate because we can produce an infinite number of sentences; the system requires a finite inventory of units. Furthermore, we desire a speech segment that is simple enough that it can can be specified by a single target value for each synthesis control parameter. Words or even syllables, although finite in number, are too complex because they cannot be represented by just a single set of control values throughout. In the most basic CV syllable, parameter values must change significantly from the consonant to the vowel. Most phonemes, on the other hand, can be reasonably specified by a single control value for all of the synthesis dimensions of interest. We have therefore adopted the phonemic approach. Phoneme units are attractive because of their relatively small number. Our inventory of phoneme units for English includes 13 vowels, 25 consonants, and a resting state. There are also segment slots for creating ambiguous tokens between any two segments; for example, in the experiments described in chapter 2 we created a set of five intermediate articulations between /b/ and /d/.

In this scheme, speech is realized by a concatenation of phoneme units. Any utterance can be represented as a string of successive phonemes, and each phoneme is represented as a set of target values for the control parameters such as jaw rotation, mouth width, and so forth, mentioned earlier. (These sets of target values are somewhat analogous to "feature matrices" in segmental phonology; note, however, that in this case the "features" are continuously valued rather than categorical.) A critical question is how we change from the target values of one phoneme to those of the next. As has been emphasized almost since the beginning of speech research, a simple concatenation of phonemes is a poor representation of real speech, because speech is smooth and continuous rather than (overtly) segmented. An obvious solution to the concatenation problem is to interpolate between the target values of adjacent phonemes. Simply interpolating between two adjacent phonemes, however, is inadequate, because it would imply that each phoneme value exerts the same influence on the intermediate values between phonemes, which is not true; some phonemes will spread their characteristics to their neighbors, others will more passively assimilate to the environment. Furthermore, this interpolation scheme forces a phoneme to be blind to all but its immediate neighbors, when in reality it can be influenced by a phoneme several segments away.

Phonemes are a linguistic abstraction and are not necessarily represented in the mind of the talker (although there is a reasonable case for the psychological reality of phonemes in speech production; see Allen, Hunnicutt & Klatt, 1987). Even if they were, it would not be possible to utter all of them in isolation or to speak them independently of one another when they are uttered together. Hockett (1955) used the vivid metaphor of a neat row of eggs on a conveyor belt moving under a rolling squasher. They are easily separable on the input but not on the resulting output. This is true of speech because, for the sake of economy (or laziness), we tend to begin one articulation before completing the last. The resultant melding of adjacent phonemes is especially evident in rapid, informal speech—as, for example, when the question, "Did you eat yet?" is uttered as "Jeet jet?" Other examples are "Whacha dune?" uttered for "What are you doing?" and "Juwana eat?" for "Do you want to eat?"

The first challenge to synthesizing continuous concatenative speech is to solve the problem of the lack of invariance of the same phoneme placed in different contexts or presented at different rates. In contrast to printed text, in which the same letter is represented identically in different contexts, speech is highly context-dependent. This context dependency means that the actual parameter values for a given phoneme cannot be constant across different speech contexts. For example, figure 12.2 illustrates how upper lip protrusion measured from cineradiographs (Perkell, 1969) differs throughout the utterances /həti/ and /hətu/. As can be seen, the degree of lip protrusion associated with the final vowel has a large influence on protrusion during earlier segments. Band 12.4 shows these two utterances from the cineradiograph analyzed by Perkell (1969). The influence of adjacent segments on articulation is called coarticulation.

COARTICULATION

Coarticulation refers to changes in the articulation of a speech segment due to the influence of preceding segments (perseverative coarticulation) and upcoming segments (anticipatory coarticulation). An example of perseverative coarticulation is a difference in articulation of a final consonant in a word depending on the preceding vowel, for example, the lip shape of /t/ in *boot* versus *beet*. An example of anticipatory coarticulation is the lip rounding of the consonants at the beginning of the word *stew* (see figure 12.10 later in this chapter). These examples relate to how the characteristics of one segment may migrate to adjacent segments, but coarticulation also encompasses other types of effects, including the deletion of segments and other modifications resulting from variations in speaking rate. In the following sections we will survey some of the research that has been done regarding the types

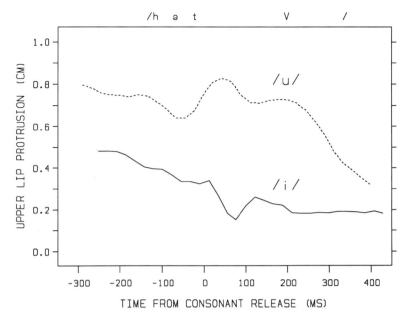

Figure 12.2 Lip protrusion for the utterances /həti/ and /hətu/ as a function of time from /t/ consonant release. Measurements from Perkell (1969).

of coarticulation found in speech, the models for these phenomena, the effects of coarticulation on speech perception, and how we may instantiate coarticulation in our visual speech synthesis algorithms. Great improvement of more recent auditory speech synthesizers, such as MITalk (Allen, Hunnicutt & Klatt, 1987) and DECtalk (1985), over the previous generation of synthesizers such as VOTRAX (1981), is partly due to the inclusion of rules specifying the coarticulation among neighboring phonemes. We expect the same to be true for visual speech.

Patterns and General Models of Coarticulation

Although there have been many studies of coarticulation (e.g., Öhman, 1966; Benguerel & Cowan, 1974; Bladon & Al-Bamermi, 1976; Lubker & Gay, 1982; Al-Bamerni & Bladon, 1982; Recasens, 1984; Perkell, 1990), little consensus has been achieved with regard to a theoretical explanation of the phenomenon (Öhman, 1967; Kent & Minifie, 1977; Bell-Berti & Harris, 1979). The goal of a model of coarticulation is that it be capable of simulating the type of coarticulation found in natural speech. Three main classes of models have been developed. Figure 12.3 illustrates the three model classes in two typical coarticulation situations. A VCV sequence (top curves) or VCCV sequence (bottom curves) is shown with the initial vowel unprotruded (e.g., /i/) and the final vowel protruded (e.g., /u/). In all three cases, the lip protrusion begins prior to voicing onset (marked by the solid vertical line) of

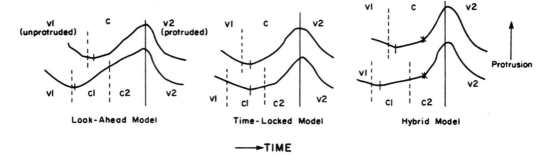

Figure 12.3 Schematic representations of lip protrusion curves consistent with the look-ahead model (left panel), the time-locked model (center panel), and the hybrid model of coarticulation. From Perkell (1969). The solid vertical line is the voicing onset of the protruded vowel V_2, with dashed lines for other segment acoustic boundaries. Short vertical ticks correspond to the onset of protrusion, and Xs mark transitional inflection points.

the protruded final vowel. What discriminates the models is the onset time and dynamics of the anticipatory movement.

In the look-ahead model (Kozhevnikov & Chistovich, 1965, Henke, 1967; (Öhman, 1967), illustrated in the left panel of figure 12.3, the movement toward protrusion starts (indicated by the solid vertical tick) as soon as possible following the unprotruded vowel V_1. Thus, the time interval between the beginning of protrusion and the onset of V_2 differs depending on the number of intervening units. A variant of this model has been used by Pelachaud, Badler, and Steedman (1991) for visual speech synthesis. In their system, phonemes are assigned high or low deformability rank. Anticipatory and perseverative coarticulation rules are applied such that a phoneme takes the lip shape of a less deformable phoneme occurring earlier or later. Their algorithm occurs in three passes. First, the ideal lip shape is computed for each phoneme; then, in two additional passes, muscle actions over time are computed based on the deformability of each phoneme and the movement constraints of the muscles involved, such as contraction and relaxation times. Conflicting muscle actions are resolved through the use of a table of action unit (AU) similarities.

In the time-locked model, also known as coproduction (Bell-Berti & Harris, 1979, 1982), illustrated in the center panel of figure 12.3, the movement toward protrusion begins a fixed time prior to V_2 onset. This model assumes that gestures are independent entities that are combined in an approximately additive fashion.

The right panel of figure 12.3 illustrates a hybrid model typical of Al-Bamerni and Bladon (1982) and Perkell and Chiang (1986). In this type of model there are two phases of movement. The first phase begins gradually and as early as possible, as in the look-ahead model. A second phase begins at a fixed time prior to V_2, analogous to the time-locked model. During this second phase, more rapid change occurs. In experimental data this model has been supported by an inflection (acceleration) point at the hypothetical phase transition indicated by the x marks in the two curves (Perkell, 1990). One example of supporting data can be seen in figure 12.10 of Cathiard, Lallouache, and Abry (1996), which shows such inflection points for upper lip protrusion and lip area during an /i#y/ sequence.

It should be pointed out that an important reason for the different theories of coarticulation is the differences among empirical results, depending on a number of experimental (see Gelfer, Bell-Berti & Harris, 1989) and linguistic factors. In one recent study, Abry and Lallouache (1991) tested the three co-articulation models against physical measurements of lip rounding in French /ikstsky/ (from the difficult phrase "Ces deux Sixte sculpterent") sequences. What they found was that none of the three models could account for the observed patterns of rounding anticipation, which instead may have depended on suprasegmental prosodic effects. In an example of cross-linguistic differences, Lubker and Gay (1982) compared talkers of American English and Swedish and found that the Swedish talkers start anticipatory rounding earlier, perhaps to preserve contrasts among the vowels, which are more numerous in that language. Similarly, Boyce (1990) describes differences between Turkish and American talkers in intervocalic protrusion. For the string /utu/, for example, American talkers show a trough pattern (a decrease in protrusion for /t/ between two peaks for /u/) versus a plateau pattern shown by the Turkish talkers (no decrease in protrusion for the /t/ between the vowels). She explained this in terms of the American speakers using a coproduction, or time-locked, strategy whereas the Turkish speakers use a look-ahead strategy. (Alternatively, Boyce also considers a grammatical explanation: the Turkish behavior might be related to a rounding harmony constraint among vowels in Turkish phonology.) Thus it may be that a single one of the three theories cannot account for coarticulation in all situations, and perhaps a more flexible general framework is called for.

Coarticulation and Speech Perception

An interesting question is to what degree coarticulation affects the visual perception of speech. Benguerel and Pichora-Fuller (1982) examined whether speechreading of consonants would be influenced by the adjacent vowels in hearing-impaired and normally hearing individuals. The test items were nonsense syllables of the form $/V_1CV_2/$. The researchers assessed the influence of coarticulation by contrasting consonant recognition in vowel contexts that produce large coarticulatory influences with consonant recognition in vowel contexts that produce small influences. The vowels /u/, /i/, and /æ/ were used. Coarticulation influenced speechreading for both groups of speech-readers. For example, the identity of V_2 had a significant effect on visible consonant recognition. Fewer consonants were recognized correctly when they were followed by /u/ than when they were followed by /i/ or /æ/. By reversing the stimuli and finding the same results, the experimenters demonstrated that the effect was due to articulation differences between the three vowels rather than to their actual position in the stimulus as presented. Differences in consonant visibility as a function of vowel context have also been found in a diminished McGurk effect for consonants adjacent to the vowel /u/ relative to those occurring with /a/ (Green, Kuhl & Meltzoff, 1988).

It should be noted that Benguerel and Pichora-Fuller's results show only that coarticulation factors influence speechreading. They do not address the question of whether speechreaders actually use coarticulatory information. For auditory speech perception, the results are more mixed (see Massaro & Oden, 1980b). More recently, Cathiard and colleagues (1991) showed that observers can use the visual information produced by anticipatory rounding. In their study, sequences of the vowels /i/ and /y/ were recorded in a French carrier sentence, with /i/ at the end of one word and /y/ at the beginning of the next. (Note that /y/ symbolizes a vowel that is just like /i/ but with lip rounding.) Both long and short sequences were recorded. Thirty-one still frames of the first vowel of the sequence were selected from the recorded video. Single frames were presented to subjects, who were asked to decide whether the second vowel was /i/ or /y/. Their judgments changed systematically as the stimulus frame was nearer in time to that of the second vowel. For both the short and long sequences, the identification changed from /i/ to /y/ identification at a point well before what would have been the acoustic onset of the second vowel. Thus, subjects were able to identify the upcoming vowel on the basis of the visual anticipatory coarticulation.

Gestural Models of Coarticulation

The speech control algorithm that we have developed at the University of California at Santa Cruz falls into the general class of gestural models of speech articulation, developed by researchers associated with Haskins Labs (Browman & Goldstein, 1989; Kelso et al., 1985; Saltzman & Kelso, 1987; Saltzman et al., 1987). Browman and Goldstein (1989) provide a good exemplar of this approach. In their model, the basic atoms of phonological structures are taken to be neither features nor segments, but primitive actions of the vocal tract called gestures. A prototypical gesture might be the formation and release over time of some constriction by one of several relatively independent sets of articulators. One example might be an alveolar stop action, performed by the articulator set made up of the tongue tip, tongue body, and jaw. The mechanics of temporal relations between gestures have been useful in accounting for a number of speech production and speech perception phenomena. Such phenomena can be accounted for on the basis of whether the coordinated gestures are performed by the same articulator set or by different articulator sets. Different articulator sets can carry out gestures in synchrony (or asynchronously) without influencing one another (e.g., the simultaneous actions of the velum and lips in producing /m/). However, the independent gestures may overlap in time, which can lead to interesting perceptual effects. An example is seen when we compare the citation and conversational forms of the phrase *perfect memory*. The /t/, which is audible in citation form, seems to get deleted in more fluent speech: /p ɝ f ə k m ɛ m ɝ r i/. The deletion is only apparent, however; the alveolar closure does occur but is hidden from auditory (not to mention visual) perception by the fact that it is completely overlapped by the preceding velar and following labial closures. On the other hand, when conflicting gestures are required of a single articulator set, some sort of blending is predicted to occur. For example, in fluent production of *ten themes*, in which the same articulator (tongue tip) must perform the alveolar constriction of /n/ followed by the dental constriction of /θ/, the result is a compromise: /n/ becomes more dental and /θ/ becomes more alveolar. The lesson of these examples is that fast speech is not simply a speeded-up version of slow speech, and fairly sophisticated theories are needed to account for the observed results both for speech production and for speech perception (e.g., Massaro & Cohen, 1983b).

Looking specifically at how speech changes with speaking rate, Munhall and Löfqvist (1992) measured the glottal opening gestures that occurred for two speakers as they produced the phrase *Kiss Ted* over a wide range of speaking rates. What they found was that the glottal openings for the voiceless consonants /s/ and /t/ merged into (effectively) a single gesture at faster rates (possibly by summation).

An interesting recent variant of the gesture model has been given by Löfqvist (1990). The central theme of this model, illustrated in figure 12.4, is that every segment has a certain *dominance* over the articulators, which increases and then decreases over time. The segment has not just one dominance function but a separate one governing each articulator. The target value of the segment for a given articulator is modulated by the corresponding dominance function, which is peaked somewhere in the middle of the segment and can spread into neighboring segments. Given this scheme, adjacent segments will have overlapping dominance over the articulators. A

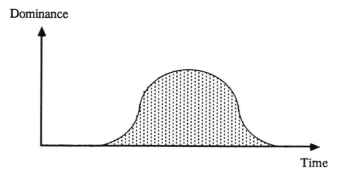

Figure 12.4 A representation of the speech segment over time in terms of its dominance over one of the articulators. From Löfqvist (1990).

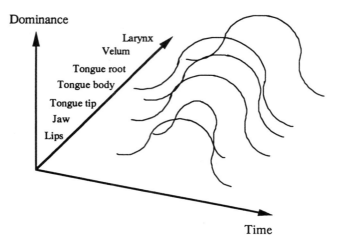

Figure 12.5 A representation of the speech segment over time in terms of its dominance on the articulators. Traces with differing characteristics are shown for different articulators. From Löfqvist (1990).

blending function is then necessary to coordinate the dominance functions of neighboring segments. That function will produce articulator values that reflect the combined influence of the segments' targets. In the property of overlapping influence, the model shares the coproduction (Bell-Berti & Harris, 1992) view of gesture combination.

Because the various articulators are independent of one another, this process occurs independently for each articulator. As can be seen in figure 12.5, the different articulators can have dominance functions that differ in magnitude, time offset, and duration. Different time offsets, for example, between lip closure and glottal pulsing (voicing) could produce differences in the VOT of bilabial stops. The magnitude of each function represents the relative importance of the articulator reaching its target value for a segment. For example, a consonant could have a low dominance on lip rounding, which would allow the intrusion of values of that characteristic from adjacent vowels.

The adjustability of these functions results in a large variety of independent dominance functions that specifically model the influence of each segment over each articulator. This provides the model with greater adaptability than models that have a single rule governing all coarticulation, as in the case of look-ahead, time-locked, and hybrid models. A number of other theories (e.g., Benguerel & Cowan, 1974) do differentiate the influence that particular segments have over particular features, but they are limited to binary settings (influential or passive) as opposed to using continuous numerical coefficients, which capture degrees of dominance. Furthermore, in our adaptation of the Löfqvist model, not only the magnitude but also the shape of the dominance curve is subject to adjustment.

The Löfqvist dominance model reflects the idea of using a numerical coefficient for "coarticulation resistance," associated with some phonetic features in the theory of Bladon and Al-Bamerni (1976). This approach also bears some similarity to Elson's (1990) use of Reynolds' (1985) S-Dynamics animation control. In Elson's facial animation system, multiple layers were used to control all dynamic attributes of a model of the human body. Overlapping time-varying displacement magnitudes were used to interpolate between ten possible phoneme targets, but this interpolation scheme was not linguistically motivated.

Our Speech Control Algorithm

We have adapted and expanded the Löfqvist gestural production model to drive our synthetic visual speech. Each segment is specified with a target value for each facial control parameter. To each segment–control parameter pair, there is also a dominance function dictating the influence that that segment exerts over the control parameter. The dominance function will determine how much weight the segment's target value carries against those of neighboring segments, which in turn will decide how the target values are blended.

To instantiate this dominance model it is necessary to select particular dominance and blending functions. One general form for dominance is given by the negative exponential function

$$D = e^{-\theta \tau^c}. \tag{12.1}$$

In this function, dominance D falls off according to the time distance τ from the peak of the dominance function, to the power c modified by the rate parameter θ. Later in this section we will discuss some other general dominance functions that are possible.

As noted, there is an individual dominance function corresponding to each segment–control parameter pair. We manipulate four parameters to shape the dominance function: the peak magnitude, the rate of magnitude increase prior to peak, the rate of falloff after peak, and the time offset between the peak and the center of the segment. To incorporate the parameter of peak magnitude, the general form of equation 12.1 is expanded to

$$D_{sp} = \alpha_{sp} e^{-\theta \tau^c}. \tag{12.2}$$

Quantity D_{sp} is the dominance of speech segment s over facial control parameter p. The parameter α_{sp} gives the peak magnitude of the dominance function for that segment-parameter pair.

Since there are two rate parameters θ, one for time prior to the peak and the other for time after the peak, equation 12.2 must branch into two separate formulas. In the case of time prior to the dominance peak, the dominance function is

$$D_{sp} = \alpha_{sp}e^{-\theta_{\leftarrow sp}|\tau|^c}, \quad \text{if } \tau \geq 0, \tag{12.3}$$

where $\theta_{\leftarrow sp}$ represents the rate parameter on the anticipatory side. Similarly, the dominance after the peak is given by

$$D_{sp} = \alpha_{sp}e^{-\theta_{\rightarrow sp}|\tau|^c}, \quad \text{if } \tau < 0. \tag{12.4}$$

In both cases, the temporal distance τ from the peak of the dominance function is given by

$$\tau = t_{csp} + t_{osp} - t \tag{12.5}$$

where t is the running time, t_{osp} is the parameter of time offset between the center of segment s and its dominance peak for facial control parameter p, and

$$t_{csp} = t_{starts} + \frac{duration_s}{2} \tag{12.6}$$

gives the time of the center of segment s given its starting time and duration.

In addition to the two θ rate parameters, the power c can be modified to alter the rate of transition on either side of the dominance peak, but this modification is mainly used for altering the rates of transition generally, not for particular segments. In practice, we usually set $c = 1$.

For a given control parameter, by using the dominance functions and target values of all segments in an utterance we can determine what the actual value of that control parameter should be at any given time, using the weighted average

$$F_p(t) = \frac{\sum_{s=1}^{N} (D_{sp}(t) \times T_{sp})}{\sum_{s=1}^{N} D_{sp}(t)} \tag{12.7}$$

where $F_p(t)$ is the value of parameter p at time t, D_{sp} is the dominance of segment s over parameter p, T_{sp} is the target value of segment s for parameter p, and N is the number of segments in the utterance.

Figure 12.6 illustrates a simple case of how the algorithm works. Dominance functions are shown for a single control parameter for two speech segments over time, with the resulting control parameter function. For this example, $\theta_{\leftarrow sp} = \theta_{\rightarrow sp} = .035$, $c = 1$, duration = 100 ms for both segments, the target values of the control parameter are .1 and .9, both α values are 1, and both t_{osp} values are 0. As shown in figure 12.6, a gradual transition occurs between the two targets, although neither target is reached. Figure 12.7 illustrates how the control parameter function changes with changes in the magnitude of the dominance function parameter α_{sp} of segment 1. As the α value of segment 1 decreases, segment 1 allows more of the intrusion of the target value from segment 2.

Figure 12.8 illustrates how the anticipatory θ parameter of segment 2 controls the transition speed between the segments. As θ of segment 2 increases,

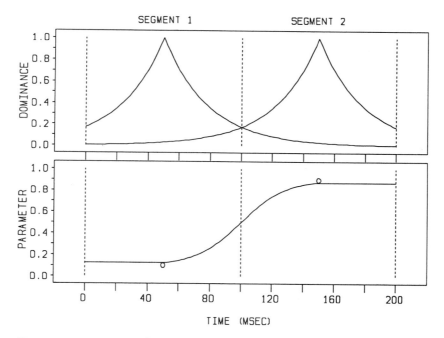

Figure 12.6 Dominance of two speech segments over time (top panel) and the resulting control parameter function (bottom panel). Circles in the bottom panel indicate target control parameter values.

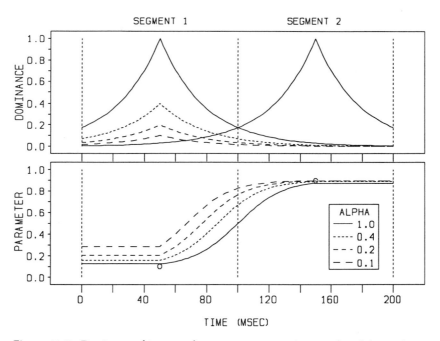

Figure 12.7 Dominance of two speech segments over time (top panel) and the resulting control parameter function (bottom panel) with α of the first segment as a parameter.

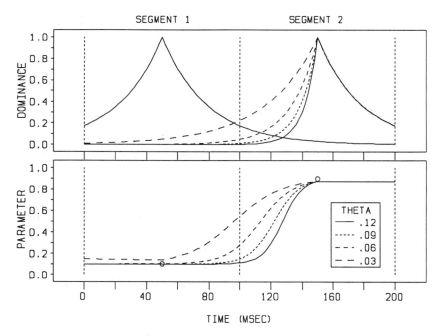

Figure 12.8 Dominance of two speech segments over time (top panel) and the resulting control parameter function (bottom panel) with anticipatory θ of the second segment as a parameter.

the transition between the two segments moves toward segment 2 and becomes steeper. Similarly, figure 12.9 illustrates how changes in the power c of the dominance function control the sharpness of transition and the transition duration between segments. As c increases, control functions come closer to the target values and the transitions become more abrupt, approaching a steplike change between segments.

The top panel of figure 12.10 illustrates the dominance functions for the word *stew*. As can be seen, the /s/ and /t/ segments have very low dominance ($\alpha = .06$) with respect to lip protrusion compared to /u/ ($\alpha = 1$). Also, the low $\theta_{\leftarrow sp}$ value of /u/ (.07) causes its dominance to extend far forward in time. The bottom panel gives the resulting control function for lip protrusion. One can see how the lip protrusion extends forward in time from the vowel. Note that the figure illustrates the dynamics only for the control of lip protrusion. For other control parameters, such as tongue angle, /t/ and /u/ have equal dominance ($\alpha = 1$). This allows the tongue to reach its proper location against the back of the upper teeth for /t/.

As we have noted, other dominance functions are possible in the algorithm. For example,

$$D = e^{-\omega \tau}(1 + \omega \tau) \tag{12.8}$$

more closely approximates a physical transition process as an oscillation curve with critical damping stiffness characteristic ω. Experimentation with

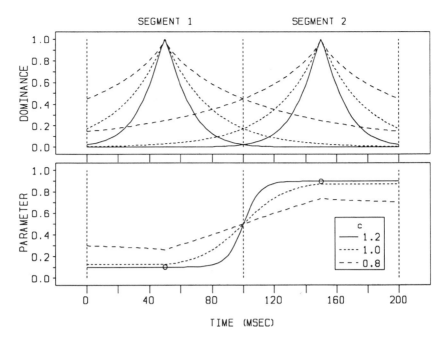

Figure 12.9 Dominance of two speech segments over time (top panel) and the resulting control parameter function (bottom panel) with *c* as a parameter.

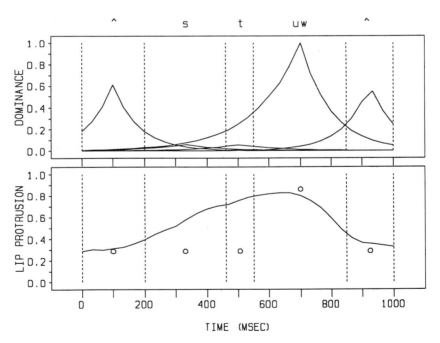

Figure 12.10 Dominance functions (top panel) and parameter control functions (bottom panel) for lip protrusion for the word *stew*.

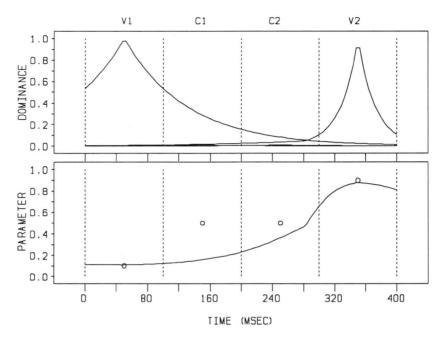

Figure 12.11 Dominance and parameter control functions for a VCCV sequence using an inflected dominance function for V_2.

this version shows rather subtle differences from those produced with equation 12.1. Figures 12.11 and 12.12 illustrate VCCV and VCV sequences with low-dominance consonants when the dominance function of V_2 contains a change in $\theta_{\leftarrow sp}$ 68 ms prior to the V_2 center. In this case both graphs show an acceleration at about 280 ms, in accord with Perkell's hybrid model, as opposed to the more look-ahead-like behavior using equation 12.1. Thus, the general scheme can be configured to account for a variety of production strategies. In addition, language-specific differences can be captured in the segment definitions. For example, recall the distinction reported by Boyce (1990) between English and Turkish speakers' pronunciation of the utterance /utu/: the English speakers exhibited a trough pattern in lip protrusion and the Turkish speakers exhibited a plateau. The difference can be represented by a much lower α value in the lip protrusion dominance of /t/ for the Turkish speakers than for the English speakers. If α is low enough, the high lip protrusion of the /u/ vowels will simply bridge across the /t/.

Another finding of Boyce (1990) was that the depth of the intervocalic trough was positively related to the duration of the consonant or consonants occurring between the two rounded vowels. Thus, short intervowel intervals led to a reduction in the trough. This finding is consistent with the coproduction model and also with Löfqvist's gesture model (Munhall & Löfqvist, 1992) because shorter durations between the vowels should lead to greater overlap of the vowel gestures. This effect of plateauing across intervowel

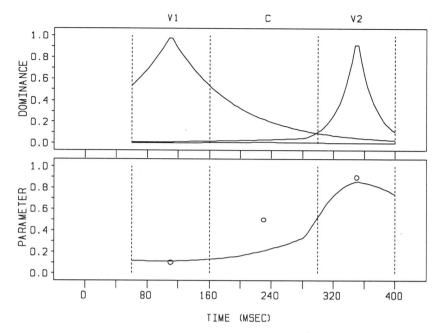

Figure 12.12 Dominance and parameter control functions for a VCV sequence using an inflected dominance function for V_2.

intervals can also be viewed as an aggregation of the two vowel gestures into a single gesture. Such aggregation, varying with speaking rate, has also been demonstrated for glottal gestures associated with a voiceless fricative-stop cluster /s#k/ across a word boundary (Löfqvist & Yoshoika, 1981). For slow speech rates, two laryngeal gestures were observed versus only a single gesture for fast rates. Interestingly, a blend of the two gestures occurred for intermediate rates.

This effect of speaking rate is also captured by our visual speech synthesis algorithm. Returning to the /utu/ example, figure 12.13 shows the lip protrusion parameter over time as a function of speaking rate. In changing the speaking rate, we simply rescale the intrinsic durations for each segment without changing other dynamic parameters (e.g., $\theta_{\leftarrow sp}$). As we shrink segment durations, the dominance functions move closer to each other and overlap more. For a slow (2×) speaking rate, the two lip-rounding gestures are clearly seen. A smaller trough is seen for the normal (1×) speech rate, and for a faster (.5×) speaking rate the two gestures have almost merged into one. Thus, the model can handle changes in speaking rate in a natural fashion.

In summary, our approach to the synthesis of coarticulated speech gives a speech segment a certain amount of dominance over the vocal articulators. Adjacent segments have overlapping dominance functions; the overlap leads to a blending over time of the articulatory commands related to these segments. We have instantiated this model in our synthesis algorithm using

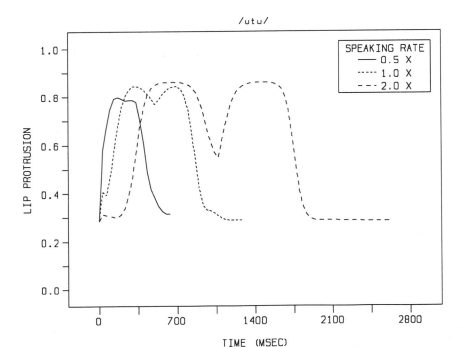

Figure 12.13 Parameter control functions for lip protrusion for /utu/ as a function of time for three speaking rates.

negative exponential functions for dominance. Because articulation of a segment is implemented by many articulators, there is a separate dominance function for each control parameter. Each phoneme is specified in terms of the speech control parameter target values and the dominance function characteristics of magnitude, time offset, and leading attack and trailing decay rates. In chapter 13 we evaluate how well this control strategy works in producing realistic speech. In conclusion of this section we note that the UCSC control strategy has now been successfully used in American English, Mexican Spanish (see band 12.5), and French (Le Goff & Benoit, 1996). Although the French version (see band 12.6) uses the same dominance function approach, it should be noted that the parameterization of the face has evolved somewhat differently. In particular, this face uses only eight parameters for speech: five parameters to control the lips (inner lip width, height, contact protrusion, and upper and lower protrusions), jaw rotation, and two parameters for a simple tongue. We now address an important issue in synthesis and perception: variability in the speech of different individuals.

SYNTHESIZING MANY FACES

Because speechreaders are faced with a variety of talkers in everyday communication, it is important both to consider how this variability affects perception and to model this variability in our visual speech synthesis. In the study of perception, the use of a variety of talkers is necessary to achieve a true picture of which cues are used. Concentration on too small a sample of natural (or synthetic) faces can lead to lack of generality and ecological validity. Therefore, in research based on synthetic visual speech one should be able to simulate the same variety of talkers that speechreaders face in the real world.

One technique that has been used to simulate a variety of faces is texture mapping. An early example of this technique was reported by Yau and Duffy (1988). The investigators used a light striping technique to construct a face of 450 polygons. This mask then received a texture map from a photo of a real face, using a software algorithm. It should be noted that more recent texture-mapped faces, such as our own, have not required implementation of much of the low-level algorithmic detail. Texture mapping is now a standard feature of high-powered graphic workstation (e.g., SGI) hardware and software capabilities. Some interesting work has been done regarding the images used for texture mapping. Kurihara and Arai (1991) reported on a method for combining a series of shots taken as the face is rotated for application to a 3-D facial surface. Another method is to use a 3-D Cyberware scan, which simultaneously records a 3-D surface geometry and a 3-D surface image.

In order to create a variety of faces, we have used texture mapping from both single frontal views and Cyberware scans of real faces in conjunction with adjustment of facial shape parameters for best fit to the source faces. For example, the size of the head, the relative sizes of the jaw, cheeks, neck, and nose, and the relative heights of mouth, nose, eyes, and forehead in the face can all be adjusted. Of special interest for speechreading, we can adjust characteristics such as overall mouth size and lip thickness. Band 12.7 illustrates a sample of our texture-mapped faces, which show differences in sex, race, build, and facial hair. One important issue to be resolved is whether the speech intelligibility of our neutral synthetic face is comparable to that of a texture-mapped face. The question to be answered by this comparison is whether having the additional facial information might help performance (e.g., by focusing attention on the critical facial features) or, alternatively, hurt performance (e.g., by obscuring the pure, abstract facial features).

It may be the case that speechreaders are more prone to errors when faced with talkers having certain facial characteristics. Lesner (1988) summarizes research revealing a variety of facial properties and speaking characteristics that influence visual intelligibility. These include lip thickness; deformations of teeth, lips, and jaw; facial hair; emotional expressiveness; and of course, speech production. The effects of all of these properties can be evaluated systematically when they are manipulated in a synthetic talking head. For example, Lesner states that thin lips are easier to speechread than thick lips. We can test this hypothesis directly by parametrically manipulating the thickness of our synthetic talker's lips. Given the parametric control of synthetic speech, all other features of the face can be held constant or manipulated independently of lip thickness. The manipulations can be done either on the standard face or on the texture-mapped faces of different racial types, allowing us to analyze the effects of the manipulated characteristics either separately or within a racial configural complex. Such research will help us determine how well our results generalize across facial variety.

DEVELOPMENT ENVIRONMENT

Our facial synthesis is being carried out on a Silicon Graphics 4D/CRIMSON-Reality Engine workstation under the IRIX operating system. The software consists of roughly 20,000 lines of C code and uses the SGI GL calls and Overmars' (1990) Forms Library to construct the graphical user interface (GUI). A smaller version of the visual speech software, with the same functionality but without the GUI, is available for use under FORTRAN f77 main programs for perceptual experiments incorporating auditory speech and the collection of responses from participants.

Band 12.8 illustrates the GUI for visual speech development. The master panel in the lower right part of the screen has facial controls; facilities for editing speech segment definitions, sentence input, and speaking rate; controls for parameter tracking; call-ups for subsidiary control panels; and other miscellaneous controls. The upper right panel is a text-based interface that can control the face using files of commands. Also in the upper right portion of the screen is a menu panel for the selection of members of a set of tokens for synthesis. In this example, the menu is set to call one of 27 CV syllables whose definitions have been read in from a file. The lower left panel is the display output. This area can also be output in NTSC video using the SGI broadcast video output option. The upper left area contains the replay controls with cursors for temporal zooming and for viewing frames of the face forward or backward in time, as well as three plots displaying the time course of selected control parameters (bottom), dominance functions (middle), and derived facial measures (top). The two lower displays currently show the plots for the example *stew*, also seen in figure 12.10.

Band 12.9 is a closeup of the display panel showing the face articulating /ða/. The tongue that is visible here is a new addition, which has been implemented as a shaded surface made of a polygon mesh, controlled by several parameters: tongue length, angle, width, and thickness. This is a considerable simplification compared to a real tongue, which has many more degrees of freedom, but it contributes a great deal to visual speech and can be computed very quickly (allowing 60 frames/sec animation of the face). We have recently created a more complex 14-parameter tongue model, based in part on magnetic resonance imaging (MRI) scans, which is currently undergoing testing in perceptual experiments.

Band 12.10 shows a close-up of the GUI master panel. The yellow slides relate to speech control, the blue slides relate to face viewing parameters, and the pink slides control nonspeech facial characteristics. To the left of each slide control is a row of buttons used to select functions for plotting. The far left buttons are for selecting which control parameters to plot. When pressed they will show the color used in the plot for the chosen parameter. The center buttons are for selecting which parameter's dominance function to plot. In addition to the tongue control parameters, a number of other new parameters (added since the earlier Parke models) are used in speech control, including parameters to raise the lower lip, roll the lower lip, and translate the jaw forward and backward. Some parameters have more global effects than in the original Parke model. For example, as the lips are protruded the cheeks pull inward somewhat, and raising the upper lip causes some parts of the face above the upper lip to rise as well.

Because the positions of some articulators, most notably the tongue, are obscured in normal viewing, one can cause the face to be displayed with varying degrees of transparency using one of the GUI control slides. This is illustrated in band 12.11 with a side view of a transparent face.

English text entered into the interface can be automatically translated into phonemes using the Naval Research Laboratory letter-to-phoneme rule algorithm (Elovitz et al., 1976). In addition, we can utilize TTS systems such as MITalk or the AT&T/Lucent Flextalk to produce the phoneme information as well as synchronized auditory speech. Alternatively, phoneme strings in arpabet (one- to two-letter codes for phonetic symbols) can be entered.

Band 12.12 shows one of the subsidiary panels called up from the master panel, the one responsible for editing materials, lighting, and other display characteristics. Standard settings can be read in from files and the new versions saved.

Band 12.13 shows another subsidiary panel used for controlling a laser videodisc via a serial line. The Bernstein and Eberhardt (1986) speechreading corpus disks can be played to compare natural and synthetic visual speech side by side. The natural video can be displayed on a monitor adjacent to the SGI console or imported to the computer using a video I/O board under the control of that panel. Band 12.14 shows a typical frame from the videodisc. Using the controls on the panel one can cause the facial synthesis to play in synchrony with the videodisc, either in real time or one frame at a time, forward or backward, and with or without audio.

Adjustments can be made and maintained in the delay between the synthetic and natural articulations to bring the two into close agreement. This process is also useful in refining the target values and temporal characteristics that define the synthetic speech segments.

Band 12.15 further illustrates the use of texture mapping with our talking head, with a rendition of Saint Teresa's vision of angels (which inspired Bernini's Baroque sculpture). For each texture, selectable from a menu in a texture control panel, information is stored regarding scaling and centering coefficients for the texture image, facial control parameter settings to bring the face shape into conformity with the image, and materials settings. Once assignments have been made between facial vertices and points in the textures, they are maintained as the face is manipulated. Various texture-mapping modes can be selected, and for some faces, mapping of texture to the eyes can be enabled. In the texture-mapped mode the maximum rendering rate is limited to 30 frames per second.

We have seen in this chapter that synthetic visual speech is an important tool in speech science, having experimental, theoretical, and applied value. There are many approaches to the encoding of facial information—from expensive, low-level image reproduction to more abstract approaches that use parametric description to translate images. Among these, the field branches into the physically based and terminal-analog routes, of which we have taken the later for its economy, speed, and ease of use. Our synthesis design incorporates polygon topology with parametric controls of vertices, a gestural model of coarticulation, and the capacity for synthesizing personalized faces using face-shape parameters and texture mapping. In the next chapter we focus on the realism and naturalness of our synthesis. All of the various uses to which the synthetic talking head can be put—from perceptual research to aids for the hearing impaired—share one paramount requirement for success: that the synthetic talking head be close to reality. We will look at a series of experiments that compare the intelligibility of the talking head to that of a real human speaker, and we will discuss some of the work we have done to improve the synthetic speech in response to the results of these evaluations.

13 Evaluating Talking Faces

*You know, this applied science is just as interesting as pure science, and what's
more it's a damn sight more difficult.*
—Sir Henry Tizard, Haldane Memorial Lecture, 1955

In the previous chapter we argued that synthetic visual speech is a valid and
even preferable substitute for real human faces in the research of perceptual
issues. Of course, varying degrees of naturalness and realism can be achieved
in synthesis, and our goal is to bring our talking head as close as possible
to the real thing. In this chapter we discuss the process of evaluating and
improving the synthetic speech—aware of the sobering fact that auditory
speech synthesis is still far short of natural speech even after 30 years of
intensive research and development. Although psychologists should know
better, we have in the past been easily swayed by the subjective comments
of many viewers, who claim that "Baldi seems so natural." These positive
assessments might reflect, in part, the lesser informativeness of visible speech
relative to audible speech: people can be less discriminating about a modality
that is on the whole less informative. To obtain a more objective evaluation
we have been performing, in parallel with our more traditional theoretical
experiments, an ongoing series of experiments aimed at evaluating the realism of our speech synthesis through comparison with natural speech. Realism of the visible speech is measured in terms of its intelligibility to
speechreaders. So our experiments are concerned with providing a comparative measure of intelligibility. The goal of the research is to learn how
Baldi falls short of natural talkers and to modify the synthesis accordingly to
bring it ever closer to natural visible speech.

It is important to stress that Baldi has been evolving continuously in our
attempt to achieve as realistic a synthesis as possible. Our story of Baldi's
tongue is a good example. He arrived without a tongue, which is not
uncommon in facial animation. None of the characters in *Toy Story* had a
moving tongue—although the animation of the mouth area was very convincing and very accurately synchronized with the natural auditory speech.

We added a tongue, which is implemented as a shaded surface made of a
polygon mesh, controlled by four parameters: tongue length, angle, width,

and thickness. Although this tongue model contributes a great deal to visual speech and can be computed very quickly, it is considerably simpler than a real tongue—merely a rigid grooved paddle with simple movements. It soon became obvious that our model allowed very little flexibility for mimicking the movements of a natural tongue. For instance, in natural speech certain consonants cause cupping or grooving of the tongue, which also coarticulates to following vowels. In the articulation of the stridents /s/ and /z/, a deep groove typically occurs down the center of the tongue (see, e.g., Hardcastle, 1975; Ladefoged & Maddieson, 1986), and for /ð, θ/ we observe that there is a cupping action. In addition, tongue articulations generally involve raising a specific part of the tongue, such as the tongue tip or body. In order to simulate these characteristics, it was necessary to develop a completely new tongue. The new model is based on B-spline curves controlled by seven sagittal and seven coronal parameters including tip, body, and overall thickness; tip and top height; tip, body, and top advancement; width; grooving; edge height and thickness; and tip shape. We believe this new design succeeds in improving the intelligibility of several of Baldi's consonantal articulations.

Development of the tongue illustrates just one aspect of the continuing evolution of our synthetic head. More incremental changes take the form of minute adjustments to the control parameters and to the parameters of the corresponding dominance functions. Our initial development of these parameter values was based on simple observation of natural speech. Empirical tests provide a more objective assessment of the settings and help to indicate where further adjustments are needed. We turn now to a review of some of the empirical tests that were used to evaluate Baldi's speech at different stages of development, and the improvements that were initiated by the results.

TEST ITEMS

There is a small cottage industry that has been involved with the evaluation of auditory speech synthesis (Benoit & Pols, 1992; Carlson, Granström & Nord, 1992; Falaschi, 1992; Greene, Logan & Pisoni, 1986; van Santen, 1993). Several decisions had to be made about the test items and data analysis (Bernstein, Demorest & Eberhardt, 1994). As with most decisions of this type, trade-offs and conflicting constraints dictate that there is no apparently correct solution. With regard to what test items should be presented to subjects, arguments can be made for the use of speech segments, words, or sentences. Speech segments in the form of nonsense words have the advantage of being purely sensory information with little possible contribution from top-down context. Sentences, in contrast, represent a situation that is more analogous to the use of speech in real-world contexts. For a number of reasons we chose the intermediate level of single words. Words are the main currency of spoken language (Cole & Jakimik, 1978, 1980). Test words make use of the text-to-speech component of the synthesis and permit the testing of consonant and vowel segments as well as consonant clusters and diphthongs. Also, we wanted a list of stimuli that would generate straightforward and easily analyzed responses from speechreaders. One limiting factor in the testing of isolated speech segments is that the subjects must use some type of phonetic notation to report their speechreading. When subjects are asked to report complete sentences, it is not entirely clear how perceptual accuracy should be scored. Should one score accuracy at the level of speech segments or at the level of understanding the gist of the message? Test words, on the other hand, can be very easy to score if we require that subjects give only single words as responses. Finally, we sought a bimodally recorded test list in natural speech that would be available to the speech and animation communities, and such a list already existed in the form of a corpus of one-syllable words presented in citation speech on the Bernstein and Eberhardt (1986) videodisc.

The reader might be surprised to learn that the test items presented were made up of only visible speech. Band 13.1 illustrates for the reader that visible speech alone can communicate valuable messages. Given the advantages we have touted for the expanded factorial design, why didn't we continue to exploit it? In addition, other investigators have been successful in tasks that assess the advantage of adding visible speech to auditory speech presented in noise (e.g., Adjoudani & Benoit, 1996). There are many reasons for our choice, but first and foremost, limiting our study to just visible speech significantly reduces the number of trial types. This simplification allows us to make many more observations per data point, and therefore to obtain a more valid and reliable measure of accuracy and confusions. Furthermore, there is no theoretical imperative to use bimodal speech in order to determine the intelligibility of visible speech. We have seen repeatedly that the contribution of the visible speech on bimodal trials follows directly from its identification on unimodal visual trials in the manner prescribed by the FLMP. This result stands in sharp contrast to Campbell's (1996) belief that silent speechreading makes use of different processes than those employed in bimodal speech perception.

EXPERIMENT 1: INITIAL ASSESSMENT

General Method

The current studies follow the methodology of Cohen, Walker, and Massaro (1996) in which a direct comparison is made between people's ability to speechread a natural talker and our synthetic talker. We presented silently for identification monosyllabic English words (e.g., *sing, bin, dung, dip, seethe*) produced either by a natural speaker (Bernstein & Eberhardt videodisc, 1986) or by our synthetic talker, randomly intermixed. The synthetic stimuli used a specific set of parameter values and dominance functions for each phoneme and our blending function for coarticulation. The AT&T text-to-speech (TtS) module was utilized to provide the phonemic representation for each word and the relative durations of the speech segments, in addition to synthesizing the auditory speech (presented as feedback) (Olive, 1990). Other characteristics such as speaking rate and average acoustic amplitude were equated for the natural and the synthetic talker. The speech on the videodisc was articulated in citation form and thus at a relatively slow speaking rate. Band 13.2 gives some sample trials from the experiment.

College students who were native speakers of American English served as subjects in two 40-minute sessions each day for two days. Up to four subjects at a time were tested in separate sound-attenuated rooms under computer control with video from the laser disc (the human talker) or the computer being presented over 13-inch color monitors. On each trial the subjects were first presented with a silent word from one of the two faces and then typed in their answers on a terminal keyboard. Only actual monosyllabic English words (from a list of about 12,000, derived mainly from the Oxford English dictionary) were accepted as valid answers. After all subjects had responded, they received feedback by a second presentation of the word, this time with auditory speech (natural or synthetic) and with the word shown in written form on the left side of the video monitor.

There were 264 test words, and each word was tested with both synthetic and natural speech, for a total of $2 \times 264 = 528$ test trials. For the counterbalancing of the test words and presentation modes, the subjects were split into two groups. Each group received the same random order of words, but the assignment of the two faces was reversed. Five unscored practice trials using additional words preceded each experimental session of 132 test words.

Analysis

By comparing the overall proportion correct and analyzing the perceptual confusions, we can determine how closely the synthetic visual speech matches the natural visual speech. The questions to be answered are: what is the extent of confusions, and how similar are the patterns of confusions for the two talkers? We simplify the analysis by ignoring confusions that take place between visually similar phonemes. Because of the limited data available in visible speech as compared to audible speech, many phonemes are virtually indistinguishable by sight even when produced by a natural face, and so are expected to be easily confused. To eliminate these nonserious confusions from consideration, we group visually indistinguishable phonemes into categories called *visemes*. The concept of the viseme has traditionally been used to parallel that of phoneme—that is, a difference between visemes is considered significant, informative, and categorical to the perceiver, whereas a difference within a viseme is not. In general, then, we expect confusions to take place within visemes but not between them. How-

Table 13.1   Table of consonant visemes and viseme frequencies

Viseme	Description	Phonemes	Initial Frequency	Final Frequency
{p}	Labial stop	/p,b,m/	58	45
{f}	Labiodental fricative	/f,v/	20	10
{θ}	Interdental fricative	/θ,ð/	7	6
{t}	Low visibility	/t,d,n,k,g,ŋ,h,j/	83	135
{s}	Alveolar fricative	/s,z/	25	21
{l}	Lateral	/l/	15	20
{r}	Retroflex	/r/	18	2
{ʃ}	Palato-alveolar	/ʃ,ž,č,ǰ/	29	21
{w}	Labial approximant	/w/	8	0

Visemes are symbolized using representative phonemes; thus, any viseme {x} denotes the set of phonemes visually nondistinct from /x/.

Table 13.2   Table of vowel visemes and viseme frequencies

Viseme	Description	Phonemes	Frequency
{i}	High front rounded	/i,I/	75
{ε}	Non-high front	/ε,æ,eI,aI/	107
{a}	Lower back	/a,ɔ,ʌ/	55
{U}	Central	/U,ɝ,ə/	3
{u}	High back rounded	/u/	1
{ɔI}	Diphthong	/ɔI/	2
{aU}	Diphthong	/aU/	13
{oU}	Diphthong	/oU/	8

ever, some confusions do take place between viseme categories. This is partly due to the difficulty of speechreading. But also, as is true of most categories, visemes are not sharply defined (i.e., they are fuzzy), and any sharp definitions imposed are therefore somewhat arbitrary and inaccurate. Even so, it is worthwhile to use some standard viseme groupings in order to assess how well the more meaningful visible speech differences are perceived.

We group the consonants into the nine viseme categories used by Walden et al. (1977) and Massaro, Cohen, and Gesi (1993). These nine visemes are defined in table 13.1. The eight vowel visemes, based on Montgomery and Jackson (1983), are given in table 13.2. Note that our practice is to symbolize visemes using representative phonemes in alternative bracketing. In terms of this notation, any viseme {x} can be said to denote the set of phonemes visually nondistinct from /x/. As can also be seen in tables 13.1 and 13.2 the visemes occurred with widely varying frequencies in the words on the test list. This is due to a number of factors, including the different number of phonemes that each viseme subsumes, differences in the frequency of occurrence of the component phonemes in the language generally, and certain

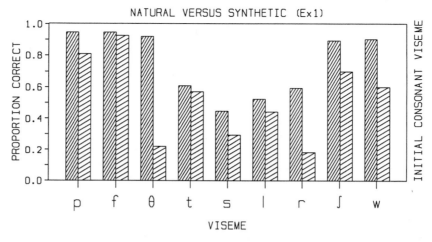

Figure 13.1 Proportion of correct responses for initial-consonant visemes for natural speech (dark bars) and synthetic speech (light bars) as a function of viseme class. (Results from experiment 1.)

idiosyncrasies of the Bernstein and Eberhardt natural speech corpus from which our own list is derived.

Using both phonemes and visemes as recognition units, a number of analyses were automatically carried out on the subjects' responses. These included derivation of confusion matrices for consonants (initial and final), vowels, consonant clusters, consonant visemes (initial and final), and vowel visemes; as well as calculation of the proportion of correct identifications of consonants and vowels, consonant and vowel visemes, and words. Our goal is to present representative analyses that are illustrative of the general pattern of results. The results were first pooled across experimental sessions and across subjects to increase their reliability. Because 264 test words were used, there were 264 × 14 subjects for a total of 3,696 observations.

Overall recognition of the initial consonant averaged about 64% correct. Figure 13.1 reveals a significant advantage for natural over synthetic speech. For consonants in initial position, performance using the natural face (.761) was superior to that for the synthetic face (.533). The synthetic speech was clearly poorer for some distinctions than others. The identification of the synthetic interdental fricatives, the viseme {θ}, was particularly poor, but the synthetic speech was also poorer for the visemes {s}, {l}, {r}, {ʃ}, and {w}. For two visemes, {f} and {t}, however, performance for the two faces is about equivalent. The major discrepancies between synthetic and natural speech occur for {θ}, {r}, {ʃ}, and {w}, the first of which (interdentals) is a particularly striking limitation of the synthetic speech.

Figure 13.2 shows the stimulus-response confusions for initial-consonant visemes for the two faces. In the figure, the correct responses fall on the main diagonal. The overall advantage of natural speech is also apparent. As expected from the poorer recognition performance, there are many more off-

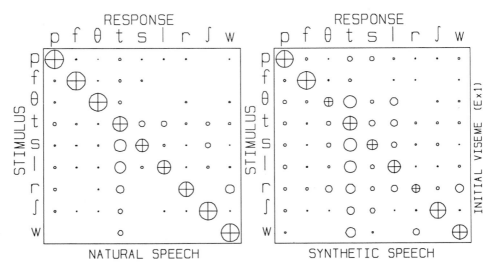

Figure 13.2 Stimulus-response confusions for initial-consonant visemes for natural (left panel) and synthetic (right panel) talkers. The area of each circle is proportional to the response probability. (Results from experiment 1.)

diagonal responses for the synthetic than for the natural speech. In some cases, the confusions are the same for both faces but occur more frequently for the synthetic. For example, {s} is generally confused with {t}, {l}, and {ʃ}, but more often with synthetic than with natural speech. On the other hand, some confusions are unique to the synthetic speech. Although the natural {b} is identified almost perfectly, the synthetic {b} is sometimes perceived as {s}. Also, the synthetic {r} is sometimes called {l}, although this seldom occurs in natural speech.

Note that synthetic {θ} is overwhelmingly mistaken for {t} and {l}. This confusion suggests that a lingual articulation is being perceived but that the distinctive characteristic of the tongue between the teeth is not being noticed in the synthetic speech as it is in the natural speech. Figure 13.3 shows this interdental fricative during articulation in both the synthetic and natural speech. It is difficult to see from this comparison what properties of the speech could account for such a large difference in perception.

These results also demonstrate that for natural as well as synthetic speech, there was a broad range of performance across the nine viseme classes. Clearly, some of the visemes are much more discriminable than others, and the actual status of some of the viseme classes might be questioned. For our purposes, however, this categorization provides a helpful simplification of the data; and, because the same classes are used for both natural and synthetic speech, it provides an accurate picture of relative performance.

Figure 13.4 shows the proportion of correct final viseme identifications for the two faces, and figure 13.5 shows the confusions. There are only eight viseme classes because {w} does not occur in final position in English. Overall

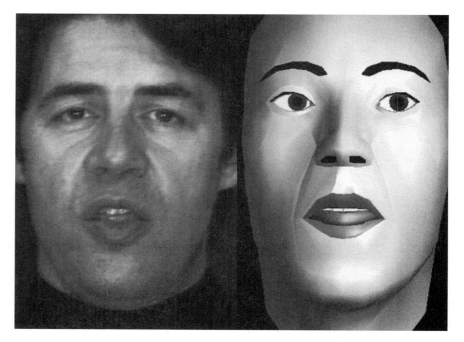

Figure 13.3 Interdental fricative during articulation for the natural and synthetic talkers.

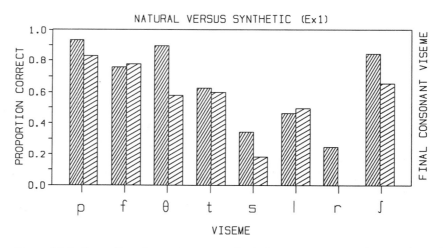

Figure 13.4 Proportion of correct responses for final-consonant visemes for natural speech (dark bars) and synthetic speech (light bars) as a function of viseme class. (Results from experiment 1.)

Creating Talking Faces

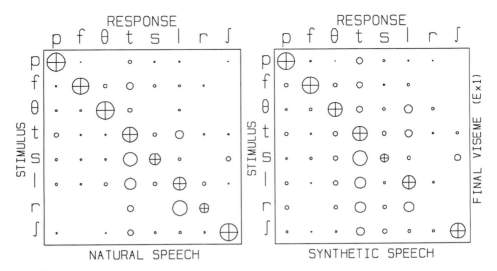

Figure 13.5 Stimulus-response confusions for final-consonant visemes for natural (left panel) and synthetic (right panel) talkers. The area of each circle is proportional to the response probability. (Results from experiment 1.)

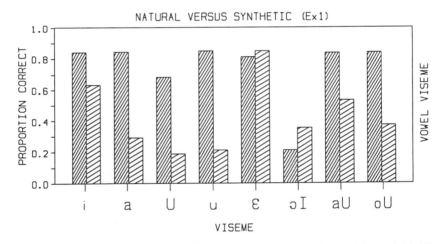

Figure 13.6 Proportion of correct responses for vowel visemes for natural speech (dark bars) and synthetic speech (light bars) as a function of viseme class. (Results from experiment 1.)

performance averaged .654 for natural speech and .520 for synthetic speech. Performance from the two faces is about equivalent for {f}, {t}, and {l}. As with initial consonants, there was a broad range of performance across the eight viseme classes.

Analysis of performance on vowel visemes shows an even larger advantage for the natural face (.747) over the synthetic (.433). Figure 13.6 shows the proportion correct vowel viseme responses, and figure 13.7 shows the confusions. As these figures show, performance on the natural face was

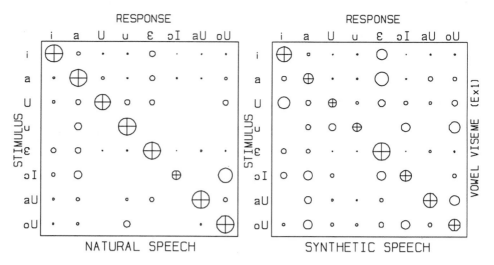

Figure 13.7 Stimulus-response confusions for vowel visemes for natural (left panel) and synthetic (right panel) talkers. The area of each circle is proportional to the response probability. (Results from experiment 1.)

better for every viseme except {i} and {ɔI}. It is clear there is still a significant distance to go to reach the degree of information present in naturally spoken vowels.

AT&T versus MITalk Synthesis

As stated in the section on method, in this experiment we employed the AT&T TtS module to derive the phoneme sequences and their durations for our test words. The control parameter values used in this experiment are the same as those used in an earlier experiment that utilized MITalk TtS (Cohen, Walker & Massaro, 1996). A direct comparison was therefore possible between the two text-to-speech systems used in the two experiments. It turned out that performance was equally good across the two experiments, which indicates that the choice between the two text-to-speech modules is not critical for the quality of the visible speech synthesis.

Improving Phoneme Specifications

In light of the results we have discussed, we can see that there is room for a great deal of improvement in our synthetic speech. Improvement of our visual speech synthesis entails revising the phoneme specifications on the basis of several sources of information, including (1) phonetic descriptions of articulation (e.g., Ladefoged, 1975), (2) visual comparisons of the synthesized speech with that of a human talker, and (3) examination of recognition errors. Although our general evaluation of the speech is based on viseme performance, the modifications are made to specific phonemes, which is the level at which parameter values are set. In most cases, however, phonemes that are under the same viseme and have the same articulatory trajectories (e.g., /b/ and /p/) will receive the same adjustments. To briefly illustrate the phoneme revision procedure, we describe the assessment of improvements needed for each phoneme (or set of phonemes) and the types of modifications made to the articulatory parameter settings and dominance functions in response to that analysis. In this cycle of revision our efforts were focused mainly on improving the consonants.

First, the labial stops /p, b, m/ were often mistaken for clusters of /s/ followed by a labial stop, a confusion that does not appear with the human talker. The articulation of /s/ involves separation of the lips whereas the labial stops have lip closure. To eliminate the confusion with an initial /s/, we emphasized the labial articulation by adjusting the targets for lip position parameters to increase lip contact and relocated the dominance peaks (time centers) of these parameters earlier in the segments to ensure an early onset of closure.

The synthetic interdental fricatives /θ, ð/ were often mistaken for /h, l/ and alveolar and velar stops, indicating that the interdental articulation was not visible enough. In these fricatives the teeth should be very close together, and the lower lip is often used to direct the airstream toward the upper teeth (Ladefoged & Maddieson, 1986). Those characteristics were emphasized in the new parameter set. Adjustments were made to the tongue length and tongue angle parameter settings as well as to those controlling mouth aperture in order to better produce an articulation between tongue and teeth. In making these modifications, we noted that finer control over different parts of the tongue would aid in the synthesis of the segments. A similar observation was made for /l/.

For the viseme group {t}, with the low-visibility phonemes /t, d, n, k, g, ŋ, h, j/, confusion data were examined separately for each place of articulation. The alveolar stops /t, d, n/ were most often confused with /s, l/, indicating that the place of articulation was being recognized but the manner of articulation—a stop—was not. Phonetic studies of alveolar stops (e.g., Kantner & West, 1960) describe these segments as involving a slight raising of the upper lip and a slight lowering of the lower lip. The jaw also lowers. We enhanced those aspects of the segments by adjusting the target parameter settings for lip and jaw height. The velar stops /k, g, ŋ/ were most systematically mistaken for /l/. More spreading at the corners of the mouth appeared to be needed, as well as some extension of the chin and cheeks and a lower tongue angle. Target parameter settings were adjusted accordingly, and dominance functions were strengthened for the appropriate facial gestures. Another member of the {t} viseme, /h/, was often mistaken for an alveolar consonant. We based the revisions of settings for this phoneme on the phonetic observation that rather than having one position for the visible articulation of /h/, the mouth should assume the position of the following vowel (Kantner & West, 1960). To realize this kind of dependent articulation, we decreased the magnitude of the dominance function for jaw rotation, so that the mouth aperture for /h/ would more closely assume that of the following vowel. The tongue angle was also set closer to that for the vowels.

The confusions indicated that /w/ needed more lip rounding, so we increased the relevant parameter settings. Also, initial /r/ was insufficiently rounded, especially before front or central unrounded vowels, so we boosted settings for parameters contributing to lip protrusion and a circular mouth aperture—both characteristics of rounding in /r/. We noted, however, that in natural speech final /r/ is not as rounded as initial /r/. To accommodate this difference, we modified the AT&T TtS to output separate allophones for initial and final /r/ and gave these two separate definitions—an approach that might be extended to some other phonemes.

The palato-alveolar group /ʃ, ž, č, ǰ/ were often confused with /s/, /t/, and in the case of the affricates /č, ǰ/ there were also confusions with an /st/ cluster. The palato-alveolar phonemes involve lip rounding, in contrast to the alveolar segments /s, t/, so rounding of the mouth aperture and protrusion of the lips were increased. To enhance the appearance of a stop followed by a fricative (as in /tʃ/) rather than a fricative followed by a stop (as in /st/), the dominance peaks of the /ʃ/, especially those for the lip parameters, were moved to a point later in the segment.

EXPERIMENT 2: SECOND GENERATION

Method and Analysis

With our new parameter set, we replicated the first experiment with 11 new subjects. All experimental conditions and procedural details were identical to those of the first experiment.

Figures 13.8 and 13.9 give the identification accuracy and the confusion matrix for performance on the initial-consonant visemes. For initial consonants, the modifications improved correct identification of the synthetic speech by almost 20%, from .534 to .643. Performance on the natural speech remained at about 76% correct. Performance on the interdentals was still very poor for synthetic speech, but every other viseme category was improved to approach that of natural speech. This result is very encouraging because it shows that our scheme for synthesis can be improved within its parameters to better represent the information found in natural visible speech. Figures 13.10 and 13.11 give the identification accuracy and the confusion matrix for performance on the final-consonant visemes. For final consonants, the modifications decreased the deficit by about half compared to the first experiment. Performance on the synthetic speech averaged .579 compared to .645 for natural speech. Performance on the the visemes {θ} and {ʃ} did not change, but recognition of the other visemes improved to

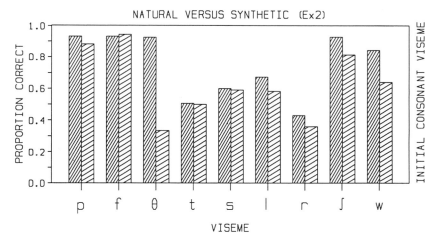

Figure 13.8 Proportion of correct responses for initial-consonant visemes for natural speech (dark bars) and synthetic speech (light bars) as a function of viseme class. (Results from experiment 2.)

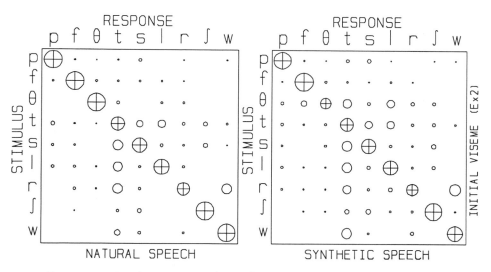

Figure 13.9 Stimulus-response confusions for initial-consonant visemes for natural (left panel) and synthetic (right panel) talkers. The area of each circle is proportional to the response probability. (Results from experiment 2.)

approach the performance levels of natural speech. Figure 13.12 shows the proportion correct vowel viseme responses and figure 13.13 shows the confusions. As revealed by comparisons with figures 13.6 and 13.7, there was very little improvement in the synthetic vowels. This is not surprising, because our efforts with the vowels in the first cycle of revisions were minor and the focus was on consonants. However, the vowels received considerable attention in the revisions that followed experiment 2.

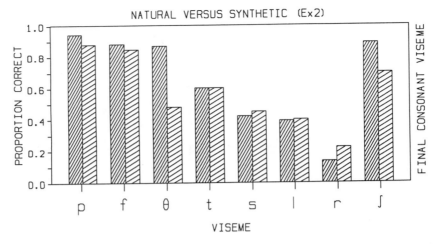

Figure 13.10 Proportion of correct responses for final-consonant visemes for natural speech (dark bars) and synthetic speech (light bars) as a function of viseme class. (Results from experiment 2.)

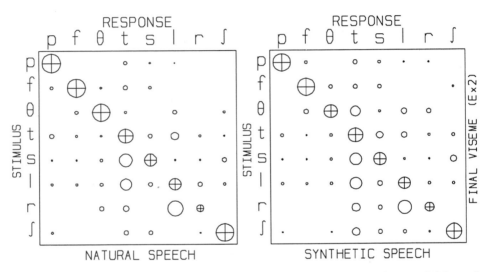

Figure 13.11 Stimulus-response confusions for final-consonant visemes for natural (left panel) and synthetic (right panel) talkers. The area of each circle is proportional to the response probability. (Results from experiment 2.)

Improving Phoneme Specifications

The high front vowels /i/ and /I/ (the viseme {i}) tended to be confused with the mid-front vowels /eI/ and /ε/. In natural speech, distinguishing features between these two sets of front vowels are degree of mouth opening and degree of lip retraction: the high front vowels are close and retracted, whereas the mid-front vowels are more open and less retracted. It was decided that /i/ and /I/ were sufficiently retracted, but that they were not

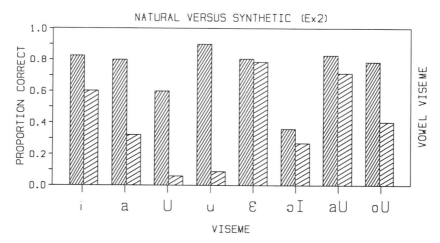

Figure 13.12 Proportion of correct responses for vowel visemes for natural speech (dark bars) and synthetic speech (light bars) as a function of viseme class. (Results from experiment 2.)

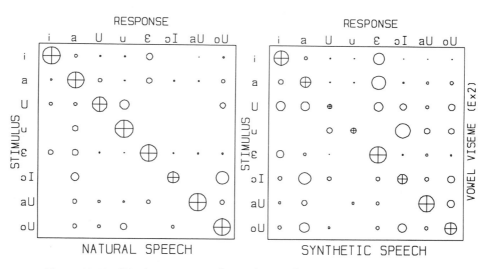

Figure 13.13 Stimulus-response confusions for vowel visemes for natural (left panel) and synthetic (right panel) talkers. The area of each circle is proportional to the response probability. (Results from experiment 2.)

closed enough to be clearly distinguishable from the mid-front vowels. To correct this problem, the target setting of jaw rotation for these two segments was reduced.

The {a} viseme consists of the lower back vowels /a/, /ʌ/, and /ɔ/. The two nonround members, /a/ and /ʌ/, were often mistaken for the lower front vowels /ɛ/, /eɪ/, and /æ/. These two classes, the (nonround) low back vowels and the low front vowels, have comparable degrees of jaw opening but differ from each other in the dimension of lip retraction: the front vowels are retracted and the back vowels are not. On inspection it became clear that our synthetic /a/ and /ʌ/ did convey a misleading suggestion of retraction. The feature of retraction involves the corners of the mouth moving outward and upward ("smiling") and the lips pulling away from each other to bare the teeth somewhat. To eliminate the appearance of retraction, therefore, we (1) decreased the settings for the parameters "mouth x" and "mouth corner x," which distend the corners of the mouth, and (2) adjusted the parameters "raise upper lip" and "raise lower lip" to bring the lips closer together so that they do not bare the teeth.

The viseme {ʊ} contains the central vowels /ʊ/, /ə/, and /ɝ/ (a syllabic /r/). Only /ʊ/ was tested. This phoneme tended to be confused with the front vowels /I/, /ɛ/, and /eI/ and with the diphthong /ɔI/. Important to the interpretation of these results is the fact that all tokens of /ʊ/ in our list of test words were k-final (e.g., *look, nook, shook*, etc.)—reflecting the majority of /ʊ/ words in the language. Our study of productions of such words suggested that the recognition problem with /ʊ/ was actually caused by the adjacent /k/, which appeared too vowel-like. The vowel-like appearance of the /k/ was due to the fact that it actually achieved *higher* jaw rotation (wider opening) than the preceding vowel; this resulted in a second opening of the mouth that could be misconstrued as the vowel. This "vowel" lacked the degree of rounding of /ʊ/, hence the confusion with front unrounded vowels.

To counter this excessive opening, we addressed the natural coarticulation behavior of /k/, which is that /k/ and other velar stops tend to assimilate in jaw rotation to whatever is adjacent rather than asserting their own peculiar degree of jaw rotation. (In this way velar stops contrast with alveolar stops, which are always articulated with the jaw closed. There is a possible physical explanation: with the jaw open the blade of the tongue cannot easily make closure against the alveolar ridge, but the back of the tongue is still within easy reach of the soft palate.) By decreasing to a low level the dominance of the velar stops /k,g,ŋ/ over jaw rotation, we smoothed away the additional jaw opening at the end of words like *took*; the velars also adapted better to the jaw rotation of wider vowels such as /a/ in *rock*.

The vowel /u/ was overwhelmingly mistaken for /ɔI/. Unfortunately, tokens of /u/ in our list of test words were limited to the one item *boot*. The fact that /u/ was commonly mistaken for /ɔI/ in this context is not so much an evaluation of /u/—for the data are not general enough—but an evaluation of the sequence /ut/. The perception of an /I/ offglide might have been produced by an excessive loss of rounding in the transition from /u/ to /t/.

The phoneme /oʊ/ was frequently confused with /ɔ/. We believe this is due not to a fault in the parameter settings of /oʊ/ but to a fault in the TtS synthesis that carries out segmentation. Currently the program outputs /oʊ/ as a monophthong (simple vowel), when actually it should be a diphthong (transitional vowel) with an /ʊ/ offglide, analogous to the diphthong /eI/ with /I/ offglide (Ladefoged, 1975). The reason synthetic /oʊ/ as a monophthong was mistaken for /ɔ/ is that /ɔ/ is the monophthongal counterpart of /oʊ/. We intend to fix this problem through a modification in the AT&T text-to-speech outputs.

Another phoneme whose performance may be corrected by changes in basic TtS segmentation is the diphthong /ɔI/, frequently mistaken for the diphthong /aI/. The TtS emits /ɔI/ as the sequence /ɔ/ + /I/ and /aI/ as the sequence /ʌ/ + /I/. Since /ɔ/ and /ʌ/ are in the same viseme class, it should come as no surprise that our /ɔI/ is easily mistaken for /aI/. However, natural /ɔI/ is visibly distinct from /aI/. Although traditional phonetic descriptions (e.g., Thomas, 1958) hold that the nucleus segment of /ɔI/ is /ɔ/, we believe that that description might be too imprecise for our purposes and that the nucleus of /ɔI/ is in fact considerably rounder and more closed than /ɔ/. Accordingly, we propose to amend the TtS program so that it outputs /ɔI/ with a nucleus vowel that is nonidentical with /ɔ/, creating a new allophone that we can then set to be rounder and more closed.

The remaining vowel visemes {ɛ} and {aʊ} performed relatively well, so no adjustments were made.

Of the consonants, the interdental fricatives {θ} still showed the weakest performance. For this reason, we placed considerable focus on that class of phonemes. Our efforts with interdentals were greatly assisted by two advances: the new tongue design, which achieves a decidedly more tongue-like shape than the previous paddle-shaped design, and the new tongue parameters, which provide greater flexibility of movement. By improving the naturalness of the tongue itself we aim to improve the recognizability of articulations involving the tongue, such as interdentals.

Through careful study of human talkers, we analyzed the visible action of the interdental articulation into four simultaneous gestures: (1) The jaw drops slightly; (2) the tip of the tongue protrudes between the teeth, and its topside (blade) makes contact with the edge of the upper teeth; (3) the central part of the upper lip rises slightly, exposing the edge of the upper teeth; (4) the lower lip rises and rounds, making contact around the underside of the protruding tongue. In less emphatic productions, some or all of these features may be attenuated or absent.

Gesture 2 is arguably the most critical to visual recognition of interdentals, because it reveals the place of constriction of the consonant. That is, recognition of interdental fricatives entails first and foremost knowing that the blade of the tongue is making contact with the edge of the upper teeth. In past attempts we had synthesized this cue by positioning the blade of the tongue immediately beneath the upper teeth. However, the fact that interdentals are most often confused with alveolar consonants /d, t, n, l/ and with the retroflex approximant /r/ shows that the perception is often that the blade of the tongue is at a point farther back in the mouth, in the area of alveolar or retroflex articulations, rather than at the interdental position. The problem is thus failure to perceive the depth of the tongue relative to the upper teeth.

One solution to this problem may be to correlate depth of the tongue with brightness. From human speakers under normal lighting conditions it can be observed that differences in tongue depth correlate with differences in the degree of brightness of the tongue: during the articulation of back vowels, for instance, the inside of the mouth is pitch black, whereas during articulation of front vowels the tongue reflects more light. Likewise, in the production of interdentals, it can be observed that the tip of the tongue gains progressively in brilliance as it moves forward to the interdental position. It emerges quite markedly from the semidarkness of the mouth's alveolar region to the full brightness shared by all of the external features of the face, such as the lips and skin.

Because our system lacks a shadowing function, however, we are as yet unable to create a true brightness gradient within the mouth. An alternative solution to the depth perception problem, which we have applied, is to have the tip of the tongue partially eclipse the edge of the upper teeth to emphasize contact. That is, the tongue tip does not merely come adjacent to the edge of the upper teeth, as before, but now it rises to cross that edge slightly. This way, the tongue is less likely to be perceived as being at a position posterior to the teeth.

Besides being confused with alveolar and retroflex articulations, the interdentals were also frequently confused with labiodental fricatives. In these cases it was not the place of articulation that was being mistaken, but the articulator itself: the tongue for the lower lip. However, this mistaking of the articulator should now be offset by the new tongue, which is tapered at the end whereas the old tongue was uniformly thick. Also, the parameter of tongue tip width was reduced somewhat from the neutral value.

Additional adjustments for interdentals aimed to better incorporate the lips. The lip gestures involved are the raising of the central part of the upper lip and the raising of the sides of the lower lip. However, the parameters for raising each lip currently raise all areas of the lip equally, which does not exactly produce the desired shapes. Some further work on the design of lip parameters is needed. We also sought to prevent the edges of the tongue from unnaturally cutting through the synthetic lower lip, which has been a problem in some coarticulation environments that affect tongue tip height. This problem was solved by increasing the parameter of tongue edge height for interdentals, making the underside of the tongue more curved so that it meets flush with the lower lip rather than cutting through it.

Penetrations of the upper teeth are much more problematic. In particular, when the interdental occurs adjacent to segments with very high tongue position, at the alveolar ridge or palate, the tongue is too high at the transition with the interdental, causing it to break through the upper teeth. This occurs adjacent to alveolars, as in *baths*, palato-alveolars, as in *watch this*, and the palatal vowel /iy/, as in *these* or *teethe*. Interpenetration not only is unrealistic but also degrades recognizability. The standard manipulation of control parameters and dominance functions has failed to solve the problem in this case. Currently we are working on a different strategy, which is to build in a procedure for detecting and deterring collisions between articulators.

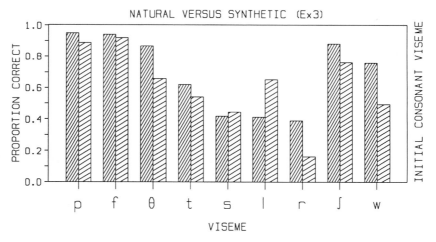

Figure 13.14 Proportion of correct responses for initial-consonant visemes for natural speech (dark bars) and synthetic speech (light bars) as a function of viseme class. (Results from experiment 3.)

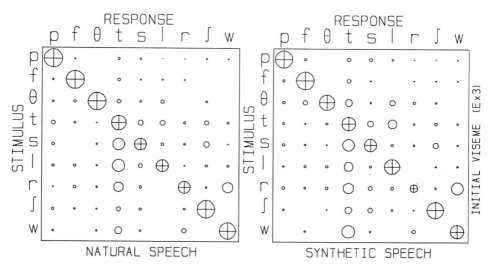

Figure 13.15 Stimulus-response confusions for initial-consonant visemes for natural (left panel) and synthetic (right panel) talkers. The area of each circle is proportional to the response probability. (Results from experiment 3.)

EXPERIMENT 3: THIRD GENERATION

After the second round of parameter revisions, we repeated the same experiment again with 14 new subjects. All experimental conditions and procedural details were the same as in the previous two tests.

Figures 13.14 and 13.15 give accuracy and the observed confusions for the initial consonants in experiment 3, with our third-generation parameter set. Although it is not quickly apparent, we closed the distance between synthetic

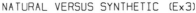
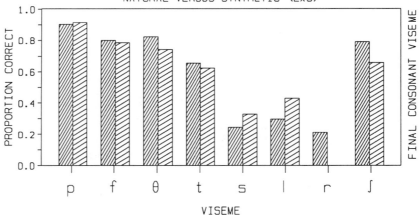

Figure 13.16 Proportion of correct responses for final-consonant visemes for natural speech (dark bars) and synthetic speech (light bars) as a function of viseme class. (Results from experiment 3.)

and natural speech even more. The overall 12% deficit in experiment 2 was reduced to 8% in the present task. Performance on the initial consonants averaged .700 for natural speech and .620 for synthetic speech. Synthetic {l} actually performed better than its natural counterpart whereas synthetic speech was poorer for {θ}, {r}, and {w}. Performance for the two faces was close to parity on the other five visemes.

Figures 13.16 and 13.17 give accuracy and the observed confusions for the final consonants. The changes were even more successful for final consonants; the new synthetic speech showed only a 3% deficit relative to natural speech (.566 versus .597). For final consonants, the interdental fricatives almost equaled their natural speech counterparts. The synthetic speech showed a significant deficit only on {r} and {ʃ}.

Figure 13.18 shows the proportion correct vowel viseme responses, and figure 13.19 shows the confusions. Performance on the synthetic vowels also improved with the new control parameters. The 33% deficit in experiment 2 was reduced to 20% in the present study; performance averaged .478 for synthetic speech and .681 for natural speech. The synthetic speech was comparable to the natural speech for the {i} and {a} visemes and close for {ʊ} and {ε}. A significant gap remains for the other vowel visemes, but we are confident that they too can be improved in future iterations.

OVERALL ASSESSMENT AND FUTURE IMPROVEMENTS

Table 13.3 summarizes performance across the three experiments. As the table shows, we were somewhat successful in closing the gap between the quality of our synthetic speech and that of a natural talker. We cut the overall gap by more than one-half, and our rate of improvement does not appear

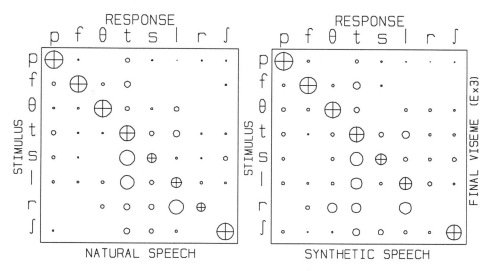

Figure 13.17 Stimulus-response confusions for final-consonant visemes for natural (left panel) and synthetic (right panel) talkers. The area of each circle is proportional to the response probability. (Results from experiment 3.)

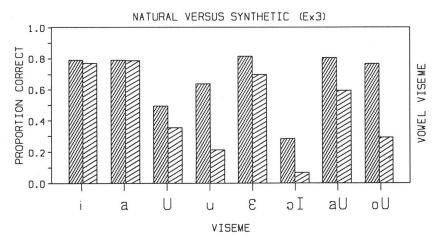

Figure 13.18 Proportion of correct responses for vowel visemes for natural speech (dark bars) and synthetic speech (light bars) as a function of viseme class. (Results from experiment 3.)

to be decreasing. We expect to reach the level of a natural talker in just a few more iterations of parameter modification and psychological testing.

We have mentioned in passing several proposals for changes more far-reaching than adjustments to parameters. These include changes in the basic text-to-speech outputs of some phonemes, such as /oʊ/ and /ɔɪ/; changes in lighting to simulate shadowing within the mouth and thus bring frontness of the tongue into relation with brightness; and development of a collision procedure to avert impossible tongue-teeth transits. We are also working on a more correct lip model with a greater number of polygons and a more natural

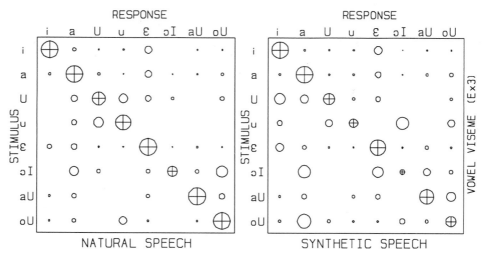

Figure 13.19 Stimulus-response confusions for vowel visemes for natural (left panel) and synthetic (right panel) talkers. The area of each circle is proportional to the response probability. (Results from experiment 3.)

Table 13.3 Overall performance on experiments 1–3

| | Experiment | | | | | |
| | 1 | | 2 | | 3 | |
Talker	N	S	N	S	N	S
Initial	.761	.533	.760	.634	.700	.620
Vowel	.747	.433	.747	.411	.681	.478
Final	.645	.520	.654	.579	.597	.566
Average	.717	.495	.720	.541	.659	.555
Difference	.222		.179		.104	

contour, and planning a set of better lip parameters to improve rounding, retraction, and other lip gestures. We also plan to broaden the range of our test items. We are in the process of compiling a list of test words that provides more optimal coverage of the phonemes. Such a list should balance the often conflicting criteria of representing segments with equal frequency, representing each segment in each of its phonetic environments, and maintaining a manageable corpus size. Before leaving the topic of evaluation, we should address the question of how intelligibility is affected by talker variability.

TALKER VARIABILITY

Because we measure the realism of our talking head through comparison with natural speech, it is important to recognize that visual intelligibility varies even across natural talkers. Lesner (1988) provides a valuable review of the importance of talker variability in speechreading accuracy. The variety across talkers is easy enough to notice in simple face-to-face conversations. But using an X-ray microbeam scanner it is possible to observe speech production more directly by tracking the movement of small gold pellets attached to the tongue. It has been discovered this way that different talkers articulate the same VCV utterance in considerably different ways (Johnson, Ladefoged & Lindau, 1993). In a classic study, Kricos and Lesner (1982) found large differences in visual intelligibility across six different talkers. These talkers may be considered to represent the extremes in intelligibility because they were selected with that goal. Unfortunately, the study does not indicate how representative the talkers are of the population as a whole.

Observers were asked to speechread the six talkers, who spoke single syllables and complete sentences. Significant differences, but also some similarities, were found across talkers. Using a hierarchical clustering analysis, the experimenters determined viseme groups for each talker based on the criterion that at least 75% of responses fell within the group. All talkers had the distinctive viseme category containing /p, b, m/. Four of the six talkers had the viseme /θ, ð/; for one other talker /r, w/ was grouped with /θ, ð/; and /θ, ð/ was not a distinctive viseme category for the sixth talker. Four of the six talkers had a unique viseme category /r, w/, whereas /r/ was grouped with /v, f/ for one of the talkers. It might have been interesting to assess viseme categories with a somewhat less stringent criterion, considering that visible speech can be influential even if it is relatively ambiguous.

Even with talkers who were chosen to represent extreme differences in intelligibility, the actual speechreading scores varied by only about 17% on consonant recognition. We studied four randomly chosen talkers (Gesi, Massaro & Cohen, 1992) and found that speechreading accuracy varied across only a smaller 5% range. It was surprising that visual intelligibility differed so little across the four talkers even though two of the four talkers were nonnative speakers of English.

It may be the case that much of the variability inherent in visible speech is overcome by perceivers. Montgomery and Jackson (1983) measured the videotaped images of four talkers speaking 15 vowels and diphthongs. They found significant differences across the four talkers, so that it was not possible to categorize the vowels simply on the basis of a physical measure of overall lip opening. The good recognition performance of human perceivers, however, seems to indicate that sufficient information is present in the overall visible configuration to overcome the variability across talkers. As Lesner observes, perhaps visible speech perception involves a spatial normalization analogous to the normalization used by listeners to account for differences in frequency arising from vocal tract length. Differences between the visible speech of our synthetic talking head and that of a natural speaker would no doubt be handled by observers in a similar manner. Nonetheless, there remains an intelligibility gap. This gap is probably in excess of what should be expected from normal speaker variability. However, this gap is minor and we consider Baldi fit for use in psychological research and beyond.

14　Applying Talking Faces

No style of thinking will survive which cannot produce a usable product when survival is at stake.
—Thomas Favill Gladwin, *East Is a Big Bird: Navigation and Logic on Puluwat Atoll*

There appears to be no shortage of potential applications for our animated talking head. We explore some of them in this chapter, and the reader is free to speculate about other possible worlds of talking heads. Technology advocates have always hoped that spoken language would be the primary medium of communication between people and machines. The talking head takes us one step closer to the realization of that hope. In the spirit of modern efficiency, each of us could have our own agent (in our image if we wish) to handle communications when we are unavailable. A talking head does not get tired or bored, isn't waylaid by a sore throat or any other human ailment, belongs to no union (as yet)—in short, is a perpetual-motion machine. As the technology improves, talking heads will be able to speak in any language, at any rate or level of complexity, and with the appropriate emotional affect.

We envision applications of this technology in a variety of domains, including but not limited to language skills, education and entertainment, and human-machine interaction. Specifically, Baldi could serve as a useful aid in second-language acquisition, the acquisition of spoken language by the hearing-impaired, improving the phonological and reading skills of dyslexic children, and in some capacity, as an influence in first-language acquisition. Baldi could pursue a career as a synthetic actor in entertainment and education, or as an educational tool in linguistics and speech science; serve as an enhancer of auditory synthetic speech; and play an integral role in machine-to-human communication. These examples in no way exhaust the possibilities. We will discuss some of these application ideas in the following final pages. Another area we will explore is the supplementation of visual speech for the hearing-impaired, a branch of visual speech technology that we have begun pursuing in parallel to our research in face synthesis.

POTENTIAL APPLICATIONS OF TALKING FACES

Second-Language Learning

Whereas learning a first language from the crib onward is typically a miracle, second-language learning is usually a sweat-and-tears affair, especially if we wait until schooling—or worse, until after adolescence. A talking head could be valuable in this situation. We firmly believe that both seeing and hearing spoken language can better guide its learning than either modality presented alone. There is some evidence that nonsighted children acquire some speech distinctions more slowly and less accurately than their sighted cohorts (Mills, 1987). In English, for example, /v/ versus /ð/ is a very difficult distinction to perceive auditorily but a relatively easy one to see. The sighted child would have an advantage when she could both see and hear these segments. Similarly, for a second-language learner, seeing articulations in face-to-face communication would make their identification more reliable and accordingly facilitate the learning of both the auditory and visual cues.

Second-language learners may have some face-to-face communication with their instructors or through immersion in a speech community, but there is often a shortage of visual input, which could be alleviated by synthetic means. In addition to providing ordinary visual speech, our talking head can also perform outstanding maneuvers that no mortal can—graphical tricks that can be utilized to facilitate language learning. One of the limitations of natural visible speech is that the face hides much of what is happening inside the mouth. There isn't much that mortal talkers can do about that. Our talking head, on the other hand, can be made transparent or displayed in a half-sagittal view. Either of those displays would make the actions inside the mouth completely visible. Band 14.1 presents a short monologue by Baldi in transparent mode.

Hearing Impairment

I am just as deaf as I am blind. The problems of deafness are deeper and more complex, if not more important, than those of blindness. Deafness is a much worse misfortune. For it means the loss of the most vital stimulus—the sound of the voice that brings language, sets thoughts astir and keeps us in the intellectual company of man.
—Helen Keller

Although visual information should be helpful for language acquisition by people with normal hearing, it should be a godsend for the hearing-impaired. Notwithstanding our enthusiasm for speech, we by no means imply that it should supplant sign language as a native language for the deaf. In terms of our framework, sign language provides a domain rich in information, and thus acquisition of sign can be accomplished as easily as the hearing learn spoken language. For hearing-impaired people, oral language is deficient in information, making its acquisition difficult to say the least. Competence in the oral language of society, however, gives every individual an invaluable competence in the dominant language and facilitates access to phonetic written language and its inherent advantages.

A variety of training programs have been devised to aid the deaf in the acquisition of spoken language (Povel & Arends, 1991; Arends et al., 1991). These current schemes only provide deaf learners with more or less symbolic feedback about the accuracy of their speech production. For example, a vowel's acoustic quality might be represented by the location of a marker in a two-dimensional space corresponding to the first two formants. With our talking head, on the other hand, we could vastly accelerate this trial-and-error learning method by demonstrating the articulation directly. For example, we could show the correct position and height of the tongue in a side view of a half-face or a side view of the transparent face for each vowel category. Figure 14.1 shows an example of the half-face view, and band 14.2

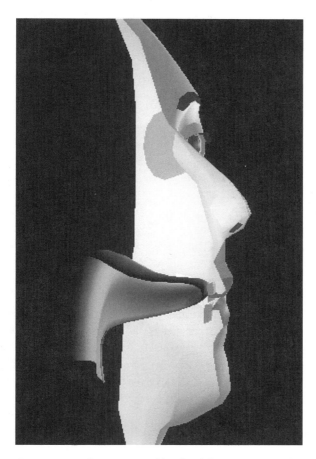

Figure 14.1   The position and height of the tongue in a midsagittal view of a half-face.

presents a half-face Baldi conducting a simulated vowel-learning exercise. Needless to say, the same type of scheme could be used not only in second-language learning but also in courses in phonetics and phonology.

We could embellish the synthetic face further by including other characteristics not normally apparent in visible speech. The velum could be raised or lowered to convey visible information about nasality. A visible breath stream could be presented during the occurrence of bursts, aspiration, and frication. Because the pitch of the voice is also an informative cue, another possibility is to add movement in the neck of the animated talker to signify vocal cord vibration. In previous training programs, pitch has been represented by the height of a balloon on a screen. In our version, we might use the height of the eyebrows, because there is evidence for a positive correlation between eyebrow height and pitch (Ohala, 1984, 1994, 1996; Cave et al., 1996). Cave and coworkers (1996), for example, found that 71% of F0 rises were accompanied by eyebrow raising. Some linguists have remarked that doing their transcriptions as students was made easier by surreptitiously watching their teachers' eyebrows. Along these lines, Pelachaud, Badler, and Steedman (1996) have extended the Facial Action Coding System (FACS; Ekman & Friesen, 1977) approach to simulate facial expressions conveying information that is normally correlated with intonation of the voice.

Training in Visible Speech Production

One question of interest is to what extent talkers can be taught to improve their visible articulations in order to become more intelligible to speech-readers. We do know that speechreaders can be taught to improve their understanding, obtaining an increase in the number of meaningful distinctions, or visemes, they can perceive in the speech (Massaro, Cohen & Gesi, 1993; Walden et al., 1977; see also chapter 6). Would it also be feasible to teach speakers to generate a better-articulated set of viseme categories? Such training would be valuable to all who struggle to communicate with hearing-impaired individuals, and even to those who simply need to be more clearly understood in general, whether because they speak in front of a camera, work in a noisy industry, or simply have a low voice. As noted in the previous chapter, the information value of visible speech appears to differ significantly across individual talkers (Johnson, Ladefoged & Lindau, 1993; Kricos & Lesner, 1982). Lesner (1988) lists several factors that can be controlled and modified during training: articulatory skills, verbal support strategies, nonverbal support strategies, and supplemental input. Recent encouraging findings indicate that talkers can become more intelligible after training based on an oral-interpreting curriculum (Stoker & French-St. George, 1987). Once such a curriculum is implemented on a small computer, persons in need of practice to improve their speechreading intelligibility could have easy access to instruction via auditory-visual speech synthesis at any time.

Pedagogy of Reading

We now turn from speechreading to reading: the out-of-the-ordinary problems that a number of children encounter in learning to read and spell. "Dyslexic" is a category used to pigeonhole children who have much more difficulty in reading and spelling than would be expected from their other perceptual and cognitive abilities (Fleming, 1984; Willows, Kruk & Corcos, 1993). Psychological science has established a tight relationship between the mastery of written language and the child's ability to process spoken language (de Gelder & Morais, 1995; Morais & Kolinsky, 1994; Taylor & Olson, 1995; Venezky & Massaro, 1987). That is, it appears that many dyslexic children also have deficits in spoken language perception. It is possible to alleviate the difficulty with spoken language by improving children's perception of phonological distinctions and transitions, which in turn improves their ability to read and spell. In a recent and well-publicized study, dyslexic children given the opportunity to practice with modified spoken language showed an improvement in their spoken language processing (Tallal et al., 1996). The researchers transformed the (auditory) speech to slow down the rapid-frequency transitions that occur between several consonants and vowels. Practice with this transformed speech facilitated the learning of various speech distinctions, which supposedly would improve reading skill. Although it is still uncertain which aspects of the speech signal are a stumbling block for these children, experience with segmentation and labeling small segments might be sufficient for improvement. If this is the case, visible speech could provide another dimension of information for the children to use in identifying segments.

Researchers have already begun to develop interactive speech and reading systems to improve children's phonological and spelling skills (Olson & Wise, 1992; Wise & Olson, 1992). A strikingly short period—only a week or so—is needed to see some improvement. At this point in time, the speech used in such systems is only auditory, and we believe that the visual component would add considerably to the remedial experience. In a year or two, fairly standard personal computers should have the capability to support a bimodal text-to-speech system, which would make it possible to incorporate decelerated visual speech. This method holds great promise, and we believe that adding visual speech will significantly enhance the positive results that have already been demonstrated with audible speech alone.

First-Language Acquisition

Children can certainly be taught to read, but can they be taught to speak? The reader might easily conclude that we have been carried away by our excitement about our talking head when we propose it as an aid to language acquisition by children. What child ever required assistance in learning language, particularly the phonology of his or her native one? It is true that most children have no need for any pedagogy and master their language perfectly with no effort. There are, however, many children who experience obstacles such as hearing impairments, production deficiencies, and slow word learning, and such children might benefit from deliberate teaching and influence. Of course, it might be questioned whether pedagogy in first-language acquisition, even when attempted, can be effective at all. A provocative conclusion recently reached by psycholinguists is that a kind of teaching does take place as a result of "motherese" (or "parentese," to be more precise), the simple efforts of parents to impart linguistic knowledge to their babies and toddlers (Fernald & Kuhl, 1987). Such findings encourage exploration of the potential for other forms of pedagogy in child language acquisition.

It seems evident that a major source of education for children in our culture is television. The muppets on *Sesame Street*, for example, teach spelling and counting and other basic but non-innate skills. However, these and legions of other animated and puppet characters that engross our children on a daily basis have very unrealistic visible speech, usually no more than an opening and closing of the mouth roughly synchronized with auditory syllables. For a more effective employment of such artificial talkers, animated figures with precise visible speech could impart articulatory instruction alongside the more commonly taught subjects. This approach could be of immense value to a variety of children. At the very least, even if it is not used with pedagogical intent, realistic visible speech should assume greater priority in commercial animation. *Toy Story*'s high-quality visible speech certainly sets a new and valuable benchmark for animated faces.

An Intelligent Agent in Human–Machine Interaction

Although we are becoming increasingly oriented toward the visual media, as a putatively literate society we are disheartened when we see video chosen over a book. There seems to be nothing inherently inferior about video in comparison to books, other than the fact that most if not all good literature in our culture is written rather than spoken aloud. However, some scientists believe that there is something unique about written literacy that cannot be had in oral language (Olson, 1994). We are hard-pressed on the other hand to envision what that difference might be. The field of psycholinguistics has not implemented an empirical research agenda that compares the two modes of language input, and so all we have is popular sentiment. Some argue that reading is active but listening—and watching—are merely passive. Others claim that oral communication is more natural. Whatever the case, we all appreciate a good book when it is read to us. The rapid proliferation of books on tape is only one sign of this desire to be read to; readings on public radio are another. Therefore, we don't see any reason why people should not be able to have machines read to them aloud, and in the guise of a particular person, if the machines are capable of it.

Although we value the spoken word, we are also an impatient species. Most people read on the order of 300 words per minute whereas spoken communication seldom reaches one-half that rate. Talking at a fast rate would be in great demand if the spoken medium were to replace the written one. Although people have some physical limitations on their ability to speak quickly, machines are another matter. Like auditory speech synthesizers, our talking head can be made to talk at different rates. Furthermore, we can understand speech spoken at much faster rates, rates comparable to reading written language (Foulke & Orr, 1973; see also the following section). So we can imagine, in the not too distant future, having our electronic mail read to us; or even relaxing in the garden while watching Baldi rattle off the news of the day, stock quotations, or the latest novel on everyone's coffee table. In summary, we are limited only by our imagination as to how a synthetic talking head might become part of our worlds of communication, education, and entertainment. We now turn to an application of synthetic visible speech in the related field of auditory synthesis.

ENHANCING PERCEPTION OF AUDITORY SYNTHESIS

It is well known that the perception and memory of synthetic auditory speech is still well below that of natural speech (Duffy & Pisoni, 1992). Accordingly, it is possible that visible speech from a talking head might increase the intelligibility of the synthetic message. To address this issue, we carried out a series of experiments to assess whether speech perception of synthetic auditory speech is improved when the audible speech is supplemented with our talking head.

Method

Sixty-one students from the University of California at Santa Cruz participated in four experiments featuring a two-alternative phoneme recognition task. The numbers of subjects in the four experiments were 12, 11, 22, and 16. respectively. Text selection was identical to that used by van Santen (1993). The test stimuli consisted of 256 sentences with the following structure:

The <adjective> <plural noun> <plural verb> a <singular noun>.

Each sentence contained a critical test word that was one word of a minimal pair. A minimal pair is defined as two words that differ only by a single phoneme. In the experiment, the phoneme could differ by a contrast of one or two phonetic features or by the complete absence of the phoneme in one of the two words. On presentation of the sentence, subjects were to decide which of the two words of the minimal pair had occurred. Nonsense sentences were used so that subjects were not influenced by semantic or pragmatic contextual factors in making the word choice. For example, the sentence *The heartless swerves study a simulator* could be presented, and the two choices would be *simulator* and *stimulator*. To eliminate any attention strategies, the test word could occur anywhere in the sentence, and the critical phoneme that differed could be either word-initial, word-medial, or word-final. Subjects were thus uncertain about which was the critical phoneme being tested until the test alternatives were presented (see van Santen, 1993, for details). Band 14.3 gives some example test sentences.

The experiment was a $4 \times 2 \times 3 \times 2 \times 3 \times 2$ within-subject design. The six variables were part of speech of the minimal pair, visual distinctiveness of the pair, the type of phoneme difference between the two words, the number of linguistic features that differed, the position of the contrasting phoneme in the word, and modality of presentation. The four levels of part of speech were plural verb, plural noun, singular noun, and adjective. The two levels of visual distinctiveness were visually distinctive or not; a minimal pair was considered visually distinct if the contrasting phonemes belonged to different viseme classes. The type of phoneme difference had three levels: the two words differed by a consonant, a vowel, or by the absence of a phoneme in one of the words. The number of phonetic features that differed could be one or two. Position of the differing phoneme in the word had three levels: initial, medial, or final. And lastly, the two modalities of presentation were auditory or bimodal. In the bimodal condition our synthetic talking face was added to the auditory speech synthesis.

Speech rate was varied across the four experiments. In the first three experiments, sentences were presented at 180, 250, and 345 words per minute, which are all very fast; in the fourth experiment the speech rate was 250 words per minute and white noise was added to the auditory speech. Within each experiment, the presentation conditions and the test sentences were counterbalanced across subjects. Up to four subjects could be tested simultaneously in separate sound-attenuated rooms with video monitors and keyboards. The synthetic face was displayed in the center of the screen; it subtended a visual angle of about 10 degrees. The loudness level of the auditory speech was 67 dB A (B & K 2231). Each subject was tested in one block of 260 trials, with a short break after the 130th trial. On each trial, a test sentence was presented after a warning tone. For the bimodal condition, each trial started with a 100 ms, 1,000 Hz warning tone presented simultaneously with a 700 ms neutral face. For the auditory-alone condition, each trial started with the same tone presented with a 700 ms black screen. In both conditions, the presentation of the sentence was followed by a display of the two alternative test words, presented side by side at the center of the screen. Subjects responded by hitting a left or right button corresponding to their choice. They received a warning tone if a response was not recorded within 5 seconds after the presentation of the test alternatives. After all of the subjects responded, feedback was given by highlighting the correct word in yellow for 1 second. The screen was then cleared and there was a two-second pause before presentation of the next trial.

Results

In the first three experiments, in which the rate of presentation was 180, 250, and 345 words per minute, respectively, overall performance averaged .895, .842, and .770. Although accuracy declined somewhat with faster rates of presentation, speech perception remained remarkably good even at a rate much faster than that of normal speaking. However, adding the talking face did not aid performance at any rate. The bimodal and auditory-only presentation conditions gave very similar performance even for the visually distinctive items. Perhaps we should be disappointed in this outcome, but we were encouraged that the visible speech didn't lower performance in a situation where the speech rates were so high.

Previous research has found an advantage of visible speech in sentence processing only when noise is added to the auditory speech (Benoit, Mohamadi & Kandel, 1994; Sumby & Pollack, 1954). In our fourth experiment, the rate of presentation was 250 words per minute and +10 dB of white noise was added to the auditory speech. Overall performance averaged .696. Performance in the conditions in which the two test items were visually distinct was .030 better in the bimodal condition than in the auditory-alone condition. There was no difference between the presentation conditions for the visually indistinctive items. Thus, there is a small but significant advantage of bimodal speech with a noisy auditory input, as has been found in previous studies. The new result is that the advantage occurs even at a fast speech rate and with a synthetic talker.

In summary, we found evidence that adding a talking head to synthetic speech does not degrade speech perception even when the speech is presented at a very fast rate. When the auditory speech is degraded, as it would be in many realistic situations, there is some evidence that visible speech can enhance perception for those features that are visually distinctive. It is possible that the forced-choice task is relatively insensitive to normal influences in sentence processing. Subjects are asked to make a fine phonetic distinction rather than to recall the words or to understand the meaning of a sentence. We plan to repeat our studies using several new tasks that require such higher-order processing.

Even if visible speech did not improve the intelligibility of synthetic speech by a large amount at these fast rates, at normal rates it is sufficient to provide a valuable addition in terms of the user's experience. After we licensed Baldi to AT&T in exchange for their text-to-speech system, the company's speech group demonstrated Baldi mouthing their speech synthesis. The vice president's first remark was, "Gee, you sure have improved the synthesis." The speech group suggested that he close his eyes and listen again. Sure enough, his impression was that the *auditory* synthesis had not improved at all. This anecdote captures most observers' experience that the synthetic speech seems so much more realistic when it is accompanied by a talking face. This affirms what has been one of our central claims, that visible speech is a valuable supplement to the auditory channel. Indeed, that belief motivates most of the foregoing application ideas: the information value of visible speech in conversation is analogous to the applied value of visible speech technology in various fields of communication. We now provide further justification for the claim that visible speech is a significant information source by appraising its information value in light of the properties of complementarity and robustness.

TWO TOUCHSTONES FOR VISIBLE SPEECH

One of the functional attributes of auditory speech is that we can talk and listen with our hands full and our eyes closed. Of course, we would argue that although successful, this type of communicating is less favorable than face-to-face exchanges. Visible speech, on the other hand, seems to require attentive looking on the part of the perceiver. We have the impression that we can't help but hear speech whereas speechreading requires greater effort. In addition, we might expect that speechreading requires actively focusing on the talker's mouth. In fact, we will present a series of experiments illustrating that speechreading is robust, in the sense that visible information is obtained even in what might be considered to be nonoptimal situations. Before that presentation, we emphasize another positive quality of visible speech: the so-called complementarity of audible and visible speech. It is more profitable to provide a complementary source of information rather than simply to enhance the information that is already available. One way to enhance the information would be to duplicate it in some manner, that is, to give the perceiver two observations of the same information. For purposes of argument, we now demonstrate that audible *and* visible speech is more valuable than a duplication of either audible *or* visible speech.

Complementarity

Complementarity simply means that a distinction is differentially conveyed by two sources of information. That is, two segments that are conveyed distinctly in one modality are relatively ambiguous in the other modality. For example, the difference between /ba/ and /da/ is easy to see but relatively difficult to hear. On the other hand, the difference between /ba/ and /pa/ is relatively easy to hear but very difficult if not impossible to see. The fact that two sources of information are complementary makes their integration much more informative than would be the case if the two sources were noncomplementary, or redundant. One way to see this is to generate some hypothetical results of a case where the two sources are not complementary and compare them to the case of typical speech with audible and visible sources of information.

We carried out such a hypothetical analysis on the results of Erber (1972), which were analyzed and fit by the FLMP in chapter 5. These results, repro-

RESPONSE

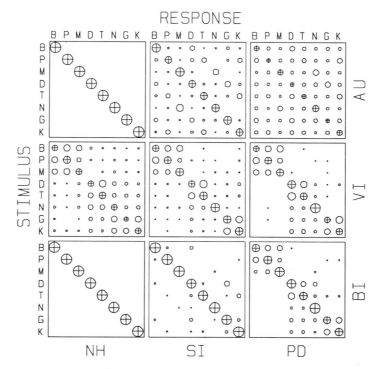

Figure 14.2 Confusion matrix for three populations of teenagers: normal hearing (NH), severely impaired (SI), and profoundly deaf (PD). The area of the circle is proportional to response probability. The results in the SI and PD groups show complementarity of auditory and visual speech because performance on the bimodal condition is so much better than it is for either the unimodal auditory or the unimodal visual condition.

duced in figure 14.2, are a quintessential demonstration of the complementarity of audible and visible speech. In Erber's experiment, speechreading performance was compared between normal hearing (NH), severely impaired (SI), and profoundly deaf (PD) teenagers under visual-alone, auditory-alone, and bimodal conditions. Although the unimodal conditions revealed that the SI and PD groups got poor information from both auditory and visual sources, the bimodal condition, in which these two deficient sources were combined, revealed a huge gain in performance relative to the unimodal conditions.

The antithesis of complementarity is the case in which the two sources of information provide equivalent information in terms of the degree of support for each of the test alternatives. The easiest way to implement such a situation is to duplicate the information from one modality as the contribution of the second source of information. Thus, we simply took the observations for the unimodal auditory condition and duplicated it to create our second hypothetical source of information. The two sources were combined according to the algorithm of the FLMP to generate the predicted results for the auditory-duplicated condition. These results are shown in figure 14.3. The

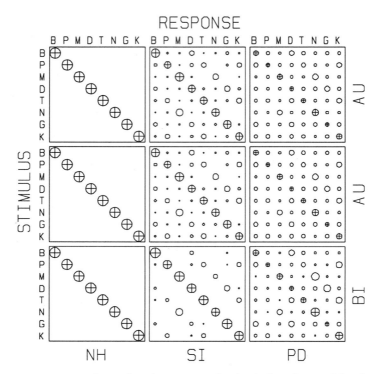

Figure 14.3 Observed confusion matrix for the duplicated unimodal auditory condition for three populations of teenagers: normal hearing (NH), severely impaired (SI), and profoundly deaf (PD). The area of the circle is proportional to response probability. The bimodal results are the FLMP's predictions for the auditory condition integrated with its duplicate. The results of this simulation show an advantage of two sources even when there is a lack of complementarity, but one that is much smaller than when complementarity exists (see figure 14.2).

same exercise was carried out with the unimodal visual condition, the results for which are shown in figure 14.4. As can be seen in figures 14.3 and 14.4, there is some advantage from having one source of information duplicated. Even in the noncomplementary cases, two sources are more valuable than just one. However, the actual situation, with complementary auditory and visual speech, gives much more of an advantage than what would be provided if observers had two independent sources of the same auditory information or two independent sources of the same visual information.

One way to assess the added bonus of complementarity is to compare performance between unimodal, duplicated unimodal, and complementary bimodal conditions. Averaged across the three groups of observers, overall accuracy was .57, .67, and .83 for the auditory, auditory-duplicated, and auditory-visual conditions. For the visual comparison, overall accuracy was .42, .52, and .83 for the visual, visual duplicated, and auditory-visual conditions. Thus, when the same information was provided by a second source and combined in FLMP fashion, we observed a .10 gain in accuracy (.57 to .67 and .42 to .52). But when the two complementary sources are combined

RESPONSE

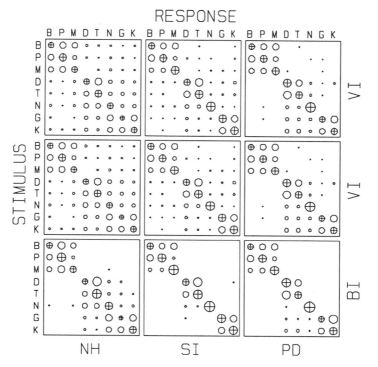

Figure 14.4 Observed confusion matrix for the duplicated unimodal visual condition for three populations of teenagers: normal hearing (NH), severely impaired (SI), and profoundly deaf (PD). The area of the circle is proportional to response probability. The bimodal results are the FLMP's predictions for the visual condition integrated with its duplicate. The results of this simulation show an advantage of two sources even when there is a lack of complementarity, but one that is much smaller than when complementarity exists (see figure 14.2).

according to the FLMP algorithm, there was a .26 gain relative to the more informative source (.57 to .83). Thus, a second source of information helps in both cases but much more when it has the complementarity found in natural speech. It is clear, then, that supplementing the auditory signal with visible speech provides a distinct advantage to the hearer. We now turn to the question of whether that advantage holds even under nonoptimal viewing conditions.

Robustness of Visible Speech

One might argue that our claim for the value of visible speech in communication is based on perceptual experiments carried out only under optimal viewing conditions, in which the subjects can train their focus directly on the speaker's mouth and in which distance and lighting do not impede clarity. If this limitation applied to all our experiments, then our conclusions might be falsified under real-world conditions. Our answer is that speechreading is indeed sufficiently robust to be helpful even under significantly degraded viewing conditions. To document its robustness, we tested speechreading performance under conditions of different peripheral views, levels of distortion, viewing angles, and simulated distances.

Speechreading in Peripheral Vision   To pursue the question of whether it is possible to derive information from the mouth without direct fixation, we conducted two experiments using our computer-animated talker (Smeele et al., 1994). We presented subjects with the animated face articulating one of four syllables without sound. The face appeared in one of five locations in the visual field. The subject's task was to identify the test syllable in a speechreading task. To prevent subjects from making eye movements during the presentation, we created a central dot-counting task. Subjects had to detect and count changes in the size of a test dot, presented at the fixation point, simultaneously with the speechreading task. Band 14.4 gives some sample trials from this experiment. Figure 14.5 shows the average correct performance of the subjects at the five spatial locations for each of the four test syllables.

Replicating previous results (see chapter 1), there were overall differences in performance as a function of the test syllable. Performance on the speechreading task also decreased somewhat when the presentation was in the periphery relative to the center. But even with a face presented 9 degrees in the periphery, performance was only about 20% poorer than with a central view.

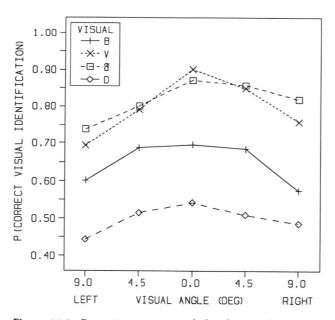

Figure 14.5 Proportion correct visual identification of the test syllables /ba/, /va/, /ða/, and /da/ as a function of the side of presentation and the visual angle between the center of the face and the fixation point.

There was also very little influence attributable to which side of the periphery the syllable was presented on. In a second study, the same task was repeated with the syllables presented for shorter durations. Similar results were found, indicating that speechreading is relatively robust across peripheral viewing. Our results are consistent with those of Vatikiotis-Bateson et al., (1996), who found that perceivers tended to focus on either the eyes or the mouth of the talker. If noise intensity was increased they tended to fixate more on the mouth, but never more than 55% of the time. Intelligibility scores also did not decline as the face was made larger. All of these findings substantiate the idea that visible speech can be an important influence even when the perceiver is not looking directly at the mouth of the talker.

Spatial Quantization of the Face A second result favoring the hypothesis that only fairly coarse visual information is necessary for successful speechreading comes from a speechreading task involving distortion of the face (Campbell & Massaro, in press). Participants were asked to speechread representatives from nine viseme consonant categories occurring before /a/. The visible CV syllables were presented under various levels of distortion as shown in figure 14.6 and on band 14.5. The spatial distortion method chosen for this experiment was the spatial quantization method first used by Harmon and Julesz (1973) and later elaborated by Costen, Parker, and Craw (1994). Spatial quantization is the process of reducing the resolution of an image through the local averaging of pixels into larger blocks. The process

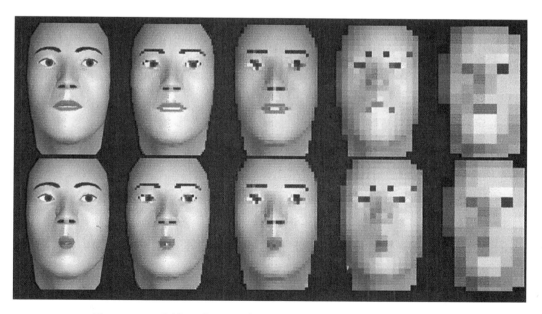

Figure 14.6 Baldi in the control condition (323 c/face) at far left through the highest level of distortion (4 c/face) at the far right. Points of extreme articulation are shown for two visemes, /va/ (top) and /wa/ (bottom).

is sometimes referred to as pixelization. These blocks eliminate the higher spatial frequency information in the image while preserving lower spatial frequency information. Also, the edges of the blocks reintroduce high spatial frequencies into the image that mask spatial frequencies immediately above the frequency of quantization. Because spatial quantization includes this masking characteristic, it tends to be more devastating to performance than other methods of removing spatial frequencies.

Spatial quantization was varied at five steps, from a normal display with 300 cycles per face to 31, 16, 8, and 4 cycles per face. Figure 14.6 shows the synthetic head in the normal presentation and at the four levels of distortion. The number of cycles per face was calculated by dividing by 2 the number of quantized blocks that run horizontally at eye level. Cycles per face, or cycles per image, is a common measure in spatial frequency research; it has the advantage of being independent of viewing distance (Riley & Costall, 1980).

Figure 14.7 gives average speechreading performance as a function of the presentation conditions. Speechreading was fairly robust across the intermediate levels of quantization. As can be seen in the figure, the relationship between the dependent measure, percent correct identification, and spatial quantization is a positively decelerating function. Figure 14.8 gives the same plot for each of the nine viseme classes. At the first level of distortion (32 cycles/face) only /da/, /la/, and /za/ showed a substantial decrease in

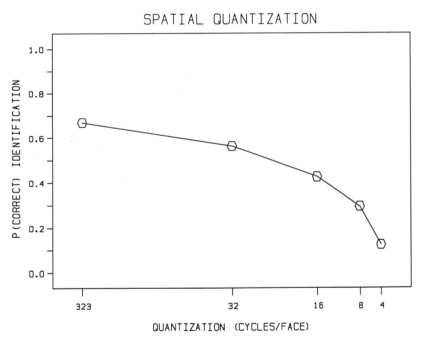

Figure 14.7 Average percentage correct identification across subjects and visemes for each level of spatial quantization.

speechreading. Performance on the visemes /ða/, /ra/, and /ǰa/ began to break down at the second level of distortion (16 cycles/face) followed by /va/, /wa/, and /ba/ as the distortion was further increased. Chance performance was reached at 4 cycles/face. These results reveal that speechreading is robust with fairly low spatial frequency information.

Variable Views of the Face   All of our experiments have used Baldi in a frontal view. In the everyday world, of course, we encounter speakers' faces from many different viewpoints. To explore speechreading accuracy when the face is rotated toward a profile view, we presented Baldi at both a 45- and a 90-degree rotation in depth. We also presented the face so that it was seen from 35.4 degrees above and from −24.6 degrees below. (Our normal presentation of Baldi is actually a view from 5.4 degrees above.) Given three horizontal rotations and three vertical rotations, there were nine possible facial presentations. As in the spatial quantization study, subjects speechread the nine consonant visemes. Some sample trials from this experiment are given on band 14.5. Figure 14.9 gives the accuracy of identification for the nine types of presentation and the nine viseme types. As the figure shows, performance remains fairly good but in some cases is degraded

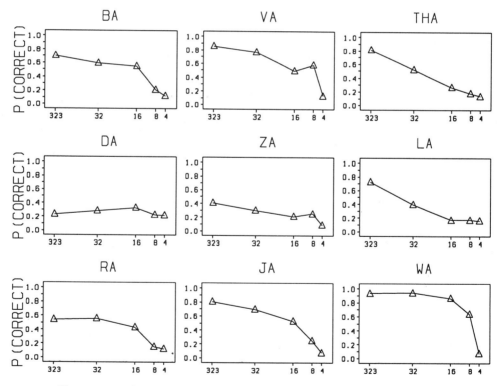

Figure 14.8   Average percentage correct identification across subjects for each viseme category for each level of spatial quantization.

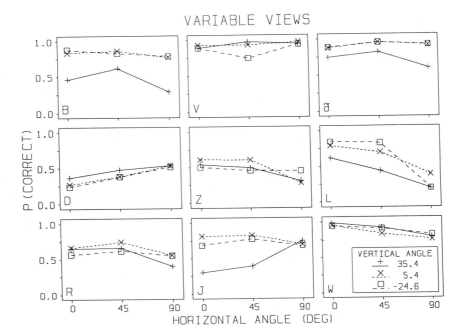

Figure 14.9 Average percentage correct identification across subjects and visemes as a function of the horizontal and vertical angles of presentation. Negative numbers refer to the view from below.

somewhat when the face is viewed in a complete profile and from above. Performance on the visemes /ba/, /ja/, and /la/ was degraded somewhat when the face was viewed from above, and /ba/ and /la/ were degraded from the profile view. Similar to the earlier findings of Erber (1974) and Wozniak and Jackson (1979), this research reveals that visible speech is also obtained from nonfrontal views of the talker.

Distance from the Talker The standard size of Baldi on the video monitor is roughly the size of an adult head. Subjects are usually about 0.5 meters from the screen. In normal encounters, the distance between talker and listener can be much greater. To explore the influence of distance away, we varied the size of Baldi to depict situations involving greater distances. In addition to the standard size, the presentation size depicted the face as being either 2, 4, or 8 times the normal viewing distance away. Subjects were again asked to speechread the nine consonant visemes. Some sample trials from this experiment are given in band 14.7. Figure 14.10 gives the accuracy of identification across four distances for the nine visemes. As can be seen in the figure, performance decreases but remains fairly good across increasing distance. Only the syllables /da/ and /wa/ did not show a decrement. Thus, like nonfrontal views, somewhat greater distances from the talker do not preclude pickup of visible speech.

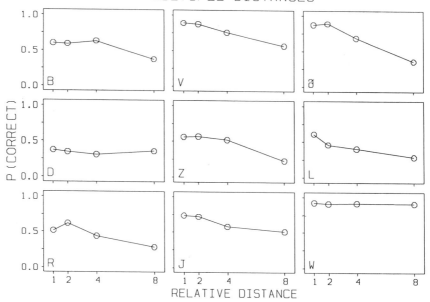

Figure 14.10 Average percentage correct identification across subjects and visemes as a function of the distance between the viewer and the talker.

Summary Our most recent findings show that speechreading, or the ability to obtain speech information from the face, is not significantly compromised by a number of variables. Humans are fairly good at speechreading even if they are not looking directly at the talker's lips. Furthermore, accuracy is not dramatically reduced when the facial image is blurred (because of poor vision, for example), when the image is rotated toward a profile view, when it is viewed from above or below, or when there is a large distance between the talker and the viewer. In chapter 3 we saw another example of the robustness of the influence of visible speech: people naturally integrate visible speech with audible speech even when the temporal occurrence of the two sources is displaced by about one-fifth of a second. These findings indicate that speechreading is highly functional in a variety of nonoptimal situations. To return to the theme of this chapter, it follows that the pursuit of visible speech technology could be of great practical value in many spheres of communication.

SUPPLEMENTING VISIBLE SPEECH

Even though visible speech can be a valuable supplement to auditory communication, it is by itself deficient for many aspects of speech perception. When used only as a supplement to the auditory channel, that deficiency is resolved by complementarity, as discussed earlier. But for people with hearing impairments, the insufficiency of the visual information remains a severe handicap. For this reason, although our main concern in visual synthesis is with creating talking faces, we have also been interested in how to supplement talking faces with the information that is ordinarily conveyed by auditory means. For hearing-impaired individuals, we can supplement the acoustic information that is lost in visible speech by transforming it into additional visual, or perhaps tactile, information. This is an exciting venture in visual speech technology that we have begun pursuing in parallel with our main work in facial synthesis. The goal is to implement a device that will perform acoustic analysis of speech and transform the acoustic features into features perceivable in another modality, which the speechreader would use in conjunction with watching the speaker's face. Our theoretical framework supports the idea that people could easily integrate these new features with the incomplete visual information to achieve productive outcomes. The featural supplementation could be applied to both natural and synthetic talkers; but because increasing natural speech intelligibility would be much more relevant to the daily lives of the hearing-impaired, that has been our focus. We now describe our initial work on the problem of supplementing visual speech.

Transforming Nonvisible Features

Visual information does not guarantee language understanding, as documented in a sad story about a deaf man who met a friend and asked what was new. The friend remarked, "Well, my brother was buried yesterday." The deaf man replied, "Oh, you must be very happy," because he thought his friend had said, "Well, my brother was married yesterday." This anecdote illustrates that visual speech is informationally deficient, and consequently speechreading does not well serve the communication needs of hearing-impaired people. The aim of this research project is to transform the auditory speech properties, which would normally complement visible speech, into informative visual cues in order to augment speechreading performance. For example, acoustic features of nasality, voicing, frication, and pitch prosody can be mapped into visible characteristics presented in conjunction with the talking face.

This general approach has been used successfully in the technique known as cued speech (Cornett, 1988; Morais & Kolinsky, 1994), in which the talker uses his or her hands to indicate additional information not available by speechreading alone. One drawback to cued speech, however, is that both communicating parties need to know the system of cues. Although being hearing-impaired might be motivation enough to learn a system of cues, we cannot expect most normal-hearing individuals to be similarly motivated. Another drawback is that cued speech is based on discrete rather than continuous speech features, and we know that speech is perceived continuously.

An interesting question is whether automated systems of cued speech would be feasible, both in terms of perceptibility and the simplicity of extraction from auditory speech. Although cued speech is optimally designed to supplement visible speech, it is difficult to implement via analysis of the auditory signal. The difficulty with automatically mapping the acoustic signal into cued speech is that the cues are essentially phoneme distinguishers and so the artificial recognition system must achieve phoneme identification. For example, the appropriate use of the thumb-up cue requires that the phoneme be identified as /t/, /m/, or /f/—a difficult task. On the other hand, determining some acoustic characteristic of the speech signal is much easier.

A more feasible system to implement would be one that requires the resolution of only some (nonvisible) features of a speech segment rather than its phoneme category. For example, determining if a segment is voiced is easier than determining what phoneme it is. Some evidence in favor of this approach comes from a prototype system constructed by Upton (1968). Relatively simple circuitry extracted three features from the acoustic signal: voicing, frication, and stop. These three simple features, plus two combination features, voiced fricative and voiced stop, were conveyed to the user via five tiny lamps, which were cemented to the lens of a pair of glasses so as to appear near the mouth of the talker being viewed. With a "considerable" training period, the user (Upton) was able to use the transformed acoustic cues to disambiguate speechreading information. Although Upton's initial paper gives only his subjective report, later papers (Pickett et al., 1974; Gengel, 1976) document positive results (with somewhat modified versions of the original device). Related research with laryngeal, nasal, and total intensity feature information presented tactilely (Miller, Engebretson & DeFilippo, 1974) and with voicing and stop features presented visually and tactilely (Martony, 1974) was reported at about the same time, though not much has been done in the two ensuing decades. As pointed out by Risberg (1982) and by Martin (1985), this promising area has not been sufficiently pursued.

We have continued this line of research, using both synthetic and natural facial video displays to transform acoustic information into visual cues, with the aim of creating successful prosthetic devices for the hearing-impaired. Our finished product would be a portable acoustic processor, with output display built into a pair of glasses, following Upton (1968). Of course, presenting additional visible cues raises the question of the extent to which subjects can simultaneously process a talking face and other visible cues. However, through our findings on the robustness of visible speech perception, discussed in the preceding section, we learned that perceivers do not have to look directly at the mouth in order to obtain visible speech information. In light of that conclusion, it seems unlikely that watching supplementary visual cues alongside the face will hinder speechreading.

We now move on to a description of our attempts at applying the idea of supplementary visual cues. Currently we have separated the research into two areas, which will be discussed in the next two sections: (1) getting a neural network to perform real-time analysis of certain acoustic features for visual display, and (2) determining how well subjects perform in learning to use these selected cues to their advantage in speechreading.

Acoustic Feature Analysis

The goal of feature analysis is to recognize the acoustic features in real time and to transform them into continuous visual displays. We developed and trained a neural network to recognize three auditory speech characteristics: nasality, voicing, and frication. In a typical experiment we sampled 2,607 analysis frames from 23 words in the Bernstein & Eberhardt (1986) corpus. The data provided to the neural network consisted of classification of each of the speech frames as 0 or 1 in terms of each of the three features, coupled with acoustic analysis of the frame. The frames were analyzed by a fast Fourier transform (FFT), which gave the amount of energy in each of 20 bark bands. These measures, together with overall amplitude and number of zero-crossings, gave a 22-valued input vector. Each frame was 7.8 ms (Hanning windowed), and a new frame was sampled every 1.6 ms. These data were then used to train a neural net model to identify the three features on the basis of acoustic input. The net included 22 input units, 8 hidden-layer units, and 3 output units with thresholds. The weights of the neural net were adjusted until an RMSD of .057 was achieved on the training frames.

Thus, in principle we have learned that we can use a network to transform the bark scale energies from each speech frame into features for presentation (see Bourland & Morgan, 1994). The current approach for analysis of feature information can be carried out in real time on the SGI-Crimson. We believe it will also be possible to carry out the analysis in real time using a compact, low-cost portable unit constructed from band-pass filter analysis chips and neural nets instantiated by an inexpensive central processing unit.

Additional work will probably be necessary, however, before it is possible to achieve good feature classification performance on a speaker-independent basis. This can be done by including speech samples from a variety of talkers in the training set, and several good databases are available. Other problems that must be overcome before such a device could be widely applicable are background noise and the presence of multiple speakers. To eliminate background noise from the input, noise-canceling or directional microphones will be employed. Multiple speakers might be separated on the basis of source localization, using stereo microphones, or through higher-level analyses that track pitch, voice quality, or semantic content. However, much research is yet to be done in these areas, and we will concentrate for the time being on relatively good listening conditions. Success under such conditions will still be a large step forward.

Visual Feature Perception

To date, our perceptual studies of supplementary visual feature information have been done using simulated rather than real-time analyzed features. We wished to see how difficult it would be for subjects to learn to use the features we had selected to their advantage in speechreading. In a five-day experiment, subjects performed again on each day the speechreading of 318 one-syllable words from the Bernstein & Eberhardt (1986) corpus presented visually. The visual speech was presented by a human speaker whose facial image was 14 degrees horizontal and 20 degrees vertical on a 30.5 cm diagonal screen located 50 cm from the viewer. One group of subjects were presented with feature information along with the silent talking head, and a control group received no feature information.

For the feature group, the features nasal, voiced, and fricative were presented at the left side of the screen (centered 10 degrees from face midline) as colored bars (5.1 degrees horizontal by 2 degrees vertical in size, spaced 3 degrees apart vertically). Figure 14.11 gives an example of the display with the features. A series of trials is given on band 14.8. The top bar indicated the nasal sounds by lighting up orange while they occurred. The middle

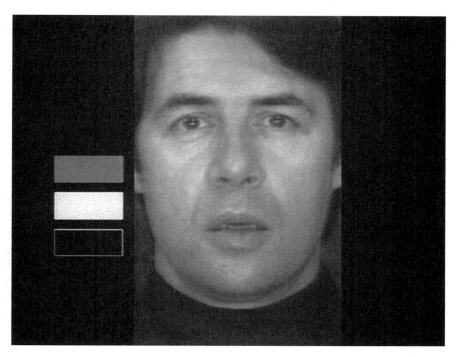

Figure 14.11 An example of the display with the visual features. The top (nasal) bar indicates the nasals by lighting up orange during the period they occur. The middle (voicing) bar indicates voiced sounds by lighting up white when they occur. The bottom (frication) bar lights up yellow for voiceless fricatives and purple for voiced fricatives.

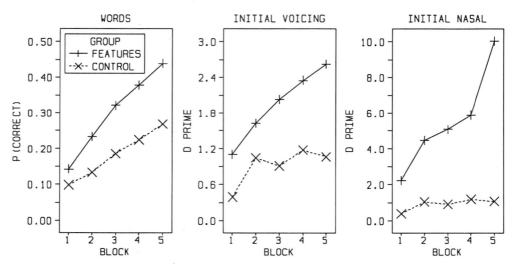

Figure 14.12 Proportion correct word identification (left panel), identification (*d'*) of initial voicing (center panel), and identification (*d'*) of initial nasality (right panel) as a function of experimental block, for feature and control groups.

bar indicated voiced sounds by lighting up white while they occurred. The bottom bar corresponded to frication, lighting up yellow for voiceless fricatives and purple for voiced fricatives. The distinction between voiced and voiceless fricatives meant that the bottom bar in some cases overlapped in information with the middle (voicing) bar. The frication bar also provided a much quicker yellow or purple flash in the event of the release burst of a stop consonant. Subjects made their speechreading responses by entering a word on a keyboard. After each identification, we gave the subjects feedback by again presenting the word (with features for the feature group) with the sound on and showing the word in print on the left side of the screen.

A number of analyses were carried out, including accuracy of word identification; accuracy in identifying initial consonants, vowels, and final consonants; consonant and vowel confusions; and accuracy of feature identification for initial and final consonants. The left panel of figure 14.12 shows the proportion of correct word identifications as a function of the five successive experimental blocks. Both groups improved with experience, but the feature group was significantly better overall and improved faster. The center and right panels of figure 14.12 show accuracy for identification of initial voicing and nasality respectively for the two groups in terms of the *d'* signal detection metric. (Note that these two panels have different scales because of the different ranges of performance.) Relative to the control group, the feature group was able to learn quickly and to utilize the supplementary visual feature information.

Figures 14.13 and 14.14 present the initial-consonant confusions for the control and feature groups respectively at the end of five blocks of trials. The

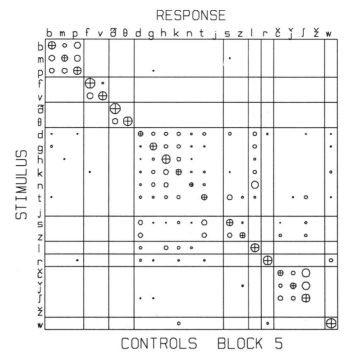

Figure 14.13 Stimulus-response confusions for initial consonant for the control group on block 5 of the visual word-identification task. The area of a circle indicates the proportion of responses for a given stimulus. Correct responses are indicated by a plus sign inside the circle. Viseme classes are indicated by horizontal and vertical lines.

feature group was able to make subviseme discriminations that were not possible for the controls. For example, within the labial viseme {b,m,p}, the feature group could discriminate between the three members of the class, whereas the control group split their responses equally among the three alternatives.

This experiment demonstrates that speechreading with specific visual features is learnable and greatly improves speechreading accuracy. However, the implementation of this idea in the form of a portable device that will provide real-time analysis and display of acoustic features, is still in its prenatal stage. First and foremost, we must test whether it is feasible to teach a neural network to recognize the acoustic features from auditory speech consistently and on a speaker-independent basis. The problems of screening background noise from the input and coping with multiple speakers must also be overcome. As for the features themselves, additional work is necessary to determine the best feature information to present and how best to present it. One type of featural information that we anticipate adding to the set presented is some representation of voice fundamental frequency, to make accessible the stress and intonation patterns in words and sentences. It has been shown that this information is a valuable addition to the silent face,

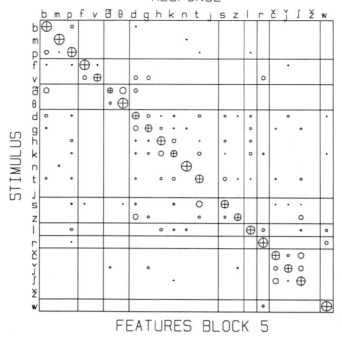

RESPONSE

STIMULUS

FEATURES BLOCK 5

Figure 14.14 Stimulus-response confusions for initial consonant for the feature group on block 5 of the visual word-identification task. The area of a circle indicates the proportion of responses for a given stimulus. Correct responses are indicated by a plus sign inside the circle. Viseme classes are indicated by horizontal and vertical lines.

both for recognizing words and for interpreting higher-level sentential information, when presented auditorily as buzzing (Rosen, Fourcin & Moore, 1981; Boothroyd, 1988; Boothroyd et al., 1988) or tactilely as vibration (Hanin, Boothroyd & Hnath-Chisolm, 1988). Visually, both color and spatial position can be used to represent absolute and relative voice fundamental frequency. For example, pitch could be represented by the height of a vertical bar.

Another feature that we will work on adding to the system is place of articulation. Although some place distinctions (e.g., labial vs. nonlabial) are easy to see in facial articulation, others (e.g., alveolar vs. velar) are almost impossible to see without special lighting inside the mouth. It has been found that place of articulation is the most difficult feature to convey by analog or by the low-level acoustic signal processing used for cochlear implants (Eddington, 1980; Tyler & Moore, 1992). Our higher-level approach using neural nets may provide a solution. To achieve good place detection, we plan to employ time-delay neural nets (TDNNs), which take into account a number of power spectrum frames across time.

Regarding the presentation of the features in visual form, one must know the optimal spatial offset of the cue information for the perceiver to integrate the features while still attending to the speaker's lips. Our subjects initially reported some difficulty in attending to both the facial and feature information (the difficulty decreased with practice), but speechreading performance is still fairly good for facial information 9 degrees from where subjects are attending. Another unanswered question concerns whether temporal, spatial, colorized, or some combination of these cues can best convey the feature information to the observer. We also plan to evaluate transparent feature indicators via a video special effects generator and also in a heads-up display. It might also be valuable to show the feature information continuously scrolled across the horizontal bar over time, in correspondence with the speech event.

One final issue is weighing the visual against the tactile modality for the presentation of the supplementary features. For example, instead of the three colored bars described earlier, the same information could be mapped into three vibratory transducers. In light of our initial success with our visual features, it is important to evaluate whether the visual presentation mode is better or worse than the more commonly used tactile modality. The outcome of such a comparison is by no means certain, given the commonalities between these sensory systems (Freides, 1974; Hirsh & Sherrick, 1961; Loomis & Lederman, 1986; Loveless, Brebner & Hamilton, 1970; Sherrick & Cholewiak, 1986). For example, it may be that observers will be at a disadvantage dividing their attention between two visual sources of information and would find it less of a strain to coordinate two sources from separate modalities. Significantly, we have not noticed any discrepancy between subjects' ability to integrate auditory and visual speech and their ability to integrate two sources of auditory speech.

Furthermore, there may be an advantage to using two sources from the same modality because of an increased ability to perceive asynchrony between the sources. We saw in chapter 3 that for asynchronous auditory and visual events, people naturally integrate the two events as long as they occur within roughly one-fourth of a second of each other. One cost of this robustness, however, is a lack of sensitivity to the onset differences between the two modalities, which precludes the use of a temporal interval between audible and visible speech to simulate such cues as voice onset time to indicate voicing. Presumably, a temporal interval between tactile and visible sources would likewise be poorly perceived. On the other hand, using two visual sources might allow subjects to more easily detect temporal relation cues such as voice onset time (which would in this case be realized as a relation between some visible facial articulation and the activation of the voicing bar). Although these initial considerations favor the use of visual over tactile features, a thorough comparison of the two techniques is called for.

Some initial evidence on this question is given by Martony's (1974) work using voicing and stop features. In an experiment with CV syllables, better performance was found for visual than for tactile presentation of features, and both performed better than unaided speechreading. For voiced stops, there was no improvement with tactile input but a significant improvement with visual feature presentation. Martony suggested that this was due to an inability of subjects to perceive the exact temporal relation between the visual and tactile information. However, the fact that the tactile modality was better than the visual for voiceless stops clouds the issue somewhat.

It is also important to look at perception of longer materials such as sentences. This comparison is important because with short stimuli, subjects may be able to employ perceptual strategies that are difficult to use with longer materials. Martony (1974) reports just such a result, finding a reversal of the visual-over-tactile advantage for recognition of whole sentences that were previously trained with a closed response set method. For sentences not previously trained, however, only a small, nonsignificant advantage over unaided speechreading was observed for both types of aids. Clearly, further work is needed to explore the potential of feature-based aids, in terms of the effectiveness and learnability of the various features and modes of presentation.

CONCLUSION

In the course of studying the problems in applied visual feature supplementation, we confronted no conflict between the interests of theory and application. Our theoretical motive throughout this book has been to explain how humans use multiple sources of information in pattern recognition. We proposed and extensively demonstrated an algorithm that assumes independent feature evaluation, multiplicative integration of support measures, and decision making based on relative degrees of support. Adding supplementary features to visual speech provides a practical demonstration of how easily we can adapt to new sources of information and integrate them to achieve better recognition. The use of the visual features in conjunction with visible speech could in fact serve as an additional test of the FLMP. For example, it would be valuable to test perception of visible speech supplemented by features in a within-subject expanded factorial design incorporating facial-alone, feature-alone, and facial-plus-feature conditions. Subjects could be tested after they had been extensively trained on the features (e.g., in a five-day word perception study), but it would be also of great interest to study the results across learning. Beyond theory, however, we would also be immensely pleased if this aspect of multimodal perception research resulted in technological aids that would benefit people in their daily lives.

Our talking-head technology has also had the double intent of refining perceptual research while potentially leading to useful products that could enhance our lives in the areas of communication, education, and entertainment. Thus, in the quiltwork of this book we have sewn together the issues of speech perception by humans and speech production by machines. The former we captured in the general pattern recognition algorithm of the FLMP, and the latter we provided in the form of Baldi, our synthetic talking head, whose fully controllable productions formed the basis for much of the perceptual data that drove our theoretical discussions. Synthesis makes it possible to test our assumptions about pattern recognition in precise ways that would not be possible otherwise.

The assumptions of the FLMP are testable because they are expressed in quantitative form. The keystone assumption of this model is the division of perception into the twin levels of information and information processing. Adhering to this fundamental dichotomy are a number of other assumptions. One is the idea that, at the information level, sources are evaluated independently. We saw in chapter 4 that independence of sources is motivated by the principle of category-conditional independence: it isn't possible to predict the evaluation of one source on the basis of the evaluation of another, so the independent evaluation of both sources is necessary to make an optimal category judgment. Although sources are thus kept separate at evaluation, they are then integrated to achieve perception and interpretation.

Multiplicative integration yields a measure of total support for a given category identification. That operation, implemented in the model, allows the combination of two imperfect sources of information to yield better performance than would be possible using either source by itself. However, the output of integration is an absolute measure of support; it must be relativized to account for the observed factor of relative influence (the influence of one source increases as other sources become less influential, i.e., more ambiguous). Relativization is effected through an assessment stage that divides the support for one category by the summed support for all other categories. Finally, categorization is achieved via the response selection operations.

An important empirical claim about this algorithm is that, although information may vary from one perceptual situation to the next, the manner of combining that information—that is, information processing—is invariant. With our algorithm, we thus propose an invariant law of pattern recognition that describes how continuously perceived (fuzzy) information is processed to achieve the perception of a category.

References

Abry, C., & Lallouache, T. (1991). Audibility and stability of articulatory movements: Deciphering two experiments on anticipatory rounding in French. *Proceedings of the Twelfth International Congress of Phonetic Sciences, 1*, 220–225.

Adams, E., & Messick, S. (1957). The axiomization of Thurstone's successive intervals and paired comparison scaling models.

Ades, A. E. (1977). Vowels, consonants, speech, and nonspeech. *Psychological Review, 84*, 524–530.

Adjoudani, A., & Benoit, C. (1996). On the integration of auditory and visual parameters in an HMM-based ASR. In D. G. Stork & M. E. Hennecke (eds.), *Speechreading by humans and machines* (pp. 463–471). New York: Springer.

Al-Bamerni, A., & Bladon, R. A. (1982). One-stage and two-stage temporal patterns of velar coarticulation. *Journal of the Acoustical Society of America, 72*, Abstract CCC8, S104.

Allen, J., Hunnicutt, M. S., & Klatt, D. (1987). *From text to speech: The MITalk system.* Cambridge: Cambridge University Press.

Allen, V. L., & Atkinson, M. L. (1981). Identification of spontaneous and deliberate behavior. *Journal of Nonverbal Behavior, 5*, 224–237.

Allen, W. (1976). *Without feathers.* New York: Random House.

Anderson, J. R. (1990). *Adaptive character of thought.* Hillsdale, NJ: Erlbaum.

Anderson, N. H. (1981). *Foundations of information integration theory.* New York: Academic Press.

Anderson, N. H. (1982). *Methods of information integration theory.* New York: Academic Press.

Anderson, N. H. (1996). *A functional theory of cognition.* Hillsdale, NJ: Erlbaum.

Archer, D. (producer), & Silver, J. (director). (1991). *A world of gestures: Culture and nonverbal communication.* Videorecording available from the University of California Extension Media Center, Berkeley, CA.

Arends, N., Povel, D. -J., Van Os, E., Michielsen, S., et al. (1991). An evaluation of the Visual Speech Apparatus. *Speech Communication, 10*, 405–414.

Bailly, G., Benoit, C., & Sawallis, T. R. (eds.) (1992). *Talking machines: Theories, models, and designs.* Amsterdam: North-Holland.

Banks, W. P., & Krajicek, D. (1991). Perception. *Annual Review of Psychology, 42*, 305–331.

Batchelder, W. H., & Riefer, D. M. (1990). Multinomial processing models of source monitoring. *Psychological Review, 97*, 548–564.

Bell-Berti, F., & Harris, K. S. (1979). Anticipatory coarticulation: Some implications from a study of lip rounding. *Journal of the Acoustical Society of America, 65,* 1268–1270.

Bell-Berti, F., & Harris, K. S. (1982). Temporal patterns of coarticulation: Lip rounding. *Journal of the Acoustical Society of America, 71,* 449–459.

Benguerel, A. P., & Cowan, H. A. (1974). Coarticulation of upper lip protrusion in French. *Phonetica, 30,* 41–55.

Benguerel, A. P., & Pichora-Fuller, M. K. (1982). Coarticulation effects in lipreading. *Journal of Speech and Hearing Research, 25,* 600–607.

Bennett, B. M., Hoffman, D. D., & Prakash, C. (1989). *Observer mechanics: A formal theory of perception.* San Diego: Academic Press.

Benoit, C. (1990). An intelligibility test using semantically unpredictable sentences towards the quantification of linguistic complexity. *Speech Communication, 9,* 293–304.

Benoit, C., Mohamadi, T., & Kandel, S. (1994). Effects of phonetic context on audio-visual intelligibility of French. *Journal of Speech and Hearing Research, 37,* 1195–1203.

Benoit, C., & Pols, L. C. W. (1992). On the assessment of synthetic speech. In G. Bailly, C. Benoit & T. R. Sawallis (eds.), *Talking machines: Theories, models, and designs* (pp. 435–441). Amsterdam: North-Holland.

Bergeron, P., & Lachapelle, P. (1985). Techniques for animating characters. *SIGGRAPH' 85 Tutorial: Advanced Computer Graphics Animation 2.*

Bernstein, L. E. (1989). Independent or dependent feature evaluation: A question of stimulus characteristics. *Behavioral and Brain Sciences, 12,* 756–757.

Bernstein, L. E., Demorest, M. E., & Eberhardt, S. P. (1994). A computational approach to analyzing sentential speech perception: Phoneme-to-phoneme stimulus-response alignment. *Journal of the Acoustical Society of America, 95,* 3617–3622.

Bernstein, L. E., & Eberhardt, S. P. (1986). *Johns Hopkins lipreading corpus video-disk set.* Baltimore, MD: Johns Hopkins University.

Bertelson, P., & Radeau, M. (1976). Ventriloquism, sensory interaction, and response bias: Remarks on the paper by Choe, Welch, Gilford, and Juola. *Perception and Psychophysics, 19,* 531–535.

Bertelson, P., & Radeau, M. (1981). Cross-modal bias and perceptual fusion with auditory-visual spatial discordance. *Perception and Psychophysics, 29,* 578–584.

Bertelson, P., Vroomen, J., Wiegeraad, G., & de Gelder, B. (1994). Exploring the relation between McGurk interference and ventriloquism. In Proceedings of the 1994 International Conference on Spoken Language Processing, Sept. 18–22, Yokohama, Japan, Vol. II, 559–562.

Beskow, J. (1995). Rule-based visual speech synthesis. *Proceedings of Eurospeech '95,* Madrid, Spain, 299–302.

Best, C. T. (1995). A direct realist view of cross-language speech perception. In W. Strange (ed.), *Speech perception and linguistic experience: Issues in cross-language research* (pp. 171–204). Baltimore: York Press.

Binnie, C. A., Montgomery, A. A., & Jackson, P. L. (1974). Auditory and visual contributions to the perception of selected English consonants for normally hearing and hearing-impaired listeners. In H. B. Nielsen & E. Kampp (eds.), *Visual and audio-visual perception of speech* (pp. 181–209). Stockholm: Almquist & Wiksell.

Blackburn, J. M. (1936). Cited by Crossman (1959). *Acquisition of skill: An analysis of learning curves.* IHRB Report no. 73.

Bladon, R. A., & Al-Bamerni, A. (1976). Coarticulation resistance of English. *Journal of Phonetics, 4*, 135–150.

Blumstein, S. E. (1986). On acoustic invariance in speech. In J. S. Perkell & D. H. Klatt (eds.), *Invariance and variability in speech processes* (pp. 178–197). Hillsdale, NJ: Erlbaum.

Blumstein, S. E., & Stevens, K. N. (1979). Acoustic invariance in speech production: Evidence from measurements of the spectral characteristics of stop consonants. *Journal of the Acoustical Society of America, 66*, 1001–1017.

Boothroyd, A. (1988). Perception of speech pattern contrasts from auditory presentation of voice fundamental frequency. *Ear and Hearing, 9*, 313–321.

Boothroyd, A., Hnath-Chisolm, T., Hanin, L., & Kishon-Rabin, L. (1988). Voice fundamental frequency as an auditory supplement to the speechreading of sentences. *Ear and Hearing, 9*, 306–312.

Boothroyd, A., & Nittrouer, S. (1988). Mathematical treatment of context effects in phoneme and word recognition. *Journal of the Acoustical Society of America, 84*, 101–114.

Bourland, H. A., & Morgan, N. (1994). *Connectionist speech recognition: A hybrid approach*. Boston: Kluwer.

Boves, L., & Cranen, B. (1996). Modelling approaches in speech production. In T. Dijkstra & K. De Smedt (eds.), *Computational psycholinguistics* (pp. 360–385). London: Taylor & Francis Ltd.

Boyce, S. E. (1990). Coarticulatory organization for lip rounding in Turkish and English. *Journal of the Acoustical Society of America, 88*, 2584–2595.

Braida, L. D. (1991). Crossmodal integration in the identification of consonant segments. *Quarterly Journal of Experimental Psychology, 43*, 647–677.

Braida, L. D., & Durlach, N. I. (1972). Intensity perception. II: Resolution in one-interval paradigms. *Journal of the Acoustic Society of America, 51*, 438–502.

Breeuwer, M., & Plomp, R. (1984). Speechreading supplemented with frequency-selective sound-pressure information. *Journal of the Acoustical Society of America, 76*, 686–691.

Breeuwer, M., & Plomp, R. (1986). Speechreading supplemented with auditorily presented speech parameters. *Journal of the Acoustical Society of America, 79*, 481–499.

Bregman, A. S. (1990). *Auditory scene analysis: The perceptual organization of sound*. Cambridge, MA: MIT Press.

Broadbent, D. (1987). Simple models for experimental situation. In P. Morris (ed.), *Modelling cognition* (pp. 169–185). Chichester, England: Wiley.

Brooke, N. M. (1989). Visible speech signals: Investigating their analysis, synthesis and perception. In M. M. Taylor, F. Neel, & D. G. Bouwhuis (eds.), *The structure of multimodal dialogue* (pp. 249–258). Amsterdam: North-Holland.

Brooke, N. M. (1992). Computer graphics synthesis of talking faces. In G. Bailly, C. Benoit, & T. R. Sawallis (eds.), *Talking machines: Theories, models and designs* (pp. 505–522). Amsterdam: North-Holland.

Brooke, N. M., & Summerfield, A. Q. (1983). Analysis, synthesis, and perception of visible articulatory movements. *Journal of Phonetics, 11*, 63–76.

Browman, C. P., & Goldstein, L. (1989). Articulatory gestures as phonological units. *Phonology, 6*, 201–251.

Brown, S. D., & Dooling, R. J. (1993). Perception of faces by budgerigars (*Melopsittacus undulatus*). II: Synthetic models. *Journal of Comparative Psychology, 107*, 48–60.

Brunswik, E. (1955). Representative design and probabilistic theory in a functional psychology. *Psychological Review, 62,* 193–217.

Brunswik, E. (1956). *Perception and the representative design of psychological experiments.* Berkeley: University of California Press.

Bryan, W. L., & Harter, N. (1897). Studies in the physiology and psychology of the telegraphic language. *Psychological Review, 4,* 27–53.

Bryan, W. L., & Harter, N. (1899). Studies on the telegraphic language: The acquistition of a hierarchy of habits. *Psychological Review, 6,* 345–375.

Cahn, J. E. (1990). The generation of affect in synthesized speech. *Journal of the American Voice Input/Output Society, 8,* 1–19.

Campbell, C. S., & Massaro, D. W. (in press). Visible speech perception: Influence of spatial quantization. *Perception.*

Campbell, H. W. (1974). Phoneme recognition by ear and by eye: A distinctive feature analysis. Ph.D. diss., University of Nijmegen, Holland.

Campbell, R. (1988). Tracing lip movements: Making speech visible. *Visible Language, 22,* 32–57.

Campbell, R. (1994). Audiovisual speech: Where, what, when, how? *Current Psychology of Cognition, 13,* 76–80.

Campbell, R. (1996). Seeing brains reading speech: A review and speculations. In D. Stork & M. Hennecke (eds.), *Speechreading by humans and machines* (pp. 115–133). Berlin: Springer.

Campbell, R., & Dodd, B. (1980). Hearing by eye. *Quarterly Journal of Experimental Psychology, 32,* 85–99.

Carey, S., & Diamond, R. (1994). Are faces perceived as configurations more by adults than by children? *Visual Cognition, 1,* 253–274.

Carlson, R., Granström, B., & Nord, L. (1992). Segmental evaluation using the Esprit/SAM test procedures and monosyllabic words. In G. Bailly, C. Benoit, and T. R. Sawallis (eds.), *Talking machines: Theories, models and designs* (pp. 443–453). Amsterdam: North-Holland.

Carlson, R., Granström, B., & Nord, L. (1993). Synthesis experiments with mixed feelings: A progress report. *Fonetik-93: Papers from the Seventh Swedish Phonetics Conference* (pp. 65–68).

Carterette, E. C., Friedman, M. P., & Wyman, M. J. (1966). Feedback and psychophysical variables in signal detection. *Journal of the Acoustical Society of America, 39,* 1051–1055.

Cassell, J. C., Pelachaud, C., Badler, N. I., Steedman, M., Achorn, B., Becket, T., Dourville, B., Prevost, S., & Stone, M. (1994). Animated conversation: Rule-based generation of facial expression, gesture, and spoken intonation for multiple conversational agents. *Computer Graphics Annual Conferences Series,* 413–420.

Casti, J. L. (1994). *Complexification: Explaining a paradoxical world through the science of surprise.* New York: HarperCollins.

Cathiard, M., Lallouache, M., & Abry, C. (1996). Does movement on the lips mean movement in the mind? In D. Stork & M. Hennecke (eds.), *Speechreading by humans and machines* (211–219). Berlin: Springer.

Cathiard, M. A., Tiberghien, G., Cirot-Tseva, A., Lallouache, M. T., and Escudier, P. (1991). Visual perception of anticipatory rounding during acoustic pauses: A cross-language study. In *Proceedings of the Twelfth International Congress of Phonetic Sciences (ICPhS),* vol. 4, 50–53. Aix-en Provence: Universite' de Provence.

Cave, C., Guaitella, I., Bertrand, R., Santi, S., Harlay, F., & Espesser, R. (1996). About the relationship between eyebrow movements and F0 variations. *Proceedings of the International Conference on Spoken Language Processing 1996* (2175–2178). Wilmington: University of Delaware.

Chalmers, D. J. (1996). *The conscious mind: In search of a fundamental theory.* New York: Oxford University Press.

Chandler, J. P. (1969). Subroutine STEPIT: Finds local minima of a smooth function of several parameters. *Behavioral Science, 14,* 81–82.

Cheeseman, P. (1986). Probabilistic versus fuzzy reasoning. In L. N. Kapal & J. F. Lemmer (eds.), *Uncertainty in artificial intelligence* (pp. 85–102). New York: Elsevier.

Clarke, F. R. (1957). Constant-ratio rule for confusion matrices in speech communication. *Journal of the Acoustical Society of America, 29,* 715–720.

Cohen, J. (1994). The earth is round (*p* < .05). *American Psychologist, 49,* 997–1003.

Cohen, M. M. (1979). Three cues to the voicing of intervocalic velar stops. Master's thesis, University of Wisconsin.

Cohen, M. M., & Massaro, D. W. (1990). Synthesis of visible speech. *Behavioral Research Methods, Instrumentation, and Computerss, 22,* 260–263.

Cohen, M. M., & Massaro, D. W. (1992). On the similarity of categorization models. In F. G. Ashby (ed.), *Multidimensional models of perception and cognition* (pp. 395–447). Hillsdale, NJ: Erlbaum.

Cohen, M. M., & Massaro, D. W. (1993). Modeling coarticulation in synthetic visual speech. In N. M. Thalmann & D. Thalmann (eds.), *Models and techniques in computer animation* (pp. 139–156). Tokyo: Springer.

Cohen, M. M., & Massaro, D. W. (1994). Development and experimentation with synthetic visible speech. *Behavioral Research methods, Instrumentation, and Computer, 26,* 260–265.

Cohen, M. M., & Massaro, D. W. (1995). Perceiving visual and auditory information in consonant-vowel and vowel syllables. In C. Sorin, J. Mariani, H. Meloni & J. Schoentgen (eds.), *Levels in speech communication: Relations and interactions* (pp. 25–38). Amsterdam: Elsevier.

Cohen, M. M., Walker, R. L., & Massaro, D. W. (1996). Perception of synthetic visual speech. In D. G. Stork & M. E. Hennecke (eds.), *Speechreading by humans and machines* (pp. 153–168). New York: Springer.

Cole, R. A., & Jakimik, J. (1978). Understanding speech: How words are heard. In G. Underwood (ed.), *Strategies of information-processing,* London: Academic Press.

Cole, R. A., & Jakimik, J. (1980). A model of speech perception. In R. A. Cole (ed.), *Perception and production of fluent speech* (pp. 133–163). Hillsdale, NJ: Erlbaum.

Cole, R. A., & Scott, B. (1974). Toward a theory of speech perception. *Psychological Review, 81,* 348–374.

Collier, G. (1985). *Emotional expression.* Hillsdale, NJ: Erlbaum.

Cornett, R. O. (1988). Cued speech, manual complement to lipreading for visual reception of spoken language: Principles, practice and prospects for automation. *Acta Oto-Rhino-Laryngologica Belgica, 42,* 375–384.

Corso, J. (1959). Age and sex differences in pure-tone thresholds. *Journal of the Acoustical Society of America, 31,* 498–507.

Corso, J. (1963). Age and sex differences in pure-tone thresholds. *Archives in Oto-laryngology, 77,* 385–405.

Costen, N. P., Parker, D. M., & Craw, I. (1994). Spatial content and spatial quantisation effects in face recognition. *Perception, 23,* 129–146.

Cowan, N. (1984). On short and long auditory stores. *Psychological Bulletin, 96,* 341–370.

Crossman, E. R. F. W. (1959). A theory of the acquisition of speed-skill. *Ergonomics, 2,* 153–166.

Crowder, R. G. (1973). Representation of speech sounds in precategorical acoustic storage. *Journal of Experimental Psychology, 98,* 14–24.

Crowder, R. G., & Cheng, C.-M. (1973). Phonemic confusability, precategorical acoustic storage, and the suffix effect. *Perception and Psychophysics, 13,* 145–148.

Crowder, R. G., & Morton, J. (1969). Precategorical acoustic storage, *Perception and Psychophysics, 5,* 365–371.

Crowley, J. L., & Demazeau, Y. 1993. Principles and techniques for sensor data fusion. *Signal processing, 32,* 5–27.

Crowther, C. S., Batchelder, W. H., & Hu, X. (1995). A measurement-theoretical analysis of the Fuzzy Logical Model of Perception. *Psychological Review, 102,* 396–408.

Cutler, A., Mehler, J., Norris, D., & Segui, J. (1986). The syllable's differing role in the segmentation of French and English. *Journal of Memory and Language, 25,* 385–400.

Cutting, J. E. (1987). Perception and information. *Annual Review of Psychology, 38,* 61–90.

Cutting, J. E., Bruno, N., Brady, N. P., & Moore, C. (1992). Selectivity, scope, and simplicity of models: A lesson from fitting judgments of perceived depth. *Journal of Experimental Psychology: General, 121,* 364–381.

Cytowic, R. E. (1993). *The man who tasted shapes: A bizarre medical mystery offers revolutionary insights into emotions, reasoning, and consciousness.* New York: Putnam.

Darwin, C. ([1859] 1968). *On the origin of species by means of natural selection.* London: Murray.

Darwin, C. (1872). *The expression of the emotions in man and animals.* London: Murray.

Davison, M., & McCarthy, D. (1988). *The matching law: A research review.* Hillsdale, NJ: Erlbaum.

De Gelder, B., & Morais, J. (eds.) (1995). *Speech and reading: A comparative approach.* Hove, England: Erlbaum.

De Gelder, B., & Vroomen, J. (1992). Auditory and visual speech perception in alphabetic and non-alphabetic Chinese-Dutch bilinguals. In R. J. Harris (ed.), *Cognitive processing in bilinguals* (pp. 413–426). Amsterdam: Elsevier.

DECtalk (1985). *Programmers Reference Manual.* Maynard, MA: Digital Equipment Corporation.

Delattre, P. C., Liberman, A. M., Cooper, F. S., & Gerstman, L. J. (1952). An experimental study of the acoustic determinants of vowel color: Observations of one- and two-formant vowels synthesized from spectrographic patterns. *Word, 8,* 195–210.

Denes, P. (1955). Effect of duration on the perception of voicing. *Journal of the Acoustical Society of America, 27,* 761–764.

Dennett, D. C. (1988). Quining qualia. In A. Marcel & E. Bisiach (eds), *Consciousness in comtemporary science* (pp. 42–77). New York: Oxford University Press.

Dennett, D. C. (1991). *Consciousness explained.* Boston: Little, Brown.

Dennett, D. C. (1995). *Darwin's dangerous idea: Evolution and the meanings of life.* New York: Simon & Schuster.

Derr, M. A., & Massaro, D. W. (1980). The contribution of vowel duration, F0 contour, and frication duration as cues to the /jus/–/juz/ distinction. *Perception and Psychophysics, 27,* 51–59.

DeYoe, E. A., & Van Essen, D. C. (1988). Concurrent processing streams in monkey visual cortex. *Trends in Neurosciences, 11,* 219–226.

Diehl, R. L., & Kluender, K. R. (1987). On the categorization of speech sounds. In S. Harnad (ed.), *Categorical perception* (pp. 226–253). Cambridge: Cambridge University Press.

Diehl, R. L., & Kluender, K. R. (1989). On the objects of speech perception. *Ecological Psychology, 1,* 121–144.

Dijkstra, T., & de Smedt, K. (1996). Computer models in psycholinguistics: An introduction. In T. Dijkstra & K. De Smedt (eds.), *Computational psycholinguistics* (pp. 3–23). London: Taylor & Francis Ltd.

Dixon, N. F., & Spitz, L. (1980). The detection of auditory visual desynchrony. *Perception, 9* 719–721.

Doenges, P. K., Chiariglione, L., Kaneko, I., & Reader, C. (1996). MPEG-4 synthetic/natural hybrid coding: Call for proposals. International Organization for Standardization, ISO/IEC JTC1/SC29/WG11N1195-MPEG96, March 1996.

Donovan, F. (1962). *The Benjamin Franklin papers.* New York: Dodd, Mead.

Dorman, M. F., Studdert-Kennedy, M., & Raphael, L. J. (1977). Stop-consonant recognition: Release bursts and formant transitions as functionally equivalent, context-dependent cues. *Perception and Psychophysics, 2,* 109–122.

Dowell, R. C., Martin, L. F. A., Tong, Y. C., Clark, G. M., Seligman, P. M., & Patrick, J. F. (1982). A 12-consonant confusion study on a multiple-channel cochlear implant patient. *Journal of Speech and Hearing Research, 25,* 509–516.

Dretske, F. (1995). Meaningful perception. In S. M. Kosslyn & D. N. Osherson (eds.), *An invitation to cognitive science.* Vol. 2: *Visual cognition* (2d ed., pp. 331–352). Cambridge, MA: MIT Press.

Driver, J. (1996). Enhancement of selective listening by illusory mislocation of speech sounds due to lip-reading. *Nature, 381,* 66–68.

Duchenne de Boulogne, G. B. ([1862] 1990). *The mechanism of human facial expression.* Cambridge: Cambridge University Press.

Duffy, S. A., & Pisoni, D. B. (1992). Comprehension of synthetic speech produced by rule: A review and theoretical interpretation. *Language and Speech, 35,* 351–389.

Easton, R. D., & Basala, M. (1982). Perceptual dominance during lipreading. *Perception and Psychophysics, 32,* 562–570.

Eddington, D. K. (1980). Speech discrimination in deaf subjects with cochlear implants. *Journal of the Acoustical Society of America, 68,* 885–891.

Ekman, P. (ed.). (1973). *Darwin and facial expresion: A century of research in review.* New York: Academic Press.

Ekman, P. (1984). Expression and the nature of emotion. In K. Scherer & P. Ekman (eds.), *Approaches to emotion* (pp. 319–343). Hillsdale, NJ: Erlbaum.

Ekman, P. (1993). Facial expression and emotion. *American Psychologist, 48,* 384–392.

Ekman, P. (1994). Strong evidence for universals in facial expressions: A reply to Russell's mistaken critique. *Psychological Bulletin, 115,* 268–287.

Ekman, P., & Friesen, W. (1975). *Pictures of facial affect*. Palo Alto, CA: Consulting Psychologists Press.

Ekman, P. & Friesen, W. (1977). *Manual for the Facial Action Coding System*. Palo Alto, CA: Consulting Psychologists Press.

Ekman, P., Friesen, W., & Ellsworth, P. (1972). *Emotion in the human face: Guidelines for research and an integration of findings*. New York: Pergamon.

Ekman, P., Hager, J. C., & Friesen, W. (1981). The symmetry of emotional and deliberate facial action. *Psychophysiology, 18*, 101–106.

Ellison, J. W., & Massaro, D. W. (1997). Featural evaluation, integration, and judgment of facial affect. *Journal of Experimental Psychology: Human Perception and Performance, 23*, 213–226.

Elovitz, H. S., Johnson, R. W., McHugh, A., & Shore, J. E. (1976). *Automatic translation of English text to phonetics by means of letter-to-sound rules*. NRL Report 7948, document AD/A021 929. Washington, DC: NTIS.

Elson, M. (1990), Displacement facial animation techniques. *ACM SIGGRAPH Facial Animantion Course Notes, 21*–42.

Enderton, H. B. (1972). *A mathematical introduction to logic*. New York: Academic Press.

Erber, N. P. (1972). Auditory, visual, and auditory-visual recognition of consonants by children with normal and impaired hearing. *Journal of Speech and Hearing Research, 15*, 423–422.

Erber, N. P. (1974). Effects of angle, distance, and illumination on visual reception of speech by profoundly deaf children. *Journal of Speech and Hearing Research, 17*, 99–112.

Erber, N. P., & De Filippo, C. L. (1978). Voice-mouth synthesis of /pa, ba, ma/. *Journal of the Acoustical Society of America, 64*, 1015–1019.

Estes, W. K. (1984). Global and local control of choice behavior by cyclically varying outcome probabilities. *Journal of Experimental Psychology: Learning, Memory, and Cognition, 10*, 258–270.

Etcoff, N. L., & Magee, J. J. (1992). Categorical perception of facial expressions. *Cognition, 44*, 227–240.

Ewertsen, H. W., & Nielsen, H. B. (1971). A comparative analysis of the audioisual, auditive and visual perception of speech. *Acta Otolaryngologica, 72*, 201–205.

Falaschi, A. (1992). Segmental quality assessment by pseudo-words. In G. Bailly, C. Benoit & T. R. Sawallis (eds.), *Talking machines: Theories, models and designs* (pp. 455–472). Amsterdam: Elsevier.

Farah, M. J. (1995). Dissociable systems for visual recognition: A cognitive neuropsychology approach. In S. M. Kosslyn & D. N. Osherson (eds.), *An invitation to cognitive science*. Vol. 2: *Visual cognition* (2d ed., pp. 101–119). Cambridge, MA: MIT Press.

Farah, M. J., Tanaka, J. W., & Drain, H. M. (1995). What causes the face inversion effect? *Journal of Experimental Psychology: Human Perception & Performance, 21*, 628–634.

Farrimond, T., (1959). Age differences in the ability to use visual cues in auditory communication. *Language and Speech, 2*, 179–192.

Fernald, A., & Kuhl, P. K. (1987). Acoustic determinants of infant preference for motherese speech. *Infant Behavior and Development, 10*, 279–293.

Finger, S. (1994). *Origins of neuroscience: A history of explorations into brain function*. New York: Oxford University Press.

Fisher, B. (1991). *Integration of visual and auditory information in perception of speech events,*. Ph.D. diss. University of California, Santa Cruz.

Flanagan, J. L., Ishizaka, K., & Shipley, K. L. (1975). Synthesis of speech from a dynamic model of the vocal cords and vocal tract. *Bell System Technology Journal, 54,* 485–506.

Fleming, E. (1984). *Believe the heart.* San Francisco: Strawberry Hill Press.

Fodor, J. A. (1983). *Modularity of mind.* Cambridge, MA: Bradford Books.

Foulke, E., & Orr, D. B. (1973). The perception of time-compressed speech. In D. L. Horton & J. J. Jenkins (eds.), Columbus, Ohio: Charles-Meuill. *Perception of Language* (pp. 79–119).

Fourcin, A. J. (1989). Links between voice pattern perception and production. In B. A. Elsendoorn & H. Bouma (eds.), *Working models of human perception* (pp. 67–91). London: Academic Press.

Fowler, C. A. (1996). Listeners do hear sounds, not tongues. *Journal of the Acoustical Society of America, 99,* 1730–1741.

Fowler, C. A., & Dekle, D. J. (1991). Listening with eye and hand: Cross-modal contributions to speech perception. *Journal of Experimental Psychology: Human Perception and Performance, 17,* 816–828.

Frank, H., & Althoen, S. C. (1994). *Statistics: Concepts and applications.* Cambridge: Cambridge University Press.

Freides, D. (1974). Human information processing and sensory modality: Cross-modal functions, information complexity, memory, and deficit. *Psychological Bulletin, 81,* 284–310.

Fridlund, A. J. (1991). Evolution and facial action in reflex, social motive, and paralanguage. *Biological Psychology, 32,* 3–100.

Fridlund, A. J. (1994). *Human facial expression: An evolutionary view.* San Diego: Academic Press.

Friedman, D., Massaro, D. W., Kitzis, S. N., & Cohen, M. M. (1995). A comparison of learning models. *Journal of Mathematical Psychology, 39,* 164–178.

Fujisaki, H., & Kawashima, T. (1970). Some experiments on speech perception and a model for the perceptual mechanism. *Annual Report of the Engineering Research Institute, 29,* 206–214. Tokyo: University of Tokyo, Faculty of Engineering.

Ganong, W. F. (1980). Phonetic categorization in auditory word recognition. *Journal of Experimental Psychology: Human Perception and Performance, 6,* 110–125.

Garner, W. R. (1974). *The processing of information and structure.* Hillsdale, NJ: Erlbaum.

Gelfer, C. E., Bell-Berti, F., & Harris, K. S. (1989). Determining the extent of coarticulation: Effects of experimental design. *Journal of the Acoustical Society of America, 86,* 2443–2445.

Gengel, R. W. (1976). Upton's wearable eyeglass speechreading aid: History and current status. In S. K. Hirch, D. H. Eldredge, I. J. Hirsh & R. S. Silverman (eds.), *Hearing and Davis: Essays honouring Hallowell Davis.* St. Louis: Washington University Press.

Gesi, A. T., Massaro, D. W., & Cohen, M. M. (1992). Discovery and expository methods in teaching visual consonant and word-identification. *Journal of Speech and Hearing Research, 35,* 1180–1188.

Gibson, J. J. (1979). *The ecological approach to visual perception.* Boston: Houghton Mifflin.

Gigerenzer, G., & Goldstein, D. G. (1996). Reasoning the fast and frugal way: Models of bounded rationality. *Psychological Review, 103,* 650–669.

Gigerenzer, G., & Hoffrage, U. (1995). How to improve Bayesian reasoning without instruction: Frequency formats. *Psychological Review, 102,* 684–704.

Gigerenzer, G., & Murray, D. J. (1987). *Cognition as intuitive statistics.* Hillsdale, NJ: Erlbaum.

Gilovich, (1991). *How we know what isn't so: The fallibility of human reason in everyday life*. New York: Free Press.

Gladwin, T. (1970). *East is a big bird: Navigation and logic on Puluwat atoll*. Cambridge, MA: Harvard University Press.

Goodale, M. A., & Milner, A. D. (1992). Separate visual pathways for perception and action. *Trends in Neurosciences, 15*, 20–25.

Goodglass, H. (1993). *Understanding aphasia*. San Diego: Academic Press.

Goodman, N. (1984). *Of mind and other matters*. Cambrdige, MA: Harvard University Press.

Gordon, P. C., Eberhardt, J. L., & Rueckl, J. G. (1993). Attentional modulation of the phonetic significance of acoustic cues. *Cognitive Psychology, 25*, 1–42.

Gouraud, H. (1971). Continuous shading of curved surfaces. *IEEE Transactions on Computer, 20*, 623–628.

Grant, D. A. (1956). Analysis-of-variance in the analysis and comparison of curves. *Psychological Bulletin, 53*, 141–154.

Grant, D. A. (1962). Testing the null hypothesis and the strategy and tactics of investigating theoretical models. *Psychological Review, 69*, 54–61.

Grant, K. W., & Walden, B. E. (1995). Predicting auditory-visual speech recognition in hearing-impaired listeners. *Proceedings of the Thirteenth International Congress of Phonetic Sciences, 3*, 122–129.

Green, D. M., & Swets, J. A. (1966). *Signal detection theory and psychophysics*. New York: Wiley.

Green, K. P. (1994). The influence of an inverted face on the McGurk effect. *Journal of the Acoustical Society of America, 95*, 3014 (Abstract).

Green, K. P., Kuhl, P. K., & Meltzoff, A. N. (1988). Factors affecting the integration of auditory and visual information in speech. *Journal of the Acoustical Society of America, 84*, S155 Abstract.

Green, K. P., Kuhl, P. K., Meltzoff, A. N., & Stevens, E. B. (1991). Integrating speech information across talkers, gender, and sensory modality: Female faces and male voices in the McGurk effect. *Perception and Psychophysics, 50*, 524–536.

Greene, B. G., Logan, J. S., & Pisoni, D. B. (1986). Perception of synthetic speech produced automatically by rule: Intelligibility of eight text-to-speech systems. *Behavior Research Methods, Instruments, and Computers, 18*, 100–107.

Greenwald, A. G., Pratkanis, A. R., Leippe, M. R., & Baumgardner, M. H. (1986). Under what conditions does theory obstruct research progress? *Psychological Review, 93*, 216–229.

Gregory, R. L. (1987). *Odd perceptions*. London: Methuen.

Hanin, L., Boothroyd, A., & Hnath-Chisolm, T. (1988). Tactile presentation of voice fundamental frequency as an aid to the speechreading of sentences. *Ear and Hearing, 9*, 335–341.

Harashima, H., Aizawa, K., & Saito, T. (1989). Model-based analysis coding of videotelephone images. *Thans. Inst. Elect. Inform. Commun. Eng. Jpn. E72, 5*, 452–459.

Hardcastle, W. J. (1975). Some aspects of speech production under controlled conditions of oral anesthesia and auditory masking. *Journal of Phonetics, 3*, 197–214.

Harmon, L. D., & Julesz, B. (1973). Masking in visual recognition: Effects of two-dimensional filtered noise. *Science, 180*, 1194–1196.

Henke, W. L. (1967). Preliminaries to speech synthesis based on an articulatory model. *Proceedings of 1967 IEEE Speech Conference*, 170–171, Boston.

Henton, C., & Litwinowicz, P. C. (1994). Saying and seeing it with feeling: Techniques for synthesizing visible, emotional speech. *Proceedings of the Second ESCA/IEEE Workshop on Speech Synthesis* (pp. 73–76). New Paltz, New York.

Hirsh, I. J., & Sherrick, C. E. (1961). Perceived order in different sense modalities. *Journal of Experimental Psychology, 62*, 423–432.

Hockett, C. F. (1955). *A manual of phonology.* Baltimore: Waverly Press.

Hornik, K., Stinchcombe, M., & White, H. (1989). Multilayer feedforward networks are universal approximators. *Neural Networks, 2*, 259–366.

Huber, L., & Lenz, R. (1993). A test of the linear feature model of polymorphous concept discrimination with pigeons. *Quarterly Journal of Experimental Psychology: Comparative and Physiological Psychology, 46*, 1–18.

Isenberg, D., Walker, E. C. T., & Ryder, J. M. (1980). A top-down effect on the identification of function words. *Journal of the Acoustical Society of America, 68*, Abstract AA6, S48.

Iverson, P., & Kuhl, P. K. (1995). Mapping the perceptual magnet effect for speech using signal detection theory and multidimensional scaling. *Journal of the Acoustical Society of America, 97*, 553–562.

Johnson, K., Ladefoged, P., & Lindau, M. (1993). Individual differences in vowel production. *Journal of the Acoustical Society of America, 94*, 701–714.

Johnson, N. F. (1975). On the function of letters in word identification: Some data and a preliminary model. *Journal of Verbal Learning and Verbal Behavior, 14*, 17–29.

Johnson, N. F., & Blum, A. J. (1988). When redundancy hurts letter detection: An attempt to define one condition. *Perception and Psychophysics, 43*, 147–155.

Johnson, W. F., Emde, R. N., Scherer, K. R., & Klinnert, M. D. (1986). Recognition of emotion from vocal cues. *Archives of General Psychiatry, 43*, 280–283.

Jordan, T. R., & Bevan, K. (1997). Seeing and hearing rotated faces: Influence of facial orientation on visual and audio-visual speech recognition. *Journal of Experimental Psychology: Human Perception and Performance, 23*, 388–403.

Kahneman, D., & Treisman, A. (1984). Changing views of attention and automaticity. In R. Parasuraman & D. R. Davies (eds.), *Varieties of attention* (pp. 29–61). New York: Academic Press.

Kallman, H. J., & Massaro, D. W. (1983). Backward masking, the suffix effect, and preperceptual storage. *Journal of Experimental Psychology: Learning, Memory, and Cognition, 9*, 312–327.

Kalra, P., Mangili, A., Magnenat-Thalmann, N., & Thalmann, D. (1991). SMILE: A multilayered facial animation system. *Proceedings of the IFIP Conference on Modeling in Computer Graphics*, Tokyo: Springer.

Kantner, C. E., & West, R. W. (1960). *Phonetics: An introduction to the principles of phonetic science from the point of view of English speech.* New York: Harper.

Kass, M., Witkin, A., & Terzopoulous, D. (1988). Snakes: Active contour models. *International Journal of Computer Vision*, 321–331.

Kelso, J. A. S., Vatikiotis-Bateson, E., Saltzman, E. L., & Kay, B. (1985). A qualitative dynamic analysis of reiterant speech production: Phase portraits, kinematics, and dynamic modeling. *Journal of the Acoustical Society of America, 77*, 266–280.

Kent, R. D., & Minifie, F. D. (1977). Coarticulation in recent speech production models. *Journal of Phonetics, 5*, 115–133.

Klatt, D. H. (1979). Synthesis by rule of segmental durations in English sentences. In B. Lindblom & S. Öhman, (eds.), *Frontiers of speech communication research* (pp. 287–299). London: Academic Press.

Klatt, D. H. (1980). Software for a cascade/parallel formant synthesizer. *Journal of the Acoustical Society of America, 67,* 971–995.

Klatt, D. H. (1987). Review of text-to-speech conversion for English. *Journal of the Acoustical Society of America, 82,* 737–793.

Klein, W., Plomp, R., & Pols, L. C. W. (1970). Vowel spectra, vowel spaces, and vowel identification. *Journal of the Acoustical Society of America, 48,* 999–1009.

Kleiser, J., & Walczak, D. (1989). *Sextone for President.* Computer Graphics video. Kleiser-Walczale Construction Co., 87 Maskhall St., North Adams, MA 01247.

Kohfeld, D. L. (1971). Simple reaction time as a function of stimulus intensity in decibels of light and sound. *Journal of Experimental Psychology, 88,* 251–257.

Kozhevnikov, V. A., & Chistovich, L. A. (1965). *Rech: Artikulatsiya i Vospriatatie* (Moscow-Leningrad). Trans. *Speech: Articulation and Perception, 30,* 543. Washington, DC: Joint Publication Research Service.

Kramer, E. (1963). Judgment of personal characteristics and emotions from nonverbal properties of speech. *Psychological Bulletin, 60,* 408–420.

Kreul, E. J., Nixon, J. C., Kryter, K. D., Bell, D. W., Lang, J. S. & Schubert (1968). A proposed clinical test of speech discrimination. *Journal of Speech and Hearing Research, 11,* 536–552.

Kricos, P. B., & Lesner, S. A. (1982). Differences in visual intelligibility across talkers. *Volta Review, 84,* 219–225.

Kurihara, T., & Arai, K. (1991). A transformation method for modeling and animation of the human face from photographs. In N. M. Thalmann & D. Thalmann (eds.), *Computer Animation'91.* (45–58). Tokyo: Springer.

Ladefoged, P. (1975). *A course in phonetics.* New York: Harcourt Brace Jovanovich.

Ladefoged, P., Harshman, R., Goldstein, L., & Rice, L. (1978). Generating vocal tract shapes from formant frequencies. *Journal of the Acoustical Society of America, 64,* 1027–1035.

Ladefoged, P., & Maddieson, I. (1986). Some of the sounds of the world's languages (preliminary version). *UCLA Working Papers in Phonetics,* Vol. 64. Los Angeles: University of California at Los Angeles, Department of Linguistics.

Lasseter, J., & Daly, S. (1995). *Toy Story: The art and making of the animated film.* New York: Hyperion.

Le Goff, B., & Benoit, C. (1996). A text-to-audiovisual-speech synthesizer for French. *Proceedings of ICSLP 96,* Philadelphia, Oct. 1996.

Le Goff, B., Guiard-Marigny, T., Cohen, M. M., & Benoit, C. (1994). Real-time analysis-synthesis and intelligibility of talking face. *Proceedings of the Second ESCA/IEEE Workshop on Speech Synthesis.* New Paltz, New York.

Leon, M., & Anderson, N. H. (1974). A ratio rule from integration theory applied to inference judgments. *Journal of Experimental Psychology, 102,* 27–36.

Lesner, S. A. (1988). The talker. *Volta Review, 90,* 89–98.

Lesner, S. A., & Kricos, P. B. (1981). Visual vowel and diphthong perception across speakers. *Journal of the Academy of Rehabilitative Audiology, 14,* 252–258.

Levine, S. C., Banich, M. T., & Koch-Weser, M. P. (1988). Face recognition: A general or specific right hemisphere capacity? *Brain and Cognition, 8,* 303–325.

Lewis, J. P., & Parke, F. I. (1987). Automated lipsynch and speech synthesis for character animation. *Proceedings Computer-Human Interaction and Computer Graphics '87,* Tornoto, 143–147.

Liberman, A. M. (1996). *Speech: A special code.* Cambrdige, MA: MIT Press.

Liberman, A. M., Cooper, F. S., Shankweiler, D. P., & Studdert-Kennedy, M. (1967). Perception of the speech code. *Psychological Review, 74,* 431–461.

Liberman, A. M., Delattre, P. C., & Cooper, F. S. (1958). Distinction between voiced and voiceless stops. *Language and Speech, 1,* 153–167.

Liberman, A. M., & Mattingly, I. G. (1985). The motor theory of speech perception revised. *Cognition, 21,* 1–33.

Liederman, J. (1995). A reinterpretation of the split-brain syndrome: Implications for the function of corticocortical fibers. In R. J. Davidson & K. Hugdahl (eds.), *Brain asymmetry* (pp. 451–490). Cambridge, MA: MIT Press.

Lindau, M., & Ladefoged, P. (1986). Variability of feature specifications. In J. S. Perkell & D. H. Klatt (eds.), *Invariance and variability in speech processes* (pp. 464–477). Hillsdale, NJ: Erlbaum.

Lindblom, B. (1996). Role of articulation in speech perception: Clues from production. *Journal of the Acoustical Society of America, 99,* 1683–1692.

Link, S. W. (1992). *The wave theory of difference and similarity.* Hillsdale, NJ: Erlbaum.

Lisker, L. (1978). Rabid vs. rapid: A catalog of acoustic features that may cue the distinction. *Haskins Laboratories, Status Report on Speech Research, SR-54,* 127–132. New Haven.

Löfqvist, A. (1990). Speech as audible gestures. In W. J. Hardcastle & A. Marchal (eds.), *Speech production and speech modeling* (pp. 289–322). Dordrecht, Netherlands: Kluwer.

Löfqvist, A., & Yoshioka, H. (1981). Laryngeal activity in Icelandic obstruent production. *Nordic Journal of Linguistics, 4,* 1–18.

Loftus, G. R., & McLean, J. E. (1997). Familiar old wine: Great new bottle. *American Journal of Psychology, 110,* 146–153.

Loomis, J. M., & Lederman, S. J. (1986). Tactual perception. In K. R. Boff, L. Kaufman & J. P. Thomas (eds.), *Handbook of perception and human performance.* Vol. 2: *Cognitive processes and performance* (pp. 31–1 to 31–41). New York: Wiley.

Loveless, N. E., Brebner, J., & Hamilton, P. (1970). Bisensory presentation of information. *Psychological Bulletin, 73,* 161–199.

Lubker, J., & Gay, T. (1982). Anticipatory labial coarticulation: Experimental, biological, and linguistic variables. *Journal of the Acoustical Society of America, 71,* 437–448.

Luce, R. D. (1959). *Individual choice behavior: A theoretical analysis.* New York: Wiley.

Luria, A. R. (1968). *The mind of a mnemonist: A little book about a vast memory.* New York: Basic Books.

MacLeod, A., & Summerfield, Q. (1987). Quantifying the contribution of vision to speech perception in noise. *British Journal of Audiology, 21,* 131–141.

Macmillan, N. A. (1987). Beyond the categorical/continuous distinction: A psychophysical approach to processing modes. In S. Harnad (ed.), *Categorical perception* (pp. 53–85). New York: Cambridge University Press.

Macmillan, N. A., & Creelman, C. D. (1991). *Detection theory: A user's guide.* New York: Cambridge University Press.

MacWhinney, B., & Bates, E. (1989). *The crosslinguistic study of sentence processing.* New York: Cambridge University Press.

Maddieson, I. (1984). *Patterns of sounds.* New York: Cambrdige University Press.

Marslen-Wilson, W., & Welsh, A. (1978). Processing interactions and lexical access during word recognition in continuous speech. *Cognitive Psychology, 10,* 29–63.

Martin, M. C. (1985). Alternatives to cochlear implants. In R. A. Schindler & M. M. Merzenich (eds.), *Cochlear implants* (pp. 549–561). New York: Raven.

Martony, J. (1974). Some experiments with electronic speechreading aids. *KTH Speech Transmission Laboratory: Quarterly Progress and Status Report, 2–3,* 34–56. Stockholm: Royal Institute of Technology.

Massaro, D. W. (1969). The effects of feedback in psychophysical tasks. *Perception and Psychophysics, 6,* 89–91.

Massaro, D. W. (1970a). Preperceptual processes and forgetting in memory tasks. *Psychological Review, 77,* 557–567.

Massaro, D. W. (1970b). Preperceptual auditory images. *Journal of Experimental Psychology, 85,* 411–417.

Massaro, D. W. (1972). Preperceptual images, processing time, and perceptual units in auditory perception. *Psychological Review, 79,* 124–145.

Massaro, D. W. (1974). Perceptual units in speech recognition. *Journal of Experimental Psychology, 102,* 199–208.

Massaro, D. W. (1975a). *Experimental psychology and information processing.* Chicago: Rand McNally.

Massaro, D. W. (ed.) (1975b). *Understanding language: An information processing analysis of speech perception, reading, and psycholinguistics.* New York: Academic Press.

Massaro, D. W. (1979a). Letter information and orthographic context in word perception. *Journal of Experimental Psychology: Human Perception and Performance, 5,* 595–609.

Massaro, D. W. (1979b). Reading and listening (tutorial paper). In P. A. Kolers, M. Wrolstad & H. Bouma (eds.), *Processing of visible language,* vol. 1 (pp. 331–353). New York: Plenum.

Massaro, D. W. (1984). Children's perception of visual and auditory speech. *Child Development, 55,* 1777–1788.

Massaro, D. W. (1985a). Attention and perception: An information-integration perspective. *Acta Psychologica, 60,* 211–241.

Massaro, D. W. (1985b). Brunswik and Gibson: Similarities and contrasts with implications for contemporary psychology (*Report 61/185 Perception and Action*). Bielefeld, Germany: Universität Bielefeld, Zentrum für interdisziplinäre Forshung.

Massaro, D. W. (1986). The computer as a metaphor for psychological inquiry: Considerations and recommendations. *Behavior Research Methods, Instruments, and Computers, 18,* 73–92.

Massaro, D. W. (1987a). Categorical partition: A fuzzy logical model of categorization behavior. In S. Harnad (ed.), *Categorical perception: The groundwork of cognition* (pp. 254–283). New York: Cambridge University Press.

Massaro, D. W. (1987b). Information-processing theory and strong inference: A paradigm for psychological inquiry. In H. Heuer & A. F. Sanders (eds.), *Perspectives on perception and action* (pp. 272–299). Hillsdale, NJ: Erlbaum.

Massaro, D. W. (1987c). Integrating multiple sources of information in listening and reading. In A. Allport, D. Mackay, W. Prinz & E. Scheerer (eds.), *Language perception and production: Shared mechanisms in listening, speaking, reading, and writing* (pp. 111–129). San Diego: Academic Press.

Massaro, D. W. (1987d). Psychophysics versus specialized processes in speech perception: An alternative perspective. In M. E. H. Schouten (ed.), *The psychophysics of speech perception* (pp. 46–65). Boston: Kluwer.

Massaro, D. W. (1987e). Speech perception by ear and eye. In B. Dodd & R. Campbell (eds.), *Hearing by eye: The psychology of lip-reading* (pp. 53–83). Hillsdale, NJ: Erlbaum.

Massaro, D. W. (1987f). *Speech perception by ear and eye: A paradigm for psychological inquiry.* Hillsdale, NJ: Erlbaum.

Massaro, D. W. (1988a). Ambiguity in perception and experimentation. *Journal of Experimental Psychology: General, 117,* 417–421.

Massaro, D. W. (1988b). Some criticisms of connectionist models of human performance. *Journal of Memory and Language, 22,* 213–234.

Massaro, D. W. (1989a). *Experimental psychology: An information proceeding approach.* San Diego: Harcourt Brace Jovanovich.

Massaro, D. W. (1989b). Multiple book review of *Speech perception by ear and eye: A paradigm for psychological inquiry,* by D. W. Massaro. Behavioral and Brain Sciences, 12, 741–794.

Massaro, D. W. (1989c). Testing between the TRACE model and the Fuzzy Logical Model of Perception. *Cognitive Psychology, 21,* 398–421.

Massaro, D. W. (1990). A fuzzy logical model of speech perception. In D. Vickers & P. L. Smith (eds.) *Human information processing: Measures, mechanisms, and models* (pp. 367–379). Amsterdam: North-Holland.

Massaro, D. W. (1991a). Connectionist models of speech perception. *Processings of the Twelfth International Congress of Phonetic Sciences, 2,* 94–97.

Massaro, D. W. (1991b). Language processing and information processing. In N. H. Anderson (ed.), *Contributions to information integration theory.* Vol. I: *Cognition* (pp. 259–292). Hillsdale, NJ: Erlbaum.

Massaro, D. W. (1992a). Broadening the domain of the fuzzy logical model of perception. In H. L. Pick Jr., P. Van den Broek & D. C. Knill (eds.), *Cognition: Conceptual and methodological issues* (pp. 51–84). Washington, DC: American Psychological Association.

Massaro, D. W. (1992b). Computational models of speech perception. In R. G. Reilly & N. E. Sharkey (eds.), *Connectionist approaches to language processing* (pp. 321–350). Hillsdale, NJ: Erlbaum.

Massaro, D. W. (1992c). The fuzzy logical model of speech perception: A framework for research and theory. In Y. Tohkura, E. Vatikiotis-Bateson & Y. Sagisaka (eds.), *Speech perception, production, and linguistic structure* (pp. 79–82). Tokyo: Ohmsha Ltd.

Massaro, D. W. (1994a). A pattern recognition account of decision making. *Memory and Cognition, 22,* 616–627.

Massaro, D. W. (1994b). Bimodal speech perception across the lifespan. In D. J. Lewkowicz & R. Lickliter (eds.), *The development of intersensory perception: Comparative persepctives* (pp. 371–399). Hillsdale, NJ: Erlbaum.

Massaro, D. W. (1994c). Modularity of information, not processing. *Current Psychology of Cognition, 13,* 97–102.

Massaro, D. W. (1994d). Psychological aspects of speech perception: Implications for research and theory. In M. Gernsbacher (ed.), *Handbook of Psycholinguistics* (pp. 219–263). New York: Academic Press.

Massaro, D. W. (1996a). Bimodal speech perception: A progress report. In D. G. Stork & M. E. Hennecke (eds.), *Speechreading by humans and machines* (pp. 79–101). New York: Springer.

Massaro, D. W. (1996b). Modelling multiple influences in speech perception. In T. Dijkstra & K. De Smedt (eds.), *Computational psycholinguistics* (pp. 85–113). London: Taylor & Francis Ltd.

Massaro, D. W. (1996c). Integration of multiple sources of information in language processing. In T. Inui & J. L McClelland (eds.), *Attention and Performance XVI: Information integration in perception and communication* (pp. 397–432). Cambridge, MA: MIT Press.

Massaro, D. W. (in press). Models for reading letters and works. In S. Sternberg & D. Scarborough (eds.), *Invitation to Cognitive Science, Vol. 4.* Cambridge, MA: MIT Press.

Massaro, D. W., & Burke, D. (1991). Perceptual development and auditory backward recognition masking. *Developmental Psychology, 27,* 85–96.

Massaro, D. W., & Cohen, M. M. (1976). The contribution of fundamental frequency and voice onset time to the /zi/–/si/ distinction. *Journal of the Acoustical Society of America, 60,* 704–717.

Massaro, D. W., & Cohen, M. M. (1977). Voice onset time and fundamental frequency as cues to the /zi/–/si/ distinction. *Perception and Psychophysics, 22,* 373–382.

Massaro, D. W., & Cohen, M. M. (1983a). Categorical or continuous speech perception: A new test. *Speech Communication, 2,* 15–35.

Massaro, D. W., & Cohen, M. M. (1983b). Consonant/vowel ratio: An improbable cue in speech. *Perception and Psychophysics, 33,* 502–505.

Massaro, D. W., & Cohen, M. M. (1983c). Evaluation and integration of visual and auditory information in speech perception. *Journal of Experimental Psychology: Human Perception and Performance, 9,* 753–771.

Massaro, D. W., & Cohen, M. M (1983d). Phonological context in speech perception. *Perception and Psychophysics, 34,* 338–348.

Massaro, D. W., & Cohen, M. M. (1987). Process and connectionist models of pattern recognition. *Proceedings of the Ninth Annual Conference of the Cognitive Science Society* (pp. 258–264). Hillsdale, NJ: Erlbaum.

Massaro, D. W., & Cohen, M. M. (1990). Perception of synthesized audible and visible speech. *Psychological Science, 1,* 55–63.

Massaro, D. W., & Cohen, M. M. (1991). Integration versus interactive activation: The joint influence of stimulus and context in perception. *Cognitive Psychology, 23,* 558–614.

Massaro, D. W., & Cohen, M. M. (1992). Speech by eye. In G. Bailly, C. Benoit & T. R. Sawallis (eds.), *Taling machines: Theories, models, and designs* (pp. 479–484). New York: North-Holland.

Massaro, D. W., & Cohen, M. M. (1993a). Perceiving asynchronous bimodal speech in consonant-vowel and vowel syllables. *Speech Communication, 13,* 127–134.

Massaro, D. W., & Cohen, M. M. (1993b). The paradigm and the fuzzy logical model of perception are alive and well. *Journal of Experimental Psychology: General, 122,* 115–124.

Massaro, D. W., & Cohen, M. M. (1994). Visual, orthographic, phonological, and lexical influences in reading. *Journal of Experimental Psychology: Human Perception and Performance, 20,* 1107–1128.

Massaro, D. W., & Cohen, M. M. (1995a). Continuous versus discrete information processing in pattern recognition. *Acta Psychologica, 90,* 193–209.

Massaro, D. W., & Cohen, M. M. (1995b). Perceiving talking faces. *Current Directions in Psychological Science, 4,* 104–109.

Massaro, D. W., & Cohen, M. M. (1995c). Modeling the perception of bimodal speech. *Proceedings of the Thirteenth International Congress of Phonetic Sciences, 3,* 106–113.

Massaro, D. W., & Cohen, M. M. (1996). Perceiving speech from inverted faces. *Perception and Psychophysics, 58,* 1047–1065.

Massaro, D. W., Cohen, M. M, & Gesi, A. T. (1993). Long-term training, transfer, and retention in learning to lipread. *Perception and Psychophysics, 53,* 549–562.

Massaro, D. W., Cohen, M. M., & Smeele, P. M. T. (1995). Cross-linguistic comparisons in the integration of visual and auditory speech. *Memory and Cognition, 23,* 113–131.

Massaro, D. W., & Cohen, M. M., & Smeele, P. M. T. (1996). Perception of asynchronous and conflicting visual and auditory speech. *Journal of the Acoustical Society of America, 100,* 1777–1786.

Massaro, D. W., Cohen, M. M., & Thompson, L. A. (1988). Visible language in speech perception: Lipreading and reading. *Visible Language, 22,* 9–31.

Massaro, D. W., & Cowan, N. (1993). Information processing models: Microscopes of the mind. *Annual Review of Psychology, 44,* 383–425.

Massaro, D. W., & Egan, P. B. (1996). Perceiving affect from the voice and the face. *Psychonomic Bulletin and Review, 3,* 215–221.

Massaro, D. W., & Ellison, J. W. (1996). Perceptual recognition of facial affect: Cross-cultural comparisons. *Memory and Cognition, 24,* 812–822.

Massaro, D. W., & Ferguson, E. L. (1993). Cognitive style and perception: The relationship between category width and speech perception, categorization, and discrimination. *American Journal of Psychology, 106,* 25–49.

Massaro, D. W., & Friedman, D. (1990). Models of integration given multiple sources of information. *Psychological Review, 97,* 225–252.

Massaro, D. W., & Friedman, D. (1991a). Adaptive rationality and identifiability of psychological processes. *Behavioral and Brain Sciences, 14,* 499–501.

Massaro, D. W., & Friedman, D. (1991b). Review of *Adaptive character of thought,* by R. Anderson. *American Journal of Psychology, 104,* 467–474.

Massaro, D. W., & Hary, J. M. (1986). Addressing issues in letter recognition. *Psychological Research, 48,* 123–132.

Massaro, D. W., & Klitzke, D. (1977). Letters are functional in word identification. *Memory and Cognition, 5,* 292–298.

Massaro, D. W., & Loftus, G. (1996). Sensory and perceptual storage: Data and theory. In E. L. Bjork & R. A. Bjork (eds.). *Handbook of perception and cognition.* Vol. 10: *Memory* (pp. 67–99). San Diego: Academic Press.

Massaro, D. W., & Oden, G. C. (1980a). Evaluation and integration of acoustic features in speech perception. *Journal of the Acoustical Society of America, 67,* 996–1013.

Massaro, D. W., & Oden, G. C. (1980b). Speech perception: A framework for research and theory. In N. J. Lass (ed.), *Speech and language: Advances in basic research and practice,* vol. 3 (pp. 129–165). New York: Academic Press.

Massaro, D. W., & Oden, G. C. (1995). Independence of lexical context and phonological information in speech perception. *Journal of Experimental Psychology: Learning, Memory, and Cognition, 21*, 1053–1064.

Massaro, D. W., & Sanocki, T. (1993). Visual information processing in reading. In D. M. Willows, R. S. Kruk & E. Corcos (eds.), *Visual processes in reading and reading disabilities* (pp. 139–161). Hillsdale, NJ: Erlbaum.

Massaro, D. W., Thompson, L. A., Barron, B., & Laren, E. (1986). Developmental changes in visual and auditory contributions to speech perception. *Journal of Experimental Child Psychology, 41*, 93–113.

Massaro, D. W., Tsuzaki, M., Cohen, M. M., Gesi, A., & Heredia, R. (1993). Bimodal speech perception: An examination across languages. *Journal of Phonetics, 21*, 445–478.

Massaro, D. W., Weldon, M. S., & Kitzis, S. N. (1991). Integration of orthographic and semantic information in memory retrieval. *Journal of Experimental Psychology: Learning, Memory, and Cognition, 17*, 277–287.

Mattingly, I. G., & Studdert-Kennedy, M. (eds.) (1991). *Modularity and the motor theory of speech perception.* Hillsdale, NJ: Erlbaum.

McClelland, J. L. (1991). Stochastic interactive processes and the effect of context on perception. *Cognitive Psychology, 23*, 1–44.

McClelland, J. L. (1996). Integration of information: Reflections on the theme of Attention and Performance XVI. In T. Inui & J. L McClelland (eds.), *Attention and Performance XVI: Information integration in perception and communication* (pp. 633–656). Cambridge, MA: MIT Press.

McClelland, J. L., & Elman, J. L. (1986). The TRACE model of speech perception. *Cognitive Psychology, 18*, 1–86.

McDowell, B. D., & Oden, G. C. (1995). Categorical decisions, rating judgments, and information preservation. Manuscript, University of Iowa, Iowa City.

McGill, W. J. (1961). Loudness and reaction time. *Acta Psychological, 19*, 193–199.

McGrath, M., & Summerfield, Q. (1985). Intermodal timing relations and audiovisual speech recognition by normal-hearing adults. *Journal of the Acoustical Society of America, 77*, 678–685.

McGurk, H., & MacDonald, J. (1976). Hearing lips and seeing voices. *Nature, 264*, 746–748.

McNeill, D. (1985). So you think gestures are nonverbal? *Psychological Review, 92*, 350–371.

McNeill, D., & Freiberger, P. (1993). *Fuzzy Logic: The discovery of a revolutionary computer technology—and how it is changing our world.* New York: Simon & Schuster.

Meehl, P. E. (1967). Theory testing in psychology and physics: A methodological paradox. *Philosophy of Science, 34* 103–115.

Meltzoff, A. N., & Moore, M. K. (1977). Imitation of facial and manual gestures by human neonates. *Science, 198*, 75–78.

Meredith, M. A., & Stein, B. E. (1985). Descending efferents from the superior colliculus relay integrated multisensory information. *Science, 227*, 657–659.

Meredith, M. A., & Stein, B. E. (1986). Visual, auditory, and somatosensory convergence on cells in superior colliculus results in multisensory integration. *Journal of Neurophysiology, 56*, 640–662.

Michon, J. A., & Jackson, J. L. (eds.) (1985). *Time, mind and behavior.* Berlin: Springer.

Miller, G. A. (1956). The magical number seven, plus or minus two: Some limits on our capacity for processing information. *Psychological Review, 63*, 81–97.

Miller, G. A., Galanter, E., & Pribram, K. H. (1960). *Plans and the structure of behavior*. New York: Holt, Rinehart & Winston.

Miller, G. A., & Isard, S. (1963). Some perceptual consequences of linguistic rules. *Journal of Verbal Learning and Verbal Behavior, 2*, 217–228.

Miller, G. A., & Nicely, P. E. (1955). An analysis of perceptual confusions among some English consonants. *Journal of the Acoustical Society of America, 27*, 338–352.

Miller, J. D., Engebretson, A. M., Defilippo, C. L. (1974). Preliminary research with a three-channel vibrotactile speech-reception aid for the deaf. In G. Fant (ed.), *Speech communication: Proceedings of the Speech Communication Seminar, Stockholm, April 1–3, 1974*. New York: Wiley.

Miller, J. L. (1995). On the internal structure of phonetic categories: A progress report. In J. Mehler & S. Franck, (eds.) *Cognition on cognition*. (pp. 333–347). Cambridge, MA: MIT Press.

Mills, A. E. (1987). The development of phonology in the blind child. In B. Dodd & R. Campbell (eds.), *Hearing by eye: The psychology of lip-reading* (pp. 145–161). Hillsdale, NJ: Erlbaum.

Mills, A. E., & Thiem, R. (1980). Auditory-visual fusions and illusions in speech perception. *Linguistische Berichte, 68/80*, 85–108.

Mohay, H. (1983). The effects of cued speech on the language development of three deaf children. *Sign Language Studies, 38*, 25–49.

Montgomery, A. A. (1980). Development of a model for generating synthetic animated lip shapes. *Journal of the Acoustical Society of America, 68*, Abstract FF13, S58.

Montgomery, A. A., & Jackson, P. L. (1983). Physical characteristics of the lips underlying vowel lipreading performance. *Journal of the Acoustical Society of America, 73*, 2134–2144.

Montgomery, A. A., & Soo Hoo, G. (1982). ANIMAT: A set of programs to generate, edit, and display sequences of vector-based images. *Behavioral Research Methods and Instrumentation, 14*, 39–40.

Moore, J. J., & Massaro, D. W. (1973). Attention and processing capacity in auditory recognition. *Journal of Experimental Psychology, 99*, 49–54.

Morais, J., & Kolinsky, R. (1994). Perception and awareness in phonological processing: The case of the phoneme. *Cognition, 50*, 287–297.

Movellan, J. R., & Chadderdon, G. (1996). Channel separability in the auditory visual integration of speech: A Bayesian approach. In D. G. Stork & M. E. Hennecke (eds.), *Speechreading by humans and machines* (pp. 473–487). New York: Springer.

Muliak, S. A., James, L. R., Van Alstine, J., Bonnett, N. Lind, S., & Stillwell, C. D. (1989). An evaluation of goodness-of-fit indices for structural equation models. *Psychological Bulletin, 105*, 430–445.

Munhall, K. G., Gribble, P., Sacco, L., & Ward, M. (1996). Temporal constraints on the McGurk effect. *Perception and Psychophysics, 58*, 351–362.

Munhall, K. G., & Löfqvist, A. (1992). Gestural aggregation in speech: Laryngeal gestures. *Journal of Phonetics, 20*, 111–126.

Murray, D. J. (1966). Vocalization-at-presentation and immediate recall, with varying recall methods. *Quarterly Journal of Experimental Psychology, 18*, 9–18.

Murray, I. R., & Arnott, J. L. (1993). Toward the simulation of emotion in synthetic speech: A review of the literature on human vocal emotion. *Journal of the Acoustical Society of America, 93*, 1097–1108.

Myers, J. L. (1976). Probability learning and sequence learning. In W. K. Estes (ed.), *Handbook of learning and cognitive processes* (pp. 171–205). Hillsdale, NJ: Erlbaum.

Myung, I. J., Pitt, M. A. (in press). Applying Occam's razor in modeling cognition: A Bayesian approach. *Psychonomic Bulletin and Review.*

Nachson, I., Moscovitch, M., & Umilta, C. (1995). The contribution of external and internal features to the matching of unfamiliar faces. *Psychological Research, 58,* 31–37.

Nagel, T. (1974). What is it like to be a bat? *Philosophical Review, 83,* 435–450.

Nahas, M., Huitric, H., & Saintourens, M. (1988). Animation of a B-spline figure. *Visual Computer, 3,* 272–276.

Nearey, T. M. (1992). Context effects in a double-weak theory of speech perception. Special Issue: Festschrift for John J. Ohala. *Language and Speech, 35,* 153–171.

Neisser, U. (1976). *Cognition and reality.* San Francisco: Freeman.

Newell, A. (1973). You can't play 20 questions with nature and win: Projective comments on the papers of this symposium. In W. E. Chase (ed.), *Visual information processing* (pp. 283–308). New York: Academic Press.

Newman, C. W., & Spitzer, J. B. (1987). Monotic and dichotic presentation of phonemic elements in a backward recognition–masking paradigm. *Psychological Research, 49,* 31–36.

Noller, P. (1985). Video primacy: a further look. *Journal of Nonverbal Behavior, 9,* 28–47.

Norman, D. A. (1969). *Memory and attention: An introduction to human information processing.* New York: Wiley.

Norman, D. A., & Wickelgren, W. (1969). Strength theory of decision rules and latency in retrieval from short-term memory. *Journal of Mathematical Psychology, 6,* 192–208.

Norton, S. J., Schultz, M. C., Reed, C. M., Braida, L. D., Durlach, N. I., Rabinowitz, W. M., & Chomsky, C. (1977). Analytic study of the Tadoma method: Background and preliminary results. *Journal of Speech and Hearing Research, 20,* 574–595.

Nosofsky, R. M. (1990). Relations between exemplar-similarity and likelihood models of classification. *Journal of Mathematical Psychology, 34,* 393–418.

Nusbaum, H. C., & Goodman, J. C. (1994). Learning to hear speech as spoken language. In H. C. Nusbaum & J. C. Goodman (eds.), *The development of speech perception: The transition from speech sounds to spoken words* (pp. 299–338). Cambridge, MA: MIT Press.

Oden, G. C. (1977a). Fuzziness in semantic memory: Choosing exemplars of subjective categories. *Memory and Cognition, 5,* 190–204.

Oden, G. C. (1977b). Integration of fuzzy logical information. *Journal of Experimental Psychology: Human Perception and Performance, 3,* 565–575.

Oden, G. C. (1978). Integration of place and voicing information in the identification of synthetic stop consonants. *Journal of Phonetics, 6,* 83–93.

Oden, G. C. (1981). A fuzzy propositional model of concept structure and use: A case study in object identification. In G. W. Lasker (ed.), *Applied systems and cybernetics* (Vol. VI, pp. 2890–2897). Elmsford, NY: Pergamon Press.

Oden, G. C., & Massaro, D. W. (1978). Integration of featural information in speech perception. *Psychological Review, 85,* 172–191.

Ohala, J. J. (1981). The nonlinguistic components of speech. In J. Darby (ed.), *Speech evaluation in psychiatry* (pp. 39–49). New York: Grune & Stratton.

Ohala, J. J. (1984). An ethological perspective on common cross-language utilization of F0 of voice. *Phonetica, 41,* 1–16.

Ohala, J. J. (1994). The frequency code underlies the sound symbolic use of voice pitch. In L. Hinton, J. Nichols & J. Ohala (eds.), *Sound symbolism* (pp. 325–347). New York: Cambridge University Press.

Ohala, J. J. (1996). Ethological theory and the expression of emotion in the voice. *Proc. ICSLP 96* (1812–1815). Wilmington: University of Delaware.

Öhman, S. (1966). Coarticulation in VCV utterances: Spectrographic measurements. *Journal of the Acoustical Society of America, 39,* 151–168.

Öhman, S. (1967). Numerical model of coarticulation. *Journal of the Acoustical Society of America, 41,* 310–320.

Olive, J. P., Greenwood, A., & Coleman, J. (1993). *Acoustics of American English speech: A dynamic approach.* New York: Springer.

Olson, D. R. (1994). *The world on paper.* Cambridge: Cambridge University Press.

Olson, R. K., & Wise, B. W. (1992). Reading on the computer with orthographic and speech feedback: An overview of the Colorado remediation project. *Reading and Writing, 4,* 107–144.

O'Shaughnessy, D. (1996). Critique: Speech perception: Acoustic or articulatory? *Journal of the Acoustical Society of America, 99,* 1726–1729.

Osherson, D. N., & Smith, E. E. (1981). On the adequacy of prototype theory as a theory of concepts. *Cognition, 9,* 35–58.

Osherson, D. N., & Smith, E. E. (1982). Gradedness and conceptual combination. *Cognition, 12,* 299–318.

Overmars, M. (1990). Forms Library. Dept. of Computer Science, Ultrecht University, Ultrecht, The Netherlands.

Palmer, S. E. (1992). Common region: A new principle of perceptual grouping. *Cognitive Psychology, 24,* 436–447.

Palmer, S. E., & Kimchi, R. (1986). The information processing approach to cognition. In T. J. Knapp & L. C. Robertson (eds.), *Approaches to cognition: Contrasts and controversies* (pp. 37–77). Hillsdale, NJ: Erlbaum.

Palmer, S. E., & Rock, I. (1994). Rethinking perceptual organization: The role of uniform connectedness. *Psychonomic Bulletin and Review, 1,* 29–55.

Palmer, S. E., Norman, J., Beck, D., & Massaro, D. W. (1995). Unpublished results.

Pandey, P. C., Kunov, H., & Abel, S. M. (1986). Disruptive effects of auditory signal delay on speech perception with lipreading. *Journal of Auditory Research, 26,* 27–41.

Parke, F. I. (1972). Computer-generated animation of faces. *Proc. ACM National Conference, 1,* 451–457.

Parke, F. I. (1974). *A parametric model for human faces.* Technical Report. UTEC-CSc-75-047. Salt Lake City: University of Utah.

Parke, F. I. (1975). A model for human faces that allows speech synchronized animation. *Computers and Graphics Journal, 1,* 1–4.

Parke, F. I. (1982). Parameterized models for facial animation. *IEEE Computer Graphics, 2 (9),* 61–68.

Parke, F. I. (1991). Control parameterization for facial animation. In N. M. Thalmann and D. Thalmann (eds.), *Computer Animation '91* (pp. 3–14). Tokyo: Springer.

Pastore, R. E. (1987). Categorical perception: Some psychophysical models. In S. Harnad (ed.), *Categorical perception* (pp. 29–52). New York: Cambridge University Press.

Patel, M., & Willis, P. J. (1991). FACES: Facial Animation, Construction, and Editing System. *Eurographics '91, 33–45.*

Patterson, E. C., Litwinowicz, P. C., & Greene, N. (1991). Facial animation by spatial mapping. In N. M. Thalmann and D. Thalmann (eds.), *Computer Animation '91,* Tokyo: Springer.

Pearce, A., Wyvill, B., Wyvill, G., & Hill, D. (1986). Speech and expression: A computer solution to face animation. Paper presented at Graphics Interface '86.

Pelachaud, C., Badler, N. I., & Steedman, M. (1991). Linguistic issues in facial animation. In N. M. Thalmann and D. Thalmann (eds.), *Computer Animation '91* (pp. 15–30). Tokyo: Springer.

Pelachaud, C., Badler, N. I., & Steedman, M. (1996). Generating facial expressions for speech. *Cognitive Science, 20,* 1–46.

Pelachaud, C., Badler, N., I, Viaud, M-L. (1994). *Final report to NSF of the standards for facial animation workshop.* (NSF Final Report. no. 9314898).

Penrose, R. (1989). *The emperor's new mind: Concerning computers, minds, and the laws of physics.* Oxford: Oxford University Press.

Penrose, R. (1994). *Shadows of the mind: A search for the missing science of consciousness.* Oxford: Oxford University Press.

Perkell, J. (1969). *Physiology of speech production: Results and implications of a quantitative cineradiographic study.* Cambridge, MA: MIT Press.

Perkell, J. S. (1990). Testing theories of speech production: Implications of some detailed analyses of variable articulatory data. In W. J. Hardcastle & A. Marchal (eds.), *Speech production and speech modeling* (pp. 262–288). Dordrecht, Netherlands: Kluwer Academic Publishers.

Perkell, J. (1991). Models, theory, and data in speech production. *Proceedings of the Twelfth International Congress of Phonetic Sciences, 1,* 182–191.

Perkell, J. S., & Chiang, C. (1986). Preliminary support for a "hybrid model" of anticipatory coarticulation. *Proceedings of the Twelfth International Conference of Acoustics,* A3–6.

Petajan, E. (1985). Automatic lipreading to enhance speech recognition. *Proceedings of the IEEE Conference on Computer Vision and Pattern Recognition,* 40–47.

Petajan, E., & Graf, H. P. (1996). Robust face feature analysis for automatic speechreading and character animation. In D. Stork & M. Hennecke (eds.), *Speechreading by humans and machines* (425–436). Berlin: Springer.

Peterson, G. E., & Barney, H. L. (1952). Control methods used in a study of the vowels. *Journal of the Acoustical Society of America, 24,* 175–184.

Pettigrew, T. W. (1958). The measurement and correlates of category width as a cognitive variable. *Journal of Personality, 26,* 532–544.

Pettigrew, T. F. (1982). Cognitive style and social behavior: A review of category width. In L. Wheeler (ed.), *Review of Personality and Social Psychology,* vol. 3 (pp. 199–223). Beverly Hills, CA: Sage.

Pickett, J. M., Gengel, R. W., Quinn, R., & Upton, H. W. (1974). Research with the Upton eyeglass speechreader. In G. Fant (ed.), *Speech communication: Proceedings of the Speech Communication Seminar, Stockholm, April 1–3, 1974.* New York: Wiley.

Pisoni, D. B. (1973). Auditory and phonetic memory codes in the discrimination of consonants and vowels. *Perception and Psychophysics, 13,* 253–260.

Pitt, M. A. (1955). The locus of the lexical shift in phoneme identification. *Journal of Experimental Psychology: Learning, Memory, and Cognition, 21,* 1037–1052.

Platt, J. R. (1964). Strong inference. *Science, 146,* 347–353.

Platt, S. M. (1985). A structural model of the human face. Ph.D. diss., University of Pennsylvania.

Platt, S. M., & Badler, N. I. (1981). Animating facial expressions. *Computer Graphics, 15,* 245–252.

Pollack, I., Rubenstein, H., & Horowitz, A. (1960). Communication of verbal modes of expression. *Language and Speech, 3,* 121–130.

Popper, K. (1959). *The logic of scientific discovery.* New York: Basic Books.

Poulton, E. C. (1989). *Bias in quantifying judgments.* Hillsdale, NJ: Erlbaum.

Povel, D.-J., & Arends, N. (1991). The Visual Speech Apparatus: Theoretical and practical aspects. *Speech Communication, 10,* 59–80.

Pylyshyn, Z. W. (1984). *Computation and Cognition.* Cambridge, MA: MIT Press.

Raney, L., Dancer, & Bradley, R. (1984). Correlation between auditory and visual performance on two speech reception tasks. *Volta Review, 86,* 134–141.

Real, L. A. (1991). Animal choice behavior and the evolution of cognitive architecture. *Science, 253,* 980–986.

Recasens, D. (1984). Vowel-to-vowel coarticulation in Catalan VCV sequences. *Journal of the Acoustical Society of America, 76,* 1624–1635.

Reed, C. M., Durlach, N. I., Delhorne, L. A., Rabinowitz, W. M., & Grant, K. W. (1989). Research on tactual communication of speech: Ideas, issues, and findings. *Volta Review, 91,* 65–78.

Reeves, W. T. (1990). Simple and complex facial animation: Case studies. *SIGGRAPH 90 Course Notes, Course 26, State of the Art in Facial Animation,* 88–106.

Reisberg, D., McLean, J., & Goldfield, A. (1987). Easy to hear but hard to understand: A lip-reading advantage with intact auditory stimuli. In B. Dodd & R. Campbell (eds.), *Hearing by eye: The psychology of lip-reading* (pp. 97–113). Hillsdale, NJ: Erlbaum.

Remez, R. E. (1996). Critique of auditory form and gestural topology in the perception of speech. *Journal of the Acoustical Society of America, 99,* 1695–1698.

Remez, R. E., Rubin, P. E., Berns, S. M., Pardo, J. S., & Lang, J. M. (1994). On the perceptual organization of speech. *Psychological Review, 101,* 129–156.

Repp. B. H., Manuel, S. Y, Liberman, A. M., & Studdert-Kennedy, M. (1983). Exploring the McGurk effect. Paper presented at the 24th meeting of the Psychonomic Society, San Diego, California, November 1983. Abstract in *Bulletin of the Psychonomic Society,* 366–367.

Restle, F., & Greeno, J. G. (1970). *Introduction to mathematical psychology.* Reading, MA: Addison-Wesley.

Reynolds, C. W. (1985). Description and control of time and dynamics in computer animation. *SIGGRAPH Advanced Computer Animation Course Notes,* 21–42.

Riley, D., & Costall, A. (1980). Comments on "Recognition of faces in the presence of two-dimensional sinusoidal masks" by Tieger and Ganz. *Perception and Psychophysics, 27,* 373–374.

Risberg, A. (1982). Speech coding in aids for the deaf: An overview of research from 1924 to 1982. *KTH Speech Transmission Laboratory Quarterly Progress and Status Report, 4/1983* (pp. 65–98). Stockholm: Royal Institute of Technology.

Robert-Ribes, J., Piquemal, M. Schwartz, J.-L., & Escudier, P. (1996). Exploiting sensor fusion architectures and stimuli complementarity in AV speech recognition. In D. G. Stork & M. E. Hennecke (eds.), *Speechreading by humans and machines* (pp. 193–210). Berlin: Springer.

Robert-Ribers, J., Schwartz, J.-L., & Escudier, P. (1995a). A comparison of models for fusion of the auditory and visual sensors in speech perception. *Artificial Intelligence Review, 9*, 323–346.

Robert-Ribers, J., Schwartz, J.-L., & Escudier, P. (1995b). Auditory, visual, and audiovisual vowel representations: Experiments and modelling. *Proceedings of the Thirteenth International Congress of Phonetic Sciences, 3*, 114–121.

Roberts, M., & Summerfield, Q. (1981). Audiovisual presentation demonstrates that selective adaptation in speech perception is purely auditory. *Perception and Psychophysics, 30*, 309–314.

Rock, I. (1983). *The logic of perception.* Cambridge, MA: MIT Press.

Roll, J. P., Gilhodes, J. C., Roll, R., & Harlay, F. (1996). Are proprioceptive sensory inputs combined into a "Gestalt"? In T. Inui & J. L. McClelland (eds.), *Attention and Performance XVI: Information integration in perception and communication* (pp. 291–314). Cambridge, MA: MIT Press.

Rönnberg, J., Arlinger, S., Lyxell, B., & Kinnefords, C. (1989). Visual evoked potentials: Relation to adult speechreading and cognitive function. *Journal of Speech and Hearing Research, 32*, 725–535.

Rosen, S. M., Fourcin, A. J., & Moore, B. C. (1981). Voice pitch as an aid to lipreading. *Nature, 291*, 150–152.

Rosenberg, E. L., & Ekman, P. (1995). Conceptual and methodological issues in the judgment of facial expressions of emotion. *Motivation & Emotion, 19*, 111–138.

Rosenblum, L. D., & Fowler, C. A. (1991). Audiovisual investigation of the loudness-effort effect for speech and nonspeech events. *Journal of Experimental Psychology: Human Perception and Performance, 17*, 976–985.

Rudnicky, A. I., & Cole, R. A. (1977). Adaptation produced by connected speech. *Journal of Experimental Psychology: Human Perception and Performance, 3*, 51–61.

Russell, J. A. (1994). Is there universal recognition of emotion from facial expressions? A review of the cross-cultural studies. *Psychological Bulletin, 115*, 102–141.

Rutherford, E. (1937). *The newer alchemy; based on the Henry Sidwick memorial lecture delivered at Newnham College, Cambridge, November, 1936, by Lord Rutherford.* Cambridge: The University Press.

Saldana, H. M., & Rosenblum, L. D. (1994). Selective adaptation in speech perception using a compelling audiovisual adaptor. *Journal of the Acoustical Society of America, 95*, 3658–3661.

Saltzman, E., & Kelso, J. A. S. (1987). Skilled actions: A task dynamic approach. *Psychological Review, 94*, 84–106.

Saltzman, E. L., Rubin, P. E., Goldstein, L., & Browman, C. P. (1987). Task-dynamic modeling of interarticulator coordination. *Journal of the Acoustical Society of America, 82.* Abstract H2, S15.

Samar, V. J., & Sims, D. G. (1983). Visual evoked-response correlates of speechreading performance in normal-hearing adults: A replication and factor analytic extension. *Journal of Speech and Hearing Research, 26*, 2–9.

Sams, M., Aulanko, R., Hämäläinen, M., Hari, R., Lounasmaa, O. V., Lu, S., & Simola, J. (1991). Seeing speech: Visual information from lip movements modifies activity in the human auditory cortex. *Neuroscience Letters, 127*, 141–145.

Sams, M., & Levänen, S. (1996). Where and when are the heard and seen speech integrated: Magnetoencephalographical (MEG) studies. In D. G. Stork & M. E. Hennecke (eds.), *Speech-reading by humans and machines* (233–238). Berlin: Springer.

Samuel, A. G. (1981). Phonemic restoration: Insights from a new methodology. *Journal of Experimental Psychology: General, 110,* 474–494.

Saulnier, A., Viaud, M-L., Geldreich, D. (1995). Real-time facial analysis and synthesis chain. *Proceedings of International Workshop on Automatic Face and Gesture Recognition,* Zurich, Switzerland.

Savage-Rumbaugh, E. S., Jurphy, J., Sevcik, R. A., Brakke, K. E., Williams, S. L., & Rumbaugh, D. M. (1993). *Language comprehension in ape and child.* Monographs of the Society for Research in Child Development, vol. 58, nos. 3–4.

Scherer, K. R. (1986). Vocal affect expression: A review and a model for future research. *Psychological Bulletin, 99,* 143–165.

Scherer, K. R. (1995). Expression of emotion in voice and music. *Journal of Voice, 9,* 235–248.

Scherer, K. R., Banse, R., Wallbott, H. G., & Goldbeck, T. (1991). Vocal cues in emotion encoding and decoding. *Motivation and Emotion, 15* 123–148.

Schindler, R. A., & Merzenich, M. M. (1985). *Cochlear implants.* New York: Raven.

Searle, C. L. (1982). Speech perception from an auditory and visual viewpoint. *Canadian Journal of Psychology, 36,* 402–419.

Searle, J. R. (1990). Minds, brains, and programs. In M. A. Boden (ed.), *The philosophy of artificial intelligence.* (pp. 67–88). Oxford: Oxford University Press.

Searle, J. R. (1992). *The rediscovery of the mind.* Cambridge, MA: MIT Press.

Sekiyama, K., & Tohkura, Y. (1991). McGurk effect in non-English listeners: Few visual effects for Japanese subjects hearing Japanese syllables of high auditory intelligibility. *Journal of the Acoustical Society of America, 90,* 1797–1805.

Sekiyama, K., & Tohkura, Y. (1993). Inter-language differences in the influence of visual cues in speech perception. *Journal of Phonetics, 21,* 427–444.

Selfridge, O. G. (1959). Pandemonium: A paradigm for learning. In *Mechanization of thought processes* (pp. 511–526). London: Her Majesty's Stationery Office.

Sergent, J. (1994). Cognitive and neural structures in face processing. In A. Kertesz (ed.), *Localization and neuroimaging in neuropsychology* (pp. 473–494). San Diego: Academic Press.

Sergent, J., Ohta, S., MacDonald, B., & Zuck, E. (1994). Segregated processing of facial identity and emotion in the human brain: A PET study: *Visual Cognition, 1,* 349–369.

Shannon, R. V. (1983). Multichannel electrical stimulation of the auditory nerve in man. I: Basic psychophysics. *Hearing Research, 11,* 157–189.

Shepard, R. N. (1957). Stimulus and response generalization: A stochastic model relating generalization to distance in psychological space. *Psychometrika, 22,* 325–345.

Shepard, R. N. (1962). The analysis of proximities: Multidimensional scaling with an unknown distance function. *Psychometrika, 27,* 125–140.

Shepard, R. N. (1987). Toward a universal law of generalization for psychological science. *Science, 237,* 1317–1323.

Shepard, R. N. (1988). George Miller's data and the development of methods for represecting cognitive structures. In W. Hirst (ed.) *The making of cognitive science: Essays in honor of George A. Miller* (pp. 45–70). Cambridge: Cambridge University Press.

Shepherd, D. C. (1982). Visual-neural correlate of speechreading ability in normal-hearing adults. *Journal of Speech and Hearing Research, 25,* 521–527.

Sherrick, C. E., & Cholewiak, R. W. (1986). Cutaneous sensitivity. In K. R. Boff, L. Kaufman & J. P. Thomas (eds.), *Handbook of perception and human performance.* Vol. 2: *Cognitive processes and performance* (pp. 12-1 to 12-58). New York: Wiley.

Shoop, C., & Binnie, C. A. (1979). The effects of age upon the visual perception of speech. *Scandinavian Audiology, 8,* 3–8.

Sidman, M. (1952). A note on functional relations obtained from group data. *Psychological Bulletin, 49,* 263–269.

Simmons, F. B. (1985). History of cochlear implants in the United States: A personal perspective. In R. A. Schindler & M. M. Merzenich (eds.), *Cochlear implants* (pp. 1–11). New York: Raven.

Simon, H. (1991). *Models of my life.* New York: Basic Books.

Smeele, P. M. T., Massaro, D. W., Cohen, M. M., & Sittig, A. C. (1994). Laterality and visual speech perception. Manuscript.

Smits, R., ten Bosch, L., & Collier, R. (1996). Evaluation of various sets of acoustic cues for the perception of prevocalic stop consonants. I: Perception experiment. *Journal of the Acoustical Society of America, 100,* 3852–3864.

Stein, B. E. (1995). A neural basis for the synthesis of sound, sight, and touch. *Journal of the Acoustical Society of America, 97.* Abstract, 3309.

Stein, B. E., & Meredith, M. A. (1993). *The merging of the senses.* Cambridge, MA: MIT Press.

Stein, B. E., Meredith, M. A., & Wallace, M. T. (1994). Development and neural basis of multisensory integration. In D. J. Lewkowicz & R. Lickliter (eds.), *The development of intersensory perception: Comparative perspectives* (pp. 81–105). Hillsdale, NJ: Erlbaum.

Stoker, R. G., & French-St. George, M. (1987). Effects of short-term training on lipreadability of speakers. Paper presented at the meeting of the American Speech and Hearing Association. New Orleans, LA.

Stork, D. G., & Hennecke, M. E. (eds.) (1996). *Speechreading by humans and machines.* New York: Springer-Verlag.

Studdert-Kennedy, M. (1976). Speech perception. In N. J. Lass (ed.), *Contemporary issues in experimental phonetics* (pp. 243–293). New York: Academic Press.

Studdert-Kennedy, M. (1989). Reading gestures by light and sound. In A. W. Young & H. D. Ellis (eds.), *Handbook of research on face processing* (pp. 217–222). New York: Elsevier.

Sumby, W. H., & Pollack, I. (1954). Visual contribution to speech intelligibility in noise. *Journal of the Acoustical Society of America, 26,* 212–215.

Summerfield, A. Q. (1979). Use of visual information in phonetic perception. *Phonetica, 36,* 314–331.

Summerfield, A. Q. (1983). Audio-visual speech perception, lipreading and artificial stimulation. In M. E. Lutman & M. P. Haggard (eds.), *Hearing science and hearing disorders* (131–182). London: Academic Press.

Summerfield, A. Q. (1987). Some preliminaries to a comprehensive account of audio-visual speech perception. In B. Dodd and R. Campbell (eds.), *Hearing by eye: The psychology of lip-reading* (pp. 3–51). Hillsdale, NJ: Erlbaum.

Summerfield, A. Q., MacLeod, A., McGrath, M., & Brooke, M. (1989). Lips, teeth, and the benefits of lipreading. In A. W. Young & H. D. Ellis (eds.), *Handbook of research in face processing* (223–233). Amsterdam: North-Holland.

Summerfield, A. Q., and McGrath, M. (1984). Detection and resolution of audio-visual incompatibility in the perception of vowels. *Quarterly Journal of Experimental Psychology, 36*, 51–74.

Suppes, P., Pavel, M., & Falmagne, J. (1994). Representations and models in psychology. *Annual Review of Psychology, 45*, 517–544.

Takeuchi, A., & Franks, S. (1992). *A rapid face constuction lab*. Sony Computer Science Lab Technical Report SCSL-TR-02-010.

Tallal, P., Miller, S. L., Bedi, G., Byma, G., Wang, X., Nagarajan, S. S., Schreiner, C., Jenkins, W. M., & Merzenich, M. M. (1996). Language comprehension in language-learning impaired children improved with acoustically modified speech. *Science, 271*, 81–84.

Tanaka, J. W., & Farah, M. J. (1993). Parts and wholes in face recognition. *Quarterly Journal of Experimental Psychology: Human Experimental Psychology, 46*, 225–245.

Tartter, V. C., & Braun, D. (1994). Hearing smiles and frowns in normal and whisper registers. *Journal of the Acoustical Society of America, 96*, 2101–2107.

Taylor, I., & Olson, D. R. (eds.) (1995). *Scripts and literacy: Reading and learning to read alphabets, syllabaries and characters*. Dordrecht, Netherlands: Kluwer.

Terzopoulous, D., & Waters, K. (1990). Muscle parameter estimation from image sequences. ACM *SIGGRAPH Facial Animation Course Notes*, 146–155.

Terzopoulous, D., & Waters, K. (1991). Techniques for realistic facial modeling and animation. In M. Thalmann & D. Thalmann (eds.), *Computer Animation '91* (pp. 115–127). Tokyo: Springer.

Thomas, C. K. (1958). *An introduction to the phonetics of American English*. New York: Ronald Press Company.

Thomas, E. A. C., & Legge, D. (1970). Probability matching as a basis for detection and recogniton decisions. *Psychological Review, 77*, 65–72.

Thomas, E. A. C., & Myers, J. L. (1972). Implications of latency data for threshold and non-threshold models of signal detection. *Journal of Mathematical Psychology, 9*, 253–285.

Thompson, L. A., & Massaro, D. W. (1986). Evaluation and integration of speech and pointing during referential understanding. *Journal of Experimental Child Psychology, 42*, 334–362.

Thompson, L. A., & Massaro, D. W. (1989). Before you see it, you see its parts: Evidence for feature encoding and integration in preschool children and adults. *Cognitive Psychology, 21*, 334–362.

Thompson, L. A., & Massaro, D. W. (1994). Children's integration of speech and pointing gestures in comprehension. *Journal of Experimental Child Psychology, 57*, 327–354.

Thurstone, L. L. (1927). A law of comparative judgment. *Psychological Review, 34*, 273–286.

Townsend, J. T., Hu, G. G., & Ashby, F. G. (1981). Perceptual sampling of orthogonal straight line features. *Psychological Research, 43*, 259–275.

Townsend, J. T., & Landon, D. E. (1982). An experimental and theoretical investigation of the constant-ratio rule and other models of visual letter confusion. *Journal of Mathematical Psychology, 25*, 119–162.

Tukey, J. W. (1962). *The citation index and the information problem: Opportunities and research in progress, annual report for 1962*. Princeton, NJ: Princeton University, Statistical Techniques Research Group.

Tukey, J. W. (1977). *Exploratory data analysis*. Reading, MA: Addison-Wesley.

Tversky, A., & Kahneman, D. (1983). Extension versus intuitive reasoning: The conjunction fallacy in probability judgment. *Psychological Review, 90*, 293–315.

Tyler, R. S., & Moore, B. C. (1992). Consonant recognition by some of the better cochlear-implant patients. *Journal of the Acoustical Society of America, 92*, 3068–3077.

Upton, H. W. (1968). Wearable eyeglass speechreading aid. *American Annals of the Deaf, 113*, 222–229.

Utley, J. (1946). A test of lipreading ability. *Journal of Speech and hearing Disorders, 11*, 109–116.

Uttal, W. R. (1990). On some two-way barriers between models and mechanisms. *Perception and Psychophysics, 48*, 188–203.

Valentine, T. (1988). Upside-down faces: A review of the effect of inversion upon face recognition. *British Journal of Psychology, 79*, 471–491.

Van Rooij, J. C., Plomp, R., & Orlebeke, J. F. (1989). Auditive and cognitive factors in speech perception by elderly listeners. I: Development of test battery. *Journal of the Acoustical Society of America, 86*, 1294–1309.

Van Santen, J. P. H. (1993). Perceptual experiments for diagnostic testing of text-to-speech systems. *Computer Speech and Language, 7*, 49–100.

Vatikiotis-Bateson, E., Munhall, K. G., Hirayama, M., Lee, Y. V., & Terzopoulous, D. (1996). The dynamics of audiovisual behavior in speech. In D. G. Stork & M. E. Hennecke (eds.), *Speechreading by humans and machines* (pp. 221–232). New York: Springer.

Venezky, R. L., & Massaro, D. W. (1987). Orthographic structure and spelling-to-sound mappings in reading English words. In A. Allport, D. MacKay, W. Prinz & E. Scheerer (eds.), *Language perception and production: Shared mechanisms in listening, speaking, reading and writing* (pp. 159–179). San Diego: Academic Press.

VOTRAX (1981). *User's Manual*. Votrax, Division of Federal Screw Works.

Vroomen, J. H. M. (1992). Hearing voices and seeing lips: Investigations in the psychology of lipreading. Ph.D. diss. Katholieke Universiteit Brabant, Tilburg, Netherlands.

Walden, B. E., Busacco, D. A., & Montgomery, A. A. (1993). Benefit from visual cues in auditory-visual speech recognition by middle-aged and elderly persons. *Journal of Speech and Hearing Research, 36*, 431–436.

Walden, B. E., Montgomery, A. A., Prosek, R. A., & Hawkins, D. B. (1990). Visual biasing of normal and impaired auditory speech perception. *Journal of Speech and Hearing Research, 33*, 163–173.

Walden, B. E., Prosek, R. A., Montgomery, A. A., Scherr, C. K., & Jones, C. J. (1977). Effects of training on the visual recognition of consonants. *Journal of Speech and Hearing Research, 20*, 130–145.

Waldrop, M. M. (1992). *Complexity: The emerging science at the edge of order and chaos*. New York: Simon & Schuster.

Waldstein, R. S., & Boothroyd, A. (1995). Speechreading supplemented by single-channel and multichannel tactile displays of voice fundamental frequency. *Journal of Speech and Hearing Research, 38*, 690–705.

Wandell, B. A. (1995). *Foundations of vision*. Sunderland, MA: Sinauer Associates.

Wang, C. L-Y., & Forsey, D. R. (1994). Langwidere: A new facial animation system. *Proceedings of Computer Animation '94* (pp. 59–68).

Warren, R. M., & Warren, R. P. (1970). Auditory illusions and confusions. *Scientific American, 223*, 30–36.

Waters, K. (1987). A muscle model for animating three-dimensional facial expression. *IEEE Computer Graphics, 21*, 17–24.

Waters, K., & Levergood, T. M. (1993). DECface: An automatic lip-synchronization algorithm for synthetic faces. Digital Equipment Corporation, Cambridge Research Laboratory. Technical Report CRL 93/4, September 23, 1993.

Waters, K., & Terzopoulous, D. (1990). A physical model of facial tissue and muscle articulation ACM *SIGGRAPH Facial Animation Course Notes, 130*–145.

Waugh, N. C., & Norman, D. A. (1965). Primary memory. *Psychological Review, 72*, 89–104.

Weldon, M. S., & Massaro, D. W. (1996). Integration of orthographic, conceptual, and episodic information on implicit and explicit tests. *Canadian Journal of Experimental Psychology, 50*, 72–85.

Wenger, M. J., & Payne, D. G. (1997). Cue integration across study tasks and direct and indirect retrieval instructions: Implications for the study of retrieval processes. *Journal of Experimental Psychology: Learning, Memory, and Cognition, 23*, 102–122.

Whitehead, A. N. (1925). *An enquiry concerning the principles of natural knowledge.* Cambridge: Cambridge University Press.

Wickens, T. D. (1982). *Models for behavior: Stochastic processes in psychology.* San Francisco: Freeman.

Williams, C. E., & Stevens, K. N. (1972). Emotions and speech: Some acoustic correlates. *Journal of the Acoustical Society of America, 52*, 1238–1250.

Willows, D. M., Kruk, R. S., & Corcos, E. (eds.), *Visual processes in reading and reading disabilities.* Hillsdale, NJ: Erlbaum.

Wise, B. W., & Olson, R. K. (1992). How poor readers and spellers use interactive speech in a computerized spelling program. *Reading and Witing, 4*, 145–163.

Working Group on Speech Understanding and Aging. (1988). Speech understanding and aging. *Journal of the Acoustical Society of America, 83*, 859–893.

Wozniak, V. D., & Jackson, P. L. (1979). Visual vowel and diphthong perception from two horizontal viewing angles. *Journal of Speech and Hearing Research, 22*, 354–365.

Yau, J. F. S., & Duffy, N. D. (1988). 3D facial animation using image samples. In N. M. Thalmann & D. Thalmann (eds.), *New trends in computer graphics.* Tokyo: Springer.

Yellott, J. I. (1977). The relationship between Luce's choice axiom, Thurstone's theory of comparative judgment, and the double exponential distribution. *Journal of Mathematical Psychology, 15*, 109–144.

Zadeh, L. A. (1965). Fuzzy sets. *Information and Control, 8*, 338–353.

Zadeh, L. A. (1982). A note on prototype theory and fuzzy sets. *Cognition, 12*, 291–297.

Zeki, S. (1993). *A vision of the brain.* Oxford: Blackwell.

Appendix: CD-ROM Selections

Dominic W. Massaro and Michael M. Cohen

Band 1.1 Baldi describes himself. Baldi is a superficial person, to say the least. As he puts it, there is little beneath his attractive exterior.

Band 1.2 Watch and listen. There are four sets of four syllables, and you should keep track of whether your auditory experience changes from syllable to syllable.

Band 1.3 Watch and listen. There are four sets of four syllables, and you should keep track of whether your auditory experience changes from syllable to syllable.

Band 1.4 Five levels of synthetic audible speech varying between /ba/ and /da/ are crossed with five levels of visible speech varying between the same alternatives. The visible speech is the fastest-moving variable. We also included the unimodal test stimuli to implement the expanded factorial design, as shown in figure 1.9.

Band 1.5 Watch and listen to the sentence, and ascertain what is being said. If you don't succeed, repeat the demonstration a few times.

Band 1.6 You might not be able to understand the words of this synthetic speech. Having them written or simply knowing them gives you the impression of *hearing* them better.

Band 2.1 Sinewave speech can be heard as speech and even understood, but it is easier to comprehend when accompanied by a talking face.

Band 3.1 Sample trials from the experiment in which a visual /ba/ or /da/ was combined with an auditory /ba/ or /da/ with an SOA of −200, −100, 0, 100, or 200 ms. The SOA in a bimodal syllable is defined as the difference between the onset of the auditory and visual syllables. Participants were instructed to watch the talker and listen to what was spoken and to identify what was *heard*.

Band 3.2 The SOA is varied to give the impression of either one or two perceptual events. The auditory and visual speech are synchronous in the first four syllables. The visual speech is /ba/ or /da/, and the auditory speech is /ba/ or /da/. The auditory speech is the fastest-moving variable. The next set of four syllables is the same except that the visual speech leads by 800 ms. Finally, the auditory speech leads by 800 ms in the last four syllables.

Band 3.3 Sample trials from the short SOA experiment, in which the asynchronous SOAs were created by offsetting the auditory and visual syllables by the specified duration relative to their normal co-occurrence at the simultaneous SOA condition.

Band 3.4 Sample trials from the long SOA experiment, in which the asynchronous SOAs were created by offsetting the auditory and visual syllables by the specified duration relative to their normal co-occurrence at the simultaneous SOA condition.

Band 3.5 The visible syllable is always the viseme /ba/. The auditory vowel /a/ is played at three different times relative to the visible syllable. The auditory and visual syllables are always terminated at the same time. Across the three syllables, the auditory syllable initially occurs well before the visual syllable and is gradually delayed. This onset difference can be used to distinguish /ma/, /ba/, and /pa/.

Band 4.1 George Miller's face was texture-mapped onto Baldi's wire-frame head, so that he could read the introduction to his seminal article on the magical number 7 plus or minus 2.

Band 6.1 The experimental setup and a few example trials from the gesture-speech experiment. The task was to indicate whether a ball or a doll was intended by the talker. An auditory continuum of five levels was made between the words *ball* and *doll*. The gestural information, also with five levels, was varied between pointing to the ball or doll objects.

Band 7.1 The different faces in the expanded factorial design. Five levels of the upper face and five levels of the lower face were factorially combined, along with the ten half-face conditions presenting the upper face or lower face alone. The levels change from the most happy to the most angry. The upper half is the fastest-moving variable. Theses factorial conditions are followed by the half-face conditions.

Band 7.2 This band demonstrates the same expanded factorial design as band 7.1, but with the lower-half of the face as the fastest-moving variable.

Band 7.3 The different faces in the expanded factorial design with the American face. The upper face is the fastest-moving variable. This experiment employed dynamic facial expression rather than the static expressions used in the previous experiments shown in band 7.1 and band 7.2. Each face stimulus began with a neutral expression and moved to the target feature value(s) during the first 600 ms, and remained on, without motion, for an additional 400 ms.

Band 7.4 The different faces in the expanded factorial design with the Japanese face. The upper face is the fastest moving variable. This experiment employed dynamic facial expression rather than the static expressions used in the previous experiments shown in band 7.1 and band 7.2. Each face stimulus began with a neutral expression and moved to the target feature value(s) during the first 600 ms, then remained on, without motion, for an additional 400 ms.

Band 8.1 Our talking head repeatedly says the word *please*. Try to determine the affect being conveyed during each articulation. There are four sets of the four words, and you should keep track of whether your perception of affect changes from syllable to syllable. If it does, then the audible speech had a substantial influence on your experience. Within each set of four words, the auditory word was articulated to be happy, angry, surprised, and fearful. The first set of four always had a happy face, the second set always had an angry face, the third surprised, and the fourth fearful. Auditory speech is the fastest-moving variable.

Band 8.2 This band demonstrates the same expanded factorial design as band 8.1, but with visible speech as the fastest-moving variable.

Band 8.3 This band illustrates the 15 test stimuli in the expanded factorial design, with the face as the fastest-moving variable.

Band 8.4 This band repeats the design shown in band 8.3 but with the voice as the fastest-moving variable.

Band 11.1 This band illustrates sample trials from the same-different task. On each trial, a pair of syllables is presented. Simply watch and listen and determine whether either the audible or visible speech differed for a given pair. There are four trials. The answers to the four trials are different, different, same, and same.

Band 12.1 The same demonstration of the influence of visible speech as given in band 1.2, but with a real face rather than a synthetic one.

Band 12.2 An example of musculoskeletal synthesis. This animation was done using Takeuchi and Franks's (1992) version of Waters's algorithm.

Band 12.3 Some examples of the original Parke synthesis. Parke (1974) selected and refined the control parameters used for several demonstration sentences by studying his own articulation frame by frame and estimating the control parameter values.

Band 12.4 The two utterances (/həti/ and /hətu/) from the cineradiograph analyzed by Perkell (1969).

Band 12.5 The UCSC control strategy also allows Baldi to speak Mexican Spanish.

Band 12.6 The UCSC control strategy has been successfully used in French (Le Goff & Benoit, 1996).

Band 12.7 Examples of the use of texture mapping to create a variety of faces. Note the differences in head shape, facial hair, mouth size and lip thickness.

Band 12.8 Graphical user interface for visual speech development. Master panel in lower right has facial controls; facilities for editing speech segment definitions, sentence input, and speaking rate; controls for parameter tracking; call-ups for subsidiary control panels; and other miscellaneous controls. Upper right panel is text interface. Lower left panel is display output. In the upper left are replay controls with cursors for zooming and for moving backward and forward in time, and plots of control parameters (bottom), dominance functions (middle), and derived lip measures (top).

Band 12.9 Close-up of the display panel showing the face articulating /ða/.

Band 12.10 Close-up of GUI master panel. Yellow slides relate to speech control, the blue slides relate to viewing, and the pink slides control other facial characteristics. Side view of transparent face. Close-up of materials, lighting, and display edit control panel.

Band 12.11 Side view of transparent face.

Band 12.12 One of the subsidiary panels called up from the master panel, the one responsible for materials and lighting editing and other display characteristics. Standard settings can be read in from files and new versions saved.

Band 12.13 Subsidiary panel used for controlling a laser videodisc via a serial line. The Bernstein and Eberhardt (1986) speechreading corpus discs can be played to compare natural and synthetic visual speech side by side. The natural video can be displayed on a monitor adjacent to the SGI console or imported to the computer using a video I/O board under the control of that panel.

Band 12.14 A typical frame from the videodisc. Using the controls on the panel one can cause the facial synthesis to play in synchrony with the videodisc, either in real time or one frame at a time, forwards or backwards, and with or without audio.

Band 12.15 This band illustrates the use of texture mapping with our talking head to give a rendition of Saint Teresa's vision of angels (which inspired Bernini's Baroque sculpture).

Band 13.1 Speechreading can be important in matters of love. The woman is mouthing "I love you."

Band 13.2 Sample trials from the experiments in which a direct comparison is made between people's ability to speechread a natural talker and our their ability to speechread our synthetic talker. Each trial consists of a visible word followed by the same word presented bimodally and in written form.

Band 14.1 Dialog with Baldi in transparent mode.

Band 14.2 Baldi conducting a vowel-learning exercise while displaying half of the face.

Band 14.3 Sample trials from the experiments evaluating the contribution of visible speech to the perception of synthetic auditory speech sentences. Each sentence contained a critical test word which was one word of a minimal pair. After presentation of the sentence, subjects were to decide which of the two words of the minimal pair had occurred.

Band 14.4 Sample trials from the experiment on speechreading a peripheral stimulus.

Band 14.5 Sample trials from the experiment on speechreading a quantized stimulus.

Band 14.6 Sample trials from the experiment on speechreading a stimulus from above or below or in profile view.

Band 14.7 Sample trials from the experiment on speechreading a face at different simulated distances.

Band 14.8 Sample trials from the experiment on presenting supplementary features along with the face.

Source Notes

The following colleagues were kind enough to contribute to this project:

Anders Löfqvist and Kluwer Academic Publishers for permission to reprint figures 12.4 and 12.5.

Fred Parke, for his original facial synthesis software and for permission to show the original facial animation in Band 12.3.

The natural face on Bands 12.1, 12.7 (upper right), 12.14, 13.2, and 14.8 were recorded with permission from Johns Hopkins University, Baltimore, Maryland.

The AT&T system used to drive our facial animation and the auditory speech output are used with permission from AT&T Bell Laboratories.

Bertrand Legoff and Christian Benoit of ICP Grenoble for the French animation given in Band 12.6.

Keith Waters and Steve Franks for the muscle model animation given in Band 12.2.

Alan Kawamoto, George Miller, and Lawrence Rabiner for permitting us to texture map their faces appearing in Band 7.3, Band 4.1, and Band 7.4, respectively.

Andee Rickey, who acted in Band 13.1.

Phillip Rubin, Haskins Laboratories, for the sine wave speech used in Band 2.1.

Dr. Joseph Perkell for permission to include Band 12.5, which shows the two utterances "hatih" and "hatuh" from the cineradiograph analyzed by Perkell (1969), originally recorded in 1962 at the cineradiographic facility of the Werner-Gren Research Laboratory at Nortull's Hospital in Stockholm Sweden under the direction of Drs. K. Stevens and S. Ohman, and later archived by Munhall, Vatikiotis-Bateson and Tohkura (1994).

Author Index

Subject Index

Categorization. *See* Pattern recognition

Category-conditional independence, 117–119

Category width, 163

Chaos theory, 46

Cluster judgments, 16, 75–76, 87–88, 147, 184–185
  and change with aging, 147
  and change with SOA, 75–76, 87–88
  compatibility description of, 75–76

Coarticulation, 372–386
  definition, 372
  dominance model of, 377–386
  gestural models of, 376–379
  models of, 373–375
  and speaking rate, 384–386
  and speech perception, 375–376
  and speech production, 371–379
  UCSC control algorithm of, 379–386

Cochlear implants, 170
  and integration, 172

Complementarity, 10, 160, 236, 424–427
  definition of, 424

Computational modeling, 39–42
  representation in, 41–42
  in speech perception, 40–42

Concepts. *See* Pattern recognition

Confusion matrices, 14–16

Confusions, 10, 14–16, 101–102

Conjunction. *See* Integration

Conjunction fallacy, 174, 271–272

Connectionist models. *See* TRACE model

Consciousness, 28–29. *See also* Qualia

Consonants. *See also* Phoneme; Viseme
  clusters (*see* Cluster judgments)
  vs. vowels, 180–182

Context
  and development, 143
  lexical, 281–283, 330–335
  phonological, 331
  syntactic, 336–338, 361–362,

Continuous information. *See* FLMP

Continuous model. *See* FLMP

Continuous perception, vs. categorical perception, 52–53, 281–285

Control parameter, communication coding, 369–370

Convergence theory, 67–69

Convergent integration, 123–124

Criterion rule, 274–276
  vs. probability matching rule, 276–281

Cross-linguistic contrasts, 148–158

Cultural influences, 148
  on emotion recognition, 224–229

Cued speech, 170, 434–435
  and continuous perception, 434

Databases, 49, 318–321

Deaf. *See* Hearing impairment

DECface, 367

DECtalk, 373

Decision heuristics, 174–179

Decision making, 174–179, 271–272

Decision stage, 263–289

DeMorgan's law, 348

Deterministic behavior, 274
  vs. probabilistic behavior, 270–271

Developmental differences, 141–143
  in information, 145–146

Dimensions. *See also* Features
  integral, 346

Direct perception, 33–34, 69
  vs. FLMP, 352–355

Disabled perceivers. *See* Hearing impairment

Discrimination, 347–350
  vs. meaningful perception, 106

Disjunction, 347–350

Dominance. *See* Coarticulation

Ecological cue, 7

Emotion perception, 111–113
  cultural influences, 224–228
  in face, 203–229
  vs. face recognition, 244–250
  facial vs. vocal cues, 232–233
  models of, 219–224
  tree of wisdom, 219
  in voice, 231–252

Equation length, 327–329

Evaluation. *See* Feature evaluation

Exemplar-based representation, 174–179

Expanded factorial design. *See* Factorial design

Experience, 165–168

Explanation, levels of, 103–104

Exponential law of forgetting, 98–100

External validity, 7, 362

Facial animation. *See* Speech synthesis

Face recognition, 205–206
  vs. emotion recognition, 244–250, 320–321
  vs. object recognition, 205–206

FACS, 367

Factorial design, 6–7
  definition, 7
  and ecological validity, 7
  expanded, 8, 17–19, 107, 153–158, 233–241, 345–346, 393
  vs. single factor, 6–7

Falsification, 111
Feature evaluation. *See also* FLMP; Information
  dynamic, 259–266
  independence vs. dependence, 218–224
Features, 61–64
  acoustic, 196–198, 436
  binary (*see* Categorical perception)
  categorical (*see* Categorical perception)
  continuous (*see* FLMP)
  discrete (*see* Categorical perception)
  multimodal, 89–93
  phonetic, 434–442
  visible, 361
FLMP, 61–66, 293–294
  application of, 61–65
  assessment in, 264–270
  and Bayes' theorem, 343–345
  brain implementation, 121–126
  and cognitive functioning, 174–179
  component processes in, 61–62
  and connectionist models, 339–341
  cross-linguistic fit, 148–158
  decision, 263–281
  and developmental changes, 141–142
  discrimination task, 347–350
  disjunction in, 347–349
  dynamic, 256–263
  evidence for, 173
  features in, 61–62
  fit across instructions, 244–250
  fit of emotion perception, 209–218, 225–
    228, 238–239, 242–243
  fit of expanded factorial design, 313–315
  fit of factorial design, 313–315
  fit of hearing impaired, 158–161
  fit of reaction times, 189–194
  and information, 135
  and information processing, 135
  learning in, 165–167
  mathematical equivalence to Bayes' theorem,
    115–117
  multimodal feature, 91–93
  and noise, 318, 324–326
  nonconvergent temporal integration, 124–
    126
  and number of responses, 184–188
  prototypes in, 61–62
  rating task, 183
  relative goodness rule in, 64
  tests of, 84–88, 146
  and TRACE model, 66–67, 331–334, 339–
    341
  truth values vs. probabilities, 119–120
  two-alternative, 120–121

Free parameter
  estimation of, 45–48
  identifiability of, 341
Free response task, 153–158
Functional cue, 7
Fuzzy logic
  conjunction of attributes, 61–65
  vs. probabilities, 119–120
  psychological reality, 347–350
  truth values in, 119–120
Fuzzy logical model of perception. *See* FLMP
Fuzzy sets. *See* Fuzzy logic
Fuzzy truth values. *See* Fuzzy logic

Gesture, perception, 170–172
Gesture theory. *See* Direct perception
Gestural models. *See* Coarticulation
GUI, 388–390

Hearing impairment, 158–161, 416–418
  and bimodal speech perception, 158–161
  and complementarity, 425–427
Hindsight bias, 106–107
Holistic models, 219–222, 350–352
  critique of, 219–222
Horse-race models. *See* RACE model

Identifiability, 341–347
  model, 341
  parameter, 341–347
Identification, 11. *See also* Bimodal speech
    perception; Pattern recognition
Identification tasks, 9
  and discrimination tasks, 347–350
  relationship to rating tasks, 286–289
Illusions, 23–26
  graph, 19
  McGurk effect, 24–26
Independence, category-conditional, 117–119
Infants, speech perception, 61
Inference, in perception, 38
Information, 199–201. *See also* Features
  and aging, 145–146
  bottom-up, 37–38, 52, 331–338
  categorical vs. continuous sources, 52–52,
    281–285
  cross-modal, 89–93
  discrete, 37 (*see also* Categorical perception)
  evaluation of, 61–66
  format, 174–179
  independence of sources, 195–196
  vs. information processing, 135, 199–201
  top-down, 31–38, 52, 331–338
Information integration. *See* Integration

Phonetic features, 434–442
Phonological context, 331
Phonotactics, 149
Pointing gesture, 170–172
Postperceptual guessing model, 50–52, 110
Power law, 97–98
PPG. See Postperceptual guessing model
Predictive power, 323–329
Prelabeling model, 66
PRLM. See Prelabeling model
Probabilistic behavior, vs. deterministic, 270–271
Probability
  vs. frequency, 174–179
  vs. truth value, 63, 119–121
Probability matching rule, 272–274
  vs. criterion rule, 276–281
Probability judgments, 271–272
Prototypes, 61–64
Psychoacoustic theory, 31–32
Psychophysics, Weber's law of, 96–97, 106, 292

Qualia, 28–29

RACE model, 52–55, 110
Rating judgments, 281–289
  distribution of, 283–288
  FLMP description of, 183–184
  relationship to identification, 286–289
  in test of TRACE model, 339–341
Reaction times, 189–194
  and ambiguity, 189–194
  and conflict, 190–191
Reading, 260–263, 281–283, 419, 420
  dual route model of, 52
  and speechreading, 153
  vs. spoken language, 420
Relative goodness rule, 63, 64
  vs. absolute goodness, 264–268
  and integration, 269–270
  in pandemonium, 270
  in semantic judgments, 268–269
Representation, 41–42
  vs. information, 167–168
Response alternatives. See also Prototypes
  number of, 184–188
Response bias. See Bias
Response selection. See Probability matching rule; Criterion rule
RGR. See Relative goodness rule
RMSD, 48
  benchmark, 296–322

definition of, 48
and statistics, 296–297
Robustness
  of integration, 198–201
  of visible speech, 427–433
Root mean squared deviation. See RMSD
RT. See Reaction time

SCM. See Single channel model
Selective adaptation, 195–196
Sense perception, vs. meaningful perception, 36–38
Sensory cues, 38–39
Sensory penetration, 121–122
Sensory storage, and integration, 89, 124
Shepard's law of generalization, 100–102
Sign language, 316–317
Simulation. See Monte Carlo simulation
Sine wave speech, 67–69
Single channel model, 42–50, 78–80, 109–110, 126, 135–136, 326, 343
  and noise, 318
SOA. See stimulus onset asynchrony
Sound localization, 25
Speech perception. See also Bimodal speech perception; Pattern recognition
  context in, 330–338, 361–362
  theories of, 31–34
Speech production, 371–379. See also Coarticulation
  and speaking rate, 385–386
  training in, 418
Speechreading, 5. See also Visible speech perception
  vs. bimodal perception, 144–148, 393
  developmental differences in, 141–143
  in Japanese, 149–153
  and reading, 153
  robustness in, 427–433
  with supplementary visual cues, 437–442
  with synthetic vs. natural speech, 11–12
Speech synthesis. See also Coarticulation
  applications, 415–424
  AT&T vs. MITalk, 420
  auditory, 17, 371
  control mechanism for, 369–372
  development environment for, 388–390
  evaluation of, 391–413
  physically based, 364–367
  research applications, 311–362
  talker variability in, 412–413
  terminal analog, 367–369
  texture mapping in, 386–388

Speech synthesis (cont.)
tongue in, 391–392
units of, 371–372
validity of, 362–364
value of, 360–364
Statistics
critique of, 338–339
and free parameters, 301–302
transformations, 329–330
STEPIT, 48
Stimulus onset asynchrony
in backward recognition masking, 256–263
and integration, 72–89
and multimodal feature, 91–93
Summary-based representation. *See*
Prototypes
Superior colliculus, 123–124
Superpower, 323–329
Syllables, 21
adaptation to unimodal and bimodal, 195–196
recognition of (*see* Pattern recognition)
Synesthesia, 28
Synthetic speech. *See* Speech synthesis
vs. natural speech, 11–12, 362–364, 393–413

Tadoma method, 352–355
Top-down information, 37–38, 52, 331–338
TRACE model, 66–67, 331–334, 339–341
and the FLMP, 339–341
Trading relations. *See* Integration
Training effects. *See* Learning
Truth values. *See* Fuzzy logic
Two-alternative task. *See* Response alternatives

Unconscious logic. *See* Inference
Universal principle
falsifiability of, 111
illustration of, 107–109
optimality of, 115–117

Variability, 45–46, 270–271, 279–281, 296–304, 316–321, 324–326
ecological, 169–201
individual, 131–168, 292, 334–335
instructions, 194, 244–250
language, 148–158
sampling, 278–279, 296–300
sensory impairment, 158–161
statistical (*see* Model testing)
talker, 412–413

Ventriloquism, 25
Viseme, 394–413
definition of, 394–395
Visible speech perception, 391–413
and hearing-impairment, 158–161
robustness of, 427–433
supplementation of, 433–443
and training, 166–167
Visible speech synthesis. *See* Speech synthesis
Visual capture, 25
Voice onset time, 89–91, 336–338, 363
VOT. *See* Voice onset time
Votrax, 373
Vowel, vs. consonant, 180–182

Weber's law, 96–97, 106
Word recognition
in evaluation of synthesis, 391–413
sentential context in, 336–338, 361–362
and supplementary cues, 434–442
and visual information, 22

Table of Phonetic Symbols

Phonetic symbol	Key world	Phonetic symbol	Key word
i	eve	d	day
I	it	k	key
ɛ	met	g	go
æ	at	h	he
a	father	f	for
ɔ	all	v	vote
U	foot	θ	thin
u	boot	ð	then
ɝ	word	s	see
Λ	up	z	zoo
ə	about	ʃ	shė
eI	say	ž	azure
aI	I	č	church
ɔI	boy	ǰ	judge
aU	out	m	me
oU	go	n	no
Iu	cute	ŋ	sing
p	pay	j	you
b	be	r	read
t	to	l	let
		w	we

CD-ROM Installation and Use Instructions

MACINTOSH

Check your Extensions folder in your System folder for any existing versions of Quicktime and Quicktime Power Plug. If these are earlier than version 2.5, install the two Quicktime extensions from the CD-ROM extensions folder in your Mac's Extensions folder in the System folder. You may need to manually remove any older versions and should reboot after installing the new ones. You should also copy the Movie Player (version 2.5) and SimpleText from the CD-ROM to your hard disk if they are newer than your current versions.

To play a Quicktime movie (*.mov) from the CD-ROM, simply click on it. To view a JPEG image (*.jpg), drag its icon onto the SimpleText icon.

WINDOWS 3.1, WINDOWS 95, WINDOWS NT

For Windows 3.1, click on QTINSTAL.EXE (if you don't have at least Quicktime for Windows version 2.1.1), or for Windows 95 or Windows NT click on QT32INST.EXE (if you don't have at least Quicktime for Windows version 2.1.2) to install Quicktime.

To play a Quicktime movie (*.mov) or view a JPEG image (*.jpg) from the CD-ROM, simply click on it. If the Quicktime movie player is not already associated with the .mov filetype you may have to set this manually. To do this, once in the CD-ROM movies folder, select "options" from the "view" pulldown menu. Then, at the "File Types" tab, scroll down to "QuickTime Movie" and doubleclick on it. The action should be set to "open." Hitting the "Edit" button, set the "Application used" to "C:\WINDOWS\Play32.exe", then hit OK to that window and its two parents. For Windows NT, you would substitute WINNT40 for WINDOWS above. Similarly, "QuickTime Pictures" (for viewing .jpg images) should be set to open with the application "C:\WINDOWS\View32.exe". Often, however, the .jpg images will be displayed using some other application, e.g., Internet Explorer or Adobe Photoshop as the default viewer.